W9-AUR-466
EDITION

*Benda
216-8692*

Peak Performance
SUCCESS IN COLLEGE AND BEYOND

Sharon K. Ferrett, Ph.D.

Humboldt State University

Boston   Burr Ridge, IL   Dubuque, IA   Madison, WI   New York   San Francisco   St. Louis
Bangkok   Bogotá   Caracas   Kuala Lumpur   Lisbon   London   Madrid   Mexico City
Milan   Montreal   New Delhi   Santiago   Seoul   Singapore   Sydney   Taipei   Toronto

Mc Graw Hill | Higher Education

*A Division of **The McGraw-Hill** Companies*

PEAK PERFORMANCE: SUCCESS IN COLLEGE AND BEYOND, ANNOTATED INSTRUCTOR'S EDITION
Published by McGraw-Hill, an imprint of The McGraw-Hill Companies, Inc., 1221 Avenue of the Americas, New York, NY 10020.
Copyright ©2008, 2006, 2002. All rights reserved. No part of this publication may be reproduced or distributed in any form or by any means, or stored in a database or retrieval system, without the prior written consent of The McGraw-Hill Companies, Inc., including, but not limited to, in any network or other electronic storage or transmission, or broadcast for distance learning.

This book is printed on acid-free paper.

2 3 4 5 6 7 8 9 0 CCI/CCI 0 9 8 7

ISBN: 978-0-07-312549-7
MHID: 0-07-312549-0

Vice President and Editor in Chief: *Emily Barrosse*
Publisher: *Beth Mejia*
Executive Editor: *David S. Patterson*
Developmental Editor: *Vicki Malinee, Van Brien & Associates*
Editorial Coordinator: *Emily Pecora*
Marketing Director: *Sharon Loeb*
Marketing Manager: *Sarah Martin*
Senior Project Manager: *Catherine R. Iammartino*
Designer: *Marianna Kinigakis*
Cover and Interior Designer: *Ellen Pettengell Design*
Photo Research Manager: *Brian Pecko*
Senior Production Supervisor: *Carol Bielski*
Media: *Ron Nelms*

Composition: 11/14 Minion, Carlisle Publishing Services
Printing: Courier Kendallville

Cover: ©Greg Epperson

Credits: The credits section for this book begins on page A-1 and is considered an extension of the copyright page.

Library of Congress Cataloging-in-Publication Data
Ferrett, Sharon K.
    Peak performance: success in college and beyond / Sharon K. Ferrett.—6th ed.
       p. cm.
    Includes bibliographical references and index.
    ISBN-13: 978-0-07-312549-7 (alk. paper)
    ISBN-10: 0-07-312549-0 (alk. paper)
      1. Academic achievement. 2. Performance. 3. Career development.
    4. Success. I. Title.

LB1062.6F47 2008
370.15'2—dc22

                                                                                    2006046874

The Internet addresses listed in the text were accurate at the time of publication. The inclusion of a website does not indicate an endorsement by the authors or McGraw-Hill, and McGraw-Hill does not guarantee the accuracy of the information presented at these sites.

www.mhhe.com

Brief Table of Contents

Contents

Preface

Why I Wrote This Book

I have spent more than 25 years working with students as a college professor, an advisor, and a dean and more than 15 years as a management consultant. I began my research into personal productivity and human relations early in my teaching career and began compiling data from years of teaching classes in organizational behavior and giving hundreds of workshops to managers and executives. I have always been interested in transitions, which led me to teaching classes to help students successfully make the transition from high school to college and from college to the world of work.

It is apparent that there is a strong connection between the world of college and the world of work, yet college is often viewed as separate from the real world. This text, more than any other, presents the relationship of college with the larger systems of work and life. It focuses on responsibility and the consequences of one's decisions and actions. It goes further and shows how decisions and actions can affect others and the larger world.

I contend that it is the nature of people to love learning and to strive for peak performance. As educators, we have the unique opportunity to provide our students with the knowledge and skills they will use in their journey to becoming a peak performer. This book provides the strategies, personal qualities, and habits that will help students put knowledge into action.

As I have developed this edition, I have kept a number of definite goals at the forefront. Essentially, to be successful, students need to

◆ **Learn how they learn best—and incorporate new ways to learn.** Throughout this text, students are given the opportunity to explore learning styles and to develop personal strategies that work for them. Features throughout the text reinforce the core principles and give students the opportunity to practice their critical thinking skills.

◆ **Maximize their available resources and seek out new opportunities.** Often, students overlook what is already available to them. Thus, throughout the text we provide strategies for making the most of surrounding resources and tips for seeking out new resources and opportunities.

◆ **Relate what they are exploring and learning now to future success on the job.** Students are more motivated when they can make the connection between school and job success. Throughout this text, we provide numerous examples and features that directly tie the knowledge, skills, and habits learned in class today to what they will experience in their career.

◆ **Be challenged to strive to become the best individuals they can be.** Our hope is not only that students become successes in the business world but also that they are productive contributors to their communities. Throughout this text, we focus on the key personal qualities, habits, and strategies that will help students become peak performers in all facets of life.

Additionally, it is critical that we

◆ **Provide you, the instructor, with the most useful and practical teaching tools possible.** The goals of your course may vary and you may be dealing with a variety of students—from incoming freshmen straight out of high school, to returning students coming from the workforce, to transferring students coming from other schools. Thus, we have developed a number of teaching tools to suit your situation and your ultimate goals.

New to the Sixth Edition

The sixth edition of *Peak Performance: Success in College and Beyond* has been thoroughly updated and refined based on the many helpful comments and suggestions of adopters and reviewers of the previous edition. Revised with our main objectives in mind, following are a number of features and concepts that are new to this edition. (For a complete list of all the text's changes, please contact your McGraw-Hill sales representative.)

Throughout the Text

- The overall themes of **self-management and personal responsibility** are even more thoroughly integrated, beginning with the retitled "Self-Management" scenario and "Journal Entry" critical thinking exercise at the outset of every chapter. A chapter worksheet is provided to record the journal entry and further explore the self-management process. In addition, Chapter 1 includes a new discussion on self-management, with the addition of key components, such as self-assessment, critical thinking, reflection, visualization, and the creation of a personal mission statement. The chapter-concluding "Re-visualization" feature has been moved to the web site in a new section, "Self-Management Workbook," allowing students to explore personal reflection further.

- An ever-increasing issue on college campuses, **academic honesty** continues to be addressed, including new discussions on the topics of cheating, plagiarism, the citing of sources, and paraphrasing.

- All **chapter titles** have been rewritten using active verbs, reinforcing that the content needs to be put into action in order to be effective.

- All definitions of **key terminology** have been examined and revised for clarity. Key terms are now boldfaced at their first discussion, and all terms appear in a new end-of-text glossary.

- A new **"Check It Out" activity in every "Peak Performer Profile"** provides web sites related to the profiled individual or his or her profession or personal cause, supporting that true peak performers impact society in a number of ways.

Chapter-by-Chapter Highlights

Chapter 1: Discover How You Learn Best

- A new discussion on **self-management** introduces the text's main theme of personal responsibility and reviews the core tools one can use and practice to become more personally responsible: self-assessment, critical thinking, visualization, and reflection. (page 3)

- A section on **reflection** has been added, including the benefits of journaling. (page 6)

- Revised definitions and descriptions of each step in the **ABCDE Method of Self-Management** more clearly explain how to put the method into practice. (page 7)

- A new discussion on **drafting a personal mission statement** reinforces that life must have a purpose and each person has to determine that for him- or herself. (page 7)

- The discussion of **brain dominance** has been revised and moved to the beginning of the discussion on learning preferences, reinforcing that the brain is the learning center. A new Figure 1.2: Left-Brain Versus Right-Brain Traits gives a number of understandable examples of the difference between left- and right-brain dominance. (page 11)

- The classifications within the **Other Intelligences** section have been renamed. "To learn best" tips have been added, as well as Personal Evaluation Notebook 1.3: Multiple Intelligences, giving students concrete tips on how to maximize learning based on their "intelligences." (pages 16–17)

- The **Adult Learning Cycle** steps have been revised to include "Reflect" as the third step. This more accurately explains that the student must go beyond thinking about what is being learned by making connections to prior knowledge and learning experiences. (page 29)

- A new section on **adjusting your learning style to your instructor's teaching style** explains the importance of coping skills—in class and on the job—and provides tips on how to adapt to various classroom situations and lecture styles. (page 31)

Chapter 2: Achieve Emotional Intelligence

- **Maturity** is defined within the discussion of Emotional Intelligence, emphasizing that emotional intelligence and maturity are very closely related and critical to long-term success. (page 44)

◆ A new discussion of **cheating and plagiarism** is introduced in the ethics discussion. (page 46)

◆ The **"Seven Positive Attitudes of Peak Performers"** is now included in this chapter, coinciding with the discussion on attitude and personal motivation. (page 55)

◆ New **Peak Progress 2.4: Setting Goals** within the discussion of motivation continues the mission statement discussion from Chapter 1, explaining to the reader how to set goals and use them as personal motivators. (page 59)

◆ A discussion of **internal and external locus of control** has been added, asking the reader to determine what type of attitude he or she approaches challenges with. (page 59)

◆ **Figure 2.4: Annual Earnings in Education** is updated with the latest statistics from the U.S. Department of Commerce. (page 63)

◆ New **Peak Performer Profile: Christiane Amanpour** highlights one of the most respected journalists covering today's issues of terrorism and war throughout the world. The new "Check It Out" section explores some of the personal sacrifices journalists must make—and safety measures they must take—in order to report international tensions accurately. (page 71)

Chapter 3: Manage Your Time

◆ The **daily time log** has been increased to 24 hours, so the student can more accurately plan a full day, including budgeting time for sleep and recreation. (page 83)

◆ A new discussion of **priorities** (urgent, important, ongoing, trivial) helps the student realize what priorities must be accomplished and plan time accordingly. (page 84)

◆ Revised **Personal Evaluation Notebook 3.3: Looking Ahead: Your Goals** follows the progression of creating a personal mission statement and drafting goals and then pulling it all together to determine short-, middle-, and long-term goals. (page 85)

◆ **Peak Progress 3.1: Invest Your Time in High-Priority Items: The 80/20 Rule** includes additional

examples to help clarify that one must focus on the few tasks in the day that provide the most desired results. (page 87)

◆ New topics in the **Time–Management Strategies** include more detailed information on keeping a calendar, developing a daily to-do list, creating a project board for long-term projects, and realizing that one can't do it all (or at least right now). (page 88)

◆ A new discussion on **time-management strategies for right-brain people** provides concrete tips for students who usually have more difficulties using structured planners and systems. (page 91)

◆ An enhanced section on **procrastination** includes additional strategies to stay motivated and on task. (page 92)

◆ New **Worksheet 3.4: Practice Goal-Setting** and new **Worksheet 3.5: Map Out Your Goals** provide handy templates to use when writing out specific goals and timelines. (pages 112–113)

◆ New **Worksheet 3.6: Daily Prioritizer and Planner: Your To-Do List** provides a 24-hour template, including sections for recording and checking off priorities. (page 114)

◆ New **Worksheet 3.7: Weekly Planner** and new **Worksheet 3.8: Month/Semester Calendar** are more tools for mapping out priorities and tasks and include sections for upcoming projects, tests, and appointments. (pages 115–116)

Chapter 4: Maximize Your Resources

◆ This chapter is now **presented earlier in the text**, logically following time management—another precious resource. (page 119)

◆ The college and community **resources are reorganized** into "People," "Program," and "On-Line and Informational Resources." Although many informational resources can still be found in print, today's student will more than likely access information on line and needs to know key things to search for and resources that provide assistance. All financial resources are then combined into one complete section, appearing in the second half of the chapter. (page 121)

◆ New discussions of important **"people" resources** include academic advisors, mentors, peers, and tips on connecting with instructors. (page 121)

- A new section instructs the student on starting a **network of contacts** who can help him or her succeed in college, begin career planning, and possibly assist in future job hunting. (page 123)

- New **"program" resources** are included that may be available to the student, such as learning centers and the student activities office (including multicultural centers). (page 124)

- New **Personal Evaluation Notebook 4.1: Activities and Clubs** provides a handy worksheet for students to fill out when reviewing opportunities on campus for getting involved, learning about career fields, building contacts, and meeting new people. (page 127)

- More detailed discussions on **how to use a school catalog** (both print and on-line) and the **schedule of classes** provide tips on using some of the school's key but often overlooked resources. (pages 128–130)

- New **Peak Progress 4.1: Using Technology at School** provides essential tips on using technology to your advantage, including taking on-line courses, using computer labs and assistance, setting up a campus e-mail account, asking about discounts, and using technology that accompanies textbooks. (page 129)

- A revised discussion of **students with disabilities** includes mention of the Americans with Disabilities Act, along with more examples of recognized disabilities and additional tips. (page 130)

- A new section on **protecting yourself from identity theft and fraud** in the financial management section sends a clear warning with important tips to follow. (page 137)

- New **Peak Performer Profile: Matt Friedman and Adam Scott** introduces two entrepreneurs who started a small business while getting their degrees and what the National Minority Franchise Initiative is doing to spur ownership by minorities. (page 145)

- New **Worksheet 4.2: Exploring Your School's Resources** provides a comprehensive checklist of the vast number of resources that may be available on campus, encouraging students to research and record services they find. (page 149)

Chapter 5: Listen and Take Effective Notes

- **"Attentive Listening"** more accurately describes the intent and message of the chapter. The strategies are now organized into three major sections: prepare, stay attentive, and review what you have heard. This reinforces that listening is a process and includes a new critical component of reviewing for comprehension and retention. (page 156)

- New **Peak Progress 5.2: Formal (Traditional) vs. Informal (Creative) Outlines** clearly explains how learning style plays a role in selecting an effective outline to use. (page 160)

- The note-taking discussion now starts with a more detailed discussion of the **Cornell System of Note Taking,** providing a clearer explanation of the elements of the popular system and how to use it. (page 162)

- Since no two people take notes in the same way, more information is provided on **how to combine note-taking systems,** showing how to combine favorite elements from various styles to create a system that works best. (page 165)

- **Using note cards** has been added to the strategies section, introducing a convenient way to take notes and study, which is revisited in appropriate places in the text. (page 169)

- **Figure 5.5: Note-Taking Shortcuts** includes more of the most commonly–used abbreviations and their definitions. (page 169)

- A new **"review schedule"** within the Assess and Review strategies provides handy time frames and tips for reviewing and retaining information. (page 170)

- Three **new worksheets** provide instruction, examples, and opportunities for the student to practice using the various note-taking systems. (pages 179–181)

Chapter 6: Actively Read

- Additional examples within the **Five-Part Reading System** more clearly explain how to use this system. (page 187)

- A more detailed discussion of the **SQ3R Reading System** also includes examples of "Questions." (page 190)

- Additional **reading strategies** are included, such as determining your purpose, setting reading goals, concentrating, comparing notes, and using the entire text. (page 193)

- New **Peak Progress 6.2: Reading for Different Courses** provides tips on tackling reading assignments in literature, history, and math and science. (page 193)

◆ New **Peak Progress 6.3: Using Your Textbook** encourages the student to make full use of this and other texts by reviewing the preface, preview features, applications, review material, and other resources. (page 196)

◆ New **Peak Progress 6.5: Reading with Children Around** provides useful tips on how to accomplish your reading while juggling parental responsibilities, including instilling a love of reading in your children. (page 203)

Chapter 7: Improve Your Memory Skills

◆ The **memory process** discussion has been revised as intention, attention, association, retention, and recall. This reinforces that one must be attentive and focused to remember—not simply observant—and that memorization also takes making associations and connections with previous information. New definitions of *mindfulness* and *memorization* are included. (page 220)

◆ New **Peak Progress 7.2: Short-Term and Long-Term Memory** provides a detailed discussion on how we process and store information. (page 223)

◆ Additional **mnemonic devices** include acrostics, chunking, and the stacking technique. (page 228)

◆ The **memory strategies** have been reorganized and revised, including a new strategy on notecards—a simple and essential tool for studying and reviewing. (page 231)

◆ Revised **Personal Evaluation Notebook 7.5: A Walk Down Memory Lane** includes a more detailed discussion on how to complete the activity and use the memory techniques. (page 232)

Chapter 8: Excel at Taking Tests

◆ The **test-taking strategies** have been reorganized into before the test, during the test, and after the test. *Before the test* includes new strategies, such as creating a sample test, using available resources, and assembling what you need. *During the test* is organized in the order the tasks should be accomplished and includes new strategies: write down key information, determine which questions are worth the most, answer objective questions, and answer essay questions. *After the test* includes new analysis and assessment strategies: confirm your grade, determine common types of mistakes, learn what to do differently next time, review with your instructor, and review with your study team. This encourages the student to learn from the results and mistakes, including recognizing patterns in wrong answers, and to discuss concerns with the instructor. (pages 252–258)

◆ A revised **Peak Progress 8.2: Special Strategies for Math and Science Tests** includes many more concrete tips the student can apply and watch for. (page 256)

◆ New **Peak Progress 8.3: Checklist for Incorrect Test Answers** provides a handy list of common reasons for mistakes on tests that the student can use to determine areas for improvement. (page 259)

◆ **Peak Progress 8.5: Important Words in Essay Questions** includes clarified definitions and many more words the student may come across when taking essay exams. (page 265)

◆ The **test anxiety** section has been revamped to include new, specific strategies. (page 268)

◆ A new **discussion on cheating** reinforces that cheating is never acceptable and has a number of negative repercussions. (page 269)

Chapter 9: Express Yourself in Writing and Speech

◆ The **writing process includes a new, fifth step—review**—detailing the tasks the student must accomplish just prior to submitting a paper and how to use the results for improvement. (page 286)

◆ Revised **Figure 9.3: Writing Pyramid** more clearly shows how the writer starts with a main topic, moves to main points, uses supporting points, then makes a conclusion. (page 293)

◆ A new editing strategy on **citing sources** includes a discussion of plagiarism and examples of paraphrasing. (page 295)

◆ New **Peak Progress 9.4: Writing Citations** discusses the various citation styles, including examples of APA and MLA styles. (page 298)

- New **Peak Progress 9.6: Evaluating On-Line Information** provides specific evaluation questions the student can use to determine if on-line information is credible, accurate, timely, and objective. (page 302)
- The **public speaking** section includes many additional strategies: understand the occasion, think about your topic, know your audience, get the audience's attention, outline your speech, and write a good conclusion. (page 303)

Chapter 10: Become a Critical Thinker and Creative Problem Solver

- **Bloom's Taxonomy** and the six levels of critical thinking skills are now included, showing how the various levels of thinking relate to what the student needs to master in college. New Peak Progress 10.1: From Knowledge to Evaluation gives a step-by-step example that shows the student how to apply Bloom's Taxonomy, and new Worksheet 10.2: Apply Bloom's Taxonomy asks the student to determine what level of skill is necessary to accomplish different tasks in a variety of course subjects. (page 320)
- The **four problem-solving steps** have been revised as (1) state and understand the problem; (2) gather and interpret information; (3) develop and implement a plan of action; and (4) evaluate the plan or solution. (page 322)
- The **critical thinking and problem-solving strategies** have been reorganized and include new detail on the importance of attitude, persistence, creativity, attention to details, seeing all sides of the issue, and reasoning (including a new discussion of inductive and deductive reasoning). (page 322)
- The **common errors in judgment** section includes new discussions of all-or-nothing thinking, negative labeling, and a more detailed definition of the halo effect. (page 325)

Chapter 11: Create a Healthy Mind, Body, and Spirit

- A new opening focus and discussion on **connecting the mind, body, and spirit** includes a new definition of wellness and explains that a healthy lifestyle involves more than being physically fit. (page 360)
- The **healthy eating strategies** include the latest Dietary Guidelines for Americans. Also included is new information on refined carbohydrates and Type II Diabetes, and the discussion on caffeine has been relocated to this section. (page 361)
- A revised Peak Progress 11.1: Eating for Health and Energy includes a discussion and illustration of the **USDA's MyPyramid.** (page 364)
- A new discussion on **eating disorders,** including anorexia nervosa and bulimia nervosa, and a new Peak Progress 11.2: Eating Disorders provide a case example, definitions and signs to look for, statistics, and resources for help. (pages 366 and 368)
- A revised discussion of **stress management** appears earlier in the chapter and includes additional examples of stressful situations and poor coping skills, along with new strategies of disputing negative thoughts and practicing deep relaxation activities. (page 370)
- New **Peak Progress 11.5: Party with a Plan** gives a concrete 0–3 formula for drinking sensibly. (page 376)
- **Figure 11.3: The Costs of Alcohol** provides the latest government statistics on alcohol use and its negative effects. (page 377)
- An expanded discussion of **depression** includes additional causes, such as accidents, peer pressure, and daily demands. (page 380)
- **Statistics on AIDS cases in the United States** have been added, reinforcing that AIDS is a serious problem at home as well as throughout the world and that people under 25 represent 50 percent of new cases. (page 383)
- A new section with strategies on **how men can prevent sexual violence** has been included. (page 387)

Chapter 12: Build Healthy and Diverse Relationships

- New **strategies for building rapport** include building common ground, paying attention to body language, and recognizing the importance of being a team player. (page 400)
- The discussion on **assertive communication** now directly follows building rapport and includes

more tips and examples of assertive statements. (page 402)

- A new strategy of **networking** explains the importance of establishing positive relationships with instructors and advisors, who can be helpful with personal recommendations and job hunting. (page 406)

- New **Peak Progress 12.1: E-Mail Etiquette with Instructors** gives concrete tips on respectfully and effectively communicating with instructors by e-mail. (page 406)

- **Conflict and criticism** are now discussed separately. The conflict section includes new strategies, such as using "I" statements, apologizing, and focusing on the problem. (page 406)

- The revised section on **constructive criticism** includes new strategies on how to give criticism and how to receive it. (page 410)

- Additional **strategies for dealing with shyness** include focusing on benefits and taking action. (page 411)

- The discussion of **diversity** is organized and presented in the second half of the chapter, including a new strategy for studying abroad. A revised Figure 12.2: Understanding the Meaning more accurately describes the concepts of attitude and behavior in regard to stereotypes, prejudice, and discrimination. (page 418)

Chapter 13: Develop Positive Habits

- A more streamlined discussion of the **Ten Habits of the Peak Performer** is included. (page 438)

- The section on **changing habits** includes new discussions of changing attitude first, understanding the "big picture," and adapting to change (with business-related examples, such as "Who Moved My Cheese?")—reinforcing that a positive attitude is fundamental to making changes and that the ability to adapt is one of the most important qualities employers value in their employees. (page 441)

- New **strategies** added to the creating positive change discussion explain that major changes don't come overnight. (page 442)

- The section on **resistors to change** includes more examples and reasons, such as lack of awareness and difficulties in making changes. (page 446)

- An expanded section on **writing a contract for change** highlights how putting a commitment in writing can be an effective motivator. (page 448)

Chapter 14: Explore Majors and Careers

- A new section on **exploring and choosing a major** discusses the reasons for being undeclared and specific strategies and school resources available for exploring majors. (page 462)

- New sections on **values, interests, abilities, and skills** includes Holland's theory of occupational personality types, reinforcing that the student must understand what his or her values and priorities are, what he or she likes to do, and what he or she is good at to help the student determine optimal career choices. A new Personal Evaluation Notebook 14.1: Your Values asks the student to explore a variety of personal and work-related values to determine which are important. (page 464)

- New **Peak Progress 14.1: Service Learning** discusses the benefits of service learning and how the student can build service learning into coursework, a resume, and networking. (page 465)

- A new section on **exploring careers** includes strategies and resources on campus, through professional organizations, and from the government. (page 468)

- A revised and reorganized section on **building a Career Development Portfolio** provides a clearer description of the essential elements in a portfolio, including easier-to-read illustrations of sample documents, and connects with the mission statement and related content from previous chapters. (page 469)

- **Figure 14.1: Career Development Portfolio Planning Guide** has been revised and a two-year option is also provided on the text's website. (page 471)

- A revised section on **planning the job hunt** includes creating and submitting a cover letter and interviewing. (page 484)

Successful Features

A number of features throughout this text reinforce learning, critical thinking, and the main goals of the text, and all have been fine-tuned to support the chapter material more succinctly.

◆ **Student preface.** This unique introduction not only walks the student through the numerous beneficial features that reinforce the text's goals but also includes "As You Get Started in Your New School: What You Need to Know and Should Not Be Afraid to Ask." This section helps students explore the reasons they are attending college, provides a checklist of the tasks to accomplish the first week of school, and gives the critical questions that they should get answers to in their situation and school (including the top questions asked of advisors). It also includes information on topics such as graduation requirements, registering, adding and dropping classes, incomplete grades, taking a leave of absence, and transferring. Also included are the top 50 strategies for success in college.

◆ **The ABCDE Method of Self-Management.** Introduced in Chapter 1, the ABCDE Method of Self-Management will help students manage thoughts, feelings, and behaviors, so that they create positive results and achieve goals. This five-step process (A = Actual event; B = Beliefs; C = Consequences; D = Dispute; E = Energized) uses visualization to show the connection among thoughts, feelings, and actions and empowers the reader to dispel negative thoughts and replace them with realistic and positive thoughts and behaviors. Each chapter begins with a "Self-Management" exercise, which includes a scenario that students can relate to. The student is then given the opportunity to reflect on personal experiences in the follow-up journal entry. A chapter worksheet is provided to record the journal entry and helps the student practice critical thinking by using the ABCDE Method of Self-Management to work through difficult situations and determine positive solutions.

◆ **The Adult Learning Cycle.** Introduced in Chapter 1 and carried throughout each chapter, the Adult Learning Cycle is a five-step process that demonstrates that learning comes from repetition, practice, and recall. This process offers a critical fifth stage not included in other learning theories: (1) relate, (2) observe, (3) reflect, (4) do, and (5) teach. Each chapter provides the reader an opportunity to apply the chapter material to the Adult Learning Cycle within a Peak Progress box.

◆ **Secretary's Commission on Achieving Necessary Skills (SCANS).** Found on pages xxv–xxvi and introduced in Chapter 1, this is the list of the competencies employees need to be able to demonstrate on the job. Included in this handy chart are the corresponding chapters in this text. The many exercises, strategies, case studies, and guidelines throughout the text correlate with several SCANS requirements, as well as systems thinking, diversity, and critical thinking.

◆ **Chapter objectives.** Rewritten in an active voice, clear and concise objectives at the beginning of each chapter identify the chapter's key concepts.

◆ **Self-Management and Journal Entry.** Each chapter begins with a retitled Self-Management scenario that students can relate to. The reader is then given the opportunity to reflect on personal experiences in the follow-up journal entry. An end-of-chapter worksheet is provided to record the journal entry.

◆ **Success Principle.** Each chapter begins with a Success Principle that succinctly communicates the important lesson to be learned from the chapter. Many of the Success Principles have been rewritten to more closely reflect the core message of the chapter, providing the student with a quick and meaningful take-away message.

◆ **Words to Succeed.** Found throughout the text, these quotes provide insight, motivation, and food for thought and are tied to the chapter's content. Many new quotes are included that are from pioneers and personalities the student will quickly recognize.

◆ **Personal Evaluation Notebook.** Appearing in every chapter, these exercises provide opportunities to practice critical thinking and decision-making skills. Many have been revised to avoid closed questions (simple yes/no answers). Spaces are provided for recording answers and thoughts directly within the activity. The new PEN name—along with the pen icon—helps the student quickly identify the feature.

◆ **Peak Progress.** The Peak Progress boxed feature demonstrates the themes and concepts of each chapter and includes helpful suggestions to accelerate and assess progress.

◆ **Taking Charge end-of-chapter summary.** Every chapter concludes with a summary of the main points presented in the chapter. Written as "I" statements, they reinforce that the chapter presents a number of potential strategies to implement and master.

◆ **Career in Focus.** This feature provides real-world career profiles that illustrate examples of the relationship between the study skills necessary for college success and the skills needed for career success. Work situations that directly call on chapter skills are highlighted to show the relationship between school and career skills.

◆ **Peak Performer Profile.** Each chapter presents a noted person in the area of business, education, the arts, or public service. These peak performers have overcome obstacles and challenges to become successful. Each profile includes a new "Check It Out" section, with web sites related to the profiled individual or his or her profession or personal cause.

◆ **Performance Strategies.** Included in every chapter is a recap of the top 10 strategies for success in applying the chapter's concepts.

◆ **Review Questions.** Each chapter includes five basic application and critical thinking questions to help the student review the chapter's main concepts. Space is now included for students to write their responses or include key terms.

◆ **Tech for Success.** Now appearing with the end-of-chapter applications section, this feature has been updated to offer tips for making the most out of technology applications in school and on the job. New tips include how to use emoticons and the 60/60 IPod rule for preserving your hearing.

◆ **Case Study.** Each chapter includes a case study activity that presents college students dealing with real-life situations that reflect the chapter's con-

cepts. Additional case study opportunities are provided on the text's web site.

◆ **Worksheet activities.** Each chapter concludes with numerous activities that are perforated and thumb-tabbed for ease of use. New worksheets have been added to offer more critical thinking opportunities as well as handy planning forms. Scoring and/or explanations have been provided where applicable. Many of the useful forms are also available on the book's web site, www.mhhe.com/ferrett6e, so they can be customized.

◆ **Career Development Portfolio worksheet.** Found at the end of every chapter, the Career Development Portfolio gives the student the opportunity to track and showcase skills, competencies, accomplishments, and work. Chapter 14: Explore Majors and Careers shows the student how to develop a personal Career Development Portfolio to use during career planning and maintenance.

Ancillaries

We have designed an extensive and convenient ancillary package that focuses on course goals, allows you to maximize your time with students, and helps students understand, retain, and apply the main principles.

◆ **Annotated Instructor's Edition (AIE) (0-07-312550-4).** The AIE contains the full text of the student edition of the text, along with instructional strategies that reinforce and enhance the core concepts. Notes and tips in the margin provide topics for discussion, teaching tips for hands-on and group activities, and references to materials provided in the Instructor's Resource Manual and the Online Learning Center web site.

◆ **Instructor's Resource Manual, Test Bank, and Student Retention Kit (0-07-331688-1).** Included in this extensive resource are chapter goals and outlines, teaching tips, additional activities, essay exercises, and transparency masters. Also provided is an extensive section on course planning, with sample syllabi. The extensive test bank includes matching, multiple choice, true/false, and short answer questions. The test bank is also available in an electronic format that can be downloaded from the text's website. The kit also includes unique resource guides that give instructors and administrators the tools to retain students and maximize the success of the course, using topics and principles that last a lifetime. Specialized sections include

- ◆ Facilitator's Guide
- ◆ Tools for Time Management
- ◆ Establishing Peer Support Groups
- ◆ Developing a Career Portfolio
- ◆ Involving the Faculty Strategy
- ◆ Capitalizing on Your School's Graduates

◆ **Implementing a Student Success Course CD-ROM (0-07-310690-9).** This innovative CD assists you in developing and sustaining your Student Success course. The features include a "how to" guide for designing and proposing a new course, with easy-to-use templates for determining budget needs and resources. Examples of model programs are provided from two-year, four-year, and career schools. The CD explores course goals, such as orientation and retention, and provides research data to support your proposal. Also included are materials to help sustain your course, such as faculty development programs and on-line resources.

◆ **Online Learning Center web site (www.mhhe.com/ferrett6e).** The book's web site includes features for both instructors and students—downloadable ancillaries, web links, student quizzing, additional information on topics of interest, and much more. Access to the web site is provided free to students.

◆ **PageOut, WebCT, Blackboard, and more.** The Online Learning Center content of *Peak Performance* is supported by WebCT, eCollege.com, and Blackboard. Additionally, our PageOut service, free to qualified adopters, is available to get you and your course up and running on-line in a matter of hours! To find out more, contact your McGraw-Hill representative or visit www.pageout.net.

◆ **Customized text options.** *Peak Performance* can be customized to suit your needs. The text can be abbreviated for shorter courses or can be expanded to include semester schedules, campus maps, additional essays, activities, or exercises, along with other materials specific to your cur-

riculum or situation. Contact your McGraw-Hill sales representative for more information or:

Canada: 1-905-430-5034
United States: 1-800-446-8979
E-mail: FYE@mcgraw-hill.com

More Resources for Teaching and Learning

◆ **LASSI: Learning and Study Strategies Inventory.** The LASSI is a 10-scale, 80-item assessment of students' awareness about and use of learning and study strategies related to skill, will, and self-regulation components of strategic learning. The focus is on both the covert and the overt thoughts, behaviors, attitudes, and beliefs that relate to successful learning and that can be altered through educational interventions. Research has repeatedly demonstrated that these factors contribute significantly to success in college and that they can be learned or enhanced through educational interventions, such as learning and study skills courses.

The LASSI provides standardized scores and national norms for 10 different scales. The LASSI is both diagnostic and prescriptive. It provides students with a diagnosis of their strengths and weaknesses, compared with other college students in the areas covered by the 10 scales, and it is prescriptive in that it provides feedback about areas where students may be weak and need to improve their knowledge, attitudes, beliefs, and skills.

The LASSI student assessment is available in print and packaged with *Peak Performance* (Package ISBN: 0-07-360450-X). Please contact your local McGraw-Hill sales representative for details.

◆ **Student Planner.** Updated annually, this convenient organizational tool is available as a stand-alone or with the student text. The planner provides daily tips for success, time-management techniques, a daily calendar, and contact information. Contact your McGraw-Hill sales representative for the latest order information.

◆ **Study Smart: Study Skills for Students 2.0 (Online at www.mhhe.com/studymart2 or on**

CD-ROM 0-07-245515-2). Developed by Andrea Bonner and Mieke Schipper of Sir Sanford Fleming College, this innovative study skills tutorial teaches students essential note-taking methods, test-taking strategies, and time-management secrets. Study Smart can be ordered free when packaged with new copies of *Peak Performance*.

◆ **Random House Webster's College Dictionary (0-07-366069-8).** Updated for the twenty-first century, this dictionary is available for a nominal cost when packaged with the text.

Acknowledgments

We would like to thank the many instructors whose insightful comments and suggestions provided us with inspiration and the ideas that were incorporated into this new edition:

Erskine Ausbrooks	Dyersburg State Community College
Kristi Brock	Northern Kentucky University
Ashley Chance Fox	Bowling Green Community College
Phyllis Curtis-Tweed	Medgar Evers College/City University of New York
Bill Donley	Spokane Community College
Connie Gulick	Albuquerque Technical-Vocational Institute
Bob Holdeman	University of South Carolina
Cathi Kadow	Purdue University Calumet
Richard Kirk	Central Florida Community College
J. Kelly Lyles	Florida Metropolitan University
Judith Lynch	Kansas State University
Margaret S. McClain	University of Arkansas–Little Rock
Venetia Miller	Tougaloo College
Sharon Occhipinti	Florida Metropolitan University
Jacqueline Phillips	Capital Community College
Angela M. Reeves	Mott Community College
Sherry Rhoden	Grand Rapids Community College
Jennifer Robb	Scott Community College
Kevin Salisbury	Community College of Rhode Island
Juliet Scherer	St. Louis Community College–Meramec
Casey Thomas	Florida Atlantic University
Glen Tourville	Hendrix College
Patricia Twaddle	Moberly Area Community College

A very special thank you goes to TC Stuwe from Salt Lake Community College, who provided additional excellent suggestions on specifically the text's activities, as well as the new discussions of goal setting and critical thinking throughout the text.

Also, we would like to thank Allice Allen of the Academy of Professional Careers in Boise, Idaho, for her excellent suggestion of renaming the in-text activities to "Personal Evaluation Notebooks," who asks her students to "get out your PENS!"

Also, I would like to gratefully acknowledge the contributions of the McGraw-Hill editorial staff—specifically, Vicki Malinee, for her considerable effort, suggestions, ideas, and insights.

Dedication

To the memory of my father, Albert Lawrence Ferrett, for setting the highest standards.

To my mother, Velma Mary Hollenbeck Ferrett, for her seamless expression of love.

To my husband, Sam, and my daughters, Jennifer Katherine and Sarah Angela, for making it all worthwhile.

—Sharon K. Ferrett

Competency Chart

Competencies and Foundations	*Peak Performance* Chapters That Address SCANS Competencies
Resources: Identifies, Organizes, Plans, and Allocates Resources	
• Managing time	Chapter 3
• Managing money	Chapter 4
• Managing space	Chapters 3, 13
• Managing people	Chapter 12
• Managing materials	Chapters 3, 4, 5, 6, 9
• Managing facilities	Chapters 4, 5, 9, 11
Information: Acquires and Uses Information	
• Acquiring information	Chapters 4, 5, 6
• Evaluating information	Chapters 7, 8
• Organizing and maintaining information	Chapters 3, 4, 7, 8, 9, 10
• Using computer to process	Chapter 10
Systems: Understands Complex Interrelationships	
• Understanding systems	All chapters, with a strong emphasis in Ch. 11
• Designing systems	Chapters 5, 6
• Monitoring systems	Chapters 3, 5, 6, 11
• Correcting systems	Chapters 3, 4, 5, 10
Interpersonal Skills: Works with Others	
• Positive attitudes	Chapters 2, 13
• Self-control	Chapters 2, 13
• Goal setting	Chapters 1, 2, 3
• Teamwork	Chapters 2, 13
• Responsibility	Chapter 2
• Stress management	Chapter 11
Technology: Works with a Variety of Technologies	
• Selecting technology	Chapters 9, 14, Tech for Success
• Applying technology	Chapters 9, 14, Tech for Success
• Maintaining technology	Chapters 9, 14
• Solving problems	Chapter 10
• Staying current in technology	Chapter 14

(continued)

Competencies and Foundations	*Peak Performance* Chapters That Address SCANS Competencies
Personal Qualities	
Responsibility, character, integrity, positive habits, self-management, self-esteem, sociability	Chapters 2, 13
Basic Skills	
• Reading—locates, understands, and interprets written information in prose and in documents, such as manuals, graphs, and schedules	Chapter 6
• Writing—communicates thoughts, ideas, information, and messages in writing and creates documents, such as letters, directions, manuals, reports, graphs, and flow charts	Chapter 9
• Arithmetic/mathematics—performs basic computations and approaches practical problems by choosing appropriately from a variety of mathematical techniques	Chapter 10
• Listening—receives, attends to, interprets, and responds to verbal messages and other cues	Chapter 5
Thinking Skills	
• Creative thinking—generates new ideas	Ch. 10, Personal Evaluation Notebooks
• Decision making—specifies goals and constraints, generates alternatives, considers risks, and evaluates and chooses best alternative	Ch. 10, Case Study, Personal Evaluation Notebooks
• Listening—receives, attends to, interprets, and responds to verbal messages and other cues	Chapters 5, 12
• Seeing things in the mind's eye—organizes and processes symbols, pictures, graphs, objects, and other information	All chapters, with a strong emphasis in Ch. 10
• Knowing how to learn—uses efficient learning techniques to acquire and apply new knowledge and skills	Chapter 1
• Reasoning—discovers a rule or principle underlying the relationship between two or more objects and applies it when solving a problem	Chapter 10

Student Preface

Getting the Most Out of This Book

Congratulations! You are about to start or restart an amazing journey of opportunity, growth, and adventure. You may be at this point in your life for a number of reasons: You may be furthering your education right after high school; you may be focusing on a specific career or trade and want to acquire the appropriate skills or certification; or you may be returning to school after years in the workforce, needing additional skills or just looking for a change.

Whatever your reasons, this is an opportunity for you to learn new things, meet new people, acquire new skills, and better equip yourself both professionally and personally for the years ahead. This book is designed to get you started on that journey by helping you (1) learn how you learn best—and incorporate new ways to learn; (2) maximize available resources and seek out new opportunities; (3) relate what you are exploring now to future success on the job; and (4) strive to become the best person you can be.

Learn How You Learn Best—and Incorporate New Ways to Learn

We Learn

Ten percent of what we read
Twenty percent of what we hear
Thirty percent of what we see
Fifty percent of what we see and hear
Seventy percent of what we discuss with others
Eighty percent of what we do and experience
Ninety-five percent of what we teach others

In this text, you will find a number of features and discussion topics that will help you become a better learner:

- **Exploration of learning styles and personality types.** As you will discover in Chapter 1, each person has a preferred learning style and dominant personality type(s). However, the truly successful learner not only maximizes current preferences but also incorporates other styles and applications, thus becoming a more well-rounded learner. As you complete the exercises in this chapter, you will discover how you learn best and what strategies you can incorporate to maximize your learning efforts and environment.

- **The Adult Learning Cycle.** This is introduced in Chapter 1 and carried throughout each chapter. This is a five-step process that demonstrates that learning comes from repetition, practice, and recall: (1) Relate, (2) Observe, (3) Reflect, (4) Do, and (5) Teach. You can apply this method to any new skill or information you want to learn and master. In each chapter, you will find a Peak Progress box that helps you see how the Adult Learning Cycle applies the chapter's content. This exercise will help you increase your awareness of how you learn best and how to explore and practice other learning styles. It will also help you overcome obstacles to learning in many different settings by giving hands-on, practical examples.

- **Critical thinking and creative problem solving.** Introduced in Chapter 1, critical thinking is more than just an educational buzzword—it is an important skill you will use and practice in situations in life. Chapter 10 further explores how to solve problems creatively, including new and extended examples and applications to use in relation to

RORDT

math and science concepts. You will learn to overcome any anxieties you may have in these course areas by focusing on problem-solving techniques.

- **Personal Evaluation Notebook.** The Personal Evaluation Notebook exercises that appear in every chapter give you opportunities to practice your critical thinking and decision-making skills. You are asked to observe, evaluate, and apply chapter concepts to your life. Spaces are provided for you to record your answers and thoughts directly within the activity.

- **Chapter Objectives.** Clear and concise objectives at the beginning of each chapter aid you in identifying and mastering each chapter's key concepts.

- **Peak Progress.** In every chapter, the Peak Progress boxes demonstrate the themes and concepts of the chapter and include helpful suggestions to accelerate and assess your progress.

- **Taking Charge end-of-chapter summary.** Every chapter concludes with a summary of the main points presented in the chapter. Written as "I" statements, they reinforce that the chapter presents a number of potential strategies for you to implement and master.

- **Review Questions.** Each chapter includes five basic questions to help you review the chapter's main concepts.

- **Worksheet activities.** Each chapter concludes with numerous activities that help you apply what you have learned to other classes and situations. The worksheets are perforated and thumb-tabbed for ease of use. Many of the useful forms are also available on the book's web site, www.mhhe.com/ferrett6e, so you can customize them and make multiple copies.

Maximize Available Resources and Seek Out New Opportunities

Often, we overlook the obvious resources and opportunities available to us. Some areas of the text that will guide you in maximizing your resources and seeking out new ones include

- **Time is money and vice versa.** In Chapter 3, you will explore time management, prioritizing, and where your time is spent—and where it should be spent. Also included is a discussion of how to use your short- and long-term goals to determine your priorities. Chapter 4 then explores external resources and tips on handling money and financial opportunities. Also included are strategies for commuter students, students with disabilities, and returning and transfer students.

- **Web site for this text.** The book's web site, www.mhhe.com\ferrett6e, offers a number of activities and resources for mastering and applying each chapter's content and for further study and exploration. Access to the web site is provided free with the text.

- **Tech for Success.** The Tech for Success feature appears in every chapter and has been updated to offer tips for making the most out of technology applications for both school and job.

Relate What You Are Exploring Now to Future Success on the Job

Chances are, one of your main reasons for attending college is to better your career opportunities. Throughout this text, you will find numerous features and examples that directly relate your experiences in college to your future success on the job. Just a few examples include

- **Secretary's Commission on Achieving Necessary Skills (SCANS).** Found on pages xxv–xxvi and introduced in Chapter 1, this is a list of the ideal competencies you will need to be able to demonstrate on the job and the corresponding chapters in this text. The many exercises, strategies, case studies, and guidelines throughout the text correlate with several SCANS requirements, as well as systems thinking, diversity, and critical thinking.

- **Creating a Career Development Portfolio.** Chapter 14 walks you through the process of choosing a major, career exploration, and the development of a personal Career Development Portfolio. It is critical for you to create an ongoing account of your experiences, skills, and achievements. Additionally, you will learn to develop an effective resume and cover letter and to prepare for a successful interview.

◆ **Career Development Portfolio worksheet.** Found at the end of every chapter, the Career Development Portfolio presents the best of your skills, competencies, accomplishments, and work. When completed, the portfolio will contain sections on self-analysis, an inventory of skills and competencies, goals, educational and career plans, an inventory of interests, cover letters, resumes, and samples of work. You can use the portfolio to create and update your resume, to help you prepare for an interview, and to advance your career. The portfolio will give you the opportunity to assess your strengths, set goals, and possess an organized system of important documents. It will also help you explore possible majors and careers.

◆ **Career in Focus.** This feature provides real-world career profiles that illustrate examples of the relationship between the study skills necessary for college success and the skills you will need for career success. Work situations that directly call on chapter skills are highlighted, so that you can see the interrelationships.

◆ **Case Study.** Each chapter includes a case study activity that presents college students dealing with real-life situations that reflect the chapter's concepts. This feature stresses that the same issues that you deal with in school also exist in the workplace; the same skills and strategies that you use in the classroom can be adapted to your job. Additional case study opportunities are provided on the text's web site.

Strive to Become the Best Person You Can Be

In this text, you are introduced to the concept of a "peak performer" (Chapter 1) and are provided strategies for maximizing your success in school, career, and life. Our hope is that you are empowered to "walk the talk" and put these strategies and perspectives into practice, starting today. To be successful, you must not only adapt to college and the larger community but also acquire the necessary skills, personal qualities, habits, and motivation to face the challenges of tomorrow's workplace and the tremendous opportunities provided by a world that is increasingly rich in its demographic and cultural diversity.

This preface includes a number of features that provide you with handy guides for future success (such as the "Best Strategies for Success in School"). Additional features in the text include

◆ **The essential personal qualities.** Chapter 2 explores Emotional Intelligence and focuses on character first, stressing that good character, integrity, and ethics are the hallmarks of truly successful leaders in both business and the community.

◆ **Good habits.** Chapter 13 follows up on how to translate and support essential personal qualities with everyday habits. Included are the top 10 habits of a peak performer.

◆ **The ABCDE Method of Self-Management.** Introduced in Chapter 1, the ABCDE Method of Self-Management will help you manage your thoughts, feelings, and behavior, so that you create the results you want and achieve your goals. This five-step process (A = Actual event; B = Beliefs; C = Consequences; D = Dispute; E = Energized) helps you see the connection among your thoughts, feelings, and actions and empowers you to dispel negative thoughts and replace them with realistic and positive thoughts and behaviors.

◆ **Self-Management exercise.** As discussed in Chapter 1, self-management involves using many, many powerful tools you can use, such as self-assessment, critical thinking, visualization, affirmations, and reflection, to imagine your success and critically think through difficult situations. A scenario is presented at the beginning of every chapter that asks you to think about your own experiences. A worksheet is provided at the end of the chapter to record your thoughts and help you practice the ABCDE Method of Self-Management.

◆ **Success Principle.** Each chapter begins with a Success Principle that succinctly communicates the important lesson to be learned from the chapter. The Success Principles in total provide a unique and powerful guide to striving for success in school, career, and life.

- **Peak Performer Profile.** Each chapter presents a noted person in the area of business, education, the arts, or public service. These peak performers have overcome obstacles and challenges to become successful. You will see that having a positive attitude and perseverance is important for success. Each profile includes a new "Check It Out" section, with web sites related to the profiled individual or his or her profession or personal cause.
- **Words to Succeed.** Found throughout the text, these quotes provide you with insights, motiva-

tion, and food for thought and are tied to the chapter's content.
- **Performance Strategies.** Included in every chapter is a recap of the top 10 strategies for success in applying the chapter's concepts.

The Text at a Glance

Here are many of the features we just explored and where they can be found throughout the text.

At the Beginning

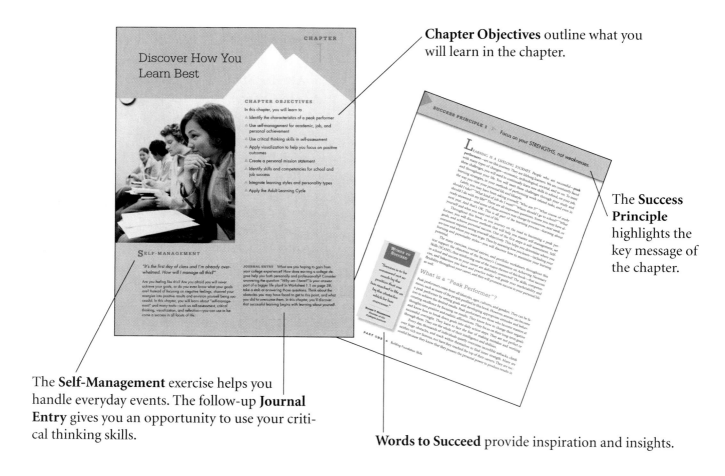

Chapter Objectives outline what you will learn in the chapter.

The **Success Principle** highlights the key message of the chapter.

The **Self-Management** exercise helps you handle everyday events. The follow-up **Journal Entry** gives you an opportunity to use your critical thinking skills.

Words to Succeed provide inspiration and insights.

Throughout the Chapter

The **Peak Progress** feature provides important strategies, lists, and further discussion of a key topic.

The **Personal Evaluation Notebook** provides opportunity for self-assessment and critical thinking.

The **Peak Performer Profile** highlights someone who has achieved success by overcoming the odds, setting goals, and being a peak performer.

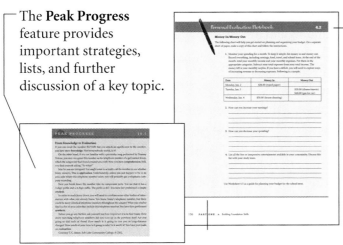

The **Career in Focus** feature shows that the strategies you are learning now are essential to your on-the-job success.

At the End of the Chapter

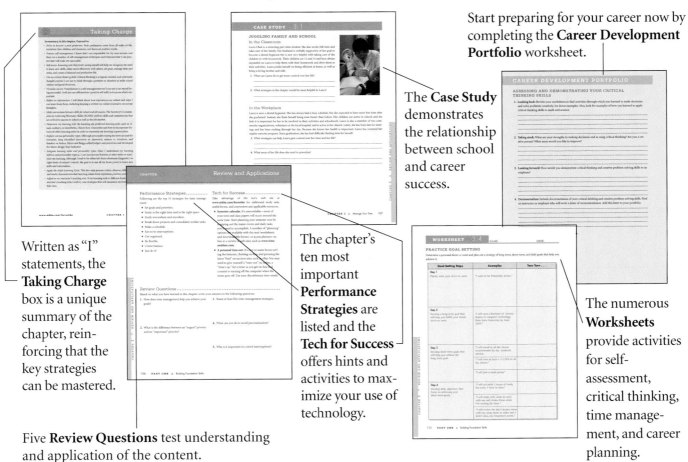

Written as "I" statements, the **Taking Charge** box is a unique summary of the chapter, reinforcing that the key strategies can be mastered.

Five **Review Questions** test understanding and application of the content.

The chapter's ten most important **Performance Strategies** are listed and the **Tech for Success** offers hints and activities to maximize your use of technology.

The **Case Study** demonstrates the relationship between school and career success.

Start preparing for your career now by completing the **Career Development Portfolio** worksheet.

The numerous **Worksheets** provide activities for self-assessment, critical thinking, time management, and career planning.

As You Get Started in Your New School: What You Need to Know and Should Not Be Afraid to Ask

Now that you have your book in hand, you are ready to get started. Or are you really ready? What else should you be aware of at this point? You may have already attended a basic orientation session, offered by most schools, which reviews campus and community resources and school requirements. Going through orientation, meeting with your advisor, and reviewing your catalog will help you get oriented. Additionally, the quick review provided in this text is designed to outline the essentials that you will want to know, so that you not only survive but also make your first year a success. **Peak Progress P.1** provides a handy checklist for the essential tasks you need to consider and accomplish the first week of school. Add to this list any tasks that are unique to your situation or school.

Why Are You Here?

College success begins with determining your goals and mapping out a plan. A good place to start is to have you reflect on why you are in college and what is expected of you. You will be more motivated if you clarify your interests and values concerning college. You will read in Chapter 2 the reasons students don't graduate from college, including poor study skills and habits and a lack of preparation, motivation, and effort. College is a commitment of many precious resources you can't afford to waste—time, money, and mental energies. Consider the following statements and your reasons for being in college and share this in your study group or with students whom you meet the first few weeks of class:

- ◆ I value education and want to be a well-educated person.
- ◆ I want to get a good job that leads to a well-paying career.

PEAK PROGRESS　　　　　　　　　　　　　　　P.1

Tasks to Accomplish the First Week of School

- Attend orientation and meet with an advisor. Ask questions and determine available resources. (See **Peak Progress P.2** for questions to ask.)
- Register and pay fees on time.
- Set up an e-mail account.
- Check deadlines and procedures. *Never* just quit going to class.
- Buy books and keep receipts. Establish a record-keeping system.
- Find out the location of classrooms, parking, and campus resources.
- Go to all classes on time and sit in the front row.
- Know expectations and requirements. Get a syllabus for each class. E-mail instructors for clarification.
- Create an organized study area. Post instructors' names, office locations, and hours, as well as important deadlines.
- Form study teams and exchange e-mails and phone numbers. Get to know instructors and other students.
- Explore resources, such as the library, learning skills center, health center, and advising center.

- I want to learn new ideas and skills and grow as a person.
- I want to get away from home and be independent.
- I want to make new friends.
- I want to have new experiences and stretch myself.
- I want to fulfill my goal of being a college-educated person.

Jot down what you want from college and why you're motivated to get it.

List four values that are most important to you and how college will help you achieve them.

1. Study Skill
2. Education
3. Mastering techniques
4. Learning skills.

What Should You Be Asking?

You don't want to learn the hard way that you need one more class to graduate, only to find it's offered only once a year (and you just missed it). Make your time with your advisor productive by getting answers to important questions that will help you map out your coursework. **Peak Progress P.2** provides a handy checklist of common questions to get you started.

What Do You Need to Do to Graduate?

You will be more motivated and confident if you understand graduation requirements. If you are a transfer student, requirements vary among schools. Don't rely on the advice of friends. Go to orientation and meet with your advisor early and often. Check out the catalog and make certain you know what is required to graduate. Fill in the following:

Graduation Requirements

- Number of units required:
- General education requirements:
- Curriculum requirements:
- Residency at the school:
- Departmental major requirements:
- Cumulative GPA required:
- Other requirements, such as special writing tests and classes:

How to Register for Classes

Find out if you have an access code and the earliest date you can register. Meet with your advisor, carefully select classes, and review general education and major requirements. Add electives that help keep you active and interested, such as an exercise or a weight-training class. Make certain that you understand why you are taking each class and double-check with your advisor that it is meeting certain requirements.

Many colleges have a purge date and, if you miss the deadline to pay your fees, your class schedule is canceled. You may not be able to get into classes and may have to pay a late fee.

Know the Grading System

Learn the minimum grade point average that you need to maintain good standing. If your GPA falls below 2.0, you may be placed on academic probation. The GPA is calculated according to the number of credit hours each course represents and your grade in the course. In the traditional system, $A = 4$ points, $B = 3$ points, $C = 2$ points, $D = 1$ point, and $F = 0$ points (your school may have a different system, so ask to be sure). To calculate your GPA, first determine your total number of points. Following is an example:

Course	Grade Achieved	Number of Credit Hours	Points
Political Science	C	2	$2 \times 2 = 4$
Psychology	B	3	$3 \times 3 = 9$
English	A	3	$4 \times 3 = 12$
Personal finance	A	1	$4 \times 1 = 4$
TOTAL		9	29

The Most Common Questions Students Ask Advisors

1. What classes do I need to take for general education?
2. Can a course satisfy both a general education and a major requirement?
3. Can I take general elective (GE) courses for Credit/No Credit if I also want to count them for my major?
4. How can I remove an *F* grade from my record?
5. What is the deadline for dropping courses?
6. Can I drop a course after the deadline?
7. What is an "educational leave"?
8. What is the difference between a withdrawal and a drop?
9. Do I need to take any placement tests?
10. Are there other graduation requirements, such as a writing exam?
11. Where do I find out about financial aid?
12. Is there a particular order in which I should take certain courses?
13. Are there courses in which I must earn a *C–* or better?
14. How do I change my major?
15. Which of my transfer courses will count?
16. What is the minimum residency requirement for a bachelor's degree?
17. Is there a GPA requirement for the major?
18. Is there a tutoring program available?
19. If I go on exchange, how do I make sure that courses I take at another university will apply toward my degree here?
20. What is a major contract and when should I get one?
21. When do I need to apply for graduation?
22. How do I apply for graduation?
23. What is a degree check?
24. What is the policy for incomplete grades?
25. Can I take major courses at another school and transfer them here?
26. As a nonresident, how can I establish residency in this state?
27. How do I petition to substitute a class?
28. Once I complete my major, are there other graduation requirements?
29. What is academic probation?
30. Is there any employment assistance available?
31. Is there a mentor program available in my major department?
32. Are there any internships or community service opportunities related to my major?

Then, to arrive at your GPA, you must divide your total points by your total number of credit hours:

GPA = Total points divided by total number of credit hours

Thus, in this example,

GPA = 29 divided by 9 = 3.22

Monitor your progress and meet with your instructors often, but especially at midterm and before final exams. Ask what you can do to improve your grade.

Adding or Dropping Classes

Make certain that you know the deadlines for adding and dropping classes. This is generally done in the first few weeks of classes. A withdrawal after the deadline could result in a failing grade. Also make certain before you drop the class that

◆ You will not fall below the required units for financial aid.

◆ You will not fall below the required units for playing sports.

◆ If required, the class is offered again before you plan to graduate.

◆ You don't need the class or units to meet graduation requirements.

◆ You are meeting important deadlines.

◆ You talk with the instructor first.

◆ You talk with your advisor.

If you choose to withdraw from all your classes, take an academic leave. Don't just walk away from your classes. Remember, it is your responsibility to drop or withdraw from a class. The instructor will not drop you, nor will you be dropped automatically if you stop going to class at any time during the semester. You must complete required forms.

An Incomplete Grade

If you miss class due to illness or an emergency, you may be able to take an incomplete if you can't finish a project or miss a test. Check out this option with your instructor before you drop a class. Make certain you have a written agreement to finish the work at a specific time

and that you stay in touch with the instructor through e-mail and phone.

Withdrawing or Taking a Leave of Absence

Some students withdraw because they don't have the money, they can't take time off from work, they lack child care, or they are having difficulty in classes. Before you drop out of college, talk with your advisor and see if you can get the support and motivation to succeed. If you want to take a leave to travel, want to explore other schools, are ill, or just need to take a break, make certain that you take a leave of absence for a semester, a year, or longer. Taking a leave means that you do not have to reapply for admission, and generally you fall under the same category as when you entered school.

Transferring

Before you transfer to another school, make certain you understand the requirements, which courses are transferable, and if there is a residency requirement. If you plan to transfer from a two-year school to a four-year school, your advisor will help you clarify the requirements.

Expectations of Instructors

Most instructors will hand out a syllabus that will outline their expectations for the class. Make certain you understand and clarify expectations and have a good understanding of the course requirements. **Worksheet P.1** on page 00 is a convenient guide to complete when checking your progress with your instructor.

The Best Strategies for Success in School

In this text, we will focus on a number of strategies that will help you determine and achieve your goals. **Peak Progress P.3** provides a comprehensive list of the proven strategies you will find woven throughout this text. Apply these to your efforts in school now and through your course of study. You will find that not only are they key to your progress in school, but also they will help you develop skills, behaviors, and habits that are directly related to success on the job and in life in general.

The Best Strategies for Success in School

1. **Attend every class.** Going to every class engages you with the subject, the instructor, and other students. Think of the tuition you are paying and what it costs to cut a class.

2. **Be an active participant.** Show that you are engaged and interested by being on time, sitting in front, participating, asking questions, and being alert.

3. **Go to class prepared.** Preview all reading assignments. Highlight key ideas and main concepts and put question marks next to anything you don't understand.

4. **Write a summary.** After you preview the chapter, close the book and write a short summary. Go back and fill in with more details. Do this after each reading.

5. **Know your instructors.** Choose the best instructors, call them by their preferred names and titles, e-mail them, and visit them during office hours. Arrive early for class and get to know them better.

6. **Know expectations.** Read the syllabus for each course and clarify the expectations and requirements, such as tests, papers, extra credit, and attendance.

7. **Join a study team.** You will learn more studying with others than reading alone. Make up tests, give summaries, and teach others.

8. **Organize your study space.** Create a quiet space, with a place for school documents, books, catalogs, a dictionary, a computer, notes, pens, and a calendar. Eliminate distractions by closing the door and focus on the task at hand.

9. **Map out your day, week, and semester.** Write down all assignments, upcoming tests, meetings, daily goals, and priorities on your calendar. Review your calendar and goals each day. Do not socialize until your top priorities are completed.

10. **Get help early.** Know and use all available campus resources. Go to the learning center, counseling center, and health center; get a tutor; and talk with your advisor and instructors about concerns. Get help at the first sign of trouble.

11. **Give school your best effort.** Commit yourself to being extra disciplined the first three weeks—buy your textbooks early; take them to class; get to class early; keep up on your reading; start your projects, papers, and speeches early; and make school a top priority.

12. **Use note cards.** Jot down formulas and keywords. Carry them with you and review them during waiting time and right before class.

13. **Review often.** Review and fill in notes immediately after class and again within 24 hours. Active reading, note taking, and reviewing are the steps that improve recall.

14. **Study everywhere.** Review your note cards before class, while you wait for class to begin, while waiting in line, before bed, and so on. Studying for short periods of time is more effective than cramming late at night.

15. **Summarize out loud.** Summarize chapters and class notes out loud to your study team. This is an excellent way to learn.

16. **Organize material.** You cannot remember information if it isn't organized. Logical notes help you understand and remember. Use a mind map for outlining key facts and supporting material.

17. **Dig out information.** Focus on main ideas, keywords, and overall understanding. Make questions out of chapter headings, review chapter questions, and always read summaries.

18. **Look for associations.** Improve memory by connecting patterns and by linking concepts and relationships. Define, describe, compare, classify, and contrast concepts.

19. **Ask questions.** What is the obvious? What needs to be determined? How can you illustrate the concept? What information is the same and what is different? How does the lecture relate to the textbook?

20. **Pretest yourself.** This will serve as practice and reduces anxiety. This is most effective in your study team.

21. **Study when you are most alert.** Know your energy level and learning preference. Maximize reviewing during daytime hours.

22. **Turn in all assignments on time.** Give yourself an extra few days to review papers and practice speeches.

23. **Make learning physical.** Read difficult textbooks out loud and standing up. Draw pictures, write on a chalkboard, and use visuals. Tape lectures and go on field trips. Integrate learning styles.

24. **Review first drafts with your instructor.** Ask for suggestions and follow them to the letter.

25. **Pay attention to neatness.** Focus on details and turn in all assignments on time. Use your study team to read and exchange term papers. Proofread several times.

26. **Practice!** Nothing beats effort. Practice speeches until you are comfortable and confident and visualize yourself being successful.

27. **Recite and explain.** Pretend that you are the instructor and recite main concepts. What questions would you put on a test? Give a summary to others in your study group. Make up sample test questions in your group.

28. **Take responsibility.** Don't make excuses about missing class or assignments or about earning failing grades. Be honest and take responsibility for your choices and mistakes and learn from them.

29. **Ask for feedback.** When you receive a grade, be reflective and ask questions: "What have I learned from this?" "How did I prepare for this?" "How could I improve this grade?" "Did I put in enough effort?" Based on what you learn, what new goals will you set for yourself?

30. **Negotiate for a better grade before grades are sent in.** Find out how you are doing at midterm and ask what you can do to raise your grade. Offer to do extra projects or retake tests.

31. **Always do extra credit.** Raise your grade by doing more than is required or *expected*. Immerse yourself in the subject and find meaning and understanding.

32. **Take responsibility for your education.** You can do well in a class even if your instructor is boring or insensitive. Ask yourself what you can do to make the class more effective (study team, tutoring, active participation). Be flexible and adapt to your instructor's teaching style.

33. **Develop positive qualities.** Think about the personal qualities that you need most to overcome obstacles and work on developing them each day.

34. **Stay healthy.** You cannot do well in school or in life if you are ill. Invest time in exercising, eating healthy, and getting enough sleep and avoid alcohol, cigarettes, and drugs.

35. **Dispute negative thinking.** Replace it with positive, realistic, helpful self-talk and focus on your successes. Don't be a perfectionist. Reward yourself when you make small steps toward achieving goals.

36. **Organize your life.** Hang up your keys in the same place, file important material, and establish routines that make your life less stressful.

37. **Break down projects.** Overcome procrastination by breaking overwhelming projects into manageable chunks. Choose a topic, do a rough draft, write a summary, preview a chapter, do a mind map, and organize the tools you need (notes, books, outline).

38. **Make school your top priority.** Working too many hours can cut into study time. Learn to balance school, your social life, and work, so that you're effective.

39. **Meet with your advisor to review goals and progress.** Ask questions about requirements, and don't drop and add classes without checking on the consequences. Develop a good relationship with your advisor and your instructors.

40. **Be persistent.** Whenever you get discouraged, just keep following positive habits and strategies and you will succeed. Success comes in small, consistent steps. Be patient and keep plugging away.

41. **Spend less than you make.** Don't go into debt for new clothes, a car, CDs, gifts, travel, or other things you can do without. Education is the best investment in future happiness and job success that you can make. Learn to save.

42. **Use critical thinking and think about the consequences of your decisions.** Don't be impulsive about money, sex, smoking, or drugs. Don't start a family until you are emotionally and financially secure. Practice impulse control by imagining how you would feel after making certain choices.

43. **Don't get addicted.** Addictions are a tragic waste of time. Ask yourself if you've ever known anyone whose life was better for being addicted. Do you know anyone whose life has been destroyed by alcohol and other drugs? This one decision will affect your life forever.

44. **Know who you are and what you want.** Visit the career center and talk with a career counselor about your interests, values, goals, strengths, personality, learning style, and career possibilities. Respect your style and set up conditions that create results.

45. **Use creative problem solving.** Think about what went right and what went wrong this semester. What could you have done that would have helped you be more successful? What are new goals you want to set for next semester? What are some creative ways to overcome obstacles? How can you solve problems instead of letting them persist?

46. **Contribute.** Look for opportunities to contribute your time and talents. What could you do outside of class that would complement your education and serve others?

47. **Take advantage of your texts' resources.** Many textbooks have accompanying web sites, CDs, and study materials designed to help you succeed in class. Visit this book's web site at www.mhhe.com/ferrett6e.

48. **Respect yourself and others.** Be supportive, tolerant, and respectful of people who are different from you. Look for ways to learn about other cultures and different views; and to expand your friendships. *Respect yourself.* Surround yourself with people who are positive and successful, who value learning, and who are sup- portive and respectful of you and your goals.

49. **Focus on gratitude.** Look at the abundance in your life—your health, family, friends, and opportunities. You have so much going for you to help you succeed.

50. **Just do it.** Newton's first law of motion says that things in motion tend to stay in motion, so get started and keep working on your goals!

PROGRESS ASSESSMENT

Course: _____

Instructor: _____

Office: _____   Office hours: _____

Phone: _____   E-mail: _____

1. How am I doing in this class?

_____

_____

_____

2. What grades have you recorded for me thus far?

_____

_____

_____

3. Are there any adjustments that I should make?

_____

_____

_____

4. Am I missing any assignments?

_____

_____

_____

5. Do you have any suggestions as to how I can improve my performance or excel in your class?

_____

_____

_____

Discover How You Learn Best

CHAPTER OBJECTIVES

In this chapter, you will learn to

▲ Identify the characteristics of a peak performer

▲ Use self-management for academic, job, and personal achievement

▲ Use critical thinking skills in self-assessment

▲ Apply visualization to help you focus on positive outcomes

▲ Create a personal mission statement

▲ Identify skills and competencies for school and job success

▲ Integrate learning styles and personality types

▲ Apply the Adult Learning Cycle

SELF-MANAGEMENT

"It's the first day of class and I'm already overwhelmed. How will I manage all this?"

Are you feeling like this? Are you afraid you will never achieve your goals, or do you even know what your goals are? Instead of focusing on negative feelings, channel your energies into positive results and envision yourself being successful. In this chapter, you will learn about "self-management" and many tools—such as self-assessment, critical thinking, visualization, and reflection—you can use to become a success in all facets of life.

JOURNAL ENTRY What are you hoping to gain from your college experience? How does earning a college degree help you both personally and professionally? Consider answering the question *"Why am I here?"* Is your answer part of a bigger life plan? In Worksheet 1.1 on page 38, take a stab at answering those questions. Think about the obstacles you may have faced to get to this point, and what you did to overcome them. In this chapter, you'll discover that successful learning begins with learning about yourself.

LEARNING IS A LIFELONG JOURNEY. People who are successful—**peak performers**—are on this journey. They are lifelong learners. We are constantly faced with many types of changes—economic, technological, societal, and so on. To meet these challenges, you will need to continually learn new skills in school, on your job, and throughout your life. You will meet these challenges through your study and learning strategies, in your methods of performing work-related tasks, and even in the way you view your personal life and lifestyle.

Lately, you may have been asking yourself, "Who am I?" "What course of study should I take?" "What kind of job do I want?" "Where should I go to school?" "What should I do with my life?" These are all important questions. Some you may have already answered—and some of those answers may change by tomorrow, next week, or next year. And that's OK. This is all part of the learning process—learning about yourself and what you want out of life.

Throughout this book, as you journey on the road to becoming a peak performer, you will discover methods that will help you master self-management, set goals, and achieve personal success. One of the first steps is self-assessment. Self-assessment requires seeing yourself objectively. This helps you determine where you are now and where you want to go. Then by assessing how you learn—including your learning and personality styles—you will discover how to maximize your learning potential.

The many exercises, journal entries, and portfolio worksheets throughout this text support the objectives of the Secretary's Commission on Achieving Necessary Skills (SCANS), thus reinforcing one of the major themes of this book—that success in school and success in your career are definitely connected! The skills, competencies, and behaviors you learn and practice today will guide your marketability and flexibility throughout your career, and they will promote success in your personal life as well.

What is a "Peak Performer"?

Peak performers come from all lifestyles, ages, cultures, and genders. They can be famous, such as many of the people profiled in this book. However, anyone can become a peak performer by setting goals and developing appropriate attitudes and behaviors to achieve the desired results. Peak performers are those who become masters at creating excellence by focusing on results. They know how to change their negative thoughts into positive and realistic affirmations. They focus on their long-term goals and know how to break down goals into daily action steps. They are not perfect or successful overnight. They learn to face the fear of making mistakes and working through them. They use the whole of their intelligence and abilities.

Every day, thousands of individuals quietly overcome incredible setbacks, climb over huge obstacles, and reach within themselves to find inner strength. Many are neither rich nor famous, nor have they reached the top of their careers. They are successful because they know that they possess the personal power to produce results in

WORDS TO SUCCEED

"Success is to be measured not so much by the position that one has reached in life as by the obstacles which he has overcome."

BOOKER T. WASHINGTON,
Founder of the Tuskegee Institute

their lives and find passion in what they contribute to life. They are masters, not victims, of life's situations. They control the quality of their lives. In short, they are their own best friend.

Peak performers

- Apply self-management in all areas of their lives
- Know their learning styles and preferences and how to maximize their learning
- Take risks and move beyond secure comfort zones
- Use critical thinking to solve problems creatively
- Make sound judgments and decisions
- Are effective at time and self-management
- Take responsibility for their actions, behaviors, and decisions
- Involve themselves in supportive relationships
- Continually acquire new skills and competencies
- Remain confident and resilient
- Are motivated to overcome barriers
- Take small, consistent steps that lead to long-term goals

Self-Management: The Key to Reaching Your Peak

What is a primary strength of every peak performer? A positive attitude! First and foremost, peak performers have a positive attitude toward their studies, their work, and virtually everything they do in their lives. This fundamental inclination to view life optimistically as a series of opportunities is a key to their success. Having a positive attitude involves more than positive thinking. It also involves clear and critical thinking. The good news is that anyone can develop the attitude of a peak performer, and it is not even difficult. It simply involves a restructuring of thought patterns. For example, instead of dwelling on problems, you can embrace challenges. Challenge drives the human spirit. Redirecting your thought patterns in this way will not only give you more drive, but it will also make every task you approach seem more meaningful and less daunting.

A positive attitude is one of the many components of self-management. Are you responsible for your own success? Do you believe you can control your own destiny? Think of self-management as a toolkit filled with many techniques and skills you can utilize to keep you focused, overcome obstacles, and help you succeed. Along with a positive attitude (which we will discuss further in Chapter 2), some very important techniques in this toolkit that we will begin to explore in this chapter are *self-assessment, critical thinking, visualization,* and *reflection.*

Self-Assessment

One of the first steps in becoming a peak performer is self-assessment. Out of self-assessment comes recognition of the need to learn new tasks and subjects, relate more effectively with others, set goals, manage time and stress, and create a balanced and productive life. Self-assessment requires facing the truth and seeing yourself objectively. For example, it is not easy to admit that you procrastinate or lack certain skills. Even when talking about your strengths, you may feel embarrassed. However, honest self-assessment is the foundation for making positive changes in your life. Self-assessment can help you

◆ Understand how you learn best
◆ Work with your strengths and natural preferences
◆ Learn to balance and integrate your preferred learning style with other styles
◆ Learn to use critical thinking and reasoning
◆ Make sound and creative decisions about school and work
◆ Learn to change ineffective patterns of thinking and behaving
◆ Create a positive and motivated state of mind
◆ Work more effectively with diverse groups of people
◆ Learn how to handle stress and conflict
◆ Achieve better grades
◆ Determine and capitalize on your strengths
◆ Recognize irrational and negative thoughts and behavior
◆ Most important, focus on self-management and develop strategies that maximize your energies and resources. The world is full of people who believe that, if only the other person would change, everything would be fine. This book is not for them. Change is possible if you take responsibility for your thoughts and behaviors and are willing to practice new ways of thinking and behaving.

WORDS TO SUCCEED

"Who looks outside, dreams; who looks inside, awakes."

CARL JUNG, *Psychologist*

Self-assessment is very important for job success. Self-assessment and feedback are tools for self-discovery and positive change. Keep a portfolio of your awards, letters of appreciation, training program certificates, and projects you have completed. Assess your expectations with the results achieved and set goals for improvement. At the end of each chapter in this text, you will find a Career Development Portfolio worksheet, which will help you begin to relate current activities to future job success. This portfolio will furnish you with a lifelong assessment tool for learning where you are and where you want to go and with a place for documenting the results. This portfolio of skills and competencies will become your guide for remaining marketable and flexible throughout your career. Chapter 14 further explores how to develop an effective portfolio and how to prepare for your future career.

Critical Thinking Skills

Throughout this book, you will be asked to apply critical thinking skills to help you with college courses and life situations. Self-management involves using your critical thinking skills to make the best choices and decisions and to solve problems. What exactly is critical thinking? Critical thinking is a logical, rational, systematic thought process that is necessary in understanding, analyzing, and evaluating information in order to solve a problem or situation. Since critical thinking determines the quality of the decisions that you make in all areas of your life, it is an important theme throughout this book. Self-management exercises will help you dispute irrational thoughts and fears and overcome self-destructive behavior. Chapter 9 in this text is entirely devoted to honing your critical thinking skills and practicing creative problem solving. However, it's obvious that you need to use critical thinking every day—from analyzing and determining your learning styles to communicating effectively with family members, classmates, or co-workers.

To help you fine-tune your critical thinking skills, make a habit of assessing your thinking skills regularly. Use the following guidelines in your journey to becoming a more critical thinker:

◆ Suspend judgment until you have gathered facts and reflected on them.
◆ Look for evidence that supports or contradicts your initial assumptions, opinions, and beliefs.
◆ Adjust your opinions as new information and facts are known.
◆ Ask questions, look for proof, and examine the problem closely.
◆ Reject incorrect or irrelevant information.
◆ Consider the source of the information.
◆ Recognize and dispute irrational thinking.

Make sure to complete the exercises and activities throughout this book, including the **Personal Evaluation Notebook** exercises and the end-of-chapter **Worksheets**. You will also enhance your critical thinking skills by practicing visualization and reflection.

Visualization and Affirmations

Visualization and affirmations are powerful self-management tools that help you focus on positive action and outcomes. **Visualization** is using your imagination to see your goals clearly and to envision yourself successfully engaging in new, positive behavior. **Affirmations** are the positive self-talk—the internal dialogue—you carry on with yourself. Affirmations counter self-defeating patterns of thought with more positive, hopeful, and realistic thoughts.

Using visualization and affirmations can help you relax, boost your confidence, change your habits, and perform better on exams, in speeches, or in sports. They can be used to rehearse for an upcoming event, and you can practice coping with obstacles. Visualization and affirmations are even part of the curriculum at the U.S. Olympic training campus.

Through self-management, you demonstrate that you are not a victim or passive spectator; you are responsible for your self-talk, images, thoughts, and behaviors. When you observe and dispute negative thoughts and replace them with positive, appropriate, and realistic thoughts, images, and behaviors, you are practicing your critical thinking and creativity skills. You are taking charge of your life, focusing on what you can change, and working toward your goals.

You can practice visualization anytime and anywhere throughout the day. For example, between classes, find a quiet place and close your eyes. It helps to use relaxation techniques, such as taking several deep breaths and seeing yourself calm, centered, and focused on your goals. This is especially effective when your mind starts to chatter and you feel overwhelmed, discouraged, or stressed. Visualize yourself graduating and walking across the stage to receive your diploma. See yourself achieving your goals. Say to yourself, "I am calm and centered. I am taking action to meet my goals. I will use all available resources to be successful."

Reflection

Reflection is an important self-management tool, whether you consider yourself a reflective person or not. To reflect is to think about something in a purposeful way with the intention of creating new meaning. Sometimes the process causes us to reconsider our previous knowledge and to explore new alternatives and ideas.

Don't confuse reflection with daydreaming—the two have little in common. Reflection is a conscious, focused, purposeful activity; it is not simply letting your mind wander. When you reflect, you direct your thoughts and use imagination. Think of your mind as an ultra-powerful relational database. To reflect upon a new experience is to search through this vast mental database in an effort to discover—or create—relationships between experiences: new and old, new and new, old and old. Reflection, then, is the process of reorganizing countless experiences stored in your mental database. As you do so, your mind's database becomes more complex, more sophisticated, and ultimately more useful. This ongoing reorganization is a key component of your intellectual development; it integrates critical thinking, creative problem solving, and visualization.

A convenient way to reflect is to simply write your thoughts down. Carry a notepad or journal with the main intent of writing down your thoughts. Or keep your thoughts on your computer. In this text is ample opportunity to practice reflection and critical thinking, including a Journal Entry exercise at the beginning of each chapter, with a follow-up Worksheet at the end of each chapter.

Throughout the text, we'll explore additional self-management techniques that focus on certain aspects of your schoolwork, employment, or personal life. See which techniques work best for you. **Peak Progress 1.1** explores the ABCDE Method of Self-Management, a unique process to help you work through difficult situations and achieve positive results. It utilizes skills such as critical thinking, visualization, and reflection to find positive outcomes.

WORDS TO SUCCEED

"It's not the load that breaks you down, it's the way you carry it."

Lou Holtz, *College Basketball Coach*

PEAK PROGRESS   1.1

The ABCDE Method of Self-Management

You may have noticed that your mood affects how your day will go. By using visualization, disputing negative thoughts, and incorporating affirmations, you become aware of patterns of thoughts that may be keeping you from achieving your goals. Clear thinking leads to positive emotions. Let's say you have to give a speech in a class and speaking in public has caused you a lot of anxiety in the past. You might be saying to yourself, "I have failed at speaking before and I find it terrifying. I feel awful. I will always fail at speaking." These negative beliefs and irrational thoughts can cause severe anxiety and are not based on clear thinking. You can direct your thoughts with positive statements that will dispel anxiety: "Public speaking is a skill that can be learned with practice and effort. I will not crumble from criticism and, even if I don't do well, I can learn from constructive feedback."

Self-management can be as easy as ABC (and D and E). These five simple steps help you manage your thoughts, feelings, and behaviors, so that you can create the results you want.

The ABCDE Method of Self-Management (continued)

A = Actual event: State the actual situation, goal, or objective.

B = Beliefs: Describe your thoughts and beliefs about the situation.

C = Consequences: Indicate the consequences of your feelings and behaviors.

D = Dispute: Challenge any negative thoughts by countering with accurate and positive statements.

E = Energized: Become focused and energized by using visualization and affirmations and looking for creative alternatives, resources, and positive actions that you can take.

Let's use another example. When you read the quote on page 2 of this chapter, you may have felt the same way—overwhelmed. You are in a new situation with many new expectations—of you and by you. Let's apply the ABCDE method to focus your energies on developing a positive outcome. For example, you might say,

A = Actual event: "It is only the first week and I already have an overload of information from this class."

B = Beliefs: "Maybe this was a bad idea. What if I fail? What if I can't keep it all straight—learning styles, personalities, temperaments? These other people are probably a lot smarter than me."

C = Consequences: "I'm feeling overwhelmed and depressed. I'm panicking and totally stressed out. I'm going to drop out."

D = Dispute: "Stop these negative thoughts! Going to college is a big change, but I have handled new and stressful situations before. I know how to overcome feeling overwhelmed by breaking big jobs into small tasks. Everyone tells me I'm hardworking, and I know I'm talented and smart in many different ways. I know that going to college is a very good idea and I want to graduate. I've handled transitions in the past and I can handle these changes too."

E = Energized: "I'm excited about discovering my learning and personality styles and how I can use them to my advantage. There are so many resources available to me—my instructor, my classmates, the book's web site, and so on. I will get to know at least one person in each of my classes, and I will take a few minutes to explore at least one resource at school that can provide support. I see myself confident and energized and achieving my goals."

In the end-of-chapter Worksheets throughout this text, you will find opportunities to practice the ABCDE Method of Self-Management, as well as the Self-Management exercises at **www.mhhe.com/ferrett6e**.

Draft a Personal Mission Statement

At the beginning of the chapter, you were asked to write about why you're in school and how it relates to your life plan. In the Preface to the Student, you also explored many reasons you are attending college, such as to learn new skills, to get a well-paying job, to make new friends, and so on. (If you haven't read the Preface to the Student, now is the perfect time to review that section.) Thinking about the answers to these and related questions gets you started on creating and writing your **mission statement.**

A mission statement looks at the "big picture" of your life, from which your goals and priorities will flow. This written statement (which can be one sentence or a number of sentences) focuses on the contributions you want to make based on your values, philosophy, and principles. When you have a sense of purpose and direction, you will be more focused and your life will have more meaning.

In one sense, what you are doing is looking at the end result of your life. What kind of a person do you want to be when you're 95? What legacy do you want to leave? What do you want to be remembered for as a person? What do you think will be most important to you?

Here is one example of a mission statement: "I commit to developing my full potential in writing, speaking, and communicating respectfully with others. My focus is to develop programs to help people succeed at school, at work, and in their personal lives. I seek to balance career and family and to integrate body, mind, and spirit for total wellness. I want my life to be a seamless expression of love and service."

You will want your mission statement to reflect your unique individuality. You may want to think about how a college education will help you fulfill your mission in life. Focusing on your mission statement will help you overcome obstacles that will inevitably challenge you.

To write your mission statement, begin by answering these (or similar) questions:

1. What do I value most in life? (List those things.)

   To have stable and happy life

2. What is my life's purpose?

   To be Successful.

3. What legacy do I want to leave?

   Hard worker and warm person.

   Now, considering the answers to those questions, draft a personal mission statement.

   My mission statement: *I am seeking a life of hard work now and ease later. I want a education to prepare for life's hurdles.*

In Chapter 2, we will discuss how you can use your personal goals to motivate you. In Chapter 3, we will then explore how your mission statement and personal goals will guide you to use your time effectively. You will also be asked to review your mission statement at the end of this text. Over the years, you will want to review and update your mission statement as you change and grow personally and professionally.

Skills for School and Job Success

Have you ever asked yourself, "What does it take to be successful in a job?" Many of the skills and competencies that characterize a successful student can also apply to the successful employee. Becoming aware of the connection between school success and job success helps you see how the skills learned in the classroom will eventually apply to the skills needed in the workplace.

Over the years, employers have told educators what skills they want employees to have. In 1990, Elizabeth Dole, who was then the Secretary of Labor, created the Secretary's Commission on Achieving Necessary Skills (SCANS). The commission members included business and industry leaders, human resource personnel, and other top advisors in labor and education. The Peak Performance Competency Wheel in **Figure 1.1** illustrates the skills and competencies recommended by SCANS for job success. These skills and competencies are necessary not only for job success but also for school success. You can apply and practice them now by completing the Peak Performance Self-Assessment Test in **Personal Evaluation Notebook 1.1** on page 10. Be honest and use critical thinking skills as you complete the test.

Discover Your Learning Style

As a lifelong learner, you need to know *how* to learn to maximize your learning potential. Everyone processes information differently and not everyone learns the same way. There is no single right way to learn, but knowing your preferred learning style

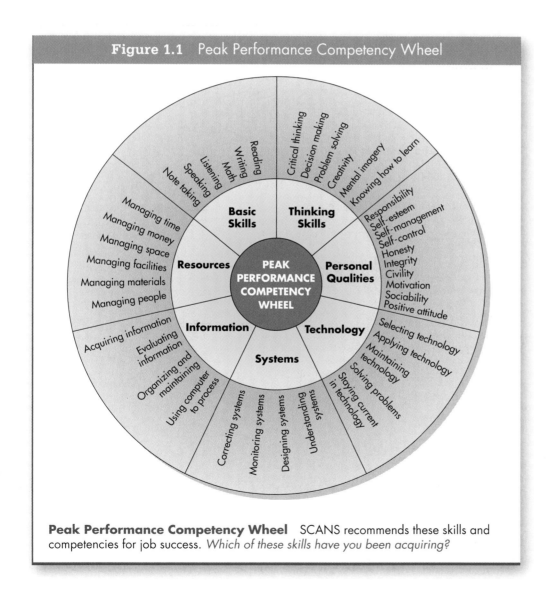

Figure 1.1 Peak Performance Competency Wheel

Peak Performance Competency Wheel SCANS recommends these skills and competencies for job success. *Which of these skills have you been acquiring?*

Peak Performance Self-Assessment Test

Assess your skills on a scale of 1 to 5 by placing a check mark. Then review your answers to discover your strongest skills and weakest skills.

Area	Good 5	4	OK 3	2	Poor 1
1. Reading	____	____	____	____	____
2. Writing	____	____	____	____	____
3. Speaking	____	____	____	____	____
4. Mathematics	____	____	____	____	____
5. Listening and note taking	____	____	____	____	____
6. Critical thinking and reasoning	____	____	____	____	____
7. Creative problem solving	____	____	____	____	____
8. Positive visualization	____	____	____	____	____
9. Knowing how you learn	____	____	____	____	____
10. Honesty and integrity	____	____	____	____	____
11. Positive attitude and motivation	____	____	____	____	____
12. Responsibility	____	____	____	____	____
13. Flexibility/ability to adapt to change	____	____	____	____	____
14. Self-management and emotional control	____	____	____	____	____
15. Self-esteem and confidence	____	____	____	____	____
16. Time management	____	____	____	____	____
17. Money management	____	____	____	____	____
18. Management and leadership of people	____	____	____	____	____
19. Interpersonal and communication skills	____	____	____	____	____
20. Ability to work well with culturally diverse groups	____	____	____	____	____
21. Organization and evaluation of information	____	____	____	____	____
22. Understanding technology	____	____	____	____	____
23. Commitment and effort	____	____	____	____	____

can increase your effectiveness in school or at work and can enhance your self-esteem. Knowing how you learn best can help you reduce frustration, focus on your strengths, and help you integrate various styles.

Integrate Both Sides of the Brain

Do you use both sides of your brain? "I use my whole brain!" you might answer—and indeed you do. However, you may have a preference for using the left or right side of the brain for many mental and physical functions. In the 1960s, Dr. Roger Sperry and his colleagues discovered that the left and right sides of the brain specialize in different modes of thinking and perception. Dominant brain function may play a significant role in how you learn.

Studies show that the brain has two systems by which it classifies information. One is linguistic and factual (left brain), and one is visual and intuitive (right brain). Although they are interconnected, one is usually more dominant. For example, if you are left-brain dominant, you probably like facts and order and think in a concrete manner. You use a logical, rational, and detailed thought process. If you are right-brain dominant, you are more inclined to use an intuitive and insightful approach to solving problems and processing new information. You are more comfortable with feelings and hunches and like to think abstractly and intuitively. **Figure 1.2** lists a number of traits that are considered either left-brain or right-brain dominant.

Figure 1.2   Left-Brain Versus Right-Brain Traits

Left-Brain Dominant	Right-Brain Dominant
Feels more comfortable with facts	Feels more comfortable with feelings
Thinks rationally based on reason and logic	Thinks intuitively based on hunches and feelings
Uses concrete thinking	Uses abstract thinking
Likes a sense of order	Likes a sense of space
Uses linear, step-by-step thinking	Uses holistic, visual thinking
Uses speech and words	Uses pictures and drawings
Is more "cerebral"	Is more "physical"
Makes lists and notes	Uses visuals and colors
Is concerned about time	Lives in the moment
Analyzes parts of the whole	Looks at the whole for patterns
Likes traditional outlines	Likes mind maps or creative outlines
Likes well-organized lectures	Likes group work and open-ended class discussion

Left-Brain Versus Right-Brain Traits   Put a check mark next to the descriptions that apply to you. *Would you consider yourself more of a left-brain dominant person, or a right-brain dominant person?*

Although you may find that you favor one side of your brain, definitely the key is to use all your brain power and integrate a variety of learning styles (which you will explore next). By doing this, you enhance learning, memory, and recall.

Are You a Reader, a Listener, or a Doer?

Your brain allows you to experience the world through your many senses. One way to explore how you learn best is to ask yourself if you are a reader, a listener, or a doer. Do you get more information from reading and seeing, talking and listening, or doing? Of course, you do all these things, but your learning strength or preferred style may be in one of these areas. For example, you may organize information visually favoring right-brain activities. Although such classifications may oversimplify complex brain activity and are not meant to put you in a box or category, the goal is to help you be more aware of your natural tendencies and habits and how you can use these preferences and learn new ways to enhance your success.

A person who learns better by reading possesses a visual learning style. Someone who learns better by listening is considered an auditory learner. A kinesthetic learner learns by touch and physical activity. The **Personal Evaluation Notebook 1.2** starting on page 13 has a Learning Style Inventory that will help you discover your learning style.

Visual Learners

Visual learners prefer to see information and read material. They learn more effectively with pictures, graphs, illustrations, diagrams, time lines, photos, pie charts, and visual design. They like to contemplate concepts, reflect, and summarize information in writing. They might use arrows, pictures, and bullets to highlight points. Visual learners are often holistic in that they see pictures in their mind that create feelings and emotion. They often use visual descriptions in their speech, such as "It is clear . . . ," "Picture this . . . ," or "See what I mean?" Visual learners tend to

- Be right-brain dominant
- Remember what they see better than what they hear
- Like to see charts and pictures
- Try to sit close to the instructor
- Prefer to have written directions they can read
- Learn better when someone shows them rather than tells them
- Like to read, highlight, and take notes
- Keep a list of things to do when planning the week
- Be fast thinkers and gesture frequently while talking
- Communicate clearly and concisely and watch facial expressions
- Like to read for pleasure and to learn

Visual learners may enjoy being an interior designer, a drafter, a proofreader, a writer, or an artist.

Auditory Learners

Auditory learners prefer to rely on their hearing sense. They like tapes and music, and they prefer to listen to information, such as lectures. They like to talk, recite, and summarize information aloud. Auditory learners may create rhymes out of words

Learning Style Inventory

Name _____Anne Jeter_____ Date __8/1/08__

Determine your learning preference. Complete each sentence by checking a, b, or c. No answer is correct or better than another.

1. I learn best when I
   - _____ **a.** see information.
   - __✓__ **b.** hear information.
   - _____ **c.** have hands-on experience.

2. I like
   - __✓__ **a.** pictures and illustrations.
   - _____ **b.** listening to tapes and stories.
   - _____ **c.** working with people and going on field trips.

3. For pleasure and relaxation, I love to
   - __✓__ **a.** read.
   - _____ **b.** listen to music and tapes.
   - _____ **c.** garden or play sports.

4. I tend to be
   - __✓__ **a.** contemplative.
   - _____ **b.** talkative.
   - _____ **c.** a doer.

5. To remember a ZIP code, I like to
   - _____ **a.** write it down several times.
   - __✓__ **b.** say it out loud several times.
   - _____ **c.** doodle and draw it on any available paper.

6. In a classroom, I learn best when
   - __✓__ **a.** I have a good textbook, visual aids, and written information.
   - _____ **b.** the instructor is interesting and clear.
   - _____ **c.** I am involved in doing activities.

7. When I study for a test, I
   - __✓__ **a.** read my notes and write a summary.
   - _____ **b.** review my notes aloud and talk to others.
   - _____ **c.** like to study in a group and use models and charts.

8. I have
   - __✓__ **a.** a strong fashion sense and pay attention to visual details.
   - _____ **b.** fun telling stories and jokes.
   - _____ **c.** a great time building things and being active.

(continued)

Learning Style Inventory–continued

9. I plan the upcoming week by
   _____ **a.** making a list and keeping a detailed calendar.
   __✓__ **b.** talking it through with someone.
   _____ **c.** creating a computer calendar or using a project board.

10. When preparing for a math test, I like to
   _____ **a.** write formulas on note cards or use pictures.
   __✓__ **b.** memorize formulas or talk aloud.
   _____ **c.** use marbles, LEGO® blocks, or three-dimensional models.

11. I often
   __✓__ **a.** remember faces but not names.
   _____ **b.** remember names but not faces.
   _____ **c.** remember events but not names or faces.

12. I remember best
   __✓__ **a.** when I read instructions and use visual images to remember.
   _____ **b.** when I listen to instructions and use rhyming words to remember.
   _____ **c.** with hands-on activities and trial and error.

13. When I give directions, I might say,
   _____ **a.** "Turn right at the yellow house and left when you see the large oak tree. Do you see what I mean?"
   __✓__ **b.** "Turn right. Go three blocks. Turn left onto Buttermilk Lane. OK? Got that? Do you hear what I'm saying?"
   _____ **c.** "Follow me," after giving directions by using gestures.

14. When driving in a new city, I prefer to
   __✓__ **a.** get a map and find my own way.
   _____ **b.** stop and get directions from someone.
   _____ **c.** drive around and figure it out by myself.

Score: Count the number of check marks for all your choices.

Total a choices ____ (visual learning style)

Total b choices ____ (auditory learning style)

Total c choices ____ (kinesthetic learning style)

The highest total indicates your dominant learning style. You may find that you are a combination and that's good. It means you are integrating styles already.

and play music that helps them concentrate. When they take study breaks, they listen to music or chat with a friend. They are usually good listeners but are easily distracted by noise. They often use auditory descriptions when communicating such as "This rings true . . . ," "It's clear as a bell . . . ," or "Do you hear what you're saying?" Auditory learners tend to

- Be left-brain dominant
- Remember what they hear better than what they see
- Prefer to listen to instructions
- Like lectures organized in a logical sequence
- Like to listen to music and talk on the telephone
- Plan the week by talking it through with someone
- Use rhyming words to remember
- Learn best when they hear an assignment as well as see it

Auditory learners may enjoy being a disc jockey, trial lawyer, counselor, or musician.

Kinesthetic Learners

Kinesthetic learners are usually well coordinated, like to touch things, and learn best by doing. They like to collect samples, write out information, spend time outdoors, and relate to the material they are learning. They like to connect abstract material to something concrete. They are good at hands-on tasks. They often use phrases such as "I am getting a handle on . . . ," "I have a gut feeling that . . . ," and "I get a sense that . . ." Kinesthetic learners tend to

- Be right-brain dominant
- Create an experience
- Use hands-on activities
- Build things and put things together
- Use models and physical activity
- Write down information
- Apply information to real-life situations
- Draw, doodle, use games and puzzles, and play computer games
- Take field trips and collect samples
- Relate abstract information to something concrete

Kinesthetic learners may enjoy being a chef, a surgeon, a medical technician, a nurse, an automobile mechanic, an electrician, an engineer, a forest ranger, a police officer, or a dancer.

Redefining Intelligence: Other Learning Styles

Because each of us has our own unique set of abilities, perceptions, needs, and ways of processing information, learning styles vary widely. Besides visual, auditory, and

Know How You Learn
Everyone has his or her own way of learning. *What type of learning style do you think best suits this person?*

kinesthetic learning styles, there are other, more specific styles, and some people have more than one learning style.

Plus, intelligence has been redefined. We used to think of intelligence as measured by an IQ test. Many schools measure and reward linguistic and logical-mathematical modes of intelligence; however, Thomas Armstrong, author of *7 Kinds of Smart: Identifying and Developing Your Many Intelligences*, and Howard Gardner, who wrote *Frames of Mind: The Theory of Multiple Intelligences*, illustrated that we all possess many different intelligences. (See **Personal Evaluation Notebook 1.3**, which includes a number of traits associated with each "intelligence.")

1. **Verbal/linguistic.** Some people are **word smart.** They have verbal/linguistic intelligence and like to read, talk, and write about information. They have the ability to argue, persuade, entertain, and teach with words. Many become journalists, writers, or lawyers. **To learn best:** talk, read, or write about it.

2. **Logical/mathematical.** Some people are **logic smart.** They have logical/mathematical intelligence and like numbers, puzzles, and logic. They have the ability to reason, solve problems, create hypotheses, think in terms of cause and effect, and explore patterns and relationships. Many become scientists, accountants, or computer programmers. **To learn best:** conceptualize, quantify, or think critically about it.

3. **Spatial.** Some people are **picture smart.** They have spatial intelligence and like to draw, sketch, and visualize information. They have the ability to perceive in three-dimensional space and re-create various aspects of the visual world. Many become architects, photographers, artists, or engineers. **To learn best:** draw, sketch, or visualize it.

4. **Musical.** Some people are **music smart.** They have rhythm and melody intelligence. They have the ability to appreciate, perceive, and produce rhythms and to keep time to music. Many become composers, singers, or instrumentalists. **To learn best:** sing, chant, rap, or play music.

5. **Bodily/kinesthetic.** Some people are **body smart.** They have physical and kinesthetic intelligence. They have the ability to understand and control their bodies; they have tactile sensitivity, like movement, and handle objects skillfully. Many become dancers, physical education teachers or coaches, or carpenters and enjoy outdoor activities and sports. **To learn best:** build a model, dance, use note cards, and do hands-on activities.

6. **Environmental.** Some people are **outdoor smart.** They have environmental intelligence. They are good at measuring, charting, and observing plants and animals. They like to keep journals, to collect and classify, and to participate in outdoor activities. Many become park and forest rangers, surveyors, gardeners, landscape architects, outdoor guides, wildlife experts, or environmentalists. **To learn best:** go on field trips, collect samples, go for walks, and apply what you are learning to real life.

7. **Intrapersonal.** Some people are **self-smart.** They have intrapersonal and inner intelligence. They have the ability to be contemplative, self-disciplined, and introspective. They like to work alone and pursue their own interests. Many become writers, counselors, theologians, or self-employed businesspeople. **To learn best:** relate information to your feelings or personal experiences or find inner expression.

Multiple Intelligences

Put a check mark on the line next to the statement that is most often true for you.

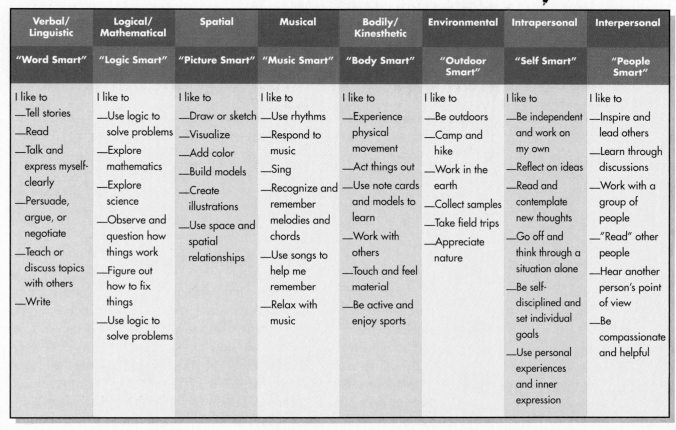

Verbal/ Linguistic	Logical/ Mathematical	Spatial	Musical	Bodily/ Kinesthetic	Environmental	Intrapersonal	Interpersonal
"Word Smart"	"Logic Smart"	"Picture Smart"	"Music Smart"	"Body Smart"	"Outdoor Smart"	"Self Smart"	"People Smart"
I like to —Tell stories —Read —Talk and express myself-clearly —Persuade, argue, or negotiate —Teach or discuss topics with others —Write	I like to —Use logic to solve problems —Explore mathematics —Explore science —Observe and question how things work —Figure out how to fix things —Use logic to solve problems	I like to —Draw or sketch —Visualize —Add color —Build models —Create illustrations —Use space and spatial relationships	I like to —Use rhythms —Respond to music —Sing —Recognize and remember melodies and chords —Use songs to help me remember —Relax with music	I like to —Experience physical movement —Act things out —Use note cards and models to learn —Work with others —Touch and feel material —Be active and enjoy sports	I like to —Be outdoors —Camp and hike —Work in the earth —Collect samples —Take field trips —Appreciate nature	I like to —Be independent and work on my own —Reflect on ideas —Read and contemplate new thoughts —Go off and think through a situation alone —Be self-disciplined and set individual goals —Use personal experiences and inner expression	I like to —Inspire and lead others —Learn through discussions —Work with a group of people —"Read" other people —Hear another person's point of view —Be compassionate and helpful

Multiple Intelligences Your goal is to try new strategies and create learning opportunities in line with each category. *What are some strategies you could easily incorporate?*

For more information, see

Frames of Mind: The Theory of Multiple Intelligences by Howard Gardner, Basic Books, 1983.

Their Own Way: Discovering and Encouraging Your Child's Personal Learning Style by Thomas Armstrong, Tarcher/Putnam, 1987.

8. **Interpersonal.** Some people are **people smart.** They have interpersonal intelligence. They like to talk and work with people, join groups, and solve problems as part of a team. They have the ability to work with and understand people, as well as to perceive and be responsive to the moods, intentions, and desires of other people. Many become mediators, negotiators, social directors, social workers, motivational speakers, or teachers. **To learn best:** join a group, get a study partner, or discuss with others.

Learning Styles
There is no one best way to learn. *How do you think you can develop and integrate different learning styles?*

Discover Your Personality Type

Your learning style is often associated with your personality type—or your "temperament." The concepts of learning styles, personality, and temperament are not new. Early writings of ancient Greece, India, the Middle East, and China addressed various temperaments and personality types. The ancient Greek founder of modern medicine, Hippocrates, identified four basic body types and the personality type associated with each body type. Several personality typing systems grew out of this ancient view of body/mind typing, including Ayurvedic Types, William Sheldon's Body-Mind Types, and Human Design. One of the most noted researchers on personality types was Carl Jung.

Carl Jung's Typology System

In 1921, psychologist Carl Jung proposed, in his book *Psychological Types*, that people are fundamentally different but also fundamentally alike. He identified three main attitudes/psychological functions, each with two types of personalities:

1. First, Jung classified *how people relate to the external or internal world.* **Extroverts** are energized and recharged by people, tending to be outgoing and social. They tend to be optimistic and are often uncomfortable with being alone. **Introverts** are energized by time alone, solitude, and reflection, preferring the world of ideas and thoughts. They tend to have a small but close set of friends and are more prone to self-doubt.

2. Next, Jung developed an assessment of *how people perceive and gather information.* **Sensors** learn best from their senses and feel comfortable with facts and concrete data. They like to organize information systematically. **Intuitives** feel more comfortable with theories, abstraction, imagination, and speculation. They respond to their inner intuition and rely on hunches and nonverbal perceptions.

3. Then, Jung characterized *how people prefer to make decisions.* **Thinkers** like to analyze problems with facts, rational logic, and analysis. They tend to be unemotional and use a systematic evaluation of data and facts for problem solving. **Feelers** are sensitive to the concerns and feelings of others, value harmony, and dislike creating conflict.

Jung suggested that differences and similarities among people can be understood by combining these types. Although people are not exclusively one of these types, he maintained that they have basic preferences or tendencies.

The Myers-Briggs Type Indicator

Jung's work inspired Katherine Briggs and her daughter, Isabel Briggs Myers, to design a personality test, the Myers-Briggs Type Indicator (MBTI), which has become the most widely used typological instrument. They added a fourth attitude/psychological function (judgment/ perception), which they felt was implied in Jung's writings, focusing on *how people live.* **Judgers** prefer orderly, planned, structured learning and working environments. They like control and closure. **Perceivers** prefer flexibility and spontaneity and like to allow life to unfold. Thus, with the four attitudes/psychological functions (extroverts vs. introverts, sensors vs. intuitives, thinkers vs. feelers, and judgers vs. perceivers), the MBTI provides 16 possible personality combinations. Although we may have all 8 preferences, 1 in each pair tends to be more developed. (See **Figure 1.3** on page 20, which lists many characteristics of *extroverts, introverts, sensors, intuitives, thinkers, feelers, judgers,* and *perceivers.*)

Understanding Personality Types
Psychologists have developed a variety of categories to identify how people function best. *What personality type or types might apply to the person in this photograph?*

Connect Learning Styles and Personality Types: The Four-Temperament Profile

You now are aware of your preferred learning styles and have a sense of your personality type. How are these connected? How can you use this information to improve your learning skills and participate in productive group and team situations?

The simple Four-Temperament Profile demonstrates how learning styles and personality types are interrelated. **Personal Evaluation Notebook 1.4** on page 21 includes a number of questions that will help you determine your dominant temperament.

The following descriptions elaborate on the four temperaments in Personal Performance Notebook 1.4. Which was your dominant temperament: analyzer, creator, supporter, or director? Did the answer surprise you? Please keep in mind that inventories only provide clues. People change over time and react differently in different situations. However, use this knowledge to discover your strengths and to become a well-rounded and balanced learner. Peak performers know not only their dominant style but also the way to integrate other styles when appropriate.

Figure 1.3   Characteristics of Personality Types

Extroverts (E) vs. Introverts (I)		Sensors (S) vs. Intuitives (iN)	
Gregarious	Quiet	Practical	Speculative
Active, talkative	Reflective	Experience	Use hunches
Speak, then think	Think, then speak	See details	See the big picture
Outgoing, social	Fewer, closer friends	Sequential, work steadily	Work in burst of energy
Energized by people	Energized by self	Feet on the ground	Head in the clouds
Like to speak	Like to read	Concrete	Abstract
Like variety and action	Like quiet for concentration	Realistic	See possibilities
Interested in results	Interested in ideas	Sensible and hardworking	Imaginative and inspired
Do not mind interruptions	Dislike interruptions	Good and precise work	Dislike precise work
Thinkers (T) vs. Feelers (F)		**Judgers (J) vs. Perceivers (P)**	
Analytical	Harmonious	Decisive	Tentative
Objective	Subjective	Closure	Open-minded
Impersonal	Personal	Plan ahead	Flexible
Factual	Sympathy	Urgency	Open time frame
Want fairness	Wants recognition	Organized	Spontaneous
Detached	Involved	Deliberate	Go with the flow
Rule	Circumstances	Set goals	Let life unfold
Things, not people	People, not things	Meet deadlines	Procrastinate
Lineal	Whole	Just the facts	Interested and curious

Characteristics of Personality Types   This chart reflects information influenced by psychologists Carl Jung and Myers and Briggs. *How can understanding your own personality and temperament help you succeed in school and life?*

The Four-Temperament Profile

The following statements indicate your preference in working with others, making decisions, and learning new information. Read each statement, with its four possible choices. Mark 4 next to the choice MOST like you, 3 next to the choice ALMOST ALWAYS like you, 2 next to the choice SOMEWHAT like you, and 1 next to the choice LEAST like you.

1. I learn best when I
   _____ a. rely on logical thinking and facts.
   _____ b. am personally involved.
   _____ c. can look for new patterns through trial and error.
   _____ d. use hands-on activities and practical applications.

2. When I'm at my best, I'm described as
   _____ a. dependable, accurate, logical, and objective.
   _____ b. understanding, loyal, cooperative, and harmonious.
   _____ c. imaginative, flexible, open-minded, and creative.
   _____ d. confident, assertive, practical, and results-oriented.

3. I respond best to instructors and bosses who
   _____ a. are factual and to the point.
   _____ b. show appreciation and are friendly.
   _____ c. encourage creativity and flexibility.
   _____ d. expect me to be involved, be active, and get results.

4. When working in a group, I tend to value
   _____ a. objectivity and correctness.
   _____ b. consensus and harmony.
   _____ c. originality and risk taking.
   _____ d. efficiency and results.

5. I am most comfortable with people who are
   _____ a. informed, serious, and accurate.
   _____ b. supportive, appreciative, and friendly.
   _____ c. creative, unique, and idealistic.
   _____ d. productive, realistic, and dependable.

6. Generally, I am
   _____ a. methodical, efficient, trustworthy, and accurate.
   _____ b. cooperative, genuine, gentle, and modest.
   _____ c. high-spirited, spontaneous, easily bored, and dramatic.
   _____ d. straightforward, conservative, responsible, and decisive.

7. When making a decision, I'm generally concerned with
   _____ a. collecting information and facts to determine the right solution.
   _____ b. finding the solution that pleases others and myself.
   _____ c. brainstorming creative solutions that feel right.
   _____ d. quickly choosing the most practical and realistic solution.

The Four-Temperament Profile—continued

8. You could describe me in one word as
   _____ **a.** analytical.
   _____ **b.** caring.
   _____ **c.** innovative.
   ___✓___ **d.** productive.

9. I excel at
   ___✓___ **a.** reaching accurate and logical conclusions.
   _____ **b.** being cooperative and respecting people's feelings.
   _____ **c.** finding hidden connections and creative outcomes.
   _____ **d.** making realistic, practical, and timely decisions.

10. When learning at school or on the job, I enjoy
   ___✓___ **a.** gathering facts and technical information and being objective.
   _____ **b.** making personal connections, being supportive, and working in groups.
   _____ **c.** exploring new possibilities, tackling creative tasks, and being flexible.
   _____ **d.** producing results, solving problems, and making decisions.

Score: To determine your style, mark the choices you made in each column below. Then add the column totals. Highest number in

- a column, you are an analyzer.
- b column, you are supporter.
- c column, you are a creator.
- d column, you are a director.

	Choice a	Choice b	Choice c	Choice d
1.	C			
2.				
3.				
4.				
5.				
6.				
7.				
8.				
9.				
10.				
Total				
	Analyzer	**Supporter**	**Creator**	**Director**

Figure 1.4 Profile of an Analyzer

Effective Traits	Ineffective Traits	Possible Majors	Possible Careers	How to Relate to Analyzers
Objective	Too cautious	Accounting	Computer programmer	Be factual
Logical	Abrupt	Bookkeeping	Accountant	Be logical
Thorough	Unemotional	Mathematics	Bookkeeper	Be formal and thorough
Precise	Aloof	Computer science	Drafter	
			Electrician	Be organized, detached, and calm
Detail-oriented	Indecisive	Drafting	Engineer	
Disciplined	Unimaginative	Electronics	Auto mechanic	Be accurate and use critical thinking
			Technician	
		Auto mechanics	Librarian	State facts briefly and concisely

Profile of an Analyzer   Analyzers want things done right. Their favorite question is "What?" *Do you recognize any analyzer traits in yourself?*

Analyzers

Analyzers tend to be logical, thoughtful, loyal, exact, dedicated, steady, and organized. They like following direction and work at a steady pace. The key word for analyzers is *thinking*. (See **Figure 1.4.**)

Strengths: Creating concepts and models and thinking things through

Goal: Intellectual recognition; analyzers are knowledge seekers

Classroom style: Analyzers relate to instructors who are organized, know their facts, and present information logically and precisely. They dislike the ambiguity of subjects that do not have right or wrong answers. They tend to be left-brained and seem more concerned with facts, abstract ideas, and concepts than with people.

Learning style: Analyzers often perceive information abstractly and process it reflectively. They learn best by observing and thinking through ideas. They like models, lectures, textbooks, and solitary work. They like to work with things and analyze how things work. They evaluate and come to a precise conclusion.

Supporters

People who are supporters tend to be cooperative, honest, sensitive, warm, and understanding. They relate well to others. They value harmony and are informal, approachable, and tactful. In business, they place emphasis on people and are

Figure 1.5 Profile of a Supporter

Effective Traits	Ineffective Traits	Possible Majors	Possible Careers	How to Relate to Supporters
Understanding	Overly compliant	Counseling or therapy	Elementary teacher	Be friendly
Gentle	Passive	Social work	Physical therapist	Be positive
Loyal	Slow to act	Family and consumer science	Social worker	Be sincere and build trust
Cooperative	Naive	Nursing	Therapist	Listen actively
Diplomatic	Unprofessional	Medical assisting	Counselor	Focus on people
Appreciative	Can be overly sensitive	Physical therapy	Nurse	Focus on personal values
		Education	Medical assistant	Create a comfortable, relaxed climate
				Create an experience they can relate to

Profile of a Supporter   Supporters want things done harmoniously and want to be personally involved. Their favorite question is "Why?" *Do you recognize any supporter traits in yourself?*

concerned with the feelings and values of those around them. The key word for supporters is *feeling*. (See **Figure 1.5.**)

> **Strengths:** Clarifying values, creating harmony, and being a loyal team player
>
> **Goal:** To create harmony, meaning, and cooperation; they are identity seekers
>
> **Classroom style:** Supporters tend to learn best when they like an instructor and feel accepted and respected. They are easily hurt by criticism. They like to integrate course concepts with their own experiences. They relate to instructors who are warm and sociable, tell interesting stories, use visuals, and are approachable. They learn best by listening, sharing ideas and feelings, and working in teams.
>
> **Learning style:** Supporters perceive information through inner intuition and process it reflectively. They like to deal with their feelings. They prefer learning information that has personal meaning, and they are patient and likeable. They are insightful; they are imaginative thinkers and need to be personally involved.

Creators

Creators are innovative, flexible, spontaneous, creative, and idealistic people. Creators are risk takers; they love drama, style, and imaginative design. They like fresh ideas and are passionate about their work. The key word for creators is *experience*. (See **Figure 1.6.**)

> **Strengths:** Creating visions that inspire people
>
> **Goal:** To make things happen by turning ideas into action; they are experience seekers

Figure 1.6 Profile of a Creator

Effective Traits	Ineffective Traits	Possible Majors	Possible Careers	How to Relate to Creators
Imaginative	Unrealistic	Art	Writer	Be enthusiastic
Creative	Unreliable	English	Politician	Be involved
Visionary	Inconsistent	Music	Travel agent	Be flexible
Idealistic	Hasty	Design	Hotel manager	Be accepting of change
Enthusiastic	Impulsive	Hospitality	Cartoonist	
Innovative	Impatient	Travel	Musician	Focus on creative ideas
	Fragmented	Theater	Composer	
		Communications	Artist	Talk about dreams and possibilities
			Journalist	
			Craftsperson	
			Florist	
			Costume designer	
			Salesperson	
			Scientist	

Profile of a Creator Creators want things done with a sense of drama and style. Their favorite question is "What if?" *Do you recognize any creator traits in yourself?*

Classroom style: Creators learn best in innovative and active classrooms. They relate to instructors who have a passion for their work; who are challenging, imaginative, and flexible; who present interesting ideas; and who make the topic exciting.

Learning style: Creators learn by doing and being involved in active experiments. They perceive information concretely and process it actively. They like games, role-playing, stories, plays, illustrations, drawings, music, and visual stimuli. They ask questions and enjoy acting on ideas. They are usually good public speakers. They are future-oriented and good at seeing whole systems.

Directors

Directors are dependable, self-directed, conscientious, efficient, decisive, and results-oriented people. They like to be the leader of groups and respond to other people's ideas when they are logical and reasonable. Their strength is in the practical application of ideas. Because of this ability, they can excel in a variety of careers, such as law enforcement, banking, and legal professions. The key word for directors is *results*. (See **Figure 1.7.**)

Strengths: Integrating theory with practical solutions

Goal: To find practical solutions to problems; they are security seekers

Figure 1.7 Profile of a Director

Effective Traits	Ineffective Traits	Possible Majors	Possible Careers	How to Relate to Directors
Confident	Aggressive	Business	Lawyer	Set deadlines
Assertive	Pushy	Law enforcement	Police officer	Be responsible for your actions
Active	Insistent	Construction	Detective	Focus on results
Decisive	Overpowering	Woodworking	Consultant	Focus on achievements
Forceful	Dominating	Carpentry	Banker	Do not try to take control
Effective leader		Business management	Park ranger	Do not make excuses
Results-oriented		Wildlife conservation	Forest ranger	Have a direction
		Forestry	Administrator for outdoor recreation	Make known time or other changes in schedule

Profile of a Director   Directors want to produce results in a practical manner. Their favorite question is "How?" *Do you recognize any director traits in yourself?*

Classroom style: Directors relate to instructors who are organized, clear, to the point, punctual, and results-oriented. They prefer field trips and hands-on activities.

Learning style: Directors learn by hands-on, direct experience. They learn best by practical application. They like classes that are relevant. They work hard to get things done.

Explore Learning and Personality Assessment Tools

Just as there is no one or best way to learn, there is no one instrument, assessment, or inventory that can categorize how you learn best. There are many theories about learning styles, and none of them should be regarded as air-tight explanations. Any learning style assessment or theory is, at best, a guide.

The assessment instruments discussed in this text have been adapted from various sources and involve many years of research. They are simple, yet they provide valuable clues and strategies for determining how you learn, process information, and relate to others. They also provide you with clues for possible college majors and careers that fit your personality and style.

As mentioned, the purpose of these inventories is to provide a guide, not to categorize you into a specific box. The goals are to develop positive strategies based on your natural talents and abilities and to expand your effectiveness by integrating all learning styles. You are encouraged to review many different instruments through your career or learning centers at your school.

One popular inventory is the **Learning and Study Strategies Inventory (LASSI)**, which is designed to gather information about learning and studying attitudes and practices. It is a self-assessment tool that looks at attitude, interest, motivation, self-discipline, willingness to work hard, time management, anxiety, concentration, test strategies, and other study skills. The inventory assesses areas in which you may need improvement and suggests ways to improve. The Personal Evaluation Notebook 1.1 Peak Performance Self-Assessment Test covers many of the same areas and will help you assess your study skills and attitude.

The **Enneagram** is another high-profile typing system. This nine-sided diagram is an ancient personality tool that blends Greek philosophy, Christian spirituality, Jewish mysticism, and psychology. It has been growing in popularity as a way of achieving self-awareness and spiritual growth. The Enneagram presents nine basic types of people with specific characteristics. The heart of the system is the various ways the types relate to each other. The Enneagram is currently in vogue in business circles as a way to understand and resolve workplace and personality conflicts.

Integrate Styles to Maximize Learning

Psychologist Henry James believed that people use less than 5 percent of their potential. Think of what you could accomplish if you could learn to work in alignment with your natural preferences and integrate various learning styles and techniques. **Figure 1.8** on page 28 illustrates how the many learning styles and personality types come together. **Figure 1.9** on page 29 then explores the Learning Pyramid, which illustrates how you can maximize your effectiveness by integrating learning styles. Now that you have assessed how you learn best—as well as new ways to learn—let's explore how learning is a never-ending cycle.

The Adult Learning Cycle

You can become a more effective learner, problem solver, and decision maker when you understand how you learn best and when you integrate all learning and personality styles. David Kolb, a professor at Case Western Reserve University, developed an inventory that categorizes learners based on how they process information:

1. Concrete experience: learn by feeling and personal experience
2. Reflective observation: learn by observing and reflecting
3. Abstract conceptualization: learn by thinking and gathering information
4. Active experimentation: learn by doing and hands-on activities

Kolb's theory about learning styles is similar to Carl Jung's four attitudes/psychological functions (feeling, intuition, thinking, and sensation). The crux of Kolb's theory is that you learn by practice, repetition, and recognition. Thus, do it, and then do it again, and then again.

Figure 1.8 Integrated Brain Power

ANALYZER	INTEGRATED BRAIN POWER	SUPPORTER
Logical		Gentle
Analytical		Caring
Literal		Sensitive
Factual	Less Assertive ↑	Harmonious
Precise		Peacemaker
Accurate		Emotional
Orderly		Loyal instead of sociable
Objective		Cooperative
Systematic		Understanding
Technical		Adaptable
Likes models		Seeks meaning

Learns by thinking and gathering new information
iNT Temperament

Learns by finding meaning and interests
iNF Temperament

Left-Brain Studying	**Right-Brain Studying**
Neat, organized study area	Cluttered desk
Daily schedules	Flexible study times
Work on one project at a time	Jump from project to project
Study alone	Study with others
Study consistently	Study in bursts of energy
Plan studying	Cram last minute

← Abstract Conceptual

Concrete Experimental →

DIRECTOR		CREATOR
Confident		Innovative
Practical		Imaginative
Realistic		Free-spirited
Disciplined		Visionary
Problem solver		Impulsive
Controlled		Open-minded
Dependable	More Assertive ↓	Creative
Results oriented		Curious
Pragmatic		Energetic
Traditional		Spontaneous
Wants results		Wants to create

Learns by practical application and doing
SJ Temperament

Learns by observing, reflecting, and experiencing
SP Temperament

Integrated Brain Power   Integrating both sides of the brain boosts learning, memory, and recall. *Do you think you are left- or right-brain dominant?*

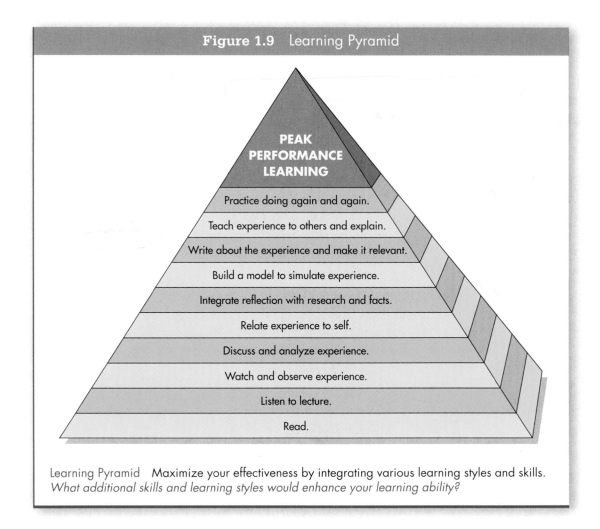

Figure 1.9 Learning Pyramid

PEAK
PERFORMANCE
LEARNING

Practice doing again and again.

Teach experience to others and explain.

Write about the experience and make it relevant.

Build a model to simulate experience.

Integrate reflection with research and facts.

Relate experience to self.

Discuss and analyze experience.

Watch and observe experience.

Listen to lecture.

Read.

Learning Pyramid   Maximize your effectiveness by integrating various learning styles and skills. *What additional skills and learning styles would enhance your learning ability?*

The following Adult Learning Cycle is an adaptation of both Kolb's and Jung's theories. It includes a fifth stage and illustrates how they are complementary to one another.

1. **RELATE. Why do I want to learn this?** What personal meaning and interest does this have for me? I learn by feeling, personal experience, and talking with others.
2. **OBSERVE. How does this work?** I learn by watching, listening, and experiencing.
3. **REFLECT. What does this mean?** I learn by thinking, gathering information, and reflecting.
4. **DO. What can I do with this?** I learn by doing, finding practical applications, and defining procedures.
5. **TEACH. How can I relay this information to others?** I learn by demonstrating and explaining, as well as by acknowledging and rewarding positive outcomes.

Depending on your learning style, the information to be learned, and the situation, you may find yourself starting the Adult Learning Cycle at different stages. *The key to learning is practice and repetition.* As you repeat the stages, meaning and recall are strengthened. To make learning long-lasting, you need to find ways to make learning meaningful and physical. For example, let's say you are taking a computer class.

1. **RELATE personal meaning, interests, and relevance.** Why do you want to use the computer? What are the benefits to you, your coursework, and your career? How does this relate to what you already know, such as typing skills? In what programs or skills would you like to become proficient? Think about the opportunities and talk with other people about the practical uses of a computer. Study and learn in a group.

2. **OBSERVE your instructor and watch other people using the computer.** Listen and ask questions. Talk, read, and write about your experiences. What is new and different? Jot down instructions, draw, sketch, and add color to your notes. Find music to illustrate ideas or use background music as you learn. Experience doing a task as your instructor or a friend helps you.

3. **REFLECT on problems critically and in sequence.** Build on information and qualify it. What works and doesn't work? Test new ways of doing things. Ask people when you get stuck. Find new ways to solve problems. Relate what you know to new information. Review instructions when you are stumped.

4. **DO it and learn by trial and error.** Jump in and try new tasks. Learning to use a computer is a great example of hands-on learning. Find new applications.

5. **TEACH it to others.** Demonstrate to someone else what you have learned. Answer questions and ask for feedback.

Then return to Stage 1 and reaffirm the benefits of learning this valuable new skill. Here's another example. Susan owns a bed and breakfast inn, which has a combination lock on the front door. Her guests need to learn how to use the lock.

1. **RELATE:** "I don't want to get locked out!" Guests have a personal interest in learning the combination, since that will be how they get in and out of the inn. It is important and relevant information.

2. **Observe:** "Here's how it works." Susan shows them how to use the combination lock and talks to them as she demonstrates. They watch and gather information. Often, they repeat what she has said.

3. **Reflect:** "Did I get it?" They integrate information and Susan offers an overview: "Don't forget to turn the knob all the way to the right."

4. **Do:** "Now I'll try it." They practice learning by doing it, and Susan offers instruction as they are doing it. "Press the 5 button four times and turn all the way to the right."

5. **Teach:** "Let me show you." They may teach it to their spouse or practice it again while they say the combination out loud.

You can adapt the Adult Learning Cycle to fit your preference, but you will be most effective if you integrate all learning styles and make learning physical and meaningful.

In each chapter, we will explore practical examples of the Adult Learning Cycle. For example, in Chapter 12, the Adult Learning Cycle will be applied to effective communication and how you can enhance your communication skills.

Overcome Obstacles

On your journey to success, more than likely you will run into stumbling blocks (or even big boulders). As mentioned before, maintain a positive attitude and make sure you are using your self-management tools.

Adjust Your Learning Style to Your Instructor's Teaching Style

One barrier is not adjusting your learning style to your instructor's teaching style. Just as we all have different learning styles, your instructors will have a variety of teaching styles. Rather than being resistant, find ways to adapt by maximizing the ways you learn best and by incorporating other techniques. For example, if you prefer a highly structured lecture, focusing on facts and taking notes, you may not feel comfortable in a student-centered course where ideas and class discussion are key and you work in small groups with little structure. Some strategies to use to help you succeed in this type of course include

- Ask questions and clarify expectations.
- Be flexible and willing to try new approaches.
- Be an active participant in class and go to every class.
- Get to know other students and form study teams.
- Be interested in other points of view.
- See exercises and class discussions as learning opportunities.
- Be friendly yet respectful and visit your instructor during office hours.
- Ask your instructor what you can do to improve.
- Do all extra credit projects.
- Try looking at the whole of a concept before breaking it into parts.
- If the instructor jumps around a lot in a lecture, or digresses, ask for main points.
- Find or ask for the theme or key points of each class.
- Focus on the learning process, not just the final product.

Let's say you prefer warm relationships and a nonstructured class. You find yourself in a traditional, content-centered, straight lecture class with few visuals or class discussion. Here are a few suggestions for adapting:

- Read the syllabus and know expectations.
- Listen attentively and take detailed notes.
- Clarify the weight of each test, paper, or project.
- Make certain you know and meet each deadline.
- Anticipate the lecture and be prepared.
- Focus on the lecture and avoid talking to others during class.
- Work in a study team, discuss lecture concepts, and predict test questions.
- Ask questions and ask for examples from the instructor and study team.
- Take advantage of the logical sequence of material and take notes accordingly.

- Add color, supporting examples, and drawings to your notes.
- Connect lectures to drawings, photographs, and diagrams in the textbook.
- Ask the instructor for visuals that help illustrate the points made in class.
- Have your questions ready when talking to your instructor during office hours.
- Use analytical thinking and focus on facts and logic.
- Be precise in definitions and descriptions.

If absolutely necessary, you can drop the class and sign up for a class with an instructor who has a teaching style that is similar to your learning style. However, since in the workplace you will be interacting with colleagues and employers with a variety of personality types and learning styles, it's important for you to learn coping and adapting skills now to help you maximize your success.

Use Critical Thinking

Another barrier to success is a lack of critical thinking, which keeps you from facing reality. Look honestly at all areas of your life. Use critical thinking to assess your performance and plan new ways to overcome discouragement and setbacks. For example, you may have discovered in your assessment exercises that you tend to be late for class or work. Create ways to help you become punctual, such as setting your clock 10 minutes early and getting organized the night before. Positive habits help you overcome counterproductive behavior. Do not get discouraged. Acknowledge and work on your shortcomings and focus on your successes. Realize that everyone gets off course sometimes, so don't dwell on mistakes. Focus on your strengths and positive habits to get back on track.

WORDS TO SUCCEED

"I have not failed. I've just found 10,000 ways that won't work."

THOMAS EDISON, *Inventor*

In summary, in this chapter, I learned to:

- *Strive to become a peak performer.* Peak performers come from all walks of life, maximize their abilities and resources, and focus on positive results.

- *Practice self-management.* I know that I am responsible for my own success, and there are a number of self-management techniques and behaviors that I can practice that will make me successful.

- *Self-assess.* Assessing and objectively seeing myself will help me recognize my need to learn new skills, relate more effectively with others, set goals, manage time and stress, and create a balanced and productive life.

- *Use my critical thinking skills.* Critical thinking is a logical, rational, and systematic thought process I can use to think through a problem or situation to make sound choices and good decisions.

- *Visualize success.* Visualization is a self-management tool I can use to see myself being successful. I will also use affirmations (positive self-talk) to focus on what's important.

- *Reflect on information.* I will think about how experiences are related and what I can learn from them, including keeping a written (or online) journal to record my thoughts.

- *Make connections between skills for school and job success.* The Secretary's Commission on Achieving Necessary Skills (SCANS) outlines skills and competencies that are critical to success in school as well as the job market.

- *Determine my learning style.* By knowing my preferred learning style, such as visual, auditory, or kinesthetic, I know how I learn best and how to incorporate features of other learning styles in order to maximize my learning opportunities.

- *Explore various personality types.* Although personality typing has been around for centuries, Jung identified extroverts vs. introverts, sensors vs. intuitives, and thinkers vs. feelers. Myers and Briggs added judgers and perceivers and developed the Myers-Briggs Type Indicator.

- *Integrate learning styles and personality types.* Once I understand my learning style(s) and personality type(s), I can incorporate features of other styles to maximize my learning. Although I tend to be either left-brain dominant (linguistic) or right-brain dominant (visual), the goal is to use all my brain power to learn new skills and information.

- *Apply the Adult Learning Cycle.* This five-step process (relate, observe, reflect, do, and teach) demonstrates that learning comes from repetition, practice, and recall.

- *Adjust to my instructor's teaching style.* If my learning style is different from my instructor's teaching style, I will try new strategies that will maximize my learning in that class.

career in focus

Louis Parker

ACCOUNTANT AND FINANCIAL PLANNER

Related Majors: Accounting, Business Administration, Economics, Finance

Setting Business Goals

Louis Parker is a certified public accountant (CPA) and financial planner. In 1984, he started his own business, Parker, Inc., by offering accounting services. Louis prepares taxes, financial reports, and payroll, and he does bookkeeping for individuals and small businesses. He employs three full-time and one part-time assistant but needs five full-time workers to help during peak tax season (January–April).

To get feedback on his services, Louis occasionally does a survey of his clients. The survey shows whether his clients are getting the services they want at prices they believe are reasonable. Louis uses the results of the survey to set goals and plan for the future.

Another of Louis' goals is to continually increase business, as Louis believes that, without marketing and growth, his business will decline. Louis has used telemarketing services to help him set up appointments with prospective clients.

A few years ago, Louis decided to add financial planning because his clients were continually asking for his advice in financial areas. Financial planners help clients attain financial goals, such as retirement or a college education for their children. Louis was able to get certified in financial planning. Because he is affiliated with a financial services organization, he sometimes helps clients invest in the stock market, mainly in mutual funds. Currently, financial planning is only 10 percent of his business, but Louis' goal is to eventually increase that amount to 30 percent.

CRITICAL THINKING How might a survey of his clients help Louis assess his personal strengths and weaknesses? What strategies should he put in place to follow up on client feedback? How can he incorporate the feedback into his long-term goals?

Peak Performer Profile

Christy Haubegger

At first glance, the glossy magazine looks like many others on the newsstands. The front cover offers a snapshot of the current issue: a profile of a famous celebrity, beauty and fashion tips, and a self-help article to improve the inner being. The big, bold letters across the top, however, spell the difference. This is *Latina*, the first bilingual magazine targeted for Hispanic-American women and the inspiration of founder Christy Haubegger.

Born in Houston, Texas, in 1968, Haubegger has described herself as a "chubby Mexican-American baby adopted by parents who were tall, thin, and blond." As a teenager during the mega-media 80s, she was especially sensitive to the lack of Hispanic role models in women's magazines. It was a void waiting to be filled. At the age of 20, Haubegger received a bachelor's degree in philosophy from the University of Texas. At 23, she went on to earn her law degree from Stanford, where she joined the editorial staff of the *Law Review,* rising to the position of senior editor. "My experience as senior editor gave me a start in the worlds of journalism and publishing."

Haubegger also took a course in marketing. In that class, she had to write a business plan for a favorite enterprise. *Latina* magazine was born. As one of the best-known publications for Hispanic-American women, *Latina* covers issues such as health, politics, family, and finance, as well as beauty and entertainment. *Latina* provides Hispanic women a voice and reminds them that they, too, are part of the American Dream.

There are more than 40 million Hispanic Americans in the United States. With numbers like that, Haubegger envisions the magazine as only "the first brick in a media empire."

PERFORMANCE THINKING If you were assessing the characteristics that make Christy Haubegger a successful publisher, which would you say are the most important?

CHECK IT OUT Go to **www.Latina.com** to see the numerous online features *Latina* offers, such as special sections devoted to Latino culture ("Our Cultura"), women ("Mujeres on the Move"), and success ("Succeed"). You can also relay your personal stories of struggle and success by clicking on the "Your Story" link.

Review and Applications

Performance Strategies

Following are the top 10 strategies for discovering how you learn best:

- ◆ Strive to become a peak performer in all aspects of your life.
- ◆ Practice self-management to create the results you want.
- ◆ Use critical thinking and honesty in self-assessment.
- ◆ Practice visualization and state affirmations that focus on positive outcomes.
- ◆ Make the connection between school and job success.
- ◆ Focus on commitment and effort.
- ◆ Discover your learning and personality styles.
- ◆ Apply the Adult Learning Cycle to maximize your learning.
- ◆ Integrate all learning styles.
- ◆ Focus on strengths and successes.

Tech for Success

Take advantage of the text's web site at **www.mhhe.com/ferrett6e** for additional study aids, useful forms, and convenient and applicable resources.

- ◆ **Electronic journal.** Sometimes, critical thinking is easier when you write down your responses. Keeping an electronic reflection and self-assessment journal allows for easy updating and gathering of information, which can be pulled into your career portfolio later.

- ◆ **Mission statement business cards.** To keep yourself motivated and focused, print your mission statement on business cards, carry them with you, and share them with family and friends. Consider chipping in with another student or your study group and buying pre-scored printer paper, or simply print on a heavier paper stock and cut the cards apart.

- ◆ **On-line self-assessments.** A number of on-line assessments can help you determine the best careers to fit your personality. Talk with your instructor, as your school may already have some available in your career center.

Review Questions

Based on what you have learned in this chapter, write your answers to the following questions:

1. What is a peak performer? List at least three potential characteristics.

   1 They Focuses on long team goals
   2 they develop Appropriate Attitudes
   3 The possess the personal power to produce results

2. Define visualization and how and when you can practice this self-management tool.

   Using your imagination to see your goal

3. Explain the differences among the three types of learners (visual, auditory, kinesthetic).

   Visual - Sees
   Auditory - hear - Listen

4. Why is it important to know your learning style and personality type?

5. How does critical thinking help you overcome barriers to self-assessment?

MAKING A COMMITMENT

In the Classroom

Eric Silver is a freshman in college. He doesn't know what major to choose and isn't even sure if he wants to continue going to college. His parents are urging him to pursue his college career, but Eric wants to go to work instead. In high school, he never settled on a favorite subject, though he did briefly consider becoming a private investigator after reading a detective novel. His peers seem more committed to college and have better study habits. Eric prefers a hands-on approach to learning, and he finds it difficult to concentrate while studying or listening to a lecture. However, he enjoys the outdoors and is creative. Once he gets involved in a project he finds interesting, he is very committed.

1. What strategies from this chapter would be most useful to help Eric understand himself better and gain a sense of commitment?

   Eric might want to examine different things that he enjoys doing and see if they are of interest, then set a goal.

2. What would you suggest to Eric to help him find direction?

   Seeing the importance of making a choice to do something. Setting time and the opportunity to just do it.

In the Workplace

Eric has taken a job as a law enforcement officer. He feels more comfortable in this job than he did in school, since he knows he performs best when actively learning. He enjoys teamwork and the exchange of ideas with his co-workers. Eric also realizes that, in order to advance in his work, he needs to continue his education. He is concerned about balancing his work, school, and family life. He does admit that he did not excel in subjects he was less interested in. Eric never learned effective study habits but realizes that he must be disciplined when returning to college.

3. What suggestions would you give Eric to help him do better in school?

   1. To plan to return to school with better habits and allowing for study time and time to get help if needed. Allowing time for friends, family

4. Under what category of learning style does Eric fall and what are the ineffective traits of this style that he needs to work on most?

   Interpersonal - Sometimes things has to be completed alone and you have to work alone

APPLYING THE ABCDE METHOD OF SELF-MANAGEMENT

In the Journal Entry on page 1 of this chapter, you were asked to think about what you are hoping to gain from your college experience. How does earning a college degree help you both personally and professionally? Essentially, "Why are you here?" On the lines provided, indicate your answers to those questions.

_____

_____

Now think about the obstacles you may have faced to get to this point and what you did to overcome them. State at least one of those obstacles:

_____

_____

Now apply the ABCDE method to one of the obstacles.

A=Actual event:

Going back to school

B=Beliefs:

That it would be hard.

C=Consequences:

had to become more discipline in study habits

D=Dispute:

E=Energized:

Looking at the value of going back to school —

Did you use this or a similar thought process when you first encountered the obstacle? Was the obstacle not really as big as it first seemed?

Practice Self-Management

For more examples of learning how to manage difficult situations, see the "Self-Management Workbook" section of the Online Learning Center web site at **www.mhhe.com/ferrett6e**.

REVIEW AND APPLICATIONS

CHAPTER 1

ASSESSING AND APPLYING LEARNING STYLES, PERSONALITY TYPES, AND TEMPERAMENTS

Learning Styles

I am a(n) (circle one):

(Visual learner)

Auditory learner

Kinesthetic learner

The following learning habits make me most like this learning style:

I like to see

What features of the two other learning styles should I incorporate to make me a well-rounded learner?

Visual, auditory ← Should work good together

Personality Types

I am a(n) (circle one for each):

Extrovert or introvert

Sensor or intuitive

(Thinker or feeler)

The following characteristics make me most like these personality types:

How can I incorporate positive features of the opposite personality types?

Temperaments

I am a(n) (circle one):

(Analyzer)

Supporter

Creator

Director

The following characteristics make me most like this temperament:

What positive behaviors/traits can I incorporate from the other three temperaments?

(continued)

Creating the Ideal Team

In school and at work, you will often be a member of a project team. In most cases, you do not have the opportunity to select your team members but, instead, need to learn how to maximize each other's strengths.

Let's pretend, however, that you have the opportunity to select a four-person team to tackle an assignment. Now that you know your preferences, indicate the characteristics of three potential teammates who would be complementary. Indicate why you think each person would be an asset to the team.

Person #1

Learning style:
Personality type:
Temperament:
What this person will add to the team:

Person #2

Learning style:
Personality type:
Temperament:
What this person will add to the team:

Person #3

Learning style:
Personality type:
Temperament:
What this person will add to the team:

And ME

What I add to the team:

CHAPTER 1 ▶ REVIEW AND APPLICATIONS

APPLYING THE FOUR-TEMPERAMENT PROFILE

You've explored your temperament and discovered your preferred learning style and personality type. Apply this knowledge by associating with people who have various styles and find ways to relate to and work more effectively with different people.

For example, let's say that you are assigned to a five-person team that will present a serious public health issue to your personal health class. You are a supporter type, and you find yourself having a conflict with Joe, a director type. You are in your first meeting, and Joe is ready to choose a topic for the group project, even though one team member is absent.

Apply the ABCDE Method of Self-Management to focus your energies on building rapport and understanding:

A = Actual event: "Joe wants to choose a topic for the group project, even though one person isn't here to voice her opinion."

B = Beliefs: "I think that we are not taking the time to be sensitive to the needs of all the team members. Everyone should be present before we make a decision. Joe is trying to take control of the group and is just impatient."

C = Consequences: "I'm worried that the absent group member will not like the decision or may even be hurt that she wasn't involved. I resent being rushed and I'm afraid that conflict will result. Maybe this person will even quit the group."

D = Dispute: "What is the worst thing that could happen if we chose a topic today? We can always refocus later if we find this topic doesn't fit our goals. Chances are the absent member would agree with the topic in question, anyhow. Joe is probably not impatient—he just wants to make a decision and get us moving."

E = Energized: "I'm glad our group is made up of different strengths and personalities. I'm psyched that our team members have complementary strengths and can respect and work well with each other. I know that Joe will keep us moving forward and that he will be sensitive to my concerns that we listen to each other and respect each other's feelings."

Are you experiencing a similar situation or conflict in your school, work, or personal life? If so, use the ABCDE method to visualize a positive solution:

A = Actual event:

B = Beliefs:

C = Consequences:

D = Dispute:

E = Energized:

REVIEW AND APPLICATIONS

CHAPTER 1

AUTOBIOGRAPHY

The purpose of this exercise is to look back and assess how you learned skills and competencies. Write down the turning points, major events, and significant experiences of your life. This autobiography, or chronological record, will note events that helped you make decisions, set goals, or discover something about yourself. Record both negative and positive experiences and what you learned from them. Add this page to your Career Development Portfolio—for example,

Year/Event	Learned Experience
1997 Moved to Michigan.	Learned to make new friends and be flexible.
1998 First job baby-sitting.	Learned responsibility and critical thinking.
1999 Grandmother became ill.	Helped with care. Learned dependability, compassion.

Year/Event	Learned Experience
1989 / Move VA	Learned to pick my places to live carefully
1990	learn to self search options
1995 / VA business	own my own business.
1997 / VA	sold business.
1998 / Sold Clothes / shoes	learn to be balance with money
2000 / VA school NURSING	learned that I had other interests
2004 / Getting A good Job	Learned that I could really do it

Achieve Emotional Intelligence

CHAPTER OBJECTIVES

In this chapter, you will learn to

▲ Strive for emotional intelligence and the key personal qualities

▲ Focus on character first, including integrity, civility, and ethics

▲ Display responsibility, self-management, and control

▲ Develop self-esteem and confidence

▲ Incorporate a positive attitude and motivation

▲ Use goal setting as a motivational tool

▲ Appreciate the benefits of a higher education

▲ Overcome the obstacles to staying positive and motivated

SELF-MANAGEMENT

"On my commute to class, a car cut me off. I was furious and yelled at the driver. I was fuming and distracted during classes, and later I blew up at a co-worker. This just ruined my entire day. How can I handle my angry feelings in a more constructive way?"

Have you ever had a similar experience? Are you easily offended by what others do or say? Have you said things in anger that have caused a rift in a relationship? In this chapter, you will learn how to control your emotions and create a positive and resourceful state of mind.

JOURNAL ENTRY In **Worksheet 2.1** on page 74, describe a time when you were angry and lost control of your emotions. How did you feel? How did others react to your outburst? What would you do differently? Visualize yourself calm and in control and realize that you have a choice in how you interpret events.

Thomer is a tendency to define intelligence as a score on an IQ test or SAT or as school grades. Educators have tried to predict who will succeed in college and have found that high school grades, achievement test scores, and ability are only part of the picture. Emotional intelligence and maturity have more effect on school and job success than traditional scholastic measures. In fact, research has indicated that persistence and perseverance are major predictors of college success. A landmark study by the American College Test (ACT) indicated that the primary reasons for first-year students' dropping out of college were not academic but, rather, were emotional difficulties, such as feelings of inadequacy, depression, loneliness, and a lack of motivation or purpose.

Employers also list a positive attitude, motivation, honesty, the ability to get along with others, civility, and the willingness to learn as more important to job success than a college degree or specific skills. In Chapter 1, you learned that SCANS identifies many personal qualities as important competencies for success in the workplace. These qualities and competencies are also essential for building and maintaining strong, healthy relationships throughout life. Essential personal qualities should be viewed as a foundation on which to build skills, experience, and knowledge.

In this chapter, you will learn the importance of emotional intelligence and why character is so important for school and job success. You will also develop personal strategies for maintaining a positive attitude and becoming self-motivated. You may realize that you are smarter than you think. You are smarter than your test scores or grades. You can maximize your success by developing emotional maturity. Success in your personal life, school, and career is more dependent on a positive attitude, motivation, responsibility, self-control, and effort than on inborn abilities or a high IQ. Peak performers use the *whole* of their intelligence—and so can you.

Emotional Intelligence and Maturity

Emotional intelligence is the ability to understand and manage yourself and relate effectively to others. **Maturity** is the ability to control your impulses, to think beyond the moment, and to consider how your words and actions affect yourself and others *before* you act. Emotional intelligence has become a popular topic as we learn more about the importance of personal qualities, communication, the management of feelings, and social competence. Researchers have demonstrated that people who have developed a set of traits that adds to their maturity level will increase their sense of well-being, help them get along with others, and enhance their school, job, and life success. Best-selling author and psychologist Daniel Goleman says that the business world rates emotional intelligence over job skill or expertise in its managers.

The ability to regulate emotions is vital for school and job success. Emotional maturity contributes to competent behavior, problem-solving ability, socially appropriate behavior, and good communication. Being unaware of or unable to control emotions often accompanies restlessness, a short attention span, negativism, impulsiveness, and distractibility. Clearly, having emotional intelligence distinguishes peak performers from mediocre ones. Becoming more emotionally mature involves three stages:

1. *Self-awareness*—tuning in to yourself
2. *Empathy*—tuning in to others
3. *Change*—tuning in to results

In Chapter 1, you explored many strategies to help you increase your self-awareness and tune into yourself. You had an opportunity to assess many skills and personal qualities in the Peak Performance Self-Assessment Test on page 10. By learning personality types, you also began to tune in to others as well. The central theme of this book is that you can use this information to begin changing your thoughts, images, and behaviors to produce the results you want in every aspect of your life. Enhancing your emotional intelligence and focusing on positive personal qualities are key to achieving those successful results.

Character First: Integrity, Civility, and Ethics

Good character is an essential personal quality for true success in school, work, and life. A person of good character has a core set of principles that most of us accept as constant and relatively noncontroversial. These principles include fairness, honesty, respect, responsibility, caring, trustworthiness, and citizenship. Recent surveys of business leaders indicate that dishonesty, lying, and lack of respect are top reasons for on-the-job difficulties. If a company believes that an employee lacks integrity, all of that person's positive qualities—from skill and experience to productivity and intelligence—are meaningless. Employers usually list honesty or good character as an essential personal quality, followed by the ability to relate to and get along with others. In short, they want people who have good character, integrity, and civility. A number of books have been written by successful top executives who claim that good character, honesty, and a strong value system are what make you an effective leader. All the corporate scandals seen in the news lately are testimonials that business leaders with poor values will eventually meet their demise.

Dr. Stephen L. Carter, Yale professor and best-selling author of *Integrity* and his follow-up book, *Civility,* suggests that following The Golden Rule (treating others as we want to be treated) is a simple way to weave integrity and civility into our everyday lives. The word integrity comes from the Latin word *integre,* meaning "wholeness." Integrity is the integration of your principles and actions. In a sense, a person who has integrity "walks the talk." They consistently live up to their highest principles. Integrity is not adherence to a rigid code but, rather, an ongoing commitment to being consistent, caring, and true to doing what is right. Not only is integrity understanding what is right; it is also the courage to do it even when it is difficult.

Civility is a set of tools for interacting with others with respect, kindness, and good manners, or etiquette. However, civility is more than good manners and politeness. As Dr. Carter said, "It is the sum of the many sacrifices we are called upon to make for the sake of living together." Empathy—understanding and compassion for

WORDS TO SUCCEED

"Character is like a tree and reputation like its shadow. The shadow is what we think of it; the tree is the real thing."

ABRAHAM LINCOLN, *U.S. President*

WORDS TO SUCCEED

"The measure of a man's character is what he would do if he knew he never would be found out."

THOMAS MACAULAY, *British writer and politician*

others—is essential for integrity and civility. You can practice civility in your classes by being on time, turning off your cell phone, staying for the entire class, and listening to the instructor and other students when they speak.

Ethics are the principles of conduct that govern a group or society. Since a company's reputation is its most important asset, most organizations have a written code of ethics that deals with how people are expected to behave and treat others. It is your responsibility to know and understand the code of ethics at your place of employment and at school. Look in your school's catalog for statements regarding academic integrity, honesty, cheating, and plagiarism. Cheating is using or providing unauthorized help in test taking or on projects. Plagiarism is considered a form of cheating, since it is presenting someone else's ideas as if they were your own. Know the consequences of your behavior, which could result in an *F* grade, suspension, expulsion, or firing from a job. You always have the choice of telling the truth, being prepared, talking with the instructor, and being responsible for your own work. If you put character first in your life, you will have a strong foundation on which to add other key elements of emotional maturity, such as motivation, a positive attitude, responsibility, confidence, and self-control. When you focus on character, integrity, and civility, you become a whole person—an emotionally mature person.

Every day, you run into situations that test your character. **Personal Evaluation Notebook 2.1** includes a number of questions and situations to get you thinking critically about your experiences. While completing this exercise, consider the personal qualities that make you smarter than you think you are, such as positive attitude, motivation, dependability, and honesty—for example, "I was raised on a farm in Michigan. What personal quality makes me smarter than my IQ or test scores?" If you answer "hard work," you're right. That one personal quality—putting in extra effort—has helped many people be more successful in life.

Personal qualities, especially honesty, are very important to consider when you think of hiring someone to work for a business that you own. Let's say that a candidate sends in an outstanding resume. She has a college degree, experience, and a great personality, and she is positive and motivated, but you find out that she stole from her last employer. No matter how bright or talented someone is, you may realize you cannot have a dishonest person working for you. Complete **Personal Evaluation Notebook 2.2** on page 48 to see what qualities you would look for in a potential employee and which of those qualities you possess.

There is no universal code of ethics and many questions about ethical issues do not have clear-cut answers. For example, taking money out of a cash drawer is clearly dishonest, but what about coming in late to work, padding your expense account, or using someone else's words without giving credit?

You will be faced with situations in your personal, school, and business lives that will force you to make decisions that will be viewed as either ethical or unethical. Sometimes it is not easy. At one time or another, everyone is faced with situations that demand tough decisions. Consider the following situations.

Peggy Lyons has a midterm test to take. This test will determine 50 percent of her final grade. She has been very busy at home and has not attended class or her study group for the past week. She knows she probably won't do well on the test, but she needs a good grade. She knows the instructor is fair and has been asking about her.

Character and Ethics

Integrity and honesty are essential qualities. It is important for you to assess and develop them as you would any skill. Use critical thinking to answer these questions.

1. What is the most difficult ethical dilemma you have faced in your life?

   _____

2. Do you have a code of ethics that helps guide you when making decisions? Explain.

   _____

3. When did you learn about honesty?

   _____

4. Who have you known that is a role model for displaying integrity and honesty?

   _____

5. Do you have a code of ethics at your college? Where did you find it? (Hint: Check your school's catalog or ask the dean of students for a copy.)

   _____

6. Does your company have a code of ethics? How do employees access it?

   _____

7. If you were the chief executive officer (CEO) or owner of a small company, what would you want to include in your code of ethics?

   _____

8. How would you make certain that employees understood and honored your company's code of ethics?

   _____

Someone Peggy met in the cafeteria tells her she can buy a copy of the test. She's tempted. What do you think she will do? What would you do?

While in college, Rey Armas has been working part-time at an electronics store. Rey's supervisor, Joe, has worked in the store for 10 years. Joe is 50 and has a family. This is his only means of support. Rey has discovered that Joe is stealing some of the electronics components to sell on the side. Rey likes Joe. What should Rey do? What would you do?

Tora Veda is up late, working on a term paper. She debates whether or not she should take the time to cite references. Her instructor warns the class about plagiarism, but, because some of her information came off the Internet, she doesn't think it should be a big deal. What should she do? What would you do?

Peggy, Rey, and Tora are all faced with tough decisions. Their final decisions will be viewed by others as either ethical or unethical and carry consequences, such as being fired, getting an *F* in the course, or even being suspended or expelled from school. They will have to call on their own personal code of ethics. When defining their code

Skills and Personal Qualities

1. Jot down the skills, personal qualities, and habits you are learning and demonstrating in each of your classes.

Skills	Personal Qualities	Habits
_____	_____	_____
_____	_____	_____
_____	_____	_____

2. Pretend that you own your own business. List the skills and personal qualities you would want in the employees you hire.

Type of business: _____

Employees' Skills	Employees' Personal Qualities
_____	_____
_____	_____
_____	_____

and their subsequent actions, they may find the following questions helpful. You, too, may find them helpful when developing a code of ethics.

- ◆ Is this action against the law?
- ◆ Is this action against company policy or code of behavior?
- ◆ How would this situation read if reported on the front page of the newspaper?
- ◆ How would you explain this to your mother? To your child?
- ◆ What could be the negative consequences?
- ◆ Are you causing unnecessary harm to someone?
- ◆ If unsure, have you asked a trusted associate outside of the situation?
- ◆ Are you treating others as you would want to be treated?

Remember, unethical behavior rarely goes unnoticed!

Responsibility

Now let's look at other personal qualities that SCANS and business leaders say are essential for success. Peak performers take responsibility for their thoughts, state of mind, and behavior. They don't blame others for their problems but, rather, use their energy to solve them. They are persistent and patient. They know they must exert a consistent amount of high effort to achieve their goals. They keep their word and agreements. When they say they are going to do something, they keep their commitment. People can depend on them.

Examples of being responsible include showing up prepared and on time for work, meetings, study teams, and so on; paying bills and repaying loans on time; and cleaning up personal messes at home and elsewhere. Responsible people own up to their mistakes and do what they can to correct them.

Other personal qualities related to responsibility include perseverance, punctuality, concentration, attention to details, follow-through, and high standards. What you do or don't do in one area of your life affects other areas of your life and other people.

Peak performers realize they are responsible for their attitudes and actions, and they know they have the power to change them. A negative attitude is sometimes the result of not coping effectively with change, conflict, and frustration. Emotional, physical, and social changes are part of the growing process at any age. Learning to adjust to frustration and discouragement can take many forms. Some people withdraw or become critical, cynical, shy, sarcastic, unmotivated, or listless. Blame, excuses, justification, and criticism of others are devices for those who cannot accept personal responsibility for their behavior and state of mind. Acknowledge your feelings and attitudes. Decide if they support your goals; if they do not, choose a state of mind and actions that support you.

Being responsible creates a sense of integrity and a feeling of self-worth. For example, if you owe money to a friend, family member, or bank, take responsibility for repaying the loan. If you have a student loan, repay it on schedule or make new arrangements with the lender. Not repaying can result in years of guilt and embarrassment, as well as a poor credit rating. It is important to your self-worth to know you are a person who keeps agreements and assumes responsibility. Go to class and be on time. A responsible person keeps commitments.

The model in **Figure 2.1** on page 50 illustrates many important interrelated personal responsibilities.

Self-Control

If anger were a disease, there would be an epidemic in this country. Road rage, spousal and child abuse, and a lack of civility are just a few examples of anger. Emotionally mature people know how to control their thoughts and behaviors and how to resolve conflict. Conflict is an inevitable part of school and work, but it can be resolved in a positive way. Following are seven tips for trying to redirect and transform your anger:

1. **Calm down.** Step back from the situation and take a deep breath. Take the drama out of the situation and observe what is happening, what behavior is triggering angry emotions, and what options you have in responding in appropriate and positive ways. If you lash out without thinking and attack verbally, you may cause serious harm to your relationship. You cannot take back words once they are spoken. Resist the urge to overreact.

2. **Clarify and define.** Determine exactly with whom or what you are angry and why. What specific behavior in the other person is causing you to feel angry or frustrated? Determine whose problem it is. For example, your instructor may

WORDS TO
SUCCEED

"Holding on to anger is like grasping a hot coal with the intent of throwing it at someone else; you are the one who gets burned."

BUDDHA

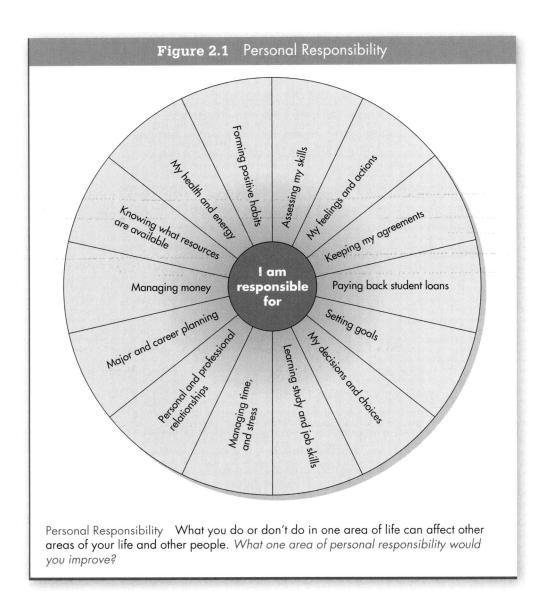

Figure 2.1 Personal Responsibility

I am responsible for

Forming positive habits
Assessing my skills
My feelings and actions
Keeping my agreements
Paying back student loans
Setting goals
My decisions and choices
Learning study and job skills
Managing time, and stress
Personal and professional relationships
Major and career planning
Managing money
Knowing what resources are available
My health and energy

Personal Responsibility   What you do or don't do in one area of life can affect other areas of your life and other people. *What one area of personal responsibility would you improve?*

have an annoying tone and style of lecturing. If a behavior annoys only you, perhaps it is something you alone need to address.

3. **Listen with empathy and respect.** Empathy includes the ability to listen, understand, and respond to the feelings and needs of others. Take the tension out of the conflict by really listening and understanding the other person's point of view. Communicate that you have heard and understood by restating the other person's position. Respect yourself as well. Ask yourself how you feel. Are you tired, hot, hungry, frustrated, rushed, or ill? If so, you may not want to deal with your anger until you feel better. Sometimes, getting a good night's sleep or having a good meal will put the situation into perspective, and your anger will dissolve.

4. **Use "I" statements.** Take ownership of your feelings. Using "I" statements—direct messages you deliver in a calm tone with supportive body language—can diffuse anger. You are not blaming another person but, rather, expressing how a situation affects you. For example, you can say, "Carlos, when *I* hear you click-

ing your pen and tapping it on the desk, *I'm* distracted from studying." This is usually received better than saying, "Carlos, *you're* so rude and inconsiderate. *You* must know that *you're* annoying me when *you* tap your pen."

5. **Focus on one problem.** Don't pounce on every annoying behavior you can think of to dump on the person. Let's continue with the example in Tip 4: "In addition to clicking your pen, Carlos, I don't like how you leave your dishes in the sink, drop your towels in the bathroom, and make that annoying little sound when you eat." Work to resolve only one behavior or conflict at a time.

6. **Focus on win-win solutions.** How can you both win? Restate the problem and jot down as many different creative solutions as possible that you can both agree on.

7. **Reward positive behavior.** As you use praise and reinforce positive behaviors, you will find that the person will exert less resistance. You can now be more direct about the specific behaviors and ask for a commitment: "Julie, if you could be here right at 8:00, we could get through this study session in two hours. Can we agree on this?" Focus on behavior, not personality or name calling, which just angers you and antagonizes the other person. Don't let anger and conflict create more stress in your life and take a physical and emotional toll. You can learn to step back automatically from explosive situations and control them, rather than let your emotions control you. **Peak Progress 2.1** on page 52 explores how you can use the Adult Learning Cycle to manage your emotions.

Self-Esteem and Confidence

Self-esteem is how you feel about yourself. Peak performers have developed confidence and believe in themselves. They assess themselves honestly and focus on their strengths. They constantly learn new skills and competencies that build their confidence. They accept responsibility for their attitudes and behavior. They know that blame and anger do not solve problems. They focus their energies on becoming a person of integrity and character.

People with a positive self-esteem have the confidence that allows them to be more open to new experiences and accepting of different people. They tend to be more optimistic. They are more willing to share their feelings and ideas with others and are willing to tolerate differences in others. Because they have a sense of self-worth, they do not find it necessary to put down or discriminate against others.

Confidence can develop from

◆ Having honesty and integrity
◆ Gaining competence and skills
◆ Accepting and respecting yourself and your work
◆ Being responsible for your choices
◆ Seeing the big picture
◆ Setting high but attainable goals and expectations

If you want to change your outer world and experiences for the better, you must begin by looking at your thoughts, feelings, and beliefs about yourself. Assess your

Applying the Adult Learning Cycle to Self-Control

The Adult Learning Cycle can help you increase your emotional intelligence. For example, you may have felt the same angry and frustrated feelings mentioned in the Self Management exercise on the first page of this chapter. It could be because someone cut you off or you've lost your keys, you may have three papers due, or you are so overwhelmed with school, work, and family that your motivation dropped and you developed a negative attitude.

1. **RELATE. Why do I want to learn this?** What personal meaning and interest does controlling my anger have for me? Has it been a challenge for me? Has it hurt important relationships in my personal life or at school or work? How will controlling my anger help me in those situations?

2. **OBSERVE. How does this work?** I can learn a lot about anger management by watching, listening, and engaging in trial and error. Whom do I consider to be an emotionally mature person? Whom do I respect because of his or her patience, understanding, and ability to deal with stressful events? When I observe the problems that people around me have in their lives, how do they exhibit their emotional maturity in general and anger specifically?

3. **REFLECT. What does this mean?** Test new ways of behaving and break old patterns. Explore creative ways to solve problems rather than getting angry. Gather and assess information about anger management and reflect on what works and doesn't work.

4. **DO. What can I do with this?** Learn by doing and finding practical applications for anger management. Practice the seven steps outlined on pages 49–51. Apply the ABCDE Method of Self-Management to specific situations to determine positive outcomes.

5. **TEACH. Whom can I share this with?** Talk with others and share experiences. Demonstrate to and teach others the methods you've learned. Model by example.

Now return to Stage 1 and realize your accomplishment in taking steps to control your anger better.

self-esteem at the end of the chapter in **Worksheet 2.3** and follow the tips in **Peak Progress 2.2**.

A Positive Attitude and Personal Motivation

There is an old story about three men working on a project in a large city in France. A curious tourist asked them, "What are you three working on?" The first man said, "I'm hauling rocks." The second man said, "I'm laying a wall." The third man said

Tips to Build Self-Esteem and Confidence

- Focus on your strengths and positive qualities and find ways to bolster them. Be yourself and don't compare yourself with others.

- Learn to be resilient and bounce back after disappointments and setbacks. Don't dwell on mistakes or limitations. Accept them, learn from them, and move on with your life.

- Use affirmations and visualizations to replace negative thoughts and images.

- Take responsibility for your life instead of blaming others. You cannot control other people's behavior, but you have complete control over your own thoughts, emotions, words, and behavior. Value civility and self-control.

- Learn skills and competencies that give you opportunities and confidence in your abilities. It is not enough to feel good about yourself; you must also be able to do what is required to demonstrate that you are a competent, honest, and responsible person. The more skills and personal qualities you acquire, the more competent and confident you will feel.

- Focus on giving, not receiving, and make others feel valued and appreciated. You will increase your self-esteem when you make a contribution.

- Create a support system by surrounding yourself with confident and kind people who feel good about themselves and who make you feel good about yourself.

with pride, "I'm building a cathedral." The third man had a sense of vision of the whole system. When college and work seem as tedious as hauling rocks, focus on the big picture.

A positive attitude is essential for achieving success in school, in your career, and in life. Your attitude influences the outcome of a task more than any other factor. **Motivation** is the inner drive that moves you to action. Even when you are discouraged or face setbacks, motivation can help you bounce back and keep on track. You may have skills, experience, intelligence, and talent, but you will accomplish little if you are not motivated to direct your energies toward specific goals.

A positive attitude results in enthusiasm, vitality, optimism, and a zest for living. When you have a positive attitude, you are more likely to be on time, aware, and alert in meetings and class and able to work well even when you have an unpleasant assignment. There is a strong link between attitude and behavior. A positive attitude encourages

- Higher productivity
- An openness to learning at school and on the job
- School and job satisfaction
- Creativity in solving problems and finding solutions

- The ability to work with diverse groups of people
- Enthusiasm and a "can do" outlook
- Confidence and higher self-esteem
- The ability to channel stress and increase energy
- A sense of purpose and direction

A negative attitude can drain you of enthusiasm and energy, and it can result in absenteeism, tardiness, and impaired mental and physical health. In addition, people who have a negative attitude may

- Feel that they are victims and are helpless to make a change
- Focus on the worst that can happen in a situation
- Blame external circumstances for their attitudes
- Focus on the negative in people and situations
- Look at adversity as something that will last forever
- Be angry and blame other people

As discussed in Chapter 1, peak performers display a positive attitude even when faced with adversity. **Peak Progress 2.3** explores the seven positive attitudes of peak

WORDS TO SUCCEED

"It is better to light a candle than curse the darkness."

ELEANOR ROOSEVELT, *U.S. First Lady and political leader*

PEAK PROGRESS   2.3

Seven Positive Attitudes of Peak Performers

1. *Having a flexible attitude* means that you are open to new ideas and situations. You are willing to learn new skills and are interested in continual growth.

2. *Having a mindful attitude* means that you are focused on lasting values. You are mindful of living in the moment, being a person of integrity and character, and acting with kindness and civility. Being is more important than acquiring or doing.

3. *Having a responsible attitude* means that you take an active role in school and work. You take responsibility for your life and don't rely on others to motivate you. You are a self-starter who takes the initiative to produce positive results.

4. *Having a supportive attitude* means that you encourage, listen, show empathy, and work well with others. You look for the best and are more concerned about understanding than persuading others. You look for win-win solutions and communicate clearly, concisely, and directly.

5. *Having a confident attitude* means that you have a balanced perspective about your strengths and limitations. You commit time and effort to grow and to renew yourself physically, mentally, emotionally, and spiritually. You are confident because you use the whole of your intelligence and you are self-disciplined.

6. *Having a follow-through attitude* means that you are aware of the big picture but are also attentive to details and follow through on essential steps. You see whole systems while attending to essential parts.

performers, explaining that having a positive attitude is more than simply seeing the glass as half full—it's a way of life.

How Needs and Desires Influence Attitudes and Motivation

One of the deepest needs in life is to become all that you can be and use all of your intelligence and potential. Abraham Maslow, a well-known psychologist, developed the theory of a hierarchy of needs. According to his theory, there are five levels of universal needs. **Figure 2.2** illustrates these levels, moving from the lower-order needs—physiological and safety and security needs—to the higher-order needs—the needs for self-esteem and self-actualization. The lower-order needs must be met first before satisfying the higher-order needs. For example, it may be difficult for you to participate in hobbies that foster your self-respect if you don't have enough money for food and rent.

For some people, the lower-order needs include a sense of order, power, or independence. The higher levels, which address social and self-esteem factors, include the need for companionship, respect, and a sense of belonging.

As your lower-order needs are satisfied and cease to motivate you, you begin to direct your attention to the higher-order needs for motivation. For example, once

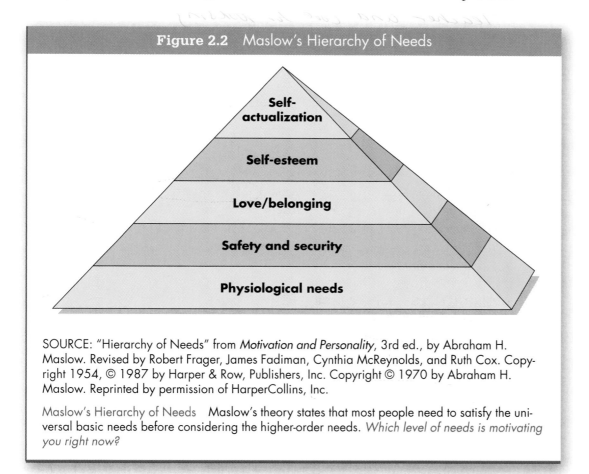

Figure 2.2 Maslow's Hierarchy of Needs

SOURCE: "Hierarchy of Needs" from *Motivation and Personality*, 3rd ed., by Abraham H. Maslow. Revised by Robert Frager, James Fadiman, Cynthia McReynolds, and Ruth Cox. Copyright 1954, © 1987 by Harper & Row, Publishers, Inc. Copyright © 1970 by Abraham H. Maslow. Reprinted by permission of HarperCollins, Inc.

Maslow's Hierarchy of Needs   Maslow's theory states that most people need to satisfy the universal basic needs before considering the higher-order needs. *Which level of needs is motivating you right now?*

Needs, Motivation, and Commitment

1. What needs motivate you at this time?

   Sucess

2. What do you think will motivate you in 20 years?

   wanting to provide A stable income.

3. Complete this sentence in your own words: "For me to be more motivated, I need . . ."

   Take And work on one thing at A time

4. Describe a time in your life when you were committed to something—such as a goal, a project, an event, or a relationship—that was important to you.

   When I was in Nursing school I had A great teacher

5. Regarding your answer to Question 4, what were the main factors that kept you motivated?

   Teacher and love for nursing

you feel confident, you find that you have more energy and focus for defining and pursuing your dreams and goals. You want to discover and develop your full potential. You not only love learning new ideas but also value emotional maturity, character, and integrity. You are well on the path to self-actualization. According to Maslow, self-actualizing people embrace the realities of the world rather than deny or avoid them. They are creative problem solvers who make the most of their unique abilities to strive to be the best they can be. Complete the **Personal Evaluation Notebook 2.3** to assess what motivates you.

Motivational Strategies

Keeping yourself motivated isn't always easy with all the pressures you may be feeling from school, work, family, and so on. However, there are some key motivational strategies you can put into action:

1. **Act as if you were motivated.** Attitude can influence behavior, and behavior can influence attitude. The way you act every day can affect your self-esteem, and your self-esteem can affect the things you do. You can attempt to change your behavior anytime. You don't need to wait until your attitude changes or until you feel motivated to begin the positive behaviors. Act as if you were already motivated.

Self-Talk and Affirmations

Listen to your self-talk for a few days. Jot down the negative thoughts you say to yourself. For example, when you first wake up, do you say, "I don't want to go to class today"?

Do your thoughts and self-talk focus on lack of time, lack of money, or other problems? Observe when you are positive. How does this change your state of mind and your physical sense of well-being? List examples of your negative self-talk and positive affirmations:

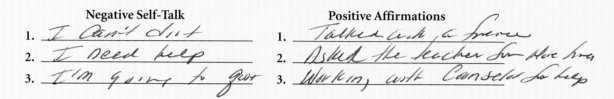

Negative Self-Talk
1. I can't do it
2. I need help
3. I'm going to quit

Positive Affirmations
1. Talked with a friend
2. Asked the teacher for more time
3. Working with Counselor for help

For example, pretend you are performing in a movie. Your character is a positive, motivated student. How would you enter the room? Would you be smiling? What would your breathing, posture, and muscle tension be like? What kinds of gestures and facial expressions would you use to create this character? What kinds of friends would this person enjoy being with? Try acting out the part when you wake up in the morning and throughout the day. If you develop positive study and work habits and do them consistently, even when you don't feel like it, you'll be successful, and this will create a positive state of mind. You are what you do consistently. Positive habits create success.

2. **Use affirmations.** Any discussion of motivation must include your self-talk, what you say to yourself throughout the day. Once you start paying attention to your self-talk, you may be amazed at how much of it is negative. Throughout the day, countless thoughts, images, and phrases go through your brain almost unnoticed, but they have a tremendous influence on your mood and attitude. Your mind is most receptive just before sleep and when first waking up. The first step, then, is to replace negative self-talk with affirmations or positive self-talk. For example, don't say, "I won't waste my time today." That just reminds you that you have a habit of wasting time. Instead, affirm, "I am setting goals and priorities and achieving the results I want. I have plenty of energy to accomplish all that I choose to do, and I feel good when I'm organized and centered." Complete the **Personal Evaluation Notebook 2.4** to determine if your self-talk needs to become more positive.

3. **Use visualization.** As we explored in Chapter 1, visualization is seeing things in your mind's eye by organizing and processing information through pictures and symbols. You imagine yourself behaving in certain ways, so that behavior will become real. For example, businessman Calvin Payne knows the power of visualization. Before he graduated from college, he bought his graduation cap

and gown and kept them in his room. He visualized himself crossing the stage in his gown to accept his diploma. This visual goal helped him when he suffered setbacks, frustration, and disappointments. He graduated with honors and now incorporates visualization techniques in his career.

Most right-brain-dominant people are visual and use imagery a great deal. They can see scenes in detail when they read or daydream. In fact, their imagery is like a movie of themselves, with scenes of how they will react in certain situations, or a replay of what has occurred in the past. These images are rich in detail, expansive, and ongoing. Left-brain dominant people tend to use imagery less, but using imagery is a technique that can be learned, developed, and practiced.

Visualization will help you see problems through formulas; read a recipe and see and taste the finished food; read blueprints and visualize the building; and see scenes and characters through narratives. You can also use mental imagery to create a positive, calm, and motivated state of mind.

4. **Use goals as motivational tools.** Just as an athlete visualizes crossing the finish line, you, too, can visualize your final goal. Working toward your goal can be a great motivator; however, you first must know what your goal is. **Peak Progress 2.4** will help you distinguish the difference between a desire and a goal and between long-term and short-term goals.

Often, peak performers not only visualize goals, but also write them down. Try keeping yours in your wallet, taping them on your bathroom mirror, or putting them on yellow sticky notes around your computer screen. Without a specific goal, it's not easy to find the motivation, effort, and focus required to go to classes and complete assignments. Make certain your goals are realistic. Achieving excellence doesn't mean attaining perfection or working compulsively toward impossible goals. If you try to be a perfectionist, you set yourself up for frustration, which can lead to decreased motivation, lowered productivity, increased stress, and failure.

5. **Understand expectations.** You will be more motivated to succeed if you understand what is expected of you in each class. Most instructors hand out a syllabus on the first day. Review it carefully and keep a copy in your class notebook. Review the syllabus with a study partner and clarify expectations with your instructor. Meet with your academic advisor to review general college and graduation requirements. College is different from high school, and, the more you understand expectations, the more focused you'll be on reaching your goals. (See **Peak Progress 2.5** on page 60.)

6. **Study in teams.** Success in the business world depends on team skills—the sharing of skills, knowledge, confidence, and decision-making abilities. The term *synergy* means that the whole is greater than the sum of the parts. It means seeing and using the whole system, not just isolated parts. You can increase your school and job success by learning, studying, and working in teams. You can also

- ◆ Teach each other material and outline main points
- ◆ Read and edit each other's reports
- ◆ Develop sample quizzes and test each other

Setting Goals

There is an old saying: "If you don't know where you are going, any road will take you there." The key, then, is to figure out where you are going, and then you can determine the best way to get there. Goal setting will help you do that. But goals provide more than direction and a clear vision for the future. When appropriately understood and applied, they are very effective motivators.

It is helpful first to distinguish between goals and desires. Identifying what you want out of life (that is, creating your mission statement, as discussed in Chapter 1) is certainly an important step in developing effective goals, but the goals themselves are not mere desires; rather, they are specific, measurable prescriptions for action. For example, if you want to be financially secure, you should start by identifying the actions that will help you fulfill that desire. Knowing that financial security is tied to education, you might make college graduation your first long-term goal. However, be careful how you construct this goal. "My goal is to have a college degree" is passive and vague. On the other hand, "I will earn my Bachelor of Science degree in computer technology from State University by June 2009" prescribes a clear course of action that can be broken down easily into sequences of short-term goals, which then can be broken down into manageable daily tasks.

Note that your long-term goal always comes first. Discomfort with long-term commitment sometimes leads people to try to address short-term goals first. Do not fall into this trap. Remember that short-term goals are merely steps toward achieving the long-term goal. As such, they cannot even exist by themselves. To understand this better, try to imagine driving to an unfamiliar city and then using a road map without having first determined where you are going. It cannot be done. You must know where you are going before you can plan your route.

Peak performers have an internal **locus of control**—they believe that they have control over their lives and that their rewards or failures are a result of their behavior, choices, character, or efforts. They are able to delay gratification and cope effectively with stress. Many people who have less school and job success have an **external locus of control**—they credit outside influences, such as fate, luck, or other people, with their success or failure. They are impulsive about immediate pleasures and are easily swayed by the influences of others. If you practice responsibility and discipline every day in small ways, your internal locus of control will grow and you will be achieving your goals and writing your own life script, rather than living the script written by your parents, circumstances, or society. In Chapter 3, we will explore using your goals to plan how to use your time effectively.

The following are some points to remember:

- Desires are not goals.
- Goals prescribe action.
- Effective goals are specific.
- Goal setting always begins with a long-term goal.
- Short-term goals are the steps in achieving the long-term goal.
- Daily tasks are the many specific actions that fulfill short-term goals.

The Differences Between High School and College

Accepting that entering college brings a new level of responsibility and expectations can be channeled into an effective motivator. For example, in college, you will be expected to

- Have more responsibilities and budget your time and money
- Express your opinions logically, not just give facts
- Motivate yourself
- Have more freedom and independence
- Have larger classes that meet for longer periods but less often
- Be responsible for knowing procedures and graduation requirements
- Write and read more than you have before
- Think critically and logically
- Receive less feedback and be tested less often but more comprehensively
- Have several textbooks and supplemental readings
- Have more work and turn in higher-quality work
- Interact with people of different values, cultures, interests, and religions
- Learn to be tolerant and respectful of diversity
- Be exposed to new ideas and critique these ideas in a thoughtful way
- Get involved in the community, school clubs, volunteer work, and internships related to your major

◆ Learn to get along with and value different people (we will explore healthy relationships in more detail in Chapter 12)

7. **Stay physically and mentally healthy.** It is difficult to motivate yourself if you don't feel well physically or emotionally. If you are ill, you will miss classes, fall behind in studying, or both. Falling behind can cause you to worry and feel stressed. Talk out your problems, eat well, get plenty of exercise and rest, and create a balance of work and play.

8. **Learn to reframe.** You don't have control over many situations or the actions of others, but you do have total control over your responses. Reframing is choosing to see a situation in a new way. For example, to pay for school, Joan Bosch works at a fast-food hamburger place. She could have chosen to see this in a negative way; instead, she sees it in a positive way. She has reframed this work situation to focus on essential job skills. She is learning to be positive, dependable, hardworking, service-oriented, flexible, and tolerant.

9. **Reward yourself.** The simplest tasks can become discouraging without rewards for progress and for completion. Set up a system of appropriate rewards and consequences. Decide what your reward will be when you finish a project.

For an easier task, the reward might be small, such as a snack, a hot shower, or a phone call to a friend. For a larger project, the reward might be listening to a new CD, going out to dinner, or throwing a small party. What are some rewards that would motivate you? The following are some additional examples of rewards:

Listen to music	Cook your favorite meal	Play sports
Read a novel	Go to a museum	Go to a movie
Go to a sporting event	Take a walk	Visit friends
Take photos	Work in a garden	Watch television

10. **Make learning relevant.** You will be more motivated if you make the connection between college and the world of work. Essentially, make sure you understand the benefits of gaining knowledge and learning new skills in your coursework and the ways they will relate to your performance on the job. You may be attending college just because you love to learn and meet new people. However, it's more likely you are enrolled to acquire or enhance your knowledge and skills, which will increase your marketability in the workforce.

The Motivation Cycle

The motivation cycle in **Figure 2.3** amplifies what you learned in Chapter 1 about the power of visualization. It illustrates how your self-esteem influences what you say to yourself, which in turn influences your physical reactions—breathing, muscular tension, and posture. These physical reactions influence your behavior—both your verbal and your nonverbal responses. Isn't it amazing how the emotions, body, and mind are interrelated? You cannot change one part without changing the whole system. Try to remember how important affirmations and visualization are for creating a resourceful state of mind.

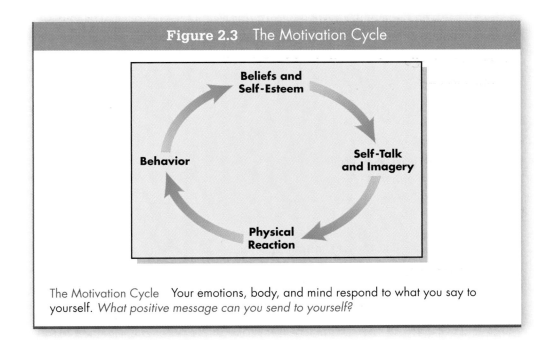

Figure 2.3   The Motivation Cycle

The Motivation Cycle   Your emotions, body, and mind respond to what you say to yourself. *What positive message can you send to yourself?*

The Benefits of Higher Education

Higher Education Encourages Critical Thinking

Higher education has its roots in the liberal arts. Many years ago, being an educated person meant having a liberal arts education. *Liberal* comes from the Latin root word *liber,* which means "to free." A broad education is designed to free people to think and understand themselves and the world around them. The liberal arts include such areas as the arts, the humanities, the social sciences, mathematics, and the natural sciences. Classes in philosophy, history, language, art, and geography focus on how people think, behave, and express themselves in our culture and in the world. The liberal arts integrate many disciplines and provide a foundation for professional programs, such as criminal justice, electronics, computer systems, business, medicine, and law.

Technology is no longer a separate field of study from liberal arts but is an important tool for educated people. Employers want professionals who are creative problem solvers, have good critical thinking skills, can communicate and work well with others, can adapt to change, and understand our complex technical and social world. Liberal arts classes can help make a skilled professional a truly educated professional by providing an integration and understanding of history, culture, ourselves, and our world.

Higher Education Is a Smart Financial Investment

As mentioned earlier, you will be more motivated to put in long hours of studying when you feel the goal is worth it. Higher education is an excellent investment. No one can take your education away from you, and it can pay large dividends. College graduates earn an average of well over $800,000 more in a lifetime than do high school graduates. (See **Figure 2.4.**) Although graduating from college or a career school won't guarantee you a great job, it pays off with more career opportunities, better salaries, more benefits, more job promotions, increased workplace flexibility, better workplace conditions, and greater job satisfaction. Many career centers at colleges make a commitment to help their students find employment.

Society and the workplace benefit when people improve their literacy. Various reports from the U.S. Department of Labor indicate that people who attend at least two years of college tend to

- Make better decisions
- Be willing to learn new skills
- Have more hobbies and leisure activities
- Have a longer life expectancy
- Be healthier
- Be more involved in the community
- Have more discipline and perseverance
- Have more self-confidence
- Learn to adapt to change

WORDS TO SUCCEED

"Education's purpose is to replace an empty mind with an open one."

MALCOLM FORBES, *Publisher*

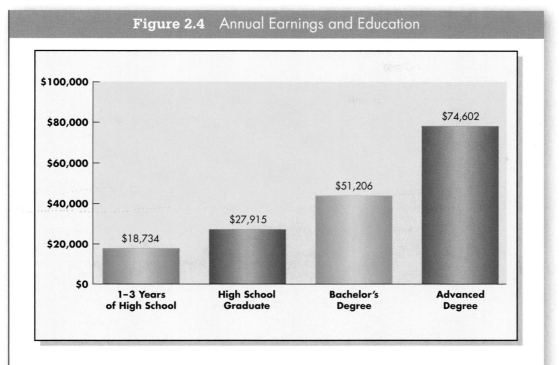

Figure 2.4 Annual Earnings and Education

SOURCE: U.S. Census Bureau, U.S. Department of Commerce, 2005.

Annual Earnings and Education   Statistically, the level of your education is directly related to your income. These figures are average earnings for the U.S. population in 2005. Incomes vary within each category. *What other advantages, besides a good job and income, do you think education offers?*

Higher Education Prepares You for Life on the Job

As you've no doubt noticed, the connection between school and job success is a major theme in this book. What you learn in school correlates directly with finding and keeping a job, as well as succeeding in a chosen career. As you go through school, think about how the skills, personal qualities, and habits you are learning and demonstrating in class are related to job and life success. **Peak Progress 2.6** on page 64 includes a number of skills and qualities you are learning, practicing, and enhancing in your coursework and indicates how you will use them on the job.

As you develop your time- and stress-management skills, which we will explore in more detail later in this text, you will see improvement in your habits in school and on the job. Time management may help you show up for class on time and be prepared every day, thus leading to better grades. Punctuality in school will carry over to punctuality for work. Stress management may help you get along better with your roommates, instructors, or co-workers. Learning how to succeed in the school or college system can serve as a model for working effectively in organizational systems. Do you think you are maximizing your strengths, skills, and personal qualities? See **Peak Progress 2.7** on page 65 to determine what kind of student/worker you are and to determine what you need to do to improve your performance.

Skills for School and Career

Keep the following skills in mind as you see the connection between school and job success.

Skills	School Application	Career Application
Basic skills	Foundation for schoolwork	Foundation for work tasks
Motivation	Motivated to attend classes	Motivated to excel at work
Thinking skills	Solve case studies, equations	Solve work problems
Creativity	Creative experiments	Creative work solutions
Control of time	Homework first	Work priorities in order
Control of money	Personal budget	Departmental budgets
Writing	Writing papers	Writing reports, memos
Speeches	Classroom speeches	Presentations
Test taking	Tests in classes	Performance reviews
Information	Selecting class information	Selecting work information
Learning	Learning for classes	Learning job skills
Systems	Learning college system	Learning organization
Resources	Using college resources	Using work resources
Technology	Using computers for papers	Using computers for work

WORDS TO SUCCEED

"I've missed more than 9000 shots in my career. I've lost almost 300 games. 26 times, I've been trusted to take the game winning shot and missed. I've failed over and over and over again in my life. And that is why I succeed."

MICHAEL JORDAN, *Professional Basketball Player*

Overcome Obstacles

Don't Get Discouraged

Discouragement is a major barrier to motivation. Even peak performers sometimes feel discouraged and need help climbing out of life's valleys. Creating and maintaining a positive state of mind and learning self-control do not happen by reading a book, attending a lecture, or using a few strategies for a day or two. It takes time and effort. Everyone gets off course now and then, but the key is to realize that setbacks are part of life. Don't allow setbacks to make you feel as if you have failed and can no longer reach your goal. Find a formula that works for you to create a positive and resourceful mind.

Don't postpone developing your personal qualities and self-control. **Peak Progress 2.8** shows that a lack of personal qualities has a direct effect on the main reasons students don't graduate. If you think, "I'll be more motivated as soon as I graduate and get a real job," you may never develop the necessary qualities and skills to achieve that. Starting today, you should

◆ Focus on being motivated and positive

◆ Focus on your successes and accomplishments

What Kind of a Student/Worker Are You?

A peak performer or an *A* student

- Is alert, actively involved, and eager to learn
- Consistently does more than required
- Consistently shows initiative and enthusiasm
- Is positive and engaged
- Can solve problems and make sound decisions
- Is dependable, prompt, neat, accurate, and thorough
- Attends work/class every day and is on time and prepared

A good worker or a *B* student

- Frequently does more than is required
- Is usually attentive, positive, and enthusiastic
- Completes most work accurately, neatly, and thoroughly
- Often uses critical thinking to solve problems and make decisions
- Attends work/class almost every day and is usually on time and prepared

An average worker or a *C* student ✓

- Completes the tasks that are required
- Shows a willingness to follow instructions and learn
- Is generally involved, dependable, enthusiastic, and positive
- Provides work that is mostly thorough, accurate, and prompt
- Misses some work/classes

A problem worker or a *D* student

- Usually does the minimum of what is required
- Has regular attendance, is often late, or is distracted
- Lacks a positive attitude or the ability to work well with others
- Often misunderstands assignments and deadlines
- Lacks thoroughness
- Misses many days of work/classes

An unacceptable worker or an *F* student

- Does not do the work that is required
- Is inattentive, bored, negative, and uninvolved
- Is undependable and turns in work that is incorrect and incomplete
- Misses a significant amount of work/classes

◆ Surround yourself with positive, supportive, and encouraging friends
◆ Tell yourself, "This is a setback, not a failure"
◆ Learn self-control and self management strategies

The Most Common Reasons Students Do Not Graduate

Between 30 and 50 percent of all college freshmen never graduate. The top 10 reasons are

1. Poor study skills and habits
2. Lack of time-management skills
3. Lack of preparation for the demands and requirements of college
4. Inability to handle the freedom at college
5. Too much partying
6. Lack of motivation or purpose
7. Failure to attend class regularly
8. Failure to ask for help early
9. Lack of effort and time spent in studying
10. Failure to take responsibility for education (such as getting to know instructors, knowing expectations, setting goals, understanding deadlines, making up tests, re-doing papers)

- Make certain you are physically renewed; get more rest, exercise more, and do something every day that you love
- Replace negative and limiting thoughts and self-talk with affirmations and positive visualization
- Collect short stories about people who were discouraged, received negative messages, and bounced back

Create Positive Mind Shifts

Having both a positive attitude and high self-esteem is important, but neither will help you reach your goals if your beliefs or perceptions are misguided. Sometimes, a mind shift is necessary to see new possibilities and adjust perceptions. Your beliefs are your mind maps, and they influence how you see life. It is important to use critical thinking to assess your beliefs to see if they are accurate and support your goals. Let's say that you are driving a car to New York. If your map is wrong, positive attitude and self-esteem won't get you to New York.

Expectations may also influence how you see yourself and others. You may let your beliefs, assumptions, or expectations get in the way of seeing a person or situation clearly. Sometimes, the closer you are to a situation, the more difficult it is to see it clearly.

Expand Your Comfort Zone

Your beliefs and expectations about yourself can either limit or expand your success. Other people's expectations of you may cause you to redefine who you think you are and what you think you are capable of achieving. You may start to believe what you tell yourself or hear from others again and again, which may be limiting your thinking.

For example, Steve Delmay comes from a long line of lumber mill workers. Although they have lived for generations in a college town, his family has never had anything to do with the college. Steve was expected to go to work at the mill right after high school. He never thought about other options. However, during his senior year in high school, he attended Career Day. He met instructors and students from the local college who were friendly, supportive, and encouraging. His world opened up, and he saw opportunities he had never considered before. Steve experienced a major mind shift. Although he had to overcome a lack of support at home, he is now a successful college student with a bright future.

Creative problem solving can expand your mind and comfort zone and shift your thinking, so that you can see new possibilities and broader and more exciting horizons. College is an ideal time to develop your natural creativity and explore new ways of thinking. Try the following guidelines:

1. **Create a support system.** Without support and role models, you may question whether you can be successful. First-generation college students, women in technical programs, and men in nursing programs may feel uncomfortable and question whether they belong. Cultural minorities, veterans, and physically challenged or returning students may feel that they don't belong. Some students may be told that they are not college material. You can find encouragement with a support system of positive and accepting people. Join a variety of clubs. Make friends with diverse groups of students, instructors, and community leaders.

2. **Reprogram your mind.** Affirmations and visualization can create a self-fulfilling prophecy. If you think of yourself as a success and are willing to put in the effort, you will be successful. Focus on your successes and accomplishments and overcome limitations. For example, if you need to take a remedial math class, take it and don't label yourself as "dumb" or "math-impaired." Instead, focus on how improved your math skills will be.

3. **Use critical thinking.** Question limiting labels and beliefs. Where did they come from and are they accurate? Be mentally active and positive.

4. **Use creative thinking.** Ask yourself, "What if?" Explore creative ways of achieving your goals. Find out how you learn best and adopt positive habits.

5. **Take responsibility.** You are responsible for your thoughts, beliefs, and actions. You can question, think, and explore. You can achieve almost anything you dream.

6. **Learn new skills.** Focus on your strengths, but be willing to learn new skills and competencies continually. Feeling competent is empowering.

7. **Use the whole of your intelligence.** You definitely are smarter than you think you are. Use all your experiences and personal qualities to achieve your goals. Develop responsibility, self-control, dependability, sociability, character, manners, and all the other qualities necessary for school, job, and life success.

In summary, in this chapter, I learned to:

- *Use the whole of my intelligence.* Developing emotional maturity and strong personal qualities is just as, if not more, important to my future success as learning new skills and information. Essential personal qualities include character, responsibility, self-management and self-control, self-esteem, confidence, attitude, and motivation.

- *Focus on character first.* Strong leaders are those who have an equally strong set of values. Having personal integrity gives me the courage to do the right thing, even when it is difficult. I display civility and empathy by interacting with family, friends, and colleagues with respect, kindness, good manners, empathy, and compassion. It's important for me to have a personal code of ethics that I follow in all facets of my life.

- *Take responsibility for my thoughts, actions, and behaviors.* I don't blame others for my setbacks, and I focus my energy on positive solutions. Others can depend on me to keep my commitments.

- *Manage and control my emotions, anger, and negative thoughts.* Conflict is an inevitable part of life, but it can be resolved in a positive way. Seven steps I can follow to redirect my negative thoughts and anger are (1) calm down; (2) clarify and define; (3) listen with empathy and respect; (4) use "I" statements; (5) focus on one problem; (6) focus on win-win solutions; and (7) reward positive behavior.

- *Develop self-esteem and confidence.* Through self-assessment, I understand my strengths and will continue to learn new skills and competencies that will build my confidence.

- *Maintain a positive attitude and keep myself motivated.* A positive attitude is essential for achieving success, and it influences the outcome of a task more than any other factor. Motivation is the inner drive that moves me to action. Working toward goals increases my motivation. Maslow's hierarchy of needs shows that I can fulfill my higher needs for self-esteem and self-actualization only when I have fulfilled my more basic needs first. The motivation cycle further demonstrates how affirmations, visualization, and self-talk affect my physical responses and behavior.

- *Realize the benefits of higher education.* Higher education has its roots in the liberal arts. Liberal arts classes can help make me a truly educated professional by providing an integration and understanding of history, culture, ourselves, and our world. My pursuit of a higher education should pay off with more career opportunities, a higher salary, more benefits, more job promotions, increased workplace flexibility, better workplace conditions, and greater job satisfaction. I will become more prepared for life on the job.

- *Overcome the barriers to staying positive and motivated.* Discouragement is the number one barrier to motivation. Setbacks will occur, but I will focus on my successes and accomplishments, surround myself with supportive and encouraging people, keep physically renewed, and replace negative self-talk with positive affirmations and visualization.

- *Create positive mind shifts and expand my comfort zone.* My beliefs and perceptions must be realistic. If they aren't, I must refocus my expectations in order to achieve my goals. I should not allow my beliefs to limit my potential, and I will use critical thinking techniques to expand my mind and comfort zone.

career in focus

Jacqui Williams

SALES REPRESENTATIVE

Related Majors: Business, Marketing, Public Relations

Positive Attitudes at Work

As a sales representative for a large medical company, Jacqui Williams sells equipment, such as X-ray and electrocardiograph (EKG) machines, to hospitals nationwide. Her job requires travel to prospective clients, where she meets with buyers to show her products and demonstrate their installation and use. Because Jacqui cannot take the large machines with her, she relies on printed materials and a laptop computer, from which she can point out the new aspects of the machines she sells. The sales process usually takes several months and requires more than one trip to the prospective client.

Jacqui works on commission, being paid only when she makes a sale. Because she travels frequently, Jacqui must be able to work independently without a lot of supervision. For this reason, being personally motivated is a strong requirement for her position. Jacqui has found that the best way to remain motivated is to believe in the products she sells. Jacqui keeps up on the latest in her field by reading technical information and keeping track of the competition. She sets sales goals and then rewards herself with a short vacation.

Because personal relations with buyers are so important, Jacqui is careful about her appearance. While traveling, she keeps a positive mind-set through affirmations, and she gets up early to eat a healthy breakfast and exercise in the hotel gym. She uses integrity by presenting accurate information and giving her best advice, even if it means not making a sale. Her clients would describe Jacqui as positive and helpful, someone whom they look forward to seeing and whose advice they trust.

CRITICAL THINKING In what way does having integrity, good character, and a code of ethics enhance a sales representative's business?

Peak Performer Profile

Christiane Amanpour

"Amanpour is coming. Is something bad going to happen to us?"[1] That's how CNN's chief international correspondent, Christiane Amanpour, says she's often greeted. Whether she appreciates the grim humor or not, Amanpour knows that her name and face have become linked in people's minds with war, famine, and death. But she has earned the respect of journalists and viewers around the world with her gutsy reporting from war-ravaged regions, such as Bosnia, Rwanda, and Iraq.

Amanpour launched her career at CNN as an assistant on the international assignment desk in 1983, when some observers mockingly referred to the fledgling network as "Chicken Noodle News." "I arrived at CNN with a suitcase, my bicycle, and about 100 dollars,"[1] she recalls. Less than a decade later, Amanpour was covering Iraq's invasion of Kuwait, the U.S. combat operation in Somalia, and the breakup of the Soviet Union as these events unfolded.

Amanpour's globe trotting began early. Born in London, Amanpour soon moved with her family to Tehran, where her father was an Iranian airline executive. Her family fled the country and returned to England during the Islamic Revolution of 1979. After high school, Amanpour studied journalism at the University of Rhode Island. She took a job after college as a graphic designer at a radio station in Providence. She worked at a second radio station as a reporter, an anchor, and a producer before joining CNN.[2]

"I thought that CNN would be my ticket to see the world and be at the center of history—on someone else's dime,"[1] she says, noting that she's logged more time at the front than most military units. Fear, she admits, is as much a part of her daily life as it is for the soldiers whose activities she chronicles: "I have spent almost every working day [since becoming a war correspondent] living in a state of repressed fear."[1]

Amanpour worries about the changes that have transformed the television news industry in recent years, as competition for ratings and profits has heated up.

But Amanpour remains optimistic. "If we the storytellers give up, then the bad guys certainly will win," she says. "Remember the movie *Field of Dreams* when the voice said 'Build it and they will come'? Well, somehow that dumb statement has always stuck in my mind. And I always say, 'If you tell a compelling story, they will watch.'"[1]

PERFORMANCE THINKING Christiane Amanpour demonstrates courage, integrity, and commitment. In what ways do you speak out for freedom, justice, and equality?

CHECK IT OUT The Committee to Protect Journalists indicates that 47 journalists were killed in 2005 because of their work. Visit their website at **www.cpj.org**, to see what's being done to safeguard the lives of journalists in the world's hotspots. Click on the manual entitled "Journalist Safety Guide" to see what precautions journalists themselves must take in high-risk situations.

[1]AIDA International, 2000 Murrow Awards Ceremony Speech, September 13, 2000. **www.aidainternational.nl**.
[2]CNN Anchors and Reporters: Christiane Amanpour. **http://edition.cnn.com**

Performance Strategies . . . .

Following are the top 10 strategies for developing emotional intelligence and personal qualities:

- ◆ Develop and practice positive personal qualities.
- ◆ Cultivate character and integrity.
- ◆ Take responsibility.
- ◆ Focus on effort, not ability.
- ◆ Use goals as motivational tools.
- ◆ Focus on the positive.
- ◆ Use affirmations and visualization.
- ◆ Reward yourself for making progress and strive for excellence, not perfection.
- ◆ Expand your comfort zone.
- ◆ Be physically active and stay healthy.

Tech for Success . . . .

Take advantage of the text's website at **www.mhhe.com/ ferrett6e** for additional study aids, useful forms, and convenient and applicable resources.

- ◆ **Ethics information on the Web.** Search for articles on ethics, business etiquette, and codes of ethics.

Check out different businesses, the military, government agencies, and colleges to find out if each has a code of ethics. Print some samples and bring them to class. What do all the codes of ethics have in common?

- ◆ **On-line discussion groups.** When you are interested in a topic or goal, it's very motivating to interact with others who have the same interests. Join a discussion group or listserv and share your knowledge, wisdom, and setbacks with others. You will learn their stories and strategies in return.

- ◆ **Goal-setting examples.** Although your goals should be personal, sometimes it helps to see how others have crafted theirs. This may inspire you to realize that setting goals isn't a difficult task—it just takes thinking critically about what you want out of life. A number of resources on the Web provide goal-setting ideas on everything from becoming more financially responsible to learning a second language.

Review Questions . . . .

Based on what you have learned in this chapter, write your answers to the following questions:

1. What personal qualities are essential to success in school and work?

   1. Time to study
   2. Rest

2. Give an example of a short-term goal versus a long-term goal.

   Short term – only provides temporary help.
   Longterm – Looking for the futures

3. List at least five motivational strategies.

   1. Having good rest
   2. Avoiding yourself which it true
   3. cleaning
   4. Completing this on time

4. Explain how affirmations and visualization affect the motivational cycle.

   1. When you affirm something you are sure about it and can see how you can accomplish it

5. Explain what a mind shift is.

   Change of plan

GETTING MOTIVATED

In the Classroom

Carol Rubino is a drafting major at a community college. In order to pay her expenses, she needs to work several hours a week. She is very organized and responsible with her school and work obligations. Most of her peers would describe Carol as motivated because she attends every class, is punctual, and works hard in both school and work. Throughout high school, Carol participated in extracurricular activities but never really enjoyed herself. She likes college but questions the connection between school and real life. As a result, Carol sometimes feels as if she is just wasting time and postponing life until graduation.

1. What strategies in this chapter can help Carol find a strong sense of purpose and motivation?

   Looking for the future and examining how school will provide for her later

2. What would you recommend to Carol for creating a more resourceful and positive attitude?

   Look at the full picture of what she will soon benefit from.

In the Workplace

Carol is now a draftsperson for a small industrial equipment company. She has been with the company for 10 years. Carol is a valuable employee because she is competent and well liked. Carol has a supportive family, is healthy, and travels frequently. Although she enjoys her job, Carol feels bored with the mundane routine of her work. She wants to feel more motivated and excited on the job, as well as in her personal life.

3. What strategies in this chapter can help Carol become more enthusiastic about work or find new interest in her personal life?

   Finding new time and also providing something to do job related while in her travels planning to see other places as a way to encourage her.

4. What would you suggest to Carol to help her get motivated?

   1. Plan where she will travel.
   2. Try to take friends along
   3. Try something social while in her travels

APPLYING THE ABCDE METHOD OF SELF-MANAGEMENT

In the Journal Entry on page 43, you were asked to describe a time when you were angry and lost control of your emotions. Describe that event below and indicate how others reacted and what you might have done differently.

_____

_____

_____

_____

_____

Now apply the ABCDE method to the situation and visualize a situation under control:

A = Actual event:

B = Beliefs:

C = Consequences:

D = Dispute:

E = Energized:

While completing this exercise, did you discover that you spend more time than you thought on negative thoughts?

Practice Self-Management

For more examples of learning how to manage difficult situations, see the "Self-management Workbook" section of the Online Learning Center website at **www.mhhe.com/ferrett6e**.

REWARDING MYSELF: A PERSONAL REINFORCEMENT CONTRACT

Use this example as a guide; then fill in the following contract for one or all of the courses you are taking this term.

Name *Sara Jones*

Course *General Accounting*   Date *September 2007*

If I *study for six hours each week in this class and attend all lectures and labs*

Then I will *reword myself with a long bike ride and picnic lunch every Saturday.*

I agree to *learn new skills, choose positive thoughts and attitudes, and try out new behaviors.*

I most want to accomplish *an "A" in this course to quality for advanced accounting courses.*

The barriers to overcome are *my poor math skills.*

The resources I can use are *my study group and the Tutoring Center.*

I will reward myself for meeting my goals by *going out to dinner with some friends.*

The consequences for not achieving the results I want will be *to find a new major.*

Reinforcement Contract

Name _____

Course _____ Date _____

If I _____

Then I will _____

I agree to _____

I most want to accomplish _____

The barriers to overcome are _____

The resources I can use are _____

I will reward myself for meeting my goals by _____

The consequences for not achieving the results I want will be _____

CHAPTER 2   REVIEW AND APPLICATIONS

SELF-ESTEEM INVENTORY

Do this simple inventory to assess your self-esteem. Circle the number of points that reflects your true feelings.

4 = all the time

3 = most of the time

2 = some of the time

1 = none of the time

1.	I like myself and I am a worthwhile person.	(4)	3	2	1
2.	I have many positive qualities.	4	(3)	2	1
3.	Other people generally like me and I have a sense of belonging.	4	(3)	2	1
4.	I feel confident and know I can handle most situations.	4	(3)	2	1
5.	I am competent and good at many things.	4	(3)	2	1
6.	I have emotional control and I am respectful of others.	4	3	(2)	1
7.	I am a person of integrity and character.	(4)	3	2	1
8.	I respect the kind of person I am.	(4)	3	2	1
9.	I am capable and willing to learn new skills.	4	(3)	2	1
10.	Although I want to improve and grow, I am happy with myself.	4	(3)	2	1
11.	I take responsibility for my thoughts, beliefs, and behavior.	4	3	(2)	1
12.	I am empathetic and interested in others and the world around me.	(4)	3	2	1

Total points   ____   ____   ____   ____

Add up your points. A high score (36 and above) indicates high self-esteem. If you have a high sense of self-esteem, you see yourself in a positive light. If your self-esteem is low (below 24), you may have less confidence to deal with problems in college or on the job. If you scored at the lower end, list some strategies you can implement that may help boost your self-esteem:

LEARNING STYLES AND MOTIVATION

You will feel more motivated and positive when you align your efforts with your learning and personality styles. Review your preference and style and think of the factors that help motivate you.

For example, *auditory learners* may find that they are more motivated when they listen to a tape of their favorite inspirational music and say affirmations. *Visual learners* may find that they are motivated when they surround themselves with pictures and practice visualizing themselves as motivated and positive. *Kinesthetic learners* may be more motivated when they work on activities, dance, hike, jog, and work with others.

Analyzers may be more motivated when they think, reflect, and organize information into sequential steps. *Supporters* may be more motivated when they work in a group and make information meaningful. *Creators* may be more motivated when they observe, make active experiments, and build models. *Directors* may be more motivated when they clearly define procedures and make practical applications.

List the ways you can motivate yourself that are compatible with your learning style and personality type:

1. *Visually — looking up information — going and seeing what's in my field.*

2. *Hand on.*

3.

4.

5.

6.

ASSESSMENT OF PERSONAL QUALITIES

Category	Assessment	Yes	No
Emotional intelligence	Do I value and practice essential personal qualities?		
Character	Do I value and practice being a person of character and integrity?		
Civility	Do I treat others with respect and courtesy?		
Ethics	Do I have a code of ethics?		
Responsibility	Do I take responsibility for my thoughts and behavior?		
Self-control	Do I have self-control and know how to manage anger?		
Self-esteem	Do I have a realistic and positive sense of myself?		
Positive attitude	Do I strive to be positive and upbeat?		
Motivation	Do I create the inner drive and determination to achieve my goals?		
Self-actualization	Am I committed to growing and realizing my full potential?		
Visualization	Do I use visualization as a powerful tool for change and growth?		
Affirmation	Do I dispute and replace negative self-talk with affirmations?		
Critical thinking	Do I use critical thinking to challenge my beliefs and see new possibilities?		

The area I most want to improve is:

Strategies I will use to improve are:

Manage Your Time

CHAPTER OBJECTIVES

In this chapter, you will learn to:

▲ Determine how you use your time

▲ Determine how you should use your time

▲ Use personal goals to identify priorities

▲ Apply time-management strategies

▲ Assess your energy level and time wasters

▲ Work in alignment with your learning style

▲ Overcome procrastination

▲ Handle interruptions

▲ Juggle family, school, and job commitments

Self-Management

"It's 7:30 A.M., I'm late for class, and I can't find my keys. It always seems like there's too little time and too much to do. I feel as if I have no control over my life. How can I manage my time and get organized?"

Have you ever had a similar experience? Do you find yourself spending hours looking for things? Do you get angry at yourself and others because you feel frustrated and unorganized? In this chapter, you will learn how to take control of your time and your life and focus on priorities. Visualize yourself going through the day organized and centered. You have a clear vision of your goals and priorities and work steadily until tasks are finished. Feel the sense of accomplishment and completion. Visualize yourself in charge of your time and your life.

JOURNAL ENTRY In **Worksheet 3.1** on page 108, describe a time or situation when you felt overwhelmed by too much to do and too little time. What were the consequences?

T his chapter looks at time management with a positive attitude. Instead of controlling, suppressing, or constricting your freedom, time management enables you to achieve the things you really want and frees up time to enjoy life. Peak performers use a systematic approach that allows them to

- Organize projects and achieve results
- Accomplish goals and priorities
- Be effective, not just efficient
- Avoid crises
- Feel calm and productive
- Feel a sense of accomplishment
- Have more free time to enjoy life

WORDS TO SUCCEED

"Time is what we want most, but what we use worst."

WILLIAM PENN, *Statesman, founder of Pennsylvania*

Everyone has the same amount of time—24 hours in each day. You can't save or steal time. When it's gone, it's gone. However, you can learn to invest it wisely. This chapter will help you learn how to get control of your life by managing your time wisely and by choosing to spend it on your main goals. It will also help you think about the contributions you want to make during your lifetime and the legacy you want to leave behind after you are gone. You will discover that there is always time to do the things you really want to do. Too many people waste time doing things that can be done in a few moments or doing things that should not be done at all and then ignoring their main goals.

As you go through this chapter, think about what you want to achieve and how you can use your time skillfully to perform at your peak level. This chapter will help you become effective, not just efficient. Being efficient is about doing things faster. Being effective is about doing the right things in the right way. As a wise time manager, you can avoid overwhelming feelings of losing control of tasks and falling behind in school, at work, or in your personal life. Whether you are an 18-year-old living on campus or a 45-year-old returning student juggling school, family, and work, the principles in this chapter can help you manage your time and your life.

Use Time Effectively

Time management is much more than focusing on minutes, hours, and days. Your attitude, energy level, and ability to concentrate have a great impact on how well you manage time. Clearly evaluate situations that may have spun out of control because of lack of planning or procrastination. Recall how these situations may have affected other people. You are part of the whole system. When you are late for class, miss a study-group meeting, or don't do your share of a team project, it affects others.

Let's look at two important questions concerning your present use of time. The answers will help you develop a plan that will fine-tune your organizational and time-management skills—ultimately leading you to become an efficient peak performer.

1. Where does your time go? (Where are you spending your time and energy?)
2. Where should your time go?

Where Does Your Time Go?

You can divide time into three types: committed time, maintenance time, and discretionary time.

Committed Time

Committed time is devoted to school, labs, studying, work, commuting, and other activities involving the immediate and long-term goals you have committed to accomplishing.

Maintenance Time

Maintenance time is the time you spend maintaining yourself. Activities such as eating, sleeping, bathing, exercising, and maintaining your home—cooking, cleaning/laundry, shopping, bill paying—use up your maintenance time.

Discretionary Time

The time that is yours to use as you please is discretionary time. Separate your commitments and maintenance from your discretionary time and put all your activities into certain categories. For example, grooming includes showering, styling your hair, cleaning your contact lenses, and getting dressed. Don't spend too much time trying to determine in which category an activity fits. You want to use your discretionary time for the things you value most in life. These important items include relationships with family and friends; service to the community; intellectual development; and activities that give you a lot of joy and relaxation and that contribute to your physical, mental, and spiritual well-being. These are important goals that tie in with your long-term goals of being healthy, feeling centered and peaceful, and having loving relationships. Make certain your discretionary activities are conscious choices and that you make them top priorities.

Remember that this section asked you where your time goes and if you are using most of the day for commitments. A good place to determine your answer is with an assessment of how your time and energy are spent. Look at the sample Time Log in **Figure 3.1** on page 82 and then complete **Personal Evaluation Notebook 3.1** on page 83. After you have recorded your activities, review your Time Log to determine how much time you are devoting to daily tasks, such as studying, commuting, and socializing. Complete **Personal Evaluation Notebook 3.2** on page 84 and tally how much time you currently spend on various activities (and add others from your Time Log). The point of these exercises is to determine where you are currently spending your time, which will then help you determine the best way to use your

Figure 3.1 Sample Time Log

Time	Activity	Notes	My Energy Level (High or Low)
12:00 – 1:00 A.M.	Sleep	Maintenance	Low
1:00 – 2:00	Sleep	Maintenance	Low
2:00 – 3:00	Sleep	Maintenance	Low
3:00 – 4:00	Sleep	Maintenance	Low
4:00 – 5:00	Sleep	Maintenance	Low
5:00 – 6:00	Sleep	Maintenance	Low
6:00 – 7:00	Shower, dress	Maintenance	Low
7:00 – 8:00	Drive kids to school	Committed	Low
8:00 – 9:00	Make to-do list	Committed	High
9:00 – 10:00	Coffee and calls	Disc./committed	High
10:00 – 11:00	Write proposal	Committed	High
11:00 – 12:00 (noon)	Meeting	Committed	Low
12:00 – 1:00 P.M.	Lunch	Maintenance	High
1:00 – 2:00			
2:00 – 3:00			
3:00 – 4:00			
4:00 – 5:00			
5:00			

Sample Time Log Knowing how you spend your time is the first step toward managing it. *Are your discretionary activities conscious choices?*

time to achieve important goals. Even if you are juggling school, work, and family and feel you have no discretionary time, this will help you use what little discretionary time that you do have to be most effective.

Where Should Your Time Go?

Peak performers know that they are responsible for their own effectiveness. The first rule of time management is to make a commitment to what you want to accomplish—in other words, to set goals. As discussed in Chapter 2, goals are not vague wishes or far-away dreams. They are specific, measurable, observable, and realistic. A goal is a target that motivates you and directs your efforts. Goal setting is not easy; you need to focus inward and think about your deepest values. You need to assess your level of commitment and believe that you can meet your goals.

It's important to have a realistic picture of what your goals are and to observe and reflect constantly on how your daily activities are leading to larger goals. Written

Time Log

Fill in this time log to chart your activities throughout the day. Under "Notes," identify activities as maintenance, committed, or discretionary. (You may want to chart your activities for more than one day to see patterns in how you spend your time.)

Time	Activity	Notes	My Energy Level (High or Low)
12:00–1:00 A.M.			
1:00–2:00			
2:00–3:00			
3:00–4:00			
4:00–5:00			
5:00–6:00			
6:00–7:00			
7:00–8:00			
8:00–9:00			
9:00–10:00			
10:00–11:00			
11:00–12:00 (noon)			
12:00–1:00 P.M.			
1:00–2:00			
2:00–3:00			
3:00–4:00			
4:00–5:00			
5:00–6:00			
6:00–7:00			
7:00–8:00			
8:00–9:00			
9:00–10:00			
10:00–11:00			
11:00–12:00 (midnight)			

How Much Time Do You Spend?

Fill in the following chart to determine how much time you spend on certain activities. Use the information you compiled in **Personal Evaluation Notebook 3.1.** Typical activities are listed. You may, of course, change or add activities to the list. Remember, the total number of hours should be 24.

Activity	Time Spent	Activity	Time Spent
Attending class		Eating	
Working		Sleeping	
Commuting		Cooking	
Studying		Shopping	
Attending meetings		Running errands	
Grooming		Socializing	
Exercising		Doing hobbies	
Doing household chores		Talking on the telephone	
Waiting in line		Watching television	
Other		Total time	

goals help clarify what you want and can give you energy, direction, and focus to put them into action. Goals can be short-term, mid-term, and long-term and are easier to identify when they flow out of a mission statement that defines what is most important to you. Placing goals within time frames can help you reach them. Complete **Personal Evaluation Notebook 3.3** to map out your goals. Then, in Chapter 14, revisit these goals when you are completing your Career Development Portfolio.

Setting Priorities

There is always time for what is most important. Prioritizing helps you focus on activities that are most important to you at any given time. You want to make certain that your days are not just a treadmill of activities, crises, and endless tasks but that you focus on what is important as well as what is urgent.

Urgent priorities are pressing, deadline-driven projects or activities, such as dropping a class, paying your fees, or turning in papers. Some urgent activities seem like busywork or distractions, but they directly affect your top goals and priorities. For example, there is a serious consequence for missing a deadline, such as paying additional fees, getting poor grades, or even missing graduation.

Important priorities are activities that support your goals and create the results you want. These activities and commitments include attending every class, creating

Looking Ahead: Your Goals

Complete this activity to help you create major targets in your life—or long-term goals. From these goals, you can write mid-term goals (two to five years), short-term goals (one year), and then immediate (or semester) goals. Save this in your Career Development Portfolio. Use additional paper if necessary, or save it on the computer.

Do it!

Nature
pg 8.

A. Mission Statement

You'll recall from Chapter 1 that your personal mission statement summarizes your most important lifetime goals and reflects your philosophy based on your deepest values and principles. In the blanks below, repeat (or revise) your thoughts from Chapter 1.

- Think of what you value most in life; then list those things:
  Being stable, Financially, physically

- What is your life's purpose?

- What legacy do you want to leave?
  that I was a go getting

Mission statement:
I am interested in Financially being able to manage my bills. and Be physically healthy while doing it

B. Long-Term Goals (Accomplish in 10 Years or So)

Brainstorm all the specific goals that you want to accomplish during your lifetime. You should include goals for all areas of your life, such as education, career, travel, financial security, relationships, spiritual life, community, and personal growth. This list will be long, and you will want to add to it and revise it every year if goals change. Following are a few incomplete statements that might help you as you brainstorm:

- My dreams include *Being in the Health field*
- I most want to accomplish *Becoming License Rn.*
- The places I most want to visit are *Staks I haven't travelled to*
- One thing I've always wanted to do is *Be financiac independant*

C. Mid-Term Goals (Accomplish in the Next 5 Years)

Then, what are the goals you want to accomplish in the next five years? Following are some examples:

- I will complete my degree.
- I will graduate with honors.
- I will buy a new sports car.
- I will take a trip to Europe.

I will Accomplish getting my degree and look frward. to owning my own business

(continued)

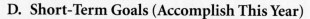

D. Short-Term Goals (Accomplish This Year)

List goals that you want to accomplish in the next year. Consider your answers to these questions:

- What is the major goal for which I am striving this year?
- How does this goal relate to my life's mission or purpose?
- Is this goal in conflict with any other goal?
- What hurdles must I overcome to reach my goal?
- What resources, help, and support will I need to overcome these hurdles?
- What specific actions are necessary to complete my goal?
- What will be my reward for achieving this goal?

E. Semester Goals

List goals you want to accomplish this semester—for example,

- I will preview chapters for 10 minutes before each lecture.
- I will go to all of my classes on time.
- I will jog for 30 minutes each day.

---

study teams, completing homework, forming healthy relationships, planning, and exercising regularly. These priorities are important not just to meet immediate goals but also to support your lifetime goals and mission. People who spend time on important items on a daily basis prevent crises in their lives. For example, if you build in a personal fitness routine every day, you will increase your energy, health, and overall sense of well-being and prevent medical problems that result from inactivity and weight gain.

Ongoing activities require continuing attention and may be urgent, but they may not be important. For example, as you go through your e-mail, open mail, and answer phone calls, you will find that some must be responded to immediately or they will fall into the urgent category, but they are not important for your goals. These activities require continual attention and follow-up and should be managed to prevent future problems. Jot down whom you need to see or call. Follow up with deadlines and determine if these activities are worthwhile and support your top goals. For example, maybe you were pressured to join a club or community group that has ended up taking a lot of time. You may need to say, "This is a worthwhile project and I appreciate being inviting to attend, but I cannot participate at this time." Ask yourself if this activity meets your highest priority at this time.

Trivial activities make up all the daily stuff of life and many are major time wasters. These unimportant activities can be fun, such as talking on the phone with friends, chatting on-line, going to parties, blogging, gossiping, shopping, and surfing the Internet. They can also be annoying, such as dealing with junk mail—both real and virtual. The key is to stay focused on your important, top-priority items and schedule a certain amount of time for trivial activities. You want a balanced life and

WORDS TO SUCCEED

"Ordinary people merely think how they shall spend their time; a man of talent tries to use it."

ARTHUR SCHOPENHAUER, *German philosopher*

you need to socialize with friends, but sometimes a phone call or quick visit can turn into an hour-long gossip session. If this happens too often, you will not accomplish your important goals.

Setting priorities helps you focus on immediate goals. These essential, small steps lead you to your big goals. Your awareness of where your time goes becomes a continual habit of assessing, planning, and choosing tasks in the order of their importance, and this leads to success. Ask yourself the following questions: Do I have a sense of purpose and direction? Are my goals clearly defined? Are any in conflict with each other? Are they flexible enough to be modified as needed? Do I forget to write priorities and phone numbers in my planner? Do I daydream too much and have a problem with concentration? Do I invest time in high-priority tasks? Do I attend to small details that pay off in a big way? See **Peak Progress 3.1** to see if the 80/20 rule applies to you.

PEAK PROGRESS — 3.1

Invest Your Time in High-Priority Items: The 80/20 Rule

Whether you are a student, an executive, or an entry-level worker, your effectiveness will increase if you focus on top-priority items. According to the 80/20 rule of time management, 80 percent of the results flow out of 20 percent of the activities—for example,

- Eighty percent of the interruptions come from 20 percent of the people.
- Eighty percent of the clothes you wear come from 20 percent of your wardrobe.
- Eighty percent of your phone calls come from 20 percent of the people you know.
- Eighty percent of a company's sales may come from 20 percent of their total customers.

Taking a look at your time wasters may reveal that you are spending too much time on low-priority activities and short-changing your top priorities. Wasting time on low-priority activities is unproductive and a major reason for not accomplishing major tasks.

If you want to produce results, you need to focus on what is important—for example,

- Twenty percent more effort can result in an 80 percent better paper or speech.
- Twenty percent more time being involved and prepared in classes could result in 80 percent better results.
- Twenty percent more time developing positive relationships could reduce conflicts by 80 percent.
- Twenty percent more time taking care of yourself—getting enough sleep, eating healthy, exercising, and controlling stress—can result in 80 percent more effectiveness.

The 80/20 rule is just a rule of thumb. The exact percentage may change based on the circumstance. However, the point is that you should spend your time on the activities that are really important and achieve the results you want.

Time-Management Strategies

Use the following strategies to improve your time-management skills and to help you achieve your goals in a balanced and effective way.

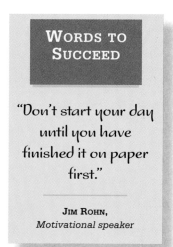

WORDS TO SUCCEED

"Don't start your day until you have finished it on paper first."

JIM ROHN,
Motivational speaker

1. **Keep a calendar.** An inexpensive pocket-size calendar is easy to carry with you and handy for scheduling commitments, such as classes, labs, and work for the entire semester. This helps you see the "big picture." Review your calendar each week and list top priorities, due dates, and important school, work, and family activities. Each day, review urgent priorities that must be done by a deadline, such as paying fees, dropping a class, returning a library book, paying taxes, or applying for graduating. Schedule important activities that support your goals, such as classes, exercise, study teams, and deadlines for choosing a topic. Jot down people to see or call, such as your instructor or advisor, or activities, such as meetings or social events. The key is to keep it simple. Remember, the shortest pencil is better than the longest memory. For example, if your advisor gives you a code for registration, put it on the date and time for your registration. Don't just write your code on your binder or toss it into your backpack. Included in the Worksheets at the end of this chapter are handy calendars to help you plan your week, month, and semester.

2. **Create a daily to-do list.** Some people like to write a to-do list for the next day, taking some time at the end of a day to review briefly what they want to focus on for the next day. Others like to write their list in the morning at breakfast or when they first get to school or work. List the tasks you need to accomplish during the day and map them out on a daily calendar. You may want to circle or place a number 1 by the most important priority to make sure it gets accomplished. Make certain you build in time for family and friends. If you have children, plan special events. Bear in mind that the schedule should be flexible; you will want to allow for free time and unexpected events. Follow this schedule for two weeks and see how accurate it is. You can follow the format of the Time Log on page 83, or see Worksheet 3.6, which includes a planner for mapping out your daily to-do list.

   Once you have written your list, get going and do your urgent, top-priority items. Keep your commitments, such as attending every class, and don't do pleasant, fun activities until the most important ones are done. When you see important items checked off, you'll be inspired. It's OK if you don't get to everything on your list. If there are tasks left over, add them to your next to-do list if they are still important. Ask yourself, "What is the best use of my time right now?"

3. **Do the tough tasks first.** You will feel a sense of accomplishment as you tackle your tough tasks first. Start out with your most difficult subjects, while you're fresh and alert. For instance, if you are avoiding your statistics homework because it is difficult, get up early and do it before your classes begin. Start projects when they're assigned.

4. **Break projects down into smaller tasks.** Begin by seeing the whole project or each chapter as part of a larger system. Then break it into manageable chunks. You may get discouraged if you face a large task, whether it's writing a major term paper or reading several chapters. Getting started is half the battle. Sometimes working for just 15 minutes before you go to bed can yield big results. For example, preview a chapter, outline or mind map the main ideas for your term

Figure 3.2 Sample Project Board

Project: Term Paper for Business Class 110

Today's date: January 23, 2007   Due date: April 23, 2007

Key Activities	Date Completed
Explore topics.	**January 23**
Finalize topic.	January 28
Mind map outline.	February 4
Initial library research	February 8
General outline	February 22
Library research	March 5
Detailed library research	March 10
Detailed outline	March 15
First draft	March 27
Do additional research and spell-check.	April 5
Proof second draft, revise.	April 10
Prepare final draft and proof.	April 15
Paper finished and turned in.	**April 23**

Sample Project Board   Making a project board is an effective time-management strategy. You can plan your tasks from start to end, or some people prefer to work backwards—starting with the end date. *How can you incorporate your project board into your daily planner?*

paper, or write a summary at the end of a chapter. You will find inspiration in completing smaller tasks, and you will feel more in control.

Some students find using a project board helpful for long-term projects, as shown in **Figure 3.2.** This doesn't need to be a complicated system. Begin with today's date (or the start date), along with the due date, clearly indicated at the top. More than likely, the end date cannot change. Your start date should also be realistic—and as soon as possible. Then separate the "board" into two columns: "Key Activities" and "Date Completed." In the date column, put today's date (or start date) at the top and the project's final due date at the bottom. (Some prefer to reverse that, putting the due date at the top and working backwards. Use whichever process works best for you.) Thus, with these two dates set, begin in the activities column by listing in order the project-related tasks that need to be accomplished between the start and end dates. Go back to the date column and start plugging in optimal dates next to the tasks, working from beginning to end. You may find that the time you think you need for each task ends up with a schedule that extends beyond your due date—obviously, that's a problem. Thus, you need to revise your dates and create a new schedule that achieves your completion date. (Make certain you allow time for proofreading and potential setbacks, such as computer problems.)

5. **Consolidate similar tasks.** If you group similar tasks, you can maximize your efforts. For example, if you need to make several calls, make them all at a specific time and reduce interruptions. Set aside a block of time to shop, pay bills,

Study Anywhere and Everywhere
Use your time between classes and while waiting for appointments to study and prepare for class. *What is something you can always carry with you, so that you are prepared for down time?*

go to the post office, and run errands. Write a list of questions for your advisor, instructor, or study team. Make certain you know expectations, so that you don't have to repeat tasks. Save your energy and use your resources by planning and combining similar activities, such as taking a walk with a friend, thus combining exercise with socializing.

6. **Study at your high-energy time.** Know your body rhythms and study your hardest subjects during your high-energy time. Review the Time Log to determine the time of day when you have the most energy. Complete **Personal Evaluation Notebook 3.4.** Guard against interruptions and don't do mindless tasks or socialize during your peak energy period. For example, if your peak time is in the morning, don't waste time by answering mail, socializing, cleaning, checking out books at the library, or doing other routine work. Use your high-energy time to do serious studying and work that requires thinking, writing, and completing projects. Use your low-energy time to do more physical work, chores, or easy reading or previewing of chapters.

7. **Study everywhere and anywhere.** Ideally, you should choose a regular study location that has few distractions, such as the library. However, you should always be prepared to study everywhere and anywhere, as you never know when you might get some unexpected down time. Carry note cards with you to review formulas, dates, definitions, facts, and important data. Bring class notes or a book with you to review during the 5 or 10 minutes of waiting between classes, for the bus, in line at the grocery store, or for appointments. Tape important material and lectures and play these tapes while commuting, exercising, dressing, walking, or waiting for class to begin. Avoid crowded times in the library and computer labs. Even if you plan well, you will occasionally get stuck in lines, but you can make the most of this time.

8. **Study in short segments throughout the day.** Studying in short segments is much more effective than studying in marathon sessions. Your brain is much more receptive to recall when you review in short sessions at various times.

9. **Get organized.** Manage your time by consistently creating good habits. Lay out your clothes and pack your lunch the night before, put your keys on the same hook, put your backpack by the door, put your mail and assignments in the same space, and keep records of bills and important information in your file. Think of the time that you waste looking for items. Getting organized saves time and reduces stress. Keep an academic file that includes your grades and transcripts. Keep a box with tests, papers, and projects. If you need to negotiate a grade, you will have the background support you will need. If you have a personal computer, take the time to learn how to save, retrieve, and back up information (to avoid losing hours of work).

Your Daily Energy Levels

Keep track of your energy levels every day for a week or more. Revisit your Time Log on page 83 to determine your daily energy levels, so that you can become more aware of your patterns.

1. What time(s) of the day are your energy levels at their peak?
   _____

2. What time(s) of the day are your energy levels at their lowest?
   _____

3. What tasks do you want to focus on during your high-energy time?
   _____

4. What can you do to increase your energy at your low-energy time?
   _____

10. **Be flexible, patient, and persistent.** Don't try to make too many changes at once, and don't get discouraged if a strategy doesn't work for you. You are striving for excellence, not perfection. Change certain aspects until a strategy fits your style. Be flexible. If it works, do it. If not, try something new. Just make sure you've given yourself at least 30 days to develop new habits. It often feels strange and uncomfortable to do any new task or vary your schedule of daily events. For example, you might discover that you have a habit of getting a donut and coffee every morning and spending an hour or so socializing with friends before your morning classes. You might try changing this habit by doing it only once a week.

11. **Realize that you can't do it all (or at least right now).** You may feel overwhelmed by too many demands and determine that some tasks are better done by others around you. This does not mean you can offload your responsibilities onto others, but focus on your important priorities and say no to activities that don't support your goals. Consider delegating certain tasks, joining a club later in the year, or participating in a fundraiser when you are on school break. Do social activities, return phone calls, and visit with friends when you have done your top-priority tasks.

Time Management and Your Learning Style

Many time-management strategies are designed for people with left-brain dominance. Left-brain dominant people like routine, structure, and deadlines. They tend to be **convergent** thinkers because they are good at looking at several unrelated items and bringing order to them. Right-brain dominant people like variety, flexibility, creativity, and innovation. They are usually **divergent** thinkers because they branch out from one idea to many. They are good at brainstorming because one idea leads to another. They are able to focus on the whole picture. However, they can also learn to break the global view of the whole project into steps, break each of these steps into

Convergent – Several Unrelated thinkers.

Divergent – branch out from one idea to many

activities, and schedule and organize activities around the big goal. If you are right-brain dominant, you should

- **Focus on a few tasks.** It is very important for right-brain dominant people to focus their efforts on one or two top-priority items instead of being scattered and distracted by busywork. Imagine putting on blinders and focusing on one step until it is completed and then move on to the next step.

- **Write it down.** A daily calendar is vital to making certain that your daily activities support your short- and long-term goals. Write down phone numbers, e-mail addresses, and office hours of instructors and study team members. Highlight in color any deadlines or top-priority activities. Besides a daily calendar, use a master calendar in your study area and allow for variety and change. Make certain you review both your daily calendar with to-do items and your master calendar before you go to bed at night, so that you see the big picture.

- **Use visuals.** Right-brain people often like to use visuals. One creative way to brainstorm, plan, and put your vision into action is to use a mind map (see Chapter 5, page 162). Use visual cues and yellow sticky notes. When you think of an activity that will help you meet your goal, write it down.

- **Integrate learning styles.** Visualize yourself completing a project. Use auditory cues by dictating ideas and planning your project on tape. Talk about the great feeling you will have when you complete this project. Make your project physical by adapting a hands-on approach and working with others to complete your project. Ask yourself, "Is there a way to simplify this task?" Planning is important, even if you are a creative person. **Peak Progress 3.2** explores the process of learning to take control of your time.

WORDS TO SUCCEED

"You may delay, but time will not."

BENJAMIN FRANKLIN,
Inventor, publisher

Overcome Obstacles

Stop Procrastinating

Procrastination is deliberately putting off tasks. It is one of the biggest obstacles to effective time management. Most of us have been guilty of putting off doing what we know should be done. However, a continual pattern of delaying and avoiding is a major barrier to time management.

There are many reasons for procrastination. Some people prefer to do the things they like to do rather than doing what should be done. Some people are perfectionists and don't want to do something or complete steps unless they feel the outcome is the best it can be. Other people are worriers and get weighed down with details or overwhelmed by the enormity of the tasks. Some people are shy and avoid working with others to accomplish a task or give a speech. Others are embarrassed because they have avoided a task for too long, so they just write it off. Other people are easily distracted, blame others, or don't want to be told what to do. Some people feel they work better under extreme pressure and use it as an excuse for waiting until the last minute. Some just simply lack the discipline to sit down and complete a task. Complete **Personal Evaluation Notebook 3.5** on page 94 to determine if you procrastinate too much and if so, why.

PEAK PROGRESS   3.2

Applying the Adult Learning Cycle to Taking Control of Your Time and Life

Applying the Adult Learning Cycle will help you establish goals and create a plan to meet them.

1. **RELATE. Why do I want to learn this?** Planning my time better and getting organized are essential for me to juggle the demands of school, work, and life. What are the areas where I need the most work?

2. **OBSERVE. How does this work?** I can learn a lot about time management by observing people who are on time, get their work done, work calmly and steadily, and seem to accomplish a lot in a short time. I'll also observe people who are unorganized, often late, miss classes, and waste a lot of time blaming, complaining, and being overly involved in other people's lives. Do their problems relate to time management and self-management? How do I manage my time?

3. **REFLECT. What does this mean?** What strategies are working for me? What are some new strategies I can try out? I will explore creative ways to solve problems rather than feeling overwhelmed.

4. **DO. What can I do with this?** Each day, I'll work on one area. For example, I'll choose one place to hang my keys and consistently put them there. If I find them in my purse or on the table, I'll put them on the hook until it becomes a habit.

5. **TEACH. Whom can I share this with?** I'll share my tips and experiences with others and find out their strategies in return. I should continue to reward myself, at least mentally, for making positive changes.

Now return to Stage 1 and think about how it feels to learn this valuable new skill of managing your time and priorities.

Self assessment is often the key to understanding why you procrastinate and developing the strategies to help you control your life and create the results you want. Once you have identified what is holding you back, you can create positive solutions and consistently apply them until they are habits. To avoid procrastination, try the following strategies.

1. **Set daily priorities.** Begin by becoming clear on your goals and the results you want to achieve. Make certain that you allow enough time to complete your goals. Review your goals often and visualize yourself completing projects and tasks and achieving your goals. For example, see yourself walking across the stage to receive your diploma and view daily tasks as stepping stones for reaching your goal. Use your to-do list to check off tasks as you complete them. This will give you a feeling of accomplishment.

2. **Break the project into small tasks.** A large project can seem overwhelming and can create procrastination. Do something each day that brings you closer to your goal. Use a project board or write down steps and deadlines that are necessary to achieve success. For example, as soon as a paper is assigned, start

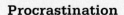

Procrastination

- What is something I should have accomplished by now but haven't?
- Why did I procrastinate?
- What are the consequences for my procrastination?
- What kind of tasks do I delay or put off?
- When do I usually procrastinate?
- Where do I procrastinate? Am I more effective in the library or at home?
- How does my procrastination affect others in my life?
- Who supports or enables my procrastination?

that day to choose a topic, the next day do research, and so on until each step leads to an excellent paper. Ask yourself, "What can I do in 10 minutes today that will get me started?"

3. **Get organized.** Gather everything you'll need to start your project. Clear off a space and get your notes and other material ready, such as pens, paper, and books. Reread the assignment and clarify expectations with your instructor or study team. Having everything ready creates a positive attitude and makes it easier to start the task. This strategy is effective whether you're doing a term paper, cleaning the garage, or making cookies.

4. **Reward yourself.** Look ahead and think about how you will feel when you complete this task versus how you'll feel if you don't. Focus on the sense of accomplishment you feel when you make small, steady steps and meet your deadlines. Reward yourself with a small treat or break when you complete activities and a bigger reward (such as a nice dinner or movie) when you complete a goal. Work first and play later. Do not allow yourself the reward of play until you have accomplished certain high-priority tasks and have met deadlines.

5. **Develop a positive attitude.** Attitude is everything. When you are positive and focused, you can accomplish a lot in a short time. Negative emotions are time wasters. Anger, jealousy, worry, and resentment can eat up hours of time and sap your energy. Instead, resolve to have a positive attitude and use affirmations. Think to yourself, "I get to work on my project today," instead of "I have to work on this project." Feel grateful that you have the opportunity to be in college. Resourceful and positive attitudes don't just happen; they are created. Once you get yourself into the action mode, you'll find that motivation builds. Most people don't feel like exercising every morning, but, once they are out for a jog, they feel great and want to complete their run. The same strategies can be used for writing, studying, and completing any project.

6. **Focus.** You can create a positive, "can do" attitude by focusing fully for a short amount of time: "I'm going to preview this chapter for 15 minutes with full

concentration." However, telling yourself you're going to study for 2 or 3 hours creates a mind set that says, "This is too difficult." Seeing how fully you can concentrate in a short amount of time builds confidence, yields success, and makes studying a game. You are using affirmations and creative discipline instead of guilt and willpower. Before you go to bed or when you have a few minutes during the day, use the same strategy: "I'm just going to spend 10 minutes writing a rough draft for my English paper." Ask yourself if you can do one more thing to get you started the next day. As you build on your success, you will increase your confidence, discipline, and concentration.

7. **Surround yourself with supportive people.** Ask for help from motivated friends, instructors, or your advisor, or visit the Learning Center for help and support. Sometimes talking out loud can help you clarify why you are avoiding a project. Study buddies or a study team can also help you stay on track. Clarify specific concerns about tasks, so that you know exactly what is expected and set deadlines. Sometimes just knowing that someone is counting on you to deliver is enough to keep you from procrastinating.

8. **Tackle difficult tasks during your high-energy time.** Do what is important first, while you are at your peak energy level and concentration is easiest. Once you get a difficult or unpleasant task done, you will feel more energy. Return phone calls, answer mail, visit with friends, and clean when your energy dips and you need a more physical, less demanding task.

9. **Eliminate distractions.** Go to the library or close your door and tell your roommates or family that you need a certain amount of time to complete a task. Set a time to socialize later. Keep breaks to a set time and do something pleasurable and different, such as a quick walk.

10. **Don't expect perfection.** You learn any new task by making mistakes. For example, you become a better writer or speaker with practice. Don't wait or delay because you want perfection. Your paper is not the great American novel. It is better to do your best than to do nothing. You can polish later, but avoiding writing altogether is a major trap. Do what you can today to get started on the task at hand.

Control Interruptions

Another major barrier to time management is interruptions. Interruptions steal your time. They cause you to stop projects, and they disrupt your thought pattern, divert your attention, and make it difficult to build momentum again. To avoid wasting time, take control. Don't let endless activities, the telephone, and other people control you. Set everyday priorities that will help you meet your goals and reduce interruptions. You may find that you spend a lot of time on the phone. Use the phone for convenience, to save time, or as a reward for accomplishing a task, but don't allow it to become an interruption. For instance, if a friend calls, set a timer for 10 minutes or postpone the call until later in the day, after you have previewed an assigned chapter or outlined a speech. Set the answering machine if you are studying, or tell the caller that you will call back in an hour. When you return a call, chat for 5 or 10 minutes

WORDS TO SUCCEED

"Time is the coin of your life. It is the only coin you have, and only you can determine how it will be spent. Be careful lest you let other people spend it for you."

CARL SANDBURG, *Author, poet*

instead of 45 minutes. Combine socializing with exercising or eating lunch or dinner. If you watch a favorite program, turn the television off right after that show. The essence of time management is taking charge of your life and not allowing interruptions to control you. Complete **Personal Evaluation Notebook 3.6** to determine the sources of your interruptions. (Also see **Worksheet 3.3** to identify your time wasters.)

Peak performers know how to live and work with other people and manage interruptions. Try these six tips to help you reduce interruptions:

1. **Create an organized place to study.** A supportive, organized study space can help you reduce interruptions and keep you focused. Have all your study tools—a dictionary, pencils, pens, books, papers, files, notes, a calendar, a semester schedule, and study-team and instructor names and phone numbers—in one place, so that you won't waste time looking for the items you need. Keep only one project on your desk at one time and file everything else away or put it on a shelf. You can increase your learning by studying in the same space and by conditioning your brain for serious studying and attention. If you have children, include a study area for them, close to yours, where they can work quietly with puzzles, crayons, or paint. This will allow study time together and create a lifelong study pattern for them.

2. **Create a good time to study.** You will find that, when you are focused, you can study anywhere, anytime. However, to increase your effectiveness, do your serious studying when your energy level is at its peak. Guard against interruptions and use this time for serious studying.

3. **Create quiet time.** Discuss study needs and expectations with your roommates or family and ask for an agreement. You might establish certain study hours or agree on a signal, such as closing your door or hanging a quiet sign, to let each other know when you need quiet time. Make certain that you balance study time with breaks to eat and socialize with your roommates or family.

4. **Study in the library.** If it is difficult to study at home or in the dorm, study in the library. Many students go to the library for quiet time. Once you enter, your brain can turn to a serious study mode. Sitting in a quiet place and facing the wall can reduce interruptions and distractions. You will find that you can accomplish far more in less time, and then you can enjoy your friends and family.

5. **Do first things first.** You will feel more in control if you have a list of priorities you work through every day. Having a clear purpose of what you want and need to do makes it easier to say no to distractions. Make certain that these important goals include your health. Taking time to exercise, eat right, and relax will not only save time but will also help increase your energy and focus.

6. **Just say no.** Hang a "Do Not Disturb" sign on your door. Tell your roommates or family when you have an important test or project due. If someone wants to talk or socialize when you need to study, say no. Set aside time each day to spend with your family or roommates, such as dinner, a walk, or a movie. They will understand your priorities when you include them in your plans. The key is balance and communication.

Interruptions!

1. Try to keep a log of interruptions for a few days. List all the interruptions you experience and their origins. Be aware of internally caused interruptions, such as procrastination, daydreaming, worry, negative thoughts, anger, and lack of concentration.

Interruptions	Frequency	Possible Solutions
Visitors		
Friends		
Family		
Telephone		
Daydreaming		
Lack of purpose		
Other		

2. Make a list of your most common time wasters. Some common time wasters are

- Socializing
- Doing what you like to do first
- Watching television
- Procrastinating
- Not setting goals and priorities
- Not keeping a calendar
- Not writing down deadlines
- Losing things and not organizing
- Failing to plan
- Having a negative attitude
- Complaining and whining
- Being overly involved with other people's problems

My common time wasters are

_____
_____
_____
_____
_____
_____
_____

Juggling Family, School, and Job

Anyone who lives with children knows how much time and energy they require. Having a family involves endless physical demands, including cleaning, cooking, chauffeuring to activities, helping with homework, and nonstop picking up. Children get sick, need attention, and just want you there sometimes for them. Focus on the big picture as you look at the following ways to juggle your many roles:

1. **Be flexible.** There are only certain kinds of studying that you can realistically expect to do around children and other kinds of studying that are hopeless even to attempt. If you expect to be interrupted a lot, use this to your advantage. Carry flash cards to use as you cook dinner or while supervising children's homework or playtime. Quiz yourself, preview chapters, skim summaries, review definitions, do a set number of problems, brainstorm ideas for a paper, outline a speech, review equations, sketch a drawing, or explain a chapter out loud. Save the work that requires deeper concentration for time alone.

2. **Communicate.** Talk with your partner and/or children about how important family is to you. Let them know that earning a college degree is an important goal and you are going to need their support and understanding. Build in quality, fun time with those you love and give them your full attention. Use every bit of time to study before you come home. Once home, let them know when you need to study and set up a specific time. Even young children can understand that you need quiet time. Make certain that they have lots of quiet activities to keep them busy when you are working. Small children can color, play with clay, or do puzzles when you are working on projects. After quiet time, you can take a walk, read, or cook dinner together. Clear communication and expectations can save you time at home, school, and work.

3. **Find good day care.** This is essential for school and job success. Line up at least two backup sources of day care. Explore public and private day-care centers, preschools, family day-care homes, parent cooperatives, baby-sitting pools, other family members, and nannies. If possible, explore renting a room in the basement or attic of your house to a child-care provider. Part of the rent can be paid with child care and light housecleaning. Trade off times with other parents.

4. **Create positive time.** Don't buy your children toys to replace spending time with them. They don't need expensive toys or elaborate outings. You can enjoy each other as you study, garden, shop, do household chores, eat, take walks, read, play games, or watch a favorite television show. The activity is secondary to your uninterrupted presence. Spend time at bedtime sharing your day, talking about dreams, reading a story, and expressing your love and appreciation to them. Make this a positive time and avoid quarrels or harsh words. They will remember and cherish this warm and special time forever, and so will you.

5. **Model successful behavior.** Returning to school is an act that sends an important message. You are saying that learning, growing, and being able to juggle

family, a job, and school are possible, worthwhile, and rewarding. It is important for children to see their parents setting personal and professional goals while knowing that the family is the center of their lives. You are modeling the importance of getting an education, setting goals and achieving them, and creating balance.

6. **Delegate and develop.** Clarify expectations with your children, so that everyone contributes to the family. Even young children can learn to be team members and important contributors to making the family unit work. Preschool children can help put away toys, fold napkins, set the table, and feel part of the team. Preteens can be responsible for cooking a simple meal one night a week and for doing their own laundry. When your children go to college, they will know how to cook, clean, do laundry, get up on time in the morning, and take responsibility for their lives. An important goal of being a good parent is to raise independent, capable, competent, and responsible adults.

7. **Create a support system.** A support system is essential for survival. Check out resources on campus through the reentry center. Set up study teams for all your classes. Make friends with other people who have children.

8. **Prepare the night before.** Avoid the morning rush of getting everyone out the door by doing tasks the night before, such as taking a shower, laying out clothes, packing lunches, organizing backpacks, and checking for keys, books, any signed notes, and supplies. Good organization helps makes the rush hour a little less stressful.

9. **Increase your energy—both physically and emotionally.** Although you are balancing school, work, and family demands, you should also make certain that you take time each day to do at least one thing you like to do. Find ways to revitalize yourself. Take time to relax, meditate, walk, and read for pleasure. Exercise, dance, do yoga, get enough sleep and rest, and eat healthy foods. Remind yourself that you are blessed with a full and rewarding life.

The Returning Student

The college classroom and workplace are changing. According to the National Center for Education Statistics, more than 40 percent of college students are over 25 years old. Reentry students are the fastest-growing group of college students. Since many reentry students have families and jobs, child care, flexible schedules, relevant classes, and financial aid are all important issues. Many colleges allow people over 60 to take courses for a nominal fee. Older students bring a wealth of experience, practical applications, and different viewpoints to the classroom.

The early baby boomers are now past 50, and this large group is changing the nature of the workplace. Many adults change jobs or careers, start working after raising a family, or do volunteer work. Older adults also bring a wealth of experience and a different perspective to the workplace. Many of these older workers are returning to school, especially to learn computer skills.

Although the following tips work for just about everyone, they are especially important for the reentry student. Think about how these tips can be applied to the workplace.

1. **Observe, read, and notice procedures, deadlines, resources, and policies.** Read the catalog and schedule of classes. Clarify expectations.
2. **Explore campus resources.** If your school has a reentry center, go there and sign up for tutoring services; check out campus day care services, the Learning Center, and the Career Center.
3. **Explore community and family resources.** Create a support system of people who can help. Have backup child care and transportation.
4. **Develop an organized record-keeping system.** Keep all your grades, transcripts, and other paperwork in one place.
5. **Join study groups.** This really works. You will be more effective when you learn to use the talents and skills of others. Studying in teams integrates learning styles, makes learning active, and creates support.
6. **Find a mentor.** Build relationships with your advisors and instructors (or bosses and co-workers). Developing positive relationships increases productivity and creates a community of learners.
7. **Integrate all learning styles.** Create experiences, write, reflect, observe, listen, read, summarize, teach, demonstrate, and do. Make learning as physical as possible.

Balance Your Life

Take time to reflect on all areas of your life and the time you are presently investing in them. Decide if you are investing too much or too little time in each area. Also, look at the roles you play in each area of your life. In the family area, you may play the role of wife, mother, daughter, and so on. In the work area, you may be a manager, a part-time worker, or an assistant.

Accompanying each role in your life are certain goals. Some goals demand greater time than others. It is OK to make a trade-off for a specific goal, but realize that you may neglect a vital area of your life. For instance, you may have a big term paper due, so you trade off a family outing to accomplish this goal. Complete **Personal Evaluation Notebook 3.7** to determine how you can achieve balance.

Balancing Your Life
Balancing family with work sometimes requires making trade-offs to have a more fulfilling life. *What can you do to create a more balanced life?*

Keeping your Life Goals in Balance

Several life areas are listed on this chart. Write one goal you have for each major area. Explain how you can commit a certain amount of time to meeting that goal and still maintain overall balance.

Life Areas	Goals
1. Career (job, earning a living)	_____
2. Education	_____
3. Spirituality (your inner being, peace of mind)	_____
4. Relationships (your family, friends, associates)	_____
5. Health (weight, exercise, food, stress, personal care)	_____
6. Recreation (hobbies, sports, interests)	_____
7. Finance	_____
8. Home	_____
9. Community involvement and service	_____
10. Personal growth and renewal	_____
11. Other	_____

In summary, in this chapter, I learned to:

- *Assess where my time goes.* Knowing where I am already spending my time is essential for time management. I assess how much time I (1) commit to school, work, and other activities; (2) spend maintaining myself and home; and (3) devote to discretionary time.

- *Determine where my time should go.* I set goals to determine what I want to accomplish. I look at my values and priorities and use them to write a mission statement. I evaluate my dreams as I write my long-term goals. I break down my tasks and goals by short-term, mid-term, and long-term. I use a daily to-do list to keep me focused on top priorities. I know what I'd like to accomplish, what I should accomplish, and what is urgent and *must be accomplished.*

- *Assess my energy level.* "Doers" are organized and know how to pace themselves. They know when their energy level is high and work on top-priority goals when they are alert and focused. Having a sense of my body rhythms and high-energy time gives me confidence that I can accomplish more in less time.

- *Break down projects.* I look at a large project and then break it into manageable chunks. I make a project board, with deadlines for each assignment, and break down the assignment into realistic steps that I can do each day. I consolidate similar tasks to maximize my efforts.

- *Study everywhere and anywhere.* I make the most of waiting time, commuting time, and time between classes. I know it is more effective to study in short segments throughout the day than to study late at night in a marathon session.

- *Get organized.* I will develop a habit of putting everything in its place and getting organized. I found that spending a few extra minutes spent organizing my space and schedule pay off later.

- *Integrate learning styles.* Visualizing myself completing a project, talking to others about the project, working in groups, working alone, and using hands-on approaches whenever possible help me integrate learning styles. I look at the whole project and break it into steps, focusing on top-priority items and setting deadlines. I observe, plan, think, and do and then evaluate and do again until the project is completed. I model successful behavior and teach others.

- *Be patient and flexible.* I reward myself for making progress and don't expect perfection. I'm flexible when appropriate and know that there is time to do whatever is most important.

- *Overcome procrastination and interruptions.* By setting daily priorities, breaking large projects into manageable tasks, being positive, creating an organized place to study, and being disciplined, I can accomplish what needs to be done. I've learned to just say no when necessary, and I reward myself when I complete projects and withhold rewards until I do first things first.

- *Take responsibility for my time.* I don't rely on others to be my alarm clock or blame others for not completing my work. I maintain a positive attitude and keep myself motivated. I manage and control my emotions, anger, and negative thoughts. Conflict and negative emotions can eat up a lot of time and energy. When I'm positive and focused, I can accomplish a lot in a short amount of time.

- *Balance my life.* I invest time in exercise and take time to rest and relax. I cannot be effective if I'm not rested and renewed. I take time to enjoy life.

Deborah Page

FOOD SCIENTIST

Related Majors: Agricultural Science, Chemistry, Microbiology, Nutrition

Focus on Tasks, Not Time

Deborah Page is a food scientist for a large company in the food-processing industry. Her job is to develop new food products and ways to preserve or store foods. To do this, she engages in research and conducts tests and experiments, keeping in mind consumer demand for safety and convenience. Occasionally, she analyzes foods to determine levels of sugar, protein, vitamins, or fat.

Because her job is task-oriented, Deborah has a great deal of freedom in structuring her day. Her company allows flexible scheduling, so Deborah arrives at work at 9:30 A.M., after her children have left for school. Deborah is able to work until 6:30 P.M., because her children are involved in after-school activities and because her husband can pick them up by 5 P.M.

Deborah finds that she does her best work in late mornings and early afternoons. She plans research and testing during those times. She schedules most calls during the first hour at work, and she uses the latter part of her day to organize tasks for the next day. Good prior planning helps her manage her time well and focus on her tasks at hand.

Deborah's job includes a fair amount of reading, and she sometimes takes work home with her for the evening. That way, she can often leave work early to take her children to an appointment or to attend one of their sports activities. Giving attention to her family and personal interests helps Deborah create a balanced life.

CRITICAL THINKING Why is it important for Deborah to organize her time wisely? What are some of the prioritization strategies she uses daily to manage her time? What are some strategies to help her balance her personal and career commitments with a healthy, fulfilling lifestyle? Explore ways for Deborah to find time for herself for personal renewal.

Peak Performer Profile

N. Scott Momaday

N. Scott Momaday has claimed many titles—dean of Native American authors, Pulitzer Prize winner, scholar, and Kiowa Indian.

Though born during the Great Depression in Oklahoma, Momaday grew up in a world rich with tradition. His childhood was spent on the reservations and pueblos of the Apache, Navaho, Pueblo, and Jemez Indians, where his parents taught school. The vast southwestern landscape that Momaday calls the "Indian world" was his playground. It was also his teacher and a colorful source of material for his future career. Horses, cowboy stories, and even comic books fed his imagination. As a boy, what did Momaday want to be when he grew up? A cowboy. "Comes with the territory," he explains.

Fortunately, Momaday followed in the footsteps of his mother and father, after pursuing his education at the University of New Mexico and then Stanford, where he received his doctorate. His mother, a descendent of American pioneers with Cherokee roots, was a writer and teacher. His Kiowa father was an artist and accomplished storyteller in the Kiowa oral tradition. One reviewer described Momaday's style as using the language of his mother to tell "his story in the manner of his father's people." He later developed his innate talent as a painter and printmaker. He settled in Arizona, where he is currently a professor at the University of Arizona.

Through his novels, plays, poems, essays, folktales, artwork, and teaching, Momaday has kept the culture and beliefs of an old world alive and relevant. In his Pulitzer Prize–winning novel *House Made of Dawn,* the central character, like Momaday, faces the conflicts of straddling both the Indian and the white worlds. Momaday, however, has always known who he is: "I am an Indian and I believe I'm fortunate to have the heritage I have."

PERFORMANCE THINKING According to N. Scott Momaday, *"I simply kept my goal in mind and persisted. Perseverance is a large part of writing."* In what ways do you think Momaday has used his goals to guide his time management?

CHECK IT OUT N. Scott Momaday is dedicated to helping preserve the rich cultural heritage he enjoyed growing up. Momaday founded the Buffalo Trust, a nonprofit organization committed to "the preservation, protection, and return of their cultural heritage to Native peoples, especially children, and founded on the conviction that the loss of cultural identity—the theft of the sacred—is the most insidious and dangerous threat to the survival of Native American culture in our time." Learn more about the goals of this organization at **www.buffalotrust.org.**

Performance Strategies............

Following are the top 10 strategies for time management:

- Set goals and priorities.
- Study at the right time and in the right space.
- Study everywhere and anywhere.
- Break down projects and consolidate similar tasks.
- Make a schedule.
- Say no to interruptions.
- Get organized.
- Be flexible.
- Create balance.
- Just do it!

Tech for Success....................

Take advantage of the text's web site at **www.mhhe.com/ferrett6e** for additional study aids, useful forms, and convenient and applicable resources.

- **Semester calendar.** It's unavoidable—most of your tests and class papers will occur around the same time. Start planning your semester now by mapping out the major events and daily tasks you'll need to accomplish. A number of "planning" options are available with this text (worksheets and downloadable forms), or access planners online at a variety of web sites, such as **www.time-anddate.com.**

- **A personal time-out.** It's easy to waste hours surfing the Internet, chatting on-line, and perusing the latest "find" on auction sites, such as eBay. You may need to give yourself a "time-out" or, rather, a "time's up." Set a timer as you get on-line and commit to turning off the computer when the timer goes off. Use your discretionary time wisely.

Review Questions ....

Based on what you have learned in this chapter, write your answers to the following questions:

1. How does time management help you achieve your goals?

1. Gives Me Sense of Worth

2. What is the difference between an "urgent" priority and an "important" priority?

Need to be done RIGHT Now
important - Soon as possible

3. Name at least five time-management strategies.

1. Prepare
2. Make enough time
3 schedule
4

4. What can you do to avoid procrastination?

By doing it Now

5. Why is it important to control interruptions?

they cause you to stop
what you are doing

JUGGLING FAMILY AND SCHOOL

In the Classroom

Laura Chen is a returning part-time student. She also works full-time and takes care of her family. Her husband is verbally supportive of her goal to become a dental hygienist but is not very helpful with taking care of the children or with housework. Their children are 12 and 14 and have always depended on Laura to help them with their homework and drive them to their activities. Laura prides herself on being efficient at home, as well as being a loving mother and wife.

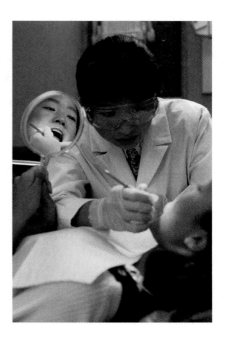

1. What can Laura do to get more control over her life?

   _____

   _____

2. What strategies in the chapter would be most helpful to Laura?

   _____

   _____

In the Workplace

Laura is now a dental hygienist. She has always had a busy schedule, but she expected to have more free time after she graduated. Instead, she finds herself being even busier than before. Her children are active in school, and she feels it is important for her to be involved in their activities and schoolwork. Laura is also a member of two community organizations, volunteers at the local hospital, and is active in her church. Lately, she has been late for meetings and has been rushing through her day. Because she knows her health is important, Laura has resumed her regular exercise program. Since graduation, she has had difficulty finding time for herself.

3. What strategies can help Laura gain control over her time and her life?

   _____

   _____

4. What areas of her life does she need to prioritize?

   _____

   _____

APPLYING THE ABCDE METHOD OF SELF-MANAGEMENT

In the Journal Entry on page 79, you were asked to describe a situation when you were overwhelmed by too much to do and too little time. Describe that event below. What were the consequences?

_____

_____

_____

_____

Now apply the ABCDE method and visualize a more organized situation:

A = Actual event:

B = Beliefs:

C = Consequences:

D = Dispute:

E = Energized:

While completing this exercise, did you determine ways you can become more organized and efficient?

Practice Self-Management

For more examples of learning how to manage difficult situations, see the "Self-Management Workbook" section of the Online Learning Center web site at **www.mhhe.com/ferrett6e.**

TIME MANAGEMENT

Complete the following statements with a Yes or No response.

		Yes	No
1.	I do the easiest and most enjoyable task first.	✓	
2.	I do my top-priority task at the time of day when my energy is the highest and I know I will perform best.		✓
3.	I use my time wisely by doing high-return activities—previewing chapters, proofreading papers.	✓	
4.	Even though I find interruptions distracting, I put up with them.	✓	
5.	I save trivial and mindless tasks for the time of day when my energy is low.		✓
6.	I don't worry too much about making lists. I don't like planning and prefer to be spontaneous and respond as events occur.		✓
7.	My work space is organized, and I have only one project on my desk at a time.	✓	
8.	I set goals and review them each semester and each year.	✓	
9.	My work space is open and I like to have people wander in and out.		✓
10.	My study team socializes first and then we work.		✓
11.	I have a lot of wasted waiting time, but you can't study in small blocks of time.		✓
12.	I block out a certain amount of time each week for my top-priority and hardest classes.	✓	

Scoring

1. Add the number of Yes responses to questions 2, 3, 5, 7, 8, 12.

2. Add the number of No responses to questions 1, 4, 6, 9, 10, 11.   5

3. Add the two scores together.   4

9

The higher the score, the more likely you are to be practicing good time management. Which areas do you need to improve?

TIME WASTERS

Getting control of your time and life involves identifying time wasters and determining your peak energy level. It also involves identifying goals, setting priorities, and creating an action plan. Determining what task should be done first and overcoming procrastination are major factors in creating success. All these steps and issues involve critical thinking skills. Use critical thinking to answer the following questions.

1. What are the major activities and tasks that take up much of your time?

_____

_____

2. What activities cause you to waste time?

_____

_____

3. What activities can you eliminate or reduce?

_____

_____

4. When is your high-energy time?

_____

_____

5. When do you study?

_____

_____

6. Look at your committed time. Does this block of time reflect your values and goals?

_____

_____

7. How can you increase your discretionary time?

_____

_____

8. Do you complete top-priority tasks first?

_____

_____

(continued)

9. Look at the common reasons and excuses that some students use for not being organized and focused. Add to this list and use creative problem solving to list strategies for overcoming these barriers.

Reasons	Strategies
I ran out of time.	
I overslept.	
I'm easily distracted.	
People interrupt me.	
Instructors put too much pressure on me.	
I feel overwhelmed and panic at deadlines.	
I forgot about an assignment.	
Other	

PRACTICE GOAL SETTING

Determine a personal desire or want and plan out a strategy of long-term, short-term, and daily goals that help you achieve it.

Goal-Setting Steps	Examples	Your Turn . . .
Step 1 Plainly state your *desire* or *want*.	"I want to be financially secure."	
Step 2 Develop a long-term goal that will help you fulfill your stated *desire* or *want*.	"I will earn a Bachelor of Science degree in computer technology from State University by June 2009."	
Step 3 Develop short-term goals that will help you achieve the long-term goal.	"I will enroll in all the classes recommended by my academic advisor.	
	"I will earn at least a 3.5 GPA in all my classes."	
	"I will join a small group"	
Step 4 Develop daily objectives that focus on achieving your short-term goals.	"I will set aside 2 hours of study for every 1 hour in class."	
	"I will make note cards to carry with me and review them when I'm waiting for class."	
	"I will review the day's lecture notes with my study team to make sure I didn't miss any important points."	

MAP OUT YOUR GOALS

Use this illustration as a visual guide for mapping out your goals. To get started, plug in your responses from Personal Evaluation Notebook 3.3.

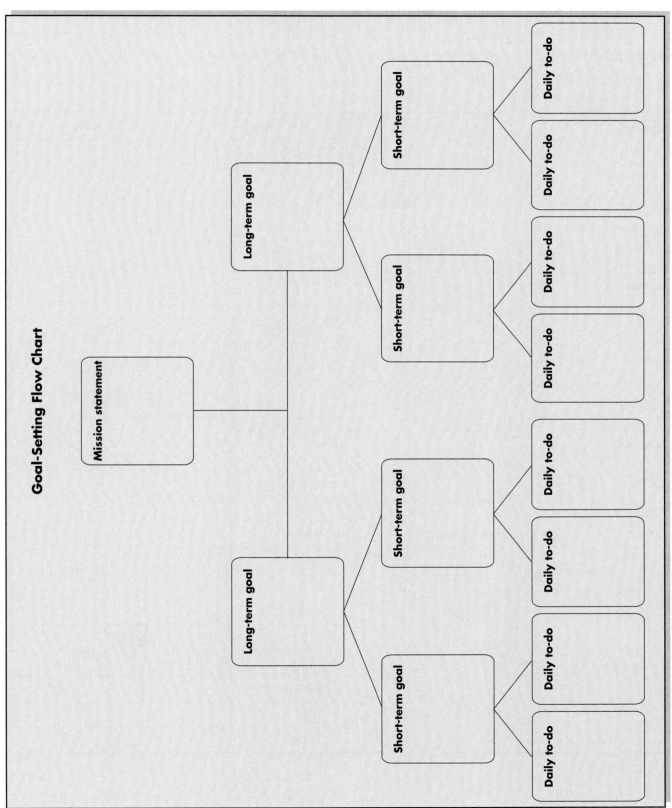

Goal-Setting Flow Chart

DAILY PRIORITIZER AND PLANNER: YOUR TO-DO LIST

Consider the 80/20 Rule on page 87 as you use this form to prioritize your tasks and schedule your daily activities. On the left side, write down the tasks you want to accomplish during the day. Then enter those tasks in the "Activity" column, focusing on urgent and important tasks first. Also make sure you include your maintenance and committed activities. Check off your tasks on the left side once they are completed. At the end of the day, see what tasks did not get accomplished and, if need be, include them on tomorrow's to-do list.

Urgent		Time	Activity
		12:00–1:00 A.M.	
		1:00–2:00	
		2:00–3:00	
		3:00–4:00	
		4:00–5:00	
Important		5:00–6:00	
		6:00–7:00	
		7:00–8:00	
		8:00–9:00	
		9:00–10:00	
		10:00–11:00	
		11:00–12:00 P.M.	
Ongoing		12:00–1:00	
		1:00–2:00	
		2:00–3:00	
		3:00–4:00	
		4:00–5:00	
		5:00–6:00	
Trivial		6:00–7:00	
		7:00–8:00	
		8:00–9:00	
		9:00–10:00	
		10:00–11:00	
		11:00–12:00	

WEEKLY PLANNER

Week of _____/_____/_____

Time	Sunday Activity	Monday Activity	Tuesday Activity	Wednesday Activity	Thursday Activity	Friday Activity	Saturday Activity
12:00–1:00 A.M.							
1:00–2:00							
2:00–3:00							
3:00–4:00							
4:00–5:00							
5:00–6:00							
6:00–7:00							
7:00–8:00							
8:00–9:00							
9:00–10:00							
10:00–11:00							
11:00–12:00 P.M.							
12:00–1:00							
1:00–2:00							
2:00–3:00							
3:00–4:00							
4:00–5:00							
5:00–6:00							
6:00–7:00							
7:00–8:00							
8:00–9:00							
9:00–10:00							
10:00–11:00							
11:00–12:00							

Urgent	Important	Ongoing

REVIEW AND APPLICATIONS

CHAPTER 3

MONTH/SEMESTER CALENDAR

Plan your projects and activities for the school term.

						Date
						Appointment
						Date
						Test
						Due date
						Project

Month of _____

DEMONSTRATING YOUR TIME-MANAGEMENT SKILLS

List all the factors involved in time management. Indicate how you would demonstrate them to employers. Add this page to your Career Development Portfolio.

Areas	Your Demonstration
Dependability	*Haven't missed a day of work in my job*
Reliability	
Effectiveness	
Efficiency	
Responsibility	
Positive attitude	
Persistence	
Ability to plan and set goals and priorities	
Visionary	
Ability to follow through	
High energy	
Ability to handle stress	
Ability to focus	
Respect for others' time	
Ability to overcome procrastination	
Reputation as a doer and self-starter	

Maximize Your Resources

ATTENTION
L STUDENTS!

CHAPTER OBJECTIVES

In this chapter, you will learn to

▲ Find and use your school's resources

▲ Seek out resources of interest to commuter students and returning students

▲ Use technology to your advantage

▲ Determine the resources available in your community

▲ Manage your financial resources and save for the future

▲ Realize that you are your greatest resource

SELF-MANAGEMENT

"Using a credit card is easy—in fact, much too easy. Before I knew it, I had rung up thousands of dollars, and I can barely handle the minimum monthly payments. In addition to credit card debt, I have student loans to pay back. I feel like I'll be in debt forever."

Are you struggling with your finances or finding it hard to make ends meet? Have you ever bought things that you didn't need or spent too much on a luxury item that you really couldn't afford? In this chapter, you will learn how to find and use your school and local resources to help you succeed in every area of your life—including financial. You will learn how to manage money, get back on a debt-free track, and find ways to participate in your school and community.

JOURNAL ENTRY In **Worksheet 4.1** on page 148, write about a time when you set a financial goal, such as buying a new car. How difficult was it to achieve? What sacrifices did you have to make?

Going to college is a big change. This is true whether you are going from high school to college, leaving home, commuting, returning, or starting college later in life. The strategies and information you learn throughout this book will help you cope with major life transitions, including the transition from college to the world of work. The more information and support you have during a transition, the more easily you'll be able to adjust and thrive. In this chapter, we will look at ways of finding and using the resources of your school and the greater community, as well as your own inner resources, to adjust to change and to meet your goals. A great deal of success in life depends on solving problems through decision making. This requires knowing what resources are available and having the good sense to use them.

When you enter college or a job, you are entering a new system and culture. It is your responsibility to understand how the system and culture work. This understanding includes knowing the system's rules, regulations, deadlines, procedures, requirements, and language. As you look through the school's catalog, you'll see terms such as *GPA, accreditation, prerequisite,* and *academic freedom*—terms that are unique to higher education. The culture is all the written and unwritten rules of any organization. It includes the work atmosphere and the way people treat each other. In a sense, you are learning *how* things are done and *who* best can solve specific problems. Knowing that information reduces stress and anxiety. Many advisors and counselors say that the top advice they would give students is to address problems as they occur and to seek help when they need it.

Explore Your School's Resources

Many students who have graduated say they regret not being more involved in school activities and not using the amazing resources available. Your college experience will be much more rewarding and successful if you take advantage of all the resources available to you. In fact, many potentially big problems can be avoided if you address situations as soon as they arise and know where to go for help.

You may have attended an orientation program, gone on a campus tour, and visited the book store and student center when you applied to or first arrived at school. You may have bought a catalog, picked up a student newspaper or map, and looked at the schedule of classes. This is a good place to start. Walking around campus, finding your classroom before classes begin, and locating your advisor's and instructors' offices can help you feel more familiar and reduce the anxiety of the unknown. You will be amazed at the support services and resources available at most schools. The resources we'll explore in this chapter include

- ◆ *People resources:* advisors, faculty, classmates, and counselors
- ◆ *Program resources:* offices for special needs, areas of study, groups, clubs, and activities
- ◆ *On-line and information resources:* catalogs, guides, and local news and events

◆ *Financial resources:* financial aid, credit agencies, and financial planning services

Use the handy form on the inside back cover of this text to record the important information for a number of key resources. **Worksheet 4.2** at the end of this chapter includes an extensive list of potential resources that may be available at your school.

People Resources

The most important resources at school are the people with whom you work, study, and relate. Faculty, advisors, counselors, study-team members, club members, sports-team members, guest speakers, administrators, and all the students with whom you connect and form relationships make up your campus community. These people will provide information, emotional support, and friendship—and may even help you find a job! We'll discuss a few key contacts, and others will be discussed in the section "Program Resources."

◆ *Academic advisor.* One of the most important contacts you will have at school is your academic advisor. This is the person who will help you navigate academic life. You will want to read the catalog first and familiarize yourself with your major's and school's requirements and procedures. Your advisor will help you clarify procedures, answer other academic concerns or questions, create a major contract, and refer you to offices on campus that can best meet your needs. Go to the departmental office and find out your advisor's name, office number, and posted office hours. It is best if you make an appointment early in the semester and develop a good relationship. Do your part to be prepared, ask questions, and follow through on suggestions. However, if your personalities clash, you may want to check with the department about changing advisors. It is important that you have an advisor who is accessible, takes time to listen, and will work closely with you to meet your academic goals. (Review **Peak Progress P-2** on page xxxvi of the Student Preface for questions to ask your advisor. Also see Chapter 12, page 403, for more tips on communicating with advisors and instructors.) You'll want to talk with your advisor about

Check Out What's Available
Your school probably offers a number of resources to help you adjust, learn, and enjoy your college experience. *What are some of the resources that you have already tapped into?*

◆ The requirements for your major and the substitutions available

◆ The best sequence of classes and when certain courses are offered

- If certain instructors are better suited to your learning style
- General education and other requirements
- Helpful suggestions concerning your academic program
- Resources at school or in the community that could be helpful
- Service learning and volunteer programs that are available
- Internships, work study programs, and opportunities beyond the classroom
- Potential career opportunities within the major

◆ *Instructors.* Most instructors enjoy teaching and getting to know their students. At most universities and many colleges, faculty are also very involved in research, professional organizations, campus committees, community projects, and academic advising. Professors and instructors are busy even when they are not in the classroom. It is important that you get to know your instructors and view them as a tremendous resource. Instructors are more supportive of students who come to class regularly, show responsibility, and stand out in class. Here are a few ways to excel:

- **Go to every class, arrive early, and sit in front.** Motivated and interested students sit close to the instructor, have good eye contact, and reduce distractions.
- **Develop a work ethic.** Work hard and show consistent effort.
- **Build rapport.** Bring in interesting articles concerning the course, visit your instructor during office hours, and join student interest clubs and informal gatherings offered by departments. Get to know instructors and find out what they are working on professionally.
- **Ask intelligent and thoughtful questions.** Show that you are a critical thinker and creative problem solver and are interested in learning. Ask questions and clarify expectations.
- **Use e-mail effectively and appropriately.** This is a great way to check in and stay connected. (See **Peak Progress 12.1** on page 406 for tips on the appropriate use of e-mail with instructors.)
- **Do more than is required.** Do extra credit and offer to help with projects. Stay open to new opportunities and show your interest and willingness to go beyond the basic requirements of a class. Your instructor may be a great person to talk to about attending a professional organization, working on a research project, or getting an internship.
- **Be supportive.** Support your instructor and acknowledge good teaching.

◆ *Mentors.* A **mentor** is a person (such as a coach, an instructor, an employer, or a colleague) who is a role model and who supports your goals, takes an interest in your professional and personal development, and helps you achieve, either directly through instruction or indirectly by example. A mentor can help open doors for you and can make a difference in your life. Check to see if your college has a formal mentoring program, whereby students are connected to faculty, staff, or more experienced students. Once you develop a supportive

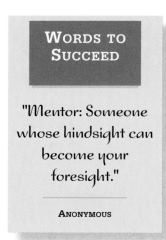

WORDS TO
SUCCEED

"Mentor: Someone
whose hindsight can
become your
foresight."

ANONYMOUS

relationship, your instructor may be willing to serve as a mentor to help you make connections in your career.

◆ *Peers.* Your fellow students may be very involved in the learning community. They are active in orientation, campus tours, information and advising centers, clubs, and almost every service area on campus. Take the initiative to organize a study team or partner for each class; get to know your lab assistant, tutor, and peers in the academic advising center, clubs' office, and so on. This is a great way to improve learning, get help, and network by building relationships. Look for ways that you can contribute your time and talents.

Networking is a term often used in business, but it simply means enriching yourself and your opportunities by building relationships with others. Sometimes you exchange professional information or services or give support and friendship. You build a large network of contacts with each person you get to know at school. Build a diverse network of instructors, advisors, and peers by staying in touch and updating phone numbers and addresses. If you're a returning student, get to know other returning students. Stretch your comfort zone by getting to know people with different backgrounds from you. Networking is one of the best strategies for overcoming isolation, getting a job, and developing long-lasting relationships. Build a wide and diverse network by using these tips:

◆ **Get to know other students in class**. Introduce yourself to other students in class. Put together a study team.

◆ **Get to know students out of class**. Smile and say "hi" to students when you see them out of class and take time to discuss lectures and assignments. Go to the student union, library, and career center, and be friendly.

◆ **Get to know your instructors.** Throughout this book, you'll find tips for building supportive relationships with instructors. Get to know them and take an interest in their research and area of expertise.

◆ **Join clubs.** Almost every academic department has a club, and there are clubs where you can meet students who have similar interests, such as chess, skiing, religion, or music. Think about attending events sponsored by various clubs. This exposes you to many different people and views.

◆ **Participate in service learning.** Find out if your class has a service learning component and ways that you can contribute what you've learned in class. Volunteer on campus. Check out the health center, learning center, and the student center to see if you can join or start a support group. (Learn more about incorporating service learning into your coursework in Chapter 14 on page 465.)

◆ **Work on campus.** A great way to meet people and earn extra money is to work on campus. Check out the career center for work study and student assistant jobs.

◆ **Perform.** Join the band, choir, jazz group, or chamber readers; perform in a play; or work in theater behind the scenes. Some campus groups impact the community by performing in local schools, or reading in library story hours.

◆ **Join the school newspaper.** Write stories or work in the office.

- ◆ **Join a political group.** Campus and community political groups are a great way to meet people, become better informed, and support a cause.
- ◆ **Attend campus events.** Go to lectures, political debates, and the many rich cultural, musical, intellectual, and fun events that are offered.

Program Resources

Depending on the type of institution you are attending, your school may have a variety of programs, departments, and offices that provide services and help, including services for specific needs. The people you meet in these offices can provide key information and help you find, evaluate, and use information of all kinds.

- ◆ *Advising center.* A central advising center is available at most colleges to provide general education advising and to answer general questions and specific concerns about policies, procedures, graduation requirements, and deadlines. The center also makes referrals and works closely with other departments, such as admissions, records, registration, learning centers, exchange and study abroad programs, and the cashier's office. In addition to your major advisor, the advising center will have **professional advisors** to help you in planning general education; professional and peer staff to answer many questions, help you register, and instruct you about deadlines and other important information; and **evaluators** to review transcripts and major contracts, and perform degree checks. If you are coming from high school, you will want to make certain that your advanced placement classes have been credited appropriately. If you are a transfer student, you need to know what upper-division and general education courses are required, what credits were transferred from your previous school, and whether they were accepted as general education or as electives.

     While your academic advisor is responsible for helping you prepare a major contract and guide you through your major's requirements, at most schools an evaluator does a degree check to make certain you have met not only your major's requirements but also all university requirements, such as general education, diversity and common ground requirements, credit and no credit guidelines, the institution's requirements, the required tests, and the number of college units. You may want to make an appointment once you have submitted your academic major contract and have applied for graduation (about three semesters before you graduate). Students report a sense of empowerment when they have a degree check, are able to plan in advance, and know exactly what they need to do to graduate. You don't want to find out a month before graduation that you are short two units or have failed to meet a basic requirement.

- ◆ *Admissions, records, and registration.* This office will have your transcripts, including information about grades, transfer credits, and the dropping or adding of classes. The registrar and staff can also assist you with graduation deadlines and requirements. Make sure, though, that you also keep copies of your transcripts, grades, grade changes, and other requirements.

◆ *Learning centers.* Many schools have a learning center or academic support services to help with academic problems and grade improvement. They offer workshops in such areas as test-taking skills; time management; reading skills; note taking; and math, vocabulary, and science study strategies. They may offer individual or group tutoring and study groups. They also do diagnostic testing to determine learning difficulties. If you are diagnosed with a learning disability, you may be eligible for additional time on tests, tutors, or other services. They often help students on probation by creating an academic success plan. Probation is a warning that you are doing substandard work. At many schools, this means less than a 2.0 GPA. If you continue to maintain a GPA below 2.0 or if it falls to a certain level, you may be disqualified. Disqualification means that you are denied further school attendance until you are reinstated. Disqualified students may petition for reinstatement, usually through the office of admissions and records. Many resources are available to help you stay in school, to avoid probation, and to raise your GPA. Tutoring is often available for all students who want to improve their grades, not just for students on probation.

◆ *Library.* When most of us think of libraries, we think of books or a great place to study. Indeed, the library is a rich source of books, periodicals (magazines and newspapers), encyclopedias, dictionaries, pamphlets, directories, and more. Libraries also offer many services besides the written and spoken word. They may vary in size and services, but they all have information, ideas, facts, and a mountain of treasures waiting to be explored. Librarians and media center staff are trained to find information about almost every subject. They can often order special materials from other libraries or direct you to other sources. Visit the library to get a good sense of all the benefits. Computer networks are now available in many libraries to retrieve information quickly. Many libraries have electronic access to books and periodicals and even more material is available via inter-library loans. Check out

◆ **The library's web site.** Look at all the links and accessible sources. Check out the collection of periodicals, audiovisual materials, and inter-library loan collections.

◆ **Computer resources.** Find out what's available on CD-ROM, as well as searchable databases. Ask about policies regarding use of the Internet on the library's computers.

◆ **Videotapes and audiotapes in the media center.** This is a wonderful way to view information, especially if you are a commuter student and you want to

Use the Library
Although you can do research on-line, your school may have an excellent library, which you should explore. *What assistance or resources can you get at the library that would be difficult to find on-line?*

WORDS TO SUCCEED

"The library is the temple of learning, and learning has liberated more people than all the wars in history."

CARL T. ROWAN, JOURNALIST, *author*

listen to tapes on your commute or watch videos of campus speakers or special events that you missed.

- **The catalog.** Look at the library's collection of encyclopedias, biographies, government works, and all the other available materials.

◆ *Career center.* The career center is not just for seniors. If you're undecided about your major and want to explore options and find out how academic majors relate to careers, this center can help. The staff can also help you with part-time jobs and **internships** related to your major. Internship opportunities are very helpful for gaining experience and getting a job. Also check out job placement services for summer or part-time work. Some schools offer a free placement service to help students find part and full-time employment. The career center offers career counseling, job fairs, interview and resume workshops, and materials and information to help you get a job. Keep a copy of inventories, materials, and possible majors and careers either in your binder or in your Career Development Portfolio.

◆ *Health center.* Take advantage of free or low-cost medical services for illnesses, eating disorders, alcohol or drug problems, anxiety, stress, birth control information, and sexually transmitted diseases. If you have a high fever, nausea, severe headache, or stiff neck, go immediately to the health center or, if closed, the emergency room, since you might have meningitis or another serious illness. Make certain you have the necessary vaccinations, or a hold may be placed on your registration.

◆ *Counseling center.* Adjusting to the demands of college life can be challenging. Most campuses have professional counselors who are trained to help you with personal problems, such as loneliness, shyness, eating disorders, addictions, depression, and relationship problems. They often offer group counseling and classes as well as individual support. They also refer students to agencies for specific problems. Many counseling centers offer classes in study skills, time and stress management, and other topics to help students succeed. Don't try to solve emotional problems by yourself when help is available on campus.

◆ *Student activities office.* Working with other offices, student services provide many programs and activities, starting with an orientation program and campus tour. Sometimes these orientation programs are offered on-line for first-time, transfer, and reentry students. There are usually many activities for students to participate in, such as

- **Multicultural centers.** Support, classes, activities, and events are offered to celebrate diversity and provide support for racial and ethnic groups and gays and lesbians. A women's center may also offer classes and support for women.

- **International and exchange programs.** Your school may offer an exchange program, which is a great way to attend a different school without transferring. You stay enrolled at your own school but study for a term or a year at a designated school, either in this country or abroad. There may also be a center for international students.

Use **Personal Evaluation Notebook 4.1** to record activities or clubs that you would like to check out, and determine which ones would work into your weekly schedule.

Activities and Clubs

Either visit the student activities office or review your school's web site to see what clubs or activities sound interesting. Look for activities that will increase your knowledge about your field of study, help you network and build business contacts, introduce you to new people with similar interests, and give you an opportunity to enjoy your discretionary time—physically and emotionally.

1. Club/activity: _____ Day/time: _____
   Contact person: _____ Phone/e-mail: _____
   Place: _____

2. Club/activity: _____ Day/time: _____
   Contact person: _____ Phone/e-mail: _____
   Place: _____

3. Club/activity: _____ Day/time: _____
   Contact person: _____ Phone/e-mail: _____
   Place: _____

4. Club/activity: _____ Day/time: _____
   Contact person: _____ Phone/e-mail: _____
   Place: _____

◆ *Student union.* Your school may have a student union or center, which may include a dining hall, a bookstore, recreational facilities, lounges, a post office, automated teller machines, and bulletin boards for information on clubs and activities, student government, and carpooling and public transportation. It may also have information on various student vacations, special classes, religious organizations, retreats, sports, and political groups. Check out all the clubs and activities available. This is a great way to stay involved, develop interests, meet new friends, and contribute your talents. The bookstore offers the school catalog, class schedule, textbooks, personal computers, and many general interest books and supplies. You will also find information about on- and off-campus housing. Check for posted lists of available apartments and houses, people requesting roommates, and so on.

◆ *Child-care center.* Child care may be provided on campus, and some schools have a children's center sponsored by the early childhood education department.

◆ *Athletic programs and centers.* Your physical health is important, and you should build exercise into your daily schedule. Check out exercise and physical activity classes, swimming, the weight room, and walking and running facilities. This is also a great way to meet other students.

◆ *Alumni association.* This organization provides discounts, travel arrangements, benefits, and information for graduates. These services are often available to all students.

◆ *Security.* Many schools have security or police departments, which provide information about safety, parking, traffic rules, and lost and found items. Some even provide safe escort for night-class students, classes in self-defense, and information on alcohol and drugs.

Additional On-Line and Information Resources

Technology affects every area of our lives, and a number of applications and resources are discussed throughout this text. You will find that schools offer many resources on-line through the school's main web site, such as the school catalog, its schedule of classes, its telephone directory, links to web sites for departments and offices, and many financial transactions, such as financial aid applications, payment of fees, and bookstore purchases. You may be able to register for classes, go through an orientation, and access your grades on-line. Many instructors distribute course materials, the syllabus, and assignments via e-mail or a course web site. On-line courses may include a blend of on-line instruction, web sites, chat rooms, on-line bulletin boards, two-way audio and visual connections, and e-mail to ask questions and respond to lectures. See **Peak Progress 4.1** for some tips on using technology to your advantage.

◆ *School catalog.* However you access resources—on-line or print—the school catalog is a key resource, which you need to review thoroughly. The catalog includes procedures, regulations, guidelines, academic areas, basic graduation requirements, and information on most services offered at your school. Begin by looking at the table of contents, the index, and maps. Most school catalogs will contain the following information:

  ◆ Table of contents
  ◆ Welcome from the president and a general description of the school and area
  ◆ Mission of the college and information about accreditation
  ◆ Support services and main offices in the campus community
  ◆ Admissions information, including placement tests and estimated expenses
  ◆ Academic regulations, such as auditing of a course, credit/no credit, class level, academic standing, educational leave, drop/add, and withdrawal
  ◆ Fees and financial aid
  ◆ List of administrators, trustees, faculty, and staff
  ◆ Academic programs, minors, credentials, and graduate degrees
  ◆ Components of the degree, such as major, general education, institutions, diversity and common ground, and electives
  ◆ Course descriptions
  ◆ Expectations on academic honesty and plagiarism, discipline for dishonesty, class attendance, disruptive behavior, student responsibility, privacy act and access policy, grievance procedures, safety and security, substance abuse policy, and so on
  ◆ Subject index

Using Technology at School

The U.S. Department of Labor's Secretary's Commission on Achieving Necessary Skills (SCANS) identified technology as a necessary competency for success in the workplace. Being competent in technology means knowing how to select, understand, and apply the appropriate program to achieve the results you want, being able to solve problems with technology, and connecting to the Internet and the World Wide Web. It also means using critical thinking to evaluate information found on line and determine if it is factual, current, and contains a credible source. Computers can help you find useful and accurate information on the Internet, create papers, stay in touch through e-mails, set goals, create calendars, keep your class schedule, create a budget, edit photos, join online groups, and create a personal web site. If you have disabilities, technology can provide voice commands and special services.

   To maximize your use of technology, you should

- Thoroughly search the school's main web site and periodically review it for recent postings.

- Register for a school e-mail account and check it often.

- Investigate if your school offers on-line courses that you may be interested in taking. (Remember, though, that taking on-line courses requires an even greater level of commitment, as you will be responsible for keeping up with assignments and reading materials on your own—just as with any class.)

- Contact or visit the computer lab and ask about support, including available hours. Does it offer courses or workshops?

- Check to see if your school offers discounts on computers for students.

- Make sure you know what and how technology will be used and required in your courses. Did your textbook come with a CD-ROM or web site that will be used in the course?

- Make sure you understand how to do quick searches on the Internet using search engines, such as Yahoo! and Google. If unclear, ask for help from another student or the computer lab.

- Don't assume that everything you see on the Internet is true. Check out sources and think through opinions versus facts. If you are unsure about the reliability of the material you find on a web site, run the web site by your instructor.

- Respect copyrights and credit all sources.

- Stretch and breathe. To reduce back pain and stress, sit up in your chair and get up and stretch periodically.

Look up questions before you ask for help and take responsibility for your own education. If someone gives you advice about a policy, ask where the rule is covered in the catalog, so that you can review it. Look under academic areas. What fields of study interest you the most or the least? Which areas are so unusual you didn't even know they existed? Sit down with a group of students and go through the catalog, so that you can build on questions, ideas, information, and understanding.

◆ *Orientation guide.* Many colleges provide a student handbook or an orientation guide that familiarizes you with the school and basic requirements. If you had the opportunity to attend an orientation program, hold on to your information packet, as you may want to refer to planning guides and requirements before you register for classes for next term.

◆ *Schedule of classes.* Buy a new schedule of classes each term. You will have not only a hard copy of classes to register for but also other up-to-date information, such as an exam schedule, deadlines, and a calendar of events. Most schools offer a schedule of classes on-line, but it is a good idea to have a copy with you when you're planning and adjusting your schedule.

◆ *School newspaper.* This publication provides information about campus events and activities, jobs, housing, and so on. Working for newspapers and other campus publications is also a great way to develop writing and job skills and to meet new people.

Students With Disabilities

Under the Americans with Disabilities Act, colleges are legally obligated to provide services and resources for students with disabilities, such as physical disabilities, mental disabilities (such as depression, anxiety, or chronic illness), physical limitations (such as visual impairment), and learning disabilities (such as dyslexia or attention deficit disorder). Students should be informed about their rights and ask for assistance.

◆ **Check out resources.** The first step is to see what is available at your school, such as a center for students with disabilities or a learning skills center. Special services may be provided by student services or counseling. The staff will help you check out services offered by the state and resources in the library. Services to ask about include
  ◆ Parking permits
  ◆ Ramps and accessibility to buildings
  ◆ Audiotapes and books in Braille
  ◆ Extended time for test taking
  ◆ Help in selecting courses, registering, and transcribing lectures
  ◆ Lab course assistance
  ◆ Availability of a Sign Language interpreter, note taker, and tutors

Some students don't think they have a disability because their problem is not a physical limitation. A learning disability is a neurological disorder that can affect reading, writing, speaking, math abilities, and social skills. If you think you have persistent problems in these areas, you can contact the learning center or student health center for a referral to a licensed professional. Students whose learning disabilities are properly documented are entitled to certain accommodations. For more information, visit the National Center for Learning Disabilities at www.ncld.org, or call 1-888-575-7373 or job services at 1-800-526-7234.

- ◆ **Meet with instructors.** Talk with all of your instructors. You are not asking for special favors or treatment but, rather, for alternatives for meeting your goals. You may want to sit in the front row, tape the lectures, have an oral test, or use a computer instead of writing assignments longhand, or you may need extra time taking a test.

- ◆ **Meet with your advisor.** Discuss your concerns with your academic advisor or an advisor from the learning center. It is critical that you get help early, focus on your strengths, get organized, and map out a plan for success.

- ◆ **Be assertive.** You have a right to services and to be treated with respect. Ask for what you need and want in clear, polite, and direct language. If you don't get results, go to the next administrative level.

- ◆ **Be positive and focus on your goals.** Realize that, even though your mountain may be steeper, you have what it takes to adapt and succeed. Use the ABCDE Method of Self-Management to help you dispute negative thinking and visualize yourself being successful.

Commuter Students

It is very important that commuter students get involved with campus events. Commuters make up the largest number of college students. Almost 80 percent of all college students are commuters. Here are some tips to help you succeed:

- ◆ **Get involved in school.** Students who get involved and join a club are more likely to graduate and have a positive college experience. Visit the student activities office and find out if there is a student newspaper or radio station and what support groups, special classes, tutorial and other activities, and support are offered. Check out the library, career center, computer center, and other available resources.

- ◆ **Get support from your family.** If you live at home, talk with your parents, spouse or partner, or children about your new responsibilities. Delegate duties and ask for help and support. Let them know when you have reports, papers, and projects due or need to study for a test.

- ◆ **Connect with others.** Build relationships with students, instructors, advisors, and staff. Find someone who cares about you. Build a connection with an instructor or advisor and join study groups.

- ◆ **Carry an emergency kit.** If you commute by car, carry a flashlight, water, snacks, medical supplies, a blanket, pen and paper, jumper cables, a towel, a few dollars and change, extra clothes, and shoes. In the winter, pack extra gloves, a hat, boots, and even a down jacket or sleeping bag. People have been stranded for hours in snowstorms. Talk with other commuters and add to your list.

- ◆ **Tape lectures.** With your instructor's permission, tape lectures or ask for tapes that would supplement your classes and make good use of your commuting time. However, never let a tape, music, or your thoughts distract you from your main job of driving safely.
- ◆ **Pack your lunch.** Also pack granola bars or packets of nuts or raisins that you can keep in your backpack or car.

Returning Students

If you are a nontraditional, returning, or reentry student, you have lots of company. Over one-third of all students are over age 25, and many are well over 40. These students are sometimes referred to as **"nontraditional" students** (with a **"traditional" student** defined as 18 to 25 years old, usually going from high school directly to college). The number of nontraditional students is growing every year as more and more people return to school to complete or further their education. Some returning students are veterans or single parents, some work full-time, and almost all have other commitments and responsibilities. Returning students often do better than younger students because they have a sense of purpose, discipline, and years of experience to draw upon.

Two of their biggest concerns are finding time and dealing with interruptions. How can they manage school as well as the demands of families and jobs? Many find that they must organize their time and use the available campus resources. More and more services are being offered for the older, returning student, such as support groups, child care, tutoring, credit for work experiences, and special classes. There are many resources that are especially important for returning students:

- ◆ Adult reentry center
- ◆ Legal aid
- ◆ Continuing education
- ◆ Adult services
- ◆ Veterans Affairs
- ◆ Office for credit for prior experience
- ◆ Women's center
- ◆ Counseling center
- ◆ Job placement center
- ◆ Information/referral services
- ◆ Financial aid office
- ◆ On-campus child care

Explore Your Community's Resources

As a college student, you have an opportunity to get to know a city and a chance to make a contribution to the campus and community. Even if you've always lived in the same city, you may not be aware of its rich resources and opportunities. When you get involved, you gain a sense of belonging and know that one person can make a difference. Many students have found enormous satisfaction in working with children, volunteering in nursing homes and hospitals, serving in a house of worship, or working with the homeless.

People Resources

Your community is made up of people who can provide you with great opportunities for growth, information, and services. Some people resources in the community include

- ◆ *Business professionals.* It is important to connect with business professionals in your field of study. They offer valuable information and advice, internships, scholarships, contacts, jobs, and career opportunities. You can make contacts by volunteering your services or joining professional organizations. Many professional groups have student memberships.
- ◆ *Government officials.* You will feel more involved in the community when you learn the names of your local political leaders. Go to a city council meeting, attend a county board of supervisors' meeting, or meet the mayor. Some city, county, and state governments have special programs, internships, and fellowships for students. Learn the names of your state senator and representative by searching on-line or calling the local political office or chamber of commerce.
- ◆ *Political parties.* Political activity is one way to meet people, become informed about local issues, and contribute your organizational talents. Political parties are always looking for volunteers.
- ◆ *Counselors.* Counselors, psychiatrists, clergy, and therapists can help with personal problems, such as depression, excessive shyness, or destructive behavior, and are available just to talk about any problem you may be having.

Program Resources

You may find a number of community programs available to you, such as

- ◆ *Chamber of commerce.* The local chamber of commerce has information about local attractions, special events, museums, bed and breakfast inns, hotels, motels, restaurants, libraries, clubs, and businesses. It also has information about economic development, the environment, political issues, clubs, and organizations.
- ◆ *Clubs and organizations.* Many clubs, such as the Rotary, Lions, Elks, Soroptimist, American Association of University Women, and Kiwanis, offer scholarships for students. Clubs such as Toastmasters and the Sierra Club offer programs for people with specific interests. Big Brothers, Big Sisters, YWCA, YMCA, Girls Clubs, and Boys Clubs are always looking for volunteers and lecturers, and they offer many services for free or at low cost.
- ◆ *Recreation centers.* Fitness centers, gyms, swimming pools, and local community education programs offer classes, programs, and opportunities to participate in enjoyable physical activity.

- *Child care.* Child care is provided by both private and public agencies. Look in the yellow pages and call your city hall, houses of worship, or local school district.

- *Health care.* Know the phone numbers of local hospitals and health clinics. They provide inexpensive vaccinations, birth control, gynecological exams, and general health care.

- *Houses of worship.* Houses of worship are also places to meet new friends. They hold social events, workshops, support groups, and conferences.

- *Job placement services.* Job placement services provide career counseling, job listings, and workshops on interviewing skills and resume writing.

- *Legal aid.* You may need free or low-cost legal aid services.

- *Crisis centers.* Hot lines are usually available 24 hours a day for such crises as suicidal feelings, physical and/or emotional abuse, rape, AIDS, and severe depression.

- *Support groups.* Whatever your needs, there may be a support group to share concerns and to offer help. Among these are support groups for alcoholism, drug addiction, friends and family of addicts or alcoholics, physical and/or emotional abuse, veterans, people making career changes, and cancer and other terminal illnesses.

- *Helping organizations.* The American Cancer Society, American Heart Association, Red Cross, and Salvation Army provide information, services, and help. These organizations are always looking for volunteers.

- *Service learning.* Many schools encourage students to incorporate internships, co-op programs, volunteering, or service learning into their education. The emphasis is on students' contributing their time and talents to improve the quality of the community and to learn valuable job skills. Students often earn college credits and obtain valuable experience while integrating what they learn in classes into practical, on-the-job problem solving. Students also have an opportunity to create their own learning experiences through directed study and field experience. Some students tutor or work with the homeless, the elderly, or people with disabilities. Many other students find that internships and co-op programs are great ways to earn college credit and contribute their talents. Businesses are looking for people who also take time to contribute to the community. Many internships offer wages, and some lead to part-time or full-time employment after graduation.

Additional On-Line and Information Resources

Other resources to explore include

- *Community telephone directories.* Scanning the yellow pages is one of the best ways to discover the services available in the area.

- *Local newspapers.* Read the local newspapers to learn about community events, services, seminars, clubs, auctions, art showings, sporting events, concerts, businesses, and entertainment. You'll also read about the local political and community leaders and the current community issues.

- *Magazines and newsletters.* Almost every community has a few newsletters or magazines describing the area, featuring local interest stories, and advertising community resources.
- *Local libraries.* Check out the city and county libraries. As already discussed, libraries are a tremendous resource. They offer a wealth of information, films, and classes.

Manage Your Financial Resources

In this section, we will analyze how to manage a very important resource—your money. Did you know the following facts, according to the Consumer Credit Counseling Service (CCCS)?

- The average student leaves college with a credit card debt of between $8,000 and $10,000 (this does *not* include student loans). At an interest rate of 18 percent, it will take 25 years of minimum payments to pay off this loan, which will ultimately cost $24,000.
- More young people filed for bankruptcy than graduated from college in 2001.
- The average college student spends more on beer than on textbooks.

If you want to be above average when it comes to handling your finances, you must be proactive and plan ahead.

- *Keep a budget.* The first step in handling your finances is to write a budget. Calculate how much money you earn and how much money you spend. Write a long-term budget for a year or more, one for the school term, and a short-term monthly budget. You will then have a big picture of large expenses, such as tuition, and you will be able to monitor and modify your expenses each month. Keep receipts, bills, canceled checks, and credit card statements in a file or box, in case you want to exchange your purchases or revise your budget for accuracy. Keep one file for taxes and file applicable receipts. Refine your budget when necessary and then stick to it. **Personal Evaluation Notebook 4.2** on page 136 provides a guide for making a budget.
- *Beware of credit card debt.* You will want to establish a good credit rating. Credit cards are convenient and a way to establish a credit rating. However, be careful not to exceed your loan limit and make certain you have the money before you charge. Thousands of students find themselves in debt every year by using a credit card without backup funds. Many students don't even know the rate of interest that they are paying. Most cards charge at least 18 percent interest. Some people blame the financial industry for making it too easy to obtain credit cards. As an adult, however, you should make a point of being informed and take responsibility for your decisions and actions.
- *Save for the future.* Once you get out of college and have a good job, save 10 percent of your income in a savings account, your company's 401k plan, an Individual Retirement Account (IRA), or a similar investment. Some sacrifices now, such as buying a used car instead of a new one, will add up later. For example, for a traditional-aged college student, $25,000 today earning 8 percent interest

WORDS TO SUCCEED

"Money is of no value, it cannot spend itself. All depends on the skill of the spender."

RALPH WALDO EMERSON, *Poet*

Money In/Money Out

The following chart will help you get started on planning and organizing your budget. On a separate sheet of paper, make a copy of this chart and follow the instructions.

1. Monitor your spending for a month. To keep it simple, list money in and money out. Record everything, including earnings, food, travel, and school items. At the end of the month, total your monthly income and your monthly expenses. Put them in the appropriate categories. Subtract your total expenses from your total income. The money left is your monthly surplus. If you have a deficit, you will need to explore ways of increasing revenue or decreasing expenses. Following is a sample.

Date	Money In	Money Out
Monday, Jan. 2	$28.00 (typed paper)	
Tuesday, Jan. 3		$20.00 (dinner/movie) $40.00 (gas for car)
Wednesday, Jan. 4	$50.00 (house cleaning)	

2. How can you increase your earnings?

_____

_____

_____

_____

3. How can you decrease your spending?

_____

_____

_____

_____

4. List all the free or inexpensive entertainment available in your community. Discuss this list with your study team.

_____

_____

_____

_____

Use Worksheet 4.5 as a guide for planning your budget for the school term.

Applying the Adult Learning Cycle to Managing Financial Resources

1. **RELATE. Why do I want to learn this?** I know if I start a habit of wise spending, successful saving, and investing now, it will pay off later. I want to stay debt-free and maintain a good credit rating.

2. **OBSERVE. How does this work?** Who do I know appears to be in good financial shape? What can I learn from resources such as investment web sites and money counselors? What are some on-line tools I can explore to determine what my goals should be?

3. **REFLECT. What does this mean?** Where can I further limit my expenses? I'll keep track of my progress and see what strategies work for me.

4. **DO. What can I do with this?** I will practice reducing my spending every chance I get. Each day, I'll work on one area. For example, instead of buying coffee and a bagel every day, I'll prepare my own at home and save about a few dollars every day. I'll also pack my lunch, rather than buying it on the run.

5. **TEACH. Whom can I share this with?** I'll ask others for tips and share my progress with a financial counselor.

Make a commitment to paying your obligations on time. Investing in a wise financial plan today will pay off with big dividends later.

will equal $800,000 at retirement. If you were to save and invest just $1 every day—the price of a small soft drink at a fast-food restaurant—you could have $90,000 in the bank at your retirement. (See **Peak Progress 4.2** for applications to the Adult Learning Cycle.)

◆ *Protect yourself.* Incidences of identify theft are increasing. Periodically check your account balances and review your bank statements, and always review your credit card statements. If you handle your transactions on-line, carefully read the procedures on the bank's or company's web site. Never respond to e-mails that ask for personal information, such as your Social Security number or bank account numbers. Report any suspicious activity to your bank or credit card company immediately.

Financial Assistance

Most schools provide many sources of jobs and financial aid. Thousands of dollars of financial aid are available and go unclaimed each year. If you are having trouble paying for your education, check the financial aid office for loans, grants, scholarships, and information on programs available to students. Generally, scholarships and grants do not have to be paid back. However, student loans must be repaid. Make certain that you know the payback policy and treat your school loan with the same respect you would treat any loan. Unpaid loans hurt the lending agency or school and, of course, other students who need loans. Defaulting on student loans may also damage your credit, because this information appears on credit reports. Some sources of financial aid include the following loans and programs.

- *School scholarships and grants.* Scholarships and grants are awarded at most schools on the basis of academic achievement, athletics, music, art, or writing and usually do not have to be paid back. Check with the financial aid office for a complete list of scholarships and grants. Also, find out if scholarships are offered by your or your parents' employer.

- *Pell grants.* This is the largest student aid program financed by the federal government. Pell grants do not have to be repaid. Check with your school's financial aid office for more information.

- *Loans.* Stafford and Perkins loans are low-interest loans to be repaid after you complete your education. Plus loans and supplemental loans for students (SLS) have variable interest rates; repayment of the principal and interest begins after the last loan payment. Check with the financial aid office for a complete list of loans.

- *Work-study.* Student employment, or work-study, is an excellent way to earn money and gain valuable experience.

- *Community scholarships and grants.* Many community organizations (such as the Rotary, Kiwanis, Lions, Elks, Soroptimist, and American Association of University Women) offer scholarships and grants, which do not have to be repaid.

- *Veterans programs.* Veterans can take advantage of money available through the Veterans Administration.

- *Programs for Native American students.* Native American students can find financial aid from the U.S. Bureau of Indian Affairs.

- *Programs for the unemployed.* Training programs, such as Work Incentive (WIN), are available for the unemployed. There are also scholarships, grants, fellowships, and loans available.

- *Other sources.* Loans, assistance programs, and aid programs may be available if you have special needs, such as visual impairments, hearing problems, speech difficulties, or a deceased parent. Search the Internet by using keywords such as "college scholarship" or "college loans" to find available programs.

Check with your school's financial aid office for a complete listing of various financial resources, or visit the U.S. Department of Education web site at **www.ed.gov.** This web site provides general information about the major federal student aid programs, who is eligible and how to apply, tax credits for education expenses, and other federal, state, and private sources of information.

Build a Savings Account

Getting in the habit of saving money is not easy for many people. The U.S. Department of Commerce reports that most Americans save less than a penny for every

$10 earned. However, there are ways to build your savings account for a sound financial future. The more money you save, the better prepared you will be to handle unexpected expenses, such as car repairs or medical costs. Increasing your savings account will help you be able to meet your financial goals. Every effort you make to save money makes a significant difference. By creating a savings plan, you will become more confident with handling your finances. Here are some tips to help you get started:

- Spend less each day by taking your lunch to school or work.
- Limit your credit card use, because interest rates are higher than what you would earn in a savings account.
- Shop around to find the bank that offers the highest interest rates for savings accounts.
- Balance your checkbook every month.
- Pay your bills and taxes on time.
- Take advantage of your employer's payroll savings deduction plan.
- Spend less money than you make.

Every time you get paid, put a sum into your savings account before paying your bills. If direct deposit is offered by your employer, make this easy by having it direct deposited.

Other Tips for Saving Money

There are many proactive ways you can cut your expenses and build your savings:

- *Shop wisely.* Refer to a list when you shop and don't buy on impulse. Don't shop as a means of entertainment. Avoid buying convenience items and snack foods. They all cost more and provide less nutrition. Pack your lunch rather than buying snacks at school or work. You can save a considerable amount of money each week.
- *Pay cash.* Don't use a credit card. If you have one, use it only for emergencies or special items, such as airline tickets. Pay off the balance on a credit card immediately. Interest charges can be expensive. You will be tempted to buy more with credit, and it is difficult to monitor how much you spend. Follow this simple rule: If you don't have the money for an item, don't buy it. Keep your money in the bank and don't carry a large sum with you, or keep it in your home. You will be less tempted to spend if money isn't readily available.
- *Use public transportation.* Buy a car only if necessary. Many cities have public transportation. Biking or walking whenever possible is cheaper and less inconvenient than searching for parking. A car is an expensive purchase, and the purchase price is only the initial cost. Make certain you have researched the cost of insurance, tires, maintenance, gasoline, and parking.
- *Exchange room and board for work.* Some students exchange room and board for lawn care, child care, or housecleaning. Since rent is an expensive item in your budget, an exchange situation can save you thousands of dollars over a

few years. Ask around or put an ad in the newspaper, local newsletter, community organization publications, and so forth. Also, look for opportunities to house-sit.

◆ *Stay healthy.* Illness is costly in terms of time, energy, missed classes, and medical bills. You can avoid many illnesses by respecting your body and using common sense. Avoid unhealthy snacks and poor eating habits. Fresh fruit, vegetables, beans, rice, and whole grains are nutritious and cost less than convenience foods. Get exercise and rest, and avoid harmful substances. Cigarette smoking is expensive, and smokers are sick more often than nonsmokers, can pay higher health premiums, and have more difficulty getting roommates.

◆ *Conserve energy.* Save money on utilities by turning down the heat, turning off lights, taking quick showers, and turning the water off while you brush your teeth.

◆ *Get a job.* Working while you go to school can help you earn extra money, but make sure you are not working long hours and neglecting your education. Check with the career center or placement office for a list of on- and off-campus jobs.

◆ *Think critically.* Expensive purchases, such as a car, stereo, or computer, should be planned carefully.

◆ *Simplify your life.* If you don't need something, don't buy it. Savor the freedom of living a simple, uncomplicated life. Look for free or inexpensive entertainment.

Communicate About Your Finances
If your financial obligations are shared by a spouse or partner, make sure you are aware of each other's spending habits. *How can financial problems affect a relationship?*

Get Financial Help If You're In Trouble

If you find that you are having financial problems and your credit rating might be damaged, get help. Don't borrow more money!

1. **First, admit to yourself that you have a problem.** Denial only makes the problem worse. There are some warning signs that you may be in financial trouble. If you experience two or more of these signs, you need to take action:

   ◆ You make only the minimum monthly payments on credit cards.

   ◆ You're having trouble making even the minimum monthly payments on your credit card bills.

   ◆ The total balance on your credit cards increases every month.

   ◆ You miss loan payments or often pay late.

   ◆ You use savings to pay for necessities, such as food and utilities.

   ◆ You receive second or third payment-due notices from creditors.

   ◆ You borrow money to pay off old debts.

   ◆ You exceed the credit limits on your credit cards.

   ◆ You've been denied credit because of a bad credit bureau report.

2. **Get professional help.** Check the yellow pages or call the local chamber of commerce and ask if your community has a consumer credit agency that helps with credit counseling. When you meet with a counselor, take all your budget information, assets, bills, resources, loans, and any other requested items. Local branches of the Consumer Credit Counseling Service (CCCS) provide debt counseling for families and individuals, and it charges only a small fee when it supervises a debt-repayment plan. Other private and public organizations, such as universities, credit unions, the military, and state and federal housing authorities, also provide financial counseling services for a nominal fee or no charge at all.

3. **Spend less than you earn.** It's as simple as that. Write a budget and be absolutely firm about sticking to it. Once the habit of living within your means is part of your life, you will reap the rewards of confidence and control.

You Are a Great Resource!

The most important resource you have is yourself. Call on your inner resources to make a difference in the world. School and community resources are available for you to become involved and to contribute your talents. Making a contribution is one of the best ways to connect to a school and community and to gain a real sense of satisfaction. What resources are you particularly interested in using? In what areas do you think you can make a contribution? Make time to get involved in at least one area of interest in school, the community, or the world.

WORDS TO SUCCEED

"If you think nobody cares if you're alive, try missing a couple of car payments."

EARL WILSON, *Professional baseball player*

WORDS TO SUCCEED

"Few men during their lifetime come anywhere near exhausting the resources dwelling within them. There are deep wells of strength that are never used."

REAR ADMIRAL RICHARD E. BYRD, *Polar explorer*

In summary, in this chapter, I learned to:

- *Explore and understand the campus system.* It is important to understand the rules, regulations, deadlines, policies, procedures, requirements, and resources for help at my school. I attend orientation sessions and find out how to register and pay fees. Exploring resources helps me create a sense of belonging and build a community of new friends, activities, and goals.

- *Determine campus resources.* I take advantage of all the resources that are available to help me succeed. I take time to go on a campus tour and go on-line to review the school's web site.

- *Seek out people resources.* I appreciate the faculty, advisors, administrators, and study-team members, as well as all the students and relationships that make up the campus community. I explore and build networks with all the people who provide information, help, and support. I meet with instructors and my advisor often to review and clarify my expectations and progress. I understand that having a mentor to look to for guidance, knowledge, and advice is essential to my growth as a person and my field of study.

- *Use program resources.* I explore various programs that offer help, support, and opportunities, such as the advising center, the career development center, counseling, the tutoring and learning center, exchange programs, the job placement office, clubs, campus events, and other activities. I spend time in the library, exploring books, magazines, and newspapers and reviewing this rich resource. I visit the bookstore and computer labs, read through the catalog, look at school material, and read the school newspaper. I explore resources available for my special needs, such as the adult reentry center and transferring student, legal aid, and veterans programs. As a commuting student, I check out carpooling boards and look for programs that can help me be more involved in campus activities.

- *Use technology to my advantage.* I determine how technology will be used in my courses and what opportunities and resources are provided by my school.

- *Explore community resources.* I appreciate the opportunity that I have to explore the community and get involved. I look into internships and part-time jobs. I go to city council meetings and become familiar with community leaders and projects. I read the local paper and am familiar with local topics and opportunities for service. I look in the yellow pages for resources and special support groups and agencies offering counseling and health services.

- *Participate in service learning.* I look for ways that I can combine learning with volunteer work. I volunteer for community projects and political parties, as well as in schools, nursing homes, hospitals, animal shelters, crisis centers, and areas of interest, such as historical buildings or environmental protection.

- *Manage my money.* I take full responsibility for my finances. I know how to make and stick to a budget, save money, and spend less than I earn. I limit my credit card use and seek help managing my money when necessary.

- *Explore financial resources.* I explore scholarships and grants, loans, work-study, and special assistance programs. I also explore campus jobs, as well as student assistance programs.

- *Realize that I am my greatest resource.* I know that I am capable of making the most of my opportunities and, in turn, I am a resource to others and my community.

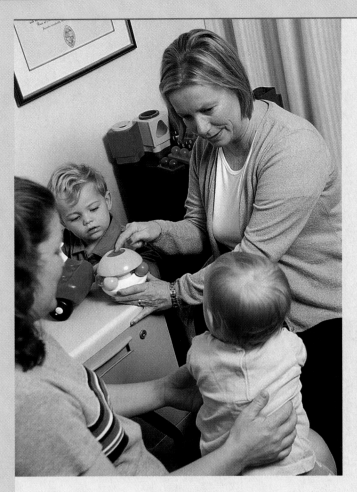

Donna Washington

SCHOOL SOCIAL WORKER

Related Majors: Social Work, Psychology, Sociology

Benefits of Community Resources

Donna Washington works as a social worker at an elementary school. School social workers help students, teachers, and parents cope with problems. Their work involves guidance and counseling regarding challenging issues in the classroom as well as in the home. They diagnose behavior problems and advise teachers on how to deal with difficult students. They work with families to improve attendance and help working parents find after-school child care. They also help recent immigrants and students with disabilities adjust to the classroom.

A long list of community resources helps Donna provide appropriate community referrals. She often uses the telephone to arrange services for children in need, such as counseling or testing. Other services on her list include legal aid societies, crisis hot lines, immigrant resource centers, and tutoring. Donna has developed her list over a 20-year career span and remains in touch with key community leaders to keep her list up-to-date.

Donna chose to be a school social worker because of a strong desire to make a difference in the lives of children. She possesses all of the qualities that make her an excellent social worker: She is responsible, emotionally stable, warm and caring, and able to relate to a wide variety of clients, and she can work independently. Because of budget cuts, agencies in her district are understaffed, and Donna struggles with a huge caseload. Although she finds the work emotionally draining at times, Donna finds tremendous satisfaction when she sees the lives of her students improve due to her care.

CRITICAL THINKING What qualities make a good social worker? Why?

Peak Performer Profile

Matthew Friedman and Adam Scott

Can a couple of college students make it in the restaurant business with no more than a few "hot" sauces, a single phone line, a beat-up hatchback car, and lots of ambition? Matthew Friedman, president and founder of Wing Zone, and his business partner, Adam Scott, senior vice president and co-founder, proved they could when they began offering delivery of chicken wings to 40,000 students at the University of Florida in the 1990s. "There were lots of options for food on campus, but there were no restaurants that served or delivered buffalo wings," recalls Friedman, age 35. "We began with $500 and tested the concept in the frat-house kitchen." The first two nights in operation, they sold out, and three weeks later they opened their first small storefront.

Today, Wing Zone is a franchise corporation with 82 locations in 25 states—and counting—throughout the Southeast and mid-Atlantic regions, as well as in Texas, Washington, and the Midwest. A high proportion of the company's franchise stores are minority-owned, and Wing Zone has been actively involved in the National Minority Franchising Initiative. This program encourages minority ownership of franchise stores, especially by employees who have come up through the ranks.

Some say Friedman's generation has had an easy ride in business, compared with industry pioneers such as Ray Kroc of McDonald's and Harlan Sanders of Kentucky Fried Chicken. But Friedman disagrees with that criticism: "I think we've had it tougher—there's more competition, customers have more choices, and they have higher expectations. We've worked hard for everything we have. It wasn't given to us on a silver platter."

Friedman has unquestionably served as a role model for young people who are interested in starting a business of any kind. But did this busy entrepreneur manage to finish his education, too? "Both Adam and I finished college with business degrees," says Friedman. "That was very important to us and to our families, and our college diplomas hang on the walls of our offices. But it was very hectic trying to run a business and take classes at the same time."

PERFORMANCE THINKING What school and community resources might Matthew Friedman and Adam Scott have tapped into when launching their business? What inner personal qualities were important to their success?

CHECK IT OUT While minorities make up more than 30 percent of the U.S. population, they represent only 8 percent to 10 percent of franchise owners in this country, according to the International Franchise Association (IFA). In an effort to improve this statistic, the IFA has established a new Diversity Institute. Visit **www.franchise.org** and enter the keyword "diversity." What efforts are underway in the franchise community to make ownership, recruiting, hiring, advancement, supplier selection, and marketing more inclusive?

Performance Strategies

Following are the top 10 tips for maximizing your resources:

◆ Explore all available resources.

◆ Join clubs and activities and widen your circle of friends.

◆ Investigate one new campus resource each week.

◆ Explore one new community resource each week.

◆ Get involved and volunteer at school and in the community.

◆ Seek help at the first sign of academic, financial, health, or emotional trouble.

◆ Know where your money goes and where you want to invest it.

◆ Use a credit card for convenience only and don't go into debt for unnecessary items.

◆ Reduce spending and increase savings.

◆ Look for creative ways to save money.

Tech for Success

Take advantage of the text's web site at **www.mhhe.com/ferrett6e** for additional study aids, useful forms, and convenient and applicable resources.

◆ **Bill paying on-line.** Many financial institutions offer a service that allows you to pay your bills through their web site. Would this feature help you keep up with your financial obligations?

◆ **Web sites and textbooks.** Many textbooks have accompanying web sites that provide additional resources and study tools, such as on-line study guides, lab manuals, resources for research projects, and materials to study for certification exams. Many of these web sites are provided free, usually when you have bought your textbook new. If you aren't sure if your textbook has an accompany web site, read the preface at the beginning of the text (usually listed under "Ancillaries," "Supplements," or "Resources"), ask your instructor, or visit the publisher's web site.

Review Questions

Based on what you have learned in this chapter, write your answers to the following questions:

1. When you hear the word *community,* what comes to mind? How would you define it based on your experiences and your culture?

2. What type of campus programs would you seek to find a full- or part-time job while attending school?

3. Name two college financial resources cited in this chapter that you would like to investigate and explain why.

4. How can staying healthy help you financially?

5. What is your most important resource? Why?

USING RESOURCES

In the Classroom

Lorraine Peterson is a returning student at a two-year business school. She also works part-time selling cosmetics at a retail store and would like to advance to a managerial position. She was away from school for several years. During that time, she started a family and is now eager to become involved in school and its activities. On returning to school, she happily discovered other returning students. Several of them get together for coffee on a regular basis. Lorraine is especially interested in foreign students and international business. She also wants to learn more about available computer services, guest speakers, marketing associations, and scholarships.

1. What suggestions do you have for Lorraine about involvement in campus and community events?

_____

_____

2. How can she find out about scholarships and explore all the resources that would increase her success as a returning student?

_____

_____

In the Workplace

Lorraine has been a salesperson for several years with a large cosmetics firm. She recently was promoted to district manager for sales. Part of her job is to offer motivational seminars on the benefits of working for her firm. She wants to point out opportunities and resources available to employees, such as training programs, support groups, demonstrations, sales meetings, and conferences. The company also donates money for scholarships and sponsors community events. An elaborate incentive system offers awards and prizes for increased sales.

3. How can Lorraine publicize these resources to her sales staff?

_____

_____

4. What strategies in this chapter would help her communicate the importance of contributing time and talents to the community and the company?

_____

_____

APPLYING THE ABCDE METHOD OF SELF-MANAGEMENT

In the Journal Entry on page 119, you were asked to write about a time when you set a financial goal. How difficult was it to achieve? What sacrifices did you have to make?

_____

_____

_____

Now think of a financial goal you may consider in the next few years and apply the ABCDE method to work through the obstacles and create a plan for achieving that goal as well.

A = Actual event:

B = Beliefs:

C = Consequences:

D = Dispute:

E = Energized:

Visualize yourself planning and saving money for investing in your goals. You feel confident about yourself, because you have learned to manage your money and your goals. See yourself feeling prosperous as you consider other aspects of wealth, such as being healthy, having supportive family and friends, having opportunities, and being surrounded by many campus and community resources.

Practice Self-Management

For more examples of learning how to manage difficult situations, see the "Self-Management Workbook" section of the Online Learning Center web site at **www.mhhe.com/ferrett6e**.

EXPLORING YOUR SCHOOL'S RESOURCES

Go on your school's web site, look through the catalog and phone directory, or go to student services to determine which resources are available—especially those that are of particular interest to you and your needs. Include additional resources that are important. In the "Notes" section of the following chart, include information such as location, contact names, and fees. Put a check mark in the "Not Available" box if this resource is not offered.

Resource	Notes	Phone/E-mail	Not Available
Activities/clubs Office			
Adult and Reentry center			
Advising center			
Alumni office			
Art gallery			
Bookstore			
Career center			
Chaplain/religious services			
Child-care center			
Cinema/theater			
Computing center/computer labs			
Continuing education			
Disability center (learning or physical disabilities)			
Distance learning			
Financial aid			
Fitness center/gymnasium			
Health center			
Honors program			
Housing center			
Information center			
Intramural sports			
Language lab			
Learning center			
Lost and found			
Math lab			
Multicultural center			
Museum			

(continued)

REVIEW AND APPLICATIONS

CHAPTER 4

Resource	Notes	Phone/E-mail	Not Available
Off-campus housing and services			
Ombudsman/conflict resolution			
Photography lab			
Police/campus security			
Post office			
Printing center			
Registration office			
School newspaper			
Student government office			
Study abroad/exchange			
Testing center			
Volunteer services			
Work-study center			
Writing lab			
Other:			
Other:			
Other:			
Other:			
Other:			

NETWORKING

Write information about your network of people on the following form. You can copy this worksheet form to extend your list of contacts.

Name _____

Company _____

Phone _____

Type of work _____

Name _____

Company _____

Phone _____

Type of work _____

Name _____

Company _____

Phone _____

Type of work _____

Name _____

Company _____

Phone _____

Type of work _____

REVIEW AND APPLICATIONS

CHAPTER 4

COMMUNITY RESOURCES

Research and list the various resources your community has to offer. Make a point to visit at least a few of them and place a check mark by those you have visited. You can copy this worksheet form to extend your list of resources.

Check

_____ Resource _____

Service offered _____

_____

Contact person _____

Phone number _____

_____ Resource _____

Service offered _____

_____

Contact person _____

Phone number _____

_____ Resource _____

Service offered _____

_____

Contact person _____

Phone number _____

_____ Resource _____

Service offered _____

_____

Contact person _____

Phone number _____

_____ Resource _____

Service offered _____

_____

Contact person _____

Phone number _____

BUDGETING EACH TERM

Creating a budget is the first step to financial success. As you plan for your expenses, take time to reflect on your spending habits. Spending within your budget will allow you to reach your financial goals. Complete the following list and review it every month to keep track of your expenses.

Budget for Each School Term

Tuition $ _____
Books and supplies $ _____
Housing $ _____
Transportation $ _____
Insurance $ _____
Clothing $ _____
Laundry $ _____
Food $ _____
Entertainment $ _____
Utilities $ _____
Phone $ _____
Health care $ _____
Household items $ _____
Savings $ _____
Miscellaneous $ _____
Total $ _____

Estimated Expenses for the Year

Tuition $ _____
Books and supplies $ _____
Housing $ _____
Transportation $ _____
Insurance $ _____
Clothing $ _____
Laundry $ _____
Food $ _____
Entertainment $ _____
Utilities $ _____
Phone $ _____
Health care $ _____
Household items $ _____
Other $ _____
Loans $ _____
Total $ _____

Estimated Resources for Each Month/Term

Parental contribution $ _____
Summer savings $ _____
Student savings $ _____
Job $ _____
Loans $ _____
Other $ _____
Total $ _____

YOUR COMMUNITY SERVICE

Exploring your personal resources and abilities is important for your career development. Answer the following questions and relate your community participation to your leadership skills. Add this page to your Career Development Portfolio.

1. Describe your ability to manage resources. What are your strengths in managing time, money, and information and in determining what resources are available to solve various problems?

   _____

   _____

   _____

   _____

   _____

2. Indicate how you would demonstrate to an employer that you have made a contribution to the community.

   _____

   _____

   _____

   _____

   _____

3. Indicate how you would demonstrate to an employer that you know how to explore and manage resources.

   _____

   _____

   _____

   _____

4. Indicate how you would demonstrate to an employer that you have learned leadership skills.

   _____

   _____

   _____

   _____

Listen and Take Effective Notes

CHAPTER OBJECTIVES

In this chapter, you will learn to

▲ Become an attentive listener

▲ Demonstrate effective note-taking strategies

▲ Take notes in alignment with your learning style

▲ Utilize the various note-taking systems

SELF-MANAGEMENT

"I am having a problem staying focused and alert in my afternoon class. The instructor speaks in a monotone and I have a hard time following his lecture. What can I do to listen more effectively and take better notes?"

Have you ever had a similar experience? Do you find yourself daydreaming during class? Do you ever leave a class and feel frustrated because you've not been focused and your notes are unreadable? In this chapter, you will learn how to be an attentive listener and to take clear and organized notes.

JOURNAL ENTRY In **Worksheet 5.1** on page 178, describe a time when you had difficulty making sense out of a lecture and staying alert. Are there certain classes in which it is more challenging for you to be an attentive listener?

Attending lectures or meetings, listening, taking notes, and gathering information are a daily part of school and work. However, few people give much thought to the process of selecting, organizing, and recording information. Attentive listening and note taking are not just tools for school. They are essential job skills. Throughout your career, you will be processing and recording information. The volume of new information is expanding in this computer age, and the career professional who can listen, organize, and summarize information will be valuable. This chapter addresses the fine points of attentive listening and note taking.

Listening to the Message: Attentive Listening Strategies

WORDS TO SUCCEED

"I only wish I could find an institute that teaches people how to listen. After all, a good manager needs to listen as much as he needs to talk....Real communication goes in both directions."

LEE IACOCCA, *Former chairman of Chrysler Corporation*

Before you can be an effective note taker, you must become an effective listener. Most people think of themselves as good listeners. However, listening should not be confused with ordinary hearing. **Attentive listening** is a decision to be fully focused with the intent on understanding the speaker. It is a consuming activity that requires physical and mental attention, energy, concentration, and discipline. It requires respect, empathy, genuine interest, and the desire to understand. Researchers say that we spend about 80 percent or more of our time communicating; and of that time, almost half—45 percent to 50 percent—is spent listening, yet few of us have been trained to listen. This helps explain why so many people are poor listeners.

Not only is listening fundamental to taking good classroom notes, but it is also directly related to how well you do in college, in your career, and in relationships. As a student, you will be expected to listen attentively to lectures, to other student presentations, and in small-group and class discussions. Attentive listening is also important for job success. Career professionals attend meetings, follow directions, work with customers, take notes from professional journals and lectures, and give and receive feedback. Many organizations have been developing listening training programs designed to improve listening and communicating habits.

You can apply the following attentive listening strategies for building effective relationships at school, at work, and in life.

Prepare to listen

◆ **Be willing to listen.** The first place to start is with your intention. You must want to be a better listener and realize that listening is an active rather than a passive process. Is your intention to learn and understand the other person? Or is your intention to prove how smart you are and how wrong the other person is? The best listening strategies in the world won't help if you are unwilling to listen and understand another's viewpoint. Prepare mentally by creating a positive and willing attitude.

- **Be open to new ideas.** Be aware of any resistance you have to learning new information. Many students resist change, new ideas, or different beliefs. This resistance gets in the way of actively listening and learning. Be open to different points of view, different styles of lecturing, and new ideas. Students sometimes have problems listening to lectures because they have already made up their minds, or they want to prove the instructor wrong and mentally challenge everything that is said. It is easy to misinterpret the meaning of a message if you are defensive, judgmental, bored, or emotionally upset. With practice and discipline, you can create interest in any subject.

- **Sit up front.** Take a seat at the front of the room. This will help you hear and focus on the message, reduce distractions, and create a more personal relationship with the speaker. It also gives you and others the message that you are serious about listening.

- **Reduce distractions.** Avoid sitting next to a friend or someone who likes to talk or is distracting. Take a sweater if it is cold in the classroom or sit by an open window if it is warm. Carry a bottle of water with you to drink when your energy starts to lag. Don't do other activities when you are listening (opening mail, doing math homework, making a to-do list, and so on.). Do whatever it takes to focus and reduce distractions.

- **Look as if you are listening.** Attentive listening requires high energy. Sit up, keep your spine straight, and uncross your legs and you will have more energy. Maintain eye contact and lean slightly forward. Participate in discussions and ask questions.

Stay Attentive

- **Be quiet.** The fundamental rule of listening is to be quiet while the speaker is talking. Don't interrupt or talk to classmates. As a listener, your role is to understand and comprehend. The speaker's role is to make the message clear and comprehensible. Don't confuse the two roles. When you are listening, listen attentively until the speaker is finished.

- **Stay focused.** Being mentally and physically alert is vital for active listening. It's true that everyone's mind wanders during a long lecture, but being mentally preoccupied is a major barrier to effective listening. It's up to you to focus your attention, concentrate on the subject, and bring your mind back to the present. Make a determined effort to stay focused and in the present moment.

- **Show empathy, respect, and genuine interest.** Focus on understanding the message and viewpoint of the speaker. Look for common views and ways in which you are alike.

- **Observe.** A large part of listening and note taking is observing. Observe your instructor and watch for obvious verbal and nonverbal clues about what information is important. If your instructor uses repetition, becomes more animated, or writes information on the board, it is probably important. Overhead transparencies or handouts may also include important diagrams, lists, drawings, facts, or definitions. Watch for examples and connect similar

WORDS TO SUCCEED

"Listening to learn isn't about giving advice-at least not until asked-but about trying to understand exactly what someone means."

ELIZABETH DEBOLD, *Businesswoman*

ideas. Observe words and phrases that signal important information or transition, such as "One important factor is . . . "

◆ **Predict and ask questions.** Keep yourself alert by predicting and asking yourself questions. Is the story supporting the main topic? What are the main points? How does the example clarify the readings? What test questions could be asked about the main points? Pretend that you are in a private conversation and ask your instructor to elaborate, give examples, or explain certain points. Make certain that you are paying attention in class, you have previewed the chapter, and you have done your homework.

◆ **Integrate learning styles** and use all your senses. If you are primarily an *auditory* learner, consider taping certain lectures (be sure to ask the instructor before you tape). Recite your book notes into a tape recorder and play the tape several times. If you are primarily a *visual* learner, the more you see, the better you remember. Visualize what your instructor is talking about and supplement your lecture notes with drawings, illustrations, and pictures. If you are a *kinesthetic* learner, write as you listen, but also draw diagrams or pictures, rephrase what you hear in your own words, and take special note of material on the board, overhead transparencies, and handouts. Shift body position, so that you're comfortable.

◆ **Postpone judgment.** Don't pass judgment too quickly or in advance. Don't judge your instructor or his or her message based on clothes, reputation, voice, or teaching style. Go to class with an open and curious mind and focus on the message, the course content, and your performance. Talk in private if you disagree or have an opposing viewpoint, but do not embarrass the person in front of others. Of course, you should use critical thinking, but be respectful and open to new ideas.

◆ **Don't get caught up in drama.** Don't let another person's emotions affect your own. Stay focused on the message and be silent when silence is needed. Speak in low, quiet tones if someone is upset. Restate what you think you heard and ask questions: "I can see you are upset. How can I help?"

Review What You Have Heard

◆ **Paraphrase.** Clarify the speaker's message. After a conversation, paraphrase what you think the speaker said to you—for example, "Professor Keys, it is my understanding that the paper should be four to five pages long, is due on Friday, and should include supporting documentation. Is that correct?" Show that you understand the speaker by reflecting and paraphrasing: "Jan, do I understand that you feel that you are doing more than your share of cleaning the apartment?" After a lecture, write a summary of the key points and main ideas. It is even more effective if you compare notes and summarize with your study team.

◆ **Assess.** Evaluate how effective your listening skills are for recall, test taking, and studying with your study group. Reflect on conflicts, misunderstandings, and others' reactions to you. Take note of accompanying nonverbal cues. If there is a misunderstanding, assess your part. Did you jump to conclusions? Did you misunderstand nonverbal clues? Did you fail to clarify the message? Did you fail to follow up? When you feel that there is a misunderstanding or something is missing, ask simple, direct questions with the intent of understanding.

◆ **Practice with awareness.** It takes time to change old habits. Choose one problem you want to work on. For example, do you continue to interrupt? Think about how you feel when that happens to you and make a commitment to change. It won't happen overnight, but with consistent practice you can learn to stop annoying habits and improve your listening skills.

Peak Progress 5.1 explores how you can become a more attentive listener by applying the Adult Learning Cycle. Then, **Personal Evaluation Notebook 5.1** on page 160 asks you to think critically about your listening skills and how you can improve them.

Recording the Message

Now that you are prepared and have sharpened your listening and observation skills, let's look at how to outline your notes so that you can organize material. **Note taking** is not a passive act of simply writing down words. It is a way to order and arrange thoughts and materials to help you remember information. You can use either a formal or an informal outline (see **Peak Progress 5.2** on page 161). The

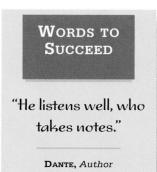

WORDS TO SUCCEED

"He listens well, who takes notes."

DANTE, *Author*

PEAK PROGRESS   **5.1**

Applying the Adult Learning Cycle to Becoming an Attentive Listener
Becoming an attentive listener and learning to take good notes take time and effort.

1. **RELATE. Why do I want to learn this?** How will being an attentive listener help me in school, work, and life? How would I rate my listening skills now? What areas do I need to improve?

2. **OBSERVE. How does this work?** I can learn a lot about attentive listening by watching others. I'll observe people who are good listeners and who take good notes. I'll also observe people who are not good listeners. Do their poor listening skills cause other problems for them?

3. **REFLECT. What does this mean?** I will gather information about listening and note taking and determine the better strategies for me to apply. What works and what doesn't seem to work? I'll explore creative ways to listen and take notes.

4. **DO. What can I do with this?** I will make a commitment to be a more attentive listener. I'll find opportunities to try my new listening skills. Each day, I'll focus on one area and work on it. For example, I'll choose one class in which I'm having trouble listening and experiment with new strategies.

5. **TEACH. Whom can I share this with?** I'll talk with others and share my tips and experiences. I'll demonstrate and teach the methods I've learned to others.

Now return to Stage 1 and think about how it feels to learn this valuable new skill of attentive listening.

Attentive Listening

Use critical thinking to answer the following questions.

1. Do you go to class prepared and in a positive and receptive state of mind? Write down one tip that you would be willing to try to improve your listening.

   _____

   _____

   _____

2. Jot down the name of a person whom you consider to be a good listener. Consider your feelings toward this person. It is usually difficult not to like someone whom you consider to be a good listener. Attentive listening shows respect and caring and is one of the best gifts one person can give to another.

   _____

   _____

   _____

3. Write a list of daily situations in which attentive listening is required. Some situations could include talking to your child about his or her day at school, listening to your spouse's or roommate's views on politics, and meeting with a community group to plan a fundraising event. What listening strategies would increase your attention and responsiveness in the situations you've listed?

   _____

   _____

   _____

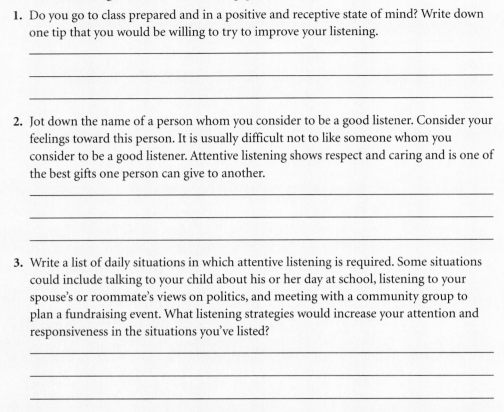

PEAK PROGRESS   **5.2**

Formal (Traditional) Versus Informal (Creative) Outlines

Your learning style, or whether you are a left-brain- or right-brain-dominant person, can affect what outline style works for you. Left-brain-dominant people tend to like a traditional outline that uses a logical, step-by-step, sequential pattern of thought and focuses on words and order. **Formal outlines** use Roman numerals and capital letters to outline headings, main topics, and points, and supporting points are highlighted with lowercase letters and numbers. This system requires consistency. For example, the rules require at least two headings on the same level; if you have a IA, you should also have IB. If you have a IIIA1, you must also have IIIA2.

Some students find that formal outlines are too time-consuming and restrictive for classroom lectures. However, they like using an outline because it organizes ideas and illustrates major points and supporting ideas. They prefer a free-form, or **informal, outline.** This system shows the same headings, main points, and supporting examples and associations, but it uses a system of dashes and indenting. Many students find an informal method to be easier for in-class note taking, since it allows them to focus on main ideas and supporting examples instead of worrying about rules.

Following are examples of formal (top) and informal (bottom) outlines.

Topic: Note taking   Jana Rosa
April 9, 2007

Effective Strategies for Taking Notes

    A. The traditional outline for note taking
        1. Advantages
           a. Occupies your attention totally
           b. Organizes ideas as well as records them
        2. Disadvantages
           a. Too structured for right-brain-dominant person
           b. Time-consuming

    B. The mapping system for note taking
        1. Advantages
           a. Presents a creative and visual model
           b. Can start anywhere on the page
        2. Disadvantages
           a. Too busy for a left-brain-dominant person
           b. Too unorganized for a left-brain-dominant person

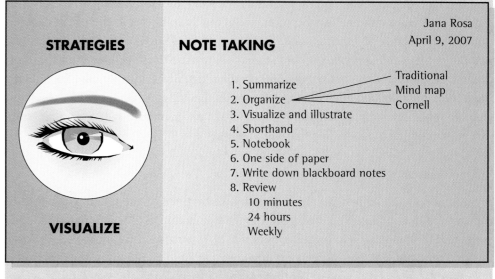

STRATEGIES

VISUALIZE

NOTE TAKING   Jana Rosa
April 9, 2007

    1. Summarize
    2. Organize   Traditional
    3. Visualize and illustrate   Mind map
    4. Shorthand   Cornell
    5. Notebook
    6. One side of paper
    7. Write down blackboard notes
    8. Review
        10 minutes
        24 hours
        Weekly

Samples of Formal and Informal Outlines A formal outline provides an orderly, sequential way to organize information. *What is one advantage of using a formal outline?* If you are right-brain dominant, you may prefer an outline that allows for illustrations, such as the informal outline. *What other items might you include on the left side of the informal outline?*

point of all note-taking systems is to distinguish between major and minor points and to add order and understanding to material. Let's start with one of the most widely used and effective note-taking systems—the Cornell System of Note Taking.

The Cornell System of Note taking

The Cornell System of Note Taking was developed by Walter Pauk at Cornell University. It has been used for more than 45 years and is effective for integrating text and lecture notes. Start with a sheet of standard loose-leaf paper and label it with the class, date, and title of the lecture. Divide your notepaper into three sections ("Notes", "Cues", and "Summary") by drawing a vertical line about 2 inches from the left-hand margin; then draw a horizontal line below that. (See **Figure 5.1** on page 163.)

◆ **Notes.** The right-hand side is the largest section. Record information from class lectures in whatever format works best for you. You can use a formal system with standard Roman numerals or an informal system of indentation to distinguish between major and minor points and meaningful facts.

◆ **Cues.** Then use the left side to jot down cues, main ideas, phrases, keywords, or clarifications. List any pertinent examples or sample test questions from the lecture or the book. Try to pose questions that are answered by your notes. When you review, cover up the right-hand side (the "Notes" section) and try to answer the questions you have written.

◆ **Summary.** On the bottom of the page, include a "Summary" section. This is a very effective way to write a summary in your own words of each class session. Fill in with details from the book and further clarify and elaborate after discussions with your study team or instructor.

The Cornell System is a great tool for reviewing and comparing notes for both lectures and books. Notes can be taken sequentially to preserve the order decided upon by the lecture. It is an effective method to review with your study team, since you can compare class notes, review summaries, and use the sample test questions on the left. One student can recite his notes on the right, while another uses the cues on the left for possible test questions and examples. Each can recite his or her class and chapter summaries. Many people who are left-brain dominant will often prefer the logical, sequential, step-by-step Cornell System.

Mind Maps

A **mind map** (or a "think link") is a visual, holistic form of note taking (see **Figure 5.2** on page 164 and **Figure 5.3** on page 165 for two examples of mind maps). The advantage is that you can see connections and the big picture. You can also see connections to the main idea. Mapping starts from the main idea, placed in the center of a page, and branches out with subtopics through associations and patterns. You may find that mapping helps you increase your comprehension, creativity, and recall. Many students find mind maps useful in brainstorming ideas for speeches or papers, in serving as a framework for recalling topics, or in helping them review, but some

Figure 5.1 The Cornell System

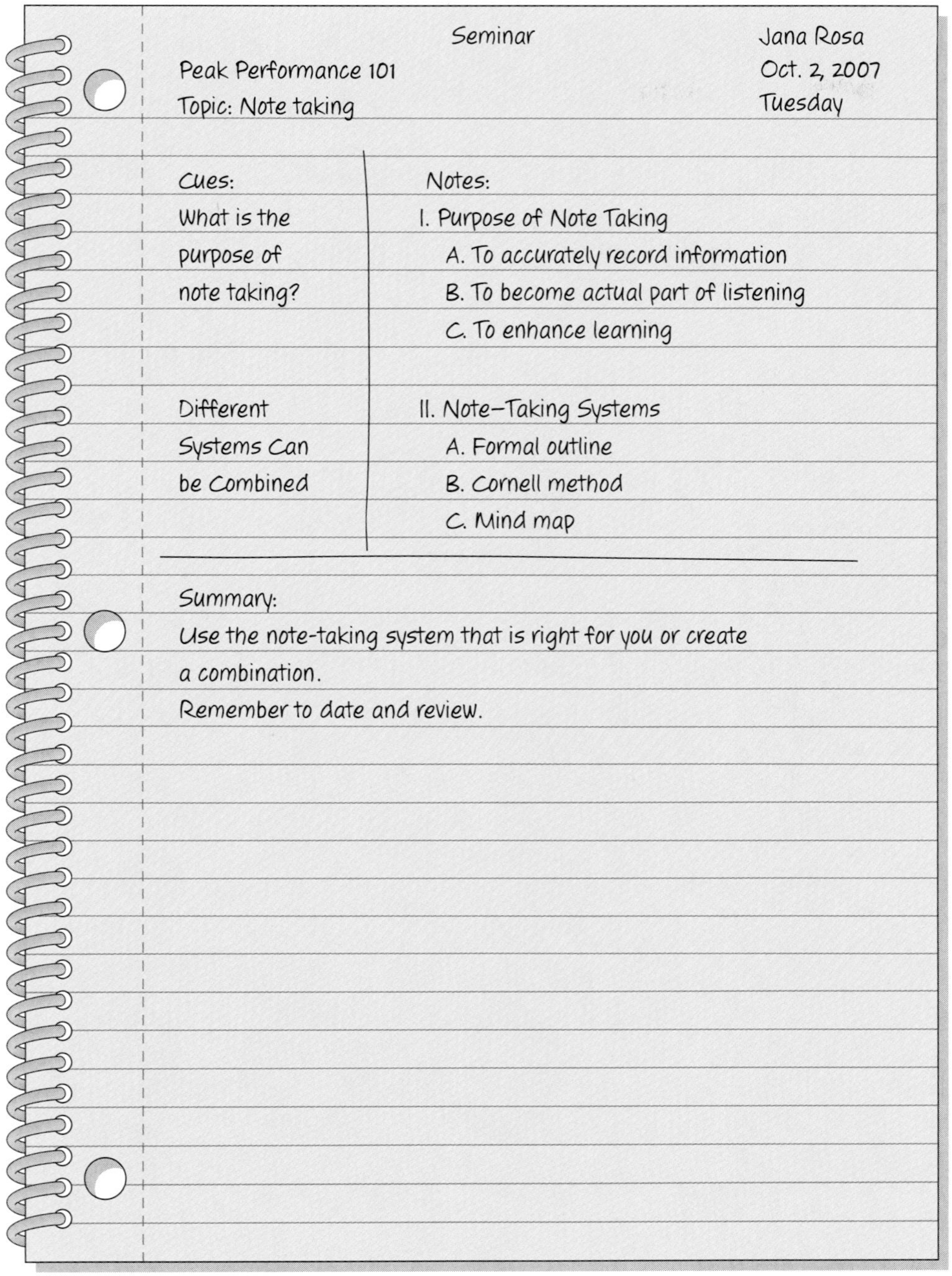

Seminar	Jana Rosa
Peak Performance 101	Oct. 2, 2007
Topic: Note taking	Tuesday

Cues:	Notes:
What is the	I. Purpose of Note Taking
purpose of	A. To accurately record information
note taking?	B. To become actual part of listening
	C. To enhance learning
Different	II. Note–Taking Systems
Systems Can	A. Formal outline
be Combined	B. Cornell method
	C. Mind map

Summary:
Use the note-taking system that is right for you or create
a combination.
Remember to date and review.

The Cornell System   This method integrates text and lecture notes and includes a summary section. *Which personality type might prefer the Cornell System?*

Figure 5.2 Sample Mind Map

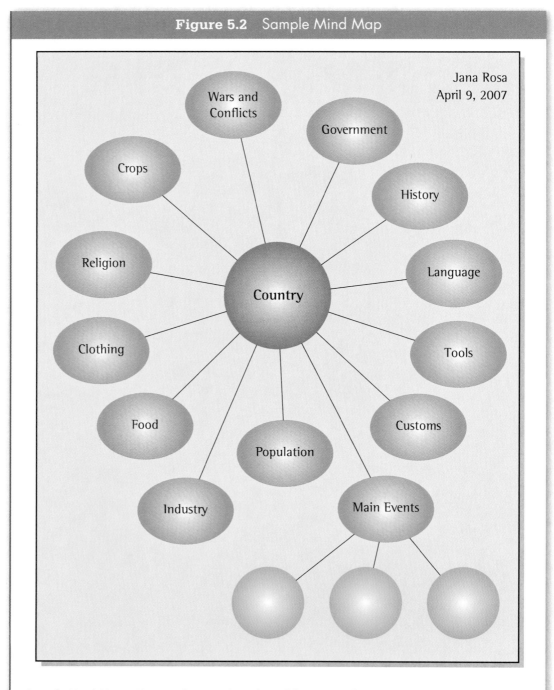

Jana Rosa
April 9, 2007

Wars and Conflicts

Government

Crops

History

Religion

Language

Country

Clothing

Tools

Food

Customs

Population

Industry

Main Events

Sample Mind Map   This template can be adapted for many subjects. *In which of your courses would this format be useful for note taking?*

find that they are not as useful as a note-taking system during class lectures, since there is not a linear or sequential order.

As we discussed earlier, right-brain-dominant learners like creative, visual patterns, and thus mind mapping may work for them. A left-brain-dominant student may be uncomfortable mapping because the outline is not sequential; it is difficult to

Figure 5.3 Another Sample Mind Map

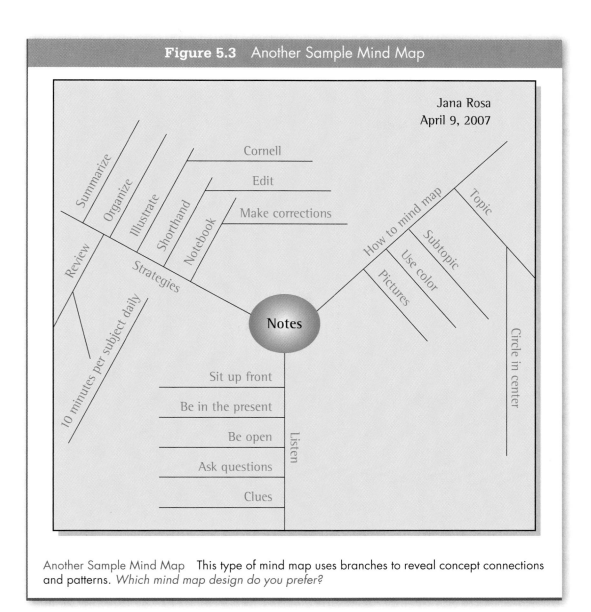

Jana Rosa
April 9, 2007

Cornell

Edit

Make corrections

Summarize

Organize

Illustrate

Shorthand

Notebook

Review

Strategies

How to mind map

Topic

Subtopic

Use color

Pictures

Circle in center

10 minutes per subject daily

Notes

Sit up front

Be in the present

Be open

Ask questions

Clues

Listen

Another Sample Mind Map   This type of mind map uses branches to reveal concept connections and patterns. *Which mind map design do you prefer?*

follow the instructor's train of thought; there is little space for corrections or additions; and the notes must be shortened to keywords and only one page. One option is to use a mind map to illustrate an entire chapter and use a traditional outline for daily notes.

In certain classes, you will study several different topics that have the same patterns. For example, you may study different cultures, and the categories or patterns are the same for each culture. See **Worksheet 5.2** at the end of this chapter for a blank mind map template that you can use or adapt for many situations.

Combination Note-Taking Systems

Since no two people take notes in the same way, you will want to experiment with several note-taking systems or a combination of systems. Effective note takers use a variety of strategies, depending on the material covered. These strategies include highlighting main ideas, organizing key points, comparing and contrasting relationships, and looking for patterns. Effective note takers listen, organize, record, and review. Find one that supports your learning and personality styles. **Figure 5.4** shows a combination note-taking system, using a formal outline, mind mapping, and the Cornell System.

Note-Taking Strategies

The following strategies will help you make the most of the note-taking system you use. Review the strategies for preparing yourself both mentally and physically for listening, which are listed at the beginning of the chapter.

1. **Preview the material.** Can you imagine going to an important class without doing your homework; being unprepared to participate; or lacking pen, paper, and necessary material? Go to classes prepared, even if you have only a few minutes to prepare the night before or right before class. Preview or skim textbook chapters for main ideas, general themes, and key concepts. Previewing is a simple strategy that enhances your note taking and learning. In a sense, you are priming your brain to process information efficiently and effectively. You will also want to review previous notes and connect what you have learned to new ideas.

2. **Go to every class and pay attention.** The most obvious and important part of being prepared is to attend all your classes. You cannot take effective notes if you are not there. Having someone else take notes for you is not the same as being in class. Of course, that you should assume this doesn't mean "If I just show up, I should get an *A*." It is important to pay attention and to be mentally aware and alert. Make a commitment that you will go to every class unless you are ill. Check bus schedules in case your car breaks down. Have several backup plans if you have children. Don't schedule other appointments when you have classes. In other words, be prepared and alert, and make a commitment to treat your education as a top priority.

3. **Be on time.** Walking in late for class indicates an attitude that class is not important and disrupts the instructor and other students. Set your watch five minutes ahead and arrive early enough to preview your notes and get settled. Punctuality also helps you prepare emotionally and mentally. You have to put forth an effort and invest in every class by showing up—on time—prepared, alert, and ready to participate.

4. **Sit up front.** You will be more physically alert, and you will see and hear better, if you sit in the front of the class. You will also be more likely to ask questions and engage the instructor in eye contact when you sit in front. You will be less likely to talk with other students, pass notes, doodle, or daydream when you sit in front.

5. **Use all your senses.** Many people view note taking not only as a passive activity but also as an auditory activity. Actually, you will find note taking more effective if you integrate learning styles and use all your senses. For example, if you

WORDS TO
SUCCEED

"Eighty-five percent
of success in life is
just showing up."

WOODY ALLEN, *Entertainer*

Figure 5.4 Combination Note-Taking System

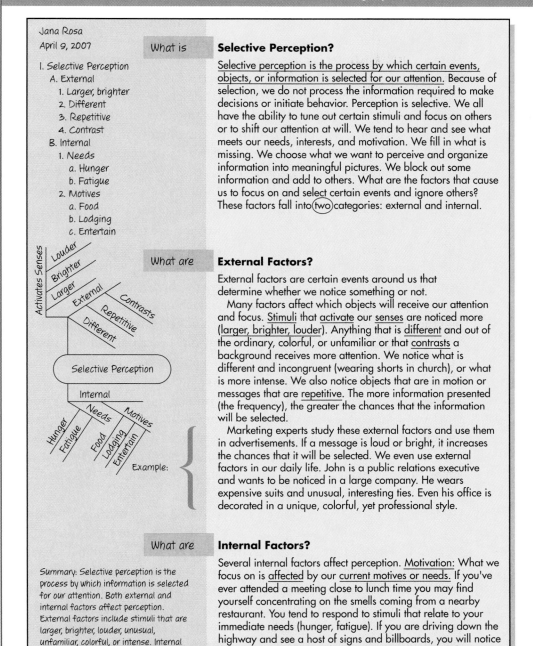

Jana Rosa
April 9, 2007

What is

I. Selective Perception
  A. External
    1. Larger, brighter
    2. Different
    3. Repetitive
    4. Contrast
  B. Internal
    1. Needs
      a. Hunger
      b. Fatigue
    2. Motives
      a. Food
      b. Lodging
      c. Entertain

Activates Senses

Louder
Brighter
Larger
External
Contrasts
Repetitive
Different

Selective Perception

Internal

Needs
Hunger
Fatigue
Food
Lodging
Entertain
Motives

Example:

What are

What are

Summary: Selective perception is the process by which information is selected for our attention. Both external and internal factors affect perception. External factors include stimuli that are larger, brighter, louder, unusual, unfamiliar, colorful, or intense. Internal factors include our motives and needs, such as hunger, anger, or attitude.

Selective Perception?

Selective perception is the process by which certain events, objects, or information is selected for our attention. Because of selection, we do not process the information required to make decisions or initiate behavior. Perception is selective. We all have the ability to tune out certain stimuli and focus on others or to shift our attention at will. We tend to hear and see what meets our needs, interests, and motivation. We fill in what is missing. We choose what we want to perceive and organize information into meaningful pictures. We block out some information and add to others. What are the factors that cause us to focus on and select certain events and ignore others? These factors fall into (two) categories: external and internal.

External Factors?

External factors are certain events around us that determine whether we notice something or not.

Many factors affect which objects will receive our attention and focus. Stimuli that activate our senses are noticed more (larger, brighter, louder). Anything that is different and out of the ordinary, colorful, or unfamiliar or that contrasts a background receives more attention. We notice what is different and incongruent (wearing shorts in church), or what is more intense. We also notice objects that are in motion or messages that are repetitive. The more information presented (the frequency), the greater the chances that the information will be selected.

Marketing experts study these external factors and use them in advertisements. If a message is loud or bright, it increases the chances that it will be selected. We even use external factors in our daily life. John is a public relations executive and wants to be noticed in a large company. He wears expensive suits and unusual, interesting ties. Even his office is decorated in a unique, colorful, yet professional style.

Internal Factors?

Several internal factors affect perception. Motivation: What we focus on is affected by our current motives or needs. If you've ever attended a meeting close to lunch time you may find yourself concentrating on the smells coming from a nearby restaurant. You tend to respond to stimuli that relate to your immediate needs (hunger, fatigue). If you are driving down the highway and see a host of signs and billboards, you will notice the ones that are directed to your current motivational state, such as those for food, lodging, or entertainment.

Combination Note-Taking System   You can use several different note-taking systems on the left, reflecting the main text on the right. *Which section on the left resembles a mind map? Which section looks like a formal outline? Which section reflects the Cornell System? Which note-making system do you prefer?*

are primarily a *kinesthetic learner,* you may want to make learning more physical by writing and rephrasing material, working with your study team or partner, collecting examples, creating stories and diagrams, using note cards, and standing when taking notes from your textbook. If you are primarily a *visual learner,* develop mental pictures and use your right-brain creativity. Draw and illustrate concepts. Practice visualizing images while the speaker is talking, form mental pictures of the topic, and associate the pictures with keywords. You might try using colored pencils, cartoons, or any other illustrations that make the material come alive. Supplement your lecture notes with drawings, and take special note of material on the board, overhead transparencies, and handouts. If you are primarily an *auditory learner,* listen attentively and capitalize on this style of processing information. You might want to tape lectures. Explain your notes to your study group, so that you can hear the material again.

6. **Make note taking active and physical.** For your mind to be alert, your body must also be alert. Physical activity gets your blood flowing throughout your body, including your brain, which is why physical activity enhances academic performance for all learning styles. Observe your body, how you hold your pen, and how your back feels against the chair. Slouching produces fatigue and signals the brain that this activity is not important. Sit straight. When you are at home, taking notes, and you feel your energy dip, take a walk, stretch, do deep knee bends or head rolls, or jog in place for a few minutes. Exercise also helps relax the body, focuses the mind, and reduces stress.

7. **Link information.** Connect ideas and link similar information. Look for patterns and information that is different. Compare and contrast; find similarities and differences. Develop associations between what you are hearing for the first time and what you already know. When you link new knowledge to what you already know, you create lasting impressions. Ask yourself how this information relates to other classes or to your job.

8. **Use creative shorthand and focus on keywords.** A common mistake students make is attempting to write down everything the instructor says. Notes are like blueprints, because they represent a larger subject and highlight main details. The essential element in taking effective notes is to jot down only main points and keywords. Illustrations, filler statements, stories, introductions, and transitions are important for depth, interest, and understanding, but you don't have to write down every word. Devise your own system for note taking that includes abbreviations and symbols. See **Figure 5.5** for examples.

9. **Organize your notes.** Use large, bold headlines for the main ideas and large print for keywords, important points, facts, places, and other supporting data. Write your name, the topic, and the date on each sheet of paper. You may want to purchase a binder for each class to organize notes, syllabi, handouts, tests, and summaries. Leave wide margins and plenty of space to make corrections, add notes, clarify, and summarize. Don't crowd your words, or the notes will be difficult to understand. Keep all handouts you receive in class. Use a question mark if you do not understand something, so that you can ask about it later.

Figure 5.5 Note-Taking Shortcuts

Symbol	Meaning	Abbreviation	Meaning
>	greater than; increase	i.e.	that is
<	less than; decrease	etc.	and so forth
?	question	lb.	pound
w/	with	assoc.	association
w/o	without	info	information
V or *	important ideas	eg.	example
+	positive; and	p.	page
—	negative	pp.	multiple pages
X	times		
~	gaps in information		
→	leads to (e.g., motivation → success)		
^	bridge of concepts; insert		
#	number		

Note-Taking Shortcuts This chart lists some common symbols and abbreviations you can incorporate into your own note-taking system. *What is the essential element in taking effective notes?*

10. **Use note cards.** Use index cards to jot down keywords, formulas, definitions, and other important information. Note cards and flash cards help you integrate all learning styles. Write down keywords and main points, use them throughout the day, and review for tests.

Assess and Review Your Notes

After you've taken your notes, reinforce your memory and understanding of the material by assessing and reviewing your notes and by using these strategies:

1. **Summarize in your own words.** When you finish taking text and lecture notes, summarize in your own words. You might want to write summaries on index cards. Summarizing can be done quickly and can cover only main concepts. This one small action will greatly increase your comprehension and learning. It is even more effective when you read your summary out loud to others; teaching is a good way to learn.

2. **Review, edit, and revise your notes.** Your review schedule should include time for adding information, clarifying, thinking critically, and summarizing.

- ◆ **Review as soon as possible**. Experts say that, unless students review soon after a lecture, much of the new information will be lost within the first half-hour after the class. Set aside a few minutes as soon as possible after the lecture to edit, revise, fill in, or copy your notes. Compare your notes with the material in the textbook. Ask yourself what questions might be on a test. Underline what the instructor has indicated is important. Fill in blanks with new material. Clean up, expand, and rewrite sections that are messy or incomplete. If you are unclear on a point, leave a space and put a question mark in the margin. You can ask for verification from other students in class or your instructor.

- ◆ **Review within 24 hours.** Research indicates that your memory is at its most receptive within 24 hours after hearing new information. You might try going to your next class early and spending 5 minutes reviewing your class notes from the previous class. Or you can review while the instructor passes out handouts, adjusts the overhead projector, or organizes the lecture.

- ◆ **Review often.** Create a regular review schedule. Reviewing right before you go to sleep is effective, since your mind is receptive to new information at that time. Make certain you review your notes with those of your study group. Keep test questions in mind as you review. Reviewing often increases your memory and helps you perform better on exams.

3. **Monitor and evaluate.** Periodically assess your note-taking system. Try different systems and strategies until you find the one that works best. Feedback from study-group members, your instructor, and tests will help you assess how well your system is working.

Overcome Obstacles

The first step in overcoming the barriers to effective note taking is to recognize its importance. Some students view note taking as a passive academic skill that they will never use once they graduate from college. As a result, their notes are often disorganized, incomplete, illegible, and of little help in preparing for tests.

Effective note taking changes the information that you hear into information that is distinctly yours. You have discarded the unessential, highlighted the essential, and organized information to give it meaning and focus. This process is an important job skill. Follow these simple steps until discipline and focus become a habit:

1. **Find meaning and interest** in the subject. Understand why taking better notes will help you in the long run. Determine specific situations in school, at work, or at home in which taking good notes will be essential.

2. **Observe** your intention and willingness to listen and learn. Observe what is on the board, in handouts, and in overhead transparencies. Sit in the front to avoid distractions and to help you focus and observe the instructor. Observe how effective students take notes.

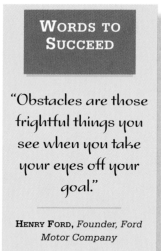

WORDS TO SUCCEED

"Obstacles are those frightful things you see when you take your eyes off your goal."

HENRY FORD, *Founder, Ford Motor Company*

3. **Listen** for understanding and for the main points and keywords. Take notes during class discussions and lectures. If you are unsure of the main points, ask your instructor.

4. **Organize** the important information. Choose a system that helps you organize and record main points and keywords. If a formal outline doesn't work for your learning style, try another method of note taking.

5. **Think** about the information and gather more if necessary. Reflect on what you know and what you don't know.

6. **Record** the date and topic, and leave room in the margins for revising.

7. **Review, revise, and practice** your notes as soon as possible. Review notes with your study team, so that you can fill in information that you missed and summarize main points. Teaching what you've learned to someone else will also help you remember and understand the material better.

8. **Evaluate** your system of taking notes. Experiment with several methods. Ask your instructor and other students for feedback.

9. **Teach** others your system. Demonstrate what works for you.

10. **Reward** yourself when you make progress. Congratulate yourself for learning and enhancing your skills.

Taking Notes on the Job
Note taking is an essential skill in many professions. *What are some jobs or professions in which taking notes is a critical, daily task?*

In summary, in this chapter, I learned to:

- *Listen attentively to the message.* Developing an interest in listening and making it meaningful to me are the first steps in becoming an attentive listener. I must want to listen and am open to new information, new ideas, and different beliefs. My intent is to understand others and to focus on the message.

- *Go to every class.* I know that it is very important to make a commitment to go to every class and form a relationship with my instructor and other students. I'm on time and sit up in front, where I'm alert and aware. I sit up straight, maintain eye contact, and act as if I'm listening and involved with the speaker. I reduce distractions and focus on listening, not talking. I'm in the present and concentrate on the subject.

- *Observe my instructor and watch for verbal and nonverbal clues.* I watch for examples, words, and phrases that signal important information or transitions. I take note of handouts and transparencies. I use critical thinking to postpone judgment. I focus on the message, not the presentation. I look beyond clothes, voice, teaching style, and reputation and focus on what the other person is saying. Using critical thinking helps me look for supporting information and facts and ask questions.

- *Prepare prior to class.* I preview chapters before class, so I have a general idea of the chapter, and make notes of questions to ask or concepts that I want the instructor to give examples of or elaborate on. I do homework and use index cards to jot down and memorize keywords, formulas, and definitions.

- *Focus on keywords.* I don't try to write down all information but, rather, look for keywords and essential information. I look for patterns, link information, and connect ideas in a way that makes sense and organizes the information. I leave space for corrections and additions and use marks, such as "?" for questions.

- *Integrate learning styles.* I not only use my preferred learning style but also integrate all styles. I make note taking active and physical. I draw pictures and make illustrations, use outlines, supplement my notes with handouts, take field trips, create models, and summarize out loud.

- *Get organized.* I know that information that is not organized is not remembered. I write the date and topic on each sheet and organize notes in a folder or binder.

- *Determine a note-taking style that works best for me.* A formal outline uses my left-brain, sequential side, while an informal outline helps me see connections and the big picture. The Cornell System of Note Taking is organized into three sections: "Notes", "Cues", and "Summary". A mind map is more visual and includes main points that are connected to supporting points or examples. I can also combine elements of various note-taking systems to determine what works best for me.

- *Summarize in my own words when I am finished taking notes in class or from the text.* This one action greatly improves my comprehension and learning. I compare this summary to the material in my book, review it with my study team, and fill in essential information. I make notes on questions to ask my instructor or study group.

- *Review, monitor, and evaluate.* I review my notes for main ideas as soon as possible after class, but within 24 hours. This increases my memory and helps me make sense out of my notes. I edit and add to my notes. I evaluate my note-taking skills and look for ways to improve.

Danielle Sievert

PSYCHOLOGIST

Related Majors: Psychology, Counseling

Listening in the Workplace

Danielle Sievert provides mental health care as an industrial-organizational psychologist for a Fortune 500 company. When most people think of psychologists, they think of clinicians in counseling centers or hospitals, but many large companies hire psychologists to tend to the needs of staff on all levels. Most industrial-organizational psychologists hold master's degrees in psychology. Psychology is the study of human behavior and the mind and its applications to mental health. Danielle and other industrial-organizational psychologists use psychology to improve quality of life and productivity in the workplace.

Danielle conducts applicant screenings to select employees who will work well within the company. She provides input on marketing research. She also helps solve human relations problems that occur in various departments. Danielle occasionally conducts individual sessions with employees who face problems within or outside of the office. Danielle works a nine-to-five schedule and is occasionally asked to work overtime. She is often interrupted to solve pressing problems.

Active listening is an important part of Danielle's job. Managers and other employees will ask for her help, she says, only when they sense that she is empathetic and desires to be of help. To hone her listening skills, Danielle asks questions to make sure she understands exactly what the person is saying. She also takes notes, either during or after a session. By using such skills, Danielle is able to fulfill her role as a psychologist in the workplace.

CRITICAL THINKING What kinds of problems might occur at the workplace that could be addressed by a firm's psychologist?

Peak Performer Profile

Anna Sui

"What should I wear?" This is a question that many people ask almost daily. For international fashion designer Anna Sui (pronounced *Swee*), the answer is simple: "Dress to have fun and feel great." Her showroom above noisy 8th Avenue in New York City illustrates her attitude with a Victorian-inspired mix of purple walls, ornate clothing racks, glass lamps, and red floors.

To the second of three children and only daughter born to Chinese immigrants, the Detroit suburbs of the early 1960s were a long way from the fashion mecca of New York City. However, even then Sui seemed to be visualizing success. Whether designing tissue-paper dresses for her neighbor's toy soldiers or making her own clothes with coordinating fabric for shoes, Sui had flair.

After graduating from high school, Sui headed for the Big Apple. She eventually opened her own business after two years of studying at the Parson's School of Design and years of working in the trenches at various sportswear companies. When Sui premiered her first runway show in 1991, the *New York Times* applauded the event as "producing a pastiche of hip and haute style." Sui's imaginative mix of styles was a hit.

To create such acclaimed designs, Sui takes note of the world around her. She continues to collect her "genius files"—clippings from pages of fashion magazines—to serve as inspiration. She listens to her clients, to music, to the street, and to her own instincts. Sui is quick to say that, although her moderately priced clothes are popular with celebrities, they are also worn by her mother. It's not about age and money, she explains, but about the "spirit of the clothing." By listening actively and staying attuned to the world around her, Sui continues to influence trends and enchant with her designs.

PERFORMANCE THINKING For the career of your choice, how would attentive listening and note taking contribute to your success?

CHECK IT OUT Look through Anna Sui's "genius files" at **www.annasuibeauty.com** (use the words "genius files" in the search box to get a complete list). Those who are profiled come from a variety of creative professions, including photographers, illustrators, filmmakers, theater and movie actors, musicians, and, of course, fashion designers and trendsetters. Consider starting your own "genius file" of people and words that inspire you.

Performance Strategies..........

Following are the top 10 strategies for attentive listening and effective note taking:

◆ Postpone judgment and be open to new ideas.

◆ Seek to understand and show respect to the speaker.

◆ Reduce distractions and be alert and focused.

◆ Maintain eye contact and look interested and alert.

◆ Observe the speaker and listen for clues, examples, signal words, and phrases.

◆ Predict and ask questions to clarify main points.

◆ Look for information that is familiar to what you already know and information that is different.

◆ Use a note-taking system that suits your learning style.

◆ Summarize in your own words and review often.

◆ Edit and revise while information is still fresh.

Tech for Success....................

Take advantage of the text's web site at **www.mhhe.com/ferrett6e** for additional study aids, useful forms, and convenient and applicable resources.

◆ **Your Instructor's Visual Presentation.** Many instructors lecture in conjunction with a PowerPoint presentation. Ask your instructor if the lecture outline is available as a handout, on a course web site, or in a bookstore. Take a copy of the printout to class with you and add notes and detail as the instructor talks. This is a handy tool for note taking that helps you follow the discussion, organize your notes, and read the text.

◆ **Summarize on Your Computer.** Some people type faster than they can write by hand. It's very important to summarize your notes as soon as possible after class to make sure you understand the main points. If that sounds like a daunting task, take a few minutes on your computer to summarize your notes. If necessary, write incomplete sentences first and then take a few minutes to flesh out the sentences. If you aren't sure if you really understood the main points of the lecture, consider e-mailing your recap to your instructor and ask him or her to review it. (This may also help your instructor determine if points presented in the lecture need clarification during the next class session.)

Review Questions ....

Based on what you have learned in this chapter, write your answers to the following questions:

1. What is attentive listening?

2. Why are listening and note-taking skills critical to job success?

3. Name two types of note-taking systems and describe how to use them.

4. Why is "Go to every class" an important note-taking strategy?

5. What should you do with your notes after attending class?

DEVELOPING ATTENTIVE LISTENING SKILLS

In the Classroom

Roxanne Jackson is a fashion design student who works part-time at a retail clothing store. She has two roommates, who are also students. Roxanne is a very social person. She is outgoing, enjoys being around people, and loves to talk and tell stories. However, Roxanne is a poor listener. In class, she is often too busy talking with the person next to her to pay attention to the class assignments. She always starts off as a popular study-group member, but it soon becomes clear that her assignments are always late and incorrect. Roxanne's roommates have finally confronted her. There is tension between them, because the roommates feel that Roxanne is not pulling her weight on household chores. Another major problem is that Roxanne does not seem to take accurate phone messages. She never seems to write down the correct information.

1. What strategies in this chapter can help Roxanne be a more effective listener?

   _____

   _____

2. What would you suggest she do to improve her relationship with others and to help her become better at taking down information?

   _____

   _____

In the Workplace

Roxanne is now a buyer for a large department store. She enjoys working with people. She is very talented and a responsible employee when she is actively aware and tuned in to others. People respond to her favorably and enjoy being around her. The problem with Roxanne is that she is often too busy or preoccupied to listen attentively or take correct notes. She often forgets directions, misunderstands conversations, and interrupts others in her haste and enthusiasm.

3. What would you suggest to help Roxanne become a better listener?

   _____

   _____

4. What strategies in this chapter would help her become more aware, more sensitive to others, and able to record information more effectively?

   _____

   _____

REVIEW AND APPLICATIONS

CHAPTER 5

APPLYING THE ABCDE METHOD OF SELF-MANAGEMENT

In the Journal Entry on page 155, you were asked to describe a time when you had a difficulty in making sense out of a lecture and staying alert. Are there certain classes in which it is more challenging for you to be an attentive listener?

_____

_____

_____

Now apply the ABCDE method to the situation and visualize yourself a more attentive listener:

A = Actual event:

B = Beliefs:

C = Consequences:

D = Dispute:

E = Energized:

Practice deep breathing, with your eyes closed, for just one minute. See yourself calm, centered, and alert. See yourself enjoying your lectures, staying alert, and taking good notes.

Practice Self-Management

For more examples of learning how to manage difficult situations, see the "Self-Management Workbook" section of the Online Learning Center web site at **www.mhhe.com/ferrett6e.**

MIND MAP YOUR TEXT

Make a mind map of a section or chapter of one of your textbooks using the format provided below (and edit/change as necessary). Use **Figure 5.2** on page 164 as a guide.

For example, let's say you will map out a section from Chapter 3 of this text: "Manage Your Time." In the middle circle, you might put "Time Management Strategies." In one of the surrounding circles, you might enter "Study everywhere and anywhere." In offshoot circles from that, you might put "Carry note cards," "Listen to taped lectures," and "Avoid peak times in the library." Compare your mind maps with those drawn by other students in your class.

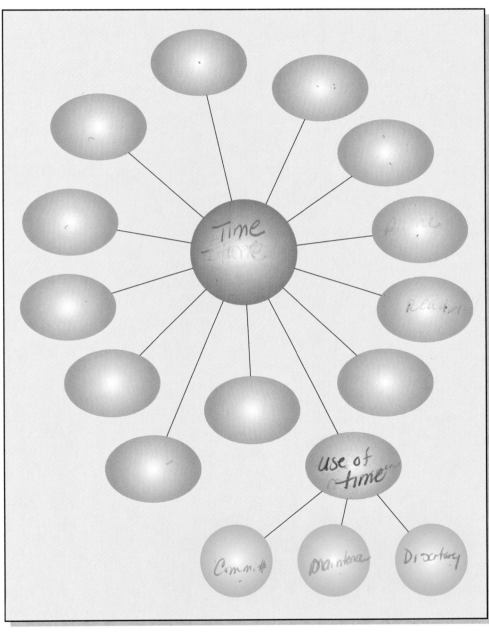

REVIEW AND APPLICATIONS

CHAPTER 5

MIND MAP A LECTURE

Create a mind map of one of your class lectures in the space provided below (see **Figure 5.2** on page 164 and **Figure 5.3** on page 165 for examples). Compare your mind maps with those drawn by other students in your class. Are there key points that you or other students have missed? Did some include too much (or too little) detail?

USE THE CORNELL SYSTEM OF NOTE TAKING

Take notes in one of your class lectures by using the Cornell System in the space provided below (see **Figure 5.1** on page 163 as a guide). Compare your notes with those from other students in your class. Are there key points that you or other students have missed? Did some include too much (or too little) detail? Did you summarize your notes?

Cues:	Notes:
what are good listening skills	1. Prepare to listen
Active List Strategy	2. Stay attentive New ideas
	3. Paraphrased
	4. Practice Awareness
Defining each.	II.
	1. Be willing to listen
	2. Eye contact
	3. Stay focus.
	4. Be open to New ideas

Summary:

Record all that you've heard in own words
Review, Edit, Revise your notes.
Review in 24° (within).
monitor and evaluate

CHAPTER 5 ▲ REVIEW AND APPLICATIONS

NAME: _____   DATE: _____

REVIEWING THE MAIN IDEAS

Review your notes and fill in this guide to create a list of the important ideas presented in a class lecture.

Class _____ Instructor _____ Date _____

Lecture topic _____

Chapters covered _____

Overall theme _____

Main ideas _____

Supporting ideas _____

Examples _____

Vocabulary terms _____

Keywords _____

Important concepts and theories _____

Applications _____

How this information is similar to known information _____

How this information is different from known information _____

CHAPTER 5 ▶ REVIEW AND APPLICATIONS

LISTENING AND NOTE TAKING IN THE WORKPLACE

Write how you will demonstrate the listed listening and note-taking skills for future employers.

1. Finding meaning and interest in new information and projects

_____

2. Showing interest and being prepared

_____

3. Listening attentively

_____

4. Observing and asking questions

_____

5. Acquiring information

_____

6. Thinking through issues

_____

7. Organizing information and taking good notes

_____

8. Staying alert and in the present

_____

9. Being willing to test new strategies and learn new methods

_____

10. Practicing attentive listening and note taking again and again

_____

11. Teaching effective methods to others

_____

REVIEW AND APPLICATIONS

CHAPTER 5

LISTENING SELF-ASSESSMENT

This simple assessment tool will give you an idea of your attentive listening skills. Read each statement. Then check Yes or No as to whether these statements relate to you.

	Yes	No
1. My intention is to be an attentive and effective listener.	✓	
2. I concentrate on meaning, not on every word.	✓	
3. I focus on the speaker and use eye contact.	✓	
4. I am aware of emotions and nonverbal behavior.	✓	
5. I withhold judgment until I hear the entire message.		✓
6. I am open to new information and ideas.	✓	
7. I seek to understand the speaker's point of view.	✓	
8. I do not interrupt, argue, or plan my response; I listen.	✓	
9. I am mentally and physically alert and attentive.	✓	
10. I paraphrase to clarify my understanding.	✓	
11. When I'm in class, I sit in the front, so that I can hear and see better.	✓	
12. I mentally ask questions and summarize main ideas.	✓	
13. I increase the value of my listening by previewing the textbook before class.		✓
14. I adapt to the instructor's speaking and teaching style.	✓	

Total Yes Responses: (12)

Count your Yes responses. If you marked Yes to 10 or more questions, you are well on your way to becoming an attentive and effective listener. If you did not, you have some work to do to improve those skills. Review this chapter. Add this page to your Career Development Portfolio.

Actively Read

CHAPTER OBJECTIVES

In this chapter, you will learn to

▲ Appreciate the benefits of active reading

▲ Determine a preferred reading system, such as the Five-Part Reading System and SQ3R

▲ Incorporate active reading strategies

▲ Build a better vocabulary

▲ Manage language courses

▲ Read technical material and complete forms

SELF-MANAGEMENT

"I usually love to read, but lately I feel like I'm on information overload. Sometimes I read several pages and realize that I haven't understood a word I've read. What can I do to read more effectively and actually remember what I've read?"

Do you ever close a book and feel frustrated because you don't remember what you've just read? In this chapter, you will learn how to become an active reader and how to maximize your reading. You will visualize yourself reading quickly, comprehending, and recalling information. You will see yourself discovering new information, building on facts and concepts, developing skills to retain and recall, and feeling the joy of reading.

JOURNAL ENTRY   Were you read to as a child? If so, use **Worksheet 6.1** on page 210 to describe a time when you enjoyed being read to by someone, such as a teacher, parent, or librarian. Why was the experience pleasurable? What types of books did you enjoy most? Did you have a favorite book or story? If you don't like to read, why? Are there specific obstacles that keep you from devoting more time to reading?

Some students express dismay at the mountain of reading they have to complete each week. You have probably discovered that it is not just the volume of reading that is required of you in college; you are also expected to comprehend, interpret, and evaluate what you read. **Comprehension** is the ability to understand the main ideas and details as they are written. **Interpreting** what you read means developing ideas of your own and being able to summarize the material in your own words. Interpretation requires several skills, such as noting the difference between fact and opinion, recognizing cause and effect, and drawing inferences and conclusions. If you are not an effective reader, you will face a major handicap both in college and on the job.

Let's approach reading as a climber approaches a towering mountain. Experienced climbers are alert and aware of the terrain and weather. They are certain of their purpose, goals, and objectives and are confident of their skills. They know the importance of concentration, and they maintain a relaxed, calm, and centered focus but never allow themselves to get too comfortable or inattentive. The same sense of adventure and purpose, concentration, and attentiveness are necessary if you are going to make reading more enjoyable and effective.

Because the amount of reading required in school can be enormous and demanding, it is easy to get discouraged and put it off until it piles up. In this chapter, you will learn to create a reading system that helps you keep up with your reading assignments and increase your comprehension.

The Importance Of Active Reading

When you were a child at home, you may have been told, "This is quiet time; go read a book," or "Curl up with a book and just relax." In school, your instructor may have said, "Read Chapters 1 through 5 for tomorrow's test," or "You didn't do well on the test because you didn't read the directions carefully." On the job, someone may have said to you, "I need your reactions to this report. Have them ready to discuss by this afternoon."

Whether you are reading material for enjoyment, for a test, or for a research project on the job, to be an effective reader you must become actively involved with what you are reading. If you approach reading with a lack of interest or importance, you read only what's required. Your ability to retain what you have read will be negatively influenced. **Retention** is the process by which you store information. If you think something is important, you will retain it.

Reading involves many important tasks, such as the following:

◆ Previewing
◆ Taking notes
◆ Outlining main points
◆ Digging out ideas
◆ Jotting down keywords
◆ Finding definitions

WORDS TO SUCCEED

"To read a writer is for me not merely to get an idea of what he says, but to go off with him, and travel in his company."

ANDREW GIDE, *Author*

- Asking and answering questions
- Underlining important points
- Looking for patterns and themes
- Summarizing in your own words
- Reviewing for recall

All of these tasks can greatly improve your comprehension and your ability to interpret material. This is active reading because you, the reader, are purposeful, attentive, and physically active.

Reading Systems

Many factors affect your reading comprehension. Your skill level, vocabulary, ability to concentrate, and state of mind, as well as distractions, all affect your comprehension and ability to recall what you have read. There are a number of proven reading systems and, over the years, you may have developed a reading system that works best for you. Two reading systems that we will explore in this chapter are the Five-Part Reading System and SQ3R.

The Five-Part Reading System

The Five-Part Reading System (see **Figure 6.1**) is similar to the Adult Learning Cycle, which is explored throughout this text (see **Peak Progress 6.1**) on page 189. The five

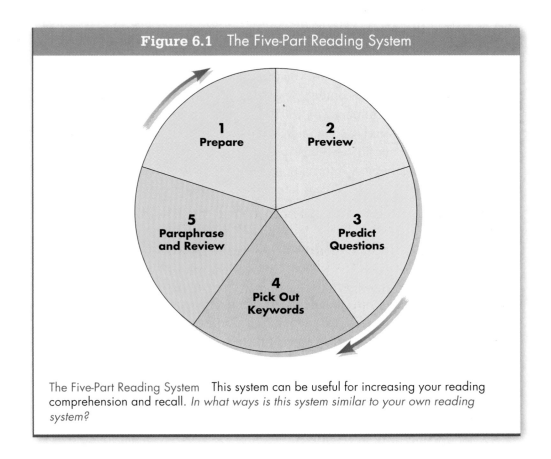

Figure 6.1 The Five-Part Reading System

1 Prepare
2 Preview
3 Predict Questions
4 Pick Out Keywords
5 Paraphrase and Review

The Five-Part Reading System   This system can be useful for increasing your reading comprehension and recall. *In what ways is this system similar to your own reading system?*

Preview Your Reading
You get the big picture by quickly scanning through a book, and you enhance your learning. *Besides identifying key concepts, what else should you look for when previewing?*

parts can be remembered easily as the five *Ps* and, as with many reading systems or strategies (and, in fact, many tasks that you will do in college), your first step is to prepare. That is then followed by preview, predict questions, pick out keywords, and paraphrase and review.

1. **Prepare.** Prepare yourself mentally for reading by creating a positive, interested attitude. Look for ways to make the subject matter meaningful. Instead of telling yourself that the book is too hard or too boring, say, "This book looks interesting," or, "The information in this book will be helpful." Focus your attention on what you are about to read. Clarify your purpose and how you will use the information. Think about what you already know about the subject before you begin reading. Prepare yourself physically by being rested and read during high-energy times. Eliminate distractions by choosing a study area that encourages concentration. Experiment and make reading physical whenever possible. For example, take notes while reading, read while standing up, and read aloud.

2. **Preview.** A quick survey of the chapter you are about to read will give you a general overview. Pay attention to the title, chapter headings, illustrations, and keywords and boldface words. Look for main ideas, connections between concepts, terms, and formulas, and try to gain a general understanding of the content. By gaining a general understanding of the assignment, you will be better prepared to read the material actively and to understand the classroom lecture. When your brain has been exposed to a subject before, it is far more receptive to taking in more information, so jot down in the margins everything you can think of that you already know about the topic, even if it is just a word or an image. Short preview sessions are effective, and you will be more motivated when there is a set goal and time for completion.

3. **Predict questions.** Next, make questions out of chapter headings, section titles, and definitions. For example, if a section is titled "Groupthink," ask the questions "What is groupthink? What conditions are required for it to occur? What is a keyword or keywords that define it? What are possible test questions?" Ask what, who, when, where, why, and how. The more questions you ask, the better prepared you will be to find answers. If there are sample questions at the end of the chapter, review them and tie them in with your other questions. Pretend you are talking with the author and jot down questions in the margin. Asking questions gets you interested and involved, keeps you focused, organizes infor-

Applying the Adult Learning Cycle to Becoming a Better Reader

Becoming an active reader and learning to like reading take time, effort, and practice.

1. **RELATE. Why do I want to learn this?** Being an effective reader can help me get ahead in school, work, and life. Through reading, I continually learn new things and explore new ideas. I can also escape through fiction, thus relieving the stress of the day. What do I want to improve overall about my reading?

2. **OBSERVE. How does this work?** I can learn a lot about active reading by watching, listening, and trying new things. I'll observe people who are avid readers and who remember information. Do I know someone who isn't a good or committed reader? I will try new techniques and strategies for active reading and mark my improvement.

3. **REFLECT. What does this mean?** Which techniques work and which ones don't work for me? Can I find creative ways to make reading more enjoyable and effective?

4. **DO. What can I do with this?** I will make a commitment to be a more active reader. I'll find practical applications for practicing my new reading skills. Each day, I'll work on one area. For example, I'll choose one class in which I'm having trouble reading and experiment with new strategies.

5. **TEACH. Whom can I share this with?** I'll talk with others and share my tips and experiences. I'll demonstrate and relay the methods I've learned to others. I'll read more for pleasure and read to others when possible.

Remember, the more you go through the cycle, the more interests and meaning reading will have for you.

mation, and helps you prepare for tests. Create possible test questions on note cards and review them as you walk to classes, eat, or wait in lines. Exchange questions with your study team or partner.

4. **Pick out keywords.** Outline, underline, and highlight keywords, main ideas, definitions, facts, and important concepts. Look for main ideas, supporting points, connections, and answers to the questions you have raised. This is the time to develop an outline, either a traditional outline or an informal one (such as a mind map), to help you organize the information. Integrate what you are reading into classroom lectures, notes, field trips, study-group discussions, models, and graphs.

5. **Paraphrase and review.** Rewrite in your own words, summarize, and review. Write a short summary and then recite it out loud or share it in your study group. Practice reciting this summary right after class and again within 24 hours of previewing the chapter. Review several times until you understand the material and can explain it to someone else. This helps you integrate

learning styles and remember the main points at the end of each major section. Review in your study teams and take turns listening to each other's summary. Remember that the best way to learn is to teach. Carry your note cards, so that you can review questions and answers and can summarize often.

The SQ3R Reading System

The SQ3R Reading System is a five-step method that has helped many students improve their reading comprehension since it was first developed by Professor Francis Robinson in 1941. It breaks reading down into manageable segments, so that you understand the material before proceeding to the next step, helping you become a more effective reader.

1. **S = Survey.** Survey the material before reading it. Quickly peruse the contents, scan the main heads, look at illustrations and captions, and become familiar with the special features in each chapter. Surveying, or previewing, helps you see how the chapter is organized and supports the main concept. You get an overview of where you're going in the material.

2. **Q = Question.** Find the main points and ask questions. Developing questions helps you determine if you really understand the material. For example, here are some questions you may ask yourself as you are reading:
   ◆ What is the main idea of this chapter?
   ◆ What is the main idea of this section?
   ◆ What are examples that support this main idea?
   ◆ Who are the main people or what key events are discussed in this chapter?
   ◆ Why are they important?
   ◆ What are possible test questions?
   ◆ What points don't I understand?

3. **R = Read.** Actively read the material and search for answers to your questions. As you read, you will be asking more questions. Even when you read a novel, you will be asking such questions as "What is the main theme of this novel? Who is this supporting character? Why did he turn up at this time in the novel? How does this character relate to the main characters? What are his motives?"

4. **R = Recite.** Recite the main ideas and key points in your words. After each section, stop and paraphrase what you just read. Recite the answers to your questions in your own words. Reciting promotes concentration and creates understanding. It also helps raise more questions.

5. **R = Review.** Review the material carefully. Go back over your questions and make certain you have answered them. Review the chapter summary and then go back over each section. Jot down additional questions. Review and clarify questions with your study group or instructor.

The exercise in **Personal Evaluation Notebook 6.1** gives you an opportunity to try out the SQ3R Reading System.

Using the SQ3R Reading System

Look at the following table for a review of the SQ3R Reading System. Then do the activity that follows.

Letter	Meaning	Reading Activity
S	Survey	Survey the assigned reading material. Pay attention to the title, boldface terms, the introduction, and the summary.
Q	Question	Find the major heads. Try to make questions out of these heads.
3R	1. Read	Read the material section by section or part by part.
	2. Recite	After reading a section or part, try to summarize aloud what you have read. Make sure your summary answers the question you formed for the section's or part's head.
	3. Review	After reading the entire assigned reading material, review your question heads. Make sure you can recall your original questions and answers. If you cannot, then go back and reread that section or part.

Use the SQ3R Reading System for the following reading selection; then complete the questions that follow.

Job Searching

Point of Departure

Before you begin to look for a job, it is important to decide what you want to do, what you like to do, and what skills and abilities you have to offer.

Self-knowledge is an understanding of your skills, strengths, capabilities, feelings, character, and motivations. It means you have done some serious reflection about what is important to you and what values you want to live your life by. It is very hard to make a career decision unless you really know yourself.

Know Yourself

The more you know about yourself—your skills, values, and attitudes and the type of work you like best—the easier it will be to market your skills. Your entire job search will be faster and smoother if you

- Identify your most marketable skills.
- Assess your strengths.
- Review your interests.
- Identify creative ways you solve problems.

(continued)

Using the SQ3R Reading System—continued

S—Survey

1. What is the title of the selection?

   _____

2. What is the reading selection about?

   _____

3. What are the major topics?

   _____

4. List any boldface terms.

   _____

Q—Question

5. Write a question for the first heading.

   _____

6. Write a question for the second heading.

   _____

3 Rs

R—Read

Read the selection section by section.

R—Recite

Briefly summarize to yourself what you read. Then share your summary with a study-team member.

R—Review

7. Can you recall the questions you had for each head?   Yes _____   No _____

8. Can you answer those questions?   Yes _____   No _____

Write your answers for each section head question on the following lines.

9. Head 1

   _____

10. Head 2

   _____

Reading Strategies

The Five-Part and SQ3R reading systems include a number of strategies, such as previewing the material and reciting or paraphrasing main concepts in your own words. Some additional overall strategies include

1. **Determine your purpose.** Clarify your purpose and how you will use the information. Your reading assignments vary in terms of difficulty and purpose. Some are technical and others require imagination. (See **Peak Progress 6.2** for tips on reading in different disciplines.) Ask yourself, "Why am I reading this?" Whether you are reading for pleasure, previewing information, enhancing classroom lectures, looking for background information, understanding ideas, finding facts, memorizing formulas and data, or analyzing and comprehending a difficult or complex subject, you will want to clarify your purpose.

2. **Set reading goals.** As mentioned, you may be assigned many chapters to read each week, preferably before walking into lecture. You do not want to wait until the day before exams to open your textbook. You want to pace your

---

PEAK PROGRESS   6.2

Reading for Different Courses

Sometimes even very successful students cringe at the thought of reading in disciplines that they are not interested in or find difficult. If you find your textbook too difficult, you might ask your instructor for supplemental reading or check out other books or sources from the library to get a different view and approach. The following are tips for different reading assignments.

Literature

Make a list of key figures and characters. Think about their personalities and motives, and see if you can predict what they will do next. Allow your imagination to expand through your senses; taste, smell, hear, and see each scene in your mind. What is the main point of the story? What are supporting points? What is the author's intent?

History

Use an outline to organize material. You may want to create a time line and place dates and events as you read. Take note of how events are related. Connect main people to key events. Relate past events to current events.

Mathematics and Science

When you are reading a math book, work out each problem on paper and take notes in the margin. You will want to spend additional time reviewing graphs, tables, notations, formulas, and the visuals that are used to illustrate points and complex ideas. These are not just fillers; they are important tools for you to review and understand the concepts behind them. Ask questions when you review each visual and use note cards to write down formulas and concepts. Come up with concrete examples when you are reading about abstract and difficult concepts. (We will further explore critical thinking and problem solving in math and science in Chapter 10.)

---

reading, not only to make sure you complete it but also to give yourself time to ask questions, make sure you understand the material, and can review it—again and again if necessary. Just as you map out the semester's exams, plan out your reading assignments in your daily planner or calendar (see Chapter 3 for many handy forms). Be realistic as to how long it takes you to read a certain number of pages, especially for courses that you find more difficult. Check off reading assignments as you complete them, and rearrange priorities if need be. Schedule blocks of time for reviewing reading assignments and preparing for exams.

3. **Concentrate.** Whether you are playing a sport, performing a dance, giving a speech, acting in a play, talking with a friend, or focusing on a difficult book, being in the present is the key to concentration. Keep your reading goals in mind and concentrate on understanding main points as you prepare to read. Stay focused and alert by reading quickly and making it an active experience. If your mind does wander, become aware of your posture, your thoughts, and your surroundings, and then gently bring your thoughts back to the task at hand. Do this consistently.

4. **Outline the main points.** Organizing information in an outline creates order and understanding. Use a traditional or informal outline to outline the main points and organize the information. (See Chapter 5 for examples of outlines.) The purpose of a brief outline is to add meaning and structure to material, as well as to simplify and organize complex information. The physical process of writing and organizing material creates a foundation for committing it to memory. Use section titles and paragraph headlines to provide a guide. Continue to write questions in the margin.

5. **Identify keywords and key concepts.** Underline and highlight keywords, definitions, facts, and important concepts. Write them in the margins and on note cards. Draw illustrations (or embellish those in the book) to help clarify the text. Use graphics and symbols to indicate difficult material, connections, and questions that you need go over again. (Refer to **Figure 5.5** on page 169 for common symbols used in note taking and reading.) You may find a highlighter useful for calling out main points and marking sections that are important to review later. Don't underline until you have previewed information. Underline just the key points and words, and think about the ideas expressed.

6. **Make connections.** Link new information with what you already know. Look for main ideas, supporting points, connections, and answers to the questions you have raised. Integrate what you are reading into classroom lectures, notes, field trips, study-group discussions, models, and graphs. Asking yourself these questions may help you make associations and jog your memory:

   ◆ What conclusions can I make as I read the material?
   ◆ How can I apply this new material to other material, concepts, and examples?
   ◆ What information does and does not match?
   ◆ What has been my experiences with reading similar subjects or with reading in general?
   ◆ What do I know about the topic that may influence how I approach the reading?

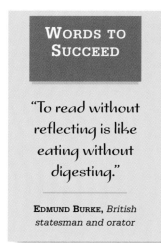

WORDS TO SUCCEED

"To read without reflecting is like eating without digesting."

EDMUND BURKE, *British statesman and orator*

7. **Talk with the author.** Pretend you are talking with the author and jot down points with which you agree or disagree. This exercises your critical thinking skills and helps you connect new information to what you already know or have learned. If there are points you disagree with, consider bringing them up with your instructor in class (if it's appropriate) and see if other students feel the same.

8. **Compare notes.** Compare your textbook notes with your lecture notes. Compare your notes with those of your study-team members and clarify questions and answers. Ask your instructor for clarifications and how much weight the textbook has on exams. Some instructors highlight important information in class and want students to read the text for a broad overview.

9. **Take frequent breaks.** Schedule short stretching breaks about every 40 minutes. A person's brain retains information best in short study segments. Don't struggle with unclear material now. Several readings may be required to comprehend and interpret the material. Go back to the difficult areas later when you are refreshed and when the creative process is not blocked.

10. **Integrate learning styles.** Read in alignment with your learning style and integrate styles. For example, if you are a *visual learner*, take special note of pictures, charts, and diagrams. Visualize and develop mental pictures in your mind and actively use your imagination. Compare what you are reading with course lectures, overhead material, and notes on the board. If you are primarily an *auditory learner*, read out loud or into a tape recorder and then listen to the tapes. If you are a *kinesthetic learner*, read with a highlighter in hand to mark important passages and keywords. Work out problems on paper and draw illustrations. Write your vocabulary, formulas, and keywords on note cards. Read while standing up or recite out loud. The physical act of mouthing words and hearing your voice enhances learning. Integrate different learning styles by using all your senses. Visualize what something looks like, hear yourself repeating words, draw, and read out loud. Review your notes and summaries with your study team. This helps you integrate learning styles and increases comprehension, critical thinking, and recall.

11. **Use the entire text.** As discussed in Chapter 4, a peak performer seeks out and uses available resources. Many textbooks include a number of resources that sometimes get overlooked such as a glossary, chapter objectives, and study questions. Make sure you read (or at least initially scan) all the elements in your textbook as they are included to help you preview, understand, review, and apply the material. (See **Peak Progress 6.3** on page 196). After all, you've paid for the text, so use it!

Reviewing Strategies

Reading isn't over with the turn of the last page. It's important to take the time to review what you have read to make sure you understand and retain the information.

1. **Summarize in writing.** After you finish reading, close your book and write a summary in your own words. Write down everything you can recall about the chapter and the main topics. In just four or five minutes, brainstorm main ideas and key points and summarize the material in your own words. Writing is an

Using Your Textbook

Textbooks are developed with a number of features to help you preview, understand, review, and apply the material. As soon as you purchase your text, take a few minutes to flip through the book to see how the text is put together. Although all textbooks are designed differently, many books include the following elements:

- **Preface.** At the beginning of the text, you will probably find a preface, and many books include two prefaces: one for the instructor who is interested in using the text in the course and the other specifically for the student. Definitely read through the student preface, as it will outline the major features of the text, explain why the information is important, describe the additional resources available with the text (such as a web site with study tools, activities, and forms), and additional information to help you get off on the right foot. For example, at the beginning of this text, you will find a preface geared for the student that not only walks you through all the features and resources but also explores many issues that you may be facing the first few weeks of school (or even prior to the first day of school).

  Even if there is a student preface, it's a good idea to review the preface designed for the instructor. This preface will give you insights into the overall approach of the text, and new developments or research in the field. It may also describe challenges that your instructor faces when teaching the course, which can be helpful for you and your fellow students to know.

- **Preview features.** Many texts include features that let you know what you will learn in the chapter, such as chapter objectives, chapter outlines, and introductory statements or quotes. *What types of preview features can you find in this text?*

- **Applications.** More effective texts not only provide the essential information but also give you opportunities to apply the information. This can be in the form of case studies, exercises, assessments, journal activities, Web sites, and critical thinking and discussion questions. *What are some of the features in this text that help you apply what you are learning?*

- **Review material.** You may find a number of features that reinforce and help you understand and review the material, such as section or chapter summaries; glossaries; key tips, key points, or keywords; bulleted lists of key information; comprehensive tables; and review questions. *What are some of the features in this text that are useful for reviewing the material?*

- **Resources beyond the text.** Many texts have accompanying Web sites, workbooks, and CD-ROMs that reinforce and apply what you are learning in the text and course. Often, connections to these resources appear in the text, reminding you to use the resource for specific information. *What resources are available with this text?*

active process that increases comprehension and recall. Write quickly and test yourself by asking questions such as these:

- ◆ What is the major theme?
- ◆ What are the main points?
- ◆ What are the connections to other concepts?

2. **Summarize out loud.** Summarizing out loud can increase learning, especially if you are an auditory or a kinesthetic reader. Some students use an empty classroom and pretend they are lecturing. If need be, recite out loud quietly to yourself, so that you don't disturb anyone, especially in the library or other populated areas. Review several times until you understand the material and can explain it to someone else. Review in your study teams and take turns listening to each other's summary. Remember that the best way to learn is to teach. You are each getting an opportunity to recite and listen to each other. You can ask questions and clarify terms and concepts.

3. **Review and reflect.** You have previewed, developed questions, outlined main points, read actively, highlighted and underlined, written keywords, and summarized in writing and aloud. Now it is important to review for understanding main ideas and to commit the information to long-term memory. You can increase your comprehension by reviewing the material within 24 hours of your first reading session. Reflect by bringing your own experience and knowledge to what you have learned with reading, lectures, field trips, and work with your study team. You will want to review your outline, note cards, keywords, and main points. Review headings, main topics, key ideas, first and last sentences in paragraphs, and summaries. Make sure that you have answered the questions that you created as you read the material. Carry your note cards with you and review them when you have a few minutes before class. Your note cards are the most effective tool for reviewing information.

4. **Read and review often.** Reviewing often and in short sessions kicks the material into long-term memory. Review weekly and conduct a thorough review a week or so before a test. Keep a list of questions to ask your instructor and a list of possible test questions. The key is to stay on top of reading, so that it doesn't pile up, which should allow you the time you will need to review effectively.

Build Your Vocabulary

You will need a fundamental vocabulary to master any subject. Developing a good vocabulary is important for reading comprehension and success in college. To succeed in a career, you must know and understand the meaning of words that you encounter in conversations, reports, meetings, and professional reading. People often judge the intelligence of another person by the ability to communicate through words. Words are the tools of thinking and communicating. Try the following methods for building your vocabulary:

- ◆ **Realize the power and value of words.** An effective speaker who has a command of language can influence others.
- ◆ **Observe your words and habits.** You may be unaware that you fill your conversations with annoying words, such as *you know, OK, like,* and *yeah.*
- ◆ **Be creative and articulate.** Use precise, interesting, and expressive words.
- ◆ **Associate with articulate people.** Surround yourself with people who have effective and extensive vocabularies.
- ◆ **Be aware and alert.** Listen for new words. Observe how they are used and how often you hear them and see them in print.

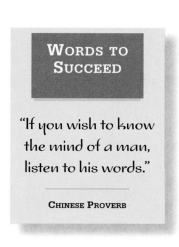

WORDS TO SUCCEED

"If you wish to know the mind of a man, listen to his words."

CHINESE PROVERB

- **Look up words you don't know.** Keep a dictionary at your desk or study area. (See **Peak Progress 6.4**, which shows you how to navigate around a dictionary.)
- **Study words.** How can you use them in conversation?
- **Write down new words.** Write new words in your journal or on note cards.
- **Practice mentally.** Say new words again and again in your mind as you read and think of appropriate settings where you could use the words.
- **Practice in conversation.** Use new words until you are comfortable using them.
- **Look for contextual clues.** Try to figure out a word by the context in which it is used.
- **Learn common word parts.** Knowing root words, prefixes, and suffixes makes it easier to understand the meaning of many new words. Also, learn to recognize syllables. When you divide words into syllables, you learn them faster, and doing so helps with pronunciation, spelling, and memory recall.

Root	Meaning	Example
auto	self	autograph, autobiography
sub	under	submarine, submerge
circum	around	circumference, circumspect
manu	hand	manuscript, manual, manufacture

- **Review great speeches.** Look at how Abraham Lincoln, Benjamin Franklin, Winston Churchill, and Thomas Jefferson chose precise words. Read letters written during the Revolutionary and Civil wars. You may find that the common person at that time was more articulate and expressive than many people today.
- **Invest in a vocabulary book.** There are a number available on the market, so you may want to ask your instructor for guidance. Also, if you have decided on your future career, you may want to see if any books are written for that field.
- **Read.** The best way to improve your vocabulary is simply to read more.

Manage Language Courses

Building vocabulary is important if you are taking an English as a second language course or learning a foreign language. Following are a number of reading and study tips for studying languages.

1. **Do practice exercises.** As with math and science, doing practice exercises is critical in learning any language.
2. **Keep up with your reading.** You must build on previous lessons and skills. Therefore, it is important to keep up with your reading; preview chapters, so that you have a basic understanding of any new words; then complete your practice sessions several times.
3. **Carry note cards with you.** Drill yourself on the parts of speech and verb conjugation through all the tenses and practice vocabulary building.
4. **Recite out loud.** Recite new words to yourself out loud. This is especially important in a language course. Tape yourself and play it back.
5. **Form study teams.** Meet with a study team and speak only the language you are studying. Recite out loud to each other, explain verb conjugation, and use words in various contexts. Recitation is an excellent strategy when studying languages.

Look It Up! Using the Dictionary

Here is a quick guide for using the dictionary.

Guide words: Boldface words at the top of the page indicate the first and last entries on the page.

Syllabication: This shows how the word is divided into syllables.

Pronunciation: The key at the bottom of right-hand page shows pronunciation.

Capital letters: The dictionary indicates if a word should be capitalized.

Part of speech: The dictionary uses nine abbreviations for the parts of speech:

n.—noun	adv.—adverb	v.t.—transitive verb
adj.—adjective	conj.—conjunction	pron.—pronoun
v.i.—intransitive verb	prep.—preposition	interj.—interjection

Etymology: This is the origin of the word, which is especially helpful if the word has a Latin or Greek root from which many other words are derived. Knowing the word's history can help you remember the word or look for similar words.

Restrictive labels: Three types of labels are used most often in a dictionary. Subject labels tell you that a word has a special meaning when used in certain fields (mus. for music; med. Medicine, etc.). Usage labels indicate how a word is used (slang, dial. for dialect, etc.). Geographic labels tell you the region of the country where the word is used most often.

Homographs: The dictionary indicates when a single spelling of a word has different meanings.

Variants: These are multiple correct spellings of a single word (*ax* or *axe*).

Illustrations: These are drawings or pictures used to help illustrate a word.

Definition: Dictionaries list the definition chronologically (oldest meaning first).

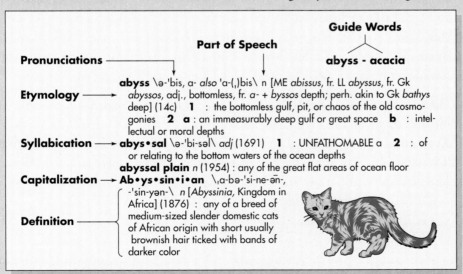

WORDS TO SUCCEED

"I was reading the dictionary. I thought it was a poem about everything."

STEVEN WRIGHT, *Comedian*

Source: By permission. From *Merriam-Websters's Collegiate® Dictionary*, 11th edition. © 2005 by Merriam-Webster, Incorporated.

Excelling in Language Courses
When learning a new language, you will find that each chapter builds on the previous chapter's lessons. Thus, it's important to keep up with your reading assignments in order to understand fully the material presented in lecture. *As this woman learns to speak Russian, what are some specific strategies she can apply?*

6. **Listen to CDs and tapes.** Play practice CDs while commuting, jogging, exercising, and so on.

7. **Visualize.** During an exam, visualize yourself listening to a CD, seeing the diagrams you have drawn and hearing yourself reciting the material.

8. **Model and tutor.** Meet with a student whose primary language is the one you are studying. Speak only his or her native language. Offer to teach the person your language in exchange for private tutoring. You can meet foreign students in classes where English as a second language is taught, usually in local schools and communities.

9. **Focus on keywords.** Study the meanings, tenses, and pronunciation of keywords. You can also keep these exercises on note cards. Carry them with you to review.

10. **Have fun.** Do research on the country of the language you're studying. Make the language come alive for you. Invite your study group over for an authentic meal, complete with music and costumes. Invite foreign students and your instructor.

The same principles and strategies you use for reading English can be applied to reading and learning a foreign language. Your efforts will be worthwhile, especially when you are able to speak, read, and understand another language as you communicate in the real world. Remember, as you become a better reader, you will enjoy the new language more and more.

Technical Reading

Some of the subjects you are taking now or will take as your course of study progresses will include technical information. Science, math, computer science, accounting, and statistics courses tend to present their data in specialized formats. You may find yourself interpreting graphs, charts, diagrams, or tables and spreadsheets. You may be reading technical material, such as the directions for a chemistry experiment, a flow chart in a computer program, the steps for administering medication, or the statistical analysis of a financial statement.

Such material can be complicated and difficult. This is why many readers—student readers, in particular—tend to skip over it or become discouraged. However, there are some reading strategies you can implement when you encounter graphics in your studies or on the job:

◆ Do not skip over any graphics.
◆ Read the
    1. Graphic title
    2. Accompanying captions
    3. Column titles
    4. Labels or symbols and their interpretations
    5. Data (percentages, totals, figures, etc.)
◆ Identify the type of graphic you are looking at. Are you looking at a table, chart, or graph?
◆ Identify the purpose of the graphic. Is it demonstrating to the reader similarities or differences, increases or decreases, comparisons or changes?
◆ See a connection between the topic of the graphic and the chapter or section topic in which it appears.
◆ Explain in your own words the information depicted on the graphic.
◆ Share your interpretation of the graphic with your study-group members. Do they feel your interpretation is clear and on target?

Reading Forms

Whether you are entering school, applying for a job, filling out medical papers, or requesting a bank loan, you will probably have to fill out some type of form. Although forms differ in many ways, there are many elements of information that are requested on all of them. You can expect to provide your name, address, Social Security number, and phone numbers.

Reading the form carefully and accurately can save time and prevent complications (see **Figure 6.2** on page 202)—for example,

◆ The directions may ask you to print your name in black or blue ink. Make sure you do not use a pencil or write your name in cursive handwriting.
◆ A job application may ask that you answer all questions in your own handwriting. Make sure you do not type the application.

In both cases, the forms would most likely be returned to you if you did not read the directions carefully, which could result in negative consequences. For example, if you typed the job application, and it is returned to you for failing to follow the directions, you may miss the deadline for submitting it and lose the job opportunity. Carelessness in reading forms can be avoided by using the following reading tips:

◆ Scan the entire form before you begin to fill it out.
◆ If you are unsure of any questions and what information is actually needed, ask or call the appropriate office or person for clarification.

Figure 6.2 Filling Out Forms

APPLICATION FOR EMPLOYMENT
SUPERIOR MARKETS

DIRECTIONS: Please use a pen and print.
Answer all sections completely and accurately.

NAME			SOCIAL SECURITY NUMBER
LAST	FIRST	MIDDLE	
Cortez	Mark	A.	032-32-3712

HOME ADDRESS				
NUMBER	STREET	CITY	STATE	ZIP
134	North Avenue	Indianapolis	IN	46268

TELEPHONE	ALTERNATE #
(317) 555-2492	

Filling Out Forms   You can apply good reading skills when filling out forms and applications. *What could happen if you were to use cursive handwriting and a pencil to fill out this form?*

Finding Time to Read
Investing time in reading pays off. Your reading skills improve when you read more. *How can you make time to read for pleasure?*

- When filling out the form, read the small print directions carefully. Often, these directions appear in parentheses below a fill-in blank.
- Fill in all questions that pertain to you. Pay attention when you read the directions that tell you what sections of the form or application you should fill out and what sections are to be completed by someone else.
- Make sure you write clearly—particularly numbers.
- When reporting somewhere to fill out forms, take with you any pertinent information that may be needed. Call ahead and ask what you are expected to have with you (for example, Social Security card; proof of citizenship; and dates of employment or schooling; names, addresses, and phone numbers of references, former employees, or teachers).
- Reread your responses before submitting your form or application.

Overcome Obstacles

One of the greatest barriers to effective reading is attitude. Many people are not willing to invest the time it takes to become a better reader. If the material is difficult, seems boring, or requires concentration, they may not complete the reading assignment. Many students have been raised in an era of videos and computer games. There is so much instant entertainment available that it is easy to watch a movie or television program or listen to the news instead of reading a newspaper or news magazine. Reading takes time, effort, concentration, and practice.

To create a positive attitude about reading, first pinpoint and dispel illogical thoughts, such as "I have way too much reading; I can never finish it all"; "I'm just not good at math"; or "I never will understand this material!" Many students have trouble reading certain subjects and may lack confidence in their abilities. It takes time and patience to learn to ski, ride a bike, drive a car, become proficient with computers, or become a more effective reader. Use affirmations to develop confidence: "With patience and practice, I will understand this material." Use the ABCDE Method of Self-Management to dispel negative thinking and create a "can do" attitude.

Some students and career professionals say that they have too much required reading and too little time for pleasure reading. Returning students have a difficult

WORDS TO SUCCEED

"My Alma mater was books, a good library... I could spend the rest of my life reading, just satisfying my curiosity."

MALCOLM X, *Civil Rights Leader*

PEAK PROGRESS 6.5

Reading with Children Around

It's true that concentrating on your reading can be challenging with children at your feet. However, it's essential that you find ways to fit reading into your daily routine (as well as theirs)—for example,

1. **Read in short segments**. Provide activities for your children and set a timer. Tell them that, when it goes off, you'll take a break from reading and will do something with them, such as have a snack or do a pleasurable activity. Then set the timer again. In 10 or 15 minutes, you can preview a chapter, outline main ideas, recite out loud, or review. Don't fall into the trap of thinking that you need 2 uninterrupted hours to tackle a chapter, or you may never get started.

2. **Read while they sleep.** Get up early and read, or consider reading at night when your kids are sleeping. Even if you're tired, read actively or outline a chapter before you turn in. Resist doing the dishes or cleaning and save those activities for when reading and concentrating would be very difficult. Do a little reading each night and notice how it pays off.

3. **Read before class.** Often, students waste time while waiting for the instructor. Use that time to preview and outline.

4. **Take reading with you**. If your children are in after-school activities, such as sports, music, or dance, take your reading with you and make the most of your waiting time. This is also a nice time to visit with other parents, but you may need to devote that time to keeping up with your reading.

5. **Exchange child care**. Find other parents and offer to watch each other's kids. Maybe you can take them to the park and read while they are playing.

6. **Read to your children**. Get your kids hooked on reading by reading to them and having them watch you read out loud. Have family reading time, when everyone reads a book. After you read your children a story, ask them to read by themselves or look at pictures while you read your assignments. Remember to approach reading with a positive attitude, so that they will connect reading with pleasure.

time juggling reading, lectures, homework, job, and kids. They can't even imagine having time to read for pleasure. However, it is important to read for pleasure, even if you have only a few minutes a day. (See **Peak Progress 6.5** for ways to fit in reading with children around.) Carry a book with you or keep one in your car. Although you shouldn't study in bed, many people like to read for pleasure each night before turning in and they find it relaxing.

The more you read, the more your reading skills will improve. As you become a better reader, you will find you enjoy reading more and more. You will also find that, as your attitude improves, so will your ability to keep up on assignments, build your vocabulary, understand and retain what you have read, and learn more about areas that interest you.

Taking Charge

In summary, in this chapter, I learned to:

- *Be an active reader.* I stay focused and alert by reading quickly and making it an active experience. I concentrate on main points and general understanding. I read difficult material out loud or standing up. I write in the margins, draw illustrations, underline, sketch, take notes, and dig out key points and keywords. I pretend that I'm giving a lecture on the chapter and that I'm taking with the author and jotting down questions.

- *Apply the Five-Part Reading System.* Very similar to the Adult Learning Cycle, this system is useful for increasing my comprehension and recall. The steps include (1) prepare, (2) preview, (3) predict questions, (4) pick out keyword, and (5) paraphase and review.

- *Apply the SQ3R Reading System.* A five-step process, this method can improve my reading comprehension: S = Survey; Q = Question; R = Read; R = Recite; R = Review.

- *Preview the material and predict questions.* Scanning chapters gives me a quick overview of main concepts and ideas. I look for information that I already know and link it to information that is new. I look for keywords, main ideas, definitions, facts, and important concepts. I make questions out of chapter headings and definitions. I go back over the chapter to find answers and jot them down in the margin or on note cards and compare my answers with those of my study team.

- *Outline main points and make connections.* Organizing information in an outline creates order, meaning, and understanding and makes it easier to recall the material. It helps simplify difficult information and make connections. I link new information with what I already know and look for connections to what I don't know. I look for similarities and differences. I look for examples and read end of chapter summaries.

- *Integrate learning styles.* I draw pictures, charts, and diagrams and use different-color pens to highlight. I read difficult material out loud and read summaries to my study group. I tape sections I want to memorize and play them back. I visualize keywords and main ideas. I integrate learning styles and make reading active.

- *Summarize.* Summarizing in writing and out loud is a powerful reading and memory strategy. I close the book at various times to write summaries, and then check my brief summaries with the book. I summarize in writing after I finish a quick read of the chapter and then fill in with details. I summarize out loud to myself and my study group.

- *Review.* I increase my comprehensions by reviewing my outline, note cards, keywords, main points, and summaries, I review within 24 hours of reading and after lectures. Teaching what I know and presenting my summaries to my study team is a great way to prepare for tests and to make recall easier.

- *Practice.* The more I read, the better reader I become. Reading becomes a pleasurable activity, and my vocabulary and knowledge base increases.

- *Build a strong vocabulary.* A good vocabulary is critical to my success in school and my career. I can improve my vocabulary by learning and incorporating new words into my writing and conversations, using resources such as a dictionary or vocabulary book, and observing my speech habits.

- *Manage language courses.* Many of the same vocabulary-building strategies work for second language courses, such as focusing on keywords, reciting out loud, carrying note cards, listening to tapes, keeping up with the reading assignments, and using practice exercises. I also take advantage of study teams, find a model or tutor, explore fun and creative ways to learn more about the language and culture, and visualize myself understanting the material.

- *Tackle technical reading and forms.* Thorough and precise-reading is critical when reading technical information, graphs, and forms. Tips for technical information include identifying the purpose of the material or graph, looking for connections, and explaining in my own words. Tips for forms include scanning before I begin, reading the small print, knowing what pertains to me, and asking questions when I'm unsure.

Brian Singer

INFORMATION TECHNOLOGY SPECIALIST

Related Majors: Computer Science, Mathematics, Information Systems

Keeping Up-to-Date

Brian Singer is an information technology specialist, or computer programmer. His job is to write instructions that computers follow to perform their functions. His programs instruct computers what to do, from updating financial records to simulating air flight as training for pilots.

When writing a program, Brian must first break the task into various instructional steps that a computer can follow. Then each step must be coded into a programming language, such as COBOL. When finished, Brian tests the program to confirm it works accurately. Usually, he needs to make some adjustments, called debugging, before the program runs smoothly. The program must be maintained over time and updated as the need arises. Because critical problems can be intricate and time-consuming and must be fixed quickly, Brian usually finds himself working long hours, including evenings and weekends. Although his office surroundings are comfortable, Brian must be careful to avoid physical problems, such as eyestrain or back discomfort.

To stay current in his field, Brian reads about 500 pages of technical materials each week. Brian also took a class on reading technical information to improve his reading skills. Because he concentrates best when he is around people, Brian likes to read and study in a coffeehouse. When he has difficulty understanding what he reads, he gets on the Internet and asks for help from an on-line discussion group. To help him remember and better understand what he has read during the week, Brian tries to implement the new information in his work.

CRITICAL THINKING What strategies might help an information technology specialist when reading technical information?

Peak Performer Profile

Oprah Winfrey

Accomplished actress, film producer, and magazine publisher, Oprah Winfrey is best known as the popular host and producer of an Emmy-award-winning talk show that aims to inspire.

Winfrey's career began when she entered Tennessee State University and soon began working in radio and television broadcasting in Nashville, Tennessee. Later, she moved to Baltimore, Maryland, where she hosted a TV talk show, which became a hit. After eight years, a Chicago TV station recruited Winfrey to host a morning show. The success of that show led her to launch the celebrated *Oprah Winfrey Show.*

A straightforward and winning approach has characterized Winfrey throughout her career. At 17, she was a contestant in a Nashville pageant for "Miss Fire Prevention." She was asked what she would do if she had a million dollars. Her response was "I would be a spending fool." She won the pageant. Over three decades later, she still displays the same bravado that propelled her from rural Mississippi to *Time* magazine's list of the 100 most influential people of the twentieth century.

However, Winfrey's success doesn't rest simply on accolades but, rather, on her connection with her audience. She shares the ups and downs of her own life and the ways in which she has overcome adversity. As an abused child and runaway teenager, Winfrey found refuge with her father, a man who expected the best from her and encouraged one of her lifelong passions—reading. Her love of books inspired her to establish a book club, which opened up the world of reading to millions of people in her audience. Winfrey credits books with saving her life and making her the person she is today. She says her goal is to help make the same kind of difference in other people's lives.

PERFORMANCE THINKING Choose a favorite book you have read and explain why you like it. Do you set time aside for reading for pleasure? Have you considered joining a book club and meeting people with similar interests? How can you inspire others to become avid readers?

CHECK IT OUT According to Oprah Winfrey, "Books gave me the idea there was a life beyond my poor Mississippi home." At **www.oprah.com**, you will find not only books recommended by Oprah's Book Club but also Oprah's personal favorites and reasons they had an impact on her. (Click on "Inside Oprah.com," scroll down, and click on "Oprah's Books.") Also included are recommended books for children of all ages. Think about books you have read, either in school or on your own, that affected you and in what ways. Consider creating your own list of personal favorites. (Note that you must register on the web site if you want to become an active member in Oprah's Book Club. Many features and book recommendations, however, are not password protected.)

Review and Applications

Performance Strategies ············

Following are the top 10 strategies for active reading:

◆ Find interest in the material.

◆ Outline the main points and identify keywords.

◆ Gather information and predict questions.

◆ Stay focused by reading quickly.

◆ Take breaks and make reading physical.

◆ Reduce distractions and stay alert.

◆ Make connections and link information.

◆ Create a relationship with the author.

◆ Summarize in writing in your own words.

◆ Teach by summarizing out loud and explaining the material to others.

Tech for Success ····················

Take advantage of the text's web site at **www.mhhe.com/ferrett6e** for additional study aids, useful forms, and convenient and applicable resources.

◆ **Books on-line.** Many of your textbooks can be purchased on-line and downloaded to your computer. Most of these books are formatted to be read on-line, rather than printed out. Does this sound appealing, or would you rather read from a printed copy of the text? List some of the advantages and disadvantages of both options.

◆ **All the news that's fit to click.** What's your source for the latest news? Most major newspapers are available on-line and archive previous articles. Take a poll of your classmates to see who still opts for newsprint, who prefers the local and cable networks, and who relies on the Web. Discuss the pros and cons. Do your classmates' preferences match their learning styles? Which sources do the more avid readers prefer?

Review Questions ·······································

Based on what you have learned in this chapter, write your answers to the following questions:

1. Name and describe each part of the Five-Part Reading System.

2. How does outlining the main points help you improve your reading?

3. Name three strategies for managing language courses.

4. Explain how building your vocabulary can be important to your career success.

5. What is the greatest barrier to effective reading?

EFFECTIVE READING HABITS

In the Classroom

Chris McDaniel has problems keeping up with her reading. She is overwhelmed by the amount of reading and the difficulty of her textbooks. She has never been much of a reader but enjoys watching television. She sometimes reads in bed or in a comfortable chair but often falls asleep. She realizes that this is not the most productive way to study, but it has become a habit. Chris has noticed that, after reading for an hour or so, she can recall almost nothing. This has caused her frustration and self-doubt her ability to succeed in college.

1. What habits should Chris change to help her improve her reading skills?

   _____

   _____

   _____

2. Suggest one or two specific strategies Chris could implement to become a better reader.

   _____

   _____

In the Workplace

Chris is now a stockbroker. She never thought that she would work in this business, but a part-time summer job led her to a career in finance, and she really likes the challenge. She is surprised, however, at the vast amount of reading involved in her job: reports, letter, magazines, and articles. She also reads several books on money management each month.

3. What strategies in this chapter would help Chris manage and organize her reading materials?

   _____

   _____

4. What are some specific reading strategies that apply to both school and work?

   _____

   _____

NAME: DATE:

APPLYING THE ABCDE METHOD OF SELF-MANAGEMENT

In the Journal Entry on page 185, you were asked to describe a time when you enjoyed being read to. Why was the experience pleasurable? What types of books did you enjoy most? Did you have a favorite book or story?

_____

_____

_____

_____

Now think about your current experiences with reading. Do you enjoy reading? If so, what are the benefits to you? Visualize either a recent positive or a recent negative reading situation. Apply the ABCDE steps to visualize how the situation can enhance your reading skills.

A = Actual event:

B = Beliefs:

C = Consequences:

D = Dispute:

E = Energized:

When you are in a positive state of mind, do you see yourself reading quickly and comprehending and recalling information effortlessly? Enjoy becoming an active reader.

Practice Self-Management

For more examples of learning how to manage difficult situations, see the "Self-Management Workbook" section of the Online Learning Center web site at **www.mhhe.com/ferrett6e.**

ATTITUDES AND READING

Read the following questions and write your answers on the lines provided.

1. What is your attitude toward reading?

   I love to read. mostly fiction. Books. I read everything.

2. What kind of books do you most like to read?

   Mostly fiction. Newspaper ads.

3. Do you read for pleasure?

   yes.

4. Do you read the daily newspaper?   Yes _____   No _____

   If yes, what sections do you read? Place a check mark.

   _____ Comics   _____ Horoscope   ✓ Weather
   _____ Sports   _____ Classified ads   ✓ World news
   ✓ Business   ✓ Entertainment   _____ Other

5. Do you read magazines?   Yes ✓   No _____

   If yes, which magazines?

   Money magazine, Jet, Good house keeping

6. How would it benefit you to read faster?

   I read a book a day

7. What techniques can you learn to read faster and remember more?

   Find quiet, special place.

DIFFERENT TYPES OF READING

Find a sample of each of the following sources of reading material:

◆ Newspaper

◆ Chapter from a textbook

◆ Instructions for an appliance, an insurance policy, or a rental contract

Read each sample. Then answer the following questions.

1. How does the reading process differ for each type of reading?

_____

_____

_____

_____

_____

_____

_____

_____

_____

2. How does knowing your purpose for reading affect how you read? Why?

_____

_____

_____

_____

_____

_____

_____

_____

_____

_____

SUMMARIZE AND TEACH

1. Read the following paragraph on predicting questions. Underline, write in the margins, and write a summary of the paragraph. Compare your work with a study partner's work. There are many ways to highlight, so don't be concerned if yours is unique. Comparing may give you ideas on creative note taking.

Predicting Questions

Dig out key points and questions. Jot down questions either in the margin or in your reading notes as you read. Asking questions gets you interested and involved, keeps you focused, organizes information, and helps you prepare for tests. As you preview the chapter, make questions out of chapter headings, sections, titles, and definitions. If there are sample questions at the end of the chapter, review them and tie them in with your own questions. What are possible test questions? List them on note cards and review them. Exchange questions with your study team or partner.

Summary

_____

_____

_____

_____

_____

2. Work with a study partner in one of your classes. Read a chapter and write a summary. Compare your summary with your study partner's summary. Then summarize and teach the main concepts to your partner. Each of you can clarify and ask questions.

Summary

_____

_____

_____

_____

_____

_____

_____

_____

_____

_____

_____

_____

_____

_____

_____

REVIEW AND APPLICATIONS

CHAPTER 6

CREATING A READING OUTLINE

Outlining what you read can be a helpful study technique. Develop the habit of outlining. Use the following form as a guide. You may also develop your own form (see Chapter 5 for examples). Outline Chapter 6 on the lines below (or select another chapter in this of one of your texts).

Course _____   Chapter _____   Date _____

I. _____

   A. _____

      1. _____

      2. _____

      3. _____

      4. _____

   B. _____

      1. _____

      2. _____

      3. _____

      4. _____

II. _____

   A. _____

      1. _____

      2. _____

      3. _____

      4. _____

   B. _____

      1. _____

      2. _____

(continued)

III. _____

   A. _____

      1. _____

      2. _____

      3. _____

      4. _____

   B. _____

      1. _____

      2. _____

      3. _____

      4. _____

IV. _____

   A. _____

      1. _____

      2. _____

      3. _____

      4. _____

   B. _____

      1. _____

      2. _____

      3. _____

      4. _____

REVIEW AND APPLICATIONS

CHAPTER 6

ANALYZING CHAPTERS

As you start to read the next chapter in this book, fill in this page to prepare for reading. You may need to add additional headings. List each heading and then phrase it as a question. Then summarize as you complete your reading. Use a separate sheet of paper if needed.

Course _____   Textbook _____

Chapter _____

Heading 1 _____

Question _____

Heading 2 _____

Question _____

Heading 3 _____

Question _____

Heading 4 _____

Question _____

Summary of Section

_____

_____

_____

_____

_____

Summary of Chapter

_____

_____

_____

_____

_____

_____

BREAKING BARRIERS TO READING

Following is a list of the common reasons that some students use for not reading effectively. Read this list; then add to it on the lines provided. Use creative problem solving to list strategies for overcoming these barriers.

Reasons for Not Reading

Strategies for Overcoming Reading Barriers

1. My textbooks are boring.

   _____
   _____
   _____

2. I can't concentrate.

   _____
   _____
   _____

3. I'm easily distracted.

   _____
   _____
   _____

4. I fall asleep when I read.

   _____
   _____
   _____

5. I never study the right material.

   _____
   _____
   _____

6. There is too much information, and I don't know what is important.

   _____
   _____
   _____

7. I read for hours, but I don't understand what I have read.

   _____
   _____
   _____

8. I don't like to read.

   _____
   _____
   _____

CAREER DEVELOPMENT PORTFOLIO

DEMONSTRATING COMPETENCIES

Follow these steps and fill in the chart to identify and demonstrate your competencies. Then add this page to your Career Development Portfolio.

1. **Looking back:** Review your worksheets from other chapters to find activities from which you learned to read and concentrate.
2. **Taking stock:** Identify your strengths in reading and what you want to improve.
3. **Looking forward:** Indicate how you would demonstrate reading and comprehension skills to an employer.
4. **Documentation:** Include documentation of your reading skills.
5. **Inventory:** Make a list of the books you've read recently, including any classics. Use a separate sheet of paper.
6. Fill in the chart; explain how you demonstrate these competencies:

Competencies	Your Demonstration
Active reading	
Critical reading	
Willingness to learn new words	
Improvement in technical vocabulary	
Articulation	
Expressiveness	
Ability to use a dictionary	
Positive attitude toward reading	
Technical reading	
Form reading	

Improve Your Memory Skills

In this chapter, you will learn to

▲ Prepare yourself mentally and physically for remembering

▲ Use your senses and learning styles to enhance memory

▲ Incorporate memory strategies

▲ Use mnemonic devices

▲ Recall names

SELF-MANAGEMENT

"I have been meeting so many new people. I wish I could remember their names, but I just don't have a good memory. What can I do to increase my memory skills and remember names, facts, and information more easily?"

Do you ever find yourself feeling embarrassed because you cannot remember the names of new people you've met? Do you ever get frustrated because you don't remember material for a test? In this chapter, you will learn how to increase your memory skills.

JOURNAL ENTRY   In **Worksheet 7.1** on page 244, describe a situation in which you needed to learn many new names or numerous facts for a test. How did you fare? What factors helped you remember?

Y ou may have heard someone say, "I just don't have a good memory." Do you have a good memory? Do you think some people are simply born with better memories? You will discover in this chapter that memory is a process. As a complex process, memory is not an isolated activity that takes place in one part of the brain; it involves many factors that you can control, such as your attitude, interest, intent, awareness, mental alertness, observation skills, senses, distractions, memory devices, and willingness to practice. Most people with good memories say that the skill is mastered by learning the strategies for storing and recalling information. This chapter will summarize and highlight specific strategies that help you remember information.

The Memory Process

The memory process involves five main steps:

1. Intention—you are interested and have a desire to learn and remember.
2. Attention—you are attentive, and you observe information and concentrate on details.
3. Association—you organize and associate information to make sense of it.
4. Retention—you practice and repeat until you know the information.
5. Recall—you recall, teach, and share information with others.

As you can see, this process is quite similar to the Adult Learning Cycle, which is explored throughout this text. (Read **Peak Progress 7.1** to see how you can use the Adult Learning Cycle to improve your memory skills.)

1. **Intention.** The first step in using memory effectively is to prepare yourself mentally. As with learning any skill, your intention, attitude, and motivation are fundamental to success. Intention means that you are interested and willing to learn. You intend to remember by finding personal meaning and interest. *You must want to remember.* Have you ever said, "I wish I could remember names," "I'm just not good at remembering facts for tests," or "I can't remember formulas for math"? Instead, say, "I really want to remember JoAnne's name."

   If you make excuses or program your mind with negative self-talk, your mind refuses to learn new information. If you think a subject is boring or unimportant, you will have difficulty remembering it. Take full responsibility for your attitude and intention. Realize that you are in control of your memory. Develop an interest in whatever you are studying or in any task or project with which you are working. Make a conscious, active decision to remember, and state your intention with positive affirmations.

WORDS TO SUCCEED

"Memory... is the diary that we all carry about with us."

OSCAR WILDE, *Dramatist*

Applying the Adult Learning Cycle to Increase Your Memory Skills

1. **RELATE. Why do I want to learn this?** I must become more proficient at remembering names, facts, and information. This is critical for success not only in school but also in the workplace and social situations. What strategies do I already use to remember and retain information?

2. **OBSERVE. How does this work?** Who do I know is good at remembering names and information? What tips can I pick up from him or her? Who do I know seems to struggle with remembering important information? I'll try using new techniques and strategies and observe how I'm improving.

3. **REFLECT. What does this mean?** What strategies seem to work the best for me? What strategies are ineffective? Have I eliminated negative and defeating self-talk? I continue to look for connections and associations. I use humor, songs, rhymes, and other mnemonic techniques.

4. **DO. What can I do with this?** I will practice memory skills in many different situations and make a conscious commitment to improving my skills. I'll make games out of my practice and have fun. I'll find practical applications and use my new skills in everyday life. Each day, I'll work on one area. For example, I'll choose one class in which I'm having trouble recalling information and experiment with new strategies. Or, for one person or group of people with whom I having trouble remembering names, I'll focus on improving.

5. **TEACH. Whom can I share this with?** I'll talk with others and share my tips and experiences. I'll ask if they have any strategies they find useful that I might also try.

Continue to congratulate yourself at least mentally when you have made improvements. The more you go through the cycle, the more interest and meaning recall will have for you, and the better your memory skills will become.

> **WORDS TO SUCCEED**
>
> "An education isn't how much you have committed to memory, or even how much you know. It's being able to differentiate between what you know and what you don't."
>
> **ANATOLE FRANCE,** *Author*

2. **Attention.** The second step in the memory process is to concentrate, observe, and be attentive to details. How many times have you physically been in one place but mentally and emotionally were thousands of miles away? **Mindfulness** is the state in which you are totally in the moment and part of the process around you. Learning occurs when your mind is relaxed, focused, receptive, and alert. Focus your attention by concentrating briefly on one thing. Visualize details by drawing mental pictures. **Personal Evaluation Notebook 7.1** on page 222 helps you practice your observation skills.

3. **Association.** Nothing is harder to remember than unconnected facts, dates, or theories. Over 2,000 years ago, Aristotle talked about the laws of association to help memory. Ask questions about how information is interconnected: *How is this information similar to other information? How is this information different?*

   By associating and linking new material with old material, you make it meaningful. You cannot retain or recall information unless you understand it.

Being Observant

How observant are you? Try the following experiments to determine if you are really observing the world around you.

Experiment 1

1. Look around the room.
2. Close your eyes.
3. Mentally picture what is in the room.
4. Open your eyes.
5. Did you remember everything? If not, what didn't you remember?

_____

_____

_____

Experiment 2

1. Look at a painting, photo, or poster for one minute.
2. Without looking back, write down the details you remember.
3. Compare your list of details with the painting, photo, or poster.
   a. What details did you remember? Colors? Faces? Clothing?

_____

_____

_____

   b. What details didn't you remember?

_____

_____

_____

   c. Did you remember the obvious things or did you remember subtle details?

_____

   d. Why do you think those were the details you remembered?

_____

_____

_____

Understanding means that you see connections and relationships in the information you are studying and you can summarize and explain this material in your own words. Make associations by looking for similarities or differences. Create understanding by finding out why this information is important and how it relates to other information. Too often, students study just enough to get by on a quiz and forget the information immediately thereafter. It is much better to learn a subject so that it becomes interesting and part of your long-term memory. (See **Peak Progress 7.2** on short-term versus long-term memory.)

PEAK PROGRESS   **7.2**

Short-Term and Long-Term Memory

People have two basic types of memory: short-term, or active, memory and long-term, or passive, memory. Each type of memory plays its own important role in learning and the ability to respond effectively to any challenge in life.

If you own a personal computer, you probably have heard references to its various types of memory. Your own short-term memory is very much like the memory in your personal computer which you know as random access memory (RAM) (see Figure 7.1).

Figure 7.1 Short-Term and Long-Term Memory

CPU

Short-term Memory
Random access memory (RAM)

hold only for ~1min
Dropping stuff off
after it's full.
Decide to remember
or let it Go.

Long-term Memory
Hard drive

—Save Paper.
retrieve when ever
you want to STAYs
leave it

Keyboard

Mouse

Information Input

Short-Term and Long-Term Memory   Think of your memory as a computer. First, you input information through your natural senses (as in inputting by way of a mouse or a keyboard.) Your short-term memory is like the random access memory in your computer, which is readily available for use but can be erased if the computer is shut down. Long-term memory is like information that has been stored onto your hard drive, which you can retrieve (or recall) for later use.

(continued)

Short-Term and Long-Term Memory (continued)

Just as the central processing unit of your computer relies on this RAM to perform all of its processing tasks, your own short-term memory is where your mind is able to apply, create, and evaluate. Short-term memory is where all of your active thinking takes place. It is a relatively limited space, yet one where tremendous potential resides.

Before short-term memory can perform its wonders, information must flow into it. This can be new information entering through your natural senses, it can be stored information that you retrieve from long-term memory, or it can be a combination of both. Using the computer analogy, you might equate your natural senses with a keyboard or mouse, while you may think of long-term memory as your hard drive or any other storage medium in which you save your work. Just as you make choices about which work you will save on your computer, you determine which information becomes stored in your long-term memory. The information you choose to save in long-term memory has great value. It can be retrieved and used as it is, or it can be retrieved and combined with other information to create something entirely new. The possibilities are endless.

When we consider the transfer of information back and forth in our memory system, think of the mind as a vast relational database. It is not enough merely to store information; for any database to be useful, the information stored in it must be organized and indexed for retrieval. This occurs naturally when we are predisposed to remember something, but what happens when we are required to memorize information we just don't care about? Not only does the information become more difficult to memorize, but also it becomes nearly impossible to recall. The good news is that we can make such information more memorable by personally relating to it. For example, we might ask ourselves questions such as "How can I use this information in my life?" Answers to such questions can create meaning, which helps our mind to naturally organize information. When it comes time to use that information, such as when we need to answer questions on an examination, it will have been naturally indexed for easier recall.

One way to organize material to look for connections is by outlining each chapter. As discussed in Chapter 5, use the Cornell System or a mind map (or whatever outline method works for you) to organize information. (See **Personal Evaluation Notebook 7.2** for a sample of a mind map.)

4. **Retention.** Repetition and practice help you retain information. Do it, and do it again. Repeat names or information aloud. Practice what you have learned, find new applications, and connect this information to other information you already know. Continue to ask questions and look for more examples.

5. **Recall.** **Memorization** is the transfer of information from short-term memory into long-term memory. Of course, the only reason to do this is so that we can retrieve it in the future for use by our short-term memory. This transfer in the other direction is known as recall. To recall information means you not only have retained it but also can remember it when you need to.

Share information with others; introduce a person you have just met; practice giving summaries of chapters to your study team. Teach it, write about it, talk about it, apply information to new situations, and demonstrate that you know it. This will

Using a Mind Map to Enhance Memory

A mind map will not only help you organize information to be memorized, but also the physical act of writing will help you commit the material to memory. Use the map figure that follows as a guide, and on the space provided create a mind map of this chapter.

- Write the main topic in the middle and draw a circle or a box around it.
- Surround the main topic with subtopics.
- Draw lines from the subtopics to the main topic.
- Under the subtopics, jot down supporting points, ideas, and illustrations.

- Be creative.
- Use different-colored ink and write main topics in block letters.
- Draw pictures for supporting points.

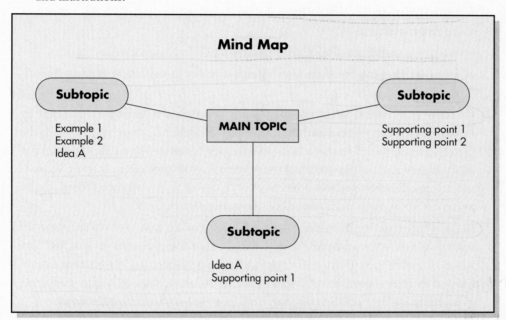

Create your own mind map.

Verbal – Words.
Visual – any thing you see
physical – any thing that you do.

help you become more interested in the information, create more meaning for you, and build your confidence. Repeating this cycle will build your memory skills.

Memory Strategies

Following are a number of strategies that will help you improve your memory skills.

1. **Write it down.** Writing is physical and enhances learning. When you write down information, you are reinforcing learning by using your eyes, hand, fingers, and arm. Writing uses different parts of the brain than do speaking and listening.

   [handwritten: General (pacific)]

   - Writing down a telephone number helps you remember it.
   - Taking notes in class prompts you to be logical and concise and fills in memory gaps.
   - Underlining important information and then copying it onto note cards reinforces information.
   - Writing a summary after reading a chapter also reinforces information.
   - Summarizing in your own words helps transfer information to long-term memory.

2. **Go from the general to the specific.** Many people learn and remember best by looking at the big picture and then learning the details. Try to outline from the general (main topic) to the specific (subtopics). Previewing a chapter gives you an overview and makes the topic more meaningful. Your brain is more receptive to specific details when it has a general idea of the main topic. Read, listen, and look for general understanding, then add details.

3. **Reduce information.** You don't have to memorize certain types of information, such as deadlines, telephone messages, and assignment due dates. You just have to know where to find this information. Write deadlines and important information in your organizer or student planner or on a calendar. Write messages in a phone log, not on slips of paper that can get lost. You can refer to any of this written information again if you need it.

   [handwritten: Right Side Brain / Creative]

   [handwritten: Left Brain / Information.]

4. **Eliminate distractions.** Distractions can keep you from paying attention and, consequently, from remembering what you're trying to learn. One way to avoid distractions is to study in a quiet study area. Libraries and designated study rooms are good places to use for quiet study. If it is noisy in class, ask the instructor to repeat information or move closer to the front. Clarify names if you are being introduced. Understand your responsibilities and avoid becoming someone else's memory support. If someone asks you to call him or her with the notes from class, ask the person to call you instead. If a study-team member asks you to remind him or her about a study meeting, suggest the use of a student planner to record important dates. You have enough to remember without taking responsibility for someone else's memory. If something is bothering you, write it down and tell yourself that, as soon as your study time is over, you will address it. In this way, you can reduce distractions and focus completely on absorbing important information.

5. **Study in short sessions.** You will use the power of concentration more fully, and the brain retains information better in short study sessions. After about 40 minutes, the brain needs a break to process information effectively. Break large

goals into specific objectives and study in short sessions. For example, if you are taking a marketing course, preview a chapter in your textbook for 20 minutes and mind map the chapter on sales for 20 minutes. Then take a 10-minute break. Stretch, drink a glass of water, or treat yourself to a small snack. Then return to complete your goal.

Even when you are working on something complex, such as completing a term paper or studying for finals, you are more effective when you take frequent, scheduled breaks.

6. **Integrate your left brain and your right brain.** Think of both sides of your brain as members of a team that can cooperate, appreciate, and support each other. Recall the discussion about right- and left-brain dominance in Chapter 1. (See **Figure 1.2** on page 11.) By using both sides of your brain, you can enhance your memory. For example, you may have a term paper assignment that constitutes 50 percent of your final grade. You want to turn in a well-researched, accurately written, neatly typed paper. The left side of your brain insists that it be error-free. Your preferred style of learning leans toward the right side, so your reaction to this assignment might be frustration, fear, and resistance. By using a word processor, you can support both sides of the brain. You satisfy the structured side, which wants a flawless paper, while allowing your creative side to correct mistakes easily by using the spell-check. Learn to integrate all learning styles and use both sides of your brain to enhance memory.

7. **Use all your senses.** Memory is sensory, so using all your senses (sight, hearing, touch, smell, and taste) will give your brain a better chance of retaining information.

Learning Memory
Focusing on your preferred learning style strengthens your memory skills. *How does your learning style affect the way in which you learn memory?*

◆ **Visualize.** Since much of what you learn and remember reaches you through sight, it is important to visualize what you want to remember. The art of retention is the art of attention. Be a keen observer of details and notice differences and similarities. Let's say that you are taking a medical terminology or vocabulary-building course. You may want to look at pictures and visualize in your mind images with the new terms or words. Look at illustrations, pictures, and information on the board.

◆ **Listen.** You cannot remember a name or information in class if you are not attentive and listen. Actively listen in class, tape lectures (ask for the instructor's permission), and play them back later. Recite definitions and information aloud.

◆ **Move.** Whether you like to learn by reading or by listening, you will retain information better if you use all your senses and make learning physical. Read aloud; read while standing; jot down notes; lecture in front of the classroom to yourself or your study team; go on field trips; draw pictures, diagrams, and models; and join a study group. Practice reciting information while doing physical activity, such as showering, walking, or jogging. The more you use all of your senses, the more likely you are to remember and retain information. Some people use aromas to remember; some people like to eat crunchy foods while they study (where appropriate).

Complete **Personal Evaluation Notebook 7.3** to see how your senses relate to your childhood memories. Complete **Personal Evaluation Notebook 7.4** on page 230 to determine how to use your learning style and all your senses.

8. **Use mnemonic devices. Mnemonic** (neh-mon-nik) **devices** are memory tricks that help you remember information. However, there are problems with memory tricks. It can take time to develop a memory trick, and it can be hard to remember the trick if you make it too complicated. Since memory tricks don't help you understand the information or develop skills in critical thinking, they are best used for sheer rote memorization. Follow up by looking for associations, making connections, and writing summaries. Some mnemonic devices include

- *Rhythm and rhymes.* In elementary school, you might have learned the rhyme "In 1492 Columbus sailed the ocean blue." It helped you remember the date of Columbus' voyage. Rhythms can also be helpful. Many people have learned to spell the word *Mississippi* by accenting all the *is* and making the word rhythmic.

- *Acronyms.* **Acronyms** are words formed from the first letters of a series of other words, such as *HOMES* for the Great Lakes (Huron, Ontario, Michigan, Erie, and Superior) and *EPCOT* (Experimental Prototype Community of Tomorrow). Consider creating your own acronyms.

- *Acrostics.* **Acrostics** are similar to acronyms but they are made-up sentences in which the first letter stands for something, such as *Every Good Boy Deserves Fun* for remembering the sequence of musical notes: E, G, B, D, F. Another is *My Very Easy Memory Jingle Seems Useful Naming Planets*, which helps you remember the order of the planets from the sun (assuming you know that the first planet is Mercury. Can you name the rest with the help of the acrostic?) Acrostics are often used in poetry, where the first letter of every line combine to spell something, such as the poem's title.

- *Association.* Suppose you are learning about explorer Christopher Columbus' three ships. Think of three friends whose names start with the same first letters as the ships' names: Pinta, Santa Maria, and Nina (e.g., Paul, Sandy, and Nancy). Vividly associate these names with the three ships, and you should be able to recall the ships' names. Using associations can also be helpful in remembering numbers. For example, if your ATM identification number is 9072, you might remember it by creating associations with dates. Maybe 1990 is the year you graduated from high school, and 1972 is the year you were born.

- *Chunking.* **Chunking**, or grouping, long lists of information or numbers can break up the memory task and make it easier for you. Most people can remember up to seven numbers in a row, which is why phone numbers are that long.

- *The stacking technique.* You simply visualize objects that represent points and stack them on top on each other. For example, if you were giving a speech on time management, you would start with a clock with a big pencil on it to represent how much time is saved if you write information down. On top of the clock is a big calendar, which reminds you to make the point that you

WORDS TO SUCCEED

"No memory is ever alone; it's at the end of a trail of memories, a dozen trails that each have their own associations."

LOUIS L'AMOUR, *Author*

Memory Assessment

A. Sometimes your perceptions differ from reality, particularly when you are assessing your skills and personal qualities. Assess your memory and your intention. Then check Yes or No as it pertains to you.

1. Do you remember names?   Yes __✓__   No _____
2. Do you remember important information for tests?   Yes ____   No _✓_
3. Did you use your senses more as a child?   Yes _✓_   No _____

B. Read each statement that follows and write your comments on the lines provided.

1. Write a few lines about your earliest memory.

   Falling down a step At home. and
   needing to go to the hospital
   _____
   _____
   _____

2. Does it help your memory to look at family photos or hear about your childhood? Why?

   Sometime I hate reviewing
   the past and it's struggle. I
   rarely look at pictures. But
   Love stories
   _____

   I — Intention   AATP.
   A — Attention.
   A — Associate
   R — Remember
   R — Recite

3. What smells do you remember most from home?

   Favorite mom foods. ← Soups, fricase
   Chicken
   _____
   _____
   _____
   _____

Learning Styles and Memory

Answer the following questions on the lines provided.

1. How can you use your preferred learning style to enhance your memory?

_____

_____

_____

_____

_____

_____

_____

_____

_____

_____

_____

2. What can you do to integrate both sides of the brain and to use all your senses to help yourself recall information?

_____

_____

_____

_____

_____

_____

_____

_____

_____

_____

_____

must set priorities in writing. On the calendar is a time log with the name Drucker on it. This will remind you to present the quote by Peter Drucker that you must know where your time goes if you are to be effective in managing your life. You stack an object to remind you of each of the key points in the speech.

◆ *The method-of-place technique.* As far back as 500 B.C., the Greeks were using a method of imagery called *loci*—the method-of-place technique. This method, which is similar to the stacking technique, is still effective today because it uses imagery and association to aid memory. Memorize a setting in detail and then place the item or information you want to remember at certain places on your memory map. Some people like to use a familiar street, their home, or their car as a map on which to place their information. The concept is the same. You memorize certain places on your street, in your home, or in your car. You memorize a specific order or path in which you visit each place. Once you have this map memorized, you can position various items to remember at different points. **Personal Evaluation Notebook 7.5 on page 232 provides an opportunity to practice this technique.**

9. **Use note cards.** Successful students use note cards. The information is condensed and written so the act of writing is kinesthetic and holding cards is tactile. Note cards are visual and, when the information is recited out loud or in a group, the auditory element enhances learning. The question can be on one side and the answer on the other side. Flashcards with keywords, formulas, and questions can help memory. Note cards are a great way to organize information and highlight keywords:

◆ Use index cards for recording information you want to memorize. Write brief summaries and indicate the main points of each chapter on the backs of note cards.

◆ Carry the cards with you and review them during waiting time, before going to sleep at night, or any other time you have a few minutes to spare.

◆ Organize the cards according to category, color, size, order, weight, and other areas.

10. **Recite.** Recite and repeat information, such as a name, a poem, a date, or formulas. Repeat again and again. When you say information aloud, you use your throat, voice, and lips and you hear yourself recite. You may find this recitation technique helpful when you are dealing with difficult reading materials. Reading aloud and hearing the material will reinforce it for you and help move information from your short-term memory to your long-term memory. Try to use the new words in your own conversations. Write summaries in your own words and read to others. Study groups are effective because you can hear each other, clarify questions, and increase understanding as you review information.

Reciting may be helpful when preparing to give a speech. Try to practice in the place you will be speaking. Visualize the audience; practice demonstrating your visual aids; write on the board; and use gestures and pauses. Tape your speech and play it back. To remember names, when you meet someone, recite

A Walk Down Memory Lane

Creating a memory map is a visual way to enhance and practice your memory skills. The key to this method is to set the items clearly in your memory and visualize them. For example, a familiar memory map involves remembering the 13 original colonies. The memory map is a garden with several distinct points. There is delicate chinaware sitting on the garden gate (Delaware); the birdbath contains a large fountain pen (Pennsylvania); in the gazebo is a new jersey calf (New Jersey); and sitting on the calf is King George (Georgia) with a cut on his finger (Connecticut). The flowerbed has a mass of flowers (Massachusetts); in the fountain, splashing, is Marilyn Monroe (Maryland); the garden sun dial is pointing south (South Carolina); a large ham is sitting on the garden bench (New Hampshire); and the gardener, named Virginia (Virginia), who is wearing an empire dress (New York), is watering the northern flowerbed (North Carolina). In the middle of the flowerbed is an island of rocks (Rhode Island) with a bottle of maple syrup. There you have the 13 original colonies in the order in which they joined the union, and it was easy to add the fourteenth state to join—Vermont.

Your Memory Garden

Think of your memory map as a garden rich in detail and full of flowers representing thoughts, images, and ideas. You always enter the garden through a white garden gate. You are actively involved, attentive to all the details, and in control of your memory. You can see each distinct point in the garden: the garden gate, the birdbath, the gazebo, the fountain, the garden bench, and the flowerbed. The key is to set the items clearly in your memory and visualize them. Draw a picture of your garden in detail with these items in the space provided at the left.

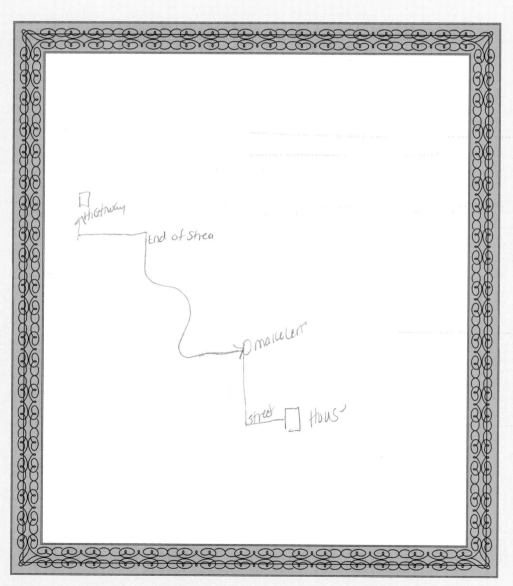

A Walk Down Memory Lane—continued

Using your drawing of the garden, let's say that you want to memorize four stories that emphasize four key points for a speech you are giving in your Speech 101 class. The first story in your speech is about a monk, so you draw a monk and place him at the garden gate. You want to tell a joke about a robin, so you place the robin in the birdbath. Your third point involves people of a bygone era, and you have chosen a Victorian woman as the image to represent this key point, so you place her in the gazebo. Your fourth point involves the younger generation, so you choose a little girl and place her playing in the fountain.

Follow the steps to the method-of-place technique:

1. Imagine your beautiful memory garden.

2. Imagine each distinctive detail of the location: the garden gate, birdbath, gazebo, fountain, garden bench, and flowerbed.

3. Create a vivid image for each item you want to remember and place it at a specific location.

4. Associate each of the images representing the items with points in the garden and see the images at each location.

5. As you mentally stroll down the garden lane, create pictures in your mind of each of your items through association.

If you have additional points you want to remember, place one at the garden bench and one at the flowerbed. If you have more than six items to remember, illustrate a rainbow over your flowerbed. Flowers in various colors of the rainbow can represent each item you wish to remember.

It is easier to remember information grouped together and associated by categories. Be creative and flexible with the method-of-place technique. If a garden doesn't work for you, use a car, the mall, or your home. Just make certain that your illustration is clear and you always start in the same place. Draw it in detail and color it.

Use a Checklist in Your Memory Garden

A checklist provides a way to review and check off each item you want to remember. You can combine it with the method-of-place technique.

Memory Checklist

1. Garden gate   Monk
2. Birdbath   Bird
3. Gazebo   Victorian woman
4. Fountain   Little girl
5. Garden bench
6. Flowerbed

Check off each memory point and the item you want to remember. Go to page 234 to see a drawn interpretation of the memory garden.

A Walk Down Memory Lane—continued

SOURCE: *The Memory Book* by Harry Lorayne, & Jerry Lucas, Stein & Day, 1996.

the person's name several times to yourself and out loud. **Peak Progress 7.3** provides a number of additional tips for remembering names.

11. **Practice, practice, practice!** You must practice information that you want to remember. For example, when you first start driver training, you learn the various steps involved in driving. At first, they may seem overwhelming. You may have to stop and think through each step. After you have driven a car for a while, however, you don't even think about all the steps required to start it and back out of the driveway. You check your mirror automatically before changing lanes, and driving safely has become a habit. The information is in your long-

Remembering Names

Here are some techniques that may help you remember someone's name.

1. Imagine the name. Visualize the name clearly in your mind: Tom Plum. Clarify how the name is spelled: P-l-u-m.

2. Be observant and concentrate. Pay attention to the person's features and mannerisms.

3. Use exaggeration. Caricaturing the features is a fun and effective way to remember names. Single out and amplify one outstanding feature. For example, if Tom has red hair, exaggerate it to bright red and see the hair much fuller and longer than it is.

4. Visualize the red hair and the name Tom. See this vision clearly.

5. Repeat Tom's name to yourself several times as you are talking to him.

6. Recite Tom's name aloud during your conversation. Introduce Tom to others.

7. Use association. Associate the name with something you know ("Tom is the name of my cat") or make up a story using the person's name and add action and color. Tom is picking red plums that match his hair.

8. As soon as you can, jot down the name. Use a keyword, or write or draw a description.

9. Use rhyming to help you recall: "Tom is not glum, nor is he dumb."

10. Integrate learning styles. It may help if you see the name (visual), hear it pronounced (auditory), or practice saying it and writing it several times and connecting the name with something familiar (kinesthetic).

11. Ask people their names. Do this if you forget or say your name first. "Hi, I'm Sam and I met you last week." If they don't offer their names, ask.

12. Reward yourself when you remember. Practice these techniques and reward yourself for your successes. Remember, the first requirements for improving your memory are a desire to remember and concentration.

term memory. The more often you use information, the easier it is to recall. You could not become a good musician without hours of practice. Playing sports, speaking in public, flying an airplane, and learning to drive all require skills that need to be repeated and practiced many times.

Repetition puts information into long-term memory and allows for recall. Improve your memory by having a desire to remember, concentrating, observing and visualizing information, thinking about associations, reciting, and repeating again and again. Use the Adult Learning Cycle to practice, think positively, and reward yourself when you see improvement.

These strategies are very effective in strengthening your memory skills. Certain strategies might work better for you than others, depending on your personality and

More Memory Affirmations

Improving your memory skills takes concentration, effort, and practice. It helps you establish stronger study habits. Integrate the following affirmations into your daily routine. These will help you as you create effective study habits and enhance your memory skills.

- I use memory techniques to help me study and recall information.
- My memory gets better every day.
- I relax, focus, and complete my project, and then I socialize.
- I take short breaks throughout my study time.
- I have a positive attitude about the information I am studying.
- I summarize material in my own words.
- I am organized and review the information often.
- I look forward to accomplishing my goals in study teams.
- I can see myself successfully remembering whatever I want.

learning styles. Everyone has his or her personal strengths and abilities. You can master the use of memory strategies with effort, patience, and practice. As you build your memory skills, you will also enhance your study habits and become more disciplined and aware of your surroundings. See **Peak Progress 7.4** about memory affirmations.

Summarize, Review, and Reflect

Summarize a lecture, a section, or a chapter of a book in your own words as soon as possible after reading it. The sooner and the more often you review information, the easier it is to recall. Ideally, your first review should be within the first hour after hearing a lecture or reading an assignment. Carry note cards with you and review them again during the first day. Studies show that, within 48 hours, you forget 85 percent of what you have learned. However, if you review right after you hear it and again within 24 hours, your recall soars to 90 percent.

Go beyond studying for tests. Be able to connect and apply information to new situations. Uncover facts, interesting points, related materials, details, and fascinating aspects of the subject. Ask your instructor for interesting stories to enhance a point. If you have time, read a novel on the subject or look for another textbook in the library that explains the subject from a different view. You will remember information more easily if you take the time to understand and apply it.

Overcome Obstacles

WORDS TO SUCCEED

"Every man's memory is his private literature."

ALDOUS HUXLEY, *Author*

One barrier to memory is disinterest. You have to want to remember. People often say, "If only I could remember names" or "I wish I had a better memory." Avoid using words such as *try, wish,* or *hope.* You can overcome the barrier of disinterest by creating a positive, curious attitude; intending to remember; using all your senses; and using memory techniques. Related to disinterest is lack of attentiveness. You must be willing to concentrate by being an attentive listener and observe. Listen for overall understanding and for details. A short period of intense concentration will help you remember more than reading for hours.

Practice becoming more observant and aware. Let's say that you want to learn the students' names in all your classes. Look at each student as the instructor takes roll, copy down each name, and say each name mentally as you look around the classroom. As you go about your day, practice becoming aware of your surroundings, people, and new information.

Finally, relax. Anxiety, stress, and nervousness can make you forget. For example, let's go back to the section on remembering names. Suppose you are with a good friend and you meet Tom. You may be so anxious to make a good impression that Tom's name is lost for a moment. Learn to relax by being totally in the moment instead of worrying about forgetting, how you look, what others may think, or your nervousness. Take a deep breath. If you still can't remember, laugh and say, "Hi, my mind just went blank. I'm Jay, please refresh my memory."

To make sure your memory skills stay sharp, review and assess your answers to the following questions periodically. Can you answer yes to them?

1. Do I want to remember?
2. Do I have a positive attitude about the information?
3. Have I eliminated distractions?
4. Have I organized and grouped material?
5. Have I reviewed the information often?
6. Have I reviewed right after the lecture? Within 24 hours?
7. Have I set up weekly reviews?
8. Have I visualized what I want to remember?
9. Have I used repetition?
10. Have I summarized material in my own words?
11. Have I used association and compared and contrasted new material with what I know?
12. Have I used memory techniques to help associate keywords?

In summary, in this chapter, I learned to:

- *Apply the five-step memory process.* Similar to the Adult Learning Cycle, the memory process consists of five steps: intention, attention, association, retention, and recall.

- *Intend to remember.* People who have better memories *want* to remember and make it a priority. It's important for me to increase my memory skills, and I take responsibility for my attitude and intention. I create personal interest and meaning in what I want to remember.

- *Be observant and alert.* I observe and am attentive to details. I am relaxed, focused, and receptive to new information. I reduce distractions, concentrate, and stay focused and mindful of the present. I look at the big picture, and then I look at details. Memory is increased when I pay attention.

- *Organize and associate information.* Organization makes sense out of information. I look for patterns and connections. I look for what I already know and jot down questions for areas that I don't know. I group similarities and look for what is different.

- *Retain information.* I write summaries in my own words and say them out loud. I jot down main points, keywords, and important information on note cards and review them often. I study in short sessions and review often.

- *Recall.* I recall everything I know about the subject. I increase my recall by writing down information, reciting out loud, and teaching others. Practicing and reviewing information often are key to increasing recall. I reward myself for concentration, discipline, and effort.

- *Go from the general to the specific.* I first look at the big picture for gaining general, overall understanding and meaning. I then focus on the details and specific supporting information.

- *Reduce information and eliminate distractions.* Some information does not have to be memorized (such as e-mail addresses and phone numbers); I just need to know where to find it easily. I also need to eliminate distractions that affect my ability to concentrate on what I'm trying to learn and remember.

- *Take frequent breaks.* I study in 40- to 60-minute sessions, since I know that the brain retains information best in short study periods. I take breaks to keep up my motivation.

- *Integrate learning styles.* I incorporate various learning styles by making learning visual, auditory, and physical.

- *Use my senses.* I draw pictures and illustrations, use color, tape lectures, play music, write out summaries, jot down questions, collect samples, give summaries to my study group, recite out loud, and go on field trips.

- *Try mnemonic devices.* I use various techniques, such as rhythms and rhymes, acronyms, acrostics, grouping, association, and the method-of-place technique to help me memorize and recall information.

- *Use note cards.* Using note cards is an easy and convenient way for me to review important facts, terms, and questions.

- *Find connections and recite.* I link new information with familiar material, and I summarize what I have learned, either out loud or in writing.

- *Practice!* If I want to understand and remember information, I must practice and review it again and again.

Marla Bergstrom

JOURNALIST

Related Majors: Journalism, English, Social Studies

Integrating Learning Styles

As a journalist, Marla Bergstrom's job is to find news-worthy local issues, collect accurate information from both sides of the story, and write an article that treats the subject fairly. As a general assignment reporter for a large newspaper, she covers stories from politics to crime, education, business, and consumer affairs.

Marla works closely with her editor when selecting a topic for an article. She often investigates leads for a story, only to realize later that she does not have enough information to make a strong story. She orga-nizes the information she gathers, not knowing how or if it will fit into the article. Marla usually works on more than one story at a time, as some stories take weeks of research. Her hours are irregular. In one week, Marla might attend an early morning political break-fast and attend a school board meeting the same evening.

Each week, Marla interviews a wide variety of peo-ple, including the mayor, the police chief, the school supervisor, and other community leaders. She always says hello to people, using their names. She prides her-self on being able to remember names after only one meeting. When conducting an interview, the first thing Marla does is write down the name of the per-son, asking for the correct spelling. By doing this, she not only checks spelling but also sees a person's name in print. Because Marla is a visual learner, this helps her remember the name. On the way home from an in-terview, Marla orally reviews the names of the people she met. After an interview, Marla types her notes and memorizes pertinent information, such as the names of people, businesses, and locations. Marla knows that having good memory skills is essential for being a ca-pable journalist.

CRITICAL THINKING Which learning styles help Marla remember pertinent information?

Peak Performer Profile

Alberto Gonzales

His rise to the top appears meteoric. In just a decade, Alberto Gonzales advanced from partner at a Houston law firm to general counsel to the governor of Texas, the 100th Texas secretary of state, a justice on the Texas Supreme Court, White House counsel, and the attorney general of the United States. However, Gonzales reached this influential position through hard work, dedication, and perseverance.

Born in San Antonio, Texas, Gonzales was raised in Houston by his parents, who had been migrant farm workers. For most of Gonzales' childhood, the family's two-bedroom house—home to eight children—had neither a telephone nor hot running water. These circumstances, however, did not diminish Gonzales' drive. Though lacking material wealth, his mother and father taught him the "value of self-responsibility." In 1975, after graduating from high school, Gonzales joined the U.S. Air Force. Originally aiming at a career as a pilot, he opted out of the military after two years, changed his career goals, and chose to study law.

Within the next five years, he earned a bachelor's degree in political science from Rice University and then a law degree from Harvard Law School. In 2001, Gonzales was appointed White House counsel. As top legal advisor, Alberto Gonzales commanded a powerful position in the administration. Not only did he advise the presidential office on all legal matters, but he also selected and evaluated judicial nominees, including those for the U.S. Supreme Court. In 2005, he was sworn in as the nation's eightieth attorney general, becoming the highest-placed Hispanic ever in the U.S. government.

PERFORMANCE THINKING The legal profession is one of many fields that requires remembering a great number of details, including the specifics of court rulings and subsequent precedents, as well as knowing how to research and locate specific information. What are some memory strategies a legal professional might use? What other professions involve remembering and understanding connections among myriad of details?

CHECK IT OUT The largest library in the world, the Library of Congress is the nation's oldest federal cultural institution and serves as the research arm of Congress. It houses more than 130 million items on approximately 530 miles of bookshelves. Visit its web site at **www.loc.gov** to search for various print, media, and on-line resources. Also available on the web site is a special section entitled "American Memory," which showcases historical information and resources on a number of topics, such as advertising, literature, conservation, and African American history.

Performance Strategies............

Following are the top 10 strategies for improving memory:

◆ Intend to remember and prepare yourself mentally.

◆ Be observant, be alert, and pay attention.

◆ Organize information to make it meaningful.

◆ Look for associations and connections.

◆ Integrate learning styles.

◆ Write down information.

◆ Study in short sessions.

◆ Use mnemonic devices.

◆ Summarize information in your own words.

◆ Practice, use repetition, and relax.

Tech for Success....................

Take advantage of the text's web site at **www.mhhe.com/ferrett6e** for additional study aids, useful forms, and convenient and applicable resources.

◆ **PDA.** Keep your notes literally on hand by using a personal digital assistant (PDA). PDAs are available in a variety of prices and with endless features. You will be motivated to take notes throughout the day to help you organize priorities and remember good ideas.

◆ **Stored memory.** Your computer is one big memory tool, storing thousands of hours of your work and contact information. For example, if you use the "Favorites" feature in your web browser to catalog web sites, consider how long it would take for you to reconstruct this information if it were suddenly wiped out. Do you have back-up plans in case your hard drive becomes inaccessible, or if you lose your cell phone containing countless stored numbers? Use these many tools and features to help you organize and save time, but don't forget to write down or keep hard copies of very important documents and contact information.

Review Questions ....

Based on what you have learned in this chapter, write your answers to the following questions:

1. What are the five main steps of the memory process?

2. Why is intending to remember so important to enhancing memory?

3. Why does writing down information help you remember it?

4. Name one mnemonic device and how it is used to help you remember. Give an example.

5. What is the purpose of reviewing information soon and often?

OVERCOMING MEMORY LOSS

In the Classroom

Erin McAdams is outgoing, bright, and popular, but she also has a reputation for being forgetful. She forgets appointments, projects, and due dates. She is continually losing her keys and important papers. She is often late and forgets meetings and even social events. She always tells herself, "I'm just not good at remembering names" and "I really am going to try harder to get more organized and remember my commitments." She blames her bad memory for doing poorly on tests and wishes that people would just understand that she's doing the best she can. She insists that she's tried but just can't change.

1. What would you suggest to help Erin improve her memory skills?

_____

_____

2. What strategies in this chapter would be most helpful?

_____

_____

In the Workplace

Erin is now in hotel management. She loves the excitement, the diversity of the people she meets, and the daily challenges. She has recently been assigned to plan and coordinate special events, which include parties, meetings, and social affairs. This new job requires remembering many names, dates, and endless details.

3. How can Erin learn to develop her memory skills?

_____

_____

4. Suggest a program for her that would increase her memory skills.

_____

_____

REVIEW AND APPLICATIONS

CHAPTER 7

APPLYING THE ABCDE METHOD OF SELF-MANAGEMENT

In the Journal Entry on page 219, you were asked to describe a situation when you needed to learn many new names or numerous facts for a test. How did you fare? What factors helped you remember?

Learning Anatomy, Phil.

Now describe a situation in which you forgot some important information or someone's name that you really wanted to remember. Work through the ABCDE method and incorporate the new strategies you have learned in this chapter.

A = Actual event: _Had to learn terms memorize it_

B = Beliefs: _Couldn't get it done unable to think_

C = Consequences: _If Don't learn I won't pass or know them_

D = Dispute: _I Can't Continue to think this way or It will make me upset And Cause distraction_

E = Energized: _I have to learn it so think so I can really Know the body Parts. I have to schedule myself better._

Relax, take a deep breath, and visualize yourself recalling facts, keywords, dates, and information easily.

Practice Self-Management

For more examples of learning how to manage difficult situations, see the "Self-management Workbook" section of the Online Learning Center website at **www.mhhe.com/ferrett6e**.

MEMORY

A. Quickly read these lists once. Read one word at a time and in order.

1	2
the	Disney World
work	light
of	time
and	and
to	of
the	house
and	the
of	packages
light	good
of	praise
care	and
the	coffee
chair	the
and	of

B. Now cover the lists and write as many words as you can remember on the lines that follow. Then check your list against the lists in Part A.

It	
And	Disney world
the	light
work	and
and	the
the	packages
of	

(continued)

1. How many words did you remember from the beginning of the list? List them.

12, and, the, work, of, Disney world, packages, light, and, the,

2. How many words did you remember from the middle of the list? List them.

and, the, packages

3. How many words did you remember from the end of the list? List them.

one, the.

4. Did you remember the term *Disney World*?   Yes ___✓___   No _____

Most people who complete this exercise remember the first few words, the last few words, the unusual term *Disney World*, and the words that were listed more than once (*of*, *the*, and *and*). Did you find this to be true about yourself?   Yes __✓__   No __✓__

C. Remembering names

1. Do you have problems remembering names?   Yes __✓__   No _____

2. What are the benefits of remembering names now and in a career?

Become a resource for me in future.

D. What memory techniques work best for you?

Writing them down and reading them

MENTAL PICTURES

Use a clock or a study partner to time you as you look at the following pictures for a duration of two minutes. As you look at these pictures, create a mental picture. After the two minutes have passed, turn the page and make up a story using all of these elements.

CHAPTER 7 ▲ REVIEW AND APPLICATIONS

1. Write your creative story on the following lines.

The picture was filled with a blue bird. The bird was enjoying his sit on a branch. I wondered why the cell phone was there was it to make a phone call? or could the bird use the phone. I thought of briefly a trip or a boat on a sunny day. But this would only be to take money. I'm afraid of alone at sea. The house was plain but the yard was well groomed nothing seemed out of place. The kitten seemed to enjoy his day. Causing me to remember to relax.

2. What memory strategies did you use to recall the information?

_____

_____

_____

_____

_____

_____

_____

3. What connections were you able to make among the photos?

_____

_____

_____

_____

_____

_____

_____

_____

_____

APPLYING MEMORY SKILLS

Assess your memory skills by answering the following questions. Add this page to your Career Development Portfolio.

1. **Looking back:** Review an autobiography you may have written for this or another course. Indicate the ways you applied your memory skills.

   _____

   _____

2. **Taking stock:** What are your memory strengths and what do you want to improve?

   _____

   _____

3. **Looking forward:** How would you demonstrate memory skills for employers?

   _____

   _____

4. **Documentation:** Include examples, such as poems you have memorized, literary quotes, and techniques for remembering names.

   _____

   _____

5. **Assessment and demonstration:** Critical thinking skills for memory include
   - Preparing yourself mentally and physically
   - Creating a willingness to remember
   - Determining what information is important and organizing it
   - Linking new material with known information (creating associations)
   - Integrating various learning styles
   - Asking questions
   - Reviewing and practicing
   - Evaluating your progress

Assess your memory skills. Review your life to discover how you learned these various skills. How do you use your memory skills in class? How would you use memory skills at work?

_____

_____

_____

_____

_____

_____

_____

Excel at Taking Tests

CHAPTER OBJECTIVES

In this chapter, you will learn to

▲ Prepare for tests

▲ Incorporate strategies for taking tests

▲ Use test results

▲ Take different types of tests

▲ Use special tips for math and science tests

▲ Prepare for performance appraisals

▲ Overcome test anxiety

▲ Practice integrity in test taking

SELF-MANAGEMENT

I studied very hard for my last test, but my mind went blank when I tried to answer the questions. What can I do to decrease my anxiety and be more confident about taking tests?

Have you ever had a similar experience? Do you find yourself feeling anxious and worried when you take tests? Do you suffer physical symptoms, such as sweaty palms, upset stomach, headaches, or inability to sleep or concentrate? Everyone experiences some anxiety when faced with a situ-ation associated with performance or evaluation. Peak performers know that the best strategy for alleviating feelings of panic is to be prepared. In this chapter, you will learn how to decrease your anxiety and learn test-taking strategies that will help you before, during, and after the test.

JOURNAL ENTRY   In **Worksheet 8.1** on page 278, describe a time when you did well in a performance, sporting event, or test. What factors helped you be calm, be confident, and remember information?

All successful athletes and performers know how important it is to monitor and measure their techniques and vary their training programs to improve results. Taking tests is part of school; performance reviews are part of a job; and tryouts and performing are part of the life of an athlete, a dancer, or an actor. In fact, there are few jobs in life that don't require you to assess skills, attitude, and behavior. The goal of this chapter is to explore specific test-taking strategies you can use in school and on the job.

Test-Taking Strategies

Before the Test

Test taking starts long before sitting down with pencil in hand to tackle the exam. The following tips will help you as you prepare for taking a test.

1. **Start on day one.** The best way to do well on tests is to begin by preparing on the first day of class. Prepare by attending all classes, arriving on time, and staying until the end of class. Set up a review schedule on the first day. Observe your instructors during class to see what they consider important and what points and keywords they stress. As you listen to lectures or read your textbook, ask yourself what questions might be on the examination. **Peak Progress 8.1** indicates important skills that you will use as you take tests.

2. **Know expectations.** The first day of class is important because most instructors outline the course and clarify the syllabus and expectations concerning

---

PEAK PROGRESS　　　　　　　　　　　　　　　　　　**8.1**

Test-Taking Skills

The factors involved in taking tests and performing well on them are

1. Preparing yourself both mentally and physically
2. Determining what information is important
3. Processing information
4. Linking new material with known information
5. Creating associations
6. Creating a willingness to remember
7. Staying focused
8. Reasoning logically
9. Overcoming fear
10. Evaluating test results

---

grading, test dates, and types of tests. During class or office hours, ask your instructors about test formats. Ask for sample questions, a study guide, or additional material that may be helpful for studying; also ask how much weight the textbook has on tests. Some instructors cover key material in class and assign reading for a broad overview. You are in a partnership with your instructors, and it is important in any relationship to understand expectations. A large part of fear and anxiety comes from the unknown. The more you know about what is expected concerning evaluations and exams, the more at ease you will be. Use your time wisely when preparing. **Personal Evaluation Notebook 8.1** on page 254 gives you a handy guide for approaching your instructors about upcoming tests and how you are currently performing in class.

3. **Ask questions.** Ask questions in class. As you read, take notes and review chapter material. Chapter summaries, key concepts, reviews, and end-of-chapter questions and exercises all provide examples of possible test questions. Save all quizzes, course materials, exercise sheets, and lab work. Ask if old tests or sample tests are available at the library.

4. **Keep up.** Manage your time and keep up with daily reading, homework, and assignments. Consolidate your class notes with your reading notes. Avoid waiting until the night before to prepare for an exam.

5. **Review early.** Start the review process by previewing chapters before classes. Take a few minutes to review your class notes immediately after class. When information is fresh, you can fill in missing pieces, make connections, and raise questions to ask later. Set up a schedule, so that you have time to review daily notes from all your classes each day. Review time can be short; 5 or 10 minutes for every class is often sufficient. A daily review should also include scanning reading notes and items that need memorization. This kind of review should continue until the final exam.

6. **Review weekly.** Spend about an hour or so for each subject to investigate and review not only the week's assignments but also what has been included thus far in the course. These review sessions can include class notes, reading notes, chapter questions, note cards, mind maps, flash cards, a checklist of items to study, and summaries written in your own words. One of the best ways to test yourself is to close your book after reading and write a summary; then, go back and fill in missing material.

7. **Do a final review.** A week or so before a test, commit to a major review. This review should include class and book notes, note cards, and summaries. You can practice test questions, compare concepts, integrate major points, and review and recite with your study team. Long-term memory depends on organizing the information. Fragmented information is difficult to remember or recall. Understanding the main ideas and connecting and relating information transfer the material into long-term memory.

8. **Create sample tests.** One of the best tips for doing well on tests is to pretest yourself by predicting questions and creating and taking sample tests. Review and rehearse until you have learned material and you are confident. Some instructors encourage students to allocate two hours per day for three days prior to the exam.

Test Taking

This exercise involves a lot of risks, and you may be tempted to avoid it—but do the exercise! Students almost always find it to be helpful. To help you prepare for tests, do the following activities and write your findings on the lines provided.

1. Go to each of your instructors and ask how you are doing in each class.
2. Discuss your expectations and the style of test questions you can expect on their tests.
3. Ask the instructors and make note of what you can do to earn a good grade.

Course _____

_____

_____

Course _____

_____

_____

Course _____

_____

_____

Course _____

_____

_____

Course _____

_____

_____

9. **Summarize.** Pretend the instructor said that you could take one note card to the test. Choose the most important concepts, formulas, keywords, and points and condense them onto one note card. This exercise highlights important material. You will do better on a test even if you cannot use the note card during the test. The number one reason that students don't do well on tests is that they don't know the material. If you can summarize in your own words, you will understand the material versus just memorizing facts.

10. **Use your study team.** You may be tempted to skip studying one night, but you can avoid temptation if you know other people are waiting for you and depending on your contribution. Have each member of the study team provide 5 to 10 questions. Share these questions and discuss possible answers. Word the questions in different formats—multiple-choice, true/false, matching, and essay.

Then, simulate the test-taking experience by taking, giving, and correcting each other's timed sample tests.

11. **Use all available resources.** If your instructor offers a review before the exam, attend and take good notes. Get a tutor or go to the learning center for additional help.

12. **Assemble what you will need.** Pack your bag with sharpened pencils, pens, paper clips, and any other items you may need, such as a watch, calculator, or dictionary. Get a good night's sleep, eat a light breakfast, and make sure you set an alarm. You don't want to be frantic and late for a test. Arrive a few minutes early.

During the Test

The following strategies will help you as you take a test.

1. **Write down key information.** As soon as you get the test, write your name on it and jot down keywords, facts, formulas, dates, principles, ideas, concepts, statistics, and other memory cues in pencil on the back of your paper or in the margins. If you wait until you are reading each question, you may forget important material while under pressure.

2. **Read and listen to all instructions.** Many instructors require that you use a pen and write on only one side of the paper. After clarifying instructions, scan the entire test briefly and make sure you understand what is expected in each section. If you are unsure, ask your instructor immediately.

3. **Determine which questions are worth the most**. Look at the point value for each question and determine the importance that should be given to each section. For example, you will want to spend more time on an essay worth 25 points than on a multiple-choice worth 5. Review subjective or essay questions to see which you can answer quickly and which will take more time. Set a plan and pace yourself based on the amount of time you have for the test. Jot down dates, keywords, or related facts, which will serve as a rough outline and may stimulate your memory for another question.

4. **Answer objective questions.** Sometimes objective questions contain details you can use for answering essay questions. Don't panic if you don't know an answer right away. Answer the questions that are easiest for you, and mark those questions that you want go come back to later.

5. **Answer essay questions.** Answer the easiest subjective or essay questions first and spend more time on the questions with the highest value. In pencil, do a quick outline, so that your answer is organized. Look for defining words and make sure you understand what the question is asking you. For example, are you being asked to justify, illustrate, compare and contrast, or explain? Write down main ideas and then fill in details, facts, and examples. Be complete, but avoid filler sentences that add nothing.

6. **Answer remaining questions.** Unless there is a penalty for guessing, answer all questions. Rephrase questions you find difficult. It may help you change the wording of a sentence. Use memory strategies if you are blocked. Draw a picture or a diagram, use a different equation, or make a mind map and write the

"'Obvious' is the most dangerous word in mathematics."

ERIC TEMPLE BELL,
Mathematician, author

Special Strategies for Math and Science Tests

During your years of study, you will probably take math and science courses. Following are some strategies for preparing to take a math or science test.

1. **Use note cards.** Write formulas, definitions, rules, and theories on note cards and review them often. Write out examples for each theorem.

2. **Write notes.** As soon as you are given the test, jot down theorems and formulas in the margins.

3. **Survey the test.** Determine the number of questions and the worth and difficulty of each question.

4. **Answer easy to hard.** Do the easy questions first. Spend more time on questions that are worth the most points.

5. **Answer general to specific.** First, read to understand the big picture. Ask, "Why is this subject in the book? How does it connect with other topics?"

6. **Write the problem in longhand.** Translate into understandable words—for example, for $A = 1/2bh$, "For a triangle, the area is one-half the base times the height."

7. **Think.** Use critical thinking and creative problem solving. Let your mind ponder possibilities.

8. **Make an estimate.** A calculated guess will give you an approximate answer. This helps you when you double-check the answer.

9. **Illustrate the problem.** Draw a picture, diagram, or chart that will help you understand the problem—for example, "The length of a field is 6 feet more than twice its width. If the perimeter of the field is 228 feet, find the dimensions of the field."

topic and subtopics. Use association to remember items that are related. (Refer back to Chapter 7 for memory skills.)

7. **Review.** Once you have finished, reread the test carefully and check for mistakes or spelling errors. Stay the entire time, answer extra-credit and bonus questions, and fill in details and make any changes necessary. (See **Peak Progress 8.2** for specific strategies for math and science texts.)

After the Test

The test isn't over when you hand it in. Successful test taking includes how you use the results.

1. **Reward yourself.** Reward yourself with a treat, such as a hot bath, a walk, an evening with friends, or a special dinner. Always reward yourself with a good night's sleep.

2. **Analyze and assess.** When you receive the graded test, analyze and assess the grade and your performance for many things, such as the following:

Special Strategies for Math and Science Tests *(continued)*

Let l = the length of the field.

Let w = the width of the field.

Then $l = 6 + 2w$

So $6w + 12 = 228$

$6w + 12 = 228$

$6w = 216$

$w = 36$

So $l = 6 + 2w = 6 + 2(36) = 78$

Translating: The width of the field is 36 ft. and its length is 78 ft.

Checking: The perimeter is $2w + 2l = 2(36) + 2(78) = 72 + 156 = 228$.

10. **Ask yourself questions.** Ask, "What is being asked? What do I already know? What are the givens? What do I need to find out? How does this connect and relate with other concepts? What is the point of the question?" Analyze and examine the problem.

11. **Show your work.** If you get stuck, try to retrace your steps.

12. **Do a similar problem.** If you get stuck, try something similar. Which formula worked? How does this formula relate to others?

13. **State answers in the simplest terms.** For example, 4/6 instead should be answered as 2/3.

14. **Pay attention to the sign.** Note if a number is actually a negative number.

15. **Be logical.** Break down the problem step by step. Look for proof of your answer.

16. **Check your work.** Does your answer make sense? Is your work correct and systematic?

17. **Review.** Review your test as soon as you get it back. Where did you make your mistakes? Did you read the problems correctly? Did you use the correct formulas? What will you do differently next time?

◆ *Confirm your grade.* Confirm that your score was calculated or graded correctly. If you believe there has been a mistake in your grade, see your instructor immediately and ask to review it.

◆ *Determine common types of mistakes.* Were your mistakes due to carelessness in reading the instructions or in lack of preparedness on certain topics? **Peak Progress 8.3** on page 259 includes a number of common themes regarding incorrect answers on tests. Do you find that there are patterns in your mistakes? If so, determine what you need to do to correct those patterns.

◆ *Learn what to do differently next time.* Your test will provide valuable feedback, and you can learn from the experience. Be a detached, curious, receptive observer and view the results as feedback. Feedback is essential for

WORDS TO SUCCEED

"We learn more by looking for the answer to a question and not finding it than we do from learning the answer itself."

LLOYD ALEXANDER, *Author*

improvement. Use the results of the test for self-assessment for future tests. Ask yourself the following questions:

1. Did my study strategy work?
2. Did I read the test before I started?
3. What were my strengths? What did I do right?
4. What questions did I miss?
5. Did I miss clues in the test? Did I ask the instructor for clarification?
6. How well did I know the content on which I was being tested?
7. What should I have studied more?
8. Did I anticipate the style and format of the questions?
9. What didn't I expect?
10. Did I have trouble with certain types of questions?
11. How was my recall?
12. Did I practice the right kind of thinking?
13. Did I test myself with the right questions?
14. Did I handle test anxiety well?
15. Would it have helped if I had studied with others?
16. What changes will I make in studying for the next test?

3. **Review with your instructor.** If you honestly don't know why you received the grade you did, ask your instructor to review your answers with you. Approach the meeting with a positive attitude, not a defensive one. Ask for clarification and explain your rationale for answers. Ask for advice on preparing for the next test.

4. **Review the test with your study team.** Review your test with your study team and compare notes. This will help you see common errors and the criteria for effective answers. Make note of how you will be able to study more effectively and answer questions better on the next test.

Remember, a test is information and feedback on how you are doing, not an evaluation of you as a person. You cannot change unless you can understand your mistakes. Learn from your mistakes and move forward. Assess what you did wrong and what you will do right the next time.

Taking Different Types of Tests

The following tips will help you as you take different types of tests.

Objective Tests

True/False Test

1. **Listen and read carefully.** Read the entire question carefully before you answer it. For the question to be true, the *entire* question must be true. If any part of the statement is false, the entire statement is false.

Checklist for Incorrect Test Answers

Following are some of the most common reasons for incorrect answers on tests. As you review your test results, see if you seem to have recurring problems in any of the following areas. Make a point to improve and prepare yourself better with these in mind.

- I did not read and/or follow the directions.
- I misread or misunderstood the question.
- I did not demonstrate reasoning ability.
- I did not demonstrate factual accuracy.
- I did not demonstrate good organization.
- My answer was incomplete.
- My answer lacked clarity.
- My handwriting was hard to read.
- I used time ineffectively.
- I did not prepare enough.
- I studied the wrong information.
- I knew the information but couldn't apply it to the questions.
- I confused facts or concepts.
- The information was not in my lecture notes.
- The information was not in the textbook.

2. **Pay attention to details.** Read dates, names, and places carefully. Sometimes the numbers in the dates are changed around (1494 instead of 1449) or the wording is changed slightly. Any such changes can change the meaning.

3. **Watch for qualifiers.** Watch for such words as *always, all, never,* and *every.* The question is often false because there are exceptions. If you can think of one exception, then the statement is false. Ask yourself, "Does this statement overstate or understate what I know to be true?"

4. **Watch for faulty cause and effect.** Two true statements may be connected by a word that implies cause and effect, and this word may make the statement false—for example, "Temperature is measured on the centigrade scale because water freezes at zero degrees centigrade."

5. **Always answer every question.** Unless there is a penalty for wrong answers, answer every question. You have a 50 percent chance of being right.

6. **Trust your instincts.** Often, your first impression is correct. Don't change an answer unless you are certain it is wrong. Don't spend time pondering until you have finished the entire test and have time to spare.

1. **Read the question carefully.** Are you being asked for the correct answer or the best choice? Is there more than one answer? Preview the test to see if an answer may be included in a statement or question.

2. **Rephrase the question.** Sometimes it helps to rephrase the question in your own words. You may also want to answer the question yourself before looking at the possible answers.

3. **Cover the potential answers.** Cover the answers (called "distractors") as you read the question and see what answer first comes to you. Then, look at the answers to see if your answer is one of the choices.

4. **Eliminate choices.** Narrow your choices by reading through all of them and eliminating those that you know are incorrect, so that you can concentrate on real choices.

5. **Go from easy to difficult.** Go through the test and complete the questions for which you know the answers. This will give you a feeling of confidence. Don't spend all your time on a few questions. With a pencil, mark the questions that you are unsure of, but make certain that you mark your final answer clearly, so that you do not leave unclear marks.

6. **Watch for combinations.** Read the question carefully and don't just choose what appears to be the one correct answer. Some questions offer a combination of choices, such as "all of the above" or "none of the above."

7. **Look at sentence structure.** Make sure the grammatical structure of the question matches that of your choice.

8. **Use critical thinking.** Make sure you have a good reason for changing an answer. Use critical thinking and clearly know you are choosing the right answer. If not, your first impulse may be right.

Matching Test

1. **Read carefully.** Read both lists quickly and watch for clues.

2. **Eliminate.** As you match the items you know, cross them out unless the directions mention that an item can be used more than once. Elimination is the key in a matching test.

3. **Look at sentence structure.** Often, verbs are matched to verbs. Read the entire sentence. Does it make sense?

Fill-In-The-Blank Test

1. **Watch for clues.** If the word before the blank is *an*, the word in the blank generally begins with a vowel. If the word before the blank is *a*, the word in the blank generally begins with a consonant.

2. **Count the number of blanks.** The number of blanks often indicates the number of words in an answer. Think of key words that were stressed in class.

3. **Watch for the length of the blank.** A longer blank may indicate a longer answer.

4. **Answer the questions you know first.** As with all tests, answer the questions you know first and then go back to those that are more difficult. Rephrase and look for key words.

5. **Answer all questions.** Try never to leave a question unanswered.

Open-Book Test

The key to an open-book test is to prepare. Students often think that open-book tests will be easy, so they don't study. Generally, these tests go beyond basic recall and require critical thinking and analysis. Put markers in your book to indicate important areas. Write formulas, definitions, keywords, sample questions, and main points on note cards. Bring along your detailed study sheet. The key is to be able to find information quickly. Use your own words to summarize. Don't copy from your textbook.

The Essay Test

Being prepared is essential when taking an essay test. Make certain that you understand concepts and relationships, not just specific facts. (See **Peak Progress 8.4** on page 262 for a sample essay test.) In addition, use the following strategies to help you take an essay test.

1. **Organize.** Organizing your notes and reading material will help you outline important topics.

2. **Outline.** An outline will provide a framework to help you remember dates, main points, names, places, and supporting material. Use **Personal Evaluation Notebook 8.2** on page 264 to practice outlining keywords and topics.

3. **Budget your writing time.** Look over the whole test, noticing which questions are easiest. Allot a certain amount of time for each essay question and include time for review when you're finished.

4. **Read the question carefully.** Make certain you understand what is being asked in the question. Respond to keywords such as *explain, classify, define,* and *compare.* Rephrase the question into a main thesis. Always answer what is being asked directly. Don't skirt around an issue. If you are being asked to compare and contrast, do not describe, or you will not answer the question correctly. **Peak Progress 8.5** on page 265 lists a number of key words used in essay questions.

5. **Organize the material.** Organize your main points in an outline, so that you won't leave out important information.

6. **Write concisely and correctly.** Get directly to the point and use short, clear sentences. Remember that your instructor may be grading a pile of other students' tests, so get to the point and avoid using filler sentences.

7. **Write neatly.** Appearance and legibility are important. Use an erasable pen. Use wide margins and don't crowd your words. Write on one side of the paper only. Leave space between answers, so that you can add to an answer if time permits.

Sample Essay Test

Steve Hackett

Intro to Economics Quiz

January 12, 2007

Question

Describe the general circumstances under which economists argue that government intervention in a market economy enhances efficiency.

Thesis Statement

Well-functioning competitive markets are efficient resource allocators, but they can fail in certain circumstances. Government intervention can generate its own inefficiencies, so economists promote the forms of government intervention that enhance efficiency under conditions of market failure.

Outline

I. Well-functioning competitive markets are efficient.

    A. Firms have incentive to minimize costs and waste.

    B. Price approximates costs of production.

    C. Effort, quality, and successful innovation are rewarded.

    D. Shortages and surpluses are eliminated by price adjustment.

II. Markets fail to allocate scarce resources efficiently under some circumstances.

    A. Externalities affect other people.

        1. Negative externalities, such as pollution

        2. Positive externalities and collectively consumed goods

    B. Lack of adequate information causes failure.

    C. Firms with market power subvert the competition.

III. Government intervention can create its own inefficiencies.

    A. Rigid, bureaucratic rules can stifle innovative solutions and dilute incentives.

    B. Politically powerful groups can subvert the process.

IV. Efficient intervention policy balances market and government inefficiencies.

8. **Focus on main points.** Your opening sentence should state your thesis, followed by supporting information.

9. **Answer completely.** Make certain that the question is answered completely, with supporting documentation. Cover the main points thoroughly and logically.

10. **Use all the available time.** Don't hurry. Pace yourself and always use all the available time for review, revisions, reflection, additions, and corrections. Proofread carefully. Answer all questions unless otherwise directed.

Sample Essay Test (continued)

Well-functioning competitive markets allocate resources efficiently in the context of scarcity. They do so in several different ways. First, in market systems, firms are profit maximizers and thus have an incentive to minimize their private costs of production. In contrast, those who manage government agencies lack the profit motive and thus the financial incentive to minimize costs. Second, under competitive market conditions, the market price is bid down by rival firms to reflect their unit production costs. Thus, for the last unit sold, the value (price) to the consumer is equal to the cost to produce that unit, meaning that neither too much nor too little is produced. Third, firms and individuals have an incentive to work hard to produce new products and services preferred by consumers because, if successful, these innovators will gain an advantage over their rivals in the marketplace. Fourth, competitive markets react to surpluses with lower prices and to shortages with higher prices, which work to resolve these imbalances.

Markets can fail to allocate scarce resources efficiently in several different situations. First, profit-maximizing firms have an incentive to emit negative externalities (uncompensated harms generated by market activity that fall on others), such as pollution, when doing so lowers their production costs and is not prevented by law. Individual firms also have an incentive not to provide positive externalities (unpaid-for benefits) that benefit the group, such as police patrol, fire protection, public parks, and roads. A second source of market failure is incomplete information regarding product safety, quality, and workplace safety. A third type of market failure occurs when competition is subverted by a small number of firms that can manipulate prices, such as monopolies and cartels.

Government intervention can take various forms, including regulatory constraints, information provision, and direct government provision of goods and services. Government intervention may also be subject to inefficiencies. Examples include rigid regulations that stifle the incentive for innovation, onerous compliance costs imposed on firms, political subversion of the regulatory process by powerful interest groups, and lack of cost-minimizing incentives on the part of government agencies. Thus, efficient government intervention can be said to occur when markets fail in a substantial way and when the particular intervention policy generates inefficiencies that do not exceed those associated with the market failure.

Last-Minute Study Tips

Cramming is not effective if you haven't studied or attended classes. You might ask yourself, however, "What is the best use of my time the night before the test?" or "What can I do right now in just a few minutes to prepare for a test?"

◆ *Focus on a few points.* Decide what is important. Focus on a few of the most important points or formulas, instead of trying to cram everything into a short study time. Preview each chapter quickly.

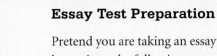

Essay Test Preparation

Pretend you are taking an essay test on a personal topic—your life history. Your instructor has written the following essay question on the board:

> *Write a brief essay on your progress through life so far, covering the highs and lows, major triumphs, and challenges.*

Before you begin writing, remind yourself of the topics you want to cover in this essay. What keywords, phrases, events, and dates would you jot down in the margin of your essay paper? List your thoughts on the lines provided.

_____

_____

_____

_____

_____

_____

_____

_____

_____

_____

_____

_____

_____

_____

_____

_____

_____

_____

_____

_____

Important Words in Essay Questions

The following words are used frequently in essay questions. Read them and become comfortable with their meanings.

Analyze   Explain the key points, parts, or process and examine each part.

Apply   Show the concept or function in a specific context.

Compare   Show similarities between concepts, objects, or events.

Contrast   Show differences between concepts, objects, or events.

Critique   Present your view or evaluation and give supporting evidence.

Define   Give concise, clear meanings and definitions.

Demonstrate   Show function or how something works; show understanding either physically or through words.

Describe   Present major characteristics or a detailed account.

Differentiate   Distinguish between two or more concepts or characteristics.

Discuss   Give a general presentation of the issue with examples or details to support main points.

Enumerate   Present the items in a numbered list or an outline.

Evaluate   Carefully appraise the problem, citing authorities.

Explain   Make an idea or concept clear, or give a reason for an event.

Identify   Label or explain.

Illustrate   Clarify by presenting examples.

Interpret   Explain the meaning of a concept or problem.

Justify   Give reasons for conclusions or argue in support of a position.

List   Enumerate or write a list of points, one by one.

Outline   Organize main points and subordinate supporting points in a logical arrangement.

Prove   Give factual evidence and logical reasons that something is true.

Summarize   Present core ideas in a brief review that includes conclusions.

◆ *Intend to be positive.* Don't panic or waste precious time being negative. State your intention of being receptive and open, gaining an overview of the material, and learning a few supporting points.

◆ *Use critical thinking.* What are the keywords and keypoints? Think logically.

◆ *Get a tutor or study partner.* Focus on main points and summarize. Do practice problems and tests. Several hours of intense study with a tutor can be far more effective than several late nights studying by yourself.

◆ *Focus on keywords.* Write on note cards formulas, keywords, dates, definitions, and important points.

- *Review your note cards.* In just a few minutes, you can review important points. Keep it simple, review quickly, and review often. Use flash cards or mind maps and review again in short segments. Carry your note cards with you.
- *Affirm your memory.* The mind is capable of learning and memorizing material in just a short time if you focus, concentrate, and apply it. Look for connections.

Preparing for a Performance Appraisal

WORDS TO SUCCEED

"It's not whether you get knocked down, it's whether you get up."

VINCE LOMBARDI, *Professional Football Coach*

Taking tests or being evaluated is part of life. If you are employed, at sometime you will probably receive a performance appraisal. For many people, performance appraisals create anxiety similar to test or public speaking anxiety. A performance appraisal can be a valuable tool to let you know how your employer perceives the quality of your work, your work ethic, and your future opportunities. It also gives you the opportunity to ask similar questions of your manager or reviewer. The following questions will help you focus on getting the most out of your performance appraisal. Also, complete **Personal Evaluation Notebook 8.3** on page 267 to review your first performance appraisal experience.

- Review your job description, including the duties you perform. What is expected of you in your job? What additional duties do you perform that are not listed?
- How do you view your job and the working climate?
- List your goals and objectives and the results achieved.
- What documentation do you have that demonstrates your results and achievements?
- What areas do you see as opportunities for improvement?
- What are your strengths and how can you maximize them?
- What are your general concerns?
- What are your advancement possibilities?
- What additional training would be helpful for you?
- What new skills could assist in your advancement?
- How can you increase your problem-solving skills?
- How can you make more creative and sound decisions?
- What can you do to prepare yourself for stressful projects and deadlines?
- Give examples of how you have contributed to the company's profits.
- What relationships could you develop to help you achieve results?
- Do you work well with other people?
- What project would be rewarding and challenging this year?
- What resources do you need to complete this project?
- Do you have open and effective communication with your supervisor and co-workers?
- How does your assessment of your work compare with your supervisor's assessment?

Performance Appraisals

Answer the following questions about your first performance appraisal.

1. Describe your first performance appraisal. Explain how you felt.

   _____

   _____

   _____

   _____

   _____

2. How did you prepare for your first performance appraisal?

   _____

   _____

   _____

   _____

3. Were you motivated by the feedback you heard? Did you become defensive after hearing criticism?

   _____

   _____

   _____

   _____

4. What would you do differently?

   _____

   _____

   _____

   _____

Overcome Obstacles

Some students see tests and performance assessments as huge mountains—one slip can cause them to tumble down the slope. Even capable students find that certain tests undermine their confidence. For example, even the thought of taking a math or science test causes some people to feel anxious, and it sends others into a state of panic. A peak performer learns how to manage anxiety and knows that being prepared is the road to test-taking success.

Test Anxiety

Test anxiety is a learned response to stress. The symptoms of test anxiety include nervousness, upset stomach, sweaty palms, and forgetfulness. Being prepared is the best way to reduce anxiety. You will be prepared if you have attended every class; previewed chapters; reviewed your notes; and written, summarized, and studied the material each day. Studying with others is a great way to rehearse test questions, summarize, and help each other learn through group interaction. Since exams, tests, quizzes, tryouts, presentations, interviews, and performance appraisals are all evaluations and part of life, it is worth the time to learn to overcome test anxiety.

The attitude you bring to a test has a lot to do with your performance. Approach tests with a positive attitude. Tests provide a chance to learn to face fear and transform it into positive energy. Tests are opportunities to show what you have mastered in a course.

Following are more suggestions that might help:

1. **Dispute negative thoughts and conversations.** Some people have negative or faulty assumptions about their abilities, especially in courses such as math and science, and may think, "I just don't have a logical mind." Replace negative self-talk with affirmations, such as "I am well prepared and will do well on this test" or "I can excel in this subject." Talk to yourself in positive and encouraging ways. Practice being your own best friend! Also avoid negative conversations that make you feel anxious—for example, if someone mentions the length of time he or she has studied.

2. **Rehearse.** Athletes, actors, musicians, and dancers practice and rehearse for hours. When performers are on stage, their anxiety is channeled into focused energy. Practice taking sample tests with your study team, and you should be more confident during the actual test.

3. **Get regular exercise.** Aerobic exercise and yoga reduce stress and tension and promote deeper and more restful sleep. Build regular exercise into your life and work out the day before a test, if possible.

4. **Eat breakfast.** Eat a light, balanced breakfast that includes protein, such as cheese or yogurt. Keep a piece of fruit or nuts and bottled water in your backpack for energy. Limit your caffeine intake, as too much can make you more nervous or agitated.

5. **Use visualization.** The power of your mind can create images of success. See yourself taking the test and doing well. Imagine being calm and focused. Before you jump out of bed, relax, breathe deeply, and visualize your day unfolding in a positive way.

6. **Stay calm.** Make your test day peaceful by laying out your clothes, books, supplies, pens, and keys the night before. Review your note cards just before you go to sleep, repeat a few affirmations, and then get a good night's rest. Last-minute,

Keeping Calm
Test anxiety can cause some people to feel overwhelmed and even panicked. *How can you reduce the feeling of anxiety before you take a test?*

WORDS TO SUCCEED

"All of us have moments in our lives that test our courage. Taking children into a house with a white carpet is one of them."

ERMA BOMBECK, *Author*

frantic cramming only creates a hectic climate and increases anxiety. Set an alarm, so that you'll be awake in plenty of time.

7. **Get to class early.** Get to class early enough that you are not rushed and can use the few minutes before the test to take a few deep breaths and review your note cards. Deep breathing and affirmations, along with visualization, can help you relax. While waiting for other students to arrive, the instructor will sometimes answer questions or explain material to students who are in class ahead of schedule.

8. **Focus.** When your attention wanders, bring it gently back. Stay in the present moment by focusing your attention on the task at hand. Focus on each question. Concentrate on answering the questions and you won't have room in your mind for worry.

9. **Keep a sense of perspective.** Don't exaggerate the importance of tests. Tests do not measure self-esteem, personal qualities, character, or ability to contribute to society. Even if the worse happens and you don't do well on one test, it is not the end of your college career. You can meet with the instructor to discuss options and possibly do additional work, take the test again, or take the class again if necessary. Keep fears in proper perspective.

10. **Get help.** If you are experiencing severe anxiety that prevents you from taking tests or performing well, seek professional help from the learning center or see a counselor at your school. Services often include support groups, relaxation training, biofeedback, and other useful techniques that can help you reduce anxiety and fear.

Reflect and use critical thinking to describe your test anxiety experiences in **Personal Evaluation Notebook 8.4** on page 270. **Peak Progress 8.6** on page 271 explores how you can apply the Adult Learning Cycle to improve your test-taking skills and reduce anxiety.

Cheating

A central theme throughout this book is that character matters. When you practice honesty during test taking, you demonstrate to your instructor, your classmates, and, most important, to yourself that you are a person of integrity and are trustworthy. Even if you haven't prepared as sufficiently for an exam as you should, there is no excuse for cheating. There is a high cost to cheating, even if you don't get caught. Cheating only hurts you because it

Cheating Only Hurts You

There is never an excuse to cheat. *If this student is caught cheating, what are some of the repercussions he could face?*

◆ **Violates your integrity.** You begin to see yourself as a person without integrity; if you compromise your integrity once, you're more likely to do it again.

◆ **Erodes confidence.** Cheating weighs on your conscience and sends you the message that you don't have what it takes to succeed. Your confidence and self-esteem suffer.

Test Anxiety

Use your critical thinking skills to answer the following questions.

1. Describe your test anxiety. Describe your emotions and thoughts associated with taking all types of tests.

   _____

   _____

   _____

   _____

2. a. Do you have different feelings about nonacademic tests, such as a driving test or a vision test, than academic tests, such as quizzes and exams?

   _____

   _____

   _____

   _____

   b. What do you think is the source of these differences?

   _____

   _____

   _____

   _____

3. a. What are your memories about your best and worst test-taking experiences?

   _____

   _____

   _____

   _____

   b. What factors contributed to your ease or discomfort during these tests?

   _____

   _____

   _____

   _____

Applying the Adult Learning Cycle to Improve Your Test-Taking Skills and Reduce Test Anxiety

1. **RELATE. Why do I want to learn this?** I need to reduce my test anxiety and I want to do better on tests. Knowing how to control my anxiety will help me not only when taking tests but also in other performance situations. Do I already apply specific test-taking strategies or habits? What are some of my bad habits, such as last-minute cramming, which I should work to change?

2. **OBSERVE. How does this work?** Who does well on tests, and does that person seem confident when taking tests? What strategies can I learn from that person? Who seems to be just the opposite—does poorly on tests or seems to be full of anxiety? Can I determine what that person is doing wrong? I can learn from those mistakes. I'll try using new techniques and strategies for test taking and observe how I'm improving.

3. **REFLECT. What does this mean?** What strategies are working for me? Have I broken any bad habits, and am I more confident going into tests? Has my performance improved?

4. **DO. What can I do with this?** I will map out a plan before each major test, determining what I need to accomplish in order to be prepared and confident going in. I won't wait until the last minute to prepare. Each day, I can practice reducing my anxiety in many different stressful situations.

5. **TEACH. Whom can I share this with?** I'll talk with others and share what's working for me. Talking through my effective strategies reinforces their purpose.

Now return to Stage 1 and think about how it feels to learn this valuable new skill. Remember to congratulate and reward yourself when you achieve positive results.

♦ **Creates academic problems.** Advanced courses depend on your learning from earlier courses, and cheating only creates future academic problems. You are paying a lot of money not to learn essential information.

♦ **Increases stress.** You have enough stress in your life without adding the intense pressure of worrying about being caught.

♦ **Brings high risks.** The consequences of cheating and plagiarism can result in failing the class, being suspended for the semester, or even being expelled from school permanently. Cheating can mess up your life for a very long time. It is humiliating, stressful, and completely avoidable.

There is never a legitimate reason to cheat. Focus on being prepared, using all the resources available to help you succeed, and practicing all the strategies offered in this book to become a peak performer.

In summary, in this chapter, I learned to:

- *Prepare for test taking.* The time before a test is critical. I must prepare early for tests, starting from the first day of class. I keep up with the daily reading and ask questions in class and while I read. I review early and often, previewing the chapter before class and reviewing the materials again after class. I save and review all tests, exercises, and notes and review them weekly. I rehearse by taking a pretest, and I predict questions by reviewing the text's chapter objectives and summaries. I summarize the chapter in my own words, either in writing or out loud, double-checking that I've covered key points. I recite my summary to my study team and listen to theirs. We compare notes and test each other.

- *Take a test effectively.* Arriving early helps me be calm and focused on doing well on the test. I get organized by reviewing key concepts and facts. I focus on neatness and getting to the point with short, clear responses. I read all the instructions, scanning the entire test briefly and writing formulas and notes in the margins. I pace myself by answering the easiest questions first, and I rephrase questions that I find difficult and look for associations to remember items. At the end, I review to make certain I've answered what was asked and check for mistakes or spelling errors. I stay the entire time that is available.

- *Follow up a test.* I should reward myself for successfully completing the test. Then I will analyze and assess how I did on the test. Did I prepare enough? Did I anticipate questions? What can I do differently for the next test? I'll use creative problem solving to explore ways to do better on future tests.

- *Be successful on different kinds of tests.* Objective tests include true/false, multiple-choice, matching, fill-in-the-blank, and open-book. I must read the question carefully, watch for clues, and look at sentence structure. Essay tests focus on my understanding of concepts and relationships. I outline my response, organize and focus on the main points, and take my time to deliver a thorough, neat, well-thought-out answer.

- *Incorporate last-minute study tips.* I know it's not smart to wait until the last minute, but a few important things I can do include focusing on a few key points and keywords, reviewing note cards, looking for connections to memorize, and not wasting time panicking—I must stay focused!

- *Prepare for a performance appraisal.* I will make the most of my performance appraisal by thinking critically about my job description and duties, as well as my goals, objectives, and results. I will focus on opportunities to advance my knowledge and skills, and I will avoid the anxiety that comes with the appraisal process.

- *Overcome test anxiety.* A positive attitude is key to alleviating anxiety before and during a test. I should prepare as much as possible and avoid last-minute cramming, practice taking a sample test, get to class early and stay calm, listen carefully to instructions, and preview the whole test and jot down notes.

- *Practice honesty and integrity when taking tests.* I know that cheating on exams only hurts me, as it lowers my self-esteem and others' opinions of me. Cheating also has long-term repercussions, including possible expulsion from school. There is never an excuse for cheating.

Carlos Fuentes

PHYSICAL THERAPIST

Related Majors: Physical Therapy, Biology

Tests in the Workplace

Carlos Fuentes is a physical therapist. A physical therapist works closely with physicians to help patients restore function and improve mobility after an injury or illness. Their work often relieves pain and prevents or limits physical disabilities.

When working with new patients, Carlos first asks questions and examines the patients' medical records, then performs tests to measure such items as strength, range of motion, balance and coordination, muscle performance, and motor function. After assessing a patient's abilities and needs, Carlos implements a treatment plan that may include exercise, traction, massage, electrical stimulation, and hot packs or cold compresses. As treatment continues, Carlos documents the patient's progress and modifies the treatment plan.

Carlos is self-motivated and an independent worker. He has a strong interest in physiology and sports, and he enjoys working with people. He likes a job that keeps him active and on his feet. Carlos spends much of his day helping patients become mobile. He often demonstrates an exercise for his patients while instructing them how to do it correctly. His job sometimes requires him to move heavy equipment or lift patients. Because Carlos is pursuing a master's degree in physical therapy, he works only three days a week.

Although he is not required to take tests as part of his job, Carlos does undergo an annual performance appraisal with his supervisor. After eight years of service, Carlos is familiar with the types of questions his supervisor might ask and keeps those in mind as he does his job throughout the year.

CRITICAL THINKING How might understanding test-taking skills help Carlos work more effectively with his patients? How would test taking skills help him prepare more effectively for performance appraisals?

Peak Performer Profile

Ellen Ochoa

When astronaut Ellen Ochoa was growing up in La Mesa, California, in the 1960s and early 1970s, it was an era of space exploration firsts: the first walk in space, the first man on the moon, the first space station. Even so, it would have been difficult for her to imagine that one day she would be the first Hispanic woman in space, since women were excluded from becoming astronauts.

By the time Ochoa entered graduate school in the 1980s, however, the sky was the limit. Having studied physics at San Diego State University, she attended Stanford and earned her Ph.D. in electrical engineering. In 1985, she and 2,000 other potential astronauts applied for admission to the National Aeronautics and Space Administration (NASA) space program. Five years later, Ochoa, 18 men, and 5 other women made the cut. The training program at the Johnson Space Center in Houston, Texas, is a rigorous mix of brain and brawn. Ochoa tackled subjects such as geology, oceanography, meteorology, astronomy, aerodynamics, and medicine. In 1991, Ochoa officially became an astronaut and was designated a mission specialist. On her first mission in 1993, Ochoa carried a pin that read "Science Is Women's Work."

From 1993 to 1999, Ochoa logged in three space shuttle missions, or about 720 hours in space. Her first and second missions focused on studying the sun and its impact on the earth's atmosphere. Her third mission involved the first docking of the shuttle *Discovery* on the International Space Station.

Between shuttle flights, Ochoa enjoys talking to young people. Aware of her influence as a woman and a Hispanic, her message is that "education is what allows you to stand out"—and become a peak performer.

PERFORMANCE THINKING Ochoa had to excel in many difficult academic courses in order to realize her dream of becoming an astronaut. What are some important personal characteristics that helped her reach the top? What are some specific testing strategies she may have used to get through her coursework as well as to prove she had the "right stuff"?

CHECK IT OUT Ochoa is among a number of space pioneers profiled by NASA at **www.nasa.gov.** This site includes a wealth of media downloads, news articles, and activities for young and old space adventurers. Also visit the "Work for NASA" section, which describes the types of internships, cooperative programs, and positions available. According to fellow astronaut Sally Ride, the "most important steps" she followed to becoming an astronaut started with studying math and science in school.

Performance Strategies . . . .

Following are the top 10 strategies for successful test taking:

- ◆ Prepare early.
- ◆ Clarify expectations.
- ◆ Observe and question.
- ◆ Review.
- ◆ Rehearse by pretesting yourself.
- ◆ Use your study team.
- ◆ Organize yourself.
- ◆ Move through the test quickly.
- ◆ Reread, recheck, rethink, and reward.
- ◆ Analyze, assess, and reprogram.

Tech for Success . . . .

Take advantage of the text's website at **www.mhhe.com/ ferrett6e** for additional study aids, useful forms, and convenient and applicable resources.

- • **On-line tutors**. A number of companies and groups provide on-line tutors and live tutorial services. Your school or public library may also offer access to this kind of service. Often, these are paid services, and you may find the assistance beneficial. However, you may be able to get limited assistance for free through a professional organization or related site. Ask your librarian for advice and explain how much assistance you think you need and in what content areas.

- • **Your resources**. Many of your textbooks have accompanying web sites that provide study materials, such as on-line study guides, animated flash cards, and possible essay questions. Often, this material is free when you purchase a new text. Take advantage of these resources to test your understanding of the information prior to taking the real test.

Review Questions . . . .

Based on what you have learned in this chapter, write your answers to the following questions:

1. Describe five strategies for preparing for a test.

2. Why is it important to pace yourself while taking a test?

3. What should you do after taking a test?

4. Describe three strategies for taking math and science tests.

5. Describe three ways in which cheating hurts you.

COPING WITH ANXIETY

In the Classroom

Sharon Oshinowa is a bright, hardworking student. She studies long hours, attends all her classes, and participates in class discussions. Sharon is very creative and especially enjoys her computer graphics course. When it comes to taking tests, however, she panics. She stays up late, cramming; tells herself that she might fail; and gets headaches and stomach pains. Her mind goes blank when she takes the test, and she has trouble organizing her thoughts. Sharon could get much better grades and enjoy school more if she could reduce her stress and apply some test-taking strategies.

1. What techniques from this chapter would be most useful to Sharon?

   _____

   _____

   _____

   _____

2. What one habit could she adopt that would empower her to be more successful?

   _____

   _____

   _____

In the Workplace

Sharon now works as a graphic designer for a large company. She likes having control over her work and is an excellent employee. She is dedicated, competent, and willing to learn new skills. There is a great deal of pressure in her job to meet deadlines, learn new techniques, and compete with other firms. She handles most of these responsibilities well unless she is being evaluated. Despite her proficiency, Sharon panics before her performance appraisals. She feels pressure to perform perfectly and does not take criticism or even advice well.

3. What strategies in this chapter would be most helpful to Sharon?

   _____

   _____

   _____

4. What would you suggest she do to control her performance anxiety?

   _____

   _____

   _____

REVIEW AND APPLICATIONS

CHAPTER 8

APPLYING THE ABCDE METHOD OF SELF-MANAGEMENT

In the Journal Entry box on page 251, you were asked to describe a time when you did well in a performance, sporting event, or test. Write about that and indicate the factors that helped you be calm, confident, and focused.

_____

_____

_____

_____

Now consider a situation in which your mind went blank or you suffered anxiety. Apply the ABCDE method to visualize a result in which you are again calm, confident, and focused.

A = Actual event:

B = Beliefs:

C = Consequences:

D = Dispute:

E = Energized:

Practice deep breathing with your eyes closed for just one minute. See yourself calm, centered, and relaxed as you take a test or give a performance. See yourself recalling information easily. You feel confident about yourself because you have learned to control your anxiety. You are well prepared and you know how to take tests.

Practice Self-Management

For more examples of learning how to manage difficult situations, see the "Self-Management Workbook" section of the Online Learning Center web site at **www.mnhe.com/ferrett6e.**

EXAM SCHEDULE

Fill in the following chart to remind you of your exams as they occur throughout the semester or term.

Course	Date	Time	Room	Type of Exam
Student Success 101	November 7	2:15 P.M.	1012A	Essay

PREPARING FOR TESTS AND EXAMS

Before you take a quiz, a test, or an exam, fill in this form to help you plan your study strategy. Certain items will be more applicable, depending on the type of test.

Course _____

Date of test _____   Test number (if any) _____

◆ Pretest(s)   Date given _____   Results _____

             Date given _____   Results _____

             Date given _____   Results _____

◆ Present grade in course _____

◆ Met with instructor   Yes _____   No _____   Date(s) of meeting(s) _____

◆ Study team members   Date(s) of meeting(s) _____

    Name _____   Phone number _____

    Name _____   Phone number _____

    Name _____   Phone number _____

    Name _____   Phone number _____

◆ Expected test format (Circle. There can be more than one test format.)

    Essay   True/false   Multiple-choice   Fill-in-the-blank

    Other _____

◆ Importance (circle one)

    Quiz   Midterm   Final exam   Other

◆ Chapters covered in the test _____

    Date for chapter review _____

◆ Chapter notes (use additional paper)

_____

_____

_____

◆ Date for review of chapter notes _____

◆ Note cards Yes _____   No _____   Date note cards reviewed _____

◆ List of keywords

    Word _____   Meaning _____

    Word _____   Meaning _____

    Word _____   Meaning _____

    Word _____   Meaning _____

◆ Possible essay questions:

1. Question _____

Thesis statement _____

Outline _____

   I. _____

      A. _____

      B. _____

      C. _____

      D. _____

  II. _____

      A. _____

      B. _____

      C. _____

      D. _____

◆ Main points

_____

_____

◆ Examples

_____

_____

2. Question _____

Thesis statement _____

Outline _____

   I. _____

      A. _____

      B. _____

      C. _____

      D. _____

  II. _____

      A. _____

      B. _____

      C. _____

      D. _____

◆ Main points

_____

_____

◆ Examples

_____

_____

REVIEW AND APPLICATIONS

CHAPTER 8

PERFORMANCE APPRAISALS

The following are qualities and competencies that are included in many performance appraisals.

Acceptance of diversity*	Safety practices
Effectiveness in working with others	Personal growth and development
Quality of work	Workplace security
Quantity of work	Technology
Positive attitude	Willingness to learn

*Diversity: Getting along with people from diverse backgrounds and cultures

1. Using this page and a separate sheet of paper, indicate how you would demonstrate each of the listed qualities and competencies to an employer.

   _____

   _____

   _____

   _____

   _____

   _____

   _____

   _____

   _____

2. Give examples of how you have used and incorporated assessment and feedback from an employer. Include sample performance appraisals in your portfolio.

   _____

   _____

   _____

   _____

   _____

   _____

   _____

   _____

ASSESSING YOUR SKILLS AND COMPETENCIES

The following are typical qualities and competencies that are included in many performance appraisals.

- Communication skills:
    Writing
    Speaking
    Reading
- Integrity
- Willingness to learn

- Decision-making skills
- Delegation
- Planning
- Organizational skills
- Positive attitude
- Ability to accept change

On the following lines, describe how you currently demonstrate each of the listed skills and competencies to an employer. Consider how you can improve. Add this page to your Career Development Portfolio.

1. How do you demonstrate the listed skills?

_____
_____
_____
_____
_____
_____
_____
_____
_____

2. How can you improve?

_____
_____
_____
_____
_____
_____
_____
_____

Express Yourself in Writing and Speech

Re...

CHAPTER OBJECTIVES

In this chapter, you will learn to

▲ Prepare research papers and speeches

▲ Use the library and take your search on-line

▲ Incorporate strategies for writing effective papers

▲ Utilize strategies for giving effective presentations

▲ Overcome writer's block

SELF-MANAGEMENT

"I put off taking the required public speaking class until the last semester. I hate getting up in front of people. My mind goes blank, I get butterflies, and my palms sweat. What can I do to decrease stage fright and be more confident about speaking in public?"

Have you ever had a similar experience? Do you find yourself feeling anxious and worried whenever you have to make a presentation or give a speech? Do you suffer physical symptoms, such as sweaty palms, upset stomach, headaches, or inability to sleep or concentrate even days before the event? In this chapter, you will learn how to deal with stage fright and learn public speaking skills.

JOURNAL ENTRY   In **Worksheet 9.1** on page 314, describe a time when you did well in a performance, sporting event, or speaking assignment. What factors helped you be calm, confident, and able to perform?

F ew things in life are as difficult as writing research papers and speaking before a group. Famed sportswriter Red Smith commented, "Writing is very easy. All you do is sit in front of a typewriter keyboard until little drops of blood appear on your forehead." Public speaking can cause even more anxiety. To some students, just the thought of speaking in front of a group produces feelings of sheer terror. In fact, research indicates that public speaking is the number one fear for most people, outranking even fear of death. For many students, writing not only produces feelings of doubt but also demands their focused attention, intense thinking, and detailed research. You can't avoid writing or speaking in school or at work, but you can learn strategies that will make them easier to do and more effective. Once you develop the skills and confidence required for speaking and writing effectively, you will experience a strong sense of accomplishment.

The Importance of Writing and Speaking

The ability to communicate clearly, both orally and in writing, is the most important skill you will ever acquire. Peter Drucker, noted management expert and author, remarked, "Colleges teach the one thing that is perhaps most valuable for the future employee to know. But very few students bother to learn it. This one basic skill is the ability to organize and express ideas in writing and speaking."

You may be asked to do research on new ideas, products, procedures, and programs and compile the results in a report. You will most likely write business letters, memos, and reports. You may have to give formal speeches before a large group, preside at meetings, or present ideas to a small group. You will be expected to present both written and spoken ideas in a clear, concise, and organized manner. Writing papers and preparing speeches in school prepare you for on-the-job reports and correspondence. These assignments give you a chance to show initiative, use judgment, apply and interpret information, research resources, organize ideas, and polish your style. Public speaking skills also help you inform and persuade others at informal meetings and presentations. Good writers and speakers are not born, and there is no secret to their success. Like other skills, speaking and writing can be learned with practice and effort.

This chapter won't tell you how to write a great novel or deliver the keynote speech at a political convention, but it will give you strategies for handling every step of the paper-writing and speech-giving process, from choosing a topic to turning in the paper or delivering the speech. Keep these five basic steps in mind as you prepare your paper or speech:

1. Prepare.
2. Organize.
3. Write.
4. Edit.
5. Review.

WORDS TO SUCCEED

"The pages are still blank, but there is a miraculous feeling of the words being there, written in invisible ink and clamoring to become visible."

VLADIMIR NABAKOV, *Author*

Figure 9.1 Sample Schedule ▲

Term Paper for Criminal Justice 101, Due April 3

Final Check. Make copy.	April 2
Edit, revise, and polish.	March 29 (Put away for one or two days)
Complete bibliography.	March 28
Revise.	March 26
Edit, review, revise.	March 24 (Confer with instructor)
Final draft completed.	March 22 (Proof and review with a good writer)
Complete second draft.	March 20
Add, delete, and rearrange information.	March 17
First draft completed.	March 15 (Share with writing group)
Write conclusion.	March 12
Continue research and flesh out main ideas.	February 16
Write introduction.	February 10
Organize and outline.	February 3
Gather information and compile bibliography and notes.	January 29
Narrow topic and write thesis statement.	January 23
Do preliminary reading.	January 20
Choose a topic.	January 16
Brainstorm ideas.	January 15
Clarify expectations and determine purpose.	January 14

Sample Schedule   This schedule for preparing a term paper starts where the paper is finished. *Why does this schedule begin at the due date of the term paper?*

Prepare for Writing

Whether you are writing a paper or a speech, there are a number of tasks you need to accomplish initially:

1. **Set a schedule.** Estimate how long each step will take and leave plenty of time for proofing. Consider working backward from the due date and allow yourself ample time for each step. See **Figure 9.1** for an example.

2. **Choose a general topic.** Choose a topic that meets your instructor's requirements, one that interests you and is narrow enough to handle in the time available. If you have any questions concerning the instructor's expectations, talk

with him or her and clarify length, format and style, purpose, and method of citation. Determine if your purpose is to entertain, inform, explain, persuade, gain or maintain goodwill, gain respect and trust, or gather information. Consider the age, education level, and size of your audience and their knowledge of the topic. Use the tips in **Peak Progress 9.1** to help you come up with a topic.

3. **Do preliminary reading**. Begin to gather general information by reviewing reference materials, such as articles or an encyclopedia. Your initial research is intended to give you an overview of the subject and key issues. Ask questions to help you begin structuring your topic and compiling a working bibliography. Make certain you check the list of related references at the end of reference books and reference book articles. You may want to develop a list of questions that can lead to new directions and additional research:

   ◆ What do I already know about the topic? What do I want to know?

   ◆ What questions do I want to explore? What interests me most?

   ◆ What is the point I want to research?

   Write these questions on note cards and include them later with your research cards.

4. **Narrow your topic**. After you have finished your preliminary reading, you can focus on a specific topic. For example, instead of "health problems in America," narrow the subject to "cigarette smoking among teenage girls" or "should cigarette advertising be banned?"

5. **Write a thesis statement**. Writing a thesis statement will help you clarify what you plan to cover in your paper. The thesis is the main point, or central idea, of a paper. In one sentence, your thesis should describe your topic and what you want to convey about it. A good thesis statement is unified and clear—for example, "Smoking among teenage girls is on the rise."

6. **Take notes**. Jot down quotations and ideas that clarify your research topic. Put this information on note cards. At the top of each card, write the topic; below that, write a summary in your own words, a brief statement, or a direct quotation. If you are quoting, use quotation marks and be sure to write the words exactly as they appear and the source. If there is an error in the text, in brackets write the term *sic*, which means "thus in the original." If you omit words, indicate missing words with ellipsis points (three dots with a space between each dot, or period). Also write down each reference source on a separate card. You will need exact information for your final bibliography and footnotes and for researching material. Put a rubber band around your cards and keep them in a small folder. Sorting these cards into subject divisions will help you prepare your outline. See **Figure 9.2** on page 290 for a sample bibliography card.

7. **Prepare a bibliography**. A bibliography is a list of books, articles, Internet sources, and other resources about a subject or by a particular author that you plan to use as support for points or information in your paper. A bibliography page or section can be found at the end of a research paper or book.

Search through the on-line catalog in the library. Most libraries have electronic access and, as with the card catalog, you can browse by subject or author. You can also

How to Generate Topic Ideas

- *Brainstorm.* Brainstorming is generating as many ideas as possible without evaluating their merit. You can brainstorm ideas by yourself, but the brainstorming process often works well in small groups. Your goal is to get a list of as many creative ideas as you can in the specific time you have set aside without defending or judging the idea. Since ideas build on each other, the more ideas the better. Within 10 minutes, you can often generate a sizable list of potential topics.

- *Go to the library.* Look in the *Reader's Guide to Periodical Literature* for possible ideas. Look through newspapers, magazines, and new books.

- *Search on-line.* The Internet is a valuable source of ideas.

- *Keep a journal.* Keeping a journal is a great way to reflect on areas of interest, generate ideas for a paper or speech, and practice your writing skills. Write down ideas, feelings, opinions, summaries of books and articles, and reactions to other speeches or papers.

- *Keep a file.* Collect articles, poems, and a list of topics you find interesting. Listen to good speeches and collect stories or ideas from current newspapers that you could research and write about from a different perspective.

- *Develop observation skills.* Be aware of life around you. Think of possible topics as you read, watch television and movies, and talk with friends. What topics are in the news? What are people talking about?

- *Complete a sentence.* This technique can help generate potential topics. Write open-ended sentences and brainstorm completions—for example,

The world would be better if _____

Too many people _____

In the future _____

A major problem today is _____

A most wondrous event in life is _____

The best thing about _____

What I enjoy most is _____

I learned that _____

It always makes me laugh when _____

The components of a perfect day are _____

If I had unlimited funds, I would buy _____

I get through a tough day by _____

- *Relax.* If you try too hard, you may become anxious and discouraged. Start to brainstorm ideas as soon as the assignment is made, so that you have plenty of time. Ask a clear question about potential topics before you go to sleep at night and let your unconscious mind solve problems. Take a moment in the morning to review your dreams, ideas, and thoughts before you jump into the day.

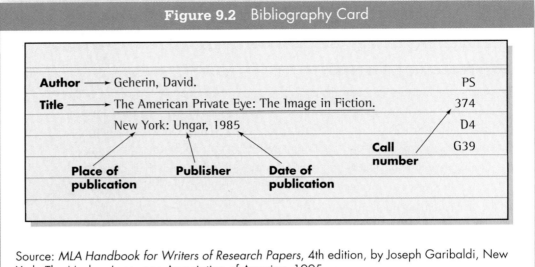

Figure 9.2 Bibliography Card

Author ——→ Geherin, David.   PS

Title ——→ The American Private Eye: The Image in Fiction.   374

New York: Ungar, 1985   D4

Call number   G39

Place of publication   **Publisher**   **Date of publication**

Source: *MLA Handbook for Writers of Research Papers*, 4th edition, by Joseph Garibaldi, New York: The Modern Language Association of America, 1995.

Bibliography Card   As you research, write down reference information for each source on a card. *What is the advantage of creating these cards?*

use the Internet to discover what is available on your topic and start putting together a preliminary bibliography by copying and pasting reference material. However, make certain that you double-check sources that you find on the Internet, as the information may have been taken from another original source.

List all materials available on your topic, put them in alphabetical order, and number them. Write down each author's full name (last name first), the exact title (underline newspapers, magazines, and book titles and put article titles in quotations marks), the place of publication, the name of the publisher, and the date of publication, and write the call number in the upper left-hand corner.

Organize a Writing Plan

Now that you have done the preliminary legwork, you'll want to create a writing plan.

1. **Organize and outline information.** Organize your note cards into a logical order using either a traditional or a mind map outline. This outline should contain main points and subtopics. An outline is a road map that illustrates your entire project. If you use a computer, check applicable software packages that offer an outline feature. Or you can use this traditional outline format:

Sample Outline

 I. Smoking among teenage girls is increasing.

    A. Smoking has increased by 24 percent.

      1. Supporting information

      2. Supporting information

B. Girls are smoking at younger ages.

II. Advertising targets young girls directly.

    A. Example of advertising

        1. Supporting information

        2. Supporting information

    B. Effects of advertising

Use **Personal Evaluation Notebook 9.1** on page 292 to help you organize your paper.

2. **Continue your research.** Look for specific information and data that support your main points and thesis. Research the books and articles you noted on your bibliography cards. Organize and separate the information.

3. **Revise your outline.** Revise your outline as you continue to research. You may also want to refine your writing strategy by focusing on how best to accomplish your purpose. What is your major topic? What subtopics do you want to include? What examples, definitions, quotations, statistics, stories, or personal comments would be most interesting and supportive? Continue to look for specific information to support your thesis.

Write Your First Draft

Now is the time to organize all your note cards according to sections and headings and write in your own words according to your revised outline. Write freely and don't worry about spelling, grammar, or format. The key is to begin writing and keep the momentum going. Both papers and speeches should have three sections: an introduction, a main body, and a conclusion.

1. **Write the introduction.** The introduction should be a strong opening that clearly states your purpose, captures the attention of your audience, defines terms, and sets the stage for the main points. Use an active rather than a passive voice. For example, "More than 450,000 people will die this year from the effects of cigarette smoking" is a stronger introduction than "This paper will present the dangers of smoking."

2. **Write the main body.** The main body is the heart of your paper or speech. Each main point should be presented logically and stand out as a unit (see **Figure 9.3** on page 293). Explain main points in your own words and use direct quotes when you want to state the original source. Refer often to your outline and your thesis statement. Your research note cards will help you find the support elements you need. If you find gaps, do more research.

3. **Write the conclusion.** Your final paragraph should tie together important points. The reader or listener should now have an understanding of the topic and believe that you have achieved your purpose. You might try using a story, a quotation, or a call to action. You may want to refer again to the introduction, reemphasize main points, or rephrase an important position. Keep your conclusion brief, interesting, and powerful. **Peak Progress 9.2** on page 294 provides some helpful hints on overcoming writer's block.

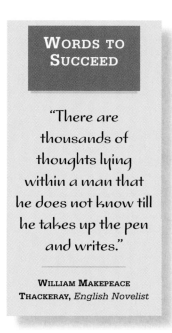

WORDS TO SUCCEED

"There are thousands of thoughts lying within a man that he does not know till he takes up the pen and writes."

WILLIAM MAKEPEACE THACKERAY, *English Novelist*

Preparing Research Papers

When you start thinking about assigned research papers, use this form to prepare and organize your paper.

Topic _____ Due date _____

Thesis _____

_____

_____

Introduction _____

_____

_____

Interest and importance _____

_____

_____

Introduce thesis in concise statement. _____

_____

_____

Review your paper and check for these elements:

Main Body

_____ Background of topic

_____ Thesis emphasized

_____ Terminology, facts, data

_____ Keywords

_____ Main points and arguments

_____ Supporting points

Conclusion

_____ Restate thesis.

_____ Summarize key points.

_____ Present a clear and strong conclusion.

Edit Your Draft

1. **Revise**.

   ◆ Revise your first draft for attention to overall meaning and effect. Revise again for punctuation, grammar, and style.

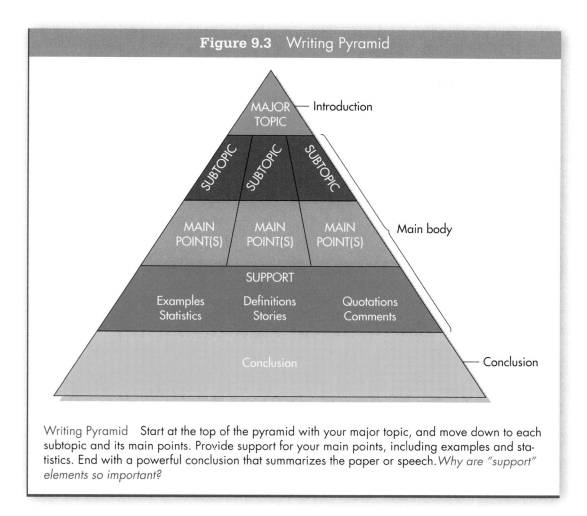

Figure 9.3 Writing Pyramid

MAJOR TOPIC — Introduction

SUBTOPIC · SUBTOPIC · SUBTOPIC

MAIN POINT(S) · MAIN POINT(S) · MAIN POINT(S) — Main body

SUPPORT
Examples Statistics · Definitions Stories · Quotations Comments

Conclusion — Conclusion

Writing Pyramid Start at the top of the pyramid with your major topic, and move down to each subtopic and its main points. Provide support for your main points, including examples and statistics. End with a powerful conclusion that summarizes the paper or speech. *Why are "support" elements so important?*

◆ Read your paper out loud to get an overall sense of meaning and the flow of your words. Vary sentence lengths and arrangements to add interest and variety. For example, don't start each sentence with the subject or overuse the same words or phrases.

◆ Rework paragraphs for clarity and appropriate transitions. Does each paragraph contain one idea in a topic sentence? Is the idea well supported? Transitions should be smooth and unobtrusive. In a speech, they should be defined clearly, so that listeners stay focused.

◆ Recheck your outline. Have you followed your outline logically? Have you included supporting information in the correct places? Break up the narrative with lists if you are presenting series of data. As you revise, stay focused on your purpose rather than on the ideas that support your conclusion. Make sure your points are clearly and concisely presented with supporting stories, quotes, and explanations.

◆ Confirm that the paper is concise and clear. Information should contribute, not just fill in space. Take out excess and unnecessary words. Ask yourself if a phrase or sentence contributes to your purpose. Revision also involves deleting and/or moving information from one section to another. If you are using

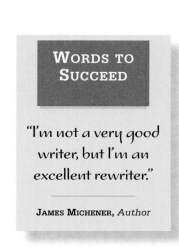

WORDS TO SUCCEED

"I'm not a very good writer, but I'm an excellent rewriter."

JAMES MICHENER, *Author*

Overcoming Writer's Block

- **Read**. Reading will give you ideas and improve your writing. Read novels, classic literature, biographies, and newspapers. Read other students' papers and exchange papers with your study team.

- **Write e-mail and letters**. Write e-mail and letters every day. Nothing improves your writing like daily practice.

- **Keep a journal**. Again, there is no better way to become a writer than to practice writing.

- **Write in a conversational tone**. Don't use technical, artificial, or stilted language. Use everyday, common words as if you were talking to someone. Try using a tape recorder to hear how your words sound.

- **Write in short blocks of time**. Like any other large task, you'll become discouraged if you try to write a large paper in one sitting. Write a little every day—anywhere you happen to be. Write for five minutes before bed, in the morning, or between classes.

- **Review your purpose**. Have a clear understanding of your purpose. Make a list of key points you want to make. In one or two words or phrases, write what you want to accomplish. What do you want to say?

- **Go to a restaurant**. Go out for a cup of coffee or tea and give yourself an hour of uninterrupted time to outline or mind map your paper or speech. If you are a visual learner, you may find that a mind map breaks your writing block. Start with your central purpose and topic. Outline main points, subtopics, and so on and fill in with additional ideas. A map allows your ideas to flow freely and allows you to see the connections between topics. You can then use this visual map as you type your paper. Don't feel that you must start with the introduction and work in a linear fashion.

- **Find a conference room or classroom**. You may need space to be alone, spread out papers, and work without interruptions.

- **Free write**. After you have completed your map outline, write for 30 or 40 minutes. Don't worry about spelling, organization, or grammar; just keep writing. Timed free writing is a powerful writing tool to break a writing block. Free writing is especially useful if you start early, allow the first draft to sit for a few days, and then revise.

- **Take a break or vary your routine**. If you get frustrated, take a short break or change the pace and work on your conclusion instead of starting with the introduction. Write your conclusion in one sentence to check for clarity. Then you can go back and write your paper.

- **Set a deadline**. Write a schedule and stick to it. Complete each task, even if it isn't what you would like it to be. You can revise later.

a computer or word processor, you can cut and paste with your word processing program. Save often and make a copy on a disk.

◆ Review sentence structure, punctuation, grammar, and unity of thought. Check carefully for typographical and spelling errors, grammatical mistakes, and poor transitions.

2. **Revise again**. Often, the difference between an *A* paper and a *B* paper, or speech, is that extra polish. If you can set it aside for a day or two before you give it a final revision, you can approach what you have written with a fresh view. Go through your entire paper or speech. Is your central theme clear and concise? Read your paper out loud. Recite your speech to a friend or tape it. Does it flow? Could it use more stories or quotes to add flair? Is it too wordy or confusing? Can you make it more concise? Does it have an interesting introduction and conclusion? Share your paper with a friend or member of your study team. Ask one of them to proofread your work. Other people can sometimes see errors that you can't, and they can provide a fresh viewpoint.

3. **Confer with your instructor**. Make an appointment with your instructor to review your paper. Some students make an appointment when they have completed their outline or first draft. Other students like to wait until they have proofed their second draft. Most instructors will review your paper with you and give you suggestions. Discuss what to add and what to revise and the preferred method of citation.

4. **Prepare your final draft**. Following your instructor's guidelines and suggestions, prepare your final draft. Leave a margin of 1 inch on all sides, except for the first page, which should have a 3-inch margin at the top of the paper. Double-space your entire paper, except for the footnotes and the bibliography, which are often single-spaced. Make corrections, revise, run a spell-check, and print out a clean, corrected copy on good-quality paper. It's always a good idea to proofread this hard copy, because it's easy to miss errors on a computer screen. See **Peak Progress 9.3** on page 296 for writing tips.

5. **Cite your sources**. Always cite your sources when you quote or use another person's words or ideas. **Plagiarism** is using someone else's words or ideas and trying to pass them off as your own. It can have serious consequences, such as a failing grade or expulsion from school. You can put the person's exact words in quotation marks, or you can **paraphrase** and use your own words to restate the author's ideas. You can give credit in the text of the paper or in a note, either at the bottom of the page as a footnote or at the end of the paper as an endnote. (See **Peak Progress 9.4** on page 298 for a discussion of the various citation styles.)

For example, you may choose to use the following source when writing a paper on the history of the funeral industry. This is the exact quote from the text along with one method of citation:

"Simplicity to the point of starkness, the plain pine box, the laying out of the dead by friends and family who also bore the coffin to the grave—these were the hallmarks of the traditional funeral until the end of the nineteenth century."[1]

[1] Mitford, Jessica. <u>The American Way of Death</u>. New York: Simon & Schuster, 1963.

Writing Do's: The Seven *C*s of Effective Writing

Be concise. Eliminate unnecessary words. Write in plain language and avoid wordiness. Cut any phrases that do not add to your purpose.

Be concrete. Emphasize verbs for active, powerful writing. Use vivid action words rather than vague, general terms. The sentence "Jill wrote the paper" is in the active voice and is easy to understand; "The paper was written by Jill" is in the passive voice and sounds weak. Favor familiar words over the unfamiliar. Include stories and quotes for interest and support. Avoid vague adjectives and adverbs, such as *nice, good, greatly,* and *badly.*

Be clear. Keep in mind the purpose of your writing. Make certain that your message is complete and includes all the information the audience needs to understand your intent. Never assume that the audience has any prior information. Use simple words and avoid stuffy, technical terms; clichés; slang; and jargon. If you must be technical, include simple definitions for your audience.

Be correct. Choose precise words and grammatically correct sentences. Make sure your supporting details are factual and that you interpret them correctly. Make certain you cite another's work. Check spelling and punctuation carefully. It is easy to miss errors with only one proofing, so proof at least twice and don't rely completely on your computer's spell-check feature. Have a detail-oriented friend proof your paper.

Be coherent. Your message should flow smoothly. Transitions between topics should be clear, logical, and varied in word choice. Also vary the length of sentences for interest and a sense of rhythm. Include stories, examples, and interesting facts.

Be complete. Make certain you have included all necessary information. Will your listeners or readers understand your message? Reread your speech or paper from their point of view. What questions might the audience have? If there are any unanswered questions, answer them.

Instead, you may choose to paraphrase the information from the book:

> In her book <u>The American Way of Death</u>, Jessica Mitford says one myth that is sold by the funeral industry is that today's elaborate and expensive funeral practices are part of the American tradition. In truth, prior to the end of the nineteenth century, the average American funeral was inexpensive and often consisted of a pine box and a simple ceremony.

You do not need to credit general ideas that are considered to be part of common knowledge, such as the suggestion that people who exercise reduce their stress levels. However, when in doubt, it's best to cite your source.

6. **Number your pages.** Number all pages except the first page, or the cover page. You can number the pages in the upper right-hand corner 1/2 inch from the top of the page. Number your endnotes and bibliography as part of the text. (Refer to any specific guidelines your instructor may have given you regarding formatting preferences.)

Writing Do's: The Seven *C*s of Effective Writing (continued)

Be considerate. Respect your reader by presenting a professional paper. Neatness counts and papers should always be typed. If you find an error in the final draft, it's OK to use white-out fluid or pen to make a correction. A word processor or computer, of course, can help you make the correction quickly and print out a flawless page. Use a respectful tone and don't talk down to your audience or use pompous or biased language. Always write with courtesy, tact, and consideration. Language is so powerful that it is important to avoid using words that are biased in terms of sex, disabilities, or ethnic groups:

Instead Of	You Can Substitute
mankind	humanity, people, humankind
manmade	manufactured, handcrafted
policeman	police officer
fireman	firefighter
housewife	homemaker
crippled	disabled, a person with disabilities
Indian (American)	Native American
Negro	African American
Oriental	Asian
Chicano	Hispanic

7. **Add a title page.** To create a title page, center the title one-third of the page from the top. Two-thirds from the top, center your name, the instructor's name, the course title, and the date. Do not number this page. See **Figure 9.4** on page 300 for a sample of a title page.

Review Your Completed Paper

1. **Final review.** Do a final check of your paper by reading through all of it one more time. You want your paper to be error-free. **Peak Progress 9.5** on page 301 provides a handy checklist to use as you finalize your paper.

2. **Make a copy.** Copy your final paper or speech in case your instructor loses the original. You should also keep copies of your major research papers in your Career Development Portfolio to show documentation of your writing, speaking, and research skills.

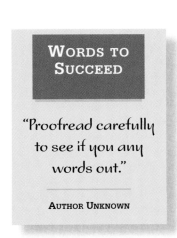

WORDS TO SUCCEED

"Proofread carefully to see if you any words out."

AUTHOR UNKNOWN

Writing Citations

There are many ways to write citations. Make sure you ask your instructor which documentation style is preferred. Each academic discipline has its preferred way of documenting sources. The Modern Language Association (MLA) of America format is often the preferred method for English and classical languages. The American Psychological Association (APA) format is commonly used for social science, psychology, and education topics. The CBE Style was developed by the Council of Biology Editors and is often used with science papers.

Computer programs are available to format according to the style you need to use. Reference footnotes can be placed at the bottom of a page or listed at the end of the paper, where they are referred to as endnotes. The bibliography is a list of books and articles, and it is found at the end of a paper after the endnotes. In the MLA format, this list is called "Works Cited."

The various citation formats are similar. The MLA is a basic style of citation that uses the simplest punctuation and can be used in most situations. It includes author, book title, publisher, place of publication, year of publication, and page number, if you choose to reference a specific page. For example, a footnote may appear as

1. Michael Heim, *The Metaphysics of Virtual Reality*, Oxford University Press, New York, 1993, p. 40.

The APA style generally uses bibliographies rather than footnotes. Included are the author's last name, the year of publication, the title of the work, the page number of the citation, the place of publication, and the publisher—for example,

Smith, R. J., & Jones, A. M. (1990). *Current trends in higher education* (p. 170). Englewood Cliffs, NJ: Prentice Hall.

A number of excellent on-line sites can guide you through the proper way to cite sources. (See **www.mhhe.com/ferrett6e** for links to a number of useful sources.) Your local or school library may also post citation information on their web sites.

Using the MLA Style

Following is a handy guide for the majority of types of sources you will cite:

For Footnotes

1. Lee, Ann. *Office Reference Manual.* New York: Irwin, 1993.

For Bibliography or Works Cited

- **Book: one author**

  Allen, James D. *Coming of Age.* New York: Macmillan, 1992.

- **Book: two or more authors**

  Arkin, Terry C., and Nancy A. Kelly. *Smoking Too Soon.* New York: Basic Books, 1991.

- **Government publication**

  U.S. Congressional Quarterly Service. A Review of Smoking. Washington, D.C.: 1989, 28.

Writing Citations (continued)

- **Journal**

   "Risking the Future Adolescent." *National Research Council Journal.* Washington, D.C.: National Academy Press, 1990.

- **Nonprint source (CD-ROM)**

   Morgan, David E. *Reference Software for Smoking Studies.* DOS Version. CD-ROM. New York: Macmillan, 1995.

- **Editorial**

   "Some Better Ways to Curb Teen Smoking." Editorial. *Los Angeles Times* 14 August 1995: sec. 1–2.

- **Encyclopedia or other reference work**

   Walton, Tom E. "Smoking." *World Book Encyclopedia.* 2001 ed.

- **Web site**

   Knapp, Susan. E. "Movie Smoking Linked to Teens Trying First Cigarette" Daily University Science News. 17 Dec. 2001. **http://unisci.com/stories/20014/1217015.htm.**

3. **Present your paper or speech on time**. Deliver your paper on time and be prepared to give your speech when it's due. Delaying the date just adds to the anxiety and may result in a lower grade.

4. **Assess and evaluate**. Review your graded paper or speech when it is returned to you. Ask your instructor for tips on improving your work.

Using the Library for Research

As we discussed in Chapter 4, the library contains a wealth of information. Besides books, libraries have newspapers, magazines, encyclopedias, dictionaries, indexes, audiovisual equipment, telephone directories, maps, catalogs, research aids, computer software, and computers. Librarians are trained to find information about every subject. They can often order special materials from other libraries or direct you to other sources. Asking for their guidance at the beginning of your search can save you hours of time and frustration. When planning your research strategy, remember the three basic types of sources found in most libraries: books, periodicals, and reference materials.

A Good Source
Libraries provide the most research options, with books, periodicals, reference materials, on-line access, and trained librarians.
What's the best source for recent data?

- *Books.* Books make up a large part of every library. Books are designed to treat a subject in depth and offer a broad scope. In your research project, use books for historical context; thorough, detailed discussions of a subject; or varied perspectives on a topic.

Figure 9.4 Sample Title Page

The Importance of Learning

Public Speaking

Karena R. Davis
Ms. J. Williams
Verbal Communications 102
December 2, 2007

Sample Title Page   Most standard styles require a title page. *Do you know how to prepare a title page?*

WORDS TO SUCCEED

"Perhaps no place in any community is so totally democratic as the town library. The only entrance requirement is interest."

LADY BIRD JOHNSON,
U.S. First Lady

◆ *Periodicals.* A periodical is anything published regularly, such as daily or weekly newspapers, weekly or monthly news magazines, professional and scholarly journals, and trade and industry magazines. Articles in periodicals provide current printed information. For your research, use periodicals when you need recent data.

◆ *Reference materials.* Reference materials may be in print or on the computer. Examples of reference materials include encyclopedias, dictionaries, chronologies, abstracts, indexes, and compilations of statistics. In your research strategy, use reference materials when you want to obtain or verify specific facts.

The *Reader's Guide to Periodical Literature* is a helpful source for locating articles. Other standard reference materials that may give you a general understanding of specific topics and help you develop questions include the *Encyclopedia Americana*, the *Encyclopaedia Britannica*, the *New York Times* index, and the *Wall Street Journal* index.

Checklists for Writing Papers and Giving Speeches

Review these checklists before submitting a paper or giving a speech.

Papers and Speeches

_____ Appropriate and focused topic   _____ Good examples

_____ Attention-getting introduction   _____ Good visuals

_____ Clear thesis statement   _____ Sources credited

_____ Appropriate word choice   _____ Smooth transitions

_____ Plenty of factual support   _____ Effective summary/conclusions

Papers

_____ Spelling and grammar checked   _____ Neat appearance/format

_____ Proofread at least twice   _____ Deadline met

_____ Pages numbered   _____ Copies made

Speeches

_____ Eye contact   _____ Relaxed body language

_____ Appropriate voice level and tone   _____ Appropriate attire

_____ No slang or distracting words   _____ Access to watch or clock

Check these sources for historical speeches:

◆ *Speech Index*

◆ *Index to American Women Speakers, 1828–1978*

◆ *Representative American Speeches, 1937*

◆ *Facts on File, 1941*

◆ *Vital Speeches of the Day, 1941*

◆ *Historic Documents of* [Year]

◆ *Public Papers of the Presidents of the United States*

Taking Your Search On-Line

The **Internet** is the world's largest information network. It is often referred to as the information superhighway, because it is a vast network of computers connecting people and resources worldwide. The Internet was developed in the 1960s because the U.S. Department of Defense was interested in creating a network through which leaders could communicate after a nuclear attack. The RAND Corporation, a military think tank, worked on the system that evolved into the Internet.

The Internet is an exciting medium to help you access the latest information. You can access data and resources such as dictionaries, encyclopedias, and library catalogs; news publications and electronic journals; and databases from universities and government agencies. You can learn about companies by visiting their web sites. Anyone with a computer and a modem can use the Internet.

Evaluating On-line Information

Since the Internet has become a source for news and information, it's important to be able to distinguish credible sites from those that may be biased or inaccurate. With millions of web pages to choose from, how do you know which sites are more reliable? Following is a checklist to use when evaluating information on the Internet for both research and personal use.

Is it credible?

- Is the author of the page clearly identified? Do they have the credentials for writing about this topic?
- Is the author affiliated with an organization? If so what is the nature or purpose of this organization?
- Is there a link back to the organization's page or some other way to contact the organization and verify its credibility? (a physical address, phone number, or email address)
- Are the purposes of the page clear?
- Is it geared for a particular audience or level of expertise?
- Is the primary purpose to provide information? To sell a product? To make a political point? To have fun?
- Is the page part of an edited or peer-reviewed publication?
- Does the domain name provide you with clues about the source of the page?
- Does the site provide details that support the data?
- Is there a bibliography or other documentation to corroborate the information? When facts or statistics are quoted, look to see whether their source is revealed.

The **World Wide Web** is a collection of mechanisms used to locate, display, and access information available on the Internet. A **web site**, or web page, is multimedia and can use colored pictures, video, sound, images, and text. You can use browser software, such as Netscape or Explorer, and click on highlighted words, called hyperlinks, to investigate additional information. The World Wide Web is a popular way to advertise businesses, departments, and products.

File Transfer Protocol (FTP) is a tool used to transfer files between two Internet sites. You can send (upload) or retrieve (download) a file from a remote site to your own. Thus, thousands of files of information and research are available to any Internet user.

Although searching for information on the Internet by using keywords or key phrases may seem relatively easy and efficient, it's important for you to make certain what you choose to use comes from a reliable source. See **Peak Progress 9.6** for some quick tips on how to evaluate on-line material. As with other sources, you must also cite material you find on the Internet.

Evaluating On-line Information (continued)

Is it accurate?

- Are there obvious typographical or spelling errors?
- Based on what you already know or have just learned about this subject, does the information seem credible?
- Can factual information be verified?
- Is it a comprehensive resource or does it focus on a narrow range of information? Is it clear about its focus?
- Has the site been evaluated?

Is it timely?

- Is it clear when the information was published? Is it current?
- When was the page last updated?
- If there are links to other Web pages, are they current?

Is it objective?

- Is the source of factual information consistent and stated clearly?
- Does the page display a particular bias? Is it clear and forthcoming about its view of a particular subject?
- If the page contains advertisements, are the ads clearly distinguishable from the content of the information?

Source: Used by permission of the University of Texas System Digital Library, The University of Texas at Austin.

Public Speaking Strategies

Public speaking is an important school and job skill. In school, you will ask and answer questions in class, lead discussions, summarize topics, introduce other students, present your academic plan or thesis, and interview for internships or jobs. On the job, you may be asked to introduce a guest, present the results of a group project, make a sales pitch, present a speech on your department's services, present goals and objects, interview clients, talk with board members, or accept an award.

Many of the strategies for choosing a topic and organizing a speech are similar to those for writing papers. Following are a few additional strategies specifically for public speaking:

- *Understand the occasion.* Why are you speaking? Is the occasion formal or informal? How much time do you have? What is your purpose? Do you want to inform, entertain, inspire, or persuade?

- *Think about your topic.* Is there a specific topic? What are you interested in talking about? Prepare a thesis statement, such as "My purpose is to inform the Forestry Club on the benefits of our organization."

- *Know your audience.* This doesn't mean you need to know them personally, but you should have a sense of their backgrounds and why they are in the room. What are their ages, interests, and knowledge? What do they already know? What do they want to know? For example, if you are giving a speech on cutting-edge technology and the majority of your audience barely knows how to turn on a computer, chances are you are going to lose them quickly unless you present the topic at a level they can relate to, with benefits they can appreciate.
- *Get the audience's attention.* Write an introduction that gets the attention of your audience, introduces the topic, states the main purpose, and briefly identifies the main points.
- *Look at the audience.* Establish eye contact and speak to the audience members. Smile, develop rapport, and notice when your audience agrees with you or looks puzzled or confused.
- *Outline your speech.* You want to organize the body of your speech to include supporting points and interesting examples.

Eye Contact
When you look at the audience as you speak, you create a rapport that makes everyone more comfortable. *What other strategies could help you become a good speaker?*

- *Write a good conclusion.* You want the audience to have a clear picture of your main point, why it's important, and what they should do about it. You may want to end with a story, a strong statement, or a question.

- *Develop visuals.* When appropriate, use overheads, slides, PowerPoint, handouts, and demonstrations. They can focus audience attention, add drama, reduce your stress, and reinforce your speech. Make sure that the type on your visuals is large enough to read, the projector works, and you have practiced working with the visual aids.

- *Prepare your prompters.* Don't memorize the speech but be well acquainted with your topic, so that you are comfortable talking about it. Prepare simple notes to prompt yourself. Write key phrases in large letters. Write key phrases, stories, and quotes on note cards.

- *Practice.* Rehearsal is everything! Practice the speech aloud several times in front of a mirror, an empty classroom, or friends. Practice speaking slowly and calmly but louder than usual. Vary the pitch and speed for emphasis. Practice will also help you overcome stage fright. Complete **Personal Evaluation Notebook 9.2** on page 306 to determine how you handle stage fright and writer's block.

- *Relax.* Take a deep breath as you walk to the front of the room. During the speech, don't rush, speak loudly and clearly, and gesture when appropriate to help you communicate.

- *Be in the present.* Look at your audience and smile. Keep your purpose in mind and stay focused on the message and the audience. Remember to pause at important points for emphasis and to connect with your audience.

- *Avoid unnecessary words.* Use clear, concise words. Don't use pauses as fillers, irritating nonwords, or overused slang, such as *uh, ur, you know, stuff like that, sort of,* and *like.* Become aware of using these distractions even in everyday conversation and work to eliminate them.

- *Review your performance.* Ask your instructor and fellow students for feedback. Be open to learning and strive to improve. You will never be sorry that you have spent time and energy in learning to become a better speaker. Review the sample speech evaluation form shown in **Figure 9.5** on page 308.

See **Peak Progress 9.7** on page 307 to explore how you can apply the Adult Learning Cycle to become more proficient at public speaking.

Controlling Stage Fright and Writer's Block

A. Use your critical thinking skills to answer the following questions. Be prepared to discuss your answers in your study teams.

1. Describe your typical physical reaction to giving a speech.

   _____

   _____

2. What has helped you control stage fright?

   _____

   _____

3. Describe the processes of writing that are easiest for you and those that are the hardest.

   _____

   _____

B. Read the following common reasons and excuses that some students use for not writing effective speeches. Add to this list. Use creative problem solving to list strategies for overcoming these barriers.

Reasons/Excuses

1. I have panic attacks before I write or give speeches.

   Strategy: _____

   _____

2. I can't decide on a topic.

   Strategy: _____

   _____

3. I don't know how to research.

   Strategy: _____

   _____

4. I procrastinate until the last minute.

   Strategy: _____

   _____

5. I don't know what my instructor wants.

   Strategy: _____

   _____

6. My mind goes blank when I start to write or give a speech.

   Strategy: _____

   _____

Applying the Adult Learning Cycle to Improve Your Public Speaking

Increasing your public speaking skills takes time, effort, and practice.

1. **RELATE. Why do I want to learn this?** I've always admired people who are confident speaking in front of others, and I want to feel that confident, poised, and in control. Becoming an effective public speaker will be a valuable skill for both school and career. What areas do I need to work on? What are my physical systems of anxiety?

2. **OBSERVE. How does this work?** I can learn by observing people who are effective and confident at giving speeches. What makes them successful? Do I understand the message? I'll also analyze ineffective speeches. Did stage fright play a role? Did the speaker seem uncomfortable and nervous? I'll try using new techniques and strategies for dealing with fear and stage fright and observe how I'm improving.

3. **REFLECT. What does this mean?** What strategies are working for me? Am I more confident and relaxed? Am I reducing anxiety and negative self-talk?

4. **DO. What can I do with this?** I will practice my public speaking skills whenever possible. I'll find practical applications to use my new skills in everyday life. Each day, I'll work on one area. For example, I'll choose less stressful situations, such as my study group or a club meeting, and offer to give a presentation on an interesting topic. I will ask for feedback.

5. **TEACH. Whom can I share this with?** I'll talk with others and share my tips and experiences and listen to theirs in return. I'll volunteer to help other students in my study group.

Now, return to Stage 1 and think about how it feels to learn this valuable new skill. Remember, the more you practice speaking in front of others, the more relaxed and confident you will become.

Figure 9.5 Speech Evaluation Form

Name _____ Topic _____

Introduction
__ Gained attention and interest
__ Introduced topic
__ Topic related to audience
__ Established credibility
__ Previewed body of speech

Body
__ Main points clear
__ Organizational pattern evident
__ Established need
__ Presented clear plan
__ Demonstrated practicality
__ Language clear
__ Gave evidence to support main points
__ Sources and citations clear
__ Reasoning sound
__ Used emotional appeals
__ Connectives effective

Delivery
__ Spoke without rushing and at an appropriate rate
__ Maintained eye contact
__ Maintained volume and projection
__ Avoided distracting mannerisms
__ Used gestures effectively
__ Articulated clearly
__ Used vocal variety and dynamics
__ Presented visual aids effectively
__ Departed appropriately
__ Other: _____

Conclusion
__ Prepared audience for ending
__ Reinforced central idea
__ Called audience to agreement/action
__ Used a vivid ending

Suggestions
_____
_____
_____
_____
_____
_____
_____
_____
_____
_____

General Notes
_____
_____
_____
_____
_____
_____
_____
_____
_____

Key: Superior (1), Effective (2), Average (3), Weak (4)

Speech Evaluation Form   Feedback on your speaking skills can help you improve. *How would you assess your last speech in a class?*

In summary, in this chapter, I learned to:

- *Become a more effective writer and speaker.* Being a good communicator is essential in all facets of life. It is the most important skill I will ever acquire. Although public speaking can be stressful, I can learn to reduce my anxiety and become more successful if I prepare, organize, write, edit, and review my presentation carefully.

- *Prepare effectively.* When writing a paper or presentation, I need to first set a schedule for accomplishment. I carefully and thoughtfully choose my topic and do the preliminary reading and information gathering. I can then narrow my topic and write a thesis statement that helps me clarify what I plan to cover. I prepare a bibliography of references and original sources, and I take notes that support my topic.

- *Organize my writing plan.* I must organize my thoughts and research into a coherent outline. I continue to look for specific data that support my main points. I revise my outline as necessary as I consider the subtopics that support my main theme. I include examples, definitions, quotations, and statistics that are interesting and supportive.

- *Write a draft of my paper or presentation.* Now that I have done the preliminary research and outline, I prepare a draft, writing freely and with momentum. My draft includes (1) an introduction, (2) the main body, and (3) a conclusion. The introduction clearly states the purpose or theme, captures attention, and defines terms. The main body includes the subtopics that support the main theme, as well as visual aids. The conclusion ties the important points together and supports the overall theme of the presentation.

- *Revise and edit my paper or presentation.* Now that I have prepared a draft, I must revise it often. I check to make sure that the overall theme and supporting points are clear and revise my outline when necessary. I correct spelling and grammatical mistakes and review my transitions and sentence structure. It helps to read it out loud to make sure the writing is varied and interesting. I will make sure I have accurately prepared the bibliography, and I will ask my instructor to review my paper. I will then finalize my paper, number the pages, and add a title page.

- *Review and assess my paper or presentation.* After a final check of my paper, I make additional copies and include one in my Career Development Portfolio. I deliver it on time, go over my graded results, and ask my instructor for tips for improvement.

- *Use the library and Internet for research.* The library provides a wealth of resources, including books, periodicals, and reference materials. Originally conceptualized by a military think tank, the Internet has become the world's largest information network, providing access to a myriad of resources, databases, and content.

- *Incorporate new strategies for effective public speaking.* When I speak in public, it's important for me to be prepared, establish eye contact with my audience, develop visual aids, and prepare simple notes or cues to prompt myself. I avoid unnecessary words and fillers, and I connect with my audience. Rehearsing is key to a successful presentation, and I review my performance by asking others for feedback.

career in focus

Lori Benson

HUMAN RESOURCES DIRECTOR

Related Majors: Human Resources, Personnel
Administration, Labor Relations

Communication Skills

Lori Benson is the human resources director for a small advertising firm. Lori is her company's only human resources employee. Besides recruiting and interviewing potential employees, Lori also develops personnel programs and policies. She serves as her company's employee benefits manager by handling health insurance and pension plans. Lori also provides training in orientation sessions for new employees and instructs classes that help supervisors improve their interpersonal skills.

Possessing excellent communication skills is essential for Lori's job. To recruit potential employees, Lori sends letters to colleges to attract recent graduates. She also places want ads in newspapers and magazines. In addition, Lori often sends memos and e-mails to the employees at her company regarding parking or a change in health insurance coverage. This kind of writing must be clear, accurate, and brief. Lori first writes a draft and then sets it aside for a few days before doing revisions. She usually asks the CEO to review the ads and letters sent to the media.

Lori does research to find out what programs and policies other companies are offering. She uses public speaking strategies when preparing for training and other classes. First she makes notes and then writes prompts to help her remember what she wants to say. Lori practices her lecture several times and reviews her notes before each class. She keeps her notes in a file for the next time she gives a class on the same subject.

CRITICAL THINKING How does Lori incorporate the communication skills she learned in college into the workplace?

Peak Performer Profile

Toni Morrison

er books have been described as having "the luster of poetry" illuminating American reality. However, one reader once commented to acclaimed novelist Toni Morrison that her books were difficult to read. Morrison responded, "They're difficult to write." The process, Morrison sums up, "is not [always] a question of inspiration. It's a question of very hard, very sustained work."

An ethnically rich background helped provide Morrison's inspiration. The second of four children, she was born Chloe Anthony Wofford in a small Ohio steel town in 1931 during the Great Depression. The family's financial struggle was offset by a home strengthened by multiple generations and traditional ties. Storytelling was an important part of the family scene and black tradition.

In the late 1940s, Morrison headed to the East Coast. After earning a bachelor's degree in English from Howard University and a master's degree from Cornell University, she was still years away from literary recognition. While working as an editor at Random House in New York City, she began her writing career in earnest, and in 1970 her first novel, *The Bluest Eye*, was published.

Since then, Morrison has produced a body of work described as standing "among the 20th century's richest depictions of Black life and the legacy of slavery." Her dedication was rewarded in 1987, when Morrison's fifth novel, *Beloved*, won the Pulitzer Prize. Based on a true incident that took place in 1851, this novel has been read by millions. Then, in 1993, Morrison was awarded the Nobel Prize in Literature. She is the first black woman and only the eighth woman to receive this supreme honor.

Through Morrison's writing skills and self-expression, she has provided insight into American cultural heritage and the human condition.

PERFORMANCE THINKING The novel *Beloved* is dedicated to "Sixty Million and more." What is Morrison trying to express?

CHECK IT OUT "Toni Morrison's novels invite the reader to partake at many levels, and at varying degrees of complexity. Still, the most enduring impression they leave is of empathy, compassion with one's fellow human beings," said Professor Sture Allén as he presented Toni Morrison with the Nobel Prize for Literature for 1993. At **www.nobelprize.org**, select the Literature section and read about the many laureates who have received this highest honor. You can also listen to acceptance speeches and Nobel lectures, including Morrison's eloquent prose, "We die. That may be the meaning of life. But we do language. That may be the measure of our lives."

Performance Strategies...........

Following are the top 10 strategies for writing papers and giving speeches:

◆ Determine your purpose and set a schedule.

◆ Choose and narrow your topic.

◆ Read and research. Prepare a bibliography.

◆ Organize information into an outline and on note cards.

◆ Write a draft.

◆ Refine your purpose and rewrite the draft.

◆ Edit and proof.

◆ Use your study team to practice and review.

◆ Revise and polish.

◆ Practice. Practice. Practice.

Tech for Success...................

Take advantage of the text's web site at **www.mhhe.com/ferrett6e** for additional study aids, useful forms, and convenient and applicable resources.

◆ **Visual aids**. As many of your instructors facilitate their lectures with handouts, overhead transparencies, and PowerPoint presentations, you, too, will want to consider enhancing your presentations with visual aids. Many employers do not provide training for such programs, but knowing how to incorporate them into business meetings and presentations is often expected. Thus, learning at least the basics of PowerPoint or a similar program now will be a valuable skill you can use both in school and on the job.

◆ **Spell-check, spell-check, spell-check**. As e-mail has replaced the traditional memo, it's much easier to send out correspondence quickly to a group of people at one time. However, it's not uncommon to receive important e-mails that are riddled with typos and grammatical mistakes. Get in the habit of using the spell-check function prior to sending all e-mails or documents. The few seconds it takes to check your outgoing correspondence can save you from unnecessary embarrassment (and more e-mails) later on.

Review Questions...................

Based on what you have learned in this chapter, write your answers to the following questions:

1. What is the one basic skill taught in college that Peter Drucker feels is the most valuable for the future employee to know?

2. How should you establish a schedule to research and write a paper?

3. What are three questions to ask when evaluating information on the Internet?

4. Describe four strategies you can use to overcome writer's block.

5. What are five public speaking strategies?

LEARNING COMMUNICATION SKILLS

In the Classroom

Josh Miller is a finance student at a business college. He likes numbers and feels comfortable with order, structure, and right-or-wrong answers. As part of the graduation requirements, all students must take classes in speech and writing. Josh becomes nervous about writing reports or giving speeches and doesn't see the connection between the required class and his finance studies. One of Josh's biggest stumbling blocks is thinking of topics. He experiences writer's block and generally delays any project until the last possible minute.

1. What strategies in this chapter would help Josh think of topics and meet his deadlines?

   _____

   _____

2. What would you suggest to help him see the value of speaking and writing well?

   _____

   _____

In the Workplace

Josh has recently been promoted to regional manager for an investment firm. He feels very secure with the finance part of his job but feels pressure with the new promotion requirements. He will need to present bimonthly speeches to top management, run daily meetings, and write dozens of letters, memos, and reports. He must also give motivational seminars at least twice a year to his department heads. Josh would like to improve his writing skills and make his presentations clear, concise, and motivational.

3. What suggestions would you give Josh to help make his presentations more professional and interesting?

   _____

   _____

4. What strategies could he use to improve his writing?

   _____

   _____

REVIEW AND APPLICATIONS

CHAPTER 9

APPLYING THE ABCDE METHOD OF SELF-MANAGEMENT

In the Journal Entry box on page 285, you were asked to describe a time when you did well in a performance, sporting event, or speaking assignment. What factors helped you be calm, confident, and able to perform?

Being prepared to talk on a subject. Preparing a talk assignment by writing out materials needed.

Now describe a situation in which your mind went blank or you suffered stage fright. How would increasing your presentation or public speaking skills have helped you? Apply the ABCDE method to visualize a result in which you are again calm, confident, and focused.

A = Actual event:

1st time during group activity.

B = Beliefs:

that I could wing it on my own, without material as if I was a expert.

C = Consequences:

started to talk Froze up.

D = Dispute:

Not Asking for help

E = Energized:

Took me deep breath, and introduced myself as new and went on from there

Practice deep breathing with your eyes closed for just one minute. See yourself calm, centered, and relaxed as you give a performance or make a speech. See yourself presenting your ideas in a clear, concise, and confident manner. You feel confident about yourself because you have learned to control stage fright, you're well prepared, and you know how to give speeches.

Practice Self-Management

For more examples of learning how to manage difficult situations, see the "Self-Management Workbook" section of the Outline Learning Center web site at **www.mhhe.com/ferrett6e.**

REHEARSING

Today your boss asked you to give an important presentation to the management staff about a program you have been developing for budgeting. You want to start preparing for the presentation and give yourself enough time to create a unique way to present your new ideas and information. You want to enhance your own delivery style and improve your performance, so that management will understand your budget program fully.

The following are some ideas about presentations. Read this list and then add your own ideas on the lines provided.

1. Begin gathering materials and taking notes.
2. Practice visualizing yourself speaking successfully.
3. Prepare a rough draft of your presentation.
4. List the main points you want to make.
5. Prepare your handouts and overheads or visuals.
6. Recite material out loud.
7. Listen to how your presentation sounds.
8. Practice while you are jogging.
9. Give the presentation to a friend.
10. Go to the room where the presentation will be given.
11. Write a summary of the material on the board.
12. Integrate different learning styles as you explain material to your audience.
13. Time yourself.
14. Get a sense of the room, where you should stand, how you would arrange the chairs, and so on. Then sit and review.
15. Eat a light meal, take a walk, or do a few jumping jacks before your presentation. Eat a light nutritious breakfast.
16. Wear a professional outfit and follow good grooming habits.
17. Walk to the front of the room with confidence.
18. _____
    _____
19. _____
    _____
20. _____
    _____

ESSAY WRITING TIPS

An essay needs more than the right topic, thorough research, and a finely tuned thesis statement. It also requires *good writing*. Good writing involves using these elements:

- Good grammar
- Complete sentences
- Accurate punctuation

- Active verbs instead of passive verbs whenever possible
- Appropriate vocabulary

Several areas of grammar can present problems for writers. Check yourself.

Subject-Verb Agreement

In sentences, subjects and verbs should always agree. This means that, when the subject in a sentence is singular (such as *John*, *girl*, or *car*), the verb also is singular (such as *walks*, *sings*, or *is*). However, if the subject in a sentence is plural (such as *John and Mary*, *girls*, or *cars*), the verb also is plural (such as *walk*, *sing*, or *are*).

Subject-Verb Examples

John walks to school.

The girl sings very well.

The car is old.

John and Mary walk to school.

The girls sing together.

The cars are old.

Write in the correct verb that agrees with the subject:

1. Parents often __give__ their children nicknames. (give, gives)
2. A baby might __get__ the nickname Red because of his hair color. (get, gets)
3. Most people __enjoy__ their nicknames. (enjoy, enjoys)
4. Nicknames __intrest__ people. (interest, interests)
5. The seats __are__ very uncomfortable in the stadium. (is, are)

Proper Use of Pronouns

In most cases, the pronouns *I* and *we* should be used as subjects. The pronouns *me* and *us* should be used as objects.

Subject Examples

Joe and I went to the concert.   We also went to the concert.

Object Examples

The usher stood between the stage and me. The music sounded wonderful to us.

Write in the correct verb that agrees with the subject:

6. The boss gave raises to __us__ (us, we)
7. __We__ couldn't wait to begin. (We, Us)
8. __We__ watched the sunset. (We, Us)
9. Marge and __I__ enjoyed the party. (I, me)
10. The next day, she told __me__ about the party. (I, me)

(continued)

REVIEW AND APPLICATIONS   CHAPTER 9

Indefinite Pronoun and Verb Agreement

Do you know indefinite pronouns? Indefinite pronouns can be either singular or plural, depending on the meaning of the sentence. But they must always agree with the verb in the sentence. Use singular verbs with singular indefinite pronouns. Use plural verbs with plural indefinite pronouns. Following are lists to help you. You can refer to them when you are writing. Use them to fill in the exercise.

Indefinite Pronouns

Singular		Plural	Singular or Plural
one	nobody	few	most
no one	anybody	both	none
each	anyone	others	
someone	anything	many	
something	everybody		
everyone	either		
	neither		

Write the correct verb on each line:

11. Every night something _knocks_ over our trash can. (knock, knocks)

12. Everybody _plays_ the game tic-tac-toe. (play, plays)

13. Most _bring_ their lunch to school. (bring, brings)

14. Others _buys_ their lunch. (buy, buys)

15. Neither of the books _are_ finished. (are, is)

Commas

A comma has many uses. Here are just a few of those uses:

◆ To set off the part of an address:

  I am going to Buffalo, New York.

◆ To set off parts of a date:

  I will be leaving on Monday, August 8, 2007.

◆ To set off introductory words or phrases:

  Wake her up, Vicki!

  No, I don't want to go.

◆ To set off a series of words:

  Bring a pen, pencil, and paper to class.

  Joe, Margo, Liz, and Pete are going to class.

Add commas where they are needed in each sentence:

16. Put those boxes in the attic, Sam.

17. On August, 10 2007 I will deliver my report.

18. I invited Jill, Mary, Tom and Sue to the party.

19. I live in Williamsburg, Virginia.

20. His sales call is at ZZZ Company 34 Putnam Street, Olean, New York.

YOUR WRITING AND SPEAKING SKILLS

Looking Back

1. Recall any activities and events through which you learned to write and speak. Jot down examples of classes, presentations, essays, journals, and papers.

_____

_____

2. What are your strengths in writing and speaking?

_____

_____

3. What would you like to improve?

_____

_____

4. What are your feelings about writing and speaking?

_____

_____

Looking Forward

5. How can you demonstrate to employers that you have effective writing and speaking skills?

_____

_____

6. Include in your portfolio samples of speeches you have given. List the titles on the following lines.

_____

_____

7. Include in your portfolio samples of your writing. List the titles.

_____

_____

8. Include in your portfolio samples of your research. List the titles.

_____

_____

Add this page to your Career Development Portfolio.

Become a Critical Thinker and Creative Problem Solver

CHAPTER OBJECTIVES

In this chapter, you will learn to

▲ Acquire critical thinking skills

▲ Explore the problem-solving process

▲ Practice critical thinking and problem-solving strategies

▲ Recognize common fallacies and errors in judgment

▲ Understand the importance of creativity in problem solving

▲ Use problem-solving strategies for mathematics and science

▲ Overcome math and science anxiety

SELF-MANAGEMENT

I dropped a class, thinking I could take it next semester, just to find out that it is only offered once a year and now I won't graduate on time. I just didn't realize how one decision could have such a major impact.

Have you ever made a decision without clearly thinking through all the consequences? How does your attitude affect your critical thinking and creative problem solving? In this chapter, you will learn to put your critical thinking and creative problem-solving skills into action and learn strategies to make sound decisions in all areas of your life.

JOURNAL ENTRY In **Worksheet 10.1** on page 350, think of a decision you made that has cost you a great deal in time, money, or stress. Maybe you failed to change the name of the responsible party on your electric bill when you moved out of your apartment, and now you have a bad credit rating. Maybe you were stopped for speeding and failed to go to traffic school, and now your license has been suspended. How would using critical thinking and creative problem solving have helped you make better decisions?

WORDS TO
SUCCEED

"A problem is a
picture with a piece
missing; the answer
is the missing piece."

JOHN HOLT, *Educator, author*

All problem solving—whether personal or academic—involves decision making. You have to make decisions to solve a problem; conversely, some problems occur because of a decision you have made. For example, in your private life you may decide to smoke cigarettes; later, you face the problem of nicotine addiction, health problems, and a lot of your budget spent on cigarettes. In your school life, you may decide not to study mathematics and science because you consider them too difficult. Because of this decision, certain majors and careers will be closed to you. You can see that many events in your life do not just happen; they are the result of your choices and decisions. In this chapter, you will learn to use critical thinking and creativity to help you make effective and sound decisions and solve problems. Mathematics and science will be discussed, as these are key areas where you can develop and improve your critical thinking and problem-solving skills. You will also learn to overcome math anxiety and develop a positive attitude toward problem solving.

Essential Critical Thinking Skills

As we discussed in Chapter 1, critical thinking is a logical, rational, and systematic thought process that is necessary to understand, analyze, and evaluate information in order to solve a problem. Critical thinking is essential for school and life success. In the 1956 text *Taxonomy of Educational Objectives,* Benjamin Bloom and his colleagues outlined a hierarchy of six critical thinking skills that college requires (from lowest- to highest-order): knowledge, comprehension, application, analysis, synthesis, and evaluation.

1. **Knowledge.** Most of your college courses will require you to memorize lists, identify facts, complete objective tests, and recognize and recall familiar terms and information.
2. **Comprehension.** You will also need to demonstrate that you comprehend ideas, and you may be asked to state ideas in your own words, outline key ideas, and translate an author's meaning.
3. **Application.** You will be asked to apply what you've learned to a new situation. You may explore case studies, solve problems, and provide examples to support your ideas. You can learn application by applying ideas to your own life. For example, how can you apply political science concepts to your community or child development ideas to your campus child-care center or to children in your life?
4. **Analysis.** You will be asked to break apart ideas and relate them to other concepts. You may be asked to write essay questions, identify assumptions, and analyze values. You may be asked to compare and contrast economic theories or two works of art.
5. **Synthesis.** You will be asked to integrate ideas, build on other skills, look for interconnections, create and defend a position, improve on an existing idea or

design, and come up with creative ideas and new perspectives. You might compose a song or dance. You may be asked to find ways that a community project affects other areas of the community. Synthesis builds on other skills, so practice is important.

6. **Evaluation.** You will be asked to criticize a position or an opinion, form conclusions and judgments, list advantages and disadvantages of a project or an idea, and develop and use criteria for evaluating a decision. You can develop your evaluation skills by using helpful criteria and standards for evaluating speeches in class, evaluating group projects, and being open to suggestions from your study group and instructors.

In order to excel in school—as well as to learn how to make important decisions and sound judgments in life—you must move beyond simple knowledge and comprehension and be able to apply, analyze, synthesize, and evaluate questions and problems you are faced with. See **Peak Progress 10.1** for an example of moving from knowledge to evaluation.

PEAK PROGRESS   **10.1**

From Knowledge to Evaluation

If you can recall the number 8675309, but you attach no significance to the number, you have mere *knowledge.* Not tremendously useful, is it?

On the other hand, if you are familiar with a particular song performed by Tommy Tutone, you may recognize this number as the telephone number of a girl named Jenny, which the songwriter had found penned on a wall. Now you have *comprehension.* Still, you find yourself asking, "So what?"

May be you are intrigued. You might want to actually call the number to see whether Jenny answers. This is *application.* Unfortunately, unless you just happen to be in an area code where this telephone number exists, you will probably get a telephone company recording.

Next you break down the number into its component parts. You see that it has a 3-digit prefix and a 4-digit suffix. The prefix is 867. You have just performed a simple *analysis.*

In order to track Jenny down, you will need to combine some other bodies of information with what you already know. You know Jenny's telephone number, but there could be many identical telephone numbers throughout the country. What you need to find is a list of area codes that include this telephone number. You have then performed *synthesis.*

Before you go any further, ask yourself just how important it is to find Jenny. How many matching telephone numbers did you turn up in the previous step? Are you going to dial each of them? How much is it going to cost you in long-distance charges? How much of your time is it going to take? Is it worth it? You have just made an *evaluation.*

Courtesy T. C. Stuwe, Salt Lake Community College, © 2002.

Problem-Solving Steps

You must exercise and apply your critical thinking skills when solving problems. The problem-solving process can be broken down into four major steps:

1. State and understand the problem.
2. Gather and interpret information.
3. Develop and implement a plan of action.
4. Evaluate the plan or solution.

1. **State and understand the problem.** What are you trying to find out? What is known and unknown? What is the situation or context of the problem? Can you separate the problem into various parts? Organize the problem, or restate the problem in your own words—for example, "Should I go on a study abroad exchange or do an internship?"

2. **Gather and interpret information.** Make certain you have all the information you need to solve the problem. How can you see the problem from different angles? Use creative problem solving and explore creative solutions. "I have visited the career center and the study abroad office. I have listed pros and cons for each choice. I have included cost and expenses."

3. **Develop and implement a plan of action.** Choose an appropriate strategy. Ask yourself what information would be helpful. "I have gathered information and talked to people in my chosen field. Most career professionals have suggested that I go on exchange as a way to broaden my world view. I found out that I can apply for an internship for the following term. Since I can learn a foreign language and take valuable classes, I am going on the study abroad exchange and will do everything possible to make this a valuable experience."

4. **Evaluate the plan or solution.** Is this the correct answer? Is there one right answer? What are the likely consequences if you choose this approach? "I made valuable contacts and am learning so much from this experience. I will do an internship when I return. This was the best choice for me at this time."

WORDS TO SUCCEED

"The value of a problem is not so much coming up with the answer as in the ideas and attempted ideas it forces on the would-be solver."

I. N. HERSTEIN,
Mathematician

Critical Thinking and Problem-Solving Strategies

There are a number of important strategies you can apply to enhance and ensure you are fully using your critical thinking and problem-solving capabilities:

1. **Have a positive attitude.** Critical thinking requires a willingness and passion to explore, probe, question, and search for answers and solutions. (See **Figure 10.1**.) Your attitude has a lot to do with how you approach and solve a problem or make a decision. Positive thinking requires a mind shift. Think of problems as puzzles to solve, rather than difficult issues or courses to avoid. Instead of avoiding, delaying, making a knee-jerk decision, or looking for the one "right answer," focus on problem-solving strategies. For example, you may have a negative attitude toward math or science, perceiving the material too difficult or

Figure 10.1   Critical Thinking Qualities

Attributes of a Critical Thinker

- Willingness to ask pertinent questions and assess statements and arguments
- Ability to be open-minded and to seek opposing views
- Ability to suspend judgment and tolerate ambiguity
- Ability to admit a lack of information or understanding
- Curiosity and interest in seeking new solutions
- Ability to clearly define a set of criteria for analyzing ideas
- Willingness to examine beliefs, assumptions, and opinions against facts

Critical Thinking Qualities.   Being able to think critically is important for understanding and solving problems. *Do you apply any of the attributes of a critical thinker when you are faced with solving a problem?*

not relevant. Choose to see a problem or situation in the best possible light. Complete **Personal Evaluation Notebook 10.1** on page 324 to practice turning negatives into positives.

2. **Persistence pays off.** Coming to a solution requires sustained effort. A problem may not always be solved with your first effort. Sometimes a second or third try will see the results you need or want. Analytical thinking requires time, persistence, and patience. Sometimes it pays to sleep on a decision and not make important choices under pressure. Effective problem solvers are not beaten by frustration but, rather, look for new ways to solve problems.

3. **Use creativity.** As we will explore in more detail later in this chapter, you should learn to think in new and fresh ways, look for interconnections, and brainstorm many solutions. Good problem solvers explore many alternatives and evaluate the strengths and weaknesses of different methods.

4. **Pay attention to details.** Effective problem solvers show concern for accuracy. They think about what could go wrong, recheck calculations, look for errors, and pay attention to details. They are careful to gather all relevant information and proofread or ask questions. They are willing to listen to arguments, create and defend positions, and can distinguish among various forms of arguments.

5. **See all sides of the issue.** Think critically about what you read, hear, and see in newspapers and on the Internet. As you read, question sources and viewpoints. For example, when you read an article in the paper about Social Security or tax cuts, ask yourself what biases politicians or special interest groups might have in how they approach such issues. Does the argument appeal to emotion rather than to logic? Learn to question your biases, beliefs, and assumptions, and try

Using Critical Thinking to Solve Problems

Stating a problem clearly, exploring alternatives, reasoning logically, choosing the best alternative, creating an action plan, and evaluating your plan are all involved in making decisions and solving problems.

Look at the common reasons or excuses that some students use for not solving problems creatively or making sound decisions, Use creative problem solving to list strategies for overcoming these barriers.

1. I'm not a creative person.

   Strategy:

   _____

   _____

2. Facts can be misleading, I like to follow my emotions.

   Strategy:

   _____

   _____

3. I avoid conflict.

   Strategy:

   _____

   _____

4. I postpone making decisions.

   Strategy:

   _____

   _____

5. I worry that I'll make the wrong decision.

   Strategy:

   _____

   _____

to see different viewpoints. Think of an issue you feel strongly about. Then try taking the opposite side of an argument and defend that side, using critical thinking and facts. Talk to people who have different opinions or belong to a different political party. Really listen to their views for understanding and ask them to explain their opinions and why they support certain issues.

6. **Use reasoning.** We are constantly trying to make sense of our world, so we make inferences as ways to explain and interpret events. Effective problem solvers are good at reasoning and check their inferences to see if they are sound and not based on assumptions, which often reflect their own experiences and biases. Ask yourself, "What makes me think this is true? Could I be wrong? Are there other possibilities?" Effective problem solvers do not jump to conclusions.

   Inductive reasoning is generalizing from specific concepts to broad principles. For example, you might have had a bad experience with a math class in high school and, based on that experience, might reason inductively that all math classes are hard and boring. When you get into your college math class, you may discover that your conclusion was incorrect and that you actually like mathematics. In contrast, **deductive reasoning** is drawing conclusions based on going from the general to the specific—for example, "Since all mathematics classes at this college must be taken for credit and this class is a math class, I must take it for credit."

Common Errors in Judgment

Some thoughts and beliefs are clearly irrational, with no evidence to support them. For example, a belief that people cannot change can cause you to stay stuck in unhealthy situations and accept that there is no solution for your problems. In order to solve problems, critical thinking and frequent self-assessment of your thoughts and beliefs are necessary. You can apply the ABCDE method of self-management you learned in this text to dispel myths and irrational and faulty thinking.

Here are some common errors in judgment or faulty thinking that interfere with effective critical thinking:

◆ *Stereotypes* are judgments held by a person or a group about the members of another group—for example, "All instructors are absentminded intellectuals." Learn to see individual differences between people.

◆ *All-or-nothing thinking* means you see events or people in black or white. You may turn a single negative event into a pattern of defeat—for example, "If I don't get an *A* in this class, I'm a total failure." Be careful about using the terms *always* and *never*.

◆ *Snap judgments* are decisions made before all necessary information or facts have been gathered. For example, you may conclude that someone doesn't like you because of one comment or because of a comment made by someone else. Instead, find out the reason for the comment as you may have misinterpreted the meaning.

◆ *Unwarranted assumptions* are beliefs and ideas that you assume are true in different situations. For example, your business instructor allows papers to be turned in late, so you assume that your real estate instructor will allow the same.

- *Projection* is the tendency to attribute to others some of your own traits in an attempt to justify your own faulty judgments or actions—for example, "It's OK if I cheat because everyone else is cheating."

- *Sweeping generalizations* are based on one experience and are generalized to a whole group or issue. For example, if research has been conducted using college students as subjects, you cannot generalize the results to the overall work population.

- The *halo effect* is the tendency to label a person good at many things based on one or two qualities or actions. For example, Serena sits in the front row, attends every class, and gets good grades on papers. Based on this observation, you decide that she is smart, organized, and nice and is a great student in all her classes. First impressions are important in the halo effect and are difficult to change. However, you can make this work for you. For example, say you start out the semester by giving it your all; you go to every class, establish a relationship with the instructor, are involved in class, and work hard. Later in the semester, you may need to miss a class or ask to take an exam early. Your instructor has already formed an opinion of you as a good student and may be more willing to give you extra help or understand your situation, since you have created a positive impression.

- *Negative labeling* is focusing on and identifying with shortcomings, either yours or others. Instead of saying, "I made a mistake when I quit going to my math study group," you tell yourself, "I'm a loser." You may also pick a single negative trait or detail and focus on it exclusively. You discount positive qualities or accomplishments. "I've lost my keys again. I am so disorganized. Yes, I did organize a successful club fundraiser, but that doesn't count."

Creative Problem Solving

Creativity is thinking of something different and using new approaches to solve problems. Many inventions have involved a break from traditional thinking and resulted in an "ah-ha!" experience. For example, Albert Einstein used many unusual approaches and "riddles" that revolutionized scientific thought. (On the Internet, you will find a number of sites that include "Einstein's Riddle." Locate one and test yourself to see if you can answer "who owns the fish?")

Use creativity at each step to explore alternatives, look for relationships among different items, and develop imaginative ideas and solutions. Use critical thinking skills to raise questions, separate facts from opinions, develop reasonable solutions, and make logical decisions. Try the following strategies to unlock your mind's natural creativity:

1. **Use games, puzzles, and humor.** Turn problems into puzzles to be solved. Rethinking an assignment as a puzzle, a challenge, or a game instead of a difficult problem allows an open frame of mind and encourages your creative side to operate. Creative people often get fresh ideas when they are having fun and are involved in an unrelated activity. When your defenses are down, your brain is relaxed and your subconscious is alive; creative thoughts can flow.

WORDS TO SUCCEED

"Imagination will often carry us to worlds that never were. But without it we go nowhere."

CARL SAGAN, *Astronomer, Author*

2. **Challenge the rules.** Habit often restricts you from trying new approaches to problem solving. Often, there is more than one solution. List many alternatives, choices, and solutions and imagine the likely consequences of each. Empty your mind of the "right" way of looking at problems and strive to see situations in a fresh, new way. How many times have you told yourself that you must follow certain rules and perform tasks a certain way? If you want to be creative, try new approaches, look at things in a new order, break the pattern, and challenge the rules. Practice a different approach by completing the Nine-Dot Exercise in **Personal Evaluation Notebook 10.2** on page 328.

3. **Brainstorm.** Brainstorming is a common creativity strategy that frees the imagination. You can brainstorm alone or with a group, which may be more effective in generating as many ideas as possible. Brainstorming encourages the mind to explore new approaches without judging the merit of these ideas. In fact, even silly and irrelevant ideas can lead to truly inventive ideas. While brainstorming ideas for a speech, one study group started making jokes about the topic, and new ideas came from all directions. Humor can generate ideas, put you in a creative state of mind, and make work fun. Top executives, scientists, doctors, and artists know that they can extend the boundaries of their knowledge by allowing themselves to extend their limits. They ask, "What if?" Complete the brainstorming exercise in **Personal Evaluation Notebook 10.3 on page 329.**

4. **Work to change mind-sets.** It is difficult to see another frame of reference once your mind is set. The exercise in **Personal Evaluation Notebook 10.4** on page 330 is an "ah-ha" exercise. It is exciting to watch people really see the other picture. There is enormous power in shifting your perception and gaining new ways of seeing things, events, and people. Perceptual exercises of this kind clearly demonstrate that you see what you focus on and when you reframe. You are conditioned to see certain things, depending on your beliefs and attitudes. Rather than seeing facts, you may see your interpretation of reality. Perceptual distortion can influence how you solve problems and make decisions. For example, John was told that his math instructor was aloof, not student-oriented, and boring. John had a mind-set as he attended the first class and, as a result, sat in the back of class and did not ask questions or get involved. He later found out that his friend was referring to another instructor. John immediately changed his opinion and could see that his mind-set was influencing how he first viewed his instructor. He reframed his impression and developed a positive relationship with the instructor.

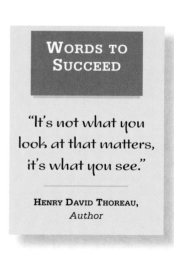

WORDS TO SUCCEED

"It's not what you look at that matters, it's what you see."

HENRY DAVID THOREAU, *Author*

5. **Change your routine.** Try a different route to work or school. Read different kinds of books. Become totally involved in a project. Stay in bed and read all day. Spend time with people who are different from you. In other words, occasionally break away from your daily routine and take time every day to relax, daydream, putter, and renew your energy. Look at unexpected events as an opportunity to retreat from constant activity and hurried thoughts. Perhaps this is a good time to brainstorm ideas for a speech assignment or outline an assigned paper. Creative ideas need an incubation period in which to develop.

6. **Allow failure.** Remember that, if you don't fail occasionally, you are not risking anything. Mistakes are stepping-stones to growth and creativity. Fear of failure

Nine-Dot Exercise

Connect the following nine dots by drawing only four (or fewer) straight lines without lifting the pencil from the paper. Do not retrace any lines. You can see the solution at the end of this chapter on page 345.

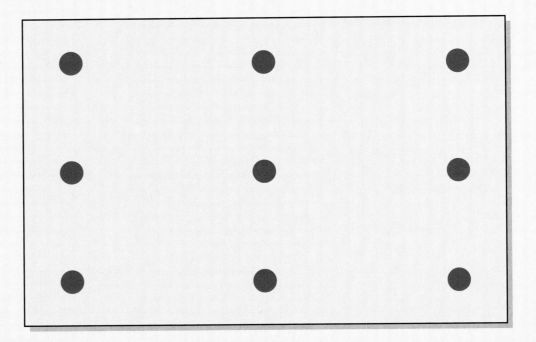

undermines the creative process by forcing us to play it safe. Eliminate the fear and shame of failure experienced in earlier years and learn to admit mistakes. Looking at your mistakes as stepping-stones and opportunities for growth will allow this shift. Ask yourself, "What did I learn from this mistake? How can I handle the same type of situation the next time? How can I prepare for a situation like this the next time?" Creative people aren't afraid to look foolish at times, to generate unusual ideas, and to be nonconformists. They tend not to take themselves too seriously. Being creative has a lot to do with risk taking and courage. It takes courage to explore new ways of thinking and to risk looking different, foolish, impractical, and even wrong.

7. **Expect to be creative.** Everyone can be creative. To be a creative person, try to see yourself as a creative person. Use affirmations that reinforce your innate creativity:

   ◆ I am a creative and resourceful person.

   ◆ I have many imaginative and unusual ideas.

   ◆ Creative ideas flow to me many times a day.

   ◆ I live creatively in the present.

Brainstorming Notes

Creating an idea is not always enough to solve a problem; it also involves convincing others that your idea is the best solution. Read the following brainstorming notes. Then, on the lines that follow, write your own brainstorming notes about how Basil can sell his ideas to his staff.

Basil's Pizza			Sept. 29, 2007
Brainstorming Notes			
Problem: Should I hire temporary employees or increase overtime of my regular employees to meet new production schedule?			
Ideas	Evaluation	Plus + or Minus –	Solution
hire temp. employees	may lack training	–	1. hire temps
	additional benefits	–	
work regular employees overtime	may result in fatigue	–	2. work overtime
	extra $ for employee	+	explore further
	higher morale	+	
	possible advancement	+	
	cross training	+	
	save on overhead and benefits	+	
turn down contract	not possible	–	
reduce hours store is open	not feasible	–	
reduce product line	not acceptable	–	

_____

_____

_____

_____

_____

_____

_____

Mind-sets

Look at the following figure. Do you see an attractive young woman or an old woman with a hooked nose?

I see an _____

If you saw the young woman first, it is very hard to see the old woman. If you saw the old woman first, it is just as hard to see the young woman.

◆ I act on many of these ideas.

◆ When in the action stage, I act responsibly, use critical thinking, check details carefully, and take calculated risks.

8. **Support, acknowledge, and reward creativity.** If you honor new ideas, they will grow. Get excited about new ideas and approaches, and acknowledge and reward yourself and others for creative ideas. Give yourself many opportunities to get involved with projects that encourage you to explore and be creative. Monitor your daily life as well. How often do you put your creative ideas into action? Is there anything you want to change but keep putting it off? What new hobby or skill have you wanted to try? If you find yourself getting lazy, set a firm deadline to complete a specific project. If you find yourself running frantically, then take an hour or so to review your life's goals and to set new priorities. If you are feeling shy and inhibited, clear some time to socialize and risk meeting new people. Reward your creativity and risk taking by acknowledging them.

WORDS TO SUCCEED

"The man who has no imagination has no wings."

MUHAMMAD ALI,
Professional Boxer

9. **Use both sides of the brain.** You use the logical, analytical side of your brain for certain activities and your imaginative and multidimensional side for others. When you develop and integrate both the left and the right sides of your brain, you become more imaginative, creative, and productive. Learn to be attentive to details and to trust your intuition.

10. **Keep a journal.** Keep a journal of creative ideas, dreams, and thoughts, and make a commitment to complete journal entries daily. Collect stories of creative people. Write in your journal about the risks you take and your imaginative and different ideas.

11. **Evaluate.** Go through each step and examine your work. Look at what you know and don't know and examine your hypotheses. Can you prove that each step is correct? Examine the solution carefully. Can you obtain the solution differently? Investigate the connections of the problem. What formulas did you use? Can you use the same method for other problems? Work with your study team to talk problems out and to see if there are other ways to solve a problem. Practice your decision-making skills by working through the case scenarios in **Personal Evaluation Notebook 10.5** and **10.6** on the following pages.

12. **Practice and be persistent.** Problem solving requires discipline and focused effort. It takes time, practice, and patience to learn any new skill. Stay with the problem and concentrate. **Peak Progress 10.2** on page 336 provides a handy checklist to help you think of new ways to find solutions.

Math and Science Applications

Critical thinking and creative problem solving are essential for success in mathematics, science, and computer science courses. A critical and creative approach is not only important in all academic classes but also vital for job and life success. For example, using logic and the analytical process can help you write papers, prepare for tests, compare historical events, and learn different theories in philosophy. By studying mathematics and science, you will learn such everyday skills as understanding interest rates on credit cards, calculating your tuition, managing your personal finances, computing your GPA, and understanding how our bodies and the world around us works. Basic arithmetic can help you figure out a tip at a restaurant, algebra can help you compute the interest on a loan, basic probability can help you determine the chance that a given event will occur, and statistics can help you with the collection, analysis, and interpretation of data. Critical thinking and creative problem solving will help you make day-to-day decisions about relationships, drugs, alcohol, which courses to take, how to find a job, where to live, how to generate creative ideas for speeches and papers, and how to resolve conflicts. Making sound decisions and solving problems are important skills for school, career, and life.

Problem-Solving Strategies for Math and Science

The basic problem-solving strategies discussed earlier in this chapter starting on page 322 also apply to math and science. There are a number of additional strategies

Anxiety About Math and Science
Some students are nervous about taking courses in math and science, even though the basic principles have many everyday applications. *What are some of the tasks you do daily that involve a working knowledge of basic math and science?*

(*continues on page 336*)

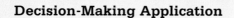

Decision-Making Application

Use critical thinking and creative problem-solving skills as you consider the following case scenario:

I am currently attending a career school and will soon earn my associate's degree in computer-aided design. Once I obtain my degree, should I continue my education or look for a full-time job? My long-term goal is to be an architect. My wife and I have been married for three years and we want to start a family soon.

- **Define the Problem.** "Should I continue my education or get a job"
- **Gather information and ask questions.** "What are the advantages and disadvantages? Whom should I talk with, such as my advisor, instructors at my current school and potential schools, family members, and career professionals?"
- **List pros and cons for each choice.** "What are the factors I should consider, such as cost, opportunities, and time?"

Consider the following pros and cons for each decision and list additional reasons that you think should be considered.

Decision: *Continue education at a local state university.*

Pros	Cons
I'll get a better job with a four-year degree.	I'll have to take out more student loans.
I'm enjoying school and the learning process.	I want to put my skills into practice in the job.
I'll meet new, diverse friends and contacts.	A lot of my time at home will be devoted to studying.

Decision: *Get a job.*

Pros	Cons
I can make more money than I am now and start paying off debts.	The opportunities would be better with a four-year degree.
We can start a family.	It will take longer to become an architect.
I get to put my skills to work.	Once I start working full-time, it may be hard to go back to school.

(continued)

Decision-Making Application—continued

- **Choose what you believe is the best solution.** "I have decided to get a job."
- **Review and assess.** "My choice is reasonable and makes sense for me now in my situation. I won't have to work such long hours and juggle both school and work, and I can pay back loans and save money. We can start our family. I can review my long-term goal and determine an alternate way to achieve it."

Would you arrive at the same decision? What would be your decision and your main reasons?

_____

_____

Now set up a problem or decision that you are facing and follow the same steps.

- Problem:

_____

_____

- Where can I get help or information?

_____

_____

Possible Solutions and Pros and Cons

Solution #1: _____

_____

Pros	Cons
1. _____	
2. _____	
3. _____	

Solution #2: _____

_____

Pros	Cons
1. _____	
2. _____	
3. _____	

Solution Chosen and Why

_____

_____

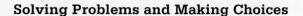

Solving Problems and Making Choices

Every day you solve problems and make choices. Some problems are easy to solve: *What's for dinner?* Some problem are harder: *Can I afford to buy a car?* Some problems change a life forever: *Should I get married?*

You will face problems and choices. You might make good or poor choices. You don't know how a choice will turn out. However, you can follow some steps to help you review your options. They may help you see changes, show you risks, and point out other choices.

Step 1   Know what the problem really is. Is it a daily problem? Is it a once-in-a-lifetime problem?

Step 2   List the things you know about the problem. List the things you don't know. Ask questions. Seek help and advice.

Step 3   Explore alternate choices.

Step 4   Think about the pros and cons for the other choices. Rank them from best to worst choice.

Step 5   Pick the choice you feel good about.

Step 6   After choosing, study what happens. Are you happy about the choice? Would you make it again?

Read the following story and apply the steps in the following exercise.

José's Choice

José is 50 years old. He has a wife and three kids. He has worked as a bookkeeper for 20 years for the same company. The company is relocating. Only a few people will move with the company. Many workers will be losing their jobs.

José's boss says he can keep his job, but he has to move. If he doesn't, he won't have a job. The family has always lived in this town. José's daughter is a senior in high school and wants to go to the local college next year. His twin boys will be in junior high and are looking forward to playing next year for the ninth-grade football team. José's wife works part-time in a bakery. She has many friends and all of her family live nearby.

The family talked about the move. His wife is afraid. His daughter doesn't want to move. The twins will miss their friends. The family has to decide about the move. What is their problem? What are the choices? Can you help them?

(continued)

Solving Problems and Making Choices—continued

Step 1   The problem is _____

_____

_____

Is it a daily problem? _____

_____

_____

Is it a once-in-a-lifetime problem? _____

_____

_____

Step 2   You know _____

_____

_____

You don't know _____

_____

_____

Step 3   The other choices are _____

_____

_____

Step 4   Rank the choices. _____

_____

_____

Step 5   Pick a choice the family might feel good about. _____

_____

_____

Step 6   What might happen? _____

_____

_____

Creative Ideas Checklist

Use this checklist of questions to challenge your usual thought patterns. When exploring alternative approaches to problem solving, you can put each category on a separate card. Here are some examples you might find helpful.

- What other idea does this situation suggest?
- How can I modify?
- What can I subtract? Can I take it apart?
- What can I streamline?
- What can I rearrange?
- Can I transfer?
- Can I combine or blend?
- What are other uses if modified?
- Have I written it out?
- Can I use another approach?
- Can I interchange components?
- Are there any opposites?
- What are the positives and negatives?
- Have I used a mind map, model, diagram, list, or chart?
- Have I used a drawing or picture?
- Have I acted it out?
- Have I talked it out?
- Have I tried it out?
- Should I sleep on it?
- List some of your own suggestions for creative problem solving:

  _____

  _____

  _____

  _____

you can use, many of them designed to get you physically involved. The following strategies integrate all learning styles and make learning physical and personal. Included are sample problems to help you practice these strategies.

1. **Make a model or diagram.** Physical models, objects, diagrams, and drawings can help organize information and can help you visualize problem situations. Use objects, cut up a model, measure lengths, and create concrete situations—for example;

   Problem: What is the length of a pendulum that makes one complete swing in one second?

Strategy: Make a model. With a 50 cm string and some small weights, make a pendulum that is tied to a pencil taped to a desk. To determine the length of the pendulum, measure the distance from the pencil to the center of the weight.

Solution: Since it is difficult to measure the time period accurately, time 10 swings and use the average. The correct answer is approximately 25 cm.

Evaluation: If the length is fixed, the amount of weight does not affect the time period. The amount of deflection does affect the period when large deflections are used, but it is not a factor for small amounts of 5 cm or less. The length of the pendulum always affects the time period.

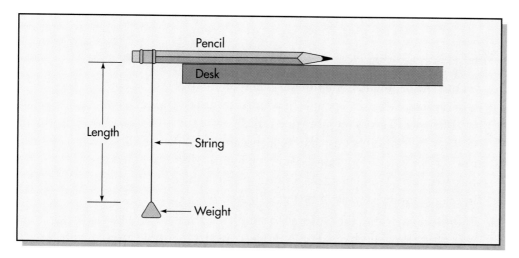

2. **Draw, illustrate, and make tables, charts, or lists.** This is a way to organize data presented in a problem, and it helps you look for patterns. For example, a fruit punch dispenser mixes 4 ml of orange juice with 6 ml of pineapple juice. How many milliliters of orange juice does it mix with 240 ml of pineapple juice?

			Answer
ml Orange juice	4	16	160
ml Pineapple juice	6	24	240

3. **Look for patterns and connections.** a pattern is a regular, systematic repetition that helps you predict what will come next. Field trips and laboratory work can help you find patterns and categorize information, and so can creating tables. For example, an empty commuter train is picking up passengers at the following rate: One passenger got on at the first stop, three got on at the second stop, and five got on at the third stop. How many passengers got on the train at the sixth stop?

Stops	1	2	3	4	5	**Answer** 6
Number of passengers	1	3	5	7	9	11

4. **Act out the problem.** Sometimes it is helpful to physically act out the problem. For example, there are 5 people in your study group and each person initiates a handshake with every member one time. How many total handshakes will there be? There will be 20 handshakes total, because each person shakes hands 4 times (since you cannot shake your own hand). Thus, 5 people times 4 handshakes equals 20 total handshakes. You multiply the total number of people times one number fewer for the handshakes.

5. **Simplify.** Sometimes the best way to simplify a problem is first to solve easier cases of the same problem. For example, consider the study group handshakes and simplify by solving it for two people instead of five. When each person initiates a handshake, two people shake hands a total of two times. Using the formula determined in number 4, you see that the equation is $2 \times 1 = 2$. Fill in the rest of the table:

Number of People	Each Person Initiates Handshake X Times	Total Number Handshakes
2	1	2
3	2	
4		
5	4	20
6		

Along the same lines, when working on homework, studying in your group, or taking a test, always do the easiest problems first. When you feel confident about your ability to solve one kind of problem, you gain enthusiasm to tackle more difficult questions or problems. Also, an easier problem may be similar to a more difficult problem.

6. **Translate words into equations.** Highlight visual and verbal learning by showing connections between words and numbers. Write an equation that models that problem. For example, Sarah has a total of $82.00, consisting of an equal number of pennies, nickels, dimes, and quarters. How many coins does she have in all? You know how much all of Sarah's coins are worth and you know how much each coin is worth. (In the following equation, p = pennies, n = nickels, d = dimes, and q = quarters).

$$p + 5n + 10d + 25q = 8{,}200$$

We know that she has an equal number of each coin, thus, $p = n = d = q$. Therefore, we can substitute p for all the other variables:

$$1p + 5p + 10p + 25p = 41p = 8{,}200, \text{ so } p = 200$$

Sarah has 200 pennies, 200 nickels, 200 dimes, and 200 quarters. Therefore, she has 800 coins.

7. **Estimate, make a reasonable guess, check the guess, and revise.** Using the example in number 6, if you were told that Sarah had a large number of coins that added up to $82.00, you could at least say that the total would be no more than 8,200 (the number of coins if they were all pennies) and no less than 328 (the number of coins if they were all quarters).

8. **Work backwards and eliminate.** For example, what is the largest 2-digit number that is divisible by 3 whose digits differ by 2? First, working backwards from 99, list numbers that are divisible by 3:

99, 96, 93, 90, 87, 84, 81, 78, 75, 72, 69, 66, 63, 60, . . .

Now cross out all members whose digits do not differ by 2. The largest number remaining is 75.

9. **Summarize in a group.** Working in a group is the best way to integrate all learning styles, keep motivation and interest active, and generate lots of ideas and support. Summarize the problem in you own words and talk through the problem out loud. Explain the problem to your group and why you arrived at the answer. Talking out loud, summarizing chapters, and listening to others clarifies, thinking and is a great way to learn.

10. **Take a quiet break.** If you still can't find a solution to the problem as a group, take a break. Sometimes it helps to find a quiet spot and reflect. Sometimes working on another problem or relaxing for a few minutes while listening to music helps you return to the problem refreshed.

Overcome Math and Science Anxiety

Many people suffer from some math and science anxiety, just as almost everyone gets a little nervous when speaking before a large group. The first step in learning any subject is to use critical thinking and creative problem solving to manage and overcome stage fright or anxiety. (See **Personal Evaluation Notebook 10.7** on page 340 to evaluate your comfort level.)

◆ **Be aware.** Observe how your body responds to anxiety and keep a journal of your thoughts and reactions. Don't suppress or deny your anxiety, but acknowledge it

The History of Your Anxiety

If you've experienced anxiety with math or science, it may be helpful to retrace the history of your anxiety. Write your responses to the following questions and exercises:

1. Try to recall your earliest experiences with math and science. Were those experiences positive or negative? Explain what made them negative or positive.

_____

_____

_____

_____

2. If you struggled with math or science, did you get help? What support did you tap into?

_____

_____

_____

_____

_____

_____

_____

_____

3. Summarize your feelings about math.

_____

_____

_____

_____

4. List all the reasons you want to succeed at math.

_____

_____

_____

_____

_____

and choose to let it go. Become aware of how you relax. Try deep breathing and relaxation techniques to help you become calm and centered.

- **Take control.** Anxiety is a learned emotional response. You were not born with it. Since it is learned, it can be unlearned. Take responsibility and don't allow unreasonable fears to control your life.

- **Be realistic.** Don't take a math or science class if you don't have the proper background. It is better to spend the summer or an additional semester to gain the necessary skills, so that you don't feel overwhelmed and discouraged.

- **Keep up and review often.** If you prepare early and often, you will be less anxious. The night before your test should be used for reviewing, not learning new material.

- **Get involved.** Focus your attention away from your fears and concentrate on the task at hand. You can overcome your math anxiety by jotting down ideas and formulas, drawing pictures, and writing out the problem. You keep your energy high when you stay active and involved. Reduce interruptions and concentrate fully for 45 minutes. Discipline your mind to concentrate for short periods. Time yourself on problems to increase speed and make the most of short study sessions.

- **Study in groups.** Learning does not take place in isolation but, rather, in a supportive environment where anxiety is reduced and each person feels safe to use trial and error methods. Creativity, interaction, and multiple solutions are proposed when you study in groups. You will build confidence as you learn to think out loud, brainstorm creative solutions, and solve problems. See **Peak Progress 10.3** on page 342 for a comprehensive checklist of questions to use as you problem solve.

- **Have a positive attitude.** As mentioned earlier, having a positive attitude is key to learning any subject. Do you get sidetracked by negative self-talk that questions your abilities or the reason for learning math skills? Choose to focus on the positive feelings you have when you are confident and in control. Replace negative and defeating self-talk with positive "I can" affirmations. Much of math anxiety, like stage fright and other fears, is compounded by this negative thinking and self-talk. Approach math and science with a positive "can do", inquisitive attitude.

- **Ask for help.** Don't wait until you are in trouble or frustrated. Get a tutor, see the instructor, and join a study group. If you continue to have anxiety or feel lost, go to the counseling center. Try enrolling in a summer refresher course. You'll be prepared and confident when you take the required course later.

- **Dispute the myths.** Many times, fears are caused by myths, such as "Men are better than women at math and science " or "Creative people are not good at math and science." There is no basis for the belief that gender has anything to do with math ability, nor is it unfeminine to be good at math and science. Success in math and science requires creative thinking. As mathematician Augustus De Morgan said, "The moving power of mathematics is not reasoning, but imagination." Use critical thinking to overcome myths. See **Peak Progress 10.4** on page 343 to apply the Adult Learning Cycle to overcoming anxiety.

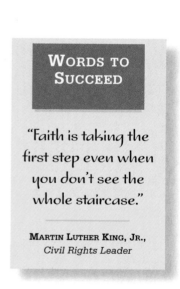

WORDS TO SUCCEED

"Faith is taking the first step even when you don't see the whole staircase."

MARTIN LUTHER KING, JR., *Civil Rights Leader*

Problem-Solving Checklist

When you enroll in any course, including a math or science course, consider these questions:

- Have you approached the class with a positive attitude?
- Have you built confidence by getting involved in problems?
- Have you clearly defined the problems?
- What do you want to know and what are you being asked to find out?
- Have you separated essential information from the unessential?
- Have you separated the known from the unknown?
- Have you asked a series of questions: How? When? Where? What? If?
- Have you devised a plan for solving the problem?
- Have you gone from the general to the specific?
- Have you explored formulas, theories, and so on?
- Have you made an estimate?
- Have you illustrated or organized the problem?
- Have you made a table or a diagram, drawn a picture, or summarized data?
- Have you written the problem?
- Have you discovered a pattern to the problem?
- Have you alternated intense concentration with frequent breaks?
- Have you tried working backwards, completing similar problems, and solving small parts?
- Have you determined if you made careless errors or do not understand the concepts?
- Do you think, apply, reflect, and practice?
- Have you asked for help early?
- Have you been willing to put in the time required to solve problems?
- Have you analyzed the problem? Was your guess close? Did your plan work? How else can you approach the problem?
- Have you brainstormed ideas on your own?
- Have you brainstormed ideas in a group setting?
- Have you rewarded yourself for facing your fears, overcoming anxiety, and learning valuable skills that will increase your success in school, in your job, and in life?

WORDS TO SUCCEED

"Man's mind, once stretched by a new idea, never regains its original dimensions."

OLIVER WENDALL HOLMES,
Author

Applying the Adult Learning Cycle to Overcoming Math and Science Anxiety

1. **RELATE. Why do I want to learn this?** I want to be confident in math and science. Avoiding math and science closes doors and limits opportunities. More than 75 percent of all careers use math and science, and these are often higher-status and better-paying jobs. This is essential knowledge I'll use in all facts of life.

2. **OBSERVE. How does this work?** I can learn a lot about applying critical thinking and creative problem solving to mathematics and science by watching, listening, and trying new things. I'll observe people who are good at math and science. What do they do? I'll also observe people who experience anxiety and don't do well and learn from their mistakes, I'll try using new critical thinking techniques for dealing with fear and observe how I'm improving.

3. **REFLECT. What does this mean?** I'll apply critical thinking to mathematics and science. What works and doesn't work? I'll think about and test new ways of reducing anxiety and break old patterns and negative self-talk that are self-defeating I'll look for connections and associations with other types of anxiety and apply what I learn.

4. **DO. What can I do with this?** I will practice reducing my anxiety. I'll find practical applications for connecting critical thinking and creative problem solving to math and science. Each day I'll work on one area. For example, I'll maintain a positive attitude as I approach math and science classes.

5. **TEACH. Whom can I share this with?** I'll form and work with a study group and share my tips and experiences. I'll demonstrate and teach the methods I've learned to others. I'll reward myself when I do well.

Remember, attitude is everything. If you keep an open mind, apply strategies you have learned in this chapter, and practice your critical thinking skills, you will become more confident in your problem-solving abilities.

Taking Charge

In summary, in this chapter, I learned to:

- *Appreciate the importance of critical thinking.* Critical thinking is fundamental for understanding and solving problems in coursework, in my job, and in all areas of my life. I have learned to examine beliefs, assumptions, and opinions against facts, to ask pertinent questions, and to analyze data. Critical thinking is especially important for mastering math and science.

- *Apply essential critical thinking skills.* Bloom's Taxonomy outlines the six critical thinking skills that college requires (from lowest- to highest-order): knowledge, comprehension, application, analysis, synthesis, and evaluation.

- *Use the problem-solving process.* When I problem solve, I will (1) state and understand the problem; (2) gather and interpret information; (3) develop and implement a plan of action; and (4) evaluate the plan or solution.

- *Incorporate problem-solving strategies.* My attitude has a lot to do with how I approach problem solving, especially in math and science classes. I have developed a positive, inquisitive attitude and a willingness to explore, probe, question, and search for answers and solutions. I have created interest and meaning in studying math and science. I will replace negative self-talk with affirmations. I will use my critical thinking skills and be persistent in solving problems. I will participate in a supportive, group environment, such as a study group.

- *Avoid errors in judgment.* I will avoid using stereotypes, snap judgments, unwarranted assumptions, sweeping generalizations, and the halo effect. I will not project my habits onto others in order to justify my behavior or decisions.

- *Define the problem.* I observe, analyze, and define the problem clearly and state it in a sentence or two. I know what is being asked and have defined the main points. I write out the problem in words and go from the general to the specific.

- *Ask questions and gather information.* I think and reflect about what I know, what I need to know, and what I am trying to find out. What is my theory or hypothesis? How is this problem similar to or different from other problems I have solved? I look for patterns, connections, and relationships.

- *Choose a strategy.* How do I set up this problem? What model, formula, drawing, sketch, equation, chart, table, calculation, or particular strategy will help? I choose the most appropriate strategy and outline a step-by-step plan.

- *Solve the problem.* I use the strategy I've selected and work the problem. I show all my work, so I can review. I make an estimate of what I think the answer will be.

- *Review and check.* I look back and see if I answered the question asked. Did I solve the problem? Is my answer reasonable and does it make sense? If not, did I make careless errors or misunderstand the concepts? I will retrace my steps.

• *Use creative problem solving.* I will use creative problem solving to approach the problem from a different direction and explore new options. What problems are similar? Is there a pattern to the problem? I will brainstorm various strategies. I will act out the problem, move it around, picture it, take it apart, translate it, and summarize it in my own words. I will solve easier problems first and then tackle harder problems.

• *Overcome anxiety for math and science.* If I am anxious about taking math and science courses, I will attempt to maintain a positive attitude, use helpful resources available to me, and take control and focus on the task at hand.

Solution to the Nine-Dot Exercise on Page 328

When confronted with this problem, most people approach it by remaining within the boundaries of the dots. However, when you move outside the confines of the dots and the boundaries are reset, you can easily solve the puzzle. This exercise helps illustrate that some problems cannot be solved with traditional thinking.

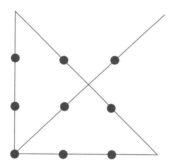

Marina and Josef Koshetz

RESTAURANT OWNERS

Related Majors: Restaurant and Food Service Management, Business

Creativity at Work

Marina Koshetz and her husband, Josef, have recently opened a small restaurant that serves foods from their homeland of Russia. Starting their restaurant was a great deal of work, requiring getting the correct permits, remodeling an existing building, purchasing equipment, and planning the menu. The couple works long hours, six days a week. Before opening the restaurant at 11 A.M., Marina makes bread while Josef mixes together the traditional dishes they will serve. Then Marina remains in the kitchen to cook and prepare dishes while Josef waits tables and runs the cash register. At the end of the day, the couple washes the dishes and cleans the restaurant together. Although the restaurant is closed on Mondays, Marina and Josef use that day to plan the next week's specials and purchase food and other supplies.

Despite their hard work, the couple has made only enough money to cover costs. On a recent Monday afternoon, the two restaurateurs brainstormed ways to attract more customers. The restaurant is located in a quiet neighborhood on the edge of a district where many Russian immigrants live. So far, almost all of their customers have been Russian. Josef and Marina realized that they needed to do more to attract other residents to their restaurant. They decided to host an open house and invite everyone who lived within a mile radius of the restaurant. Then they decided to add a couple of popular American dishes and began running ads in a local newspaper. Soon their restaurant was attracting more customers, and the business began to show a profit.

CRITICAL THINKING How did Josef and Marina use creativity and critical thinking to improve their business?

Peak Performer Profile

Scott Adams

He's been described as a techie with the "social skills of a mousepad." He's not the sort of fellow you'd expect to attract media attention. However, pick up a newspaper, turn to the comics, and you'll find him. He's Dilbert. Cartoonist Scott Adams created this comic-strip character who daily lampoons corporate America and provides a humorous outlet for employees everywhere.

Though creative at a young age, Adams' artistic endeavors were discouraged early on. The Famous Artists School rejected him at age 11. Years later, he received the lowest grade in a college drawing class. Practicality replaced creativity. In 1979, Adams earned a B. A. in economics from Hartwick College in Oneaonta, New York, and in 1986, an MBA from the University of California at Berkeley. For the next 15 years, Adams settled uncomfortably into a number of jobs that "defied description." Ironically, the frustrations of the workplace—power-driven co-workers, inept bosses, and cell-like cubicles—fueled his imagination. Adams began doodling, and Dilbert was born.

Encouraged by others, Adams submitted his work to United Media, a major cartoon syndicate. He was offered a contract in 1989, and "Dilbert" debuted in 50 national newspapers. Today, "Dilbert" appears in 2,000 newspapers in 65 countries and was the first syndicated cartoon to have its own web site.

With such mass exposure, coming up with new ideas for cartoons could be a challenge. However, Adams found the perfect source: He has made his e-mail address available. He gets hundreds of messages a day from workers at home and abroad. His hope is that, through his creative invention, solutions will develop for the problems he satirizes.

PERFORMANCE THINKING Of the Creative Problem-Solving strategies on pages 326–331, which one do you think has been most helpful for Scott Adams and why?

CHECK IT OUT According to Scott Adams, "Creativity is allowing yourself to make mistakes. Art is knowing which ones to keep." Adams is no stranger to taking chances and voicing his views on management—both in the workforce and the government. At **www.dilbert.com,** you can read (and respond to, if you like) the Dilbert.blog written by Adams, and you can sign up to receive the Dilbert Newsletter (a.k.a. the DNRC—the official publication of Dogbert's New Ruling Class). Although it's geared for entertainment, the games section includes a "Mission Statement Generator," which provides a handy list of keywords commonly used in drafting mission statements.

Review and Applications

Performance Strategies

Following are the top 10 strategies for critical thinking and creative problem solving:

◆ Create a positive attitude.

◆ Use writing to draw sketches and critically solve problems.

◆ Use flash cards to practice formulas, equations, and terms.

◆ Think about and examine similar problems that you understand and try similar ways to solve this problem.

◆ Look for patterns.

◆ Make tables, diagrams, pictures, and charts.

◆ Go step by step and then work backwards.

◆ Translate equations into words and words into equations.

◆ Analyze problems and write out what you know and what you don't know.

◆ Integrate all learning styles and practice again and again.

Tech for Success

Take advantage of the text's web site at **www.mhhe.com/ ferrett6e** for additional study aids, useful forms, and convenient and applicable resources.

◆ **Working on weak areas.** There are excellent on-line programs that help you determine the mathematical areas where you need the most work. ALEKS (**www. highedmath.aleks.com**) is a tutorial program that identifies your less proficient areas, then focuses on improvement through practice and targeted problems.

◆ **Math at your fingertips.** In your studies, you will come across many standard calculations and formulas, most of which can be found on-line and downloaded. Although this should not replace working through the formulas yourself to make sure you understand their applications, it does make incorporating math into your everyday life much easier.

Review Questions

Based on what you have learned in this chapter, write your answers to the following questions:

1. Name six essential critical thinking skills necessary for success in college.

2. What are the attributes of a critical thinker?

3. What are the four steps to problem solving?

4. Name five strategies for becoming more creative.

5. Name five strategies for problem solving in math and science.

CONQUERING FEAR OF FAILURE

In the Classroom

Gloria Ramone is a single mom who works part-time and lives and attends school in the inner city. She is eager to complete her education, begin her career, and have the opportunity to receive a higher salary. She is an electronics student who wants her classes to be practical and relevant. She is required to take a class in critical thinking, a class she is resisting because she sees no practical application to her job. Her attitude is affecting her attendance and participation.

1. Offer ideas to help Gloria see the importance of critical thinking in decision making.

_____

_____

2. Help her connect decisions in school with job decisions.

_____

_____

In the Workplace

Gloria is now a manager in a small electronics business. She is also taking evening classes, working toward a business degree. She has received promotions quickly on her job, but she knows that she needs further management training. Gloria is very interested in the electronics field and loves to solve problems. On a daily basis, she is faced with issues to solve and has decisions to make. She has lots of practice predicting results and using critical thinking for problem solving. Gloria enjoys most of the business classes, but she doesn't want to take the classes in finance and statistics. Gloria has math anxiety and is dreading the upper-division math and statistics.

3. What strategies in this chapter can help Gloria overcome math anxiety?

_____

_____

4. What are some affirmations Gloria could use to help her develop a positive attitude about math?

_____

_____

_____

REVIEW AND APPLICATIONS

CHAPTER 10

APPLYING THE ABCDE METHOD OF SELF-MANAGEMENT

In the Journal Entry on page 319, you were asked to describe a decision you made that cost you a great deal in time, money, or stress. How would using critical thinking and creative problem solving have helped you make better decisions?

_____

_____

Now that you know more strategies for critical thinking and creative problem solving, apply the ABCDE method to a difficult situation you have encountered, such as a financial dilemma, a rigorous course, or a serious personal crisis. Use your critical thinking skills to work through the situation and arrive at a positive result.

A = Actual event:

B = Beliefs:

C = Consequences:

D = Dispute:

E = Energized:

Use positive visualization and practice deep breathing with your eyes closed for just one minute. See yourself calm, centered, and relaxed, learning formulas, practicing problem solving, and using critical thinking to work through problems. You feel confident about yourself because you have learned to control your anxiety and maintain a positive attitude.

Practice Self-Management

For more examples of learning how to manage difficult situations, see the "Self-Management Workbook" section of the Online Learning Center web site at **www.mhhe.com/ferrett6e.**

APPLY BLOOM'S TAXONOMY

Different situations call for different levels of thinking. Although many, if not all, these skills are required in every course you take, jot down the classes or situations where you might use a particular thinking skill to a greater degree. For example, if you are in a speech class, you may be asked to evaluate others' speeches.

Critical Thinking Skill	Task	Class or Situation
Knowledge	Recite; recall; recognize	
Comprehension	Restate; explain; state; discuss; summarize	
Application	Apply; prepare; solve a problem; explore a case study	
Analysis	Break ideas apart and relate to other ideas; complete an essay	
Synthesis	Integrate ideas; create new ideas; improve on design	
Evaluate	Critique; evaluate; cite advantages and disadvantages	

CHAPTER 10 ▲ REVIEW AND APPLICATIONS

PROBLEM SOLVING

Write three problems you may be experiencing in the workplace or at school. Use critical thinking to find creative solutions to the problems.

Problems

1. _____
   _____
   _____

2. _____
   _____
   _____

3. _____
   _____
   _____

Possible Solutions

1. a. _____
   b. _____
   c. _____

2. a. _____
   b. _____
   c. _____

3. a. _____
   b. _____
   c. _____

PREPARING FOR CRITICAL THINKING

Brainstorm alternative approaches and solutions to the problems that arise in your day-to-day activities. By using critical thinking, you will be able to explore new ideas as you fill in this form.

Issues/Problems in Day-to-Day Activities

_____

_____

_____

_____

_____

Solution #1: _____

Pros	Cons	Potential Consequences	Costs	Timing

Solution #2: _____

Pros	Cons	Potential Consequences	Costs	Timing

Solution #3: _____

Pros	Cons	Potential Consequences	Costs	Timing

REVIEW AND APPLICATIONS

CHAPTER 10

YOU CAN SOLVE THE PROBLEM: SUE'S DECISION

Every day you solve problems. Some problems are easy to solve: *Should I do my shopping now or later?* Some problems are harder: *My car is in the shop. How will I get to work?* Some problems change your life forever: *Can I afford to go to school?*

Every day life brings problems and choices. The kinds of choices you make can make your life easier or harder. Often, you do not know which direction to take. But there are ways to help you be more certain. There are steps you can take. You can look at your choices before you make them. You can see some of the problems you may face. You may find you have other or better choices. Here are some steps to help you make choices:

Step 1   Know what the problem really is. Is it a daily problem? Is it a once-in-a-lifetime problem?

Step 2   List the things you know about the problem. List the things you don't know. Ask questions. Get help and advice.

Step 3   Explore alternate choices.

Step 4   Think about the pros and cons for the other choices. Put them in order from best to worst choice.

Step 5   Pick the choice you feel good about.

Step 6   Study what happens after you have made your choice. Are you happy about the choice? Would you make it again?

Read the following story and apply the steps in the following exercise.

Sue has been diagnosed with cancer. Her doctor has told her that it is in only one place in her body. The doctor wants to operate. He thinks that he will be able to remove all of it, but he still wants Sue to do something else. He wants her to undergo chemotherapy for four months, which will make her feel very sick. It will make her tired, but the medicine can help keep the cancer from coming back.

Sue is not sure what to do. She has two small children who are not in school. Sue's husband works days and cannot help care for the children during the day. Sue's family lives far away, and she cannot afford day care. She asks herself, "How will I be able to care for my children if I am sick?"

The doctor has told Sue that she must make her own choice. Will she take the medicine? Sue must decide. She will talk with her husband, and they will make a choice together.

What is Sue's problem? What are her choices? What would you decide? Apply the six steps to help Sue make a good choice by writing responses to the following questions and statements.

CHAPTER 10 ▸ REVIEW AND APPLICATIONS

Step 1   The problem is

_____

_____

_____

Step 2

   a. You know these things about the problem:

_____

_____

_____

   b. You don't know these things about the problem:

_____

_____

_____

Step 3   The other choices are

_____

_____

_____

Step 4   Rank the choices, best to worst.

_____

_____

_____

Step 5   Pick a choice the family might feel good about.

_____

_____

_____

Step 6   What might happen to Sue and her family?

_____

_____

_____

_____

REVIEW AND APPLICATIONS

CHAPTER 10

YOU CAN SOLVE THE PROBLEM: CASEY'S DILEMMA

You make choices and solve problems every day. Some choices are automatic and don't require much thought, such as stopping a car at a red light or stepping on the gas pedal when the light turns green. Other problems required you to make easy choices, such as which TV show to watch. Other problems are more difficult to solve—for example, what to say to your teenage son when he comes home past curfew, smelling like beer.

In your life, you will face many problems and choices. You might make good or poor choices because you don't always know how a choice will turn out.

There are some steps you can follow to help you make a good choice and solve your problem. These steps can help you think of options and improve your problem-solving skills:

Step 1   Stop and think. Take a deep breath before you say or do something you will regret.

Step 2   Write a problem statement. Be sure to include who has the problem and state it clearly.

Step 3   Write a goal statement. Check to see that it has simple, realistic, and positive words.

Step 4   List all your choices, both the good and the bad choices.

Step 5   Remove choices that don't match your goal, will hurt others, or will cause more problems than they will solve.

Step 6   Make your best choice. Check Step 3 to be sure your choice matches your goal.

Read the following story and apply the steps in the following exercise.

Casey has been divorced for three years, and her children visit their father every other weekend. When he brought the children home this weekend, he told Casey that he was planning to remarry.

Now her children will have a stepmother and Casey is worried how everyone will get along. She wants her children to continue to visit their dad and enjoy the visits.

Can you help Casey solve this problem? Follow the six steps to help Casey make a choice by writing responses to the following questions and statements.

1. What is the first thing Casey should do?

_____

_____

2. Write a problem statement.

_____

_____

3. What is Casey's goal?

_____

_____

4. List as many choices as you can for Casey.

_____

_____

5. Which choices should Casey cross off her list?

_____

_____

6. What is the best choice for Casey to make?

_____

_____

7. Does your answer in number 6 match her goal in Step 3?

_____

_____

CHAPTER 10   REVIEW AND APPLICATIONS

CAREER DEVELOPMENT PORTFOLIO

ASSESSING AND DEMONSTRATING YOUR CRITICAL THINKING SKILLS

1. **Looking back:** Review your worksheets to find activities through which you learned to make decisions and solve problems creatively. Jot down examples. Also, look for examples of how you learned to apply critical thinking skills to math and science.

   _____

   _____

   _____

   _____

   _____

2. **Taking stock:** What are your strengths in making decisions and in using critical thinking? Are you a creative person? What areas would you like to improve?

   _____

   _____

   _____

   _____

   _____

3. **Looking forward:** How would you demonstrate critical thinking and creative problem-solving skills to an employer?

   _____

   _____

   _____

   _____

   _____

4. **Documentation:** Include documentation of your critical thinking and creative problem-solving skills. Find an instructor or employer who will write a letter of recommendation. Add this letter to your portfolio.

   _____

   _____

   _____

   _____

   _____

Add this page to your Career Development Portfolio.

Create a Healthy Mind, Body, and Spirit

CHAPTER OBJECTIVES

In this chapter, you will learn to

▲ Connect the mind, body, and spirit

▲ Make healthy choices in your diet

▲ Make exercise a positive habit

▲ Manage stress and reduce anxiety

▲ Make sound decisions about alcohol and other drugs

▲ Recognize depression and suicidal tendencies

▲ Protect yourself from disease, unplanned pregnancy, and acquaintance rape

SELF-MANAGEMENT

I'm stressed out with doing so much homework and trying to juggle everything. I haven't been getting enough sleep, and I'm gaining weight from eating too much fast food and not exercising. What can I do to manage my stress and be healthier?

Do you find yourself feeling overwhelmed and stressed by too many demands? Do you lack energy from too little sleep or exercise or from excess calories? In this chapter, you will learn how to manage stress and create healthy habits to last a lifetime. You will see yourself healthy and in charge of your physical, mental, and spiritual life.

JOURNAL ENTRY In **Worksheet 11.1** on page 394, describe a time when you had lots of energy, felt healthy and rested, and was in control of your weight. What factors helped you be calm, confident, and healthy? How did your attitude help you be in control?

Creating balance, managing stress, increasing energy, and providing time for renewal are some of the keys to becoming a peak performer. In this world of multitasking, we need to slow down, become mindful of our purpose, and focus on important priorities. The purpose of this chapter is to present principles and guidelines to help you develop the most effective methods of maintaining your health while learning how to cope effectively with daily demands.

Redefining Health: Connecting the Mind, Body, and Spirit

Many people think of health as being the absence of disease. However, having optimal health—or **wellness**—means living life fully with purpose, meaning, and vitality. Your overall wellness is largely determined by the decisions you make about how you live your life and the preventative measures you take to avoid illness (such as being proactive rather than reactive). However, genetics, age, and accidents also influence your health and are beyond your control. Regardless of your genetics or age, you can optimize your health by understanding the connection among your mind, body, and spirit. The habits you develop now will affect not only how long you live but also the quality of life you enjoy.

The Mind

Peak emotional and intellectual wellness requires that you develop both the thinking and the feeling aspects of the *mind*. It is important to develop critical thinking and creative problem-solving skills, good judgment, common sense, and self-control. Besides good thinking skills and intellectual development, it's important to develop and manage your emotional qualities, such as a positive attitude, optimism, confidence, coping skills, and rapport building. For example, some people have a knack of saying the right thing at the right time. It is important that you understand and be able to express emotions, have empathy for others, manage yourself, and develop healthy relationships.

The Body

Peak *physical* wellness requires eating healthy foods, exercising, getting plenty of sleep, recognizing the symptoms of disease, making responsible decisions about sex, avoiding harmful habits, improving your immune system, and taking steps to prevent illness and physical harm. None of this information is new to us; however, many people have a difficult time putting these good habits into practice.

The Spirit

Peak *spiritual* wellness requires that you think about and clarify your values and question the purpose, beliefs, and principles that give your life meaning. Spirituality

---

WORDS TO SUCCEED

"He who has health has hope; and he who has hope has everything."

ARABIC PROVERB

---

may include your religious beliefs or a belief in a higher power, but it really encompasses a broader dimension, such as your willingness to serve others; your sense of ethics and honesty; your relationship to people, nature, and animals; how you define the purpose of life; the legacy you want to leave; and how you fit into this universe. In Chapter 2, we discussed Maslow's hierarchy of needs. At the highest level, self-actualized people achieve fulfillment, creativity, and higher levels of spiritual growth. Some physicians, such as author Bernie Siegel, believe that spirituality is the essence of wellness and wholeness. The body, mind, and spirit are interconnected. For example, if you are optimistic and live with love, honesty, and forgiveness, you are more likely to be physically well.

Understanding the connection among the mind, body, and spirit will help you develop skills for coping with the demands of school and work. Papers, reports, deadlines, tests, performance reviews, conflicts, committees, commuting, family responsibilities, and presentations are all part of school, career, and life. These demands will also create a considerable amount of stress. Stress is not an external event but part of a larger system, and it affects every part of your mind, body, and spirit.

Awareness

The first step in managing your health is awareness. Observe how your body feels, the thoughts going through your mind, and your level of stress. Be aware of negative habits. You may not even realize that you eat every time you watch television, drink several cans of soda while you study, or nibble while you fix dinner. Fast food may be part of a routine to save time, or you skip breakfast. Or you may find yourself having a drink or smoking when you're under stress instead of learning coping skills. Observe your daily habits and begin to replace unproductive ones with beneficial choices. Take a minute to observe your body's reactions by completing **Personal Evaluation Notebook 11.1** on page 362.

Have you experienced discomfort or a change in your body? If you can identify symptoms and early warning signs of an illness, you can take appropriate action to protect yourself from diseases, such as cancer. (See **Figure 11.1** on page 363.)

Strategies for Good Health Management

1. **Eat healthy foods for high energy.** Eat a nutritious diet daily to control your weight and blood pressure and to reduce depression, anxiety, headaches, fatigue, and insomnia. Many foods, such as dark leafy greens, avocadoes, berries, tomatoes, yogurt, nuts, seeds, whole grains, sweet potatoes, lean meats, and a variety of fruits and vegetables, pack a lot of nutrition.

   The *Dietary Guidelines for Americans,* published jointly every five years by the Department of Health and Human Services and the U.S. Department of Agriculture, provides authoritative advice about how good dietary habits can promote health and reduce risk for major chronic diseases. The 2005 edition can be found at **www.healthierus.gov/dietaryguidelines.** Additionally, the following general guidelines will help you make healthy choices in your diet:

   ◆ *Eat a variety of foods.* Include whole grains, lots of fruits and vegetables, milk, meats, poultry, fish, and breads and cereals in your diet. See **Peak Progress 11.1** on page 364 for suggested balanced diets illustrated by the food pyramids.

Becoming Attuned to Your Body

Set aside a few minutes of quiet, private time. Stop what you are doing and close your eyes. Try to focus on your body. Observe its reactions to these few minutes of quiet. Notice your breathing. Write your observations on the lines provided.

1. How were you sitting? _____
2. What was your state of mind? _____
3. Were you feeling rested, energetic, or tired? _____
4. Did you observe pain anywhere in your body? Where? _____
5. Was there any feeling of tension? _____ Yes _____ No
6. Were you holding your shoulders up? _____ Yes _____ No
7. Were you clenching your jaw? _____ Yes _____ No

Try to stop and discern how you're feeling several times a day.

- *Eat plenty of fresh fruits and vegetables.* Fruits and vegetables are excellent sources not only of disease-preventing fiber but also of vitamins.
- *Take a multivitamin supplement every day.* Many experts advise taking vitamin and mineral supplements for optimal health. Some recommend extra C, E, B complex, and A vitamins if you are under stress.
- *Increase whole-grain cereals and breads.* Whole grains contain fiber, vitamins, and minerals. They are also filling and keep you from snacking.
- *Reduce the amount of animal fat in your diet.* Too much animal fat can increase the level of cholesterol in your blood, which can affect your cardiovascular system, causing your body to get less oxygen.
- *Broil or bake meats rather than fry them.* If you do fry, use olive oil or other monounsaturated fat instead of butter.
- *Cut down on sugar and refined carbohydrates.* Sugar has no nutritional value and promotes tooth decay. Eating refined sugars creates a downward cycle, a sudden drop of blood sugar, shakiness, and a need for more glucose. This can lead to Type II diabetes and other health problems. Maintain an even energy level rather than a quick fix. Substitute whole grains and fresh fruit and vegetables for white bread and sweets.
- *Cut down on salt.* Salt is an ingredient in many prepared foods. Be aware of how much salt you use and if it's necessary.
- *Cut down on caffeine.* A small amount of caffeine can enhance alertness and effectiveness for some people. A cup or two of coffee in the morning can give you a burst of energy and create a sense of well-being; it does not pose a health problem for most people. Caffeine is not just found in coffee, however; it is also in tea, many soft drinks, chocolate, and some medications,

Figure 11.1 Observing Caution Signs

The American Cancer Society provides the following guidelines. See your doctor if you notice any of the following symptoms:

C Change in bowel or bladder habits

A A sore that does not heal

U Unusual bleeding or discharge

T Thickening or lump in the breast or elsewhere

I Indigestion or difficulty in swallowing

O Obvious changes in a wart or mole

N Nagging cough or hoarseness

SOURCE: The American Cancer Society, 2001.

Observing Caution Signs   Protect yourself by monitoring your health. *Do changes in your health always signal a serious condition?*

such as aspirin products. Thus, it is easy to consume too much caffeine and become anxious, nervous, jittery, irritable, and prone to insomnia. Too much caffeine may deplete your B vitamins, minerals, and other nutrients that your body needs to cope with stress. Caffeine can also be addictive: The more you consume, the more it takes to produce the desired burst of energy. If you experience caffeine-induced symptoms, reduce your intake, but do so gradually. Headaches can result from rapid caffeine withdrawal. Try substituting

Coffeehouse Blues
The caffeine in coffee can be pleasurable in moderate amounts, but, because it is addictive, there's a downside to drinking too much. *What are some other ways to increase your energy besides ingesting caffeine?*

Eating for Health and Energy

Beneficial eating and exercise habits can pay big dividends for success in life. Researchers have studied the effects of diet for years and have attempted to agree on the best diet for most people. In 1993, the Harvard School of Public Health sponsored a major conference on nutrition. Scientists and nutritionists from the United States and Europe met to look at the traditional Mediterranean diet, which may have prolonged life and prevented disease for centuries in Mediterranean countries. The experts released a model similar to that of the U.S. Department of Agriculture's (USDA's) original food guide pyramid. The Mediterranean model suggests the consumption of more beans and legumes over animal-based proteins and advocates the use of olive oil in a daily diet.

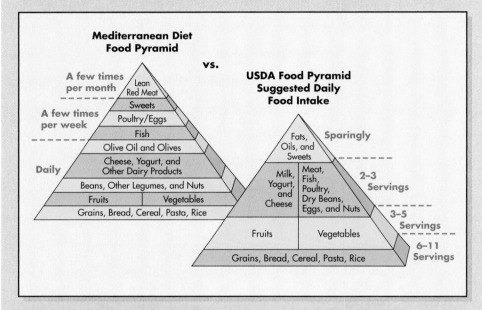

SOURCE: U.S. Department of Agriculture, U.S. Department of Health and Human Services.

My Pyramid

The food guide pyramid developed by the USDA has continued to change over the years. Because we have individual diet and exercise needs, the latest pyramid, called My

(continued)

decaffeinated coffee and tea (green tea is especially high in antioxidants) or plain water after lunch. Check labels to confirm that your substitutions are indeed caffeine-free.

◆ *Use alcohol in moderation.* If you drink alcoholic beverages, do it in moderation of one or two drinks about three times a week. Too much alcohol increases the risk for certain cancers, cirrhosis of the liver, damage to the heart and brain, and strokes. Never drink and drive.

Eating for Health and Energy (continued)

Pyramid, has been redesigned to make use of on-line technology to help you pinpoint what you should be eating based on your age, sex, and activity level. Each "color" in the pyramid is tied to a specific food group (i.e., orange = grains, green = vegetables, etc.) To determine your needs and create a good eating plan, go to **www.mypramid.gov**.

For example, the recommendations for a 25-year-old woman who exercises less than 30 minutes each day look like this (based on 2,000 calories per day):

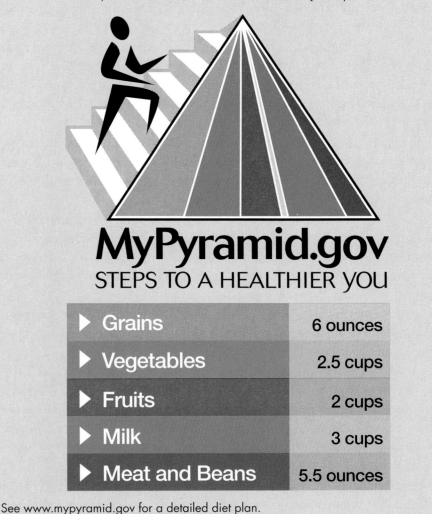

MyPyramid.gov
STEPS TO A HEALTHIER YOU

▶ Grains	6 ounces
▶ Vegetables	2.5 cups
▶ Fruits	2 cups
▶ Milk	3 cups
▶ Meat and Beans	5.5 ounces

See www.mypyramid.gov for a detailed diet plan.

2. **Maintain your ideal weight.** You will have more energy and be generally healthier when you maintain your ideal weight. Weight maintenance is a major problem for many people because they eat too much junk food and exercise too little. People spend millions of dollars every year on fad diets, exercise equipment, and promises of a quick fix. If you need to lose weight, don't try to do it too quickly with fad diets or fasting. Consult a physician to discuss the best method for you. Slow weight loss is more effective and helps you keep the

WORDS TO SUCCEED

"More die in the United States of too much food than of too little."

JOHN KENNETH GALBRAITH
Economist

weight off longer. Support groups for weight control can be very helpful. Building energy by nourishing and helping the body do its job effectively takes a long-term commitment to changing habits. Build exercise into your daily life and try taking a walk when you have the urge to snack.

The following general guidelines will help you maintain your ideal weight:

◆ *Exercise.* If you want to lose and keep weight off as well as have more energy, build exercise into your life. If you have the time and are in a safe area, park your car a little farther out in the parking lot and walk a few extra steps. Sign up for an exercise class or jog on a track. Find out what local fitness resources are offered free by your school or community.

◆ *Eat only when you're hungry.* Make sure you eat to sustain your body, not because you are depressed, lonely, bored, or worried.

◆ *Don't fast.* Fasting can lead to major health problems. When a person fasts as a way to reduce daily caloric intake, the body's metabolic rate decreases, so the body burns calories more slowly than before. Then, at a certain point, the body has an urge to binge, which is nature's way of trying to survive famine. Make small, consistent, and healthy changes.

◆ *Eat regularly.* Don't skip meals. If you are really rushed, carry a banana, an apple, raw vegetables, or nuts with you. Establish a three-meals-a-day pattern or six small meals. You need to eat regularly and have a balanced diet to lose weight and keep it off.

◆ *Create healthy patterns.* Eat slowly and enjoy your food. Eat in one or two main places. For example, eat in the dining room or at the kitchen table. Resist the urge to eat on the run, sample food while you are cooking, munch in bed, or snack throughout the day. Use critical thinking as you explore your eating patterns in **Personal Evaluation Notebook 11.2.**

◆ *Get help.* Do you have a problem with weight control or are you overly concerned with being thin? Do you have a problem with eating too little or with fasting (such as **anorexia nervosa**)? Do you eat and then vomit as a way to control your weight (as with **bulimia nervosa**)? Anorexia and bulimia are illnesses and need medical treatment. You might feel isolated and powerless, but there are many resources that can offer help. Confide in a friend or family member. Go to the counseling or health center. Look in the yellow pages or discuss your problem with your doctor or counselor. Don't wait. (See **Peak Progress 11.2** on page 368.)

3. **Renew energy through rest.** It is important for good health and energy to get enough rest. Although amounts vary from one person to the next, most people need between six and nine hours of sound sleep each night. The key is not to be concerned about the number of hours of sleep that you require but, rather, whether or not you feel rested, alert, and energized. Some people wake up rested after five hours of sleep; others need at least nine hours to feel energized and refreshed. If you wake up tired, try going to bed earlier for a night or two and then establish a consistent bedtime. Notice if you are using sleep to escape conflict, depression, or boredom. It is also important to find time to relax each day. Use critical thinking in **Personal Evaluation Notebook 11.3** on page 369 to assess your commitment to getting rest.

Reviewing Your Health

Read the following and write your comments on the lines provided.

1. Do you maintain your ideal weight? If not, what can you do to achieve your ideal weight?

   _____

   _____

   _____

2. Describe a few of your healthy eating habits.

   _____

   _____

   _____

3. Describe a few of your unhealthy eating habits.

   _____

   _____

   _____

4. Do you feel you have control over your eating? Explain.

   _____

   _____

   _____

5. What can you do to make positive and lasting changes in your eating habits?

   _____

   _____

   _____

4. **Exercise for energy.** The goal of aerobic exercise is to raise the heart rate above its normal rate and to keep it there for 20 or more minutes. Regular aerobic exercise is essential for keeping your body at peak performance. Aerobic exercise strengthens every organ in the body (especially the heart), reduces stress, strengthens the immune system, increases muscle strength, reduces excess fat, stimulates the lymph system, and increases your endurance stamina. Exercise can also alter body chemistry by changing hormones, adjusting metabolism, and stimulating the brain to release more endorphins. Endorphins are natural chemicals in the body that affect your state of mind and increase feelings of

Eating Disorders

Known as a perfectionist, 20-year-old Jill was a bright, social, college sophomore who seemed to have it all together. She was able to cope with the stress of college and part-time work. In just a few months, however, she broke up with her boyfriend, her sister married and moved away, and she felt pressured to choose a college major before the semester ended. In addition, she lost control of her car on an icy road and her car was totaled, although she wasn't seriously hurt. All these changes caused her to feel depressed and out of control. She loved to exercise, so she started running twice as much as usual. She withdrew from family and friends and didn't feel like eating, so she gradually eliminated most foods from her diet, except fruits, yogurt, and salads. She continued to lose weight until her family insisted that she get counseling and weigh in at the health center every day. Jill didn't think she had an eating disorder because she wasn't obsessed with being thin, but she was diagnosed as suffering from anorexia nervosa.

Most *anorexics* are white, young, middle-class women who have a distorted body image and want to be thin. Some anorexics are perfectionists, grew up in families with high expectations, and feel overwhelmed that they cannot meet these expectations and turn to something that they can control—their weight.

Bulimia is another eating disorder; it involves binge eating and purging through forced vomiting, or by using laxatives. It can cause long-term dental damage and chemical imbalances, which both can lead to serious health issues, organ damage and failure, bone loss, and even death. Often, people with eating disorders also suffer from depression, anxiety, or substance abuse.

The National Association of Anorexia Nervosa and Associated Disorders estimates that approximately 8 million people in the United States have anorexia nervosa, bulimia, and related eating disorders. Essentially, about 3 of every 100 people in this country eat in a way disordered enough to warrant treatment. Ninety percent of those dealing with eating disorders are women. Research suggests that about 4 of every 100 college-age women have bulimia.

If you are dealing with an eating disorder, or you suspect a friend or family member is struggling with a disorder, seek help immediately. For more information, visit the National Eating Disorders Association web site at **www.nationaleatingdisorders.org** or call 1-800-931-2237.

well-being. How much exercise you need to stay in good physical health depends on your goals, your present fitness level, your overall health, and your physician's advice. For most healthy people, a regular program of 20 to 30 minutes of aerobic exercise is needed at least three times a week for optimum health. There are many ways to exercise aerobically. Walking, swimming, bicycling, dancing, and jogging are some popular ways. The key is to start slowly, build up gradually, and be consistent! If you experience pain during aerobic exercise, stop. Assess your commitment to exercise in **Personal Evaluation Notebook 11.4** on page 370.

Getting Proper Rest

Read the following and write your comments on the lines provided.

1. Do you generally wake up in the morning feeling rested and eager to start the day or tired with little energy?

_____

_____

2. How many times do you normally hit the snooze button before getting out of bed?

_____

3. What prevents you from getting enough rest?

_____

_____

4. Besides sleep, what activities can renew your body and spirit?

_____

_____

Increasing Energy
Most people benefit from as little as 20 minutes of exercise three times a week. *What is your exercise goal?*

5. **Establish healthy relationships.** Healthy relationships can be a wonderful source of increased energy. We all know the deep satisfaction of sharing a good talk or a wonderful evening with a friend, or the sense of pride and accomplishment when

Committing to Exercise

Read the following and write your comments on the lines provided.

1. Describe your current commitment to exercising your body.

   _____

   _____

   _____

2. What are your excuses for not exercising? What can you do to overcome these barriers?

   _____

   _____

   _____

3. Set your exercise goal.

   _____

   _____

   _____

we've completed a team project. Indeed, other people can help us think through problems, develop self-confidence, conquer fears, develop courage, brainstorm ideas, overcome boredom and fatigue, and increase our joy and laughter. The following are some barriers to healthy relationships:

◆ Getting so busy at school and work or with your goals that you ignore your friends and family

◆ Being shy and finding it difficult to build friendships

◆ Approaching friendship as a competitive sport

It takes sensitivity and awareness to value others' needs. It also takes courage to overcome shyness. The key is to see the enormous value of friendships. Personal friends bring a deep sense of joy and fellowship to life. Life's sorrows and setbacks are lessened when you have friends to support and help you through difficult times. You will find yourself energized by good friends.

Manage Stress

As a college student, you are faced with many demands—papers, tests, deadlines, studying, finances, relationships, and conflicts. Coping with stress means being able to manage difficult circumstances, solve problems, resolve conflicts, and juggle the daily demands of school, work, and relationships. Developing effective coping strategies is essential for making your life productive, meaningful, and healthy. Stress is the body's natural reaction to any demand, pleasant or unpleasant. Stress is simply your body's reaction to external events (e.g., taking an exam or giving a speech) or internal events (e.g., fear, worry, or unresolved anger). Everything you experience stimulates your body to react and respond. Stress is normal and, in fact, necessary for a vital life. With too little positive stress, many people are bored and unproductive. The key is knowing how to cope with demands and channel stress instead of dealing with stress in unproductive ways, such as

◆ Denying, ignoring, or repressing your feelings or problems, so that you don't have to face them

◆ Lashing out at other people

◆ Turning to alcohol or other drugs or smoking as a way to reduce tension

◆ Eating too much or too little

◆ Thinking you can handle your problems yourself without getting help

Life is a series of changes, and these changes require adaptive responses. The death of a close family member or friend, a serious illness or accident, exams, divorce, relationship changes, financial problems, and the loss of a job are all changes that require adjustment and cause some types of stress. It is important to realize, however, that your perception of and reaction to these inescapable life events determine how they affect you. Even positive events can be stressful. Events such as marriage, a promotion, the birth of a baby, a new romantic relationship, a new roommate, graduation, even vacations and holidays may be disruptive and demanding for some people and, therefore, stressful. Public speaking may be exciting and fun for one person but may cause an anxiety attack in another. Look at the early warning signs in **Peak Progress 11.3** on page 372 to see if you are under too much stress.

You can choose to see stress as a challenge or something to avoid. You can choose a positive, optimistic outlook; use resources; and rechannel energy in positive and productive ways. Stress is something you can learn to manage with coping strategies.

A little stress can add excitement to life and even help motivate you. However, not coping effectively with prolonged stress can wear you down. Too many negative or positive changes stimulate the production of certain hormones and chemicals that affect the body. The solution is not to avoid stress but to acknowledge it directly and learn to manage and channel it. Try the following strategies:

1. **Become attuned to your body and emotions.** Many of us have been taught to deny emotions or physical symptoms and ignore stress. Become aware of your body and its reactions. Stress produces physical symptoms. Are you having physical symptoms of stress, such as frequent headaches? Are you finding it difficult to relax? Are you emotionally upset, depressed, or irritable?

    The transition to college forces you to become more self-reliant and self-sufficient. Give yourself permission to feel several different emotions, but also learn strategies to pull yourself out of a slump. (See **Figure 11.2** on page 373.) You might set a time limit: "I accept that I'm feeling overwhelmed or down today. I will allow a few hours to feel these emotions; then I will do what I know works to make me feel better." Remember that you have the power to change negative, hurtful thoughts and to create positive habits.

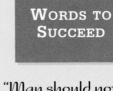

WORDS TO SUCCEED

"Man should not try to avoid stress any more than he would shun food, love, or exercise."

HANS SELYE
Endocrinologist

Stress Leads to Burnout Signs

Here are early warning signs that your body is pushing too hard and too long and may be on its way to burnout. If you have more than four of the following symptoms, you may want to consider getting help for dealing with stress overload.

- Frequent headaches, backaches, neck pain, stomachaches, or tensed muscles
- Insomnia or disturbed sleep patterns
- No sense of humor; nothing sounds like fun
- Fatigue, listlessness, or hopelessness and low energy
- Increase in alcohol or other drug intake or smoking
- Depression or moodiness
- Racing heart
- Appetite changes (eating too much or too little)
- Frequent colds, flu, or other illnesses
- Anxiousness, nervousness; difficulty concentrating
- Irritability, losing your temper, and overreacting
- Lack of motivation, energy, or zest for living
- A feeling that you have too much responsibility
- Lack of interest in relationships

2. **Exercise regularly.** Experts say that exercise is one of the best ways to reduce stress, relax muscles, and promote a sense of well-being. Most people find that they have more energy when they exercise regularly. Make exercise a daily habit and a top priority in your life.

3. **Dispute negative thoughts.** We've talked about the importance of self-management and monitoring your self-talk. Using the ABCDE Method of Self Management helps you challenge self-defeating thoughts and replace them with positive, realistic, and hopeful thoughts. Pessimists tend to describe their stressful situations with such words as *always* and *never,* and they imagine the worst possible outcomes. Negative thinking can lead to a self-fulfilling prophecy; if you say you're going to fail, you probably will. You can change these negative thoughts to confident, optimistic, and positive thoughts and actions.

4. **Rest and renew your mind, body, and spirit.** Everyone needs to rest, not only through sleep but also through deep relaxation. Too little of either causes irritability, depression, inability to concentrate, and memory loss. Yoga or pilates is a great way to unwind, stretch and tone the muscles, and focus energy. Many people find that meditation is essential for relaxation and renewal. You don't have to practice a certain type of meditation; just create a time for yourself when your mind is free to rest and quiet itself. Go for a walk, listen to music, create art, dance, or sing. Other people find that a massage relieves physical and

Figure 11.2 Student Stress Factors

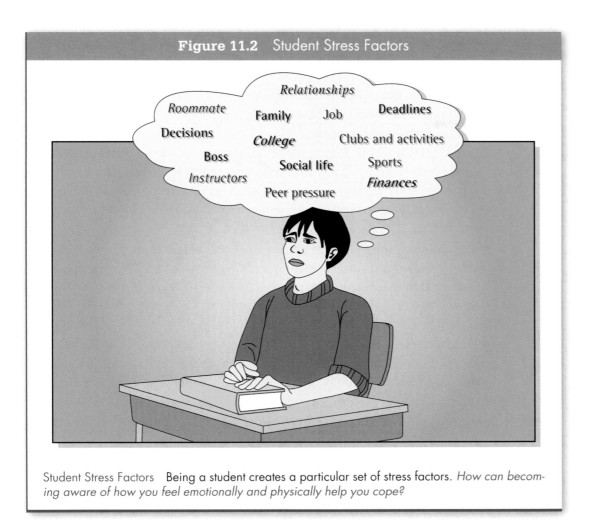

Student Stress Factors   Being a student creates a particular set of stress factors. *How can becoming aware of how you feel emotionally and physically help you cope?*

mental tension. Visualization is another powerful technique for relaxing your body and reducing anxiety.

Go to the health or counseling center and ask about a method called *deep relaxation*—activities that relax your mind, body, and spirit. Here's a simple version:

> Sit in a quiet place and breathe deeply, fill your lungs, and exhale completely. Tense and relax your body by clenching your fist and then relaxing it; now the other fist. Then shrug your shoulders, wrinkle your forehead, squint your eyes, clench your jaw, and tighten your thighs and toes, followed by relaxing each muscle.

5. **Use breathing methods.** Deep breathing reduces stress and energizes the body. If you are like many people, you breathe in short, shallow breaths, especially when under stress. Begin by sitting or standing up straight, breathe through your nose, fill your lungs completely, push out your abdomen, and exhale slowly and fully. Focus on a word, a sound, or your breathing and give it your full attention for about 10 minutes. You can do a variation of this anytime during the day, even if you can't escape to a quiet spot.

6. **Develop hobbies and interests.** Hobbies can release stress. Sports, painting, quilting, reading, and collecting can add a sense of fun and meaning to your life. Many find satisfaction and focus by developing an interest in the environment, the elderly, politics, children, animals, or the homeless. Investigate volunteering opportunities in your area.

7. **Develop a support system.** The support and comfort of family and friends can help you clear your mind, sort out confusion, and make better decisions. Express your feelings, fears, and problems to people you trust. Dozens of support groups can help you cope with stress. A group of people with similar experiences and goals can give you a sense of security, personal fulfillment, and motivation.

8. **Take mini-vacations.** Next time you are put on hold on the phone or kept waiting in line, pull out a novel and enjoy a few moments of reading. Practice deep breathing or head rolls, or visualize the tension flowing out of your body. Get up and stretch periodically while you're studying. These mini-vacations can keep you relaxed and expand your creativity.

9. **Rehearse a feared event.** When you mentally rehearse a stressful event beforehand, you are inoculating yourself against it. Your fears become known and manageable. Visualization is an excellent technique for rehearsing an event.

10. **Exercise and stretch the mind.** Mental exercise can refresh and stimulate your entire life. Reading, doing crossword puzzles, and playing challenging board games renew the spirit and stretch the mind. Attend lectures, take workshops and seminars, and brainstorm creative ideas or current subjects with well-read friends. Think of all the ways that you can renew and expand your thinking. Make friends with creative people who inspire you and renew your perspective.

11. **Create balance in your life.** Peak performers recognize the importance of balance between work and play in their lives. Assess your activities and determine if they are distractions or opportunities. Learn to say no to requests that do not enrich your life or the lives of others. Set a time limit on work, demands from other people, and study; reward yourself for tasks accomplished.

12. **Develop a sense of humor.** Nothing reduces stress like a hearty laugh or spontaneous fun. Discovering the child within helps us release our natural creativity. Laughing produces endorphins, natural chemicals that strengthen the immune system and produce a sense of well-being. Laughter also increases oxygen flow to the brain and causes other positive physiological changes. Find and delight in the joy of nature, music, art, and people.

13. **Plan; don't worry.** Leading a disorganized life is stressful. Write down what has to be done each day; don't rely on your memory. Take a few minutes the night before to lay out your clothes, pack your lunch, and jot down a list of the next day's priorities. Get up 20 minutes early, so you don't have to rush. Worrying is stressful and depletes your energy. You can have only one thought in your mind at a time, so don't allow self-defeating thoughts to enter. Set aside 20 minutes a day to plan, solve problems, and explore solutions. Get involved in the solutions, not the problem. When your time is up, leave the problems until your next scheduled session.

14. **Be assertive.** Stand up for your rights, express your preferences, and acknowledge your feelings. Assertive communication helps you solve problems, rather than build resentment and anger, and increases your confidence and control over your life.

15. **Keep a log.** A log can be helpful in gaining insight into the types of situations that are stressful for you and how you respond to them. Write journal entries in this book. Be honest with yourself and record daily events and your reactions. Writing in a journal also helps clarify your concerns and decisions and can give you a fresh perspective.

16. **Get professional help.** It is normal to experience grief after a loss or a major transition, and you should allow yourself time to grieve, so that you can experience and release your emotional pain. However, if your sadness, depression, or anger continues despite your best efforts, or if you are suicidal, get professional help. Call a crisis hot line, health center, counseling center on campus or in the community, or mental health department for a list of agencies that can provide help. With a counselor's guidance, you can gain insight into your pattern of reacting to stress and modify your perception and behavior. (See **Peak Progress 11.4** on using the Adult Learning Cycle to create a more healthy balance.)

PEAK PROGRESS   11.4

Applying the Adult Learning Cycle to Create a Healthier Lifestyle

1. **RELATE. Why do I want to learn this?** I know I must reduce my stress, control my eating habits, and exercise and maintain my ideal weight. What areas do I struggle with, and what would I like to improve? Having strong physical energy will boost my mental energy.

2. **OBSERVE. How does this work?** Who do I know that seems to "have it all together"? What behaviors do I want to emulate? What factors or benefits will motivate me to make positive changes about my health behaviors? I'll try developing new habits and using new techniques and strategies and observe how I'm improving.

3. **REFLECT. What does this mean?** What strategies are working, and where do I continue to struggle? What tools or information would keep me motivated?

4. **DO. What can I do with this?** I will make a commitment to improve my health by eating healthy and exercising. Each day, I'll work on one area. For example, I'll use my time-management skills and find ways to build exercise into my day. I'll practice reducing my stress in many different situations. I'll find practical application and use my new skills in everyday life.

5. **TEACH. Whom can I share this with?** I'll try to find a partner with similar interests and we'll keep each other motivated. I'll share my tips, experiences, and setbacks.

Living a healthy lifestyle is a life-long commitment. You will repeat the cycle many times in order to stay focused and successful.

Unhealthy Addictions

Unfortunately, many college students turn to alcohol, other drugs, or cigarettes as a way to relieve stress. One of the biggest concerns many health professionals have about students smoking marijuana or drinking every day is that you simply delay developing coping skills, which then leads to very serious problems. Rather than looking for quick fixes, practice coping strategies, such as facing your problems head on, resolving conflicts through communication, and finding creative solutions to solve problems. It is important that you develop a set of coping strategies and practice them every day. Succumbing to unhealthy behaviors will only escalate your problems.

Alcohol Abuse

Alcohol abuse can be one of the biggest energy drains on your body. Because it is a drug, alcohol can alter moods, become habit-forming, and cause changes in the body. Because alcohol is a depressant, it depresses the central nervous system.

Alcoholism can begin as early as childhood and is often influenced by peer pressure. A major life lesson is to think for yourself and be responsible for your choices and behavior. Alcoholism is considered a chronic disease that can be progressive and even fatal. For most adults, a glass of wine or a beer at dinner is not a problem, but it is important to realize that even a small amount of alcohol can cause slowed reactions and poor judgment. See **Peak Progress 11.5** on how to "party with a plan."

High school and college drinking has become a major social and health problem. Students in the United States consume more than 430 million gallons of alcohol per year. There are more than 25 million alcoholics in the United States today, and most say they began drinking in high school and college.

Students often believe that there isn't a problem if they drink just beer, but it is possible to be an alcoholic by drinking only beer. A six-pack of beer contains the

WORDS TO SUCCEED

"I made a commitment to completely cut out drinking and anything that might hamper me from getting my mind and body together. And the floodgates of goodness have opened upon me—both spiritually and financially."

DENZEL WASHINGTON
Actor

PEAK PROGRESS   11.5

Party with a Plan

Motivational speaker Randy Haveson has created Party with a Plan®—a quick guide for drinking alcohol sensibly. See **www.partywithaplan.org** for a complete description.

> 0 = if you are pregnant, driving, under age, or taking medications
> 1 = no more than one drink per hour (12 oz. beer; 4 oz. wine, 1 oz. shot)
> 2 = no more than two times per week
> 3 = no more than three drinks in one day

Used by permission from Randy Speaks, Inc. copyright 2006

Figure 11.3 The Costs of Alcohol

- In 2005, 16,972 fatalities were caused by alcohol-related crashes. That means 1 alcohol-related fatality every 33 minutes.
- Three out of 10 Americans my be involved in an alcohol-related crash.
- In 2003, 1.4 million people were arrested in the United States for driving under the influence of alcohol or narcotics rate of 1 of every 135 licensed drivers.
- According to the Department of Justice, each year 37 percent of rapes and sexual assaults involve alcohol use by the offender, as do 15 percent of all robberies, 27 percent of all aggravated assaults, and 25 percent of all simple assaults.

SOURCES: National Highway Traffic Safety Association; National Center for Statistics and Analysis; www.factsontap.org/collexp/stats.htm; U.S. Department of Justice, *Alcohol and Crime: An Analysis of National Data on the Prevalence of Alcohol Involvement in Crime.*

The Costs of Alcohol   Knowing the facts can help you make the right choices. *Would you allow yourself or a friend to drink and drive?*

same amount of alcohol as six drinks of hard liquor—or one beer is equivalent to one shot of hard liquor. Take a close look at some of the facts about alcohol and alcoholism in **Figure 11.3.**

Although one in five college students report that they don't drink at all, the Core Institute, an organization that surveys college drinking practices, reports the following:

◆ Three hundred thousand of today's college students will eventually die of alcohol-related causes, such as drunk driving accidents, cirrhosis of the liver, various cancers, and heart disease.

◆ One hundred fifty-nine thousand of today's first-year college students will drop out of school for alcohol- or other drug-related reasons.

◆ The average student spends $900 on alcohol each year, compared with $450 on textbooks.

◆ Almost one-third of college students admit to having missed at least one class because of their alcohol use.

◆ One night of heavy drinking can impair your ability to think abstractly for up to 30 days.

Cigarette Smoking

It is hard to believe that anyone would smoke after hearing and viewing the public awareness campaigns that present the risks of cigarette smoking. Perhaps the billions of dollars advertisers spend each year convince enough people that smoking makes you more attractive, sexier, cooler, and calmer. Those advertising claims are in stark contrast to the facts shown in **Figure 11.4** on page 378.

Figure 11.4 The Costs of Cigarette Smoking

- Cigarette smoking–related diseases cause about 430,700 deaths each year in the United States.
- Cigarette smoking is directly responsible for 87 percent of all lung cancer cases and causes most cases of emphysema and chronic bronchitis.
- The Environmental Protection Agency estimates that secondhand smoke causes about 3,000 lung cancer deaths and 37,000 heart disease deaths in nonsmokers each year.
- Nonsmokers married to smokers have a 30 percent greater risk for lung cancer than those married to nonsmokers.
- The effects of secondhand smoke, especially on children, include respiratory problems, colds, and other illnesses, such as cancer.
- Secondhand smoke contains over 4,000 chemicals: 200 are poisons and 63 cause cancer.
- Smoking costs the United States approximately $97.2 billion each year in health-care costs and lost productivity.

SOURCES: American Lung Association, www.lungusa.org/tobacco.

The Costs of Cigarette Smoking   Cigarette smoking causes major health problems for those who smoke, as well as for those exposed to it through secondhand smoke. *Why do you think many people still smoke, in spite of the expense and health risks involved?*

Illegal Drug Use

Almost 80 percent of people in their mid-twenties have tried illegal drugs. Drug addiction also causes major social and health problems. Here are some pertinent facts concerning drug abuse:

- Certain patterns of behavior among marijuana users, especially adolescents, show loss of memory and intellectual reasoning.
- The cost of drug abuse to American society is almost $50 billion a year.
- According to the National Council on Alcoholism and Drug Dependence, marijuana releases five times more carbon dioxide and three times more tar into the lungs than tobacco does.
- Crack addiction can occur in less than two months of occasional use.
- Intravenous drug use causes 24 percent of AIDS cases in the United States.

Critical Thinking About Addictive Substances

Drugs (both legal and illegal), including alcohol and tobacco, are everywhere. People want to feel good and forget their pain and troubles. Every drug-induced high, however, has a crashing low. Try to rely on your inner strength, not on external means, to feel good about life. Be aware of the facts about alcohol and other drug abuse and the high cost of addiction.

You need energy and concentration if you are to be successful at school and in your job. Only you can take responsibility for your life and determine if harmful substances are costing you more than the pleasure you get from them. Ask yourself if you really need to complicate your life, if using addictive substances will actually make your life better.

Overcoming Addictions

Addictive behavior comes in many forms and is not relegated to substance abuse solely. Just as an alcoholic feels happy when drinking, a food addict feels comforted when eating, a sex addict gets a rush from new partners, a shoplifter feels a thrill with getting away with something, an addictive shopper feels excited during a shopping spree, a gambler feels in control when winning, and a workaholic feels a sense of importance while working late each night or on weekends. Addiction is an abnormal relationship with an object or event and is characterized by using a substance or behavior repeatedly. Beginning as a pleasurable act or a means to escape, it progresses until it becomes a compulsive behavior and causes significant problems. Take a good look at your life to see if you have a pattern of addiction. If you don't get this under control now, it will only get worse.

If you are trying to overcome an addiction, you may experience anxiety, irritability, or moodiness. Some people switch addictions to help them cope and to give them the illusion that they have solved the problem. For example, many former alcoholics become chain smokers. Some people take up gambling as a way to have fun and get a rush, but then it becomes a problem. Compulsive gambling can leave people deeply in debt and devastate families and careers. A key question to ask is "Is this behavior causing ongoing disruption in my life or the lives of those close to me?" Warning signs include secrecy; a change in discipline, mood, or work habits; a loss of interest in hobbies or school; and altered eating and sleeping habits. You may become withdrawn, depressed, or aggressive. You must take the initiative to get help. Ask your school counselor or go to the health center.

Here are some additional steps to take to deal with an addiction:

◆ *Admit there is a problem.* The first step toward solving a problem is to face it. Denial is often a reaction for someone with an addiction. He or she may do well in school or hold down a job and, therefore, doesn't see a problem. If you think you have lost control or are involved with someone who has, admit it and take charge of your life. Look at how you handle stress and conflict. Do you solve problems, deny them, or look for an escape?

◆ *Take responsibility for addiction and recovery.* You are responsible for and can control your life. Several support groups and treatment programs are available for a number of addictions. Search the Internet or your local phone book for resources in your area, or contact

   Alcoholism: Alcoholics Anonymous: **www.alcoholics-anonymous.org**

   Drug abuse: National Institute on Drug Abuse: **www.drugabuse.gov**

   Gambling: National Council on Problem Gambling: **www.ncpgambling.org**

Sexual behavior: The Society for the Advancement of Sexual Health:
www.ncsac.org

Smoking: The Centers for Disease Control and Prevention, Tobacco Information and Prevention Source (TIPS): **www.cdc.gov/tobacco**

Codependency

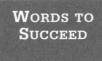

WORDS TO SUCCEED

"One trait of addictive families is that we never recognize our own addictions."

LORNA LUFT
Entertainer

Even if you are not directly involved with alcohol or other drugs, your life may be affected by someone who is involved. A common term used when discussing non-addicted people whose lives are affected by an addict is **codependency.** There are many definitions of codependency, and codependent people exhibit numerous self-defeating behaviors, such as low self-esteem; lack of strong, solid, and emotionally fulfilling relationships; lack of self-control; and overcontrolling behavior. A codependent person may

◆ *Avoid facing the problem of addiction.* Denying, making excuses, justifying, rationalizing, blaming, controlling, and covering up are all games that a codependent person plays in an effort to cope with living with an addict.

◆ *Take responsibility for the addict's life.* This may include lying; taking over a job, an assignment, or a deadline; or somehow rescuing the addict.

◆ *Be obsessed with controlling the addict's behavior.* For example, a codependent person may hide bottles; put on a happy face; hide feelings of anger; confuse love and pity; and sometimes feel that, if only he or she could help more, the addict would quit.

If you feel that you have problems in your life as a result of growing up in an alcoholic family or that you may be codependent, get help. Organizations such as Adult Children of Alcoholics (ACA) address the issues of people who grew up in alcoholic homes. There are many agencies and groups that can make a difference.

Emotional Health

Everyone has the blues occasionally. Sometimes stress and emotional problems interfere with your goals or ability to cope. A variety of emotional problems affect college students and professionals in all walks of life.

Depression

Depression is an emotional state of sadness ranging from mild discouragement to feelings of utter hopelessness. Each year, over 60 million people suffer from mild forms of depression, which is relatively short-term. Severe depression is deeper and may last months or years. Over 6 million Americans suffer serious depression that impairs their ability to function. Depression accounts for 75 percent of all psychiatric hospitalizations. Depression can occur as a response to the following situations:

◆ *Loss.* The death of a loved one, divorce, the breakup of a relationship, the loss of a job, involvement in a robbery or an assault, or any other major change, loss, disappointment, or violation can trigger depression.

- *Health changes.* Physical changes, such as a serious disease or illness, an injury, childbirth, or menopause, can result in chemical changes that may cause depression.
- *An accident.* A car accident can be a very traumatic event, leading to feelings of being out of control and depression. Even if you have not been seriously injured, feelings of hopelessness can result from an accident.
- *Conflicts in relationships.* Unresolved conflicts in relationships can cause depression.
- *Loneliness.* Loneliness can seem like a physical illness. It hurts and can feel as if someone has thrown a wet, dark blanket over your life. It is often felt by freshmen who have left home, family, and friends and haven't yet rebuilt a social network. We'll discuss loneliness in more detail in Chapter 12. Get involved in activities on campus and in the community, get a part-time job, practice listening, and attempt to develop new relationships.
- *Peer pressure.* You may feel pressured to get involved in alcohol, other drugs, smoking, or sex. When you have doubts, stop. Really think about the consequences and why you are allowing others to define your values and boundaries. If you do something that you are not comfortable doing, you may experience depression or sadness. It is as if you have lost a sense of who you really are—so don't be pressured.
- *Daily demands.* You may find yourself feeling overwhelmed and depressed by too many demands. There are deadlines, and you may feel under pressure to choose a major. Nontraditional, or re-entry, students often have to juggle school, work, family, and care of their home. Set your priorities, ask for help, and try to eliminate or reduce unimportant or routine tasks or delegate whenever possible.

Depression can be triggered by many events. Some of these events are tied to certain stages in life. For example, adolescents are just beginning to realize who they are and are trying to cope with the responsibilities of freedom and adulthood. Setting unrealistic goals can also cause depression. If you are facing middle age, you may feel the loss of youth or unrealized career success, or you may miss children who are leaving home. For an elderly person, the loss of physical strength, illness, the death of friends, and growing dependency may prompt depression.

Learn to recognize some of the common symptoms of depression:

- Sleep disturbance (sleeping too much or too little, constantly waking up)
- Increase in or loss of appetite
- Overuse of prescription drugs
- Use of nonprescription drugs
- Overconsumption of alcohol
- Withdrawal from family and friends, leading to feelings of isolation
- Recurring feelings of anxiety
- Anger and irritability for no apparent reason
- Loss of interest in formerly pleasurable activities
- A feeling that simple activities are too much trouble
- A feeling that other people have much more than you have

When depression causes persistent sadness and continues for longer than a month, severe depression may be present.

Suicide

Suicidal thoughts occur when a feeling of hopelessness sets in and problems seem too much to bear. Suicidal people think that the pain will never go away, but they usually respond to help. Be concerned if you or others exhibit the following warning signs:

♦ Excessive alcohol or other drug use
♦ Significant changes in emotions (hyperactivity, withdrawal, mood swings)
♦ Significant changes in sleeping, eating, studying patterns, or weight

Severely Depressed
If not addressed, depression can become very serious and lead to thoughts of suicide. *How can you help a friend or co-worker who is suffering from depression?*

♦ Feelings of hopelessness or helplessness
♦ Little time spent with or a lack of close, supportive friends
♦ Nonsupportive family ties
♦ Rare participation in group activities
♦ Recent loss or traumatic or stressful events
♦ Suicidal statements
♦ A close friend or family member who committed suicide
♦ Attempted suicide in the past
♦ Participation in dangerous activities
♦ A plan for committing suicide or for giving away things

You should be concerned if you know someone who exhibits several of these warning signs. If you do know someone who is suffering from depression and seems suicidal, take the following steps:

1. Remain calm.
2. Take the person seriously; don't ignore the situation.
3. Encourage the person to talk.
4. Listen without moralizing or judging. Acknowledge the person's feelings.
5. Remind the person that counseling can help and is confidential.
6. Remind the person that reaching out for help is a sign of strength, not weakness.
7. Call a suicide hot line or a counselor at school; get the name of a counselor for the person to call or make the call with him or her.
8. Stay with the person to provide support when he or she makes the contact. If possible, walk or drive the person to the counselor.
9. Seek support yourself. Helping someone who is suicidal is stressful and draining.

Protecting Your Body

Reliable information about sex can help you handle the many physical and emotional changes you will experience in life. It can also help you make better decisions about difficult choices. Although sex is a basic human drive and a natural part of life, there are also dangers, including unplanned pregnancies, sexually transmitted diseases, and rape. Your level of sexual activity is a personal choice and can change with knowledge, understanding, and awareness. Just because you were sexually active at one time does not mean you cannot choose to be celibate now. No one should pressure you into sexual intercourse. If you decide to be sexually active, you need to make responsible choices and decisions and to be aware of the risks. Know the facts and protect your body.

Sexually Transmitted Diseases (STDs)

Sexually transmitted diseases, or STDs, are spread through sexual contact (including genital, vaginal, anal, and oral contact) with an infected partner. A person may be infected yet appear healthy and symptom-free. See **Figure 11.5** on page 384 for a list of STDs and their symptoms, treatments, and risks. Despite public health efforts and classes in health and sexuality, STDs continue to infect significant numbers of young adults. Even if treated early, STDs are a major health risk and can have a devastating effect on your life. They can result in damage to the reproductive organs, infertility, or cancer.

Acquired immune deficiency syndrome (AIDS) is a fatal STD. It weakens the immune system and leads to an inability to fight infection. AIDS is transmitted through sexual or other contact with the semen, blood, or vaginal secretions of someone with human immunodeficiency virus (HIV) or by sharing nonsterile intravenous needles with someone who is HIV-positive. Occasionally, it is contracted through a blood transfusion. An estimated 1 million people are currently living with HIV in the United States, with approximately 40,000 new infections occurring each year. Half of all new infections in the United States occur in people 25 years of age or younger.

AIDS is not exclusively a homosexual disease. In fact, worldwide, it is most commonly spread by heterosexual intercourse. AIDS cannot be transmitted by saliva or casual contact, such as by sharing utensils or shaking hands. Recently, drug therapies using a combination of drugs have been successful in controlling the progression of the disease. However, there is currently no cure for AIDS.

To avoid contracting any STD, follow these guidelines:

◆ Know your partner. It takes time and awareness to develop a healthy relationship.

◆ Ask a prospective partner about his or her health. Don't assume anything based on looks, class, or behavior.

◆ No matter what the other person's health status is, explain that you always use safety precautions.

◆ Latex condoms and dental dams can help protect against most sexually transmitted diseases. However, abstinence is the only totally effective method in preventing the spread of STDs and preventing pregnancy. It is vital to know the facts, the latest treatments, and the ways you can protect your body.

Figure 11.5 STDs: Symptoms, Treatments, and Risks

Sexually Transmitted Diseases	What Are the Common Symptoms?	What Is the Treatment?	What Are the Risks?
Genital herpes — Cold sores can spread genitally via oral sex.	Ulcers (sores) or blisters around the genitals	There is no cure; antiviral medications can shorten and prevent outbreaks.	Highly contagious; become more susceptible to HIV infection
Genital warts	The virus lives in the skin or mucous membranes and usually causes no symptoms; some people get visible genital warts.	There is no cure, although the infection usually goes away on its own. Cancer-related types are more likely to persist.	Higher risk of cervical cancer
Chlamydia	Known as the "silent" disease, because most infected people have no symptoms. Others may experience discharge from genitals or burning sensation when urinating.	Antibiotics	Infertility
AIDS/HIV	No symptoms for years; some carriers can be HIV+.	There is no known cure; medical treatments can slow the disease.	Weakening of the immune system; life-threatening infections

SOURCE: Centers for Disease Control and Prevention, Division of Sexually Transmitted Diseases www.cdc.gov/std.

STDs: Symptoms, Treatments, and Risks   Because STDs are a serious health risk, it is important to separate fact from myth when considering your options for protection. *In what ways can knowing the facts about STDs protect you?*

Birth Control

If your relationship is intimate enough for sex, it should be open enough to discuss birth control and pregnancy if birth control fails. Both men and women need to stop and ask, "How would an unwanted pregnancy change my life?"

Many contraceptives are available, but you must understand that *none are 100 percent foolproof* (except abstinence). Current contraceptives include birth control pills, condoms, diaphragms, sponges, spermicidal foams, cervical caps, intrauterine devices (IUDs), and long-term implants. Douching and withdrawal do not prevent pregnancy and should not be used for birth control. Discuss birth control methods with your partner and with a qualified health professional. Make an informed decision and choose what is best for you.

Understanding and Preventing Acquaintance Rape

Katie, a sophomore living off campus, is on her third date with Jeff, who is in her English class. They have been having a great time together and Jeff is attentive and loving. In fact, Katie has told friends that he puts her on a pedestal. After a movie, they are sitting on her living room couch, drinking wine, talking, and sharing affectionate hugs and kisses. Jeff's kissing becomes more aggressive and Katie pushes his hands away several times. Finally, she tells him she feels uncomfortable, wants to take the relationship slowly, and asks him to leave. Jeff blows up, accuses her of being a tease and leading him on, holds her down, and rapes her.

A typical image about rape involves a stranger lurking around a dark corner of an apartment or a deserted street. Although this does occur and safety precautions should be taken, most rapes and sexual assaults are committed by assailants known by the victim and many are committed in the victim's home. Over 85 percent of all rapes on college campuses are acquaintance or date rapes. According to the FBI, up to 90 percent of all rapes are not reported because the victim fears retaliation and social ostracism, fears not being believed, and, like Katie, may blame herself because she had too much to drink or wonders if she said or did something to give the attacker the wrong idea. Make no mistake about it—date rape is rape.

One in three women in the United States will become a victim of sexual assault in her lifetime. All women are vulnerable to rape, no matter their age, race, class, or physical appearance. Rape is an act of aggression. A rapist is seeking a person he can dominate and control. Check with the counseling center, health center, or campus police for ways to protect yourself from date rape. Here are a few preventative measures:

1. **Make your expectations clear.** Send clear messages and make certain that your body language, tone of voice, and choice of words match your feelings. In a direct, forceful, strong, serious tone, let others know when their advances are not welcome. If you do not want to get physically intimate, don't allow anyone to talk you into it. Be aware of your own limits and feelings and communicate them assertively to your date. Say, "No," loudly and clearly. Scream for help if you need it.

2. **Meet in public places.** Until you know someone well, arrange to meet where others will be around. Double date whenever possible or go out with a group of friends. Have an agreement with friends that you will not leave a party alone or with someone you do not know well.

3. **Trust your intuition.** Be attuned to body cues, be aware of your surroundings, and trust your intuition and instincts. If the situation doesn't feel right, leave and get help as soon as you can. If you feel ill, get help immediately. If you plan to go to a movie, to a party, or for a walk, ask a friend to go with you. If you're on a date, tell others when you expect to be back, take your cell phone, and leave your date's name. If something doesn't feel right, call your roommates or a friend.

4. **Take your time.** It is impossible to spot a rapist by appearance, race, occupation, or relationship to you. The attacker might be your date, your lab partner, an instructor, a friend of a friend, or a neighbor down the hall. Take time to

know a person before you spend time alone with him or her. Don't take chances because someone looks nice or knows someone you know. Don't ask anyone to come to your home unless you really know this person well. Otherwise, make certain a roommate or friends are around. Relationships that start slowly are built on friendship and are healthier and safer.

5. **Recognize that alcohol and other drugs can be dangerous.** The dangers of sexual assault are exacerbated when alcohol and other drugs are involved. Alcohol and other drugs can inhibit resistance, increase aggression, and impair decision-making skills. If you are intoxicated, you may not be able to protect yourself or be aware of the signals that would otherwise warn you of danger. In some cases, date rapists have added what are called date rape drugs, such as Rohypnol (also called Roofies), GHB, Ecstasy, or Ketamine, to the victim's drink, causing the victim to become confused, drowsy, and dizzy; to have impaired judgment; or to experience temporary amnesia. It can lead to loss of consciousness and can result in a coma or death. Never leave your drink unattended, and do not accept drinks from a common container.

6. **Learn to read the danger signals of an unhealthy relationship.** Be concerned if you are dating someone who
   - Pressures you sexually
   - Refers to women as sex objects
   - Drinks heavily or uses drugs and pressures you to drink or take drugs
   - Doesn't respect your wants, needs, or opinions
   - Is possessive or jealous
   - Wants to make decisions for you—tells you whom you may be friends with or what clothes to wear
   - Is bossy or aggressive
   - Has a temper and acts rashly
   - Is physically abusive
   - Is verbally and emotionally abusive through insults, belittling comments, or "sulking" behavior
   - Becomes angry when you say "No"

7. **Be safe and vigilant.** Make wise choices when possible, use common sense, and do everything possible to protect yourself. Don't go jogging alone or in isolated areas, lock your doors and windows, and don't pick up hitchhikers. Make certain you know your campus and community well and stay out of dark, secluded areas. If you are taking a night class, find the safest place to park your car. Carry a cell phone and find out where campus security phones are located. If there is no campus escort policy, arrange to walk to your car with a friend or group from your class. Consider taking a self-defense course; consult a rape crisis counseling center or the campus police to learn if a course is available.

8. **Get professional help.** Unfortunately, even the most careful, diligent, and safety-minded people can be raped. Get to a safe place and call someone you

trust to be with you. Report a rape immediately by calling 911, a rape crisis center, or the local or campus police. Preserve evidence by not bathing or changing clothes. Make certain you get counseling to deal with the trauma. Remember, it is not your fault!

Rape is not just a woman's problem. Besides the fact that both men and women can become victims of rape, many men have girlfriends, wives, or relatives who may also be targets. Understand how your own attitudes and actions perpetuate sexism and violence and work toward changing them. Both men and women can become aware and speak up against such stereotypical attitudes that women who are raped ask for it, or that women are sex objects. You can challenge demeaning and cruel jokes and attitudes by taking a mature, caring stand against violence whenever possible.

1. **Take your time getting to know someone.** Rushing a relationship is a danger sign. Take your time and get to know someone as a person. Look for and create healthy and fulfilling relationships.

2. **Your date has the right to say no.** Respect another person's right to say no under any conditions and at any time. Do not misinterpret the word *no*. Don't expect sex in exchange for dinner or just because you have had sex with this person before. People have a right to change their minds, and this right should be respected. Silence does not mean consent.

3. **Understand and state your intentions.** Be clear about your feelings and intentions and respect your date's feelings and intentions. If you believe you are getting mixed messages, talk about it and clear up any miscommunication. Not only are you protecting your partner, but you are showing empathy and genuine concern and care. If you continue to get mixed messages or the situation doesn't feel right, leave. Listen to your intuition.

4. **Alcohol and other drugs can be dangerous.** Alcohol and other drugs reduce sexual inhibition and the ability to read body language and cues. Some people blame alcohol consumption for their actions that take advantage of someone else or for their own aggressive behavior. This is not an excuse for unacceptable or illegal behavior. If your partner has had too much to drink, is high on drugs, or is otherwise unable to give consent and you have sex with him or her, you have committed sexual assault.

5. **Rape is a serious crime.** Rape is a violent crime and can result in the offender spending years in prison. It is an act of violence, aggression, and force. *No one asks to be raped because of his or her clothing or behavior.* Forced sexual intercourse is degrading and humiliating—and it is rape.

6. **Get involved.** Volunteer at a rape crisis center. Find out if the school has a security escort policy for students taking a night class or using the library in the evening. (If such a service does not exist, perhaps you can organize one.) Listen carefully to women and ask them about feeling pressured, aggression, and sexist behavior. Speak up against sexism or male violence against women or oppression in all its forms.

In summary, in this chapter, I learned to:

- *Connect my mind, body, and spirit.* I envision my body and mind as a whole system and realize that everything is connected. I observe my thoughts, how my body feels, my level of stress, my negative habits, what I eat and drink, and changes or discomfort in my body.

- *Eat a variety of healthy foods in moderation.* I increase my consumption of fresh fruits and vegetables, eat whole grains, limit animal fat, cut down on sugar and caffeine, and take a multivitamin supplement every day. This helps me maintain my ideal weight, increases my self-esteem, and gives me energy.

- *Exercise regularly.* I participate in an aerobic activity for 30 minutes three times a week. I balance rest and relaxation with active sports, such as bicycling, dancing, or swimming. Being active not only helps me maintain my ideal weight but also gives me energy and increases my sense of well-being.

- *Develop healthy relationships.* Spending time with friends who are supportive and share my interests is a great source of satisfaction, and it helps increase my energy and enjoyment of life. Friendships bring a deep sense of joy and fellowship.

- *Reduce stress.* I have developed strategies for reducing stress, including exercising, doing deep breathing, disputing negative thoughts and beliefs, developing a sense of humor, rehearsing feared events, and creating balance in my life.

Taking Charge

- *Use critical thinking to avoid drugs.* Since alcohol is a toxin, heavy drinking can cause brain damage, increase the risk for heart disease, depress the immune system, and cause liver failure. Alcohol and other drugs can cause a loss of memory and intellectual reasoning.

- *Get help for addictions.* I recognize the signs of addiction to food, gambling, and alcohol and other drugs and when to seek help. I know that there are resources on campus and in the community that can help me or someone I know who has a drinking or other drug problem.

- *Observe my emotional health.* Although I know that life has its ups and downs, I am aware of times when I don't seem to bounce back after a disappointment or loss. Some of the warning signs of depression are changes in sleep patterns and appetite, the use of drugs, and feelings of anxiety, anger, isolation, and disinterest. Severe depression and suicidal tendencies occur when feelings are extreme.

- *Protect my body.* I protect myself from illness, sexually transmitted diseases, unwanted pregnancies, and rape. I am knowledgeable, aware, and proactive. I make certain that I visit the health center, use safety precautions, and learn self-defense techniques.

career in focus

Tony Ferraro

FIREFIGHTER

Related Majors: Fire Science, Public Administration

Preventing Stress and Fatigue at Work

Tony Ferraro has been a member of the fire department in his city for 25 years. Three years ago, he was promoted to captain of his station. He and the other firefighters at his station respond to fire alarms, using various techniques to put out fires. They also respond to medical emergencies by providing emergency medical assistance until an ambulance arrives. When not out on calls, Tony and his crew maintain their equipment, participate in drills and advanced fire fighting classes, and keep physically fit.

Tony works two or three 24-hour shifts a week, during which time he lives and eats at the fire station. Because fire fighting involves considerable risks for injury or even death, it is a stressful and demanding job. Being alert, physically fit, energized, calm, and clear-headed is critical for making sound decisions. To stay healthy mentally and physically, Tony studies a form of karate that helps him not only stay in shape but also remain calm and focused. In addition, he drinks no more than one to two cups of coffee a day and has given up smoking.

As captain of his fire station, Tony initiated better eating habits in the kitchen by posting a food pyramid and talking to the other firefighters about reducing fat and sugar in their diet. In addition, he observes the firefighters for signs of stress and makes suggestions when needed, such as taking time off or getting sufficient rest. The company's health insurance policy includes coverage for counseling. Once after a particularly stressful period, Tony invited a stress counselor to speak and offer services at the station.

CRITICAL THINKING Why is it important for firefighters to work toward healthy goals in physical, emotional, and mental areas?

Peak Performer Profile

Lance Armstrong

Many people bicycle for fun. For Lance Armstrong, the Olympic world-champion cyclist, it's a job he loves to do. Athletic from an early age, Armstrong grew up in the suburbs of Dallas, Texas, and was competing as a triathlete at age 16. By his senior year in high school in the late 1980s, the U.S. Olympic development team had spotted him as a world-class cyclist, and he was invited to train in Colorado. Many championships and titles followed.

However, in 1996, when Armstrong was only 25, he faced the most difficult trial of his life. Diagnosed with advanced testicular cancer that had spread to his lungs, lymph nodes, abdomen, and brain, he was given about a 50 percent chance of survival. Although shaken, Armstrong was determined to overcome the disease. He underwent surgery, changed his diet, and began months of aggressive chemotherapy. He also focused on the future: "I might have a bald head and not be as fast, but I'll be out there. I'm going to race again." He was pronounced cancer-free a year later.

July 30, 2001, was a landmark day for America's "golden boy of cycling." After pedaling more than 2,000 grueling miles, he crossed the finish line near the Champs Elysèes in Paris as winner of the prestigious Tour de France for the third consecutive year. He was the first American to have won three years in a row.

A few months later, October 2 marked the five-year anniversary of his cancer diagnosis and survival. Past this point, doctors begin using the word *cured.* As for the tour in 2002, this peak performer commented, "I'll be back. . . . And I won't be back to finish second." Armstrong did come back, and finished first.

Since then, Armstrong has won the tour three more times, totaling a record seven times. More important, Armstrong has proven that attitude and perseverance influence not only success in sports but also success in life.

PERFORMANCE THINKING Lance Armstrong has said, "If I never had cancer, I never would have won the Tour de France." Armstrong views this disease in a positive way. Do you think his attitude affected his recovery? Why?

CHECK IT OUT The Lance Armstrong Foundation is dedicated to helping people with cancer focus on living: "We believe unity is strength, knowledge is power, and attitude is everything." Visit **www.livestrong.com** to read inspiring stories of cancer survivors; to learn how cancer takes both a physical and an emotional toll on the body and on relationships, as well as ways to cope; and to access important information, including dealing with insurance companies and communicating with health-care providers. Of course, you can also order the famous "livestrong" yellow bracelet, which started an advertising trend.

Performance Strategies...........

Following are the top 10 tips for achieving a healthy lifestyle:

◆ Be aware of your body, your emotions, and the reasons you eat. Is it because you're hungry or because you're bored, anxious, lonely, or stressed?

◆ Maintain your ideal weight.

◆ Focus on healthy eating, not dieting. (Fill up on vegetables, fruits, whole grains, and a balanced diet.)

◆ Exercise for energy and health.

◆ Get enough rest and renewing time.

◆ Develop supportive and healthy relationships.

◆ Create balance in your life.

◆ Avoid harmful substances, such as cigarettes and other drugs.

◆ Protect yourself from sexually transmitted diseases and pregnancy.

◆ Get help immediately for physical and mental distress.

Tech for Success.....................

Take advantage of the text's web site at **www.mhhe.com/ferrett6e** for additional study aids, useful forms, and convenient and applicable resources.

◆ **Health on the Web**. There are more sites on the Internet devoted to the topic of health than devoted to any other subject. However, how do you know which sites are providing accurate information? Start with government, professional organization, and nonprofit sites. Many of these sites offer "questions to ask" or red flags to look for when consulting with physicians or purchasing products on the Internet.

◆ **Assess yourself**. You will find a vast array of free personal assessment tools on the Internet. You can explore everything from ideal body weight to your risk of developing a certain cancer. Use assessments to help you determine what patterns and behaviors you want to change. As with all information on the Internet, check the source or research behind the assessment tool.

◆ **Just what _Is_ in that burger?** Almost every fast-food chain provides the caloric breakdown of its most popular items on the company's web site. Before your next trip to your favorite restaurant, look up the calories and fat content of your usual order. Is it what you expected, or even higher? Does knowing this information make an impact on your selections?

◆ **Music to my ears**. You may enjoy listening to your IPod, but follow the 60/60 rule to preserve your hearing: No more than 60 percent volume for no more than 60 minutes at a stretch.

Review Questions.....................................

Based on what you have learned in this chapter, write your answers to the following questions:

1. What are five strategies for good health management?

2. What are some of the benefits of aerobic exercise?

3. Why is it important to manage your stress?

4. Cite two statistics or facts about alcohol.

5. List four symptoms of depression.

INCREASING YOUR ENERGY LEVEL

In the Classroom

Danny Mendez, a business major in marketing, works part-time at a sporting goods store, is president of his fraternity, and is on the crew team. This demanding schedule is manageable because Danny's energy is high. However, around midterm he feels overwhelmed with stress. He needs to find ways to increase his energy level, maintain his good health, and manage his stress.

1. What strategies would you suggest to Danny that would help reduce his stress?

   _____

   _____

2. What can you suggest to Danny to increase his energy level?

   _____

   _____

In the Workplace

Danny is now a marketing manager for a large advertising agency. He often travels to meet with current and prospective clients. When Danny returns, he finds work piled on his desk—advertising campaign issues, personnel problems, and production delays. Danny's energy has always been high, but lately he eats too much fast food, has started smoking again, and rarely exercises anymore. He keeps saying that he'll get back on track when his stress is reduced.

3. What habits should Danny adopt to reduce his stress and fatigue?

   _____

   _____

4. What strategies in this chapter can help him increase his energy?

   _____

   _____

APPLYING THE ABCDE METHOD OF SELF-MANAGEMENT

In the Journal Entry on page 359, you were asked to describe a time when you had lots of energy, felt healthy and rested, and were in control of your weight. What factors helped you be calm, confident, and healthy?

_____

_____

_____

Describe a situation in which you suffered from lack of sleep, were not eating healthy, or were stressed out. Apply the ABCDE method to work through the scenario and achieve a positive outcome.

A = Actual event:

B = Beliefs:

C = Consequences:

D = Dispute:

E = Energized:

Use visualization to see yourself healthy and in charge of your physical, mental, and emotional life. You feel confident about yourself because you have learned to invest time in exercising, eating healthy, and being rested.

Practice Self-Management

For more examples of learning how to manage difficult situations, see the "Self-Management Workbook" section of the Online Learning Center web site at **www.mhhe.com/ferrett6e**.

STRESS PERFORMANCE TEST

Read the following statements. Then, think back over the last few months. Have you experienced stress as described in the statements? If so, put a checkmark in the column that best indicates how you coped with the experience.

	Overwhelmed (3)	Moderately Stressed (2)	Handled Effectively (1)	Did Not Experience/ Not Applicable (0)
1. No time for goals	____	____	✓	____
2. Lack of money	____	✓	____	____
3. Uncomfortable living and study areas	____	✓	____	____
4. Long working hours	✓	____	____	____
5. Boring, uninteresting job	____	____	____	✓
6. Conflict with roommate, family, etc.	____	____	____	✓
7. Conflict with instructors	____	____	____	✓
8. Too many responsibilities	✓	____	____	____
9. Deadline pressures	✓	____	____	____
10. Boring classes	____	____	____	✓
11. Too many changes in life	____	✓	____	____
12. Lack of motivation	____	____	✓	____
13. Difficulty finding housing	____	____	____	✓
14. Little emotional support from family	✓	____	____	____

(continued)

REVIEW AND APPLICATIONS

CHAPTER 11

	Overwhelmed (3)	Moderately Stressed (2)	Handled Effectively (1)	Did Not Experience/ Not Applicable (0)
15. Poor grades	___	✓	___	___
16. Parents/partners have set standards and expectations that are too high	___	___	✓	___
17. Unclear on goals	___	✓	___	___
18. Too many interruptions	✓	___	___	___
19. Health problems	✓	___	___	___
20. Dependency on alcohol, other drugs	___	___	___	✓
21. Too much socializing	___	___	___	✓
22. Lack of career/life goals	✓	___	___	___
23. Speaking/test-taking anxiety	___	___	✓	___
24. Lack of relationships, friends	___	___	✓	___
25. Lack of self-esteem	___	___	✓	___
Subtotals	___	___	___	___

Add your 1s, 2s, and 3s to give yourself a total score:

Totals
$$\underset{7 \times 3}{\overset{21}{}} \quad + \quad \underset{5 \times 3}{\overset{15}{}} \quad + \quad \underset{6 \times 1}{\overset{6}{}} \quad = \quad \underset{\text{Total Score}}{49}$$

SCORES

25–36　Peak performer (you have learned how to function effectively under stress)

37–48　Persistent coper (you cope and handle stress in most situations, but you have some difficulty coping and feel overwhelmed sometimes)

49–60　Stress walker (you have frequent feelings of being overwhelmed and exhausted, and they affect your performance)

60+　　Burnout disaster (you need help coping; stress is taking its toll on your health and emotions and you are facing burnout)

BETTER HEALTH

On the following lines, describe four ways you can improve your health.

1. _____

   _____

   _____

   _____

   _____

   _____

2. _____

   _____

   _____

   _____

   _____

   _____

3. _____

   _____

   _____

   _____

   _____

   _____

4. _____

   _____

   _____

   _____

   _____

   _____

CHAPTER 11   REVIEW AND APPLICATIONS

INVENTORY OF INTERESTS

Developing outside interests can be a helpful way to reduce stress in your life. Interests are activities that you enjoy and pique your curiosity. Besides helping you reduce your stress level, they may help you determine your life's work and career path. For example, an interest in the outdoors may lead to a major in natural resources, which could lead to a career as a park ranger. A passion for working with cars may lead to a certificate in auto mechanics and thus to your own auto repair shop.

Fill in the following inventory to help you determine a career that coincides with activities you like to do. Review this later to see if your interests change.

1. My interests are

   _____

   _____

   _____

   _____

2. Answer the following questions:

   a. What magazines do I like to read?

   _____

   _____

   _____

   _____

   b. What kinds of books do I like to read?

   _____

   _____

   _____

   _____

   c. When I have free time, what do I like to do? (Check the areas that interest you.)

Reading	_____	Working with people	_____
Writing	_____	Working with computers	_____
Sports	_____	Building or remodeling	_____
Outdoor activities	_____	Creating artwork	_____
Traveling	_____	Public speaking	_____

Other Activities

_____

_____

_____

_____

Build Healthy and Diverse Relationships

CHAPTER OBJECTIVES

In this chapter, you will learn to

▲ Use strategies for communicating and building rapport

▲ Practice assertive communication

▲ Communicate effectively with instructors and advisors

▲ Resolve conflicts

▲ Accept and deliver criticism

▲ Overcome shyness

▲ Build strong relationships

▲ Understand and appreciate college and workplace diversity

SELF-MANAGEMENT

I never realized I would interact with so many new people at college. It's both exciting and frightening. I've been so focused on planning my coursework that I'm not prepared to think beyond my own little world.

Attending college offers many new experiences and exposes you to a wide variety of people with different backgrounds, opinions, and interests. It also gives you an opportunity to become a better communicator and an effective participant in social and group settings. In this chapter, you will learn how to create healthy relationships, solve conflicts, work effectively in a team, become more assertive, and handle criticism. You will see yourself communicating with others in a clear, concise, confident, and direct manner.

JOURNAL ENTRY In **Worksheet 12.1** on page 432, describe a difficult or confrontational situation in which you felt comfortable communicating your needs and ideas in an assertive, direct, and calm manner. What factors helped you be confident and respectful?

No one exists in a vacuum. You can learn to read more efficiently, write more fluid prose, take tests well, or memorize anything you want, but success will elude you if you don't have the ability to communicate and build rapport with different people. People spend nearly 70 percent of their waking hours communicating, listening, speaking, writing, and reading. Communication skills and the ability to build rapport and foster diverse relationships are key strengths for school and job success. SCANS lists interpersonal relationships, communication, an understanding of diversity, and team skills as important for job success.

This chapter will discuss ways to improve your ability to understand and relate to people and to solve conflicts. Developing these skills is one of the most important challenges you will face in your personal, school, and work lives.

The Importance of Effective Communication and Rapport

Communication is the giving and receiving of ideas, feelings, and information. Note the word *receiving.* Some people are good at speaking but are not effective listeners. Poor listening is one of the biggest barriers to effective communication. Miscommunication wastes billions of dollars in business and damages relationships.

Think of what you really want when you communicate with someone else. Do you want people to listen to you, understand your feelings, and relate to your message? Building **rapport** is more than just giving and receiving information. It is finding common ground with another person based on respect, empathy, and trust. Finding **common ground** is having an intent to focus on similarities in interests and objectives and appreciate core values that are diverse or cross-cultural, seeing other viewpoints and building bridges to understanding.

Some people seem to have a knack for building rapport and making others feel comfortable and accepted. They are highly sensitive to nonverbal cues and the responses they elicit from other people. They have developed empathy and make people feel valued. They are comfortable with themselves and comfortable communicating with people from different cultures and backgrounds. They can put their egos aside and focus on the other person with genuine interest and appreciation. You can learn this skill, too. People will want to be near you because you will make them feel good about themselves, give them a sense of importance, and create a climate in which they feel comfortable. People who are good at building rapport not only look for similarities in others but also appreciate, value, and celebrate differences.

Strategies for Building Communication and Rapport

Let's look at a few strategies for building communication and rapport.

1. **Be willing to find common ground.** The first step in building rapport is to assess your intention and willingness to find common ground. Your intention sets the tone and direction and often determines the results. If your goal is to build understanding, acceptance, and rapport, it will usually be reflected in your tone, body language, and style. If you are judgmental, however, this message will come through, regardless of your choice of words. You may have pasted a smile on your face and insist that you want to find common ground, but your honest intention may be to prove yourself right, scold, judge, instruct, embarrass, or put down.

2. **Be an attentive listener.** In Chapter 5, we explored how to be an effective listener by using strategies such as the following:

   ◆ *Listen; don't talk.* Don't change the subject unless the speaker is finished. Be patient and don't interrupt others. Listen for feelings, undertones, and meanings in what people are saying. You can do this by being attuned to nonverbal cues—posture, tone of voice, eye contact, body movements, and facial expressions.

   ◆ *Put the speaker at ease.* Listeners who want to build rapport put the talker at ease by creating a supportive, open climate. Being warm and friendly, showing interest, and smiling all help put others at ease.

   ◆ *Withhold criticism.* Criticizing puts people on the defensive and blocks communication. Arguing almost never changes someone's mind, and it may widen the communication gap.

   ◆ *Paraphrase.* Restating in your own words what the speaker has said shows that you are really interested in understanding the other person's point. Then ask for feedback: "Did I understand you correctly?" Encourage others to talk and explain. Ask questions and seek to understand another person's point of view.

   ◆ *Know when you cannot listen.* If you know you do not have time to pay close attention to the speaker, say so. For example, if you have a lot of studying to do and your roommate wants to talk about a date, you may want to say in a kind and respectful tone, "I'd like to know more about your date, but I have to read this chapter. Can we have a cup of coffee in an hour and talk about it?" You also may want to delay talking and listening if you are angry, tired, or stressed. Just make certain you respond in a respectful tone of voice.

3. **Pay attention to body language.** Look at the speaker and appear attentive, interested, and alert. For example, let's say that your arms are crossed, you are frowning and leaning back in your chair, you have indirect eye contact, and you are sighing and shaking your head. Your words may say, "I want to listen," but your nonverbal body language is shouting, "I don't like you, and I don't want to listen." When your eyes wander, you appear uninterested or bored. You can create an attentive, supportive climate by communicating openness with facial expressions, relaxed and uncrossed arms, and a posture of leaning slightly toward the person. Try not to sit behind a desk but closer to the other person. Some experts say that 70 percent of what is communicated is done through nonverbal communication, or body language. If you intend to build rapport, your body

language must be warm and open and convey interest and acceptance. Your words must be in alignment with your body language in order to be believed.

4. **Be respectful.** Many organizations are implementing employee-training programs that emphasize the importance of business etiquette—respect for and consideration of the feelings and needs of others. Good manners and respect are the foundation of all healthy relationships. People need to feel they are getting the consideration and appreciation they deserve, whether it is in the classroom, on the job, or at home. Therefore, if you want to build rapport with others, be respectful, kind, and thoughtful.

5. **Use warmth and humor.** You can build rapport by knowing how to use humor. Avoid sarcasm and jokes at the expense of another person's feelings, but don't take yourself too seriously. Humor puts people at ease. A joke or easy laughter can dissipate tension. Humor, wit, and a sincere smile create warmth and understanding and can open the door to further effective communication.

6. **Relate to a person's personality style.** As mentioned in Chapter 1, there are many types of people in this world, who learn, think, and relate differently. Knowing this can help you interact and work more effectively with diverse people and teams. For example, if your boss has an analyzer or a thinker type of personality, you will want to make certain that your reports are based on facts and your presentations are clear, concise, and correct.

7. **Relate to a person's learning or teaching style.** You can build rapport with your instructors, co-workers, and supervisors by relating to their personality, learning, and teaching styles. For example, perhaps your instructor prefers the visual mode. She writes on the board, shows overheads and films, and uses phrases such as "Do you see what I'm saying?" For an instructor who prefers a visual mode, enhance your visual presentation. For example, turn in an especially attractive visual paper by taking note of neatness and spelling and using pictures, diagrams, and drawings whenever appropriate. Try to maintain eye contact while this instructor is lecturing and return visual clues, such as nods, smiles, and other reassurances.

8. **Be a team player.** It is important to pull your weight on a team—whether at school or at work. You build team rapport not by being fun, charming, and a good conversationalist but, rather, by being clear on expectations, deadlines, commitment, and follow-through. Excuses do not build rapport and no one likes a "slacker." Check in often with your team and make certain that you know when you will meet again, what work should be accomplished by individual team members, and what resources each person needs in order to produce results. The foundation of teamwork is effective communication and responsibility.

Assertive Communication

You may not always feel you have the right to speak up for what you need, particularly in new situations where you see yourself as powerless and dependent. Assertive communication should help in these situations. **Assertive communication** is expressing yourself in a direct, above-board, and civil manner. Only you can take responsibility for clarifying your expectations, expressing your needs, and making your own decisions. You might find yourself acting passively in some situations, aggressively in others, and assertively in still others. In most situations, however, strive to communicate in an assertive, direct, clear, and respectful manner.

- *Passive* people rarely express feelings, opinions, and desires. They have little self-confidence and low self-esteem, have difficulty accepting compliments, and often compare themselves unfavorably with others. Sometimes they feel that others take advantage of them, which creates resentment.
- *Aggressive* people are often sarcastic, critical, and controlling. They want to win at any cost and sometimes blame others for making them angry. They sometimes resort to insults and criticisms, which breaks down communication and harms relationships.
- *Passive-aggressive* people appear to be passive but act aggressively. For example, a passive-aggressive student will not respond in class when asked if there are any questions about an assignment but will then go to the dean to complain. A passive-aggressive roommate will leave nasty notes or complain to others rather than confront a roommate directly.
- *Assertive* people state their views and needs directly; use confident body language; and speak in a clear, strong voice. They take responsibility for their actions. Assertive people respect themselves and others.

Many of the same communication strategies that we've already discussed will help you be more assertive. Here are a few more tips:

1. **State the problem in clear terms.** Be clear on your position and what you want: "I cannot study with the music so loud."
2. **Express your feelings**. Use "I" messages instead of "You" messages: "I feel frustrated when the music is too loud, because I have to study for a test tomorrow."
3. **Make your request.** "Please turn the music down. I especially need it quiet after ten o'clock."
4. **Use assertive body language.** Stay calm and centered. Use direct eye contact, square your shoulders, and speak in a clear, low tone.
5. **State the consequences**. Always start with the positive: "If you will turn down the volume on your music, I can study better and our relationship will be more positive." If you don't get the results you want, try saying, "I'm going to have to go to our landlord to discuss this problem."

Practice developing assertive responses in **Personal Evaluation Notebook 12.1** on page 404.

Communicating with Instructors and Advisors

Develop professional relationships with your instructors and advisors, just as you would with your supervisor at work. Try a few of these tips to increase rapport:

1. **Clarify expectations.** Make certain you understand the objectives and expectations of your instructors and advisors. Most instructors will give you extra help

Assertive Communication Role-Playing

Read the following situations. Then develop an assertive response for each one.

1. **Situation:** You receive a *B* on your test, and you think you deserve an *A:* What would you say to your instructor?

   Assertive response: Ask why / what's the reason.

2. **Situation:** A friend asks you to read her term paper. She tells you it is the best paper she has ever written. However, you find several glaring errors.

   Assertive response: Us you have a couple

3. **Situation:** Your roommate asks to borrow your new car. You don't want to lend it.

   Assertive response: NO.

4. **Situation:** An acquaintance makes sexual advances. You are not interested.

   Assertive response: The offer was not acceptable

5. **Situation:** You go to a party and your date pressures you to drink.

   Assertive response: I am not drinking

6. **Situation:** Your roommate's friend has moved in and doesn't pay rent.

   Assertive response: you have to pay rent it's 50/50

7. **Situation:** Your sister borrowed your favorite sweater and stained it.

   Assertive response: Replace it or clean it

8. **Situation:** A friend lights up a cigarette, and you are allergic to smoke.

   Assertive response: Walk away / I allergic to cigarette smoke

9. **Situation:** You want your roommate or spouse to help you keep the apartment clean.

   Assertive response: Please clean up behind yourself

10. **Situation:** Your mother wants you to come home for the weekend, but you have to study for a major test.

    Assertive response: I can't home because I need to study for a test

and feedback if you take the initiative. For instance, before a paper is due, hand in a draft and say, "I want to make sure I am covering the important points in this paper. Am I on the right track? What reference sources would you like me to use? What can I add to make this an *A* paper?"

2. **Clarify concerns.** If you don't understand or you disagree with a grade you have received on a test or paper, ask for an appointment with the instructor. Approach the situation with a supportive attitude: "I like this course and want to do well in it. I don't know why I got a *C* on this paper, because I thought I had met the objectives. Could you show me exactly what points you think should be changed? Could I make these corrections for a higher grade?" Make certain you are respectful and appreciative of your instructor's time and help, as your instructor may be teaching many courses with many students. Follow basic rules of etiquette when communicating with your instructor by e-mail. (See **Peak Progress 12.1** on page 406.)

Connecting with Your Instructor
Develop a rapport with your instructor by taking the initiative to ask for feedback and help when you need it and in plenty of time to put the advice into action. *Are you working on assignments or papers right now that you should be consulting with your instructor about?*

3. **Adapt to your instructor's teaching style.** Approach each class with a positive attitude and don't expect that all instructors will teach according to your learning style.

4. **Be open to learning.** Attend every class with an inquisitive, open mind. Some instructors may be less interesting, but you owe it to yourself to be as supportive of the instructor as possible. If you are a returning student, you may find that the instructor is younger than you are and may lack life experiences. Be open to learning and valuing the training, education, and knowledge the instructor brings to class. The same rule applies to the workplace. Be supportive and open to learning, and consider yourself on the same team.

5. **Take responsibility for your own learning.** Don't expect your instructor to feed you information. Take an active role in each class. You are ultimately responsible for your own learning and your own career. You may be tempted to cut classes when you don't like your instructor, but you will miss valuable class discussions, question-and-answer sessions, explanations, reviews of concepts, expectations about tests, contact with students, and structure to help you stay focused. Furthermore, you will miss the opportunity to see your instructor improve because your initial impression may be false. Students have reported that, once they gave the instructor a chance and worked hard, their attitudes changed. In fact, in some instances, this instructor became their favorite, and they excelled in the class.

6. **Take an interest in your instructors.** Visit them during office hours to discuss your work, goals, grades, and future coursework. When appropriate, ask about your instructor's academic background as a guide for yours. Ask about degrees, colleges attended, work experience, and what projects they are working on for professional growth. A large part of building rapport is showing genuine interest, appreciation, and respect.

E-Mail Etiquette with Instructors

Although you may have established a friendly, personable relationship with your instructor or advisor, you should always treat him or her with the same respect you would any employer or evaluator of your performance or behavior. Because technology has allowed us to communicate more quickly, we often forget to practice the basic rules of communication etiquette that are common in written memos and face-to-face communication.

When e-mailing your instructor for assistance, clarification, or advice, keep in mind the following:

1. **Use proper spelling, grammar, and punctuation.** Although you may be used to text messaging in lowercase letters, proper e-mail etiquette calls for writing the e-mail just as you would a memo. Thus, start each sentence with a capital letter and end each sentence with punctuation (period, question mark, etc.). It's also common e-mail knowledge that you should not write in all capital letters—which designates "shouting" or intense urgency. Always use the spell-check before sending, as well as read through the e-mail at least one more time.

2. **Avoid using slang, abbreviations, or "smileys."** Again, you wouldn't say "ADN" (for "any day now") in a memo or include little smiley faces ("emoticons"). Those are fine when e-mailing to good friends, but not to instructors or employers. Also, you may find that your instructor has lost your meaning because he or she doesn't know what "BTW" ("by the way") stands for.

3. **Use proper greetings.** You wouldn't start a memo to your instructor with "Hey, Dr. Smith." "Dear Dr. Smith" is appropriate; "Hello, Dr. Smith" is also acceptable in most cases.

4. **Make it clear who you are.** Since instructors interact with many people on a daily basis, they can't decipher who you are by your e-mail account (bhappy16@aol.com). Quickly make it clear who you are ("I'm Beatrice Jones in your English 305 course") and put your full name (and phone number, if necessary) at the end of your e-mail.

(continued)

7. **Network.** Building your professional network begins in college. You will want to form close professional relationships with other students, your advisor, your coach, a few key instructors, club advisors, the music director, administrators, and so on. Exchange e-mails and ask people on campus (who know you well) if you may use them as a reference or if they would be willing to write a letter of recommendation for graduate school, an internship, or your first job. You can help by creating a resume that includes your accomplishments and strengths.

Conflict

Some common causes of conflict are strong emotions, unsatisfied needs, misperceptions and stereotypes, miscommunication, repetitive negative behavior, and differing

E-Mail Etiquette with Instructors (continued)

5. **Be concise and to the point.** Remember that your instructor has many people to respond to during the day, such as students, other faculty members, and administrators (not to mention people involved in their research work, professional memberships, and consulting obligations). In your message subject line, clearly state the overall point: "Question about today's discussion on learning styles." In one or two paragraphs, succinctly ask your question or make your point. Include just the essential details. If you feel your point may be lost, either put your question at the very beginning or highlight it in bold or another color in the text.

6. **Respectfully include a "due date," if necessary.** Never say to an instructor, "I must hear from you by . . . " However, your question or issue may be time-sensitive for a reason, such as a registration deadline. If you need a response by a certain time, indicate that politely and write, "It would be great to have your response by this Friday, as I have to turn in my forms by that afternoon." If you haven't received a response, send a follow-up "Just checking to make sure you received my e-mail." When something is urgent, you may determine that e-mail is not the appropriate mode of communication. Call the instructor, drop by his or her office, catch him or her in class, or schedule an appointment. Do not let e-mail be an excuse for not getting an important answer.

7. **Leave in the message thread.** If there has been a string of e-mails to this point, it's always better to leave them in if you can, in case the recipient needs to refresh his or her memory about the issue.

8. **Do not use graphics.** Unless necessary, do not be creative with the typeface, graphics, or backgrounds in your e-mails. They only make the e-mail harder to read (and increase the file size).

9. **Always say, "Thank you."** Get in the habit of ending e-mails with a *thank you*, *thanks*, or *I appreciate your help*. People will respond to you more quickly and more often if their efforts are acknowledged and appreciated.

expectations, views, opinions, beliefs, and values. Conflicts can occur between spouses, parents and children, siblings, business partners, neighbors, roommates, friends, coworkers, teammates, and instructors and students. Although conflict can impede communication and damage relationships, it can also bring problems to the surface and lead to creative problem solving when it is understood and coped with in appropriate ways. Use your observation and critical thinking skills to complete **Personal Evaluation Notebooks 12.2** and **12.3** on pages 408 and 409 about conflict resolution.

The common responses to conflict are to avoid it, to compromise, to accommodate others, or to cooperate with others. Following are a few suggestions that focus on cooperation as a means of resolving conflict.

1. **Define the conflict.** Define and state the conflict as a concrete problem to be solved. Identify the issues involved. Focus on the problem, not the other

Observing Conflict

Read the following questions and write your answers on the lines provided.

1. Observe how others handle conflict, compliments, and criticism. Do you notice any ineffective behaviors? If so, list them.

   _____

   _____

2. If you were a consultant in conflict resolution, what are some conflict resolution tips you would give?

   _____

   _____

3. What behaviors do you use under stress that you would like to change?

   _____

   _____

4. What do you intend to do the next time you are in a conflict with someone?

   _____

   _____

person—for example, "The conflict is that I feel angry because Joe is doing most of the talking in my study group and I want to move on and solve the problem, so that the group can be more productive."

2. **Convert "You" statements into "I" statements.** Making "I" statements, instead of "You" statements is an effective technique for communicating information without pointing the finger at the other person and putting him or her on the defensive. Instead of saying, "You talk too much," say, "I *feel* angry *when* one person does all the talking, *because* we need to hear the opinions of other people before we can make an informed decision." Use a three part formula:

   "I FEEL (emotions) _____ WHEN (behavior) _____ BECAUSE (reason) _____."

3. **Attentively listen.** One of the best ways to resolve conflict is by attentively listening to the other person's concerns and criticism. Don't interrupt or start your defense. Really concentrate on the other person's perceptions, feelings, and expectations. Give physical cues that you are listening. Listen to *what* is said, *how* it is said, and *when* it is said, and listen with *understanding*. Listen also for what is *not* being said. Ask for clarification, avoid jumping to assumptions, and don't hurry the speaker.

Conflict Resolution

Describe a conflict you have not yet resolved. Think of resolution techniques that would be helpful. Respond to the following statements.

1. Describe the problem.

   _____

   _____

2. Express your feelings.

   _____

   _____

3. State what you want.

   _____

   _____

4. Predict the consequences.

   _____

   _____

4. **Develop empathy.** Empathy is the ability to share another's emotions, thoughts, or feelings in order to understand the person better. By taking the role of the other, you can develop the ability to see and feel the situation through his or her eyes. Sympathy is feeling *for* a person, which can border on pity or condescension. An empathetic attitude says, "I am here *with* you." Empathy allows for the distance needed to maintain objectivity, so that the problem can be solved.

5. **Stay calm.** Control your emotions and don't lose your temper. Ask the other person to calm down: "I can see that you are upset, and I really want to know what your concerns are. Please talk more slowly." It is important to listen to the message without overreacting or becoming defensive.

6. **Focus on the problem.** Focus on the problem and get to important points. Don't use detours and attack the person—for example, "You think I'm messy. Look at your room. You're a real pig." Instead, focus on the problem: "If I do the dishes the same evening I cook, will that make you feel more comfortable?" Trust that you can both speak your minds calmly and nondefensively without damaging your relationship.

7. **Clarify concerns.** Ask for specific details, and clarification: "Can you give a specific incident or time when you think I was rude?" Keep comments in perspective, and ask for clarification. The key is to understand the issue at hand.

8. **Focus on solutions.** Focus on possible solutions instead of the other person. You might say, "I can see that this is a problem. What can I do to solve it? What procedures or options can we explore?"

9. **Apologize.** If you think the situation warrants it, apologize: "I'm sorry. I was wrong." It defuses anger and builds trust and respect.

Constructive Criticism

Part of effective communication is to be open to feedback and criticism. Start with the attitude that the critic has good intentions and is offering constructive criticism—criticism that is meant to be supportive and useful for improvement. Unconstructive criticism is negative and harsh; it doesn't offer options, and can create defensiveness and tension.

Giving Constructive Criticism

Your experience and feedback will be asked for more often if you give it in an effective, nurturing way.

1. **Establish a supportive climate.** It helps if you can create an open dialogue and warm climate that invite feedback and conversation. People need to feel safe when receiving feedback or criticism. Choose a convenient time and a private place to talk. If possible, sit next to the person instead of behind a barrier, such as a desk.

2. **Focus on the behavior, not the person.** Make certain that you define the specific behavior you want to change. Don't hit the person with several issues at once.

3. **Stay calm.** Look at the person, keep your voice low and calm, use positive words, and avoid threats. Be brief and to the point.

4. **Be balanced.** Let the other person know that you like him or her and that you appreciate the person's good qualities or behaviors. Don't use words such as *always* and *never*.

5. **Explain.** Explain why the behavior warrants criticism and why a change is in order. Talk about options and offer to help.

Receiving Criticism

Learning to accept and grow from constructive criticism is important for school and job success. Here are some tips:

1. **Listen with an open mind.** Being reminded that you aren't perfect is never easy or pleasant. However, try to listen with an open mind when your instructor, boss, co-worker, roommate, spouse, or classmate points out mistakes, mentions concerns, or makes suggestions. Don't talk until you have heard all the details. Think about what is being said and evaluate if the criticism is constructive or

unconstructive. You may want to ask for time to think it through. Do others feel the same way? Have you heard similar criticism before? If so, it may be valid.

2. **Pay attention to nonverbal cues.** Sometimes people have difficulty expressing criticism and may express nonverbal criticism. If the person is aloof, angry, or sad, you might ask if you did something to offend the person. If he or she is sarcastic, perhaps there is underlying hostility. If appropriate, you can say something like, "You have been very quiet today. Did I do something to offend you?"

3. **Ask for clarification.** Make certain you understand the criticism—for example, "Professor Walker, you gave me a *B* on this paper. Could you explain what points you consider to be inadequate?"

4. **Ask for suggestions**. If the criticism is constructive, ask for suggestions—for example, "How can I improve this paper?" Summarize the discussion and clarify the next steps. Know what you need to do to correct the situation. Don't make excuses for your behavior. If the criticism is true, change your behavior.

5. **Explain your viewpoint.** If you feel that the criticism is unfair, discuss it openly. Explain your behavior from your point of view. You don't want to let resentments smolder and build. Practice saying, "Thank you. I appreciate your viewpoint and your courage in telling me what is bothering you. However, I don't think the criticism is fair." Criticism reflects how another person views your behavior at a certain time. It is not necessarily reality but an interpretation; thus, relax and put it in perspective.

Dealing with Shyness

Shyness is common, especially on college campuses, where people are adjusting to new situations and meeting new people. Behavioral experts say it affects thousands of people. Shyness is not a problem unless it interferes with your life. It is perfectly acceptable to enjoy your privacy, be quiet, be modest, prefer a few close friends to many, and even embarrass easily. However, if shyness prevents you from speaking up in class, getting to know your instructors and other students, giving presentations, or making new friends, it is keeping you from fulfilling your potential for success. Shyness can also add to feelings of loneliness. In school and in the workplace, it is important to ask questions, clarify assignments, and ask for help. The inability to ask for help is one of the biggest drawbacks to being shy. In addition, shy people may not contribute to classroom discussions, ask questions, build rapport with instructors, or offer feedback. They can appear emotionally detached and withdrawn. You can overcome your shyness, build rapport, and be an effective conversationalist by following these strategies:

1. **Use positive self-talk.** Reinforce your self-confidence and self-image by replacing negative self-talk with positive talk. Instead of saying, "I'm shy; I can't change," tell yourself, "I am confident, people like me, and I like people. I find it easy and enjoyable to get to know new people. I am accepted, appreciated, and admired."

2. **Use direct and relaxed eye contact.** Many shy people look down or avoid making eye contact. Direct eye contact reinforces your confidence and shows interest in and empathy with others. Look at your instructors and show interest in what they are presenting.

> ## WORDS TO SUCCEED
>
> *"Minds are like parachutes. They only function when they are open."*
>
> **SIR JAMES DEWAR**
> *Chemist and physicist*

3. **Ask questions and show genuine interest.** You don't have to talk a lot to be an effective conversationalist. In fact, you don't want to deliver monologues. Ask questions, show genuine interest, and give others a chance to talk and to change the subject. Asking open-ended questions shows interest and concern. For example, instead of asking Jennifer if she is finished with an assigned term paper (yes/no), ask her how she is progressing with the paper (open-ended question). If you are asking questions of an instructor, be clear and to the point and focus on understanding the concept. Focusing on others takes the pressure off you.

4. **Listen to other points of view.** You don't have to agree with other people's points of view, but you can listen and respond tactfully and thoughtfully. You have something to contribute, and exchanging different views is a great way to learn and grow. Ask others how they developed their point of view or belief.

5. **Use humor.** Most people like to laugh. Poking good-natured fun at yourself lightens the conversation, as does a funny joke or story. Just make certain to be sensitive; don't tell off-color or racial jokes or stories. Smiling at others will improve your own outlook.

6. **Focus on the benefits.** Making friends helps you develop your sense of community and belonging. It can ease the loneliness that many students feel.

7. **Take action.** Join clubs and activities. Volunteer in one of the organizations that sponsors service learning. Join study groups or ask one of your classmates to study with you. Get a part-time job or get involved in community organizations. Go to various cultural groups and activities. Try out for a play or choir—really stretch yourself. Reach out to others and make friends with a broad range of people.

Overcome Obstacles to Effective Communication

The number one barrier to effective communication is the assumption that the other person knows what you mean. It is easy to think that what you say is what the other person hears, but communication is a complex system, with so many barriers to overcome that it is a wonder anyone ever really communicates. Other barriers include

◆ Faulty perception
◆ Poor listening skills
◆ Misunderstandings
◆ The need to be right
◆ Cultural, religious, social, and gender differences

Communication is the lifeblood of personal relationships and the foundation of effective team and work groups. Learning how to work effectively with your study team, advisors, instructors, roommates, co-workers, and supervisors will help you be successful at school, at work, and in personal relationships. Many professional and personal problems involve a failure in communication.

The first step to effective communication is the desire and willingness to understand and build rapport with others. Seek to clarify intentions and be an active lis-

Patterns in Relationships

Look at the pattern of some of your relationships. Recall situations that occur again and again. For example, you may have the same problem communicating with instructors or advisors. You may have had conflicts with several roommates, co-workers, or supervisors. Once you see the pattern and consequences of your interactions, you can begin to think and act differently. When you take responsibility for changing your inner world of beliefs and thoughts, your outer world will also change. Write about what seems to be a recurring theme or pattern in your relationships.

_____

_____

_____

_____

_____

_____

_____

_____

_____

_____

_____

_____

_____

_____

_____

tener. Show that you are interested in others and establish common bonds. Paraphrase conversations to assess mutual understanding. Develop healthy relationships based on integrity, respect, trust, and honesty. Look for patterns that seem to occur in your relationships as you complete **Personal Evaluation Notebook 12.4.**

Build Good Relationships

Problems in relationships can consume a great deal of your time and energy, and they may affect your self-esteem. Because feeling good about yourself is one key to all-around success, it is important to assess how you handle relationships with partners, friends, and family.

Romantic Relationships

Being successful in life can be even more meaningful when you are part of a loving, supportive relationship. However, too often we define ourselves by success in romantic endeavors rather than understanding what we gain emotionally by a rewarding relationship. Following are a few tips to help you build healthy relationships.

1. **Progress slowly.** A healthy relationship progresses slowly. Take the time to get to know the other person and how he or she feels and reacts to situations. Relationships that move too fast or have intense and instant sexuality as a basis often end quickly. Some people go from casual to intimate in one date. Solid relationships need time to grow and develop through the stages of companionship and friendship. Take the time to know people in many different situations. Develop good acquaintances and solid friendships. Perhaps a romantic relationship will develop from one of these friendships.

2. **Have realistic expectations.** Some people think that having a good romantic relationship will magically improve their lives, even if they make no effort to change their thinking or behavior. If you are a poor student, are unmotivated, are depressed, or lack confidence, you will still have these problems even if you have a great relationship. It is unrealistic to expect a relationship to solve life's problems; only you can solve your problems. Knowing this, you can put more energy into improving your life than you do in looking for someone else to do it.

3. **Be honest.** A healthy relationship is based on commitment to the truth. You certainly don't want to reveal your entire past to a casual acquaintance or first date. At the appropriate time, however, honesty about your feelings, basic values, and major life experiences is the foundation of a healthy relationship. For example, if you are an alcoholic or have been married before, the other person should know that as your relationship progresses.

4. **Be supportive.** A healthy relationship is supportive of the growth and well-being of each partner; an unhealthy relationship is not. No one owns another person, nor does anyone have a right to harm another physically or emotionally. An unhealthy relationship is possessive and controlling. A healthy relationship is mutually supportive.

5. **Have respect.** A healthy relationship is based on respect for the feelings and rights of the other person. An unhealthy relationship is self-centered and disrespectful.

6. **Have trust and be trustworthy.** A healthy relationship works in a relaxed, loving, and comfortable way. When a problem comes up, you have an inherent trust that it will be faced and resolved. If someone in a relationship is obsessive, controlling, and distrustful, the relationship is unhealthy. When problems arise, the focus should be on solving them, not on assigning blame.

7. **Know that change can occur.** It is easy for healthy relationships to change. Emotionally healthy people know that not all relationships will develop into romantic and intimate commitments. Letting go and knowing how to end a relationship are as important as knowing how to form healthy relationships. It is acceptable

WORDS TO SUCCEED

"Lots of people want to ride with you in the limo, but what you want is someone who will take the bus with you when the limo breaks down."

OPRAH WINFREY
Talk show host, actor, publisher

and normal to say no to an acquaintance who asks you out or to decide that you don't want a romantic relationship or a friendship to continue after a few dates. No one should date, have sex, or stay in a relationship out of guilt, fear, or obligation. It is more difficult to terminate a relationship that has progressed too fast or one in which the expectations for the relationship are perceived differently. Talk about your expectations and realize that your sense of personal worth does not depend on someone's wanting or not wanting to date you.

8. **Keep the lines of communication open.** Healthy relationships are based on open communication. Trouble occurs in relationships when you think you know how the other person feels or would react to a situation. For example, you may assume that a relationship is intimate, but the other person may regard it as a casual affair. Expectations for the relationship can be vastly different. Make certain that you make your expectations clear.

Communication in a healthy relationship is open enough to discuss even sensitive topics, such as birth control, sexually transmitted diseases, and unplanned pregnancy. Take a moment to reflect on your relationships in **Personal Evaluation Notebook 12.5** on page 416.

Relationships with Roommates and Family Members

The following suggestions will help you create rapport and improve communication with your roommates and family members.

1. **Clarify expectations of a roommate.** List the factors that you feel are important for a roommate on the housing application or in an ad. If you don't want a smoker or pets, be honest about it. Think about your ideal roommate. Sometimes

Family Ties
Balancing honesty with courtesy and respect will strengthen your relationships and improve communication. *Besides communication, what other area would you want to improve in your family relationships?*

Healthy Relationships

Read the following statements and questions and respond to them on the lines provided.

1. List the factors that you believe are essential for a healthy relationship.

_____

_____

_____

2. What do you believe contributes to unhealthy relationships?

_____

_____

_____

3. Who are your friends?

_____

_____

_____

4. Describe some of your other relationships, such as support groups and study teams.

_____

_____

_____

5. List the ways that your relationships support you and your goals.

_____

_____

_____

6. List the ways that unhealthy relationships may undermine you and your goals.

_____

_____

_____

7. Describe your relationships with your instructors.

_____

_____

_____

it is best not to share a room or apartment with a good friend—rooming together has ruined more than one friendship. Plus, getting to know new people with different backgrounds and experiences is a great opportunity.

2. **Discuss expectations when first meeting your roommate.** Define what neatness means to you. Discuss how both of you feel about overnight guests, drinking, drugs, choice and volume of music, housework, food sharing, quiet times, and so on.

3. **Clarify concerns and agree to communicate with each other.** Don't mope or whine about a grievance or leave nasty notes. Communicate honestly and kindly. It's important that you understand each other's views and expectations and try to work out conflicts. If your roommate likes to have the dishes done after each meal, try to comply rather than convince him or her that he or she is a neat freak. If you like to have friends over, but your roommate goes to bed early or is studying, entertain in the early evenings, be quiet, or go out with friends in the late evenings. If you truly want to get along and you use common sense and communication, you will succeed.

4. **Treat your roommate and family members with respect.** Don't give orders or make demands. Communicate openly and calmly. Listen to each other's needs. Treat each other with courtesy and civility. Be especially respectful of your roommate's need to study or sleep. Don't interrupt or make noise. Think about your tone of voice, body language, and choice of words. Sometimes we treat family, friends, and roommates with less respect than strangers.

5. **Don't borrow unless necessary.** A lot of problems result over borrowing money, clothes, jewelry, bikes, cars, and CDs. The best advice is not to borrow. However, if you must borrow, ask permission *first* and return the item in good shape or replace it if you lose or damage it. Fill the tank of a borrowed car with gas, for instance. Immediately pay back all money you borrow.

6. **Take responsibility for your life.** It isn't anyone's responsibility to loan you money or food, clean up after you, entertain or feed your friends, or pay your bills.

7. **Keep your agreements.** Your life will improve greatly if you practice keeping your word and agreements. Make a list of chores, agree on tasks, and do your share. You should all feel that you are keeping up a fair share of the load. When you say you will do something, do it. When you agree on a time, be punctual. Try to be flexible, however, so that annoyances don't build.

8. **Accept others' beliefs.** Don't try to change anyone's beliefs. Listen openly and, when necessary, agree that your viewpoints are different.

9. **Accept others' privacy.** Don't enter each other's bedroom or private space without asking. Don't pry, read personal mail, or eavesdrop on conversations. Don't expect to share activities unless you are invited. Give each other space.

10. **Get to know each other.** Set aside time for occasional shared activities. Cook a meal, go for walks, or go to a movie. You don't need to be your roommate's best friend, but you should feel comfortable sharing a room or an apartment. Appreciate your roommate and/or family members and try not to focus on little faults or annoyances.

Appreciate Diversity

Colleges and workplaces are becoming more and more diverse. **Diversity** includes factors such as gender, race, age, ethnicity, sexual orientation, physical ability, learning styles and learning disabilities, social and economic background, and religion. We all tend to surround ourselves with people who are similar to us and to see the world in a certain way. College is an excellent place to get to know, understand, and value other cultures and people who have had different life experiences, talents, and political and social views. Make it a point to expand your horizons and have a wide variety of friends and acquaintances who see the world differently. Communication breaks down walls, stereotypes, and false beliefs and enriches your life.

Working Together
The composition of the workforce will continue to change and diversify in the twenty-first century. To be effective and get along with co-workers, people will need to deal with any prejudices they've learned. *What can companies do to help employees understand and appreciate diversity?*

More and more people travel to different countries for business or personal reasons, and they encounter varied cultures and customs. Coupled with television, newspapers, computers, the Internet, telephones, and fax machines, the opportunities to link nations and interact with many cultures are on the rise. The Bureau of Labor projects that the workforce of the twenty-first century includes more women, minorities, and part-time workers.

These diverse people bring a broad worldview to schools, society, and organizations. As a result of this cultural explosion, many organizations offer diversity awareness training to help employees relate comfortably to each other and appreciate diversity. These programs provide opportunities for employees to develop and strengthen critical thinking skills and to reduce stereotypical thinking and prejudice.

As a contributing member of society and the workforce, it is essential that you use critical thinking to assess your assumptions, judgments, and views about people who are different from you. Building cultural sensitivity will be the foundation for building common ground with diverse groups. (See **Figure 12.1.**)

Communication Strategies for Celebrating Diversity

Here are some strategies you may wish to use when developing acceptable communication with diverse groups of people. (See **Peak Progress 12.2** on page 420 on how to apply the Adult Learning Cycle to make best use of your strategies.)

1. **Be aware of your feelings and beliefs.** If you have a negative attitude or reaction to a group or person, examine it and see where it is coming from. (See **Figure 12.2** on page 421.) Be aware of how you talk to yourself about other people. Be willing to admit your own prejudices. This is the first step toward change and a willingness to build rapport.

2. **See the value in diversity.** We are a rich nation because of different races, cultures, backgrounds, and viewpoints. Knowledge and understanding can break through barriers. The value of education is the appreciation of different views and the tools for building understanding and tolerance. Learn to think instead

Figure 12.1 Cultural Understanding

Culturally Biased	Culturally in Denial	Culturally Aware	Culturally Sensitive and Respectful	Culturally Responsible and Active
Believes different groups have positive and negative characteristics as a whole	Believes there is no problem; everyone should be the same	Attempts to understand and increase awareness; is aware that experiences differ for people based on their culture	Respects people from diverse cultural and social backgrounds; seeks out contacts with people from diverse backgrounds; encourages people to value and respect their cultural identity	Acts on commitment to eliminate oppression; seeks to include full participation of diverse cultural groups in decision making

Cultural Understanding   Different categories of cultural understanding are seen in our society. *In what column do you believe you currently fit and why?*

of react. By sharing different viewpoints, you can learn new and interesting ways of seeing situations and approaching problems. Shift your thinking about diversity by reviewing **Peak Progress 12.3** on page 421. Are you accepting of others and appreciate our diversity? Complete **Personal Evaluation Notebook 12.6** on page 422 to determine your attitudes.

3. **See and treat people as individuals.** It is important to look beyond preconceived notions and see people as individuals, not members of a particular group. Try to see people as unique and valued. Use critical thinking to assess how you or others may view people in stereotypical ways. Attitudes are in the mind. Behavior is what you do and is often an outward magnification of your attitude and beliefs. You can change both your attitude and behavior. Complete **Personal Evaluation Notebook 12.7** on page 423 to determine your attitudes and behaviors.

4. **Treat people with respect.** Treat people with respect and consideration. You can be respectful even if someone's behavior is unacceptable or you don't agree with him or her.

5. **Focus on similarities.** It is important to focus on similarities and find a way to build a common bond. We are all human and experience similar emotions, fears, and needs for appreciation and respect. Don't let differences dominate your interactions. However, don't act as if people were all alike and their experiences were the same. Be aware that values and experiences differ for people based on their culture, religion, background, and experiences.

6. **Listen.** Listen and don't talk. Be supportive and don't criticize. Paraphrase, ask questions, and be willing to learn: "That is an interesting viewpoint. How did you develop it? What experiences shaped your beliefs?"

WORDS TO SUCCEED

"People are pretty much alike. It's only that our differences are more susceptible to definition than our similarities."

LINDA ELLERBEE
Journalist

Applying the Adult Learning Cycle to Become a Better Communicator

1. **RELATE. Why do I want to learn this?** Being able to communicate effectively is the most important skill I can acquire, practice, and perfect. It's not only important in my personal relationships but also essential to my success in school and career. By being more direct and assertive, I avoid negative feelings of resentment or thoughts that I'm being taken advantage of. I can succinctly express my views, wants, and impressions, as well as my innovative ideas and decisions. I want to feel confident that I can handle difficult situations and avoid over-reaching and creating unnecessary conflict.

2. **OBSERVE. How does this work?** I've always admired people who are assertive and confident when expressing themselves and their views. What makes them successful? What are specific techniques or mannerisms they use when communicating with others? I'll also observe people who are passive or aggressive and learn from their mistakes. How do others react or respond? I'll try using new techniques and strategies for dealing with fear, resentment, and upset feelings.

3. **REFLECT. What does this mean?** What seems to work for me? Do I feel more confident and comfortable interacting with others? Do I believe I'm presenting my ideas, so that others clearly understand my point of view? Am I more respectful of others' opinions and feelings? Have my personal and professional relationships improved? I'll continue to avoid negative self-talk and focus on a positive attitude and outlook.

4. **DO. What can I do with this?** I will practice being more assertive. I will make a commitment to be direct, kind, and respectful. Each day, I'll work on one area. For example, when my roommate plays music too loudly, I'll express my needs in an assertive and respectful manner.

5. **TEACH. Whom can I share this with?** I'll ask others if they have ever felt misunderstood and what they have changed to express themselves more effectively. I'll share my experiences and the strategies that have worked for me. I'll volunteer to help other students in my study group.

Now return to Stage 1 and continue to monitor your progress and think of new ways to enhance your communication skills.

7. **Get involved.** Take a cultural diversity course or workshop at college or in the community. Visit with people from other religions. Be willing to seek out people from different cultures. Go to lectures, read, and look for opportunities to become acquainted with other cultures. Visit your campus diversity center, if you have one, or seek out various clubs and activities.

8. **Take risks.** Don't avoid contact with other cultures because you are afraid of making a mistake, saying the wrong thing, or inadvertently offending someone. Cultivate friendships with people from different cultures, races, and viewpoints.

Figure 12.2 Understanding the Meaning

Attitudes are thoughts and feelings. Behaviors are what we do—how we act out those thoughts and feelings. If we work on eliminating stereotypes and prejudices, we can affect the outcome: discrimination.

Stereotype	Prejudice	Discrimination
A mental or emotional picture held in common by members of a group that represents an oversimplified belief, opinion, or judgment about members of another group	An unjustified negative feeling directed at a person or group based on preconceived opinions, judgments, and stereotypes	An unjustified negative behavior toward a person or group based on preconceived opinions, judgments, and stereotypes

Understanding the Meaning Having a better understanding of prejudice can help reduce its effect. *Have you ever felt prejudice? How have you dealt with that feeling?*

PEAK PROGRESS   12.3

Thinking About Diversity

If you could shrink the earth's population to a village of precisely 100 females and males—but maintain the existing demographic ratios—the group would look like this:

- 57 Asians
- 21 Europeans
- 14 Western Hemisphere dwellers (North and South Americans)
- 8 Africans
- 70 nonwhites
- 30 whites
- 70 non-Christians
- 30 Christians
- 70 unable to read
- 50 malnourished
- 80 living in substandard housing
- 1 university graduate
- Fifty percent of the wealth worldwide would be in the hands of 6 people–all citizens of the United States.

Appreciating Diversity

A. Read the following and write your comments on the lines provided.

1. What is your attitude toward people who are different from you in gender, race, sexual orientation, or culture? Is your attitude one of acceptance or exclusion?

   _____

2. Have you ever attended a political event for a party other than the one you support? If so, what are some of your viewpoints that differed from those of the other party?

   _____

3. Would you speak up if someone's gender, cultural, racial, sexual, or ethnic background were discussed in a stereotypical manner? How?

   _____

4. Do you consider yourself to be a sensitive, respectful person? Why or why not?

   _____

5. How do you show a sensitive, respectful attitude even when someone sees the world differently? For example, how can you discuss abortion or gay marriage with someone who has an opposite view and find common ground?

   _____

B. Look at the excuses some students use for not meeting different people. Write strategies for overcoming these excuses.

1. **Excuse:** I'm afraid of rejection or of getting into an argument.

   Strategy: _____

2. **Excuse:** People who are different want to stick with their own kind.

   Strategy: _____

3. **Excuse:** You can't change people's minds or beliefs, so what is the point?

   Strategy: _____

4. **Excuse:** I might say something embarrassing. I feel uncomfortable around people who are different from me.

   Strategy: _____

5. **Excuse:** People who are different from me wouldn't want me in their group.

   Strategy: _____

Stereotypical Thinking

Do you know someone who views people in a stereotypical way? Can you describe some stereotypical reactions you may have observed or heard concerning people such as those in the following list? Write your comments on the lines provided:

1. Welfare recipient _____

2. Asian female _____

3. Truck driver _____

4. Homemaker _____

5. Lawyer _____

6. Farmer _____

Share your own culture's traditional foods and customs with others. Knowledge of other cultures can help you appreciate your own roots. When you take a risk, you become more aware of how other people relate to you, and you become more comfortable dealing with diversity. The only way you can bridge the gaps between cultures is to risk getting involved.

9. **Apologize when you make a mistake.** Mistakes happen, even with the best intentions. Ask for clarification and apologize. However, be prepared at times for strong feelings or misunderstandings that result from past experiences with racism or sexism. Don't take it personally if someone does not respond as positively as you had hoped. Sometimes bridging the gap requires that you make an extra effort to understand. Apologize, seek to understand, and move on.

10. **Speak out.** It is not enough to be aware that values and experiences differ for people from different cultures; you must act on this knowledge. Stand up and speak out whenever you hear or see discrimination in school or at work. Encourage your school to welcome and celebrate diversity.

11. **Encourage representation.** Encourage active participation by members of diverse cultural and social groups in various clubs, student government, local government, college meetings and boards, community groups and boards, and any decision-making groups. Don't hold a self-righteous attitude that says, "I belong to the right political party, religion, or social cause." Open your mind and explore different views with a sincere willingness to learn.

12. **Study abroad.** Look into a national or an international exchange program. Spending a semester or year abroad is a tremendous learning and enriching experience. You can also get to know students on your campus who are studying from other countries or states. Attend events sponsored by the exchange programs. Volunteer to help with tutoring other students in English. Check out internships in different countries or states.

Diversity in the Workplace

The workplace has become and will continue to be more diverse than ever. Attitudes and behavior from top management set the tone for the whole company. Many top managers approach the issue by asking themselves, "How can I instruct others to tolerate differences in race, gender, religion, and sexual preference?" Perhaps a better question would be "How can I set an example, create a climate of respect, and encourage people to value differences?" Managers can create an atmosphere of respect and understanding.

Many seminars and workshops offer ideas on working successfully with people of different cultures and genders. Firm guidelines need to be established and communicated clearly about the consequences of discrimination.

Discrimination is illegal and can be grounds for court action. Organizations have a responsibility and an obligation to make certain that all employees know what behaviors are illegal and inappropriate, as well as the consequences for such behavior. Top managers are responsible for establishing procedures and need to offer a safe atmosphere for complaints. In short, companies must provide education, create guidelines and procedures, and set a tone of serious concern and respect toward all differences in the workplace. Think about what you learned about personality and team styles in Chapter 1. Diversity can have many positive effects on team effectiveness. Consider your study or work teams as you complete **Peak Progress 12.4**.

Sexual Harassment at School and at Work

Sexual harassment is behavior that is unwelcome, unwanted, and degrading. It can be destructive to the school and work climate. It is also costly. Employee turnover, loss of productivity, expensive lawsuits, and a negative work environment are just some of the consequences of sexual harassment. Think about your attitudes, beliefs, and behaviors. Err on the side of discretion and be cautious about being too chummy or touchy or disclosing too many details about your personal life. If you have doubts that a remark or joke is appropriate, don't say it.

Organizations are responsible for establishing accepted guidelines. Most campuses and companies employ someone you can talk to if you have a complaint or concern. Organizations with more than 25 employees are legally required to have written procedures concerning sexual harassment and should practice the following procedures.

◆ Define sexual harassment and the disciplinary actions that may result because of inappropriate behavior.

◆ Make certain that all employees are informed of the policy and are aware of the procedures for filing a complaint.

◆ Designate a person to handle confidential complaints and concerns.

◆ Ensure that common work practices are in compliance with the policy.

Your goal should always be to create a supportive, respectful, and productive environment—one that makes colleagues feel comfortable and valued.

Team Effectiveness

Most organizations function with teams. Even the most educated and skillful people will falter if they can't work effectively and cooperatively with one another. When you need to review the effectiveness of a work team, a study team, or any other team, use the following list of skills and score each item from 1 to 10 (10 = most effective).

Team Function

- Commitment to tasks   _____
- Oral communication skills   _____
- Listening skills   _____
- Writing skills   _____
- Conflict resolution   _____
- Decision-making skills   _____
- Creative problem solving   _____
- Openness to brainstorming and new ideas   _____
- Team spirit and cohesiveness   _____
- Encouragement of critical thinking   _____
- Interest in quality decisions   _____
- Professionalism   _____
- Team integrity and concern for ethics   _____
- Starting and ending meetings on time   _____

When a score is totaled, the team can discuss answers to these questions:

1. How can this team be more effective?

   _____

   _____

   _____

2. What can individual members do to strengthen the team?

   _____

   _____

   _____

In summary, in this chapter, I learned to:

- *Value and improve communication.* Effective communication, including the ability to build rapport with diverse people, is fundamental for school, work, and life success. It involves both the giving and receiving of ideas, feelings, and information.

- *Build rapport with others.* To build rapport effectively, I must first clarify my intention and use corresponding body language. I must be an attentive listener, including putting the speaker at ease, containing my criticisms, restating the speaker's point, and declining respectfully if the timing is not good for communicating. I should appear attentive and interested, be respectful and considerate, and use humor when appropriate. I relate to different learning and personality styles, understanding that people process and learn information and see the world in different ways. I look for the best in others and appreciate the strengths of different styles. I focus on people's strengths, not weaknesses. I am flexible and can adapt to different personality types.

- *Be assertive.* I express myself in a direct, above-board, and respectful manner. I can express feelings and opinions in a calm, confident, and authentic way that does not offend others. I do not use sarcasm or criticism to express myself. I can say no to inappropriate behavior that is unwelcome and unwanted.

- *Communicate with instructors and advisors.* I meet with my instructors often to (1) clarify expectations, (2) get help with homework, (3) consult on drafts of papers or speeches, (4) discuss ways to prepare for tests, (5) get advice about project requirements, (6) discuss grades or assignments, and (7) find additional help for studying and assignments. I attend every class, adapt to my instructor's teaching style, and am positive and open to learn. I take an interest in my instructor's research, writing, or area of expertise. Since I have built rapport with my instructor, I feel comfortable asking for a letter of reference.

- *Accept feedback and criticism.* I know that to grow and learn, I must be open to feedback and occasional criticisms. I do not take offense when it is offered in the spirit of helpfulness. I listen, stay calm, and ask for clarification and suggestions. My intent is to improve and grow in all areas of my life. If I make mistakes, I apologize and try to make amends.

- *Overcome shyness.* It is fine to be quiet, but, when shyness interferes with making friends, speaking in front of groups, working with others, or getting to know my instructors, I must learn to be more confident and outgoing. I use visualization and affirmations to dispute negative self-talk. I realize that shyness is a problem for many people and focus on making others feel comfortable and welcomed. I use direct eye contact, am warm and friendly, ask questions, and listen. I relax, am able to laugh at myself, and use humor when it is appropriate.

- *Clarify miscommunications.* I do not assume that I know what the other person thinks or says. I clear up misunderstandings by asking for clarification and paraphrase what I think I heard. I focus on listening and seek to understand rather than to be right. I want to be a better listener and improve my communication with others.

- *Develop healthy relationships.* I value friendships and take time to get to know others. My relationships are built on a foundation of honesty, trust, respect, and open communication. I am supportive of others' goals and values and I expect them to respect and support mine. I talk about expectations with friends—both casual and romantic.

- *Communicate with roommates and family.* To improve communication, I clarify and discuss expectations concerning guests, smoking, neatness, noise, borrowing, food, bills, privacy, and other issues that could cause problems. We agree to talk and get to know each other but also to respect each other's beliefs, views, and space. I take responsibility for my life and do not expect my roommate or family members to be my memory system, alarm clock, driver, or maid.

- *Appreciate diversity.* Our diversity can be expressed by our race, age, ethnicity, gender, learning and physical abilities, and social, economic, and religious backgrounds. I value different cultures and seek to understand and build rapport with diverse people. By sharing different backgrounds, experiences, values, interests, and viewpoints, I can learn new and interesting ways of seeing situations and solving problems. I look for ways to become acquainted with other cultures and opportunities to work with a variety of people.

- *Recognize sexual harassment.* Sexual harassment is behavior that is unwelcome, unwanted, degrading, and detrimental to school and work.

Kathy Brown

MARINE BIOLOGIST

Related Major: Biological Science

Team Building at Work

Kathy Brown is a marine biologist who manages teams doing research on saltwater organisms outside Monterey, California. Currently, she is head of a project to gain more knowledge on the navigation techniques of gray whales during migration.

Although Kathy is a top-rate biologist and researcher with a Ph.D., she can accomplish her project goals only by building teams of researchers who work together effectively. To do this, she carefully considers the personalities and leadership styles of each researcher while forming teams. Kathy provides pre-project training in communication skills, group decision making, diversity, and conflict resolution. She lets teams brainstorm ideas and come up with solutions for studying wild animals in a controlled experiment. To facilitate the teams, Kathy uses lots of humor. She also has teams rate their effectiveness in several key team functions, including creative problem solving and team spirit.

Finally, the teams are sent to sea to set up labs and conduct research from ocean vessels. Kathy travels from vessel to vessel to encourage teamwork, check research procedures, and help solve problems. She makes sure that each team knows how to reach her at all times, day and night.

Because teamwork is so important to the overall results, Kathy will not rehire anyone who cannot work as a part of a team. She knows that even the most educated and skillful researchers will fail if they are not able to work effectively and cooperatively with a variety of people.

CRITICAL THINKING Why do you think team building is an important part of a science research project?

Peak Performer Profile

Mia Hamm

Soccer champion Mia Hamm writes "Dream big" on the soccer balls she autographs for the kids that flock around her at games. Since age five, when she got her start on a coed peewee soccer team, Hamm has lived by that motto.

Born in 1972 in Selma, Alabama, the fourth of six children, Hamm grew up as a "military brat." She got the soccer "bug" in Italy, where her father was stationed. Hamm's mother, a former ballerina, initially tried to interest her young daughter in dancing. Instead, Hamm chose to follow in the footsteps of her father, a soccer enthusiast, who coached his children's soccer teams. The Olympic development team noticed her agility at age 14, and she was signed on. She was the youngest player ever to play on the U.S. national team. Later, Hamm attended the University of North Carolina–Chapel Hill where she continued to wow them on the field while earning a degree in political science. The UNC team held the NCAA soccer championship title while she was a student and retired Hamm's college jersey when she graduated.

The 1996 Olympics in Atlanta, Georgia, were a dream come true when Hamm's team won the gold, defeating China. Then in 1999, the U.S. soccer team again faced the Chinese team for the Women's World Cup. The final game—scoreless until the last minute—came down to a single, penalty-free kick by Hamm. For the first time in sports history, female soccer players became national heroes.

The U.S. women's team took gold in the 2004 Olympics and Hamm announced her retirement soon after. Though hailed as the greatest woman soccer play of all time, Hamm deflects individual praise: "Everything I am, I owe to this team."

PERFORMANCE THINKING When Mia Hamm writes "Dream big" on little girls' soccer balls, what is she trying to convey?

CHECK IT OUT The next chapter of Hamm's life is dedicated to giving back to the many people and organizations that have supported and inspired her. The Mia Hamm Foundation (**www.miafoundation.org**) focuses on two principle causes: support for bone marrow transplant patients and families (in honor of her brother Garrett) and young women in sports. According to Hamm, "I would not have had the life experiences to date without other pioneers who worked tirelessly to provide opportunities for women in sport." The Women's Sport Foundation (**www.womenssportfoundation.org**)—founded by Billie Jean King, another pioneer in women's sports, is also dedicated to "increasing the participation of girls and women in sports and fitness and creating an educated public that supports gender equity in sport." This site includes a number of resources, including an "inspiration station" for athletes.

Performance Strategies

Following are the top 10 tips for building healthy, diverse relationships:

- Determine your intention.
- Listen to understand.
- Show interest and empathy and ask questions.
- Use good eye contact, warmth, and humor.
- Build rapport and create common bonds.
- Communicate in an assertive, clear, calm, and direct yet kind manner.
- Make time to develop diverse, supportive, and healthy relationships.
- Take an interest in other people.
- Paraphrase to clarify.
- Ask yourself, "What is one thing that I could do to improve this relationship?"

Tech for Success

Take advantage of the text's website at **www.mhhe.com/ferrett6e** for additional study aids, useful forms, and convenient and applicable resources.

- **Relationships and computers.** If used properly, technology can help you build better relationships:

  E-mail and cell phones. Keep in touch with family, friends, and professional colleagues almost anywhere in the world.

  Chat rooms. Talk with others who share your interests.

  Blogs. Express yourself or find others who are knowledgeable about common interests.

- **Are you smiling?** If you are frustrated by e-mails that include smiley faces (emoticons) and are not sure what each one means, consult on-line sites that include mini-glossaries and instructions on how to create them. Use search words such as "e-mail smileys" and you'll receive many options.

Review Questions

Based on what you have learned in this chapter, write your answers to the following questions:

1. Describe five strategies for building rapport.

2. Describe three ways to handle conflict.

3. How do assertive people communicate?

4. Name a barrier to effective communication and how to overcome it.

5. What are five strategies for creating rapport and improving communication with roommates?

SUCCESSFUL TEAMWORK

In the Classroom

Brian Chase is an electronics student who works part-time in an electronics firm. He likes working with his hands and enjoys his technical classes. However, he has one marketing class that he finds difficult. The instructor has formed permanent class teams with weekly case studies to present to the class and a final team project to complete. Brian dislikes relying on others for a final grade and gets frustrated trying to keep the team members focused on their tasks. Some people are late for meetings, others don't do their share of the work, and two team members have personality conflicts with each other.

1. What suggestions do you have for Brian to help him work more effectively with others?

_____

_____

2. What strategies in the chapter would increase Brian's listening and team-building skills?

_____

_____

In the Workplace

Brian is now a department manager of service technicians for a large security company that provides security equipment and alarm systems for banks, hotels, and industrial firms. His department must work closely with salespeople, systems design specialists, clerical staff, and maintenance personnel. Brian is having trouble convincing his technicians that they are part of the team. Sometimes they don't listen to the advice of the salespeople, clerical staff, or each other, which results in miscommunication and frustration.

3. What suggestions do you have for Brian that would help him build rapport within and among various departments?

_____

_____

4. What strategies in this chapter could help create a solid team?

_____

_____

APPLYING THE ABCDE METHOD OF SELF-MANAGEMENT

In the Journal Entry on page 399, you were asked to describe a difficult or confrontational situation in which you felt comfortable communicating your needs and ideas in an assertive, direct, and calm manner. What factors helped you be confident and respectful?

_____

_____

_____

Now think of a confrontational situation in which you were passive or aggressive. Apply the ABCDE method to explore how you can achieve a positive outcome.

A = Actual event:

B = Beliefs:

C = Consequences:

D = Dispute:

E = Energized:

See yourself calm, centered, and relaxed as you state your needs, ideas, or rights. See yourself talking in a clear, concise, and confident manner. You feel confident about yourself because you have learned to communicate in an assertive and direct manner.

Practice Self-Management

For more examples of learning how to manage difficult situations, see the "Self-Management Workbook" section of the Online Learning Center website at **www.mhhe.com/ferrett6e.**

STUDY-TEAM RELATIONSHIPS

List some strategies for helping your study team be more organized and effective.

1. Before the Meeting

_____

_____

_____

_____

2. During the Meeting

_____

_____

_____

_____

3. After the Meeting

_____

_____

_____

_____

4. Think of effective ways to deal with the following list of challenges.

Challenges	Solutions
Latecomers or no-shows	_____
Passive members	_____
Negative attitudes	_____
Low energy	_____
Arguments	_____
Lack of preparation	_____
Socializing	_____
Members who dominate	_____

APPRECIATING DIVERSITY

Assess your appreciation for diversity and check Yes or No for each of the following comments.

	Yes	No
1. I am committed to increasing my awareness of and sensitivity to diversity.	✓	
2. I ask questions and don't assume that I know about various groups.	✓	
3. I use critical thinking to question my assumptions and examine my views.	✓	
4. I strive to be sensitive to and respectful of differences in people.	✓	
5. I listen carefully and seek to understand people with different views and perspectives.	✓	
6. I realize that I have certain biases, but I work to overcome prejudices and stereotypes.		✓
7. I do not use offensive language.		✓
8. I readily apologize if I unintentionally offend someone. I do not argue or make excuses.	✓	
9. I celebrate differences and see diversity as positive.		✓
10. I speak up if I hear others speaking with prejudice.	✓	
11. I try to read about other cultures and customs.		✓
12. I do not tell offensive jokes.	✓	
13. I encourage active participation by members of diverse cultural and social groups in clubs, groups, and any decision-making group.	✓	
	9	4

As you review your responses, think of areas where you can improve. List at least one of those areas and possible strategies you could use:

ARE YOU ASSERTIVE, AGGRESSIVE, OR PASSIVE?

Next to each statement, write the number that best describes how you usually feel when relating to other people.

3 = mostly true   2 = sometimes true   1 = rarely true

3	**1.**	I often feel resentful because people use me.
2	**2.**	If someone is rude, I have a right to be rude, too.
3	**3.**	I am a confident, interesting person.
2	**4.**	I am shy and don't like speaking in public.
2	**5.**	I use sarcasm if I need to make my point with another person.
2	**6.**	I can ask for a higher grade if I feel I deserve it.
2	**7.**	People interrupt me often, but I prefer not to bring their attention to it.
3	**8.**	I can talk louder than other people and can get them to back down.
2	**9.**	I feel competent with my skills and accomplishments without bragging.
2	**10.**	People take advantage of my good nature and willingness to help.
3	**11.**	I go along with people so they will like me or to get what I want.
3	**12.**	I ask for help when I need it and give honest compliments easily.
1	**13.**	I can't say no when someone wants to borrow something.
2	**14.**	I like to win arguments and control the conversation.
2	**15.**	It is easy for me to express my true feelings directly.
1	**16.**	I don't like to express anger, so I often keep it inside or make a joke.
1	**17.**	People often get angry with me when I give them feedback.
3	**18.**	I respect other people's rights and can stand up for myself.
1	**19.**	I speak in a soft, quiet voice and don't look people in the eyes.
3	**20.**	I speak in a loud voice, make my point forcefully, and can stare someone in the eye.
3	**21.**	I speak clearly and concisely and use direct eye contact.

Scoring

Total your answers to questions 1, 4, 7, 10, 13, 16, 19 (passive): _____

Total your answers to questions 3, 6, 9, 12, 15, 18, 21 (assertive): _____

Total your answers to questions 2, 5, 8, 11, 14, 17, 20 (aggressive): _____

Your highest score indicates your prevalent pattern.

ASSESSING YOUR RELATIONSHIP SKILLS

Developing your skills in building diverse and healthy relationships is essential for success in school and throughout your career. Take stock of your relationship skills and look ahead as you do the following exercises. Add this page to your Career Development Portfolio.

1. **Looking back:** Review your worksheets to find situations in which you learned to build rapport, listen, overcome shyness, resolve conflict, work with diversity, and be assertive. List the situations on the lines provided.

   _____

   _____

   _____

   _____

   _____

2. **Taking stock:** Describe your people skills. What are your strengths in building relationships? What areas do you want to improve?

   _____

   _____

   _____

   _____

   _____

3. **Looking forward:** Indicate how you would demonstrate to an employer that you are able to work well with a variety of people.

   _____

   _____

   _____

   _____

   _____

4. **Documentation:** Include documentation and examples of team and relationship skills. Ask an advisor, a friend, a supervisor, or an instructor to write a letter of support for you in this area. Keep this letter in your portfolio.

   _____

   _____

   _____

   _____

   _____

Develop Positive Habits

CHAPTER OBJECTIVES

In this chapter, you will learn to

▲ Recognize the top 10 habits of peak performers

▲ Focus on a positive attitude

▲ Adapt and change by developing positive habits

▲ Overcome resistors to making changes

▲ Use the peak performance success formula

SELF-MANAGEMENT

It's been a soul-searching journey to get to this point, but I now understand that I control my destiny. I make choices every day regarding what new things I will learn, how I will interact with others, and on what I will focus my energies. I will be successful because I have the power to become a peak performer in everything I do.

Are you ready for the exciting journey ahead of you? Do you know what your greatest assets are and the areas where you would like to improve? Only you can determine what kind of person—student, employee, family member,

and contributor to society—you will be. You have tremendous power to create your own success. Take a few minutes each morning before you jump out of bed or as you shower to set the tone for the day. Visualize yourself being focused and positive and successfully completing your projects and goals. Imagine yourself overcoming fear and negative habits that are self-defeating. See yourself putting all the strategies that you've learned to work for you and creating positive, long-lasting habits.

JOURNAL ENTRY In **Worksheet 13.1** on page 457, think of a time when you knew what to do but kept repeating negative habits. How would positive visualization have helped you?

Throughout this text, we have discussed many strategies and techniques for doing well in your school, career, and personal life. You know your strengths and the areas where you would like to improve. You have learned many tips to manage your time, succeed at tests, and develop healthy relationships. Acquiring knowledge and skills is one thing, but actually making these techniques and strategies part of your everyday life is another. If you have ever tried to quit smoking, you know how hard it is to kick the habit. Aside from the chemical addiction, there is the strong habit of routine: smoking while drinking a cup of coffee or having a drink with friends or as a way to soothe stress.

Habits are these thoughts, behaviors, and activities that you perform unconsciously as a result of frequent repetition. Thoughts wear a path in the neurons of your brain, and, the more you think certain thoughts and do certain actions, the deeper the path becomes until it is an unconscious habit. Habits can make life more comfortable and less stressful and threatening. Sometimes, however, you become so used to thinking and behaving in the same manner that it becomes difficult to see a better way of responding.

Knowing how to develop positive thoughts, attitudes, and behaviors will give you the confidence to take risks, grow, contribute, and overcome life's setbacks. You have what it takes to keep going, even when you feel frustrated and discouraged. This chapter will show you how to turn strategies into lasting habits.

The 10 Habits of Peak Performers

In Chapter 2, we discussed the importance of emotional maturity for school, job, and life success. You may have a high IQ, talent, skills, and experience but, if you lack emotional maturity and such important qualities as responsibility, effort, commitment, a positive attitude, interpersonal skills, and especially character and integrity, you will have difficulty in school, in the workplace, and in your relationships. However, it is not enough to review essential traits and qualities of emotional maturity. You must be committed to making them long-lasting habits. The best way to learn anything is to find personal meaning and have a willingness to learn, observe others, reflect, practice, teach, and model. To create a habit, you must practice and teach deliberately and consistently. Commit yourself to making the following 10 essential qualities long-lasting habits (see **Figure 13.1**).

1. **Be honest**. As we have stressed throughout this book, if you lack integrity, all your positive qualities—from skill and experience to intelligence and productivity—are meaningless. Practice the habit of honesty every day by being truthful, fair, kind, compassionate, and respectful. Doing the right thing is a decision and a habit.

2. **Be positive**. Greet each day and every event as an opportunity. Focus on your strengths and be your own best friend by working for and supporting yourself.

> ### WORDS TO SUCCEED
>
> "If you are going to achieve excellence in big things, you develop the habit in little matters. Excellence is not an exception, it is a prevailing attitude."
>
> COLIN POWELL
> *65th U.S. Secretary of State*

Figure 13.1   The 10 Habits of Peak Performers

THE 10 HABITS OF PEAK PERFORMERS

1. Be honest.
2. Be positive.
3. Be responsible.
4. Be resilient.
5. Be engaged.

6. Be willing to learn.
7. Be supportive.
8. Be a creative problem solver.
9. Be disciplined.
10. Be grateful.

The 10 Habits of Peak Performers   Peak performers translate positive personal qualities into action. *Do you demonstrate these habits consistently?*

Positive thinking is not wishful thinking but, rather, rational, hopeful thinking. Develop the habit of being positive and enthusiastic by looking for creative ways to create a motivated, resourceful state of mind. Look for the best in others and in every situation. Being enthusiastic about routine, uninspiring, but necessary tasks at school and work will get you noticed. Learn to be aware of the common barriers and setbacks that cause people to fail. Then set goals to focus your energy on the most appropriate path. Create the specific thoughts and behaviors that will produce the results you want.

Throughout this book, you've had an opportunity to practice the ABCDE Method of Self-Management. You have discovered that your thoughts create your feelings, which in turn can affect how you interpret events. Learn to dispel negative thoughts and replace them with realistic, optimistic, and empowering thoughts and behaviors. Developing this habit of being optimistic will keep you centered, calm, rational, productive, and peaceful, even in the midst of confusion and turmoil. You will be empowered to overcome obstacles, resistors, and fears; to maintain a positive attitude; and to reach your goals.

3. **Be responsible.** You may not always feel like keeping your commitments to yourself or your instructors, friends, co-workers, or supervisors, but meeting obligations is the mark of a mature, responsible person. For example, a major obligation for many students is the repayment of student loans after completing a course of study. Deciding to pursue higher education is a partnership with your school. Keep your commitment by paying back loans. Develop the habit of responsibility by doing what you say you're going to do, showing up, being proactive, and keeping your agreements.

4. **Be resilient**. Adversity happens to everyone. Even good students sometimes lose papers, forget assignments, miss deadlines, and do poorly on tests. Don't

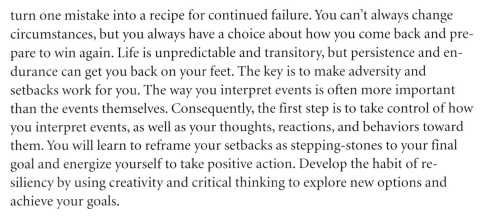

WORDS TO
SUCCEED

"We are what we
repeatedly do.
Excellence, then, is
not an act, but a
habit."

ARISTOTLE
Greek philosopher

turn one mistake into a recipe for continued failure. You can't always change circumstances, but you always have a choice about how you come back and prepare to win again. Life is unpredictable and transitory, but persistence and endurance can get you back on your feet. The key is to make adversity and setbacks work for you. The way you interpret events is often more important than the events themselves. Consequently, the first step is to take control of how you interpret events, as well as your thoughts, reactions, and behaviors toward them. You will learn to reframe your setbacks as stepping-stones to your final goal and energize yourself to take positive action. Develop the habit of resiliency by using creativity and critical thinking to explore new options and achieve your goals.

5. **Be engaged**. Peak performers do not sit back and wait for life to happen. They are engaged, are active, and have a desire to contribute. This means shifting a self-centered "what's-in-it-for-me?" attitude to a "what can I do to be more involved and useful?" attitude. One way to sabotage your classes or career is to expect your instructors or supervisor to make your life interesting. All careers are boring or monotonous at times, and some classes are less than spellbinding. Develop the habit of using your imagination and creativity to make any situation challenging and fun.

6. **Be willing to learn**. Employees can find themselves at a dead end if they refuse to learn new skills. Shifts in the economy can result in layoffs for even competent, highly educated, and skilled workers. If you are flexible and are willing to learn new skills, you can go to plan B if plan A doesn't work out. Being willing to learn and open to new ideas reflects commitment, concern, and dedication. You will get your instructor's attention if you develop the habit of curiosity and interest in every class.

Be Willing to Learn
Many are finding it necessary to further their education after a number of years in the workforce. *What percentage of your fellow students are returning students, and what are some of the reasons they are taking classes or pursuing a degree?*

7. **Be supportive**. School provides an excellent opportunity to develop the habit of understanding, supporting, and cooperating and collaborating with people with different backgrounds. Your instructors, advisors, classmates, co-workers, friends, family, and supervisors will go the extra mile to help you if you are respectful, kind, and supportive. Listen to what you say and how you say it. If your tone is brusque, others won't cooperate. Don't interrupt or criticize—people need to be heard and respected. Work to solve problems with a win/win approach. Acknowledge and be supportive of others' accomplishments and goals. Working effectively with others is fundamental for school, job, and life success.

8. **Be a creative problem solver**. Creative problem solvers have a clear vision of where they want to go and they set realistic goals. You can expand your sense of adventure and originality in problem solving and learn to think critically and creatively. You can challenge your beliefs and try new approaches. Critical thinking also helps you distinguish between an inconvenience and a real prob-

lem. Some people spend a great deal of time and energy getting angry at minor annoyances or events that they cannot change. They complain about the weather, become angry when their plane is late, become annoyed because other people don't meet their expectations, and are upset because they have to wait in line. For example, a late plane is an inconvenience; a plane crash is a real problem. A serious car accident is a problem; a fender bender is an inconvenience. Cancer or another life-threatening disease is a problem; a cold is an inconvenience. Critical thinking helps you put events in perspective and allows you to "wake up" and consciously use your creative mind. Instead of postponing, ignoring, or complaining, you actively engage in exploring solutions.

9. **Be disciplined**. Peak performers do what needs to be done—not simply what they'd like to do. They keep up on assignments, set goals and priorities, and carve out time throughout the day to focus their attention on the task at hand. Discipline demands mental and physical conditioning, planning, and effort. Using discipline and self-control, you know how to manage your time, stress, money, and emotions—especially anger. As Benjamin Franklin said, "Anger always has its reasons, but seldom good ones." Getting angry rarely solves problems, but it can create big ones. Through discipline and awareness, you can overcome impulsive reactions and learn to use critical thinking before reacting in haste. Develop the habit of discipline by being patient and by investing time, practice, and effort in your goals.

10. **Be grateful**. Life often seems like a comparison game, with competition for grades, jobs, relationships, and money. Sometimes others seem to have more, and you may feel that your own life is lacking. Reflect on your blessings, strengths, and talents, not on how your life compares with others'. Focus on what you have, not on what you don't have. Learn to listen to, appreciate, and renew your body, mind, and spirit. Appreciating your body means taking time to rest, invest in exercise, and eat good foods. Appreciating your mind means spending time reading, visualizing, creatively solving problems, writing, and challenging yourself to learn and be open to new ideas. Appreciating your spirit means finding time for quiet reflection and renewal and making an effort to listen, develop patience, and love others. The goal is to stay balanced and renewed. Develop the habit of gratitude by appreciating what you have in life and by approaching each day as an opportunity to serve and grow.

Change Your Habits By Changing Your Attitude

How can you keep a positive attitude when you are discouraged and frustrated? What if some days you have one problem after another? What if your study group or work environment is negative? Is it possible to see life differently?

In Chapter 10, we talked about the tendency to see what we already believe. Whereas we see with our eyes, we perceive with our brains. People tend to have mindsets that filter information. Each of us has attitudes or beliefs about people and

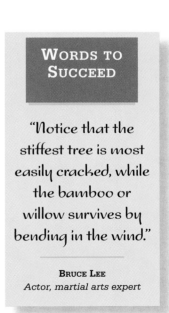

WORDS TO SUCCEED

"Notice that the stiffest tree is most easily cracked, while the bamboo or willow survives by bending in the wind."

BRUCE LEE
Actor, martial arts expert

events, and these attitudes decide for us what parts of our perception we will allow our brains to interpret and what parts we filter out. Our attitudes have a lot to do with how we relate to others and to the world and even how we see ourselves. Go back to the illustration on page 330. Some people who observed the picture saw a young women and some saw an old woman. Of course, both were actually there. Which did you see? The point is that most of us do not see the entire meaning in a situation or have difficulty seeing "the big picture."

Most people resist change. Even when you are aware of a bad habit, sometimes it is difficult to change it. However, the ability to adapt in response to new situations is not only important in school but also crucial to success in the workplace. Accountemps, a temporary staffing service for accounting professionals, asked 1,400 executives to rank the characteristics that were essential for an employee to succeed. From the list, "Adapts easily to change" and "Motivated to learn new skills" ranked #1 and #2. In a corporate world of acquisitions, mergers, and buyouts, best-selling business books such as *Who Moved My Cheese?* have spurred companies to hold employee seminars on the importance of adapting to change and growing professionally along with the company.

Strategies for Creating Positive Change

Habits can be learned—and unlearned. Adopting new habits requires a desire to change, consistent effort, time, and commitment. Try the following 10 strategies for eliminating old habits and acquiring positive new ones.

1. **Be willing to change**. As with all learning, you must desire and see the value and meaning in developing positive attitudes and habits. It's easy to find *excuses*. At some point in your life, you must be willing to find *reasons* to change. It helps to identify goals: "I really want to be more optimistic and positive and to get along with people." "I am determined to see problems as challenges and see creative alternatives." "I will no longer be a victim. I have control over my thoughts and behavior." Lasting change requires desire, effort, and commitment.

2. **Focus on the positive**. Are you a glass-half-empty or glass-half-full type of person? Practice the ability to see the good qualities in yourself and others and the positive side of any situation. Dispute negative thoughts and beliefs with critical thinking and use creative problem solving to explore the best alternatives— for example, "I missed my study group meeting. I'll e-mail my test questions to the group, apologize, and offer to do extra summaries for the next meeting. This situation has reminded me how important it is to check my calendar each morning."

3. **Develop specific goals**. Setting specific goals is a beginning for change. Statements such as "I wish I could get better grades" and "I hope I can study more" are too general and only help you continue your bad habits. Goals such as "I will study for 40 minutes, two times a day, in my study area" are specific and can be assessed and measured for achievement.

4. **Change only one habit at a time**. You will become discouraged if you try to change too many things about yourself at the same time. If you have decided to study for 40 minutes, two times a day, in your study area, then do this for a month, then two months, then three, and so on and it will become a habit. After you have made one change, move on to the next. Perhaps you want to exercise more, give better speeches, or get up earlier. When completing **Personal Evaluation Notebook 13.1** on page 444, assess your habits and put a star by the areas you most want to work on.

5. **Start small**. Realize that consistently taking small steps each day will produce major results. Sometimes the smallest changes make the biggest difference. For example, don't put off starting an exercise program because you don't have time for a long workout. Just start small by walking to class instead of driving or taking a walk at lunch. Being just a little more positive or a little more organized, finding small ways to be kind and supportive, and doing just a little more than what is expected of you are simple steps that can lead to positive change.

6. **Use visualization and affirmations to imagine success**. Imagine yourself progressing through all the steps toward your desired goal. For example, see yourself sitting at your desk in your quiet study area. Affirm, "I am calm and find it easy to concentrate. I enjoy studying and feel good about completing projects." Before you get out of bed in the morning, imagine your day unfolding effortlessly: "I am positive and focused and will accomplish everything on my to-do list."

7. **Observe and model others**. How do successful people think, act, and relate to others? Do students who get good grades have certain habits that contribute to their success? Basic success principles produce successful results. Research indicates that successful students study regularly in a quiet study area. They regularly attend classes, are punctual, and sit in or near the front row. Observe successful students. Are they interested, involved, and well prepared in class? Do they seem confident and focused? Model this behavior until it feels comfortable and natural. Form study groups with people who are good students, are motivated, and have effective study habits.

8. **Be aware of your thoughts and behaviors**. Pay attention to your behavior and reflect on ways you can be more successful. For example, you may notice that the schoolwork you complete late at night is not as thorough as the work you complete earlier in the day. Becoming aware of this characteristic may prompt you to change your time frame for studying and completing schoolwork. You may notice that you feel less stressed in the morning when you take 10 minutes at night to pack your bag with books, keys, and snacks; lay out clothes; and check the next day's events.

9. **Reward yourself**. One of the best ways to change a habit is to reward yourself when you've made a positive change. Increase your motivation with specific payoffs. Suppose you want to reward yourself for studying for a certain length of time in your study area or for completing a project. For example, you might say to yourself, "After I outline this chapter, I'll watch television for 20 minutes," or "When I finish reading these two chapters, I'll call a friend and talk for 10 minutes." The reward should always come after the results are achieved and be

Make a Commitment to Learn and Apply Positive Habits

Committing yourself to good habits is the foundation for reinforcing the cycle of success. Read the following statements concerning habits for success that we have discussed in this text. Check either Yes or No as each statement applies to you.

Success Habit	Yes	No
1. Have you created a study area that helps you concentrate?	✓	
2. Do you make learning physical?	✓	
3. Do you preview each chapter before you read it?		✓
4. Do you preview other chapters?		✓
5. Do you rewrite your notes before class?		✓
6. Do you outline your papers?	✓	
7. Do you proofread your papers several times?	✓	
8. Do you rehearse your speeches until you are confident and well prepared?	✓	
9. Do you attend every class?		✓
10. Do you sit in the front of the class?	✓	
11. Do you attentively listen and take good notes?	✓	
12. Do you review your notes within 24 hours?		✓
13. Do you monitor your work?	✓	
14. Do you get help early, if necessary?	✓	
15. Do you participate in class and ask questions?	✓	
16. Have you developed rapport with each of your instructors?	✓	
17. Have you joined a study team?		✓

Make a Commitment to Learn and Apply Positive Habits
—continued

Success Habit	Yes	No
18. Do you study and review regularly each day?	✓	
19. Do you complete tasks and assignments first and then socialize?	✓	
20. Do you recite and restate to enhance your memory skills?	✓	
21. Do you take advantage of campus and community activities?	✓	
22. Can you create a motivated, resourceful state of mind?	✓	
23. Do you know how to solve problems creatively?	✓	
24. Do you use critical thinking in making decisions?	✓	
25. Do you exercise daily?		✓
26. Do you maintain your ideal weight?		✓
27. Do you keep your body free of harmful substances and addictions?	✓	
28. Do you support your body by eating healthy foods?	✓	
29. Do you practice techniques for managing your stress?	✓	
30. Have you developed an effective budget?	✓	
31. Do you take the time for career planning?	✓	

If you find you've answered No to many of these questions, don't be alarmed. When old habits are ingrained, it's difficult to change them. Select at least one of the habits you answered No to. Determine what you can do today to turn it into a positive habit.

limited in duration. Focus on the pleasurable feelings you get when you make positive change and avoid the pain, guilt, and other bad feelings associated with negative habits.

10. **Be patient and persistent**. It takes at least 30 days to change a habit. Lasting change requires a pattern of consistent behavior. With time and patience, the change will eventually begin to feel comfortable and normal. Don't become discouraged and give up if you haven't seen a complete change in your behavior in a few weeks. Give yourself at least a month of progression toward your goal. If you fall short one day, get back on track the next. Don't expect to get all *As* the first few weeks of studying longer hours. Don't become discouraged if you don't feel comfortable instantly studying at your desk instead of lying on the couch. Lasting change requires time.

Overcome the Resistance to Change

The following are some obstacles that everyone may experience or feel, including peak performers. (See **Figure 13.2**.) Recognize and confront these resistors to create lasting change:

- *Lack of awareness.* Due to daily pressures, you may not recognize the need to make positive changes until there is a crisis. This concept is best explained by the boiled-frog syndrome. Neurobiologist Robert Ornstein, a professor from Stanford University, explained that if you put a frog in a pot of water and heated the water very slowly, the frog would remain in the pan. The frog would not detect the gradual change in temperature until it boiled to death. Sometimes you may be so busy, preoccupied, and stressed by daily pressures that you are not aware of the signals your body is giving you. In a sense, you become desensitized to the "pain." Take time each day to reflect about the state of your mind, body, and spirit and look for signs of gradual pain, such as a deterioration in grades or morale. When was the last time you felt joy? You do not have to wait for a crisis to recognize the need for change.

- *Fear of the unknown.* All change creates uncertainty. Some people even choose the certainty of misery over the uncertainty of pleasure. Fear blocks creativity, causes the imagination to run wild, and makes everyday frustrations look catastrophic: "I don't like my living situation and it's affecting my grades, but who knows what kind of roommate I would get if I asked for a change?" or "I'd like to take a computer class, but I don't know if I could do the work." When you are faced with a new and fearful situation, such as a math exam, a public speaking class, or a new roommate, be positive and optimistic.

- *Familiarity and comfort.* Old habits become comfortable, familiar parts of your life, and giving them up leaves you feeling insecure and uncomfortable. For example, you want to get better grades, and you know it's a good idea to study only in a quiet study area rather than while watching television or listening to the radio. However, you have always read your assignments while watching television. You might even try studying at your desk for a few days, but then you lapse into your old habit. Be open to trying new ideas and methods.

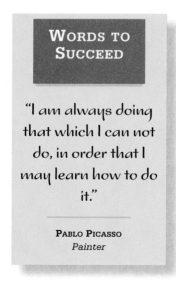

WORDS TO SUCCEED

"I am always doing that which I can not do, in order that I may learn how to do it."

PABLO PICASSO
Painter

Figure 13.2 Courage to Overcome

Elizabeth Garrett Anderson	Although rejected by medical schools because she was female, she still became the first female member of the British Medical Association.
Abraham Lincoln	Although raised in poverty and teased because of his appearance, he was still elected president of the United States.
Glen Cunningham	Although doctors believed he would never walk again after he was severely burned at age three, in 1934 he set the world's record for running a mile in just over four minutes.

Courage to Overcome   These peak performers demonstrated discipline, dedication, and a positive attitude to reach their goals despite obstacles. *What stands in your way of realizing your goals? What steps could you take to overcome obstacles?*

◆ *Independence.* You may believe that making personal changes means you are giving in to others and losing your independence. Instead, see yourself as part of the bigger picture of a team of people working together to achieve success. Understand the benefits of change and working with others to achieve a common goal.

◆ *Security.* You feel secure with your beliefs and views and may feel some of the new ideas that you are learning are so different: "I had thought through my opinions, but now I see that there are lots of ways of looking at issues. This is exciting, but it also makes me feel insecure." The old saying "knowledge is power" is definitely true and helps you overcome insecurities.

◆ *Tradition.* There may be certain preconceived notions or expectations on your future based on your experiences at home: "I was always expected to stay home, raise my family, and take a job only to help supplement the family income. My desire for a college education and career of my own contradicts family tradition. My sister-in-law says that I'm selfish and foolish to go back to school at this time in my life." If a change in direction benefits you personally (and possibly professionally), then the important people in your life will also benefit and should be supportive of your decisions.

◆ *Embarrassment.* You may think a new situation will expose you to embarrassment: "Will I feel embarrassed being in classes with younger students? Can I

WORDS TO SUCCEED

"We first make our habits, and then our habits make us."

JOHN DRYDEN
Poet and playwright

hold up my end of the team projects and class discussions? I haven't had a math course in 20 years and my study skills are rusty." Remember that learning is all about trial and error.

◆ *Responsibility.* You may feel that the demands on your time are too great to attempt making any changes: "I am overwhelmed by the responsibility of working, going to school, and caring for my family. I know I am responsible for my life, but sometimes it would be easier if someone would just tell me what to do." It's essential to put time-management strategies into practice to make sure you are accomplishing what you need to and identifying areas to adapt and change.

◆ *Environment.* You may believe that your physical environment is too constricting: "My place is not supportive for studying. Our home is noisy and there is no place where I can create my own study area. My husband and children say they are proud of me, but they complain about hurried meals and a messy house. They resent the time I spend studying." It's important to determine and negotiate when and where you can get your work done, such as at established quiet times or in the library.

◆ *Cost.* Your personal finances may limit your ability to make changes: "I am concerned about the cost of going to school. Tuition, textbooks, a computer, day care, and supplies all add up. Is it worth it? Maybe I should be saving for my children's education instead." Evaluate all your available resources and make sure you know where your money is going to determine what changes you could make.

◆ *Difficulty.* The truth is that people can and do change. Changing habits is a simple, three-step process:

  ◆ *Discard what doesn't work.* First, unlearn and discard old ideas, thoughts, and habits in order to learn more positive habits.

  ◆ *Replace with what does work.* The next step is to *replace* old habits with new habits.

  ◆ *Practice! Practice! Practice!* You can learn new habits but you must consciously apply and practice them. In a sense, you must "freeze" new patterns through consistent practice and repetition.

Making positive changes and establishing new habits is a learning process. See **Peak Progress 13.1** on applying the Adult Learning Cycle to learning new habits.

Contract for Change

Most people talk about changing, wishing they could be more positive or organized, but few actually put their commitment in writing. Many find it useful to take stock of what common resistors, or barriers, keep them from meeting their goals. Write a contract with yourself for overcoming your barriers and state the payoffs for meeting your goals. Refer back to your mission statement and goals in Chapter 3 and use them to help you determine the positive changes you want to make. Use **Personal Evaluation Notebook 13.2** on page 450 to begin drafting a personal commitment contract.

Applying the Adult Learning Cycle to Develop Positive Habits

The Adult Learning Cycle can help you increase your ability to change your behavior and adapt long-lasting positive habits.

1. **RELATE. Why do I want to learn this?** I know that practicing positive habits and creating long-lasting changes will help me succeed in school, work, and life. What are some of my positive habits, and which ones do I need to change or improve? Do I portray the 10 habits of a peak performer?

2. **OBSERVE. How does this work?** I can learn a lot about positive habits by watching others and trying new things. I will observe people who are positive, are motivated, and know how to manage their lives. What do they do? Are their positive habits obvious? I will also observe people who display negative habits and learn from their mistakes.

3. **REFLECT. What does this mean?** I will gather information by going to workshops and taking special classes. I will focus on the 10 habits of a peak performer and create strategies for incorporating them into my everyday routine. I will think about and test new ways of breaking out of old patterns, negative self-talk, and behaviors that are self-defeating. I will look for connections and associations with time management, stress and health issues, and different types of addictive behaviors.

4. **DO. What can I do with this?** I will focus on and practice one habit for one month. I will reward myself when I make progress. I will focus on my successes, and I will find simple and practical applications to use my new skills in everyday life. Each day, I will take small steps. For example, I will spend more of my social time with my friends who like to hike and do other positive things that I enjoy, instead of hanging out with friends who like to drink.

5. **TEACH. Whom can I share this with?** I will share my progress with family and friends and ask if they have noticed a difference.

Something becomes a habit only when it is repeated, have is just as the learning cycle is more effective the more times you go through it.

Commitment Contract

Complete the following statements in your own words.

1. I most want to change _____

   _____

   _____

   _____

2. My biggest barrier is _____

   _____

   _____

   _____

3. The resources I will use to be successful are _____

   _____

   _____

   _____

   _____

4. I will reward myself by _____

   _____

   _____

   _____

   _____

5. The consequences for not achieving the results I want will be _____

   _____

   _____

   _____

   _____

Date _____

Signature _____

Peak Performance Success Formula

There isn't any secret to becoming an outstanding athlete, a skilled musician, an accomplished performer, or an experienced mountain climber—or to achieving academic excellence and success. The same principles of training required to get into Olympic form apply to getting results in school and in work. **Figure 13.3** describes four components for achieving success in both your personal and career lives.

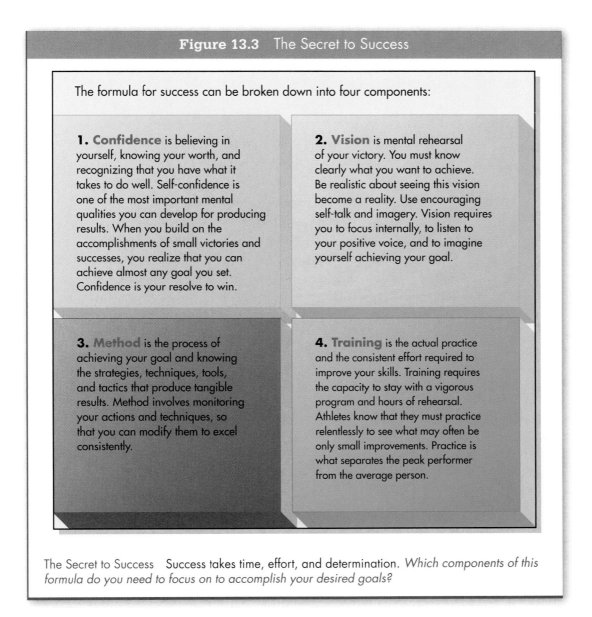

Figure 13.3 The Secret to Success

The formula for success can be broken down into four components:

1. Confidence is believing in yourself, knowing your worth, and recognizing that you have what it takes to do well. Self-confidence is one of the most important mental qualities you can develop for producing results. When you build on the accomplishments of small victories and successes, you realize that you can achieve almost any goal you set. Confidence is your resolve to win.

2. Vision is mental rehearsal of your victory. You must know clearly what you want to achieve. Be realistic about seeing this vision become a reality. Use encouraging self-talk and imagery. Vision requires you to focus internally, to listen to your positive voice, and to imagine yourself achieving your goal.

3. Method is the process of achieving your goal and knowing the strategies, techniques, tools, and tactics that produce tangible results. Method involves monitoring your actions and techniques, so that you can modify them to excel consistently.

4. Training is the actual practice and the consistent effort required to improve your skills. Training requires the capacity to stay with a vigorous program and hours of rehearsal. Athletes know that they must practice relentlessly to see what may often be only small improvements. Practice is what separates the peak performer from the average person.

The Secret to Success   Success takes time, effort, and determination. *Which components of this formula do you need to focus on to accomplish your desired goals?*

In summary, in this chapter, I learned to:

- *Strive to become a peak performer.* Peak performers are successful because they develop and practice good habits. They are honest, responsible, resilient, engaged, willing to learn, supportive, disciplined, and grateful. They have positive attitudes and creatively solve problems.

- *Develop a positive attitude.* I have learned to be my own best friend by being positive and approaching each task with a "can-do" attitude. Enthusiasm and a positive attitude help me focus on my strengths and create the thoughts and behaviors that produce the results I want.

- *Embrace change and develop positive habits.* I know that adapting to change is important to my success. I will focus on creating positive habits by developing specific goals, focusing on one habit at a time, taking small steps each day, and remaining positive and persistent. I know that developing positive habits takes time.

- *Avoid and overcome resistors and fears.* Fear of the unknown, insecurities, embarrassment, and overwhelming responsibilities are just some of the stressors that can impede my progress if I don't focus on positive outcomes.

- *Make a commitment.* I have made a commitment to turn the strategies I have learned into lasting habits. I have identified specific, meaningful goals and use affirmations and visualization to help me realize them. I observe, listen to, and model successful people and practice positive habits until they are a part of my life. I have put my commitment in writing by developing a commitment contract.

Rick Torres

CARPENTER

Related Majors: Mathematics, Bookkeeping, Computer-Aided Design

Good Habits in the Workplace

Rick Torres is a carpenter who, like one-third of carpenters in the United States, works as an independent contractor. This means that Rick is self-employed and does a variety of carpentry jobs for homeowners, from building decks to completing remodeling jobs.

The first thing Rick does is figure out how to accomplish the task. Then he provides the customer with a written time and cost estimate, purchases materials, completes the work, and hauls away construction debris. He needs good basic math skills to provide an accurate estimate and to calculate the amount of materials required for the job. Basic bookkeeping skills also help Rick keep track of his earnings and help him prepare to pay quarterly taxes. The work is often strenuous, requiring expertise with large tools, such as power saws and sanders; the handling of heavy materials; and prolonged standing, climbing, bending, and kneeling. Rick often works outdoors and enjoys the flexibility and physical activity that his work provides.

Through the years, Rick has learned that good habits are essential to his future. Rick gains new customers through word of mouth. Customers pass his name on to others because he is reliable and has excellent skills. Rick's business has been successful because he cultivates positive attitudes and is committed to providing quality service. He shows up on time for appointments, is courteous, and follows through with his commitments. Occasionally, Rick works for neighborhood low-income projects. He occasionally hires younger carpenters to work with him and enjoys teaching them old tricks and new methods of construction.

CRITICAL THINKING What might be the result of poor work habits for a carpenter working as an independent contractor?

Peak Performer Profile

Ben Carson, M.D.

Ben Carson's life is a testament to having a positive attitude, motivation, and integrity. Despite major obstacles, he has become a world-renowned neurosurgeon and author who has touched many lives.

Overcoming the disadvantages of growing up in an economically depressed neighborhood in Detroit, Carson has lived by the words "no excuses." As a child, when difficult situations would confront him or his brother, his mother would ask, "Do you have a brain? Then you can think your way out of it." Carson did just that.

During the 1950s, Carson's mother worked multiple domestic jobs to keep the family afloat. Though life at home was challenging, days at school were even more so. Carson recalls, "There was an unspoken decree that the black kids were dumb." His mother knew better. When the two brothers brought home failing grades, she turned off the TV and required the boys to read two books a week and write reports. Eventually, Carson rose to the top of his class and went on to graduate from Yale University and the University of Michigan School of Medicine.

However, one biographer wrote that, during Carson's youth, his temper made him seem "most quali-

fied for putting someone else in the hospital." It was only after a life-threatening confrontation that Carson realized his choices were "jail, reform school—or the grave."

Today Carson is the director of pediatric neurosurgery at Johns Hopkins Hospital. Even working under primitive conditions in South Africa in 1997, Carson succeeded against the odds when he separated 11-month-old conjoined twins who were joined at the head. The man who was tagged "dummy" now saves the lives of children whom others label as hopeless.

PERFORMANCE THINKING Explain how attitude played a part in Ben Carson's success. What are some of the habits he established in his childhood that contributed to his future achievements?

CHECK IT OUT Ben Carson continues his service of helping others through the Carson Scholars Fund (**www.carson-scholars.org**). The foundation's mission is to promote the joy of reading and to recognize and reward students in grades 4–11 who strive for academic excellence and demonstrate a strong commitment to their community. "THINK BIG" is Carson's philosophy, which promotes outstanding academic achievement and dedication to helping others.

Performance Strategies ....

Following are the top 10 tips for developing good habits:

◆ Commit to changing self-defeating behaviors.

◆ Set realistic goals and specify behaviors you want to change.

◆ Assess and monitor your thoughts that create feelings.

◆ Dispute irrational thoughts and describe events in an objective manner.

◆ Work on one habit at a time and focus on success.

◆ Be resilient and get right back on track after setbacks.

◆ Use affirmations and visualization to stay focused.

◆ Reward yourself for making improvements and create penalties if you do not meet realistic goals.

◆ Observe your progress and make appropriate changes until you achieve the results you want.

◆ Surround yourself with support and positive influences.

Tech for Success ....

Take advantage of the text's web site at **www.mhhe.com/ ferrett6e** for additional study aids, useful forms, and convenient and applicable resources.

◆ **Inspiration**. In this text, you have read about many peak performers who have overcome great obstacles to get where they are today. Who truly represents a peak performer to you? If it's even a relatively well-known person, chances are you will find that person's story on-line. Spend at least a few minutes searching and reading about what makes this person stand out. Do you recognize any of the 10 habits?

◆ **A log of positive habits**. Create a Word or an Excel document and use the 10 habits of peak performers. Every time you have a significant personal example in which you demonstrate a habit, log it into your document. Eventually, this will create an ideal list of personal examples, which you can relay to a future employer. Keep a copy in your Career Development Portfolio.

Review Questions ....

Based on what you have learned in this chapter, write your answers to the following questions:

1. Name the 10 habits of a peak performer.

2. What are three strategies for creating positive change in your life?

3. Why is adapting to change so critical to job success?

4. Describe one resistor to change you have experienced and how you overcame it.

5. How long does it take to change a habit?

SPREADING GOOD HABITS

In the Classroom

Craig Bradley is a welding student. He never liked high school, but his mechanical ability helped him get into a trade school. He wants to be successful and knows that this is an opportunity for him to get a good job. Both of Craig's parents worked, so he and his sister had to get themselves off to school and prepare many of their own meals. Money has always been tight, and he hardly ever received encouragement for positive behavior. He never learned positive study or work habits.

1. What kind of a study plan can you suggest to Craig to build his confidence and help him be successful?

   _____

   _____

2. What strategies in this chapter can help him develop positive, lasting habits?

   _____

   _____

In the Workplace

Craig is now working in a large farm equipment manufacturing plant. He has just been promoted to general supervisor in charge of welding and plumbing. He is a valued employee at the firm and has worked hard for several years for this promotion. Craig wants to ensure his success in his new job by getting training in motivation, team building, quality customer service, and communication skills.

3. What suggestions do you have for Craig to help him train his staff in good habits?

   _____

   _____

4. What strategies in this chapter can help him be more successful?

   _____

   _____

APPLYING THE ABCDE METHOD OF SELF-MANAGEMENT

In the Journal Entry on page 437, you were asked to think of a time when you knew what to do but kept repeating negative habits. How would positive visualization have helped you?

Not being prepared for Work

Now apply the ABCDE Method of Self-Management. How is the outcome different?

A = Actual event: Not being prepared for work

B = Beliefs: I thought I could get by on listening and just winging it

C = Consequences: Came in and felt out of place

D = Dispute: If I don't do it I won't be able to do my job

E = Energized: Take the time pomotion is in sight

Practice Self-Management

For more examples of learning how to manage difficult situations, see the "Self-Management Workbook" section of the Online Learning Center web site at **www.mhhe.com/ferrett6e.**

REVIEW AND APPLICATIONS

CHAPTER 13

DEVELOPING POSITIVE HABITS

On the following lines, list five habits you would like to change into positive behavior. It is important to focus on changing one habit at a time for a successful transition. Then, in the following chart, list the steps you will need to take, the barriers that stand in your way, and the methods by which you can overcome these barriers to reach your goal.

Positive Habits You Want to Develop

1. _____

2. _____

3. _____

4. _____

5. _____

Steps	Barriers	Methods to Overcome Barriers
1.		
2.		
3.		
4.		
5.		

OVERCOMING RESISTANCE TO CHANGE

Fill in the following.

1. I resist _____

2. I resist _____

3. I resist _____

4. I resist _____

5. I resist _____

6. I resist _____

7. I resist _____

8. I resist _____

9. I resist _____

10. I resist _____

For each item you listed above, write a strategy to overcome your resistance.

1. _____

2. _____

3. _____

4. _____

5. _____

6. _____

7. _____

8. _____

9. _____

10. _____

REVIEW AND APPLICATIONS

CHAPTER 13

PLANNING YOUR CAREER

Developing good habits in planning will benefit your career. Use the following form to create a career action plan for yourself. Then add this page to your Career Development Portfolio.

Career objective: _____

What type of job? _____

When do you plan to apply? _____

Where is this job? _____

- City _____

- State _____

- Company _____

Whom should you contact? _____

How should you contact? _____

- Phone _____

- Letter _____

- E-mail _____

- Walk-in _____

Why do you want this job? _____

Resources available: _____

Skills applicable to this job: _____

Education: _____

- Internship _____

- Courses taken _____

- Grade point average _____

- References _____

Explore Majors and Careers

CHAPTER OBJECTIVES

In this chapter, you will learn to

▲ See the connection between school and job success.

▲ Explore majors and careers.

▲ Determine your values, interests, abilities, and skills.

▲ Assemble a portfolio for career development.

▲ Adapt to workplace trends.

▲ Always practice good business ethics.

SELF-MANAGEMENT

I'm not quite certain if the major I've chosen will lead to the job I want. One of my biggest fears is that I'll be stuck in a dead end job and won't have an interesting career. What if I have spent all this time and money and I still can't get a good job?

Have you ever wondered if you are learning the skills and developing the qualities that will help you get and keep the job you want? Sometimes it's difficult to see the connection between college and the world of work. Have you ever taken a class and wondered how it relates to real life and if

it will help you be more successful? How do you integrate all that you are learning to make it meaningful and personal? In this chapter, you will learn steps for exploring college majors and careers. You will see that career planning is an exciting, lifelong process. You will also learn how to translate the information, experiences, and skills you are acquiring in school into a useful Career Development Portfolio.

JOURNAL ENTRY In **Worksheet 14.1** on page 497, write down one of the classes you are currently taking and list at least three skills you will acquire in this class that will benefit you in your career.

C areer and life planning has its roots in ancient times. Early Roman philosopher Plotinus of Delphi (A.D. 205–270) said that there are three main universal concerns:

◆ Who am I?

◆ What shall I do?

◆ What shall become of me?

We will be continually challenged to understand who we are and what we want in life. In this rapidly changing world, you may have the opportunity to do many kinds of work. Studies show that the average working American will have 3 to 5 careers and 10 to 12 jobs during his or her lifetime. And many of the career opportunities that will be available in 10 years don't even exist today. Thus, career planning involves more than just picking a profession. It involves learning about yourself and what you want out of life.

In this chapter, we will explore ways to choose a college major and explore careers. The strategies in this chapter, including step-by-step instructions on how to assemble a Career Development Portfolio, will help you create new opportunities in the world of work and help you respond to ever-changing needs, desires, and interests.

Connecting School and Job Success

The path to career success began the day you started classes. As you have read in this text, the same habits, attitudes, and personal qualities that are required for school success are also required for job success. The same strategies—assessing yourself, knowing your learning style, thinking critically, creatively solving problems, effectively communicating, and establishing healthy relationships—will be applied to career exploration and planning, no matter what your college major is.

Exploring and Choosing a Major

In our society, people are identified by their profession. For example, when adults are getting acquainted, a question that is often asked is "What do you do for a living?" In college, the question may be "What is your major?" A college major helps define who you will become professionally. It is a declaration of academic purpose and helps give many students structure and goals. It provides entry into an academic department and fellowship with other students and instructors.

Some students know from an early age what they want to major in in college. They may have known for some time that they wanted to be an engineer, a writer, a business owner, a nurse, or a computer programmer. For many students, deciding on a college major is a daunting task. Some students

WORDS TO SUCCEED

"Success is not the key to happiness. Happiness is the key to success. If you love what you are doing, you will be successful."

ALBERT SCHWEITZER
Physician

- Have many interests, so it is difficult to narrow them to one major
- Have not assessed their interests, values, or goals
- Have not explored the wide range of majors at their campus
- Have difficulty making decisions
- Fear they will get stuck with a major they won't like
- Fear a major will lead to a career they will dislike
- Are influenced by family expectations
- Are unsure of the current job market
- Know they like philosophy or a specific subject area but don't know what they can do with it

If you are unsure of your college major, you're in good company. On some campuses, "undeclared" is the largest major. The average student changes majors three times. Community colleges are experiencing a growth in students who want to change careers or learn new skills. Many students already have a four-year degree but now want to learn cooking, woodworking, real estate, nursing, firefighting, or fashion design. What you want to do at 18 may be very different from what you want to do at 40, 50, or 60. The strategies for choosing a major are similar to those for choosing a career:

1. **Assess yourself.** Since major and career planning begins with self-assessment, you will want to return to Chapter 1 and review the assessment tools. Discovering your interests, how you learn, how you process information, and how you relate to others can be useful in choosing a college major and career path. People are happiest when they do work that is consistent with their values, interests, abilities, and skills (which we will discuss further in this chapter). When your job is an extension and expression of who you are, you experience joy and fulfillment.

2. **Meet with a career counselor at your school.** Counselors are trained to offer and interpret self-assessment tools and interest inventories. They can help you clarify values, talents, and skills and offer insight into your interests, personality type, and goals. The career center often offers career fairs and can help you link majors with careers.

3. **Talk with your support system.** Discuss possible majors with family, friends, instructors, and advisors. People who know you best may shed light on your unique abilities and talents. Talk with your academic advisor and instructors. Talk with other students and ask about their majors.

4. **Explore through college classes.** Taking general education classes is a great way to experience various disciplines, get to know different instructors and students, and still meet college requirements.

5. **Explore through the course catalog.** Review the catalog to find a major that you did not know existed. What is the most unusual major or minor you come across? Determine at least two majors you'd like to research further.

6. **Go to the academic department.** Go to the departments of majors you are interested in and find out more information, such as the requirements, job

outlook, and possible careers. Ask for handouts and ask if the department has clubs or activities.

7. **Take classes or workshops.** Many campuses offer major or career exploration courses that provide assessments to determine interests, traits, and self-understanding. Sometimes alumni are invited to speak at campus events.

8. **Gain experience.** Get involved through internship possibilities, volunteer work, part-time jobs, and service learning activities that provide hands-on experience (see **Peak Progress 14.1**). On- and off-campus jobs help you explore possible major and career interests. Also join clubs, participate in extracurricular activities, seek out leadership opportunities, and travel with educational tours or programs.

9. **Be creative with your major.** Your campus may have an interdisciplinary major, a self-designed major, or a broad liberal arts major that allows you to take a broad range of courses in areas that interest you. Many employees are looking for liberal arts graduates who have strong writing, critical thinking, and reasoning skills, have creative problem-solving skills, and can work well with diverse groups of people.

10. **Relax and reflect.** Although you want to be proactive about learning about various majors, you also need to realize that you have your own inner wisdom. In Chapter 2, we reviewed Maslow's hierarchy of needs, which explains what motivates people and gives their actions meaning. Self-actualization is the process of fulfilling your potential, becoming everything that you are capable of, and experiencing satisfaction and joy. To advance to the highest level of self-actualization requires listening to your inner voice. Spend time reflecting on what makes you happy and get to know the real you.

Finally, remind yourself that getting a college degree in anything will help launch your career. There are no guarantees, but a college degree—plus hard work, additional experience and skills, and positive habits and qualities—go a long way toward creating opportunities.

Values, Interests, Abilities, and Skills

As we discussed in relation to self-assessment, it's important to determine your values, interests, innate abilities, and already acquired skills to help you decide which career direction you want to take and thus which major course of study you should pursue.

Values

Values are the worth or importance you attach to various factors in your life. They are formed in early childhood and are influenced by parents, teachers, the environment, and your culture. Your values can reflect your self-esteem, optimism, self-control, and ability to get along with others.

Your values are important when it comes to choosing a college major and career. You will be much happier if your career is in line with your values. Complete **Personal Evaluation Notebook 14.1** on page 466 to determine your overall personal values and those that are important to your career.

Service-Learning

As we discussed in Chapter 4, service-learning offers a unique opportunity for you to get involved with your community in a meaningful way by integrating service projects with classroom learning. Service-learning enables you to use what you are learning in the classroom to solve real-life problems. It is based on a reciprocal relationship in which the service reinforces and strengthens the learning, and the learning reinforces and strengthens the service. You not only learn about democracy and citizenship but also become an actively contributing citizen and community member through the service you perform.

Many colleges offer courses that provide service-learning opportunities. In these courses, there is structured time for students to reflect on their service and learning experiences through a mix of writing, reading, speaking, listening, and creating in small and large groups and individual work. This fosters the development of personal qualities—empathy, personal values, beliefs, awareness, self-esteem, self-confidence, and social responsibility—and helps foster a sense of caring for others. Credit is awarded for learning, not for a requisite number of service hours.

There are many benefits of service-learning:

- It provides students with opportunities to use newly acquired skills and knowledge in real-life situations.
- Although it fills a need for volunteer support in the community, it also uses that need as a foundation to examine ourselves, our society, and our future.
- It identifies in advance and tracks specific learning objectives and goals (as well as the intangible ones).
- Students perform a valuable, significant, and necessary service that has consequence to the community.
- Students feel empowered that they have contributed positively to their community.

Service-learning experiences can be personally rewarding and enriching, and they are also important points in a portfolio or resume. As employers review job applicants who are equally qualified, they are looking for experiences, skills, or qualities that make one candidate stand out from another. Service-learning opportunities may also allow you to work with administrators and members of your community whom you might not have otherwise met, providing you new job contacts and mentors who may help open doors for you in the future.

Interests

Interests are the activities and subjects that draw you in and cause you to feel comfortable, at ease, excited, enthusiastic, or passionate. Psychologist John L. Holland explored interests and their relationship to college major and career choice. His theory suggests that career choice is often a reflection of personality type and that most people generally fit into one of six occupational personality types, which are largely

Your Values

Your values play an important role in determining what will satisfy you in a career. By each value, rank them as

3 = most important

2 = somewhat important

1 = not that important

Overall Values	Rank
Security	_____
Helping others	_____
Recognition	_____
Collaborating with others	_____
Serving religious or spiritual beliefs	_____
Adventure	_____
Variety	_____
Serving community/national/international concerns	_____
Artistic/creative expression	_____
Personal growth and learning	_____
Focusing on family	_____
Others:	_____

Specific Factors You Value in a Career	Rank
High salary	_____
Great deal of freedom/autonomy	_____
Flexible working hours	_____
Opportunities for advancement	_____
Good vacation/benefits	_____
Supportive co-workers	_____
Working with others	_____
Working alone	_____
Telecommuting/working at home	_____
Working outdoors	_____
Social environment	_____
Job status	_____
Clean and comfortable working environment	_____
Others:	_____

determined by their interests. Revisit Chapter 1 in this text and review your personality assessments. Then read Holland's types and see if you fall into one or two of the categories:

Realistic: Realistic people have athletic or mechanical ability and prefer to work with objects, machines, tools, plants, or animals or to be outdoors. They like to work with their hands. Possible careers include architect, optician, surveyor, laboratory technician, automotive mechanic, mail carrier, engineer, chef, and bus or truck driver.

Investigative: Investigative people like to observe, learn, investigate, analyze, evaluate, or solve problems. They are observant and enjoy academic and scientific challenges. Possible careers include computer operator, airplane pilot, mathematics teacher, surgical technician, doctor, economist, and chemist.

Artistic: Artistic people have creative, innovative, or intuitive abilities and like to work in unstructured situations. They may be flamboyant and imaginative. Possible careers include actor, commercial artist, public relations representative, editor, decorator, fashion designer, and photojournalist.

Social: Social people like to work with people—to inform, enlighten, help, train, develop, or cure. They have strong verbal and written skills. Possible careers include social worker, minister, psychologist, parole officer, training instructor, school superintendent, rehabilitation therapist, and hair stylist.

Enterprising: Enterprising people enjoy working with people—influencing, persuading, performing, leading, or managing to meet organizational goals or achieve economic gain. Possible careers include small business owner, communications consultant, college department head, stockbroker, sales representative, restaurant manager, and motivational speaker.

Conventional: Conventional people like to work with data, have clerical or numerical abilities, are detail-oriented, and follow directions well. They like working with numbers and facts and enjoy bringing situations to closure. Possible careers include certified public accountant, business teacher, court reporter, credit manager, data entry operator, secretary, military officer, office manager, and title examiner.

Abilities

Abilities are the qualities that are an intrinsic part of who you are. They are innate talents or gifts, which may be enhanced and developed to reach maximum potential through study and practice. You may have the ability to understand mathematics easily or play many musical instruments. Or your ability may be as intangible as being able to resolve conflict or handle a crisis calmly.

Skills

Skills are capabilities you have learned and developed. They often have a more technical connotation than abilities. Some skills are job-specific, such as operating a bulldozer, conducting lab tests, editing manuscripts, or shoeing horses. **Transferable skills** are those that can be used in a variety of careers, such as negotiating, analyzing data, preparing presentations, effectively managing people or resources, and using technology.

It's important to identify your skills to see how they can be developed throughout your career. Following is a broad list of skills you can use to determine the areas in which you excel. What career choices might you like to explore based on these skills?

WORDS TO SUCCEED

"Mostly I just followed my inner feelings and passions...and kept going to where it got warmer and warmer, until it finally got hot...Everybody has talent. It's just a matter of moving around until you've discovered what it is."

GEORGE LUCAS
Director

People	Data	Mechanical
Instructing	Analyzing	Handling
Supervising	Coordinating	Setting up
Negotiating	Comparing	Driving/operating
Entertaining	Computing	Tending
Persuading	Compiling	Selecting

Exploring Careers

Once you have assessed your personal values and what you are looking for in a career, you can determine what opportunities are ahead for you. You may be starting out—at the bottom—or you may be taking courses to prepare for promotional opportunities or a new direction or responsibilities. A mentioned earlier, the strategies for choosing a major are applicable to determining a career path. Some additional resources include

- ◆ *Career center.* Career center personnel have many valuable resources for exploring careers. You can check out free magazines and up-to-date publications. They have information about career trends, opportunities, and data concerning growth, salaries, and the availability of jobs.

- ◆ *Library.* Your school or local library has many resources, such as the *Dictionary of Occupational Titles, The Guide for Occupational Exploration, Occupational Outlook Handbook,* and the classic *What Color Is Your Parachute?* by Richard Bowles.

- ◆ *Professional organizations.* Visit web sites of related professional organizations in your field of interest and consider joining. Student members often pay a discounted membership fee. Find out what you would receive with a membership, such as magazines, reports, journals, and access to job listings. At the web site or in the journals, look for individuals who have received promotions or have contributed to the field. Are any of them local, or do they provide their contact information and welcome correspondence? Most professionals enjoy talking to young people who are entering their profession and are happy to offer advice.

- ◆ *Your network.* Personal contacts are excellent ways to explore careers and to find a job. As we discussed in Chapter 4, networking provides access to people who can serve as mentors and can help connect you to jobs and opportunities. Personal and professional contacts must be created, cultivated, and expanded. Talk with instructors, advisors, counselors, and other students. Collect and keep business cards and e-mail addresses.

- ◆ *Government organizations.* A number of organizations, such as the U.S. Department of Labor, are dedicated to tracking job statistics, predicting future opportunities, and providing employment guidance—such as SCANS, which we discussed earlier. Besides at the library, the *Occupational Outlook Handbook* can be found at the Bureau of Labor Statistics web site at **www.bls.gov/oco**. It lists the outlook for hundreds of types of jobs and provides employment guidance, such as job search methods and where to learn about job openings, how to apply for certain jobs, and resume and job interview tips. See **Peak Progress 14.2**, on using the Adult Learning Cycle for exploring majors and careers.

Applying the Adult Learning Cycle When Exploring Majors and Careers

1. **RELATE.** Write down the top three things that are important to you in a future career, such as independence, high visibility, flexible hours, ability to work from home, and management opportunities. Now compare those wishes with your personality type. Are there certain careers that fit your personality that offer these features?

2. **OBSERVE.** Explore three potential opportunities for learning more about this career, such as acquaintances in the field, knowledgeable instructors, professional organizations, and introductory courses.

3. **REFLECT.** Based on your research and observations, does this career still sound appealing? What are the drawbacks? Are they significant enough that they outweigh the positives? Did any related professions come to light?

4. **DO.** If the career choice still looks promising, determine three ways you can gain experience and/or related skills the profession will require, such as joining a club or securing an internship. Construct a time line for accomplishing those tasks.

5. **TEACH.** Relay your impressions and reservations to your family, friends or fellow students who are also career searching. You will no doubt be asked some very good questions that will make you think about where you are in selecting a major and what your next steps should be. You will also enlighten others by relaying the various avenues and resources you are using.

If your conclusion is that you are still undecided, explore other career options and attempt some or all of the steps again. Consider practicing visualization whenever you need help focusing. Eventually, you will find the career path that suits your personality and interests.

Building a Career Development Portfolio

A Career Development Portfolio is a collection of documents that highlight your strengths, skills, and competencies. It includes grades, summaries of classes, certificates, letters of recommendation, awards, lists of activities, inventories you've taken, and samples of written work. A portfolio can help you connect what you have learned in school to your current or future work, and it is an organized and documented system demonstrating that you have the necessary skills, competencies, and personal qualities to perform a job.

Even if you have little work experience, you will have assembled examples of your skills and abilities with samples of your work and evidence of courses taken. This documentation can give you an edge when applying for a job. For example, Janet convinced an employer to hire her based on her portfolio: She showed the manager samples of her work and the certificates she had earned. Jake used his portfolio to receive a promotion: He was able to stress his strengths based on documentation of his skills and experiences in his portfolio.

Your Career Development Portfolio helps you

- Plan and design your educational program and postgraduate learning
- Record significant life experiences
- Draw attention to your accomplishments
- Describe how your experiences have helped you grow professionally
- Document skills and accomplishments in and out of the classroom
- Provide links between what you can do and what an employer is looking for in a candidate
- Apply patterns of interests, skills, and competencies to career planning
- Identify areas you want to enhance, augment, or improve
- Record and organize experiences for your resume and job interviews
- Express talents creatively and artistically
- Justify college credit for prior learning, military, internship, or life experiences
- Prepare for a job change

When Should You Start Your Portfolio?

You can start your portfolio at any time—but the sooner the better. If you completed assessments, journal entries, and worksheets at the end of each chapter in this text, then you've already started your portfolio. Ideally, you will begin your portfolio during your first term or year in school. As you go through each semester, make copies of papers or other coursework to add to your portfolio. Make note of courses that relate to your career interests. If you have a work-study job or an internship that is related to your career goal, you can keep records of your experiences, any written work, and letters of recommendation to include in your Career Development Portfolio. By the time you graduate, you will have a tool that is distinctly personal and persuasive.

A sample planning guide appears in **Figure 14.1.** Students in both two- and four-year schools can use this guide. Students in a two-year school can use freshman and sophomore years for the first year, junior and senior years for the second year. Modify the planning guide to fit your needs.

How to Organize and Assemble Your Portfolio

The exercises, Personal Evaluation Notebooks, and worksheets that you have completed throughout this book form the basis of your Career Development Portfolio. You will want to type an edited version of this information on the computer and save it, so that you can easily make changes and update it often. You will also need these items:

- Three-ring notebook
- Sheet protectors to hold documents and work samples
- Labels and tabs
- Box to store work samples and information

Figure 14.1   Career Development Portfolio Planning Guide

Freshman Year

- Begin your Career Development Portfolio.
- Explore and join clubs and get involved on campus.
- Assess your interests, skills, values, goals, and personality.
- Go to the career center at your school and explore majors and careers.
- Set goals for your first year.
- Explore college majors and minors.
- Explore the community.
- Network with professors and students. Get good grades.
- Keep a journal. Label the first section "Self-Assessment." Begin to write your autobiography.
- Label another section "Exploring Careers."

Sophomore Year

- Add to your Career Development Portfolio.
- Start a file about careers and majors.
- Choose a major.
- Review general education requirements.
- Continue to explore resources in the community.
- Build your network.
- Join clubs and take a leadership role.
- Read articles and books about your major area.
- Find a part-time job or volunteer your time.
- Start or update your resume.
- Explore internships and co-op programs.
- Add a section to your journal called "Job Skills and Qualities."

Junior Year

- Update and expand your Career Development Portfolio.
- Gain more job experience.
- Write and submit a major contract, outline your program, apply for graduation.
- Join student organizations and professional organizations and add to your network.
- Develop relationships with faculty, administrators, and other students.
- Identify a mentor or someone you can model to achieve your goals.
- Start to read the journal of your profession.
- Obtain an internship or gain additional job experience.
- Update your journal with job tips and articles about your field.
- Update your resume.
- Visit the career center on campus for help with your resume, internships, and job opportunities.

Senior Year

- Refine your Career Development Portfolio.
- Put your job search into high gear. Go to the career center for advice.
- Read recruitment materials. Schedule interviews with companies.
- Update and polish your resume and print copies. Write cover letters.
- Actively network! Keep a list of contacts and their telephone numbers.
- Join professional organizations and attend conferences.
- Start sending out resumes and attending job fairs.
- Find a mentor to help you with your job search and career planning.
- Meet with an evaluator or advisor to review graduation requirements.
- Log interviews in your journal or notebook.

Career Development Portfolio Planning Guide   This planning guide will help you review your skills and maintain your Career Development Portfolio as you move toward your career goal. This and a modified plan for a two-year degree can be found at the book's web site at **www.mhhe.com/ferrett6e**. *What are some other strategies you can use to prepare for your career?*

The steps for organizing and assembling your portfolio will vary, depending on your purpose and the school you are attending. However, they generally include procedures such as these:

- ◆ *Step 1: Determine your purpose.* You may want to keep a portfolio as a general documented system of achievements and professional growth, or you may have a specific reason, such as attempting to receive credit for prior learning experiences.
- ◆ *Step 2: Determine criteria.* The U.S. Department of Labor created the Secretary's Commission on Achieving Necessary Skills (SCANS) to identify skills and competencies needed for success in the workplace. These skills apply to all kinds of jobs in every occupation. You may add specific criteria to this list as they apply to your situation. (See page 00 for a complete list of SCANS skills.)
- ◆ *Step 3: Do your homework.* Make certain that you have completed the Career Development Portfolio exercise at the end of each chapter. Assess and review your worksheets.
- ◆ *Step 4: Assemble your portfolio.* Print computer copies using high-quality paper. It often works best to work with a study partner. The following section is a general guideline for the contents of your portfolio.

Elements of Your Portfolio

If you will need to submit your portfolio to your school for review or evaluation, there are probably established guidelines that you will need to follow. If not, the following sections describe elements that are applicable to most portfolios.

Cover or Title Page

Include a cover page, with the title of your document, your name, the name of the college, and the date. See **Figure 14.2** for an example. (If you are reproducing your portfolio to submit for evaluation, you may want to include an additional cover page printed on heavy card stock. You can also put your own logo or artwork on the cover to make it unique.)

Contents Page

The contents page lists the contents of the portfolio. You can make a draft when you start your portfolio, but it will be the last item you finish, so that the page numbers and titles are correct. See **Figure 14.2** on page 00 for an example of a contents page.

Introduction

The introduction should discuss the purpose of your portfolio and the goals you are trying to achieve with its development. This is similar to a preface in a text, which summarizes the purpose and main features. See **Figure 14.3** on page 474 for an example of an introduction page.

List of Significant Life Experiences

This section of your portfolio includes a year-by-year account of all your significant life experiences (turning points). You are preparing a chronological record, or time line. Resources that can help you are family members, friends, photo albums, and

Figure 14.2 Career Development Portfolio Elements

Sample Title Page	Sample Contents Page

CONTENTS

CAREER DEVELOPMENT PORTFOLIO

Kim Anderson
Louis College of Business

September 20, 2007

Career Development Portfolio Elements   The presentation of your Career Development Portfolio reflects your personality and makes a valuable first impression. *What are the different ways you can personalize the title or cover page?*

journals. Don't be concerned about what you learned but concentrate on experiences that are important because you

◆ Found the experience enjoyable
◆ Found the experience painful
◆ Learned something new about yourself
◆ Achieved something that you value
◆ Received recognition
◆ Expended considerable time, energy, or money

This section can also be written as an autobiography. It can include

◆ Graduation and formal education
◆ Jobs/promotions
◆ Marriage/divorce
◆ Special projects
◆ Volunteer work
◆ Training and workshops
◆ Self-study or reentry into college

Figure 14.3   Sample Introduction Page

INTRODUCTION

The Career Development Portfolio I am submitting reflects many hours of introspection and documentation. The purpose of this portfolio is to gain college credit for similar courses that I completed at Wake View Community College. I am submitting this portfolio to Dr. Kathryn Keys in the Office of Prior Learning at Louis College of Business.

I recently made a career change and want to enter the marketing field. The reason for the change is personal growth and development. I had an internship in marketing, and I know I will excel in this area. I plan to complete my degree in business administration at Louis College of Business. Eventually I want to work my way up to store manager or director of marketing at a large store.

This portfolio contains

- List of significant life experiences
- Analysis of accomplishments
- Inventory of interests, aptitudes, and values
- Inventory of skills and competencies
- Inventory of personal qualities
- Documentation
- Work philosophy and goals
- Resume
- Interview planning
- Samples of work
- Summary of transcripts
- Credentials, certificates, workshops
- Bibliography
- Appendix

Sample Introduction Page   A Career Development Portfolio is a record of your goals, progress, skills, and experience. *What are some other elements you should include in your portfolio?*

- ◆ Extensive travel
- ◆ Hobbies and crafts
- ◆ Relocation
- ◆ Military service
- ◆ Events in your family

WORDS TO SUCCEED

"When your work speaks for itself, don't interrupt."

HENRY KAISER
Industrialist

Analysis of Accomplishments

Once you have completed your list of significant life experiences, you are ready to identify and describe what you learned and how you learned it. Specifically, identify what you learned in terms of knowledge, skills, competencies, and values and how you can demonstrate the learning. Whenever possible, include evidence or a measurement of the learning. Review your list of significant experiences and look for patterns, themes, or trends. Assess your accomplishments. Did these experiences

- ◆ Help you make decisions?
- ◆ Help you clarify and set goals?
- ◆ Help you learn something new?

Figure 14.4 SCANS Skills

Basic Skills: reading, writing, listening, speaking, and math

Thinking Skills: critical thinking, creative problem solving, knowing how to learn, reasoning, and mental visualization

Personal Qualities: responsibility, positive attitude, dependability, self-esteem, sociability, integrity, and self-management

Interpersonal Skills: teaches others, team member, leadership, works well with diverse groups, and serves clients and customers

Information: acquires, evaluates, organizes, maintains, and uses computers

Systems: understands, monitors, corrects, designs, and improves systems

Resources: allocates time, money, material, people, and space

Technology: selects, applies, maintains, and troubleshoots

SCANS Skills   Acquiring these skills and competencies will help you succeed throughout your career. *Which of these skills do you need to develop?*

◆ Broaden your view of life?
◆ Accept diversity in people?
◆ Help you take responsibility?
◆ Increase your confidence and self-esteem?
◆ Result in self-understanding?
◆ Change your attitude?
◆ Change your values?

Inventory of Skills and Competencies

Use your completed Career Development Portfolio worksheets, inventories from the career center, and activities in this text to record skills and competencies. Your college may also provide you with a list of specific courses, competencies, or categories. The Department of Labor report from the Secretary's Commission on Achieving Necessary Skills (SCANS) can be a guide. (See **Figure 14.4**.) Complete **Personal Evaluation Notebook 14.2** on page 476 to determine your transferable skills.

SCANS lists several important personal qualities for success in the workplace: responsibility, a positive attitude, dependability, self-esteem, sociability, integrity, and self-management. Cultivate these qualities and apply them to your daily routine. Your personal qualities will set you apart from others in the workplace. In **Personal Evaluation Notebook 14.3** on page 477, use critical thinking to explore ways you've learned and demonstrated your personal qualities.

Documentation

For your Career Development Portfolio, document each of the SCANS skills, competencies, and personal qualities. Indicate how and when you learned each. Write the

Transferable Skills

Read the following and comment on the lines provided.

1. What transferable skills do you have?

   _____

   _____

2. What specific content skills do you have that indicate a specialized knowledge or ability, such as plumbing, computer programming, or cooking?

   _____

3. List your daily activities and determine the skills involved in each. Then consider what you like about this activity. These factors may include the environment, interactions with others, or a certain emotional reaction—for example, "I like bike riding because I am outdoors with friends, and the exercise feels great."

Activity	Skills Involved	Factors
Bike riding	Balance, stamina, discipline	Being outdoors

names of people who can vouch that you have these skills, competencies, and personal qualities. Include letters of support and recommendation. These letters can be from your employer verifying your skills, from co-workers and community members, and from clients or customers expressing thanks and appreciation. Your skills and competencies may have been learned at college, in vocational training programs, in community work, through on-the-job training, or through travel.

Work Philosophy and Goals

Your work philosophy is a statement about how you approach work. It can also include changes that you believe are important in your career field. For example, define your educational goals. The following is a sample statement defining your educational goals:

My immediate educational goal is to graduate with a certificate in fashion design. In five years, I plan to earn a college degree in business with an emphasis in marketing.

Also define your career goals—for example,

◆ To hold a leadership role in fashion design
◆ To upgrade my skills
◆ To belong to at least one professional organization

Inventory of Personal Qualities

Indicate how you have learned and demonstrated each of the SCANS qualities. Next indicate how you would demonstrate them to an employer. Add personal qualities that you think are important. Use additional pages if needed.

1. Responsibility: _____

_____

_____

2. Positive attitude: _____

_____

_____

3. Dependability: _____

_____

_____

4. Self-esteem: _____

_____

_____

5. Sociability: _____

_____

_____

6. Integrity: _____

_____

_____

7. Self-control: _____

_____

_____

Expand on your short-term, medium-range, and long-term goals. Include a mission statement and career objectives. You may also write your goals according to the roles you perform. What is it you hope to accomplish in each area of your life? **Figure 14.5** is an example of a mission statement. Ask yourself the following questions:

- Do I want to improve my skills?
- Do I want to change careers or jobs?
- Do I want to become more competent in my present job or earn a promotion?
- Do I want to obtain a college degree?
- Do I want to spend more time in one or more areas of my life?
- Do I want to learn a new hobby or explore areas of interest?
- Do I want to become more involved in community service?
- Do I want to improve my personal qualities?
- Do I want to improve my human relations skills?
- Do I want to spend more time with my family?
- Do I want to assess my interests and aptitudes? (See **Personal Evaluation Notebook 14.4** on page 480.)

Return to Chapter 3 and review **Personal Evaluation Notebook 3.3: Looking Ahead.** Reflect on what you wrote and update it. How has it changed in just a few weeks? Make it a habit to reflect and make connections between what you are learning in class and how it relates to work and life. Integrate your experiences between your coursework and your outside learning experiences. How do all of these experiences relate? How are they changing the way you see yourself, others, and the world? How are they changing your values, interests, and goals? How are they changing how you view and work with diverse people? At the end of your college experience, it is very valuable to record these questions in your portfolio and update it often.

Resume

The purpose of a resume is to show the connections between your strengths, accomplishments, and skills and the needs of a company or an employer. The resume is a critical tool because it is a first impression, and first impressions count. Your resume is almost always the first contact an employer will have with you, since many companies now initially screen potential candidates through on-line application submission. You want it to stand out, to highlight your skills and competencies, and to look professional. Computer programs and on-line services can help you format your resume, and resume classes may be offered in the career center. See **Figure 14.6** on page 481 for a sample resume.

Although you may not be actively looking for a job right now, it's good practice to have at least a draft resume in your portfolio to build on. This will make creating a polished version an easier task. You may want to include the following components in your resume:

1. **Personal information.** Write your name, address, telephone number (including cell phone, if necessary), and e-mail address. If you have a temporary or school address, also include a permanent address and phone number. Don't include

Figure 14.5 Sample Mission Statement

Name **Anna Marcos**

My mission is to use my talent in fashion design to create beauty and art. I want to influence the future development of fashion. I seek to be a lifelong learner because learning keeps me creative and alive. In my family, I want to build strong, healthy, and loving relationships. At work, I want to build creative and open teams. In life, I want to be kind, helpful, and supportive to others. I will live each day with integrity and be an example of outstanding character.

Long-Term Goals

Career goals: I want to own my own fashion design company.
Educational goals: I want to teach and lead workshops.
Family goals: I want to be a supportive parent.
Community goals: I want to belong to different community organizations.
Financial goals: I want to earn enough money to live comfortably and provide my family with the basic needs and more.

Medium-Range Goals

Career goals: I want to be a manager of a fashion company.
Educational goals: I want to earn a college degree in business and marketing.

Short-Term Goals

Career goals: I want to obtain an entry-level job in fashion design.
Educational goals: I want to earn a certificate in fashion design.

Sample Mission Statement A mission statement reveals your aspirations and your philosophy on work and life. *What other types of personal information can your mission statement reveal?*

marital status, height, weight, health, interests, a picture, or hobbies unless you think they are relevant to the job. Keep your resume simple. Adding nonessential information only clutters it and detracts from the essential information.

2. **Job objective.** It is not essential to include a job objective on your resume. The rule is to include a job objective if you will accept only a specific job. You may be willing to accept various jobs in a company, especially if you're a new graduate with little experience. If you decide not to list a job objective, you can use your cover letter to relate your resume to the specific job for which you are applying.

3. **Work experience.** List the title of your last job first, dates worked, and a brief description of your duties. Don't clutter your resume with needless detail or irrelevant jobs. You can elaborate on specific duties in your cover letter and in the interview.

4. **Educational background.** List your highest degree first, school attended, dates, and major field of study. Include educational experience that may be relevant to

Inventory of Interests and Aptitudes

Aptitudes are abilities or natural inclinations that you have in certain areas. Some people learn certain skills easily and are described by these aptitudes; for example, Joe is a natural salesman or Mary is a born speaker.

Check the following areas in which you have an aptitude. You may add to the list.

_____ Mechanical	_____ Gardening
_____ Clerical	_____ Investigative
_____ Musical	_____ Artistic
_____ Drama/acting	_____ Working with numbers
_____ Writing	_____ Working with people
_____ Persuasive speaking	_____ Working with animals
_____ Sales	_____ Working with things

the job, such as certification, licensing, advanced training, intensive seminars, and summer study programs. Don't list individual classes on your resume. If you have special classes that relate directly to the job you are applying for, list them in your cover letter.

5. **Awards and honors.** List awards and honors that are related to the job or indicate excellence. In addition, you may want to list special qualifications that relate to the job, such as fluency in a foreign language. Highlight this information prominently rather than writing it as an afterthought. Pack a persuasive punch by displaying your best qualifications at the beginning.

6. **Campus and community activities.** List activities that show leadership abilities and a willingness to contribute.

7. **Professional memberships and activities.** List professional memberships, speeches, or research projects connected with your profession.

8. **References.** You will want three to five references, including employment, academic, and character references. Ask instructors for a general letter before you leave their last class or soon after. Fellow members of professional associations, club advisors, a coach, and students who have worked with you on projects can also provide good character references. See **Figure 14.7** on page 482 for a sample request for a recommendation letter. Ask your supervisor for a letter before you leave a job. Make certain you ask your references for permission to use their names and phone numbers. Update a list of possible references and their addresses and phone numbers. Don't print your references on the bottom of your resume. List them on a separate sheet of paper, so that you can update the list

Figure 14.6 Sample Resume

KATIE J. JENSEN

Present address:
1423 10th Street
Arlin, Minnesota 52561
(320) 555-2896

Permanent address:
812 La Jolla Avenue
Burlingate, Wisconsin 53791
(414) 555-1928

JOB OBJECTIVE: To obtain an entry-level job as a travel agent

WORK EXPERIENCE

University Travel Agency, Arlin, Minnesota
Tour Guide, August 2005–present
- Arrange tours to historic sites in a four-state area. Responsibilities include contacting rail and bus carriers, arranging for local guides at each site, making hotel and restaurant reservations, and providing historical information about points of interest.

- Develop tours for holidays and special events. Responsibilities include pre-event planning, ticketing, and coordination of travel and event schedules.

- Specialized tour planning resulted in 24 percent increase in tour revenues over the preceding year.

Burlingate Area Convention Center, Burlingate, Wisconsin
Intern Tourist Coordinator, December 2004–June 2005
- Established initial contact with prospective speakers, coordinated schedules, and finalized all arrangements. Set up computerized database of tours using dBase IV.

- Organized receptions for groups up to 250, including reserving meeting rooms, contacting caterers, finalizing menus, and preparing seating charts.

EDUCATION
Arlin Community College, Arlin, Minnesota
    Associate of Arts in Business, June 2006
    Magna Cum Laude graduate

Cross Pointe Career School, Arlin, Minnesota
    Certificate in Tourism, June 2004

HONORS AND AWARDS
Academic Dean's List
Recipient of Burlingate Rotary Scholarship, 2004

CAMPUS AND COMMUNITY ACTIVITIES
Vice President, Tourist Club, 2005–2006
Co-chaired 2004 home-tour fundraising event for Big Sisters

PROFESSIONAL MEMBERSHIP
Burlingate Area Convention and Visitors Bureau

Sample Resume   An effective resume should be clear, concise, and eye-catching to create the best possible first impression. *What is the most important element of your resume?*

Figure 14.7   Request for a Letter of Recommendation

May 2, 2007

Professor Eva Atkins
Chair of the Fashion Department
Green Briar Business Institute
100 North Bank Street
Glenwood, New Hampshire 03827

Dear Professor Atkins:

I was a student of yours last term in Fashion Design and earned an A in your class. I am currently assembling my Career Development Portfolio so I can apply for summer positions in the fashion business. Would you please write a letter of recommendation addressing the following skills and competencies?

- My positive attitude and enthusiasm
- My ability to work with diverse people in teams
- My computer and technical skills
- My skills in design and art

I have also included my resume, which highlights my experience, my GPA, and selected classes. If it is convenient, I would like to stop by your office next week and pick up this letter of recommendation. Your advice and counsel have meant so much to me over the last three years. You have served as an instructor, an advisor, and a mentor. Thank you again for all your help and support. Please call or e-mail me if you have questions.

Sincerely,
Susan Sanchos
Susan Sanchos
242 Cherry Lane
Glenwood, New Hampshire 03827
Home phone: (304) 555-8293
e-mail: susans@edu.glow.com

Request for a Letter of Recommendation   Instructors, advisors, coaches, and previous employers are ideal candidates to ask for a letter of recommendation. *Who might you ask to write a letter of recommendation?*

when appropriate. Also, you may not want your references to be called until you have an interview. Include recommendations in your Career Development Portfolio. See **Figure 14.8** for an example of a letter of recommendation.

Many people put their resume on-line and create their own home page on a web site or job-listing web site. In addition, you can highlight the essential aspects of your Career Development Portfolio. Many services are available to scan your resume and help you place it in an electronic database. Some services will help you design your resume and identify trends in your field. Check with your campus career center or a job search agency for assistance.

Samples of Work

When appropriate, include samples of your work in your portfolio. Think of how you can demonstrate visually your expertise in your field. These samples can include

Figure 14.8 Letter of Recommendation

August 12, 2007

Mr. Jason Bently
University Travel Agency
902 Sunnybrae Lane
Pinehill, New Mexico 88503

Dear Mr. Bently:

It is a pleasure to write a letter of support for Ms. Mary Anne Myers. I have worked with Mary Anne for five years at Computer Divisions Corporation. We were part of the same project team for two years and worked well together. For the last year, I have been her supervisor at Computer Divisions. Mary Anne is a team player and works well with a variety of people. She is also well-prepared, knowledgeable, and hard-working. Recently, a major report was due and Mary Anne worked several weekends and nights to meet the deadline.

Mary Anne has a positive attitude and is willing to tackle any assignment. She is self-motivated and creative. In 2001 she won our Creative Employee Award for her new marketing design. Mary Anne is also an excellent listener. She takes the time to build rapport and listen to customers and, as a result, many repeat customers ask for her by name.

Mary Anne is a lifelong learner. She is attending classes for her college degree in the evenings, and she regularly takes additional training in computers.

I highly recommend Mary Anne Myers. She is an excellent employee. Call or e-mail me if you have questions.

Sincerely,
Joyce Morocco
Joyce Morocco, MBA
Computer Divisions Manager
388 Maple Street
Midland, New Mexico 85802
Office Phone: (606) 555-3948
e-mail: joycem@CDCorp.com

Letter of Recommendation In your portfolio, include letters of recommendation from a variety of people, highlighting your many strengths and experiences. *How might a letter of recommendation be instrumental in securing a job interview?*

articles, portions of a book, artwork, fashion sketches, drawings, photos of work, poetry, pictures, food demonstrations, brochures, a typical day at your job, job descriptions, and performance reviews. If you are in the music field, you can include visual samples of flyers and an audiotape.

Summary of Transcripts
Include a copy of all transcripts of college work.

Credentials, Certificates, and Workshops

Include a copy of credentials, certificates, workshops, seminars, training sessions, conferences, continuing education courses, and other examples of lifelong learning.

Bibliography

Include a bibliography of books you have read that pertain to your major, career goals, or occupation.

Appendix

Include internships, leadership experiences in clubs and sports, volunteer work, service to the community, and travel experiences that relate to your goals. You can also include awards, honors, and certificates of recognition.

Portfolio Cover Letter

If you are submitting your portfolio for review, you should include a cover letter that indicates the purpose of the submission (such as to prove previous experiences or college credit), the documents enclosed, a brief review, and a request for a response (such as an interview or acceptance). See **Figure 14.9** for an example of a portfolio cover letter.

Overcome the Barriers to Portfolio Development

The biggest barrier to portfolio development is procrastination. Maybe you're telling yourself that the idea of a portfolio sounds good but you also think of these excuses:

- ◆ I don't have the time.
- ◆ I wouldn't know where to start.
- ◆ It's a lot of work.
- ◆ I'll do it when I'm ready for a job.
- ◆ I don't have enough work samples.

A Career Development Portfolio is an ongoing process. It will take time to develop your work philosophy, goals, documentation of your skills and competencies, and work samples. If you are resisting or procrastinating, work with a partner. Together you can organize supplies, brainstorm ideas, review each other's philosophies and goals, and help assemble the contents.

Planning the Job Hunt

As discussed earlier in this chapter, there are a number of resources you can tap into when you are beginning your search for a job, such as the career center and career counselor, instructors, mentors, and alumni. There are also numerous Internet sites designed to help match employers with future employees. Most major employers list their current job openings on their web sites. Even if you aren't looking right now, it's good to look at job descriptions posted by potential employers to see what types of jobs they often have available and what types of qualifications they are looking for. This can also help you determine if you need to redesign or enhance your portfolio to fulfill certain requirements.

Figure 14.9 Portfolio Cover Letter

> ## Portfolio Cover Letter
>
> 737 Grandview Avenue
> Euclid, Ohio 43322
>
> October 2, 2007
>
> Dr. Kathryn Keys
> Director of Assessment of Prior Learning
> Louis College of Business
> 333 West Street
> Columbus, Ohio 43082
>
> Dear Dr. Keys:
>
> I am submitting my portfolio for credit for prior learning. I am applying for credit for the following courses:
>
> Marketing 201   Retail Marketing
> Management 180   Introduction to Management
> Business Writing 100   Introduction to Business Writing
>
> I completed my portfolio while taking the course Special Topics 350. My experiences are detailed in the portfolio and I believe they qualify me for six units of college credit. I look forward to meeting you to discuss this further. I will call your office next week to arrange an interview. If you have questions, please call me at (202) 555-5556.
>
> Sincerely,
> *Kim Anderson*
> Kim Anderson

Portfolio Cover Letter   Since your portfolio showcases your variety of experiences, your cover letter should pinpoint the reason you are presenting it for review at this time. *What are some reasons you may be submitting your portfolio for review?*

There is no set time to do certain activities; however, whether you are a two-year, four-year, or transfer student, you will want to put your job search in high gear during your senior or final year.

Submitting a Cover Letter

A cover letter is a written introduction; it should state the job you are applying for and what you can contribute to the company. If possible, find out to whom you should address your cover letter. Often, a call to the personnel office will yield the correct name and title. Express enthusiasm and highlight how your education, skills, and experience relate to the job and will benefit the company.

You should submit your cover letter along with your resume and, if applicable, parts of your portfolio. Follow up with a phone call in a week or two to make certain that your resume was received. This is also the time to ask if additional information is needed and when a decision will be made.

As you develop your portfolio, include good examples of cover letters that you find helpful. See **Figure 14.10** on page 486 for a sample of a cover letter.

Figure 14.10 Sample Cover Letter

July 1, 2007

Dr. Sonia Murphy
North Clinic Health Care
2331 Terrace Street
Chicago, Illinois 69691

Dear Dr. Murphy:

Mr. David Leeland, Director of Internship at Bakers College, gave me a copy of your advertisement for a medical assistant. I am interested in being considered for the position.

Your medical office has an excellent reputation, especially regarding health care for women. I have taken several courses in women's health and volunteer at the hospital in a women's health support group. I believe I can make a significant contribution to your office.

My work experiences and internships have provided valuable hands-on experience. I set up a new computer-designed program for payroll in my internship position. In addition to excellent office skills, I also have clinical experience and people skills. I speak Spanish and have used it often in my volunteer work in hospitals.

I have paid for most of my college education. My grades are excellent, and I have been on the dean's list in my medical and health classes. I have also completed advanced computer and advanced office procedures classes.

I will call you on Tuesday, July 22, to make sure you received this letter and to find out when you might be able to arrange an interview.

Sincerely,

Julia Andrews

Julia Andrews
Green Briar Business Institute
242 Cherry Lane
Chicago, Illinois 69692
Home phone: (304) 555-5593

Sample Cover Letter   A good cover letter captures the employer's attention (in a positive way) and makes connections between your qualifications and what is being sought for the position. *Who might you ask to review your cover letter before you submit it with your resume and application?*

Interviewing

Just as the resume and cover letter are important for opening the door, the job interview is critical for putting your best foot forward and clearly articulating why you are the best person for the job. Many of the tips discussed in this text about getting hired and being successful in a career center around both verbal and nonverbal communication skills. These communication skills will be assets during your job interview. Here are some interview strategies that will help you make full use of these skills and others:

1. **Be punctual.** A good first impression is important and can be lasting. If you arrive late, you have already said a great deal about yourself. Make certain you know the time and location of the interview. Allow time for traffic and parking.

2. **Be professional.** Being too familiar can be a barrier to a professional interview. Never call anyone by his or her first name unless you are asked to. Know the interviewer's name and title, as well as the pronunciation of the interviewer's name, and don't sit down until the interviewer does.

3. **Dress appropriately.** Since much of our communication is nonverbal, dressing appropriately for the interview is important. In most situations, you will be safe

if you wear clean, pressed, conservative business clothes in a neutral color. Pay special attention to grooming. Keep makeup light and wear little jewelry. Make certain your nails and hair are clean, trimmed, and neat. Don't carry a large purse, a backpack, books, a coat, or a hat. Leave extra clothing in an outside office, and simply carry a pen, a pad of paper, and a small folder with extra copies of your resume and references.

4. **Learn about the company.** Using the Internet makes researching a company very easy, as most companies have a web site, even if just for informational purposes. Be prepared and show that you are familiar with the company. What product(s) does it make? How is it doing? What is the competition? Always refer to the company when you give examples.

5. **Learn about the position.** Before you interview, request a job description from the personnel office. What kind of employee—and with what skills—is the company looking for to fill the position? You will likely be asked the common question "Why are you interested in this job?" Be prepared to answer with a reference to the company.

6. **Relate your experience to the job.** Use every question as an opportunity to show how your skills relate to the job. Use examples taken from school, previous jobs, internships, volunteer work, leadership in clubs, and experiences growing up to indicate that you have the personal qualities, aptitudes, and skills needed at the new job.

7. **Be honest.** Although it is important to be confident and to stress your strengths, it is equally important to your sense of integrity to be honest. Dishonesty always catches up with you sooner or later. Someone will verify your background, so do not exaggerate your accomplishments, grade point average, or experience.

8. **Focus on how you can benefit the company.** Don't ask about benefits, salary, or vacations until you are offered the job. During a first interview, try to show how you can contribute to the organization. Don't appear to be too eager to move up through the company or suggest that you are more interested in gaining experience than in contributing to the company.

9. **Be poised and relaxed.** Avoid nervous habits, such as tapping your pencil, playing with your hair, or covering your mouth with your hand. Watch language such as *you know, ah, stuff like that.* Don't smoke, chew gum, fidget, or bite your nails.

10. **Maintain comfortable eye contact.** Look people in the eye and speak with confidence. Your eyes reveal much about you; use them to show interest, confidence, poise, and sincerity. Use other nonverbal techniques, such as a firm handshake, to reinforce your confidence.

Maintain Eye Contact
Look the hiring manager in the eye, remain calm and confident during your interview, and be prepared to explain how you can contribute to the company. *What are some typical interview questions that you should be prepared to answer?*

11. **Practice interviewing.** Consider videotaping a mock interview. Most college campuses have this service available through the career center or media department. Rehearse questions and be prepared to answer directly.

12. **Anticipate question types.** Expect open-ended questions, such as "What are your strengths?" "What are your weaknesses?" "Tell me about your best work experience," and "What are your career goals?" Decide in advance what information and

skills are pertinent to the position and reveal your strengths. For example, you could say, "I learned to get along with a diverse group of people when I worked for the park service."

13. **Close the interview on a positive note.** Thank the interviewer for his or her time, shake hands, and say that you are looking forward to hearing from him or her.

14. **Follow up with a letter.** A follow-up letter is especially important. It serves as a reminder for the interviewer. For you, it is an opportunity to thank the interviewer and a chance to make a positive comment about the position and the company. See **Figure 14.11** for a sample follow-up letter.

Workplace Trends

WORDS TO SUCCEED

"Don't go around saying the world owes you a living. The world owes you nothing. It was here first."

MARK TWAIN
Author

As middle management jobs are eliminated, workers are expected to take more responsibility for managing themselves and their work progress. The job security of lifelong employment will be replaced by a reliance on employees' own portfolios of skills and competencies. Salary increases and advancement will tend to be based on performance and production rather than seniority or entitlement. You will be responsible for managing your own career and marketing yourself. Career planning gives you information for making sound decisions, helps you learn how to assess your skills and competencies, and creates a dynamic system that encourages you to adapt to changing jobs and careers. The Internet, computer technology, and telecommunications have fueled major changes. Being prepared, resilient, flexible, and willing to be a lifelong learner will help you overcome many barriers to career success.

Keep a section in the appendix of your Career Development Portfolio for workplace trends that relate directly to your occupation. One of the important trends will be education on the job. Some of this education will be informal and will consist of acquiring on-the-job training, acquiring new job skills, learning to complete challenging projects, and shifting your work style so that you can work more effectively with others. Other education will be formal, such as seminars, courses, and workshops designed to improve or add to your job skills. These formal courses may include training in these areas:

◆ Computers
◆ World Wide Web
◆ Grant writing
◆ Financial planning
◆ Technical skills
◆ Report writing

Other formal seminars, courses, or workshops may develop better human relations skills, covering these topics:

◆ Alcohol and other drug abuse
◆ Sexual harassment

Figure 14.11 Sample Follow-Up Letter

May 29, 2007

Mr. Henry Sanders
The Mountain View Store
10 Rock Lane
Alpine, Montana 79442

Dear Mr. Sanders:

Thank you for taking the time yesterday to meet with me concerning the position of sales representative. I enjoyed meeting you and your employees, learning more about your growing company, and touring your facilities. I was especially impressed with your new line of outdoor wear. It is easy to see why you lead the industry in sales.

I am even more excited about joining your sales team now that I have visited with you. I have the education, training, enthusiasm, and personal qualities necessary to succeed in business. I am confident that I would fit in with your staff and make a real contribution to the sales team.

Thank you again for the interview and an enjoyable morning.

Sincerely,

John A. Bennett

John A. Bennett
124 East Buttermilk Lane
LaCrosse, Wisconsin 54601
Home phone: (608) 555-4958
e-mail: johnb@shast.edu

Sample Follow-Up Letter   A follow-up letter is another opportunity to set yourself apart from other job candidates. *What should you include in your follow-up letter?*

- Cultural and gender diversity
- Team building
- Time and stress management
- Communication
- Motivation
- Negotiation
- Conflict resolution
- Basic supervision

You may decide that you need to earn an advanced degree or certificate by going to lengthy training sessions or attending college in the evenings. However you go about it, lifelong education is a new and significant job trend. An employee who learns new skills, cross-trains in various positions, and has excellent human relations skills will be sought after and promoted. Complete **Personal Evaluation Notebook 14.5** on page 490 to assess how your skills have improved even during the past few months.

WORDS TO SUCCEED

"I am learning all the time. The tombstone will be my diploma."

EARTHA KITT
Entertainer

Assessment Is Lifelong

Read the following skills. Then rate yourself on a scale of 1 to 5 (1 being poor and 5 being excellent). Refer back to **Personal Evaluation Notebook 1.1** in Chapter 1 and compare it with your answers here. Have you improved your skills and competencies?

Area	Excellent		Satisfactory		Poor
	5	4	3	2	1
1. Reading			_____		
2. Writing			_____		
3. Speaking			_____		
4. Mathematics			_____		
5. Listening			_____		
6. Critical thinking and reasoning			_____		
7. Decision making			_____		
8. Creative problem solving			_____		
9. Mental visualization			_____		
10. Knowing how to learn			_____		
11. Personal qualities (honesty, character, responsibility)			_____		
12. Sociability			_____		
13. Self-management and control			_____		
14. Self-esteem and confidence			_____		
15. Management of time, money, space, and people			_____		
16. Interpersonal, team, and leadership skills			_____		
17. Working well with cultural diversity			_____		
18. Organization and evaluation of information			_____		
19. Understanding systems			_____		
20. Understanding technology			_____		
21. Commitment and effort			_____		

Assessment Is Lifelong—continued

Assess your results. What are your most excellent skills? What are your poor skills that need improvement?

Do you have a better understanding of how you learned these skills and competencies? Do you know how to document and demonstrate these skills and competencies? Your major or career choice may include other skills. Assess additional skills that can be transferred to many situations or jobs. For example, here are six broad skill areas:

- Communication skills
- Human relations skills
- Organization, management, and leadership skills
- Technical and mechanical skills
- Innovation and creativity skills
- Research and planning skills

Business Ethics

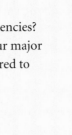

WORDS TO SUCCEED

"It's easy to make a buck. It's a lot tougher to make a difference."

TOM BROKAW
Journalist

We discussed the importance of character, integrity, and ethics in Chapter 2. It bears repeating at the close of this text, however, since business ethics are an important issue in today's business world. The go-for-it-at-any-cost attitude of corporate raiders and unethical businesspeople has tarnished the image of big business and has made us all more aware of ethical business practices. Leaders of major companies such as Enron, WorldCom, and Tyco not only face the legal ramifications of their dishonest practices but also have ruined the financial lives of many of their key stakeholders—their employees.

Top managers have a responsibility for setting an ethical code and acting as role models for all employees. They should act with integrity and model ethical behavior. Corporations must set clear guidelines for ethical behavior and insist on accountability. Many corporations have improved their images by being socially responsible and encouraging their employees to become involved in the community and contribute their time and talents to worthwhile community agencies and causes.

Each employee must make decisions based on moral values and good conscience and must follow the code of ethics provided by his or her industry. Sometimes this is an unwritten code; sometimes it is an industrywide set of rules. Whether they are written or unwritten, ethical business standards must be upheld. What Hsi-Tang Chih Tsang, renowned Zen master, said 1,200 years ago is still true today: "Although gold dust is precious, when it gets in your eyes it obstructs your vision." If you focus on your values, positive personal qualities, and mission in life, you will attain whatever you deem precious—and will become a true peak performer.

Taking Charge

In summary, in this chapter, I learned to:

- *Explore potential majors and career paths.* To determine my major course of study, I first need to assess my interests. I consult with available resources, such as the career counselor, family, and friends; explore the college catalog; visit academic departments; and participate in classes, workshops, internships, and service-learning opportunities.

- *Assess my values, interests, abilities, and skills.* What I value personally is important to determining what I will value in a future career. I have certain interests that may lead me in one occupational direction. I have innate abilities that enable me to be more successful in certain areas. I also have acquired transferable skills that can be used in many different fields.

- *See the value of career development portfolios.* My portfolio helps me assess, highlight, and demonstrate my strengths, skills, and competencies. Starting my portfolio early helps me get organized and gives me a chance to add, update, and edit throughout my college experience and into my first career.

- *Organize essential elements.* Assembling my portfolio in a three-ring notebook and box helps me collect and organize work samples, information, lists, examples, transcripts, credentials, certificates, workshops, and documentation of personal qualities.

- *List significant life experiences and accomplishments.* I include such experiences as formal education, special classes and projects, volunteer work and service-learning, jobs, self-study, travel, hobbies, military service, special recognition, and accomplishments and events that helped me learn new skills or something about myself or others. I list books I have read that pertain to my major or career or that have helped me develop a certain philosophy.

- *Document skills and competencies.* I connect essential skills to school and work, and I look for transferable skills. I document critical thinking, interpersonal, computer, financial, and basic skills that are important for school and job success. When appropriate, I include samples of my work.

- *Create an effective resume.* My resume is an essential document that helps me highlight my education, work experience, awards, professional memberships, and campus and community activities.

- *Write a cover letter and prepare for an interview.* Drafting a sample cover letter will make it easy for me to apply for a variety of jobs at a moment's notice. I save articles and tips on interviewing and practice whenever possible. I assess my performance and strive to improve.

- *Adapt to workplace trends.* I take the time to learn more about career opportunities, and I observe workplace trends, especially additional education and training needed.

- *Practice good business ethics.* I realize that character and integrity are core values that are critical to success on the job and in life.

492   **PART THREE** ▲ Application

Steven Price

SOCIAL STUDIES TEACHER/LEGISLATOR

Related Majors: Education, Social Studies, Political Science

Career Planning Is Lifelong

Steven Price taught social studies classes at a high school. With an avid interest in politics, Steven soon developed a strong curriculum for teaching government and current affairs. He was well known in the district for his innovative classes in which students researched and debated local issues and then voted on them.

Throughout the years, Steven remained active in a local political party. Each year, he could be counted on to help hand out flyers and canvass neighborhoods before the September primaries and November elections. One year, a party member suggested that Steven run for state legislator.

Steven took the offer seriously. After 21 years of teaching, he felt ready for a change. He had enjoyed being in the classroom, especially when his students had shared his passion for politics. However, he felt that being a state legislator would allow him to work more directly in bringing about changes in his community. He took a leave of absence from his teaching job. He filed the appropriate papers and worked hard with a campaign manager to get his name out to the voters in his district. Because Steven had already prepared a career portfolio over the years, the manager was able to use the collected information to promote Steven.

Using his years of experience teaching government and current affairs, Steven felt rejuvenated and excited as he worked on his political campaign. His lifelong commitment to politics paid off when he won the election! He was glad that he had taken the risk. A career change was a positive move for both Steven and his community.

CRITICAL THINKING What might have happened to Steven if he had not taken the risks of moving to a different career?

Peak Performer Profile

David Filo and Jerry Yang

It's a sure thing that anyone seeking information on the World Wide Web knows about Yahoo!—short for Yet Another Hierarchical Officious Oracle. Log on to Yahoo.com and you'll be able to track down the number of times your heart beats per year (40 million beats), search the ancient tombs of Egypt, or check out your astrological profile. What started as a spare-time activity between friends David Filo and Jerry Yang emerged as a successful business and one of the Internet's most popular search engines.

Although Filo and Yang crossed paths as Stanford doctoral candidates, they took a roundabout route. Their lives began, literally, on opposite ends of the earth. At the age of 10, Jerry Yang, born Chih-Yuan Yang, immigrated to America from Taiwan with his grandmother, widowed mother, and little brother in 1968. An only child, David Filo grew up in an alternative community in Louisiana. His family lived with six other families, sharing a garden and a single kitchen.

When Filo and Yang both went to Stanford to study electrical engineering in the early 1990s, they discovered common interests—and a great idea.

In 1994, they put together one of the first directories to help net surfers navigate the Internet. Previously, web sites had used only a domain name, such as a personal or company name, making it almost impossible to locate material by topic. Filo and Yang found a novel way to break down and organize the web sites into categories, a system not unlike a library's catalog. They also included such useful features as news and weather, shopping guides, a handy reference section, and even a personalized page, "My Yahoo," for users who wanted to keep favorite links close at hand. Today Yahoo! receives over 200 million hits each month and has transformed the Internet.

PERFORMANCE THINKING If you were preparing Filo's and Yang's resumes, what would you write in the job objective section for these "Chief Yahoos"? What are some of their personal experiences that may have contributed to their career success?

CHECK IT OUT The web site Yahoo!—which started out as "Jerry and David's Guide to the World Wide Web"—began as a hobby for two electrical engineering students, proving that your career path can take a different direction than originally planned. Many state and local governments offer help in determining what interests you and potential career directions to consider, such as **www.nycareerzone.org,** a service provided by the state of New York. You can take a personal assessment based on Holland's theory of occupational personality types, explore featured careers, and review job listings. Check to see if your community or state offers a similar site or service.

CHAPTER 14

Performance Strategies ....

Following are the top 10 tips for planning for a career:

◆ Determine what you value in life and a career.

◆ Know how to connect essential work skills and competencies to school and life and how to transfer skills.

◆ Assemble your portfolio in an organized planning guide and review, assess, update, and make additions to your portfolio often.

◆ Document skills, competencies, and personal qualities in your portfolio.

◆ Include essential elements in your portfolio, such as a resume, transcripts, and accomplishments.

◆ Value, document, and demonstrate service-learning and volunteer work on campus and in the community.

◆ Use your portfolio to reflect on your work philosophy and life mission, as well as to set goals and priorities.

◆ Prepare for the job hunting and interview process early.

◆ Observe and reflect on workplace trends.

◆ Create and live by a code of ethics.

Tech for Success ....

Take advantage of the text's web site at **www.mhhe.com/ ferrett6e** for additional study aids, useful forms, and convenient and applicable resources.

◆ **Your resume on-line.** Many potential employers are willing to receive your resume and supporting documents via a web site or CD. A number of programs and services, such as FolioLive (www. foliolive.com), are available to help you develop your resume on-line. One feature is a set amount of space for storing digital files, such as graphic images, video, and PowerPoint presentations. Your school may use a preferred source for developing a portfolio, so consult your advisor as you get started.

◆ **Job search web sites.** There are a number of job search sites, such as monster.com and hotjobs.com. These sites require you to type your resume into their format, which then feeds into their search engine. When you are ready to start your job hunt, it's worth investigating these and more specialized sites that cater to the field you are pursuing. Also, check out any professional organizations in the field, as they may also provide job listings on-line.

Review Questions ....

Based on what you have learned in this chapter, write your answers to the following questions:

1. Why is it important to determine your values during career planning?

2. Define *transferable skill* and give an example.

3. What is the purpose of your Career Development Portfolio?

4. What are the four steps for organizing and assembling your portfolio?

5. What information should be included in a resume?

EXPLORING CAREERS

In the Classroom

Maria Lewis likes to make presentations, enjoys working with children, and is a crusader for equality and the environment. She also values family, home, and community. Making a lot of money is not important to her. Her motivation comes from the feeling that she is making a difference and enjoys what she is doing. Now that her own family is grown, she wants to complete a college degree. However, she is hesitant because she has been out of school for many years.

1. How would you help Maria with her decision?

_____

_____

2. What careers would you have Maria explore?

_____

_____

In the Workplace

Maria completed a degree in childhood development. She has been a caregiver at a children's day-care center for two years. She has enjoyed her job, but she feels that it is time for a change. If she wants to stay in her field and advance, she has to travel and go into management. She wants more time off to spend with her family, write, and become more involved in community action groups. Maria would like to stay in a related field. She still likes working with children, but she also enjoys giving presentations and workshops and writing. She has thought about consulting, writing, or starting her own small business.

3. What strategies in this chapter would help Maria with her career change?

_____

_____

4. What one habit would you recommend to Maria to help her with her career planning?

_____

_____

APPLYING THE ABCDE METHOD OF SELF-MANAGEMENT

In the Journal Entry on page 461, you were asked to write down one of the classes you are currently taking and list at least three skills you will acquire in this class that will benefit you in your career:

_____

_____

_____

Now think about a class you are taking that doesn't seem to relate directly to your career plans. Use the ABCDE method to analyze what you are learning in that class and how it benefits you, either today or later on.

A = Actual event:

B = Beliefs:

C = Consequences:

D = Dispute:

E = Energized:

Use positive visualization to help you achieve the results you want. See yourself creating a portfolio that helps you organize all the information you're learning and relate it to job success. Think of the confidence you'll have when you've developed a cover letter and resume and practiced for job interviews. See yourself focused with a vision and purpose and working in a job you love.

Practice Self-Management

For more examples of learning how to manage difficult situations, see the "Self-Management Workbook" section of the Online Learning Center web site at **www.mhhe.com/ferrett6e**.

CHECKLIST FOR CHOOSING A MAJOR

Earlier in this chapter, you used the Adult Learning Cycle to explore majors and career opportunities. Follow this handy guide as you put this into practice.

Relate

◆ What are the most important criteria for my future career, such as independence, high visibility, flexible hours, ability to work from home, and management opportunities?

◆ What is my personality type and/or temperament?

◆ Are there certain careers that fit my personality that offer these features?

◆ What skills do I already have that would be useful or necessary?

Observe

◆ Whom do I know who is currently working in this field whom I could interview or talk to?

◆ Which instructors at my school would be the most knowledgeable about the field? Who are the most approachable and are available to advise me?

◆ What are the major professional organizations in this field? Have I explored their web sites for additional information? Can I join these organizations as a student? Would it be worth the investment?

◆ Which courses should I be enrolled in right now or next semester that will further introduce me to this area?

◆ I've visited the career center at my school and have talked with my advisor and/or a career counselor about:

Reflect

◆ What are the positives I am hearing?

◆ What are the drawbacks I am hearing?

◆ What education and skills will be necessary for me to pursue this major and career?

◆ Are there related professions that seem appealing?

Do

◆ I've constructed a time line for gaining experience in this area that includes tasks such as:

◆ Securing an internship; to be secured by:

◆ Joining a student club; to be involved by:

◆ Participating in related volunteer activities; to be accomplished by:

◆ Getting a related part-time job; to be hired by:

◆ Other:

Teach

◆ I have relayed my impressions to my family and/or friends. Some of the questions/responses they have given are

◆ I have talked with fellow students about their major and career search. Some tips I have learned from them are

◆ The most important resources I have found that I would recommend to others are

As of now, the major/career I would like to continue exploring is _____.

PREPARING YOUR RESUME

In anticipation of preparing your resume, start thinking about the information that will appear on it. On the following lines, summarize your skills and qualifications and match them to the requirements of the job you are seeking. Use proactive words and verbs when writing information for your resume. Here are some examples:

◆ *Organized* a group of after-school tutors for math and accounting courses

◆ *Wrote* and *published* articles for the school newspaper

◆ *Participated* in a student academic advisory board

◆ *Developed* a new accounting system

◆ *Managed* the petty cash accounts for the PTA

◆ Can *keyboard* 60 wpm

You should not be discouraged if you have only a few action phrases to write at this time. You can add to your list as you continue your studies and become an active participant on your campus and with your courses of study.

Skills and Qualifications

1. _____

2. _____

3. _____

4. _____

5. _____

6. _____

7. _____

8. _____

9. _____

10. _____

INFORMATIONAL INTERVIEW

Make a list of the types of jobs you think you would like. Then make a list of hiring managers in those types of jobs. Ask those contacts if you can interview them about their career field. The purpose of each interview is to find out about the person's career and what the job is really like, as well as establishing a contact for the future. Following is a list of questions to ask. (Remember to send a thank-you note after each interview.)

Person interviewed _____

Job title _____ Date _____

1. Why did you choose your career?

   _____

2. What do you do on a typical day?

   _____

3. What do you like best about your job?

   _____

4. What do you like least?

   _____

5. Would you mind telling me the salary range for your job?

   _____

6. When you are filling a position, what kinds of qualities or skills do you typically look for?

   _____

7. If you had to do it again, would you choose the same job? If not, what would you do differently in planning your career?

   _____

8. What advice can you give me for planning my career?

   _____

EXPLORING CAREERS

Go to the library or career center and find 10 careers you've never heard of or are interested in exploring. Do the following exercises. Then add this page to your Career Development Portfolio.

1. Use the Internet to explore at least one career.

_____

_____

_____

2. Can these careers be grouped into one field?

_____

_____

_____

3. List your skills and interests. Then list the careers that match these skills and interests. Create names for careers if they are unusual.

Skills/Interests	Possible Careers
_____	_____
_____	_____
_____	_____

4. Review your list of skills and interests. What stands out? Do you like working with people or accomplishing tasks? Think of as many jobs as you can that relate to your skills and interests. Your skills and interests are valuable clues about your future career.

_____

_____

_____

5. Describe an ideal career that involves the skills you enjoy using the most. Include the location of this ideal career and the kinds of co-workers, customers, and employees you would encounter.

_____

_____

_____

Glossary

academic advisor   an educational advisor who assists students in the development of meaningful educational plans compatible with the attainment of their life goals

acronym   a word formed from the first letter of a series of other words

acrostic   a made-up sentence in which the first letter of each word stands for something

affirmation   positive self-talk or internal thoughts that counter self-defeating thought patterns with positive, hopeful or realistic thoughts

anorexia nervosa   an eating disorder that involves a pathological fear of weight gain leading to faulty eating patterns, malnutrition, and usually excessive weight loss

assertive communication   expressing oneself in a direct and civil manner

attentive listening   a decision to be fully focused with the intent of understanding the speaker

body smart   people who have physical and kinesthetic intelligence; have the ability to understand and control their bodies; and have tactical sensitivity, like movement, and handle objects skillfully

bulimia nervosa   an eating disorder that involves binge eating and purging through forced vomiting, or by using laxatives

character   attributes or features that make up and distinguish an individual and are considered constant and relatively non-controversial by most people

cheating   using or providing unauthorized help

chunking   breaking up long lists of information or numbers to make it easier to remember

civility   interacting with others with respect, kindness, good manners, or etiquette

codependency   a psychological condition or a relationship in which a person is controlled or manipulated by another who is affected with an addictive condition

common ground   a basis of mutual interest or similarities of core values

communication   giving and receiving ideas, feelings and information

comprehension   understanding main ideas and details

convergent   the ability to look at several unrelated items and bringing order to them

creators   people who tend to be innovative, flexible, spontaneous, creative, and idealistic

critical thinking   a logical, rational, systematic thought process that is necessary to understand, analyze, and evaluate information in order to solve a problem or situation

deductive reasoning   drawing conclusions based on going from the general to the specific

depression   an emotional state marked especially by sadness, inactivity, difficulty in thinking and concentration, a significant increase or decrease in appetite and time spent sleeping, feelings of dejection and hopelessness, and sometimes suicidal tendencies

directors   people who are dependable, self-directed, conscientious, efficient, decisive, and results-orientated

divergent   the ability to break apart an idea into many different ideas

diversity   differences in gender, race, age, ethnicity, sexual orientation, physical ability, learning styles and learning disabilities, social and economic background, and religion

emotional intelligence   the ability to understand and manage oneself and relate effectively to others

empathy   understanding and having compassion for others

Enneagram   a typing system that divides people into nine basic types with specific characteristics

ethics   the principles of conduct that govern a group or society

evaluator   a person in an advising center who reviews transcripts, major contracts, and perform degree checks

external locus of control   the belief that success or failure is due to outside influences such as fate, luck, or other people

extrovert   person who is outgoing, social, optimistic and often uncomfortable with being alone

feeler   person who is sensitive to the concerns, feelings of others, values harmony, and dislikes creating conflict

file transfer protocol (FTP)   a tool to transfer files between two internet sites

formal outline   a traditional outline that uses Roman numerals and capital letters to highlight main points

informal outline   a free form of outline that uses dashes and indenting to highlight main points

integrity   firm adherence to a code of especially moral values

internal locus of control   the belief that control over life is due to behavior choices, character, and effort

internet   a vast network of computers connecting people and resources worldwide

internship   an advanced student or graduate usually in a professional field gaining supervised practical experience

interpreting   developing ideas and being able to summarize the material

introvert   person who tends to like time alone, solitude, and reflection, and prefers the world of ideas and thoughts

intuitive   people who are more comfortable with theories, abstraction, imagination, and speculation

judgers   person who prefers orderly, planned, and structured learning and working environments

Learning and Study Strategies Inventory (LASSI)   a self-assessment system that looks at attitude, interest, motivation, self-discipline, willingness to work hard, time management, anxiety, concentration, test strategies, and other study skills to gather information about learning and studying attitudes and practices

logic smart   people who have logical/mathematical intelligence; like numbers, puzzles, and logic; and have the ability to reason, solve problems, create hypotheses, and think in terms of cause and effect

maturity   the ability to control impulses, to think beyond the moment, and to consider how words and actions affect others

memorization   the transfer of information from short-term memory into long-term memory

mentor   a role model who takes a special interest in another's goals and personal and professional development

mind map   a visual, holistic form of note taking that starts with the main idea placed in the center of a page and branches out with subtopics through associations and patterns

mindfulness   the state of being totally in the moment and part of the process

mission statement   a written statement focusing on desired values, philosophies, and principles

mnemonic   memory tricks used to help remember information

motivation   an inner drive that moves a person to action

music smart   people who have rhythm and melody intelligence; the ability to appreciate, perceive and produce rhythms

networking   the exchange of information or services for the purpose of enriching individuals, groups, or institutions

non-traditional student   students who do not go directly from high school to college, but return later in life

note taking   a method of creating order and arranging thoughts and materials to help retain information

outdoor smart   people who have environmental intelligence and are good at measuring, charting and observing animals and plants

Paraphrase   reword or restate another's ideas with your own

peak performer   a person who is successful and desires to pursue a lifetime of learning

people smart   people who have interpersonal intelligence; and like to talk and work with people, join groups, and solve problems as part of a team; and have the ability to work with and understand people, as well as to perceive and be responsive to the moods, intentions and desires of other people

perceiver   a person who prefers flexibility and spontaneity, and likes to allow life to unfold

picture smart   people who have spatial intelligence and like to draw, sketch and visualize information; and have the ability to perceive in three-dimensional space and re-create various aspects of the visual world

plagiarism   to steal and pass off the ideas or words of another as one's own

procrastination   deliberately putting off tasks

professional advisors   professional and peer staff who answer questions, help students register, and instruct students about deadlines and other important information

rapport   the ability to find common ground with another person based on respect, empathy, and trust

recall   the transfer of information from long-term memory into short-term memory

reflect   to think about something in a purposeful way with the intention of creating new meaning

retention   the process of storing information

self smart   people who have interpersonal and inner intelligence; have the ability to be contemplative, self-disciplined, and introspective

self-assessment   the recognition of the need to learn new tasks and subjects, relate more effectively with others, set goals, manage time and stress, and create a balanced and productive life

self-management   a thought process that involves techniques you can utilize to help you manage your thoughts and behaviors and keep you focused, overcome obstacles, and succeed

sensors   people who learn best from their senses and feel comfortable with facts and concrete data

supporter   a person who tends to be cooperative, honest, sensitive, warm, and understanding

thinker   a person who likes to analyze problems with facts, rational logic, and analysis

traditional student   a student 18 to 25 years old, usually going from high school directly to college

transferable skills   skills that can be used in a variety of careers

visualization   using imagery to clearly see goals and successfully envision engaging in new positive behavior

web site   a collection of mechanisms used to locate, display, and access information available on the internet

wellness   to live life fully with purpose, meaning, and vitality

word smart   people who have verbal/linguistic intelligence; like to read, talk, and write about information; and have the ability to argue, persuade, entertain, and teach with words

Additional Credits

Text Credits

Chapter 14 p. 465, Peak Progress 14.1, Adapted from "What is Service-Learning?", Corporation for National and Community Service, www. learnandserve.org; "Four Things Faculty Want to Know About!", Mark Cooper, Florida International University, www.fiu.edu/~time4chg/Library/fourthings.html.

Photo Credits

Chapter 1 p. 1, Getty Images/Digital Vision; p. 15, Verve Commissioned Series/Getty Images; p. 18, BananaStock/JupiterImages; pp. 19, 34, ©Royalty-Free/Corbis; p. 35, ©James Leynse/Corbis; p. 37, ©Digital Vision

Chapter 2 p. 43, Duncan Smith/Getty Images; p. 70, PhotoDisc/Getty Images; p. 71, ©Kate Brooks/Corbis; p. 73, © Ronnie Kaufman/Corbis

Chapter 3 p. 79, © Cat Gwynn/Corbis; p. 90, Getty Images/Digital Vision; p. 100, E. Dygas/Getty Images; p. 104, Ryan McVay/Getty Images/PhotoDisc; p. 105, © Bassouls Sophie/Corbis Sygma; p. 107, Keith Brofsky/Getty Images/PhotoDisc

Chapter 4 p. 119, BananaStock/JupiterImages; p. 120, Patrick Clark/Getty Images/PhotoDisc; p. 125, ©Digital Vision; p. 140, Ryan McVay/Getty Images/PhotoDisc; p. 144, ©Royalty-Free/Corbis; p. 145, Dave Duggan/Infocus Photography; p. 147, Ryan McVay/Getty Images/PhotoDisc

Chapter 5 p. 155, ©Image100 Ltd.; p. 171, ©Royalty-Free/Corbis; p. 174, ©Ryan McVay/Getty Images/PhotoDisc; p. 175, ©Steve Azzara/Corbis; p. 177, ©Ryan McVay/Getty Images/PhotoDisc

Chapter 6 p. 185, ©Royalty-Free/Corbis; p. 188, BananaStock/JupiterImages; p. 200, Emma Lee/Life File/Getty Images; p. 202, Steve Cole/Getty Images; p. 206, Photodisc Collection/Getty Images; p. 207, © Vaughn Youtz/Zuma/Corbis; p. 209, Andrew Ward/Life File/Getty Images

Chapter 7 p. 219, The McGraw-Hill Companies, Inc./Gary He, photographer; p. 227, © Image100 Ltd.; p. 240, Ryan McVay/Getty Images; p. 241, ©Shawn Thew/epa/Corbis; p. 243, Antonio Mo/Getty Images; p. 247TL, PhotoLink/Getty Images; p. 247TM, Steve Cole/Getty Images; p. 247TR, PhotoLink/Getty Images; p. 247BL, Amanda Clement/Getty Images; p. 247BR, Kent Knudson/PhotoLink/Getty Images

Chapter 8 p. 251, ©Image100 Ltd.; p. 268, PhotoDisc/Getty Images; p. 269, ©Digital Vision; p. 274, Keith Brofsky/Getty Images; p. 275, ©Corbis; p. 277, PhotoDisc/Getty Images;

Chapter 9 p. 285, ©Charles Gupton/Corbis; p. 299, Jeff Maloney/Getty Images; p. 304, Keith Brofsky/Getty Images; p. 310, Ryan McVay/Getty Images; p. 311, © Marc Brasz/Corbis; p. 313, Keith Brofsky/Getty Images;

Chapter 10 p. 319, Getty Images; p. 331, © image100 Ltd.; p. 346, © Chuck Savage/Corbis; p. 347, ©AP/Wide World Photos; p. 349, Keith Brofsky/Getty Images

Chapter 11 p. 359, © image100/PunchStock; p. 363, ©Digital Vision; p. 369, Jeff Maloney/Getty Images; p. 382, ©BananaStock/PunchStock; p. 390, ©Royalty-Free/Corbis; p. 391, ©Alex Grimm/Reuters/Corbis; p. 393, C. Borland/PhotoLink/Getty Images

Chapter 12 p. 399, Comstock Images/Jupiter Images; p. 405, © Royalty-Free/Corbis; p. 415, Ryan McVay/Getty Images; p. 418, Keith Brofsky/Getty Images; p. 428, ©Tony Freeman/PhotoEdit; p. 429, © Duomo/Corbis; p. 431, Royalty-Free/Corbis

Chapter 13 p. 437, Doug Menuez/Getty Images; p. 440, dynamicgraphics/Jupiterimages; p. 453, Skip Nall/Getty Images; p. 454, Courtesy Carson Scholars Fund; p. 456, Adam Crowley/Getty Images

Chapter 14 p. 461, Pixtal/Superstock; p. 487, © Digital Vision; p. 493, Doug Menuez/Getty Images; p. 494, © Ed Kashi/Corbis; p. 496, Royalty-Free/Corbis

Features Guide

Index